Officials and employees of the city county of Suffolk with their residences, compensation, etc 1909

Boston

Alpha Editions

This edition published in 2020

ISBN: 9789354029042

Design and Setting By
Alpha Editions
email - alphaedis@gmail.com

[Document 105 — 1909.]

OFFICIALS AND EMPLOYEES

OF THE

City of Boston

AND

County of Suffolk

WITH THEIR

RESIDENCE, COMPENSATION, ETC.

1909

PREPARED AND PUBLISHED IN ACCORDANCE WITH THE
REVISED ORDINANCES, AND AN ORDER OF THE COUNTY
COMMISSIONERS OF THE COUNTY OF SUFFOLK

BOSTON
PRINTING DEPARTMENT
1909

"Each officer in charge of a department shall, on or before the fifth day of May, in each year, prepare and furnish to the Mayor lists of the officials and employees of the city employed in his department on the thirtieth day of April preceding. Such lists shall be arranged by divisions and districts, and shall give the names, residences, designations of, compensation of, and date of election or appointment of, each of such officials and employees; and it shall be the duty of the City Auditor to verify the said lists from the pay rolls." — *Revised Ordinances of 1898, chapter 3, section 27, as established by Ordinances of 1904, chapter 3, section 1.*

"He [the Superintendent of Printing] shall also print, on or before the first day of June in each year, a city document containing the lists of officials and employees of the city, referred to in section twenty-seven of chapter three." — *Revised Ordinances of 1898, chapter 31, section 2, as amended by Ordinances of 1904, chapter 3, section 2.*

CITY OF BOSTON,
IN BOARD OF ALDERMEN, April 5, 1909.

Ordered, That the Sheriff and other officers of Suffolk County are hereby requested to prepare and furnish to the County Auditor, on or before the fifth day of May, lists of the officials and employees appointed or employed by them and paid from the County Treasury on the weekly pay roll for the week ending Thursday, April 29, 1909, or on the monthly pay roll payable May 1, 1909. Such lists shall give the names, residences, designations of, compensation of, and date of election or appointment of, each of such officials and employees, and it shall be the duty of the County Auditor to verify the said lists from the pay rolls.

Passed.

A true copy.

Attest:

JOHN T. PRIEST,
City Clerk.

OFFICIALS AND EMPLOYEES OF THE CITY OF BOSTON.
APRIL 30, 1909.

Mayor's Office.

Name.	Residence.	Designation.	Compensation.	Date of Election or Appointment.
George A. Hibbard	35 Beaumont st	Mayor	$10,000 yr	Dec. 10, 1907
James C. White	8 Fairfax st	Secretary	4,000 "	Jan. 6, 1908
William A. Boudrot	27 Carruth st	Assistant Secretary	2,500 "	" 6, 1908
Timothy A. Butler	637 Dudley st	Chief Clerk	2,500 "	Feb. 1, 1899
John M. Casey	58 Barry st	Assistant Secretary	1,800 "	March 4, 1904
Harry Fogarty	110 Brook ave	Stenographer	1,200 "	Jan. 6, 1908
Reginald H. Mair	175 Ashmont st	Messenger	1,200 "	" 6, 1908
Edwina McCabe	11 Bushnell st	Stenographer	800 "	" 9, 1908
Josephine M. Kiley	306 Bunker Hill st	Telephone Operator	700 "	Oct. 7, 1907
Arthur F. Langley	528 Bennington st	Boy	426 "	May 11, 1908

Board of Aldermen.

Name.	Residence.	Designation.	Compensation.	Date of Election or Appointment.
George Pomeroy Anderson, 25 Cumberland st		Alderman	$1,500 yr	Dec. 15, 1908
John Joseph Attridge	118 Malden st	"	1,500 "	" 15, 1908
Walter Ballantyne	224 Dudley st., Rox.	"	1,500 "	" 15, 1908
Frederick James Brand	4 Melville ave., Dor.	"	1,500 "	" 15, 1908
Charles Lancaster Carr	13 Everett st., Dor.	"	1,500 "	" 15, 1908
William Dudley Cotton, Jr., 77 Walnut pk., Rox.		"	1,500 "	" 15, 1908
James Michael Curley	114 Mt. Pleasant ave., Rox.,	"	1,500 "	" 15, 1908
Daniel Joseph Donnelly	29 Curve st.	"	1,500 "	" 15, 1908
Thomas Joseph Giblin	517 Orleans st., E. B.	"	1,500 "	" 15, 1908
Matthew Hale	50 River st	"	1,500 "	" 15, 1908
James Frank O'Hare	600 E. Fourth st., S. B.	"	1,500 "	" 15, 1908
James Patrick Timilty	5 Sumner pl., Rox.	"	1,500 "	" 15, 1908
Daniel Aloysius Whelton	61 Allen st	"	1,500 "	" 15, 1908
Frank X. Chisholm	49 Regent st., Rox.	Secretary	2,000 "	Jan. 23, 1893

Common Council.

Ward 1.

Name.	Residence.	Designation.	Compensation.	Date of Election or Appointment.
Edward C. R. Bagley	150 Princeton st	Councilman	$300 yr	Dec. 15, 1908
Frank A. Goodwin	986 Saratoga st	"	300 "	" 15, 1908
Joseph A. Hoey	430 Bennington st	"	300 "	" 15, 1908

Ward 2.

Name.	Residence.	Designation.	Compensation.	Date of Election or Appointment.
Joseph H. Pendergast	48 Chelsea st	Councilman	$300 yr	Dec. 15, 1908
Dennis A. O'Neil	195 Havre st	"	300 "	" 15, 1908
Michael J. Brophy	268 Maverick st	"	300 "	" 15, 1908

Ward 3.

Name.	Residence.	Designation.	Compensation.	Date of Election or Appointment.
James J. Brennan	176 Chelsea st	Councilman	$300 yr	Dec. 15, 1908
Joseph A. Dart	26 Decatur st	"	300 "	" 15, 1908
William J. Murray	44 Corey st	"	300 "	" 15, 1908

Common Council.— Continued.

Name.	Residence.	Designation.	Compensation.	Date of Election or Appointment.
Ward 4.				
Francis M. Ducey	330 Bunker Hill st	Councilman	$300 yr	Dec. 15, 1908
Patrick B. Carr	560 Medford st	"	300 "	" 15, 1908
James I. Green	117 Baldwin st	"	300 "	" 15, 1908
Ward 5.				
John J. Buckley	33 Cordis st	Councilman	$300 yr	Dec. 15, 1908
William E. Carney	72 Washington st	"	300 "	" 15, 1908
Edward A. Troy	19 Ellwood st	"	300 "	" 15, 1908
Ward 6.				
Stephen Gardella	30 Hull st	Councilman	$300 yr	Dec. 15, 1908
Francis D. O'Donnell	404 Hanover st	"	300 "	" 15, 1908
Alfred Scigliano	144 North st	"	300 "	" 15, 1908
Ward 7.				
John L. Donovan	14 Noanet st	Councilman	$300 yr	Dec. 15, 1908
John T. Kennedy	35 Carver st	"	300 "	" 15, 1908
Dominick F. Spellman	31 Tyler st	"	300 "	" 15, 1908
Ward 8.				
James J. Ryan	54 Spring st	Councilman	$300 yr	Dec. 15, 1908
James A. Bragan	68 Causeway st	"	300 "	" 15, 1908
Adolphus M. Burroughs	36 McLean st	"	300 "	" 15, 1908
Ward 9.				
Isaac Gordon	77 Village st	Councilman	$300 yr	Dec. 15, 1908
Robert J. Howell	107 Union Park st	"	300 "	" 15, 1908
Thomas B. McKeagney	15 Taylor st	"	300 "	" 15, 1908
Ward 10.				
J. Henderson Allston	10 Dundee st	Councilman	$300 yr	Dec. 15, 1908
Channing H. Cox	Hotel Westminster	"	300 "	" 15, 1908
William S. Kinney	406 Columbus ave	"	300 "	" 15, 1908
Ward 11.				
Courtenay Crocker	343 Commonwealth ave	Councilman	$300 yr	Dec. 15, 1908
Theodore Hoague	75 Mt. Vernon st	"	300 "	" 15, 1908
Charles H. Moore	59 Pinckney st	"	300 "	" 15, 1908
Ward 12.				
Seth Fenelon Arnold	94 Worcester st	Councilman	$300 yr	Dec. 15, 1908
Alfred G. Davis	692 Tremont st	"	300 "	" 15, 1908
Francis J. H. Jones	625 Columbus ave	"	300 "	" 15, 1908
Ward 13.				
Leo F. McCullough	89 Auckland st	Councilman	$300 yr	Dec. 15, 1908
Stephen A. Welch	37 A st	"	300 "	" 15, 1908
Coleman E. Kelly	82 Eighth st	"	300 "	" 15, 1908
Ward 14.				
Cornelius J. Fitzgerald	4 G st	Councilman	$300 yr	Dec. 15, 1908
Thomas J. Casey	233 K st	"	300 "	" 15, 1908
Joseph L. Collins	753 E. Broadway	"	300 "	" 15, 1908

Common Council.— Concluded.

Name.	Residence.	Designation.	Compensation.	Date of Election or Appointment.
Ward 15.				
John O'Hara	10 Vale st	Councilman	$300 yr	Dec. 15, 1908
William T. Conway	5 Telegraph st	"	300 "	" 15, 1908
Joseph A. O'Bryan	9 Telegraph st	"	300 "	" 15, 1908
Ward 16.				
John D. McGivern	10 Boston st	Councilman	$300 yr	Dec. 15, 1908
Hugh M. Garrity	153 E. Cottage st	"	300 "	" 15, 1908
William D. McCarthy	18 Edison green	"	300 "	" 15, 1908
Ward 17.				
Thomas M. Joyce	25 Adams st	Councilman	$300 yr	Dec. 15, 1908
Francis J. Brennan	292 Dudley st	"	300 "	" 15, 1908
John D. Connors	100 Burrell st	"	300 "	" 15, 1908
Ward 18.				
Daniel F. Cronin	79 W. Lenox st	Councilman	$300 yr	Dec. 15, 1908
Michael F. O'Brien	82 Roxbury st	"	300 "	" 15, 1908
George Kenney	259 Cabot st	"	300 "	" 15, 1908
Ward 19.				
Peter A. Hoban	116 Parker Hill ave	Councilman	$300 yr	Dec. 15, 1908
William J. Kohler	10 Conant st	"	300 "	" 15, 1908
John J. Donovan	40 Terrace st	"	300 "	" 15, 1908
Ward 20.				
Charles T. Harding	3 Clement st	Councilman	$300 yr	Dec. 15, 1908
Harry R. Cumming	608 Park st	"	300 "	" 15, 1908
William Smith, Jr	79 Sydney st	"	300 "	" 15, 1908
Ward 21.				
William N. Hackett	5 St. James ter	Councilman	$300 yr	Dec. 15, 1908
John Ballantyne	63 Copeland st	"	300 "	" 15, 1908
Walter R. Meins	171 Humboldt ave	"	300 "	" 15, 1908
Ward 22.				
William H. Morgan	45 Oakview ter	Councilman	$300 yr	Dec. 15, 1908
George Penshorn	3 Atherton st	"	300 "	" 15, 1908
Bernhard G. Krug	7 Brookside ave	"	300 "	" 15, 1908
Ward 23.				
George W. Carruth	rear 765 South st	Councilman	$300 yr	Dec. 15, 1908
George W. Smith	4181 Washington st	"	300 "	" 15, 1908
Ward D. Prescott	34 Cohasset st	"	300 "	" 15, 1908
Ward 24.				
Frank B. Crane	61 Dracut st	Councilman	$300 yr	Dec. 15, 1908
James A. Hart	1892 Dorchester ave	"	300 "	" 15, 1908
Clifford C. Best	6 Whitney pk	"	300 "	" 15, 1908
Ward 25.				
Edward C. Webster	241 Cambridge st	Councilman	$300 yr	Dec. 15, 1908
George C. McCabe	66 Murdock st	"	300 "	" 15, 1908
Charles H. Warren	87 Etna st	"	300 "	" 15, 1908
Clerk's Office.				
Joseph O'Kane	40 Blakeville st	Clerk	$3,500 yr	Jan. 5, 1885
Alice M. McCarty	40 Blakeville st	Assistant	1,100 "	" 5, 1885
James Celeste	107 Leverett st	Messenger	800 "	July 28, 1903

Art Department.

Name.	Residence.	Designation.	Compensation.	Date of Election or Appointment.
Samuel D. Warren†	261 Marlboro st	Chairman	None	Oct. 19, 1903
Francis W. Chandler	195 Marlboro st	Commissioner	"	May 1, 1899
Alex W. Longfellow	12 Mt. Vernon st	"	"	" 11, 1900
Arthur F. Estabrook	346 Commonwealth ave	"	"	Feb. 19, 1909
J. Templeton Coolidge, Jr.	114 Beacon st	Secretary	"	May 7, 1900
Henry C. Greene	111 Chestnut st	Temporary Clerk	$300 yr	Nov. 6, 1908

Assessing Department.

Name.	Residence.	Designation.	Compensation.	Date of Election or Appointment.
John J. Murphy	541 Dudley st	Principal Ass'r, Chairman	$4,500 yr	Feb. 17, 1885
Charles E. Folsom	30 Esmond st	" Secretary	4,200 "	Aug. 2, 1898
Fred E. Bolton	26 Dunreath st	Principal Assessor	4,000 "	Oct. 27, 1907
James Buckner	80 Brighton ave	"	4,000 "	" 25, 1898*
Edward B. Daily	7 Akron st	"	4,000 "	April 28, 1891*
John H. Donovan	26 Potosi st	"	4,000 "	Aug. 1, 1898*
Frederick H. Temple	234 Bunker Hill st	"	4,000 "	Feb. 3, 1903*
William H. Allen	57 Harvest st	First Assistant Assessor	1,000 "	April, 1901*
Alonzo F. Andrews	58 Waverly st	" "	1,000 "	" 1894
Matthew Binney, Jr.	48 Winthrop st	" "	1,000 "	" 1900
Thomas H. Bond	15 Linden st., Alls	" "	1,000 "	" 1895
Benjamin F. Bowditch	20 Trenton st	" "	1,000 "	" 1899*
Alexander P. Brown	110 Draper st	" "	1,000 "	Feb. 15, 1904*
Fred W. Burleigh	33 Radford lane	" "	1,000 "	April 30, 1908
Harry C. Byrne	31 Sherman st	" "	1,000 "	" 10, 1906*
John C. Cook	12 Rockville pk	" "	1,000 "	" 1884*
David W. Creed	204 Dorchester st	" "	1,000 "	" 30, 1908
William A. Creney	3 W. Cottage st	" "	1,000 "	Feb. 11, 1904*
William H. Cuddy	22 N. Anderson st	" "	1,000 "	April, 1900
Joseph D. Dillworth	74 Harold st	" "	1,000 "	" 30, 1908*
Michael F. Dolan	715 Centre st	" "	1,000 "	" 1896
Charles J. Dowd	11 Isabella st	" "	1,000 "	" 1901*
Daniel A. Downey	92 Sheridan st	" "	1,000 "	" 1891
A. Glendon Dyar	12 Greenwich pk	" "	1,000 "	" 1899
Terence F. Feely	1112A Washington st	" "	1,000 "	Jan. 19, 1904*
Benjamin M. Fiske	124 Academy Hill rd	" "	1,000 "	April, 1895*
James P. Fox	104 Calumet st	" "	1,000 "	" 1894*
Warren F. Freeman	14 Chilton rd	" "	1,000 "	Dec. 23, 1905
John H. Giblin	33 Adams st	" "	1,000 "	April, 1872*
William N. Goodwin	26 Harley st	" "	1,000 "	" 1902*
Warren B. Hadley	Waverley House, Chsn	" "	1,000 "	" 30, 1908*
John E. Heslan	37 Arklow st	" "	1,000 "	" 1900
John H. Hout	412 E. Eighth st	" "	1,000 "	" 30, 1908
Henry J. Ireland	132 Hudson st	" "	1,000 "	" 1899*
Joseph T. Lyons	132 Thornton st	" "	1,000 "	" 1901
John Marno	37 Princeton st	" "	1,000 "	Nov. 23, 1905
Thomas O. McEnaney	417 Meridian st	" "	1,000 "	April, 1892
Frederick L. McGowan	344 Park st	" "	1,000 "	March, 1909
James I. Moore	13 Pacific st	" "	1,000 "	April, 1892
James F. Morgan	85 Albion st	" "	1,000 "	" 1902*
Timothy J. Murphy	382 Hanover st	" "	1,000 "	Feb. 5, 1903*
Timothy W. Murphy	1692 Washington st	" "	1,000 "	April, 1900*
Philip O'Brien	193 Hanover st	" "	1,000 "	Jan. 19, 1904
Frederick F. O'Doherty	364 E st	" "	1,000 "	" 19, 1904
James H. Phelan	22 Belvidere st	" "	1,000 "	April, 1905
G. Frederick Pierce	835 Adams st., Dor	" "	1,000 "	March, 1909
Frank S. Pratt	28 St. John st	" "	1,000 "	April, 1885
Joseph T. Preston	1 Ashland st	" "	1,000 "	" 1900*
Nathan P. Ryder	590 Blue Hill ave	" "	1,000 "	" 1896
Arthur W. Smith	144 Warren st	" "	1,000 "	" 30, 1908
Edwin R. Spinney	594 E. Eighth st	" "	1,000 "	" 1896*
Charles A. Tilden	108 Falcon st	" "	1,000 "	" 1895
George W. Warren	33 Chestnut Hill ave	" "	1,000 "	" 1880*
Frederick A. H. Bennett	10 E. Dedham st	Second Assistant Assessor	5.00 day	" 1895
Robert C. Bradbury	2 Madison st	" "	5.00 "	" 26, 1909*
William A. Brade	25 Cortes st	" "	5.00 "	" 30, 1908
Frederick M. Brinnick	47 Kilton st	" "	5.00 "	" 30, 1908
Michael C. Broughal	582 River st	" "	5.00 "	" 30, 1908
Louis Burkhardt	14 Highland st	" "	5.00 "	" 1897
Patrick F. Carley	224 N. Harvard st	" "	5.00 "	" 1892

* Previously in the department.   † Original appointment September 14, 1898.

Assessing Department. — Continued.

Name.	Residence.	Designation.	Compensation.	Date of Election or Appointment.
William H. Coblentz	75 Shawmut ave	Second Assistant Assessor	$5.00 day.	April 9, 1907
Jacob Cohen	8 Balfour st., Dor	" "	5.00 "	" 26, 1909
John P. Cottrell	4 Bunker Hill st	" "	5.00 "	1905
James J. Crowley	16 School st	" "	5.00 "	" 30, 1908
John J. Devlin	95 Warren ave	" "	5.00 "	" 30, 1908
James F. Dowling	77 Wenham st	" "	5.00 "	1898
Clinton P. Duryea	76 Aldrich st	" "	5.00 "	" 30, 1908
Joseph Esselen	839 Parker st	" "	5.00 "	" 30, 1908
Daniel J. Falvey	215 Harrison ave	" "	5.00 "	1903
William M. Farrington	13 Farrington ave	" "	5.00 "	1904
Richard F. Field	21 Beacon st	" "	5.00 "	" 30, 1908
Redmond S. Fitzgerald	58 Norton st	" "	5.00 "	" 30, 1908
Frederick T. Griffin	70 W. Cedar st	" "	5.00 "	" 30, 1908
Charles F. Holmes	105 Union Park st	" "	5.00 "	1905
Albert W. Huebener	159 Granite ave	" "	5.00 "	1901
Loyal L. Jenkins	312 Meridian st	" "	5.00 "	March 16, 1909
William J. Keenan	15 Warrenton st	" "	5.00 "	April, 1905
John F. Kinney	174 Ward st	" "	5.00 "	May 1, 1905
George E. Leet	208 Lexington st	" "	5.00 "	April 30, 1908
Cornelius N. Liston	272 E. Ninth st	" "	5.00 "	" 30, 1908
Ward A. Marsh	14 Edson st	" "	5.00 "	" 10, 1906
John S. McDonough	35 Howell st	" "	5.00 "	" 9, 1907
Augustus D. McLellan	670 Tremont st	" "	5.00 "	March 16, 1909
James McNulty	46 Cooper st	" "	5.00 "	April, 1901
Walter E. Merriam	394 Centre st	" "	5.00 "	" 30, 1908
James H. Mugridge	18 Vine st	" "	5.00 "	" 30, 1908
John J. O'Neil	1393 Dorchester ave	" "	5.00 "	" 30, 1908
Lucian J. Priest	2 Pearl st	" "	5.00 "	" 30, 1900
William F. Prindeville	97 Montebello rd	" "	5.00 "	" 10, 1906
Frank J. Riley	26 Savin st	" "	5.00 "	" 10, 1906
Joseph F. Ripp	238 E st	" "	5.00 "	1899
Patrick J. Roche	245 K st	" "	5.00 "	1902
Saverio R. Romano	247 Hanover st	" "	5.00 "	May 2, 1904*
Frederick F. Smith	2 Byron st	" "	5.00 "	April, 1904
Michael J. Toumey	403 Charles st	" "	5.00 "	1902
Charles H. Turner	166 W. Broadway	" "	5.00 "	1902
George Uriot	573 Beech st., Ros.	" "	5.00 "	1902
Alfred L. Whitney	285 Webster st., E. B.	" "	5.00 "	" 30, 1903
Jacob Rosenberg	81 Brighton st	" "	5.00 "	March 16, 1909
Edward T. Kelly	11 Schuyler st	Chief Clerk	3,000 yr.	Sept. 1, 1897*
Correl Kendall	26 High Rock way	Assistant Clerk	2,400 "	" 1, 1897*
Frank M. Finnegan	9 Homes ave., Dor.	Clerk	1,800 "	June 1, 1903*
Jeremiah W. Fogarty	88 Moreland st., Rox.	Conveyancing Clerk	2,500 "	May 1, 1896*
Chris. I. FitzGerald	15 Sargent st	Clerk	2,400 "	Feb. 1, 1907*
Dennis J. Gorman	62 Forest st., Rox.	"	2,400 "	" 1, 1907*
Timothy J. Crowley	37 Mt. Vernon st	Bank and Probate Clerk	2,200 "	" 13, 1907*
John H. Parker	228 Shawmut ave	Assistant Bank Clerk	Per item	May 1, 1866
John F. Sweeney	108 Draper st., Dor.	Asst. Conveyancing Clerk	$1,500 yr.	April, 1896*
Fred S. Hunter	82 Woolson st	Engineer	2,200 "	May 1, 1896
George E. Richardson	13 Tremlett street	Office and Street Clerk	2,500 "	April, 1857
Simeon Adams	80 Waumbeck st	" " "	⎫	June, 1900*
Moses Berger	21 Lambert ave., Rox	" " "		April, 1894*
Francis T. Browne	287 K st	" " "		" 27, 1905*
Harrison G. O. Browning	20 Clarkwood st	" " "		" 1896*
Edward M. J. Burke	186 Northampton st	" " "		May 1, 1908*
Michael J. Carr	14 Page st., Dor.	" " "		April 27, 1905*
Octavius Cate	19 Whiting st., Rox	" " "		" 1868
Hugh J. Crane	9 Marion st., Chsn.	" " "		" 1896*
Joseph H. Dalton	106 White st., E. B.	" " "	$5.00 per	June 16, 1874*
Joseph P. Dempsey	108 I st., S. B.	" " "	day for	May 1, 1908*
Frank F. Derby	12 Laurel st., Rox.	" " "	street work;	June 16, 1898*
John D. Fogarty	14 Savin st., Rox.	" " "	office work,	April, 1886
James E. Gallagher	96 Franklin st., Bri.	" " "	per item,	" 1894
Alban S. Green	93 Gainsboro st	" " "	on basis of	" 1875
John B. Kelley	27 Blakeville st	" " "	50 to 75	" 1898*
John H. A. Krauss	26 Walter st., Ros.	" " "	cents	April, 1902*
Edgar H. Loveren	92 Temple st., W. Rox	" " "	per hour.	" 1887*
Patrick J. Marron	45 Allen st	" " "		" 1895*
Edwin A. Millard	11 Helen st., Dor.	" " "		" 1875
John F. Miller	Meredith st., W. Rox	" " "		" 1895*
Joseph G. O'Malley	9 Fremont ave., Rox	" " "		" 1907*
William Penn	22 Rosedale st., Dor.	" " "		" 1893*
Daniel F. Ryan	109 Calumet st., Rox	" " "	⎭	May 1, 1908*

* Previously in the department.

Assessing Department. — Concluded.

Name.	Residence.	Designation.	Compensation.	Date of Election or Appointment.
Joseph E. Ryan	9 Milford st	Office and Street Clerk ... ⎫		May, 1900
William Sawyer	49 Oak square ave	" "		April, 1874
Timothy F. Sullivan	33 Sherman st., Rox	" "		June 16, 1903*
William H. Vannevar	10 Hartwell st., Rox	" "		April, 1874
Benson B. Banker	19 Cottage side	Street Clerk		" 1904
Thomas F. Carr	5 Gloucester pl	"	$5.00 per	" 1909
William O. Childs	21 Sargent st	"	day for	" 1890
Arthur L. Curry	106 Cedar st., Rox	"	street work;	March 31, 1908
Arthur H. Fogarty	88 Moreland st	"	office work,	April 30, 1906
Oscar L. Lomasney	38 Brookside ave	" ⎬	per item	" 1907
Charles J. McCarthy, Jr	50 Linwood st	"	on basis of	" 1909
Charles V. McNulty	30 Pearl st., Chsn	"	50 to 75	March 31, 1908
William M. O'Brien	48 Laurel st., Rox	"	cents	April, 1907
John P. Ogden	20 Newton st., Bri	"	per hour.	" 1892
Joseph M. Smart	237 Eustis st	"		" 1909
Alfred Spear	1098 Washington st	"		Feb. 16, 1905
Louis J. Sullivan	63 Old Harbor st	"		April, 1908
Bernard L. Watson	9 Abbotsford st	"		" 1909
Frank J. Williams	1692 Washington st	" ⎭		" 1898

Auditing Department.

Name.	Residence.	Designation.	Compensation.	Date of Election or Appointment.
J. Alfred Mitchell†	796 E. Fourth st	City Auditor	$6,000 yr	Nov. 23, 1904*
Julien C. Haynes	194 Huntington ave	Assistant City Auditor and Chief Clerk	3,600 "	" 25, 1904*
William H. Hayward	1134 Boylston st	Bond and Interest Clerk	3,000 "	July 20, 1882
Rupert S. Carven	56 Baldwin st	Income and Pay Roll Clerk	2,700 "	March 24, 1885
Henry E. Keenan	50 Wellington Hill st	Abstract Clerk	2,400 "	Aug. 1, 1886
Richard D. Cleary	52 Alleghany st	Sub-division Clerk	2,400 "	" 7, 1888
George W. Currier	147 Belgrade ave	" "	2,400 "	Feb. 11, 1874
Pierce J. O'Connell	52 Coolidge rd	" "	2,000 "	May 25, 1891
Cornelius F. Donovan	4 Calumet st	Contract Clerk	2,200 "	March 25, 1885
John J. Gateley	101 Brown ave	County and General Clerk	2,200 "	Sept. 1, 1888
Maurice H. Cobe	5 Harvard ave	Clerk	1,800 "	" 25, 1895
Arthur W. Ferreira	80 Patten st	"	1,800 "	" 19, 1898
John J. Marshall	133 Calumet st	"	1,600 "	Dec. 19, 1904
Charles L. Sullivan	78 Village st	"	1,300 "	June 1, 1907
Elmer B. Derby	3 Smith ct	"	1,100 "	Dec. 29, 1899
Joseph L. Flanagan	3 Eaton st	Messenger	1,300 "	July 2, 1896

Bath Department.

Name.	Residence.	Designation.	Compensation.	Date of Election or Appointment.
Joseph B. Maccabe	198 Trenton st., E. B	Chairman Trustees	None	Sept. 29, 1908
Lawrence M. Stockton	31 Commonwealth ave	Vice-Chairman Trustees	"	" 30, 1908
Mrs. Lawrence J. Logan	560 Broadway	Trustee	"	March 14, 1898
George B. Morison	841 Boylston st	"	"	Sept. 30, 1908
James F. Sweeney	Hotel Eastgate	"	"	" 29, 1908
Mrs. A. J. Bulger	61 Monmouth st	"	"	Dec. 2, 1908
Walter R. Mansfield	202 Huntington ave	"	"	" 29, 1908
Joseph P. O'Brien	335 Shawmut ave	General Superintendent	$2,200 yr	June 17, 1904*
James L. Walsh	56 Bakersfield st	Chief Instructor	2,000 "	Nov. 1, 1901
Mary L. MacCool	163 Devon st	Clerk	1,200 "	Oct. 25, 1901

Cabot Street Bath House and Gymnasium.

Name.	Residence.	Designation.	Compensation.	Date of Election or Appointment.
Matthew M. Leary	334 Meridian st	Instructor	$23.00 wk	June 17, 1904*
David M. Owens	4½ Sumner pl., Rox	Custodian	3.00 day	Dec. 20, 1905
Averland L. Foster	2 Chambers st	Fireman	2.84 "	Sept. 23, 1905
Kieran McManus	1177 Tremont st	"	2.84 "	Oct. 12, 1905
William C. Rowe	644 E. Fifth st	Swimming Instructor	2.75 "	June 18, 1900
Harry A. Grainger	477 Meridian st	"	2.50 "	" 25, 1906*
William Metzger	14 Day st	Assistant Custodian	2.50 "	Dec. 29, 1905*
Thomas J. Shannon	25 Phillips st., Rox	Janitor	2.50 "	Nov. 18, 1904*

* Promoted to present position on date given.   Previously in department.
† See, also, County of Suffolk and Sinking Funds Department.

Bath Department.— Continued.

Name.	Residence.	Designation.	Compensation.	Date of Election or Appointment.

Cabot Street Bath House and Gymnasium.—Concluded.

Name.	Residence.	Designation.	Compensation.	Date of Election or Appointment.
Charles Bleiler	112 Heath st	Janitor	$2.25 day	Feb. 1, 1901
Jerome S. Morris	8 Valentine st	"	2.25 "	Jan. 24, 1902
Patrick F. O'Melia	1122 Tremont st	"	2.25 "	Feb. 14, 1905*
James Kilduff	67 Cabot st	Life Guard and Helper	2.25 "	Sept. 22, 1905*
Richard P. Morrissey	1275 Massachusetts ave	" "	2.25 "	Oct. 27, 1905*
John M. O'Brien	87 Hampshire st	" "	2.25 "	Aug. 4, 1907
Henry W. Walter	4 Noble court	" "	2.25 "	June 17, 1904
Catharine Daly	21 Delle ave., Rox	Matron	1.50 "	Jan. 16, 1901
Margaret L. Hickey	1122 Columbus ave	"	1.50 "	" 15, 1904
Catharine A. Hurley	263 Ruggles st	"	1.50 "	Oct. 11, 1905
Mary A. Maher	279 Roxbury st	"	1.50 "	" 11, 1905
Mary E. O'Connor	6 Hammett st	"	1.50 "	" 11, 1905
Ellen J. Sheehan	119 Cabot st	"	1.50 "	" 11, 1905
Catharine F. Muldoon	111 Vernon st	Pianist	1.00 "	" 9, 1905
Annie J. Gurry	994 Columbus ave	Charwoman	.50 "	Feb. 25, 1907

Dover Street Bath House and Laundry.

Name.	Residence.	Designation.	Compensation.	Date of Election or Appointment.
Timothy H. Sullivan	249 Dover st	Custodian	$3.00 day	June 17, 1904
John Stevens	127 River st	Engineer	3.00 "	Oct. 14, 1898
William Earle	23 Richfield st., Dor	"	18.00 wk	Jan. 1, 1900
Charles F. McDermott	29 East st	Machinist	2.50 day	June 28, 1900
William H. Monahan	4 Regent st	Janitor	2.50 "	Nov. 1, 1898
Michael J. O'Leary	28 W. Dedham st	"	2.50 "	July 14, 1902
John J. Barry	97 Tyler st	"	2.25 "	" 12, 1900
Joseph M. Horgan	14 Emerald st	"	2.25 "	April 29, 1898
James H. McGloan	540 Bremen st	Life Guard and Helper	2.25 "	Oct. 26, 1900
Margaret T. O'Brien	61 Dearborn st	Matron	2.00 "	" 14, 1898
Louise G. Clark	129 Marion st	"	10.00 wk	June 24, 1903*
Mary E. Hallinan	29 Woodlawn st	"	10.00 "	April 29, 1899
Margaret J. Killian	59 Delle ave., Rox	"	10.00 "	Nov. 20, 1899
Catharine Sullivan	22 North ave	"	10.00 "	Oct. 21, 1898
Catharine Barry	336 Border st	"	1.50 day	Sept. 13, 1901
Lucy McLaughlin	251 Dover st	"	1.50 "	June 16, 1905
Rose A. Wogan	45 Maywood st	"	1.50 "	May 30, 1901

D Street Gymnasium.

Name.	Residence.	Designation.	Compensation.	Date of Election or Appointment.
Joseph J. McNamara	4 Valentine st	Instructor	$23.00 wk	June 17, 1904
James P. Sweeney	321 Athens st	Custodian	3.00 day	Oct. 12, 1900
Peter F. McDonough	318 D st	Engineer	2.50 "	" 12, 1900
John T. Burke	271 Broadway	Janitor	2.25 "	" 26, 1899
John L. Lane	19 Knowlton st	"	2.25 "	" 26, 1899
George A. Melledy	290 Fifth st	"	2.25 "	Dec. 8, 1905*
Thomasine Downing	8 National st	Matron	1.50 "	Nov. 9, 1899
Mary A. Lamb	180 Hamilton st., Dor	"	1.50 "	" 9, 1899
Mary J. Eide	413 W. Fourth st	Pianist	1.00 "	Oct. 16, 1905
Ellen Fitzgibbons	628 E. Second st	Charwoman	.50 "	Nov. 10, 1899
Mary McIntire	294 Bolton st	"	.50 "	" 10, 1899

Ward 16 Gymnasium.

Name.	Residence.	Designation.	Compensation.	Date of Election or Appointment.
I. George DeCost	468 Quincy st	Instructor	$23.00 wk	Oct. 3, 1904
George T. Cuddihy	573 E. Broadway	Swimming Instructor	2.50 day	" 12, 1906*
James W. Hurley	82 Chelsea st., E. B	"	2.50 "	May 27, 1898
Leo C. Kneble	202 L st	Assistant Instructor	2.25 "	Nov. 21, 1904
Frank J. Pendergast	64 Auckland st	Janitor	2.25 "	Oct. 20, 1905*
Dennis A. Sullivan	91 Minot st	Life Guard and Helper	2.25 "	Nov. 21, 1904*
John A. Long	31 Hyde Park ave	" "	2.25 "	July 7, 1898
Hannah Donnelly	16 Dromey st	Matron	1.50 "	Nov. 21, 1904
Lillian A. Graham	753 Dorchester ave	"	1.50 "	" 21, 1904
Mary A. Sullivan	102 Fellows st	"	1.50 "	March 29, 1909
Annie M. Kelly	19 Morrill st	Pianist	1.00 "	April 6, 1908

*Promoted to present position on date given. Previously in the department.

Bath Department.— Continued.

Name.	Residence.	Designation.	Compeusation.	Date of Election or Appointment.

East Boston Gymnasium.

Name.	Residence.	Designation.	Compeusation.	Date of Election or Appointment.
Henry A. Higgins	401 Saratoga st	Instructor	$23.00 wk	June 17, 1904*
Thomas Holmes	195 Webster st	Custodian	3.00 day	April 25, 1898
Thomas H. Casey	56 Patten st	Life Guard and Helper	2.50 "	Sept. 18, 1898
Samuel Carter	246 Webster st	Janitor	2.25 "	April 25, 1898
Bernard J. Maguire	152 Bremen st	"	2.25 "	June 30, 1899
Colin F. McDonald	166 Paris st	"	2.25 "	" 24, 1898
Margaret English	27 Maverick st	Matron	1.50 "	Oct. 2, 1900
Sarah Leonard	59 Newcomb st	"	1.50 "	April 27, 1898
Lillian M. Mountain	200 Lexington st	Pianist	1.50 "	" 27, 1898
Annie Belanger	12 Haynes st	Charwoman	.50 "	Jan. 1, 1899
Nellie Jones	24 Decatur st., E. B.	"	.50 "	Dec. 23, 1903
Bridget Goss	41 Chelsea st., E. B.	"	.50 "	" 10, 1905

Ward 7 Gymnasium.

Name.	Residence.	Designation.	Compeusation.	Date of Election or Appointment.
John A. Lane	468 Quincy st	Instructor	$23.00 wk	Oct. 12, 1905*
William J. Healy	322 W. Fourth st	Janitor	2.25 day	March 21, 1902
John J. Quigley	652 Saratoga st	Life Guard and Helper	2.25 "	June 1, 1898
Alice C. Bearens	30 Forest st	Matron	1.50 "	April 13, 1909
Ellen A. Collins	32 W. Fifth st	Charwoman	.50 "	Oct. 11, 1901
Mary A. Powers	86 Hudson st	"	.50 "	" 11, 1901
Rose B. Sullivan	23 Blakeville st	Pianist	1.00 "	Nov. 16, 1908

Ward 9 Gymnasium.

Name.	Residence.	Designation.	Compeusation.	Date of Election or Appointment.
John J. Driscoll	82 Bayswater st	Instructor	$23.00 wk	June 17, 1904*
Joseph R. Havey	99 Union Park st	Custodian	3.00 day	Oct. 12, 1900
Thomas M. Curley	80 Malden st	Janitor	2.25 "	Dec. 30, 1904
William E. Kennedy	19 Savoy st	Life Guard and Helper	2.25 "	Nov. 5, 1905*
Hannah McDonald	43 Woodcliff st	Matron	1.50 "	Oct. 16, 1900
Nellie A. Wigmore	94 Tyler st	"	1.50 "	" 9, 1906*
Bella E. Crawford	16 Savoy st	Pianist	1.00 "	" 16, 1900
Nora Donoghue	1466 Washington st	Charwoman	.50 "	" 16, 1900
Catharine McManus	45 E. Dedham st	"	.50 "	July 26, 1901

North Bennet Street Bath House.

Name.	Residence.	Designation.	Compeusation.	Date of Election or Appointment.
Patrick J. Sheerin	239 W. Third st	Fireman	$2.84 day	April 6, 1909
Joseph H. Weston	76 Clayton st	"	2.84 "	Aug. 30, 1908
Joseph E. Denton	36 N. Bennet st	Life Guard and Helper	2.25 "	April 6, 1909*
Daniel H. Slattery	15 Unity st	"	2.25 "	June 22, 1907*
James P. Saunders	64 Bennington st	Repairer	2.25 "	July 12, 1898
Ida Goldberg	49 Salem st	Matron	1.50 "	Oct. 15, 1901
Theresa Lagoria	1 Unity st	"	1.50 "	July 2, 1907

Copley School Baths.

Name.	Residence.	Designation.	Compeusation.	Date of Election or Appointment.
George T. Maloney	15 Beacham st	Janitor	$2.25 day	April 18, 1907*
Ellen L. Devaney†	288 Bunker Hill st	Janitress	2.00 "	" 16, 1907
Catherine Dunn	53 Tufts st	Matron	1.25 "	" 16, 1907

Sewing.

Name.	Residence.	Designation.	Compeusation.	Date of Election or Appointment.
Mary E. McCarthy	23 Border st	Sewing	$1.25 day	Dec. 21, 1908
Nellie Morley	321 Dudley st	"	1.25 "	" 17, 1908
Mary A. Moynihan	282 Fifth st	"	1.25 "	" 17, 1908*
Ellen O'Connell	69 Clarkson st	"	1.25 "	" 17, 1908*

L Street Bath House.

Name.	Residence.	Designation.	Compeusation.	Date of Election or Appointment.
Michael F. Kelly	221 L st	Custodian	$2.75 day	July 8, 1904*
Edward F. Doherty	252 Sixth st	Life Guard and Helper	2.25 "	June 15, 1906*
Theodore L. Stowe	813 Broadway	Assistant Custodian	2.25 "	" 1, 1895*

* Promoted to present position on date given. Previously in the department.
† Employed in the Bath Department during the evening for shower bathing at the Copley School.

Bath Department.— Concluded.

Name.	Residence.	Designation.	Compensation.	Date of Election or Appointment.

North End Park.

Name.	Residence.	Designation.	Compensation.	Date of Election or Appointment.
John W. Lawton	26 Havre st	Custodian	$3.00 day.	May 27, 1898
Martin J. Clougherty	71 Charter st	Life Guard and Helper	2.50 "	Jan. 2, 1906
Eugene F. O'Donnell	23 Everett st., E. B.	"	2.50 "	June 26, 1899

Floating Bath Houses and General Repairing.

Name.	Residence.	Designation.	Compensation.	Date of Election or Appointment.
William T. Bibbey	462 Meridian st	Custodian	$2.75 day.	May 12, 1890
Henry H. Griffin	36 Rockford st	Carpenter	2.75 "	April 1, 1898
John F. McQuillan	423 Bennington st	Custodian	2.50 "	May 28, 1897
Edward A. Swett	137 London st	"	2.50 "	June 1, 1872
Timothy Harrington	45 Hale st	Assistant Custodian	2.50 "	May 28, 1896
Joseph F. Hussey	11 Meridian st	Cooper	2.50 "	" 27, 1898
George P. Quinn	90 Chelsea st., E. B.	Life Guard and Helper	2.50 "	July 15, 1898
Joseph A. McIntire	58 Nashua st	Custodian	2.25 "	Aug. 24, 1893
Benjamin R. Austin	262 Bremen st	Life Guard and Helper	2.25 "	June 25, 1899
Hugh J. Conway	138 Medford st	"	2.25 "	March 29, 1907*
Joseph R. Dolan	9 Reading st	"	2.25 "	April 8, 1907
Timothy F. Keneally	5 Gould's ct	"	2.25 "	July 22, 1898
James H. Leonard	rear 152 Havre st	"	2.25 "	June 17, 1898
Daniel J. Ahern	62 Condor st	Janitor	2.25 "	Aug. 2, 1901
Joseph G. Finn	794 Saratoga st	"	2.25 "	June 29, 1905*
Frank N. Kivenaar	305 Sumner st., E. B.	"	2.25 "	" 20, 1901
Michael O'Meara	175 Maverick st	"	2.25 "	" 23, 1905
Edward O'Keefe	376 Bremen st	"	2.25 "	" 27, 1901

Automobile for Delivery of Supplies.

Name.	Residence.	Designation.	Compensation.	Date of Election or Appointment.
Frank P. Guthrie	638 E. Seventh st	Chauffeur	$2.25 day.	July 18, 1906
Robert A. Jones	95 Union Park st	Janitor	2.25 "	June 23, 1905

Employed at Gymnasiums.

Name.	Residence.	Designation.	Compensation.	Date of Election or Appointment.
Dr. Eliza A. Dadmun	483 Beacon st	Medical Examiner	$200 yr.	Dec. 5, 1905
Dr. Helen I. Doherty		"	200 "	Oct. 1, 1899
Dr. Laura A. C. Hughes	96 Huntington av	"	200 "	" 15, 1900
Dr. Edward J. Denning	246 Broadway	"	150 "	Dec. 5, 1905
Dr. James C. Donoghue	214 Newbury st	"	150 "	Oct. 15, 1901
Dr. Francis D. Donoghue	864 Beacon st	"	150 "	" 16, 1908*
Dr. Francis X. Mahoney	701 Columbia rd., Dor.	"	150 "	" 16, 1908
Dr. Daniel A. O'Shea	49 Chelsea st., E. B.	"	150 "	" 15, 1900
Dr. William R. Woodbury	175 Newbury st	Medical Director	150 "	" 15, 1900

Boston Infirmary Department.

Name.	Residence.	Designation.	Compensation.	Date of Election or Appointment.
Edward M. Gallagher	58 Lexington st	Chairman Trustees	None	April 29, 1907
Mary A. Dierkes	33 Mill st	Secretary Trustees	"	" 29, 1907
Max E. Wyzanski	46 Moreland st	Trustee	"	" 29, 1907
Mrs. Jane S. Alexander	71 Gainsboro st	"	"	" 29, 1907
James A. Dorsey	45 Crawford st	"	"	" 29, 1907
Thomas A. McQuade	82 Tuttle st	"	"	" 29, 1907
Nathaniel W. Emerson, M. D., 244 Newbury st		"	"	May 25, 1908

Visiting Medical Staff of the Long Island Hospital.

Name.	Residence.	Designation.	Compensation.	Date of Election or Appointment.
James J. Minot, M. D.	188 Marlboro st	Pres., Visiting Physician	None	1895
E. Wyllys Taylor, M. D.	457 Marlboro st	Sec., Visiting Neurologist	"	July 26, 1895
Wilder Tileston, M. D.	117 Beacon st	Asst. Visiting Physician	"	June 29, 1903
Francis W. Palfrey, M. D.	88 Beacon st	" "	"	Sept. 14, 1905
Gerald Blake, M. D.	212 Beacon st	" "	"	Dec. 4, 1908
Walter E. Paul, M. D.	104 Marlboro st	Asst. Visiting Neurologist	"	Feb. 5, 1909
John Bapst Blake, M. D.	178 Beacon st	Visiting Surgeon	"	Dec. 7, 1905
John H. Cunningham, Jr., M. D., 829 Boylston st		Asst. Visiting Surgeon	"	Aug. 20, 1904
Frank H. Leahy, M. D.	827 Boylston st	" "	"	Feb. 5, 1909
Edward H. Bradford, M. D.133 Newbury st		Consulting Ortho. Surgeon	"	May 17, 1906*
Robert Soutter, M. D.	133 Newbury st	Visiting Ortho. Surgeon	"	" 1, 1908

* Promoted to present position on date given. Previously in the department.

Boston Infirmary Department.— Continued.

Name.	Residence.	Designation.	Compensation.	Date of Election or Appointment

Visiting Medical Staff of the Long Island Hospital.—Concluded.

Edwin N. Kent, D. M. D...Brookline.............Visiting Oral Surgeon.......None......Nov. 15, 1907
Wm. T. Councilman, M. D. 78 Bay State rd..........Visiting Pathologist........ " 1895
A. Rocke Robertson, M. D.†Brookline.............Pathologist............ " ......April 6, 1907
Fred M. Spalding, M. D... 665 Boylston st.........Visiting Ophthalmologist.... " ......Feb. 4, 1901
Arthur C. Jelly, M. D.....69 Newbury st............Consulting Psychiatrist..... " ......Jan. 26, 1905
Harvey P. Towle, M. D....453 Marlboro st..........Consulting Dermatologist... " ......May 1, 1908
James R. Torbert, M. D...252 Marlboro st..........Consulting Obstetrician..... " ......Oct. 16, 1908
John J. Hurley, M. D.....416 Marlboro st..........Visiting Aurist............ " ......April 13, 1907
Percy Brown, M. D.......155 Newbury st...........Radiologist.............. " ......June 7, 1906

Boston Office, 28 Court Square.

Isabel F. Gerrish.........39 Hartwell st..........Executive Clerk..........$1,200 yr...May 7, 1902*
Mary A. McGinley........90 Pinckney st...........Bookkeeper............. 1,200 " ...Feb. 1, 1905*
Elizabeth G. Nelson.......16 Myrtle st.............Clerk................ 900 " ... " 1, 1905
Lillian F. Corr (temporary) ,46 Maywood st........... " .... 600 " ...July 13, 1909

Boston Almshouse and Hospital.

(Receive board in addition to salary.)

Charles E. Donlan, M. D..35 Esmond st.............Superintendent............$2,500 yr...May 1, 1908
George W. Holmes, M. D..Long Island...........Resident Physician......... 1,500 " ...July 1, 1907
A. Rocke Robertson, M. D.§Brookline.............Pathologist, also on Visiting
　　　　　　　　　　　　　　　　　　　　Staff................. 500 " ...April 6, 1907
Charles C. Haskell, M. D..Long Island...........House Officer............None......July 1, 1908
Gordon B. Underwood.M.D. " .... " .... " ...... " 1, 1908
William T. Graham, M. D. " .... " .... " ......Nov. 1, 1908
James S. Tomkies, M. D.. " .... " .... " ...... " 1, 1908
Arthur S. Torrey, M. D.... " .... " .... " ......April 1, 1909
Thomas M. Connell, M. D.. " .... " .... " 1, 1909
Arthur P. Moran.........39 G st................Chief Officer, Men's Building,$1,000 yr...July 1, 1906
Timothy J. O'Donnell.....4 Mt. Vernon st., Dor......Chief Clerk............... 900 " ...Sept. 23, 1907
Matthew H. Doyle........22 Gates st ....Bookkeeper............. 360 " ...April 20, 1909
Mary E. Maloney.........Long Island.............Stenographer............ 360 " ...Feb. 1, 1908*
George J. Uriot ‡ §.......190 Harrison ave.........Messenger............... 120 " ...Nov. 1, 1907
William H. Lyng.........Long Island............Druggist.............. 720 " ...Oct. 15, 1903
Edward F. Hoynes........ " ....Storekeeper............. 480 " ...Nov. 1, 1908*
John E. Keogh...........8 Curtis st..............Meat Cutter............. 480 " ...April 7, 1909
William B. Corrigan......154 Quincy st............Chief Engineer.......... 1,200 " ...Sept. 1, 1906*
Andrew F. Murphy.......498 Fourth st............First Assistant Engineer .... 720 " ... " 1, 1906*
John Corey.............Long Island.............Assistant Engineer......... 600 " ... " 1, 1906*
Luke Cunniff............1 Beach street pl., Chsn.... " .... 600 " ...Oct. 15, 1907*
John Mulcahy...........Long Island,.............Fireman.............. 600 " ...March 1, 1905
John Sheridan........... " .... " .... 600 " ...Sept. 30, 1908
Walter J. West..........256 Webster st............ " .... 600 " ...Oct. 28, 1907
Timothy R. Mahoney.....6 Coleman st.............Head Farmer............ 600 " ...March 4, 1909
David I. Bagley.........Long Island............Assistant Farmer.......... 300 " ... " 19, 1908
Willard Lee............. " .... " .... 300 " ...Feb. 1, 1907
Walter Wicks........... " .... " .... 300 " ...June 9, 1908
Daniel B. Sheehan ....1334 Dorchester ave.......Gardener............... 420 " ...April 17, 1908
Richard Carrigan.........53 Preble st.............Carpenter.............. 660 " ...June 4, 1907
Thomas E. Murphy.......115 G st................Laundry Officer.......... 540 " ...Aug. 29, 1895*
Joseph A. Browne........55 High st., Chsn.........Watchman.............. 480 " ...May 14, 1906
Daniel F. Hurley.........75 Porter st., E. B......... " .... 480 " ...Aug. 28, 1906
Thomas D. Noonau......Long Island............. " .... 480 " ...Jan. 7, 1907
Hubert Dolan...........60 Bromley st., Rox......Baker................ 720 " ... " 7, 1907
Henry Sherman.........Long Island............Cook................ 600 " ...March 6, 1907
Catherine Sherman....... " .... " .... 360 " ... " 6, 1907
Margaret Kerrigan....... " .... " .... 360 " ...Feb. 26, 1908
Amy Whalen............ " .... " .... 360 " ...Sept. 11, 1907
Mary A. Sullivan........ " .... " .... 300 " ...April 15, 1909
Mary E. MacDonald..... " .... " .... 216 " ...Oct. 21, 1908
Margie Butters.......... " ....Substitute Cook.......... 300 " ...Jan. 16, 1909
Hilda V. Johnson........ " ....Head Matron .... 480 " ...April 1, 1908*
Mary E. Sheehan........ " ....Matron, Linen Room....... 360 " ...Feb. 1, 1908

† Also salaried pathologist at Boston Almshouse and Hospital, Long Island.
* Promoted to present position on date given. Previously in the department.
‡ See, also, Institutions Registration Department and Children's Institutions Department.
§ Without board.

Boston Infirmary Department.— Continued.

Name.	Residence.	Designation.	Compensation.	Date of Election or Appointment.

Boston Almshouse and Hospital.— Continued.

Name.	Residence.	Designation.	Compensation.	Date of Election or Appointment.
Ann Allinson	Long Island	Matron	$360 yr	Jan. 4, 1906
Catherine Burke	"	"	360 "	Oct. 1, 1907
Margaret E. Coleman	"	"	360 "	Sept. 17, 1906
Abbie A. Hill	"	"	360 "	April 1, 1902
Jessie A. MacDonald	"	"	360 "	Nov. 5, 1906
Annie M. McLaughlin	"	"	360 "	Feb. 12, 1908
Rosina M. Wade	"	"	360 "	Jan. 19, 1901
Mary A. Waldron	"	"	360 "	July 31, 1905
Josephine White	"	Housekeeper	360 "	May 27, 1908
Margaret J. Chisholm	"	Superintendent of Nurses	800 "	July 1, 1907*
Anna M. Allan	"	Head Nurse	360 "	Dec. 2, 1908*
Josephine S. Byrne	"	"	360 "	March 15, 1909
Margaret J. Campbell	"	"	420 "	Dec. 4, 1907*
Marie Graham	"	"	420 "	Sept. 8, 1902*
Margaret McMillan	"	"	360 "	March 6, 1909
Genevieve L. Senna	"	"	420 "	Jan. 25, 1908
Kate Tait	"	"	360 "	March 1, 1909
Margaret I. Anderson	"	Nurse	120 "	July 14, 1908
Emma B. Arnold	"	"	120 "	April 24, 1909
Mildred F. Ashley	"	"	120 "	July 15, 1908
Sarah A. Barry	"	"	120 "	Nov. 28, 1908
Margaret M. Breslin	"	"	120 "	Feb. 27, 1909
Ethel Burton	"	"	120 "	" 15, 1909
Isabella Coffey	"	"	144 "	Aug. 14, 1907*
Margaret Connolly	"	"	120 "	Jan. 9, 1909
Laura A. Conrad	"	"	144 "	" 15, 1908
Mary H. Donovan	"	"	120 "	Sept. 26, 1908
Flora A. Ducharme	"	"	120 "	" 8, 1908
Annie Farrell	"	"	120 "	Aug. 29, 1908
Lizzie A. Frazier	"	"	144 "	April 25, 1907
Margaret E. Hare	"	"	120 "	Nov. 14, 1908
Nellie V. Horan	"	"	144 "	Aug. 8, 1907
Eunice Humphrey	"	"	120 "	Oct. 29, 1908
Anna C. Knox	"	"	144 "	April 28, 1908
Bessie MacLean	"	"	144 "	Feb. 10, 1908
Anna L. Madden	"	"	144 "	Jan. 15, 1907
Catherine Malone	"	"	144 "	April 21, 1908
Nellie G. Mitchell	"	"	120 "	Oct. 29, 1908
Catherine C. McCall	"	"	144 "	March 5, 1908
Margaret M. McCloskey	"	"	144 "	Jan. 1, 1908
Annie C. McLaughlin	"	"	120 "	Aug. 29, 1908
Helen M. McLaughlin	"	"	120 "	March 24, 1909
Alice G. O'Malley	"	"	144 "	April 25, 1907
Eleanor E. O'Toole	"	"	120 "	Nov. 12, 1908
Astrid M. Peterson	"	"	120 "	Aug. 5, 1908
Laura M. Plaisted	"	"	120 "	May 9, 1908
Catherine M. Powers	"	"	144 "	Feb. 8, 1908
Blanche M. Sarr	"	"	120 "	Sept. 22, 1908
Mary Sheehan	"	"	144 "	Dec. 26, 1907
Rachel Simpson	"	"	120 "	Aug. 17, 1908
Ida M. Sirles	"	"	144 "	April 10, 1908
Marguerite M. Sullivan	"	"	144 "	Oct. 10, 1907
Mamie Theise	"	"	144 "	Feb. 12, 1908
Agnes D. Walsh	"	"	120 "	March 2, 1909
Edna A. Watson	"	"	144 "	May 15, 1907
Helena C. Whalen	"	"	120 "	Jan. 20, 1909
Charles E. Coombs	"	Orderly	360 "	Sept. 1, 1907
Elemuel S. Duggan	2 Savin st.	"	300 "	May 7, 1908
Thomas F. Hurley	Long Island	"	360 "	Oct. 15, 1903
John W. Kinnelly	"	"	360 "	Sept. 1, 1906
Joseph McConville	"	"	360 "	May 3, 1907
George Porter	"	"	300 "	April 19, 1909
William J. Rogers	11 Marion st., Chsn.	"	300 "	" 20, 1909
Rives Tatum	57 Norway st.	"	300 "	Oct. 31, 1908
Charles C. Ware	Long Island	"	360 "	Jan. 22, 1908
Catherine Corey	"	Housemaid	240 "	June 15, 1902*
Minnie Gillis	"	"	216 "	Feb. 23, 1909
Bessie Twomey	"	"	240 "	Aug. 1, 1904*
Isabel E. Ross	"	Wardmaid	216 "	May 20, 1907
Annie Smith	"	"	216 "	Dec. 17, 1907

* Promoted to present position on date given.   Previously in the department.

Boston Infirmary Department. — Concluded.

Name.	Residence.	Designation.	Compensation.	Date of Election or Appointment.

Boston Almshouse and Hospital.—Concluded.

Name.	Residence.	Designation.	Compensation.	Date of Election or Appointment.
Margaret Corey	Long Island	Laundress	$216 yr	Oct. 14, 1908
Emma Murphy	"	"	240 "	Sept. 19, 1904
Johanna Nilsson	"	"	240 "	Nov. 7, 1907
Jane Campbell	"	Substitute Laundress	216 "	April 1, 1909
Rev. Matthew McDonald, S.J.	"	Chaplain	600 "	Aug. 4, 1904
Rev. Geo. E. Stokes, D.D.†‡	Winthrop	"	600 "	" 1, 1908
Adelaide Donohoe†§	Everett	Organist	300 "	April, 1896
Clara W. Baker†‡	Somerville	"	150 "	Oct. 15, 1898

Almshouse, Charlestown.

Name.	Residence.	Designation.	Compensation.	Date of Election or Appointment.
Mary A. Morris	Almshouse	Superintendent	$1,200 yr	July 1, 1907*
Joseph E. McDermott, M.D.†385 Main st		Visiting Physician	480 "	May 1, 1903
Patrick Twomey	23 Downing st., Rox.	Farmer	480 "	June 1, 1904*
William J. Curry||	51 Tremont st., Chsn	Engineer	540 "	Aug. 14, 1907
Alfred J. Erickson	Almshouse	Substitute Engineer	540 "	March 1, 1909
Archibald F. Scott	"	Watchman	300 "	Dec. 18, 1906
Mary J. Furlong	"	Matron	300 "	March, 1890
Beatrice Fox	"	"	300 "	Oct. 1, 1906
Eulalie E. Button	"	"	300 "	June 24, 1907
Nellie O'Keefe	"	Cook	300 "	" 1893
Thomas O. White	"	Baker	204 "	Nov. 11, 1897

Steamer "John Howard."

Name.	Residence.	Designation.	Compensation.	Date of Election or Appointment.
William H. Sampson	Long Island	Captain	$1,200 yr	Nov. 20, 1896
Charles H. Christian	"	Mate	840 "	" 3, 1904
James T. Cowan	"	Engineer	900 "	June 8, 1908
Daniel A. Barron	"	Assistant Engineer	600 "	April 5, 1909
Loring D. Johnson	"	Fireman	600 "	Sept. 15, 1908*

Building Department.

Name.	Residence.	Designation.	Compensation.	Date of Election or Appointment.
Arthur G. Everett	Chestnut Hill ave	Building Commissioner	$5,000 yr	May 1, 1908
Charles S. Damrell	Revere House	Clerk of Department	2,500 "	Oct. 1, 1881*
Frank L. Wells	504 W. Park st	Clerk	1,500 "	April 1, 1881
John F. Clark	21 Decatur st	"	1,200 "	May 1, 1903*
Max H. Levy	27 Quincy st	"	1,200 "	Jan. 10, 1899
James T. Murtagh	274A Shawmut ave	"	1,200 "	July 1, 1897*
Joseph DeMarco	49 Ottawa st	"	1,200 "	" 14, 1906*
Katherine L. Wells	17 Helen st	"	1,100 "	Jan. 1, 1880
Winnie D. Harrison	88 Pearl st., Chsn	"	1,000 "	March 20, 1883
Florence L. Preble	291 Bunker Hill st	"	600 "	June 25, 1906
Elizabeth R. Johnson	30 Sumner st	Telephone Operator	420 "	Nov. 23, 1903
Edward W. Lapworth	1606 Dorchester ave	Surveyor	1,200 "	May 1, 1899
James P. Keliher	80 Rutland st	Constable and Messenger	1,200 "	" 1, 1893
James O'Connor	192 Paris st., E. B.	Constable	1,100 "	Sept. 11, 1899
William W. K. Campbell	45 Dwight st	"	1,000 "	Jan. 4, 1902
Thomas F. Bruen	28 W. Sixth st	Laborer	900 "	Dec. 7, 1903
James A. Murray	28 Columbia rd	Chauffeur	900 "	June 26, 1908
Anna J. Harmon¶	145 Hillside st	Clerk	600 "	Dec. 7, 1908

Plan Division.

Name.	Residence.	Designation.	Compensation.	Date of Election or Appointment.
Michael W. Fitzsimmons	16 Sheridan st., J. P.	Supervisor	$2,500 yr	May 1, 1878
George Finneran	3189 Washington st	Architect	1,200 "	April 29, 1903
Richard W. Power	30 Oakley st	"	1,200 "	July 1, 1901

Construction Division.

Name.	Residence.	Designation.	Compensation.	Date of Election or Appointment.
Edwin J. Turner	692 Saratoga st	Supervisor	$2,500 yr	Oct. 28, 1903
John H. Mahoney	116 Hutchins st	"	1,800 "	Aug. 7, 1906*
John Currie	191 Neponset ave	Inspector	1,400 "	July 1, 1895

* Promoted to present position on date given.   Previously in the department.
† Without board.   ‡ See, also, Penal Institutions Department.
§ See, also, Children's Institutions Department. || On leave of absence.
¶ Temporary.

Building Department. — Concluded.

Name.	Residence.	Designation.	Com pensation.	Date of Election or Appointment.

Construction Division.— Concluded.

Name.	Residence.	Designation.	Com pensation.	Date of Election or Appointment.
John J. Dunigan	79 Tonawanda st	Inspector	$1,400 yr	July 30, 1906
Thomas H. Grinnell	47 Tower st	"	1,600 "	Aug. 1, 1904
Thomas M. Hinchey	799 Blue Hill ave	"	1,600 "	Oct. 8, 1897
Alphonsus C. Hickey	27 Cottage st., Dor	"	1,400 "	Aug. 7, 1906
Thomas F. Kearney	435 Washington st	"	1,400 "	May 26, 1904
Edwin D. Kelley	50 Tremont st	"	1,400 "	Sept. 1, 1897
Cornelius J. Murphy	351 Bowdoin st., Dor	"	1,400 "	July 30, 1906
William F. Murphy	50 Monument ave	"	1,400 "	June 1, 1896
Carl Stuetzel, Jr	743 Parker st., Rox	"	1,400 "	Aug. 27, 1908*

Egress Division.

Name.	Residence.	Designation.	Com pensation.	Date of Election or Appointment.
Levi W. Shaw	73 Chandler st	Supervisor	$1,800 yr	Jan. 24, 1878
Patrick F. Shevlin	384 Hyde Park ave	Inspector	1,600 "	Sept. 1, 1896
Thomas McCullough	57 Monument ave	"	1,600 "	May 24, 1906

Plumbing Division.

Name.	Residence.	Designation.	Com pensation.	Date of Election or Appointment.
William A. Wheater	814 E. Sixth st	Supervisor	$1,800 yr	Feb. 6, 1908*
Dennis H. Collins	234 Commercial st	Inspector	1,400 "	Jan. 10, 1883
Thomas E. Crosby	12 Oakdale st., Bri	"	1,400 "	Feb. 19, 1906
John J. Donovan	64 Clarkson st	"	1,400 "	Nov. 20, 1896
Robert W. Godfrey	30 Barry st	"	1,400 "	" 1, 1900
Richard Lynch	537 Talbot ave	"	1,600 "	Feb. 4, 1896
John H. Mulloney	1 Dunford st	"	1,400 "	May 4, 1903
Thomas C. Reiley	27 Havre st	"	1,400 "	March 1, 1899
Joseph F. Salter	441 Meridian st	"	1,400 "	Nov. 20, 1896
Patrick F. Slattery	92 Pleasant st	"	1,400 "	March 24, 1897
Thomas M. Wilson	55 Hollander st	"	1,400 "	May 1, 1896

Gas Fitting Division.

Name.	Residence.	Designation.	Com pensation.	Date of Election or Appointment.
David A. Finnegan	11 Waltham st	Supervisor	$1,600 yr	Oct. 1, 1898*
Ernest Blasser	44 Bayard st	Inspector	1,300 "	" 5, 1897
Warren Brooks	266 Vernon st	"	1,300 "	March 23, 1901
Joseph L. Curran	38 E. Canton st	"	1,300 "	Oct. 5, 1897
James W. Flynn	8 Plymouth st	"	1,300 "	" 5, 1897
Charles B. Gould	20 Hawes ave	"	1,300 "	" 5, 1897
Charles F. Gallagher	24 Chambers st	"	1,300 "	April 2, 1907
Louis Hofnauer	435 E. Seventh st	"	1,300 "	May 4, 1903
James A. O'Neil	20 Dilworth st	"	1,300 "	Oct. 25, 1898
Charles E. Phillips	298 Centre st., J. P	"	1,300 "	" 5, 1897

Elevator Division.

Name.	Residence.	Designation.	Com pensation.	Date of Election or Appointment.
Patrick H. Costello	24 Smith st	Supervisor	$1,700 yr	Jan. 31, 1888
Frederick C. Floyd	Hemenway Chambers	Inspector	1,600 "	Nov. 21, 1895
Marshall D. E. Greene	19 Park st., Chsn	Elevator Inspector	1,000 "	June 25, 1906
Thomas H. McNellis	8 Albion pl	Inspector	1,000 "	July 18, 1906

Board of Appeal.

Name.	Residence.	Designation.	Com pensation.	Date of Election or Appointment.
George R. Swasey	181 Massachusetts ave	Chairman	$10.00 day	Sept. 9, 1907
William D. Austin	23 Bellevue st., Fenway	Secretary	10.00 "	" 9, 1907
Edward H. Eldredge	44 Chestnut st	Member	10.00 "	" 9, 1907
Neil McNeil	59 Stanley st., Dor	"	10.00 "	" 9, 1907
Dennis J. Sullivan	80 Hillside st	"	10.00 "	" 9, 1907
Nellie F. Noonan	89 Union Park st	Clerk, Stenographer and Typewritist	600 yr	Oct. 1, 1908

Cemetery Department.

Board of Trustees.

Name.	Residence.	Designation.	Com pensation.	Date of Election or Appointment.
Charles E. Phipps	30 Channcy st	Chairman Trustees	None	May 19, 1902
Albert W. Hersey	4 Wellington ct	Trustee	"	" 1, 1897

* Promoted to present position on date given. Previously in the department.

Cemetery Department.— Continued.

Name.	Residence.	Designation.	Com-pensation.	Date of Election or Appointment.

Board of Trustees.— Concluded.

Fred E. Atteaux	176 Purchase st	Trustee	None	Nov. 21, 1904
Jacob R. Morse	858 Beacon st	"	"	May 4, 1908
Thomas Leavitt	137 Tonawanda st	"	"	Nov. 2, 1908

Central Administrative Force.

Leonard W. Ross	723 Harvard st	General Superintendent	$2,500 yr	Feb. 1, 1909
John Frank Keating	140 Harrison ave	Secretary, Stenographer	1,500 "	Nov. 1, 1902
Nellie V. Norton	595 Fourth st	Clerk, Assistant Secretary	1,000 "	May 2, 1895
Adelbert F. Arris	26 Danforth st	Special Officer	2.75 day	Nov. 21, 1897

Mount Hope Cemetery.

John M. Morton	106 Maple st	Assistant Custodian	$1,300 yr	Feb. 14, 1900*
Henry L. Dolan	145 Bourne st	Blacksmith's Helper	2.25 day	June 22, 1906*
Elsie C. Newcombe	50 St. Germain st	Clerk	14.00 wk	March 5, 1907
John Lippens	87 Roxbury st	Engineer	2.75 day	Nov. 13, 1906
Frank Doonan	660 Walk Hill st	Farmer	2.25 "	Aug. 29, 1907
John F. Kenny	102 Phillips st	"	2.25 "	" 5, 1907
Patrick H. Curley	53 Wellington Hill st	Gardener	3.00 "	April 24, 1888
James H. Flynn	50 Folsom st	"	3.00 "	May 9, 1882
Patrick H. Fox	75 Keyes st	"	3.00 "	April 28, 1887
Joseph Werner	30 Bridge st	"	3.00 "	Nov. 19, 1897
James T. Morton	25 Nelson st	"	2.75 "	May 4, 1904
James E. Phelan	19 Garden st	"	2.50 "	Nov. 3, 1905*
James J. Graham	163 Hyde Park ave	Gardener's Assistant	2.25 "	Dec. 4, 1903*
Michael P. McWeeny	961 Canterbury st	"	2.25 "	June 11, 1907
Francis Manning	850 Canterbury st	"	2.25 "	Oct. 25, 1907
Michael J. Mullen	684 Canterbury st	"	2.25 "	May 15, 1867
John E. Mulrey	818 Canterbury st	"	2.25 "	June 21, 1901*
David F. Sloan	794 Norfolk st	"	2.25 "	May 22, 1878*
Thomas Dolan	55 Mt. Hope st	Grader	2.25 "	" 11, 1896
Martin Butler	75 Call st	Grader and Sodder	2.25 "	July 15, 1903
Thomas J. Lavin	8 Lawn st	" "	2.25 "	May 14, 1906*
Dennis Manning	38 Mt. Hope st	" "	2.25 "	" 14, 1906*
Timothy M. Ryan	86 Norton st	" "	2.25 "	" 18, 1906
Patrick Blessington	128 Mt. Hope st	Grave Digger	2.25 "	Oct. 16, 1896
Thomas J. Burke	866 Canterbury st	"	2.25 "	" 28, 1904*
Thomas Corliss	730 Hyde Park ave	"	2.25 "	April 15, 1902*
Edward F. Curley	133 Bourne st	"	2.25 "	Feb. 28, 1902*
John J. Desmond	52 Neponset ave	"	2.25 "	May 24, 1891
William H. Egar	63 Fenwood rd	"	2.25 "	March 18, 1902*
John F. Flynn	15 Birch st	"	2.50 "	April 1, 1902
Charles T. Jesser	44 St. Rose st	"	2.25 "	March 18, 1903
Peter F. Kane	45 Worley st	"	2.25 "	April 14, 1903
William T. Kenny	22 Julian st	"	2.25 "	July 29, 1907*
Richard G. Lehman	14 Berry st	"	2.25 "	May 9, 1902*
Patrick Lennon	72 Neponset ave	"	2.25 "	" 28, 1902*
John Maloney	26 Wensley st	"	2.25 "	April 4, 1902
Henry J. Pfetzing	158 Mt. Hope st	"	2.25 "	" 21, 1879
John Riley	849 Canterbury st	"	2.25 "	May 21, 1901
James B. Dolan	21 Lee st	Grave Digger and Assistant Gardener	2.25 "	Dec. 18, 1903
Timothy Donovan	46 Bradstreet ave	Grave Digger and Grader	2.25 "	April 10, 1874
Frank T. Donovan	46 Bradstreet ave	Janitor	2.50 "	Oct. 30, 1903*
Jeremiah J. Driscoll	632 Broadway	"	2.50 "	Feb. 28, 1902
Thomas H. Brahany	321 Walk Hill st	Laborer	2.25 "	Aug. 17, 1904*
John Casey	224 Eustis st	"	2.25 "	Feb. 5, 1906
Moses Curtice	205 Bourne st	"	2.25 "	May 21, 1887
Michael Daum	205 Bourne st	"	2.25 "	" 11, 1888
Adolph H. Deichert	310 Ashland st	"	2.25 "	Feb. 10, 1903*
John J. Flynn	15 Berry st	"	2.25 "	April 29, 1868
James J. Godvin	rear 66 Mt. Hope st	"	2.25 "	Nov. 1, 1900*
Thomas J. Godvin	110 Mt. Hope st	"	2.25 "	June 18, 1903*
John Johnson	99 Mt. Hope st	"	2.25 "	April 1, 1897*
Frank Kelley	14 Neponset ct	"	2.25 "	" 17, 1870*
Michael Killion	9 Anson st	"	2.25 "	" 29, 1892
Michael J. Maloney	14 Frioburg st	"	2.25 "	July 1, 1903*
Hugh V. Markey	53 Monument ave	"	2.25 "	Aug. 11, 1898*
Edward J. Martin	158 Mt. Hope st	"	2.25 "	June 11, 1892

* Promoted to present position on date given.   Previously in the department.

Cemetery Department.— Concluded.

Name.	Residence.	Designation.	Compensation.	Date of Election or Appointment.

Mount Hope Cemetery.— Concluded.

Name.	Residence.	Designation.	Compensation.	Date of Election or Appointment.
John Mullen	19 Puritan ave	Laborer	$2.25 day	July 15, 1887
James O'Toole	93 Hyde Park ave	"	2.25 "	Oct. 24, 1896
Thomas Roach	788 Canterbury st	"	2.25 "	May 29, 1867
Aaron Vantassel	416 Harvard st	"	2.25 "	March 2, 1903*
Patrick McDonald	224 Eustis st	Ledgeman	2.25 "	April 28, 1886
Thomas F. Conniff	602 Canterbury st	Marble Rubber	2.25 "	Oct. 11, 1901
Thomas Gateley	89 Paine st	Foreman	3.00 "	March 14, 1870
Edward W. McCaffrey	71 Oak st	Moth Exterminator	2.25 "	April 6, 1905
Thomas J. Carey †	598 Canterbury st	Stableman	2.50 "	Oct. 27, 1897*
Thomas Kenny	225 W. Selden st	"	2.25 "	Feb. 8, 1902*
Patrick Lynch	92 Hyde Park ave	Teamster	2.25 "	Oct. 13, 1898*
Daniel Mahoney	800 Canterbury st	"	2.25 "	May 15, 1891
John J. Manning	1334 Blue Hill ave	"	2.25 "	Nov. 1, 1897*
Patrick H. Redding	678 Canterbury st	"	2.25 "	Oct. 10, 1902*
David H. Crowley	37 Vaughan ave	Tool Sharpener	3.00 "	May 23, 1906
George J. Duffy	572 Hyde Park ave	Treeman	2.50 "	Aug. 15, 1905*
Timothy F. Murphy	31 Buttonwood st	"	2.50 "	Oct. 6, 1905*
James J. Murray	245 Cabot st	"	2.50 "	Aug. 15, 1905*
Bridget McCartin ‡	81 Call st	Matron	1.50 "	May 17, 1906

Evergreen Cemetery.

Name.	Residence.	Designation.	Compensation.	Date of Election or Appointment.
Charles P. Harding	16 Foster st	Custodian	$1,200 yr	Dec. 10, 1897
John Harrington	27 Station st	Grader	2.25 day	May 2, 1887
James F. Connors	41 Snow st	Grader and Sodder	2.25 "	April 29, 1901
John Leonard	1101 Columbus ave	Grave Digger	2.25 "	March 19, 1902
Patrick Connors	73 Union st	Laborer	2.25 "	April 20, 1890
Michael W. Cassells	239 Eustis st	Teamster	2.25 "	May 11, 1896

Phipps Street and Bunker Hill Grounds.

Name.	Residence.	Designation.	Compensation.	Date of Election or Appointment.
Augustus M. Lydston	58 Sullivan st	Custodian	$660 yr	March 4, 1884

Copp's Hill Ground.

Name.	Residence.	Designation.	Compensation.	Date of Election or Appointment.
John Norton	595 Fourth st	Custodian	$600 yr	March 1, 1903

Bennington Street Cemetery.

Name.	Residence.	Designation.	Compensation.	Date of Election or Appointment.
Frank L. Turner	682 Saratoga st	Custodian	$720 yr	June 12, 1893

Children's Institutions Department.

Name.	Residence.	Designation.	Compensation.	Date of Election or Appointment.
Charles P. Putnam	63 Marlboro st	Chairman	None	May 1, 1906
Mary Boyle O'Reilly	39 Elliot st., J. P.	Secretary	"	Nov. 21, 1905
Mrs. Caroline S. Atherton	82 Ruthven st	Trustee	"	May 18, 1908
James P. Cleary	1493 Tremont st	"	"	Nov. 13, 1905
Lee M. Friedman	41 Winthrop st	"	"	May 1, 1905
John O'Hare	1 Garden Court st	"	"	1, 1908
Mrs. Rachel S. Thorndike	24 Marlboro st	"	"	Feb. 18, 1909

Parental School.

Name.	Residence.	Designation.	Compensation.	Date of Election or Appointment.
Dana P. Dame §	Parental School	Superintendent	$2,000 yr	Sept. 1, 1901
Hervey C. Bailey§	"	Superintendent's Assistant	600 "	Oct. 14, 1908
Alice E. Bentley	15 Maple st., W. R.	Teacher	936 "	Nov. 27, 1898
Kate E. Coney	47 Mt. Vernon st., W. R.	"	996 "	June 1, 1898
Elizabeth E. Dacey	8 Lexington st., Chsn.	"	648 "	" 1, 1906
Emma M. Gardiner	14 Billings st., W. R.	"	936 "	Nov. 19, 1898
Isabel R. Gardiner	47 Mt. Vernon st., W. R.	"	936 "	Sept. 1, 1902
Sallie C. Johnson	1 Montgomery st., W. R.	"	900 "	" 12, 1906
Mildred Kallen	28 Lynde st	"	696 "	Nov. 11, 1907

* Promoted to present position on date given. Previously in the department.
† Regularly employed 24 hours extra weekly at 31¼ cents per hour.
‡ Employed two days each week and holidays.
§ And living.

Children's Institutions Department.— Continued.

Name.	Residence.	Designation.	Com-pensation.	Date of Election or Appointment.

Parental School.— Concluded.

Name.	Residence.	Designation.	Com-pensation.	Date of Election or Appointment.
Annie L. Lynch	45 Cotton st., Ros	Teacher	$936 yr	Oct. 1, 1901
Mary L. Mahoney	Norwood	"	792 "	Sept. 12, 1906
Elizabeth M. Moody	87 Mt. Vernon st., W. R.	"	936 "	" 7, 1897
Isabel J. Mulkern	Dedham	"	936 "	April 25, 1897
Katherine Dempsey	57 Morrison st., W. R.	"	300 "	Nov. 30, 1908
James J. Grindley†	Parental School	Master	600 "	March 1, 1906
Rolla R. Horton†	"	"	600 "	" 1, 1902
John D. Lounsberry†	"	"	600 "	Dec. 28, 1896
Charles S. McQueenery†	"	"	600 "	" 4, 1906
Henry P. Smith†	"	"	600 "	June 1, 1903
L. Arthur Finley†	"	"	600 "	July 1, 1904
Horace C. Marden†	"	Relief Master	600 "	Aug. 17, 1908
Fred W. Ross†	"	"	600 "	Dec. 4, 1906
Michael J. Casey†	64 Newbury st., Ros	Asst. Master and Watchman	420 "	" 1, 1902
Annie E. Potter†	57 Morrison st., W. R.	Matron Girls' Cottage	600 "	" 1, 1907
Lizzie Horton†	Parental School	Matron	300 "	Aug. 1, 1903
Minnie C. Lounsberry†	"	"	300 "	Dec. 28, 1896
Anna E. McQueenery†	"	"	300 "	Oct. 1, 1906
Anna M. Smith†	"	"	300 "	June 1, 1903
Josie F. Finley†	"	"	300 "	Sept. 1, 1908
Sarah C. Grindley†	"	Matron, Dining Room	300 "	March 1, 1907
Joanna McKay†	"	Relief Matron	300 "	June 4, 1908
Margaret Sheehan†	"	Dormitory Matron	240 "	May 1, 1907
Janet Machon†	"	Hospital Matron	240 "	Aug. 5, 1899
Kate Chute†	"	Assistant Matron	240 "	Nov. 1, 1908
Lucy S. Newton†	"	"	240 "	Aug. 5, 1895
Florence B. Pfeiffer†	"	"	240 "	June 1, 1903
Susie A. Russell†	"	"	240 "	Jan. 1, 1908
Gertrude M. Scribner†	"	"	240 "	May 20, 1907
Ethan A. Miner†	11 Lambert ave., Rox	Chief Engineer	780 "	Sept. 24, 1908
Patrick Rooney†	Somerville	Assistant Engineer	600 "	Oct. 1, 1908
Simon P. Starrett†	Parental School	"	600 "	" 3, 1908
Effie Campbell†	"	Baker	300 "	March 1, 1907
Ann Cronin†	52 Johnson st., W. R.	Cook	300 "	Oct. 8, 1904
Mary Hughes†	Parental School	Superintendent's Cook	240 "	Feb. 19, 1908
James Snail†	"	Laundryman	600 "	Oct. 14, 1908
Grace E. Bailey†	"	Laundress	240 "	" 19, 1908
Valencia M. Bouvé†	11 Belle ave., W. R.	"	240 "	May 1, 1908
Annie B. Marden†	Parental School	"	240 "	Oct. 14, 1908
Carrie Haseufuss†	29 Billings st., W. R.	"	240 "	March 1, 1909
Evan P. Wentworth	419 Boylston st.	Dentist	300 "	Feb. 1, 1909
Edward D. Hurley	552 Broadway	Ophthalmologist	None	" 1, 1909
C. Morton Smith	437 Marlboro st	Dermatologist	"	" 1, 1909
John E. Overlander†	Parental School	Medical House Physician	50 yr	" 1, 1909
James S. Stone	234 Marlboro st	Consulting Surgeon	None	" 1, 1909
William W. Howell	1923 Centre st	Visiting Physician	"	" 1, 1909
Franklin C. Jillson	11 Hastings st	"	"	" 1, 1909
Edward N. Libby	1990 Columbus ave	"	"	" 1, 1909
Arthur M. Worthington	Dedham	"	"	" 1, 1909

Placing Out and Office Division.

Name.	Residence.	Designation.	Com-pensation.	Date of Election or Appointment.
John E. McCarthy	27 Rutland sq	General Agent	$2,000 yr	May 1, 1897*
Daniel F. Lynch	64 Regent st	Assistant Agent	1,400 "	Feb. 16, 1892
Ellen C. Dresser	12 Cumberland st	"	1,000 "	Jan., 1890
Robert E. Tracy	80 Alexander st	"	1,000 "	July 27, 1908*
Mary J. Riley	37 Belmont st	Bookkeeper	1,000 "	Aug. 29, 1898
Ellen F. McCarty	98 Day st	Stenographer	720 "	" 1, 1908
Julia V. Driscoll	13 Hull st	Stenographer and Clerk	750 "	March 1, 1906
Grace S. Hoogs	83 Pinckney st	Visitor	900 "	" 3, 1898
Jane Pratt	Cambridge	"	800 "	" 1, 1899
Lucy MacBride	12 Waban st	Visitor and Nurse	800 "	Sept. 19, 1901
Harriet A. Smith	755 Boylston st	Visitor	700 "	Dec. 31, 1906
Lillian R. Carney	2 Fremont pl	Matron	600 "	March 1, 1906
Albert A. Borofsky	96 Devon st	Messenger and Interpreter	521 "	Feb. 5, 1906
Maria A. Higgins †	Spring st	Seamstress	300 "	Oct. 1, 1887
Delia S. Peterson	14 Concord sq	Temporary Stenographer	600 "	Feb. 3, 1909

* Previously in the employ of the city.   † And living.

Children's Institutions Department.— Concluded.

Name.	Residence.	Designation.	Compensation.	Date of Election or Appointment.

Suffolk School for Boys.

Name.	Residence.	Designation.	Compensation.	Date of Election or Appointment.
Sumner D. Seave.‡	Rainsford Island	Superintendent	$2,000 yr.	Oct. 1, 1899
Alfred L. Leighton†	214 Brighton ave	Deputy Superintendent	720 "	18, 1899
Charles A. Rabetho‡	Rainsford Island	Physician and Athletic Instr.	960 "	April 15, 1906
Kate Leeds Eddy†	"	Principal of Schools	800 "	Jan. 1, 1909*
George F. Clark†	10 Union pk	Instructor of Printing	660 "	Sept. 1, 1896
Russell R. Walton†	Rainsford Island	Instructor of Shoemaking	660 "	May 1, 1897
Urban A. Wallace†	"	Sloyd Teacher	600 "	Sept. 1, 1902
Elizabeth Egan†	"	Teacher	480 "	1, 1903
Josephine Bryan†		"	420 "	Oct. 1, 1907
Antoinette Carroll†			420 "	Jan. 1, 1909
Lena E. Patten†	Somerville		420 "	March 1, 1908
Hiram W. Mellish†	Rainsford Island	Carpenter	660 "	Dec. 13, 1900
John H. Boyle†	27 Brookside ave	Cottage Master	540 "	April 4, 1907
Nelson A. Lane†	Rainsford Island	Officer	480 "	Nov. 1, 1899
Eugene Hayes†	55 Wesley ave	Supervisor	480 "	July 7, 1908
Ernest A. Lawson†	Rainsford Island		480 "	March 28, 1907
Walter M. Leighton†	55 N Beacon st	"	480 "	April 1, 1906
George W. McDonold†	Rainsford Island	"	480 "	June 1, 1908
Thomas P. Sullivan†	"		480 "	Dec. 5, 1908
Elizabeth Havender†	"	Matron	300 "	July 1, 1907
Genevieve Scribner†	"		300 "	Oct. 1, 1907
Mary E. Seavey†	"		300 "	Nov. 16, 1899
Emma J. Shaw†	"		300 "	2, 1908
Lemuel H. Needham†		Engineer	840 "	Jan. 15, 1903
William F. Lailor†	Hyde Park		480 "	4, 1909
William H. Parker†	Rainsford Island		480 "	Aug. 1, 1907
Charles C. Averill†		"	660 "	Oct. 7, 1908
Ellis F. Hermanson†	3 Riordan pl	Temporary Engineer	600 "	April 4, 1909
Bernard Downey†	3 Riordan pl	Fireman	420 "	1, 1899
Daniel H. McGunigle†	7 Monmouth st	"	360 "	Oct. 14, 1908
John Hannaford†	Milton	Temp. Farmer & Watchman	600 "	Nov. 20, 1908
Kate Kennealy †	Rainsford Island	Cook	300 "	Sept. 1, 1902
Margaret McCormick†			300 "	April 1, 1903
Catherine I. Austin†	Somerville	Temp. Cook & Housekeeper	300 "	23, 1909
Josephine McKim†	Rainsford Island	Seamstress	300 "	Sept. 1, 1907
Adelaide Donohoe	Everett	Organist	150 "	Nov. 1, 1898*
Evan P. Wentworth	419 Boylston st	Dentist	200 "	Feb. 1, 1909
George Uriot‡	190 Harrison ave	Messenger	60 "	Jan. 1, 1908

City Clerk Department.

Name.	Residence.	Designation.	Compensation.	Date of Election or Appointment.
John T. Priest	76 Homestead st	City Clerk	$5,000 yr.	Feb. 24, 1908*
Wilfred J. Doyle	73 Wellington Hill st	Assistant City Clerk	3,800 "	March 1, 1908*
John B. Lynch	63 Edwin st	Record Clerk	2,300 "	Nov. 1893
Martin W. O'Brien	10 Adelaide st	Chief Clerk Rec. Division	2,000 "	June, 1894
John J. Leary	49 Allen st	Bookkeeper	1,800 "	July, 1902
John D. Carmody	821 Fourth st	Clerk	1,800 "	1894
John L. Cates	5 Merlin st	"	1,800 "	1890
James W. Coulter	41 Leon st	"	1,200 "	Jan. 1895
Laura F. Tilton	164 Newbury st	"	1,200 "	Sept., 1874
Nellie N. Cole	146 Massachusetts ave	"	1,100 "	Feb., 1883
Katherine Kelley	115 Dale st	"	1,100 "	Dec., 1883
Frances C. Leonard	146 Massachusetts ave	"	1,100 "	Jan., 1881
Anna I. Mansfield	345 Dudley st	"	1,100 "	April, 1892
Adora L. Collison	194 Harrishof st	"	1,000 "	June, 1888*
Florence A. Howe	16 Linwood st	"	1,000 "	Feb., 1897*
Mary L. Ingalls	1761 Washington st	"	1,000 "	March, 1884
Margaret A. Leary	28 W. Fifth st	"	1,000 "	June, 1891*
Barbara J. Morrison	50 Fairview st	"	1,000 "	Sept., 1884
Kate O'Neil	115 Vernon st	"	1,000 "	Nov., 1887*
Charlotte E. Rebholz	36 Saunders st	"	1,000 "	July, 1894
Nellie G. Barnett	23 Barry st	"	800 "	1900*
Margaret T. Connell	5 Cherokee st	"	728 "	Dec., 1900
Laurania C. Ray	4 York st	"	728 "	Feb., 1902
Annie C. Riley	38 Elmira st	"	728 "	May, 1900
Mary C. Boyle	48 W. Tremlett st	"	624 "	Feb., 1904
John B. Cadigan	28 Buttonwood st	Messenger	1,200 "	1892
James F. McEttrick	453 Dudley st	"	1,200 "	1896
Edward F. McLaughlin	53 Snow Hill st	"	1,200 "	April, 1889
Thomas J. O'Neil	5 Fabyan st	"	1,000 "	May, 1896

* Previously in the employ of the city. † And living.
‡ See also Boston Infirmary Department and Institutions Registration Department.

City Messenger Department.

Name.	Residence.	Designation.	Compensation.	Date of Election or Appointment.
Edward J. Leary	351 W. Fourth st	City Messenger	$4,000 yr	May 1, 1896
Charles D. Murphy	29 Sparhawk st	Deputy City Messenger	1,900 "	" 1, 1896
Charles E. Silloway	87 Rockland st	Assistant City Messenger	1,700 "	April 1, 1878
Timothy Mooney	15 Tower st	" "	1,500 "	July 13, 1887
Fred A. Robinson	184 Webster st	" "	1,300 "	May 1, 1896
Daniel J. Sheehan	43 Silver st	Assistant City Messenger and Chief Janitor	1,300 "	June 1, 1896
Daniel E. Sullivan	391 W. Fourth st	Messenger	1,050 "	Feb. 13, 1897
Hugh W. J. McLaughlin	40 Billerica st	Assistant Chief Janitor	900 "	May 24, 1879
Atlas Skinner	2 Smith ave	Assistant Janitor	782 "	Aug. 1, 1872
William T. Dunn	9 Mt. Vernon st	"	782 "	April 1, 1876
Patrick H. Kelly	100 Bartlett st	"	782 "	" 20, 1900
George T. Perry	92 C st	"	782 "	Jan. 13, 1902
James E. McDonough	871 E. Fourth st	"	782 "	" 22, 1897
David Welch	61 Gold st	"	782 "	" 1, 1906
James A. Rahell	103 Cottage st	"	782 "	July 12, 1892
Theodore Jennings	1 Briggs pl	Elevator Attendant	782 "	Oct. 1, 1881
Frederick J. Glenn	610 E. Broadway	Furniture Polisher	782 "	June 7, 1907
Mark Ridge	71 W. Sixth st	"	3.00 day	" 7, 1907
Mary Meehan	111 W. Fifth st	Floor Washer	7.00 wk	July 1, 1896
Elizabeth Doherty	18 Causeway st	"	7.00 "	Oct. 23, 1900
Mary Isaacs	240 E st	"	7.00 "	" 2, 1901
Ellen O'Brien	13 Wharf st	"	7.00 "	Feb. 2, 1906
Mary Sullivan	110 Charles st	"	7.00 "	Sept. 14, 1906
Julia Bowman	211 W. Fifth st	"	7.00 "	March 4, 1907
Ellen McBride	58 Tudor st	"	7.00 "	April 1, 1907
Barbara Curley	50 George st	"	7.00 "	June 7, 1907
Ellen Hines	130 Leverett st	"	7.00 "	Aug. 15, 1907
Mary Whelton	188 Eustis st	"	7.00 "	" 15, 1907
Edward McHugh†	20 Charlotte st	Police Officer	200 yr	Dec. 15, 1892*
James A. Gately‡	434 Dudley st	"	200 "	May 1, 1894

Clerk of Committees Department.

John F. Dever	56 Mt. Pleasant ave	Clerk of Committees	$4,000 yr	May 1, 1896
Thomas J. Hurley§	63 Bainbridge st	Asst. Clerk of Committees	2,400 "	March 2, 1908
James W. Reed	40 Pinckney st	Bookkeeper and Clerk	1,600 "	Sept. 1, 1895
Joseph P. Dever	1 Carmen st., Dor	Constable	1,400 "	Dec. 15, 1901
P. J. A. Murphy‖	24 Athelwold st	Clerk	250 "	May 1, 1891

Licensed Minors Division.

James E. Norton	1007 Harrison ave	Supt. of Licensed Minors	$2,000 yr	March 21, 1892
William G. Dolan	70 High st., Chsn	Constable	1,200 "	April 15, 1902
Lawrence J. Kelly	41 W. Seventh st	"	1,200 "	" 15, 1902

Collecting Department.

Charles R. Brown	12 East Cottage st	City Collector	$5,000 yr	March 16, 1908*
James P. Kelly	45 Minot st., Dor	Cashier	3,000 "	Aug. 4, 1902
George D. Underwood	38 Gardner st	Bookkeeper	2,800 "	" 9, 1875
Thomas W. O'Rourke	14 Windermere rd	Teller	2,600 "	May 1, 1900
Charles E. Tucker	33 Garden st	"	2,600 "	June 22, 1908
Isaac W. Derby	12 Laurel st	Chief Deputy Collector	2,100 "	May 1, 1900
Michael W. Ahern	822 Huntington ave	Deputy Collector	1,800 "	June 22, 1908
Thomas R. Appleton	52 Townsend st	"	1,800 "	May 1, 1891
Cornelius F. Crowley	32 East Cottage st	"	1,800 "	March 16, 1904
Jeremiah J. Crowley	72 Surrey st	"	1,800 "	May 1, 1902
Crohan J. Daly	414 Newbury st	"	1,800 "	Aug. 1, 1894'
James F. Daley	13 Liverpool st	"	1,800 "	May 6, 1902
Frederick L. Donnelly	37 G st	"	1,800 "	Sept. 12, 1887
Jeremiah J. Hartnett	10 Prospect st	"	1,800 "	Jan. 10, 1906
John J. Hannon	109 Western ave	"	1,800 "	May 20, 1902
William Kells, Jr	33 East Eighth st	"	1,800 "	" 6, 1902

* Promoted to present position on date given. Previously in the department.
† Appointed on Police Force, May 5, 1873. ‡ Appointed on Police Force, December 27, 1872.
§ Original, May, 1898. ‖ See Street Department.

Collecting Department.— Concluded.

Name.	Residence.	Designation.	Compensation.	Date of Election or Appointment.
Robert Kershaw	383 K st	Deputy Collector	$1,800 yr	Feb. 1, 1909
Joseph T. Madden	54 Chestnut st	"	1,800 "	May 6, 1902
Edward F. McAdams	60 Weld Hill st	"	1,800 "	" 7, 1906
Matthew H. McFettrick	26 Woodville st	"	1,800 "	" 6, 1902
James S. McKenna	303 C st	"	1,800 "	" 6, 1902
James J. Nolan	49 Chestnut ave	"	1,800 "	" 1, 1900
John T. O'Connor	161 Ashland st	"	1,800 "	June 12, 1891
Leavitt B. Palmer	174 Lexington st	"	1,800 "	Sept. 13, 1881
William H. Pearson	205 Walnut ave	"	1,800 "	" 12, 1887
Louis P. Pfau	1019 South st	"	1,800 "	May 6, 1902
Charles E. Pierce	368 K st	"	1,800 "	" 1, 1900
William H. Spain	9 Joy st	"	1,800 "	" 6, 1902
Edwin A. Wall	89 Munroe st	"	1,800 "	Jan. 19, 1897
John J. Hennessey*	217 Millet st	Special Assessment Clerk	1,800 "	Feb. 1, 1894
Edward A. Morrissey	87 Munroe st	Water Tax Clerk	1,800 "	May 10, 1889
William E. Cunningham	32 Holborn st	Insolvency Clerk	1,800 "	June 22, 1908
Edward J. Dixon	872 East Broadway	Tax Clerk	1,600 "	March 1, 1901
Timothy J. Brinnin	354 Seaver st	Clerk	1,600 "	July 1, 1897
Daniel C. Casey	294 Dudley st	"	1,600 "	May 20, 1902
Patrick H. Conway	38 Hawthorne st	"	1,600 "	Jan. 13, 1891
William T. Gartland	20 Roslin st	"	1,600 "	March 1, 1901
James B. Machugh	20 Charlotte st	Stenographer and Clerk	1,400 "	" 1, 1901
Thomas J. Gorman	47 Tuttle st	Clerk	1,400 "	May 20, 1902
LeForrest A. Hall, Jr.	25 Leyland st	Assistant Bookkeeper	1,400 "	July 1, 1900
Abraham Levy	37 Copeland st	Clerk	1,400 "	Feb. 18, 1901
James E. Moore	16 Ballou ave	"	1,400 "	Nov. 1, 1906
Henry J. Daly	5 Arklow st	"	1,200 "	May 20, 1902
James A. Desmond	41 Everett st	"	1,200 "	March 1, 1901
Timothy F. Gorman	87 Munroe st	"	1,200 "	May 11, 1908
Frank J. McBarron	1697 Washington st	"	1,200 "	March 1, 1907
John H. McElroy	13 Auburn st	"	1,200 "	" 13, 1904
John F. Quinn	37 Oakview ter	"	1,200 "	May 20, 1902
William H. Sullivan	131 Hudson st	"	1,200 "	March 1, 1907
James Roster	27 Radford lane	"	1,100 "	Jan. 6, 1908
James G. Davis	24 Dustin st	"	1,000 "	Nov. 1, 1906
Michael F. Gearin	437 East Sixth st	"	1,000 "	May 7, 1906
John F. Grant	20 Thornley st	"	1,000 "	June 1, 1908
John T. Hayes	13 Trenton st	"	1,000 "	" 1, 1908
Joseph H. Hickey	26 River st	Assistant Stenographer and Clerk	1,000 "	May 11, 1908
Stewart E. Hoyt	121 Warwick st	Clerk	1,000 "	July 21, 1906
Michael J. Markey	1697 Washington st	"	1,200 "	Dec. 26, 1893
Paul A. Tuckerman	96 Harvard ave	"	1,000 "	July 22, 1902
Romanzo N. Wiswall	40 Mt Pleasant ave	"	1,000 "	June 1, 1908

Consumptives' Hospital Department.

Name.	Residence.	Designation.	Compensation.	Date of Election or Appointment.
Edward F. McSweeney	23 Beacon st	Chairman Trustees	None	March 19, 1906
Margaret G. O'Callaghan	119 Stoughton st	Trustee	"	Nov. 26, 1906
James J. Minot, M. D.	188 Marlboro st	"	"	March 12, 1906
Isabel F. Hyams	26 Wales st	"	"	" 12, 1906
Chandler Hovey	20 Fairfield st	"	"	May 1, 1908
John F. O'Brien, M. D.	401 Bunker Hill st	"	"	" 1, 1908
Herbert F. Price	56 Dix st	Secretary Trustees	"	April 30, 1907
Simon F. Cox, M. D.†	274 Boylston st	Superintendent	$2,500 yr	Dec. 7, 1906
Catherine A. Sullivan	114 Melville ave	Stenographer	900 "	June 8, 1906
Etta C. McNamara	401 Bunker Hill st	"	600 "	April 12, 1909
Edwin A. Locke, M. D.	311 Beacon st	Chief of Staff	2,500 "	" 30, 1907
Timothy J. Murphy, M. D.	372 Dudley st	First Asst. (Medical Staff)	1,750 "	" 30, 1907
William T. Councilman, M D.	78 Bay State rd	Pathologist	500 "	" 30, 1907
Cleaveland Floyd, M. D.	Brookline	Second Asst. Physician	1,000 "	May 3, 1907
John T. Sullivan, M. D.	324 Ashmont st	Laryngological Assistant	600 "	Oct. 4, 1907
Louis Mendelsohn, M. D.	477 Washington st., Dor.	Assistant Physician	200 "	Dec. 20, 1907
Henry I. Bowditch, M. D.	506 Beacon st	"	200 "	" 20, 1907
Bradford Kent, M. D.	798 Blue Hill ave	"	200 "	Jan. 24, 1908
Horace K. Boutwell, M. D.	665 Boylston st	"	200 "	May 29, 1908
Charles E. Shay, M. D.	132 Warren st	"	400 "	" 29, 1908
Albert Ehrenfried, M. D.	1112 Boylston st	"	200 "	June 1, 1908

* See County of Suffolk, Miscellaneous.

† Dr. Simon F. Cox receives in addition to his salary a compensation of $600 per annum for maintenance in lieu of quarters.

Consumptives' Hospital Department.— Concluded.

Name.	Residence.	Designation.	Compensation.	Date of Election or Appointment.
Walter C. Bailey, M. D..	267 Clarendon st	Assistant Physician	$200 yr	Nov. 13, 1908
Williston W. Barker, M. D.	4 Lyndhurst st	"	200 "	" 13, 1908
Michael J. Cronin, M. D.	5 Elm Hill ave	"	200 "	" 13, 1908
Andrew F. Downing, M. D.	127 Newbury st	"	200 "	" 13, 1908
Nathaniel K. Wood, M. D.	259 Beacon st	"	200 "	" 13, 1908

Out-Patient Department.

Name.	Residence.	Designation.	Compensation.	Date of Election or Appointment.
Elizabeth P. Upjohn	80 Pinckney st	Head Nurse	$1,200 yr	April 26, 1907
Margaret V. Alvaney	45 Bainbridge st	Nurse	900 "	Sept. 11, 1907
Gertrude D. Boutwell	133 W. Concord st	"	900 "	" 11, 1907
Maria A. Collins	152 W. Concord st	"	900 "	Oct. 16, 1907
Edith A. Babcock	2 Parkman pl	"	900 "	Dec. 27, 1907
Dora Deutch	11 Langdon st	"	900 "	Jan. 1, 1908
Bessie M. Mac Mullen	Newton Highlands	"	900 "	April 4, 1908
Bridget H. Conlon	4 Prospect ave	Nursing Maid	312 "	" 24, 1908
Mary F. Thompson	52 Blue Hill ave	Nurse	900 "	" 24, 1908
Zepha M. Gardner	206 Huntington ave	"	900 "	July 6, 1908
Winnifred Hernan	9 Newbury st	"	900 "	Nov. 17, 1908
Bessie Magee	44 Newbury st	"	900 "	" 17, 1908
Theresa Cullen	84 Waltham st	"	900 "	Dec. 7, 1908
Laura A. Beaton	406 Massachusetts ave	"	900 "	April 7, 1909
Leonora MacComiskey	Brookline	"	900 "	March 1, 1909
Ezra M. Rideout	13 Burroughs pl	Orderly	780 "	June 7, 1907
Mary A. B. Flynn	55 Baldwin st., Chsn	Stenographer	720 "	Aug. 22, 1907
Alice L. Byrne	68 Bradshaw st., Dor	Clerk	600 "	Mar. 25, 1909
Hannah Swanson	2 Waterford st	Cleaner	1.50 day	Sept. 3, 1907
Mary E. Warnock	88 Warrenton st	"	1.25 "	April 24, 1909

Hospital.

Name.	Residence.	Designation.	Compensation.	Date of Election or Appointment.
David Townsend, M. D.	405 Marlboro st	Assistant Physician	$1,000 yr	June 26, 1908
Richard H. Houghton, M. D.	302 Sumner st., E. B.	"	600 "	July 14, 1908
Mary E. McCue	168 River st	Head Nurse (Camp)	780 "	" 7, 1908
Mary A. Kilduff	34 Kent st	Head Nurse(Cottage Ward)	780 "	Mar. 1, 1909
Catherine McNally	479 Massachusetts ave	Nurse	480 "	July 9, 1908
Jeremiah O'Brien	249 River st	Orderly	420 "	Mar. 24, 1908
Elizabeth Reedy	249 River st	Cook	360 "	Nov. 17, 1908
Elizabeth Hogan	249 River st	Assistant Cook	300 "	April 13, 1909
Sadie Cunningham	249 River st	Maid	216 "	Feb. 7, 1909
Mrs. Elizabeth Payne	249 River st	"	216 "	April 10, 1909
Delia Healey	249 River st	"	216 "	Dec. 10, 1908
Sarah Haynes	8 Windermere rd	"	216 "	April 23, 1909
William Jutras	249 River st	Choreman	216 "	June 29, 1908
Abraham Brown	249 River st	"	216 "	Feb. 1, 1909
Cornelius Doherty	7 Jarvis pl	"	216 "	April 2, 1909
Martin Meehan	249 River st	Farmer	900 "	Nov. 7, 1908
Thomas Martin	9 Liversidge way	Assistant Farmer	360 "	Dec. 12, 1908
Thomas Melly	2214 Dorchester ave	"	360 "	Mar. 19, 1909
Patrick Flaherty	23 Monson st	"	360 "	April 12, 1909

Election Department.

Name.	Residence.	Designation.	Compensation.	Date of Election or Appointment.
John M. Minton	Orchard ave	Chairman	$4,000 yr	May 1, 1902
Melancthon W. Burlen	27 Waumbeck st	Commissioner	3,500 "	July 19, 1900
Alpheus Sanford	56 Kingsdale st	"	3,500 "	May 1, 1905
Edward A. McLaughlin	86 Walnut ave	"	3,500 "	" 4, 1908
Matthew F. Foley	15 Wabeno st	Assistant	2,000 "	Sept. 11, 1888
Frederic Eaton	1 Wadsworth st	"	1,900 "	May 10, 1900
Thomas J. McMackin	98 N. Margin st	"	1,800 "	" 18, 1907
Winsor S. Smith	495 Columbia rd	Assistant Registrar	1,900 "	Sept. 9, 1895
George W. Stevens	4 Walnut st	"	1,700 "	Oct. 2, 1891
Alexander L. Brown	480 Massachusetts ave	"	4.00 day	May, 1882
John J. Capelle	15½ Walnut pk	"	4.00 "	June 15, 1896
John W. Dolan	4 Henchman st	"	4.00 "	July 17, 1903
Frank J. Enos	122 Melville ave	"	4.00 "	Jan. 11, 1904
Allan H. Farnham	820 Beacon st	"	4.00 "	May 10, 1900
William M. Humphreys	536 Dudley st	"	4.00 "	" 18, 1907
Paul D. Kane	28 Magdala st	"	4.00 "	" 10, 1900
Henry Karle	27 Ashmont st	"	4.00 "	July 2, 1896
William E. Mahoney	436 Bunker Hill st	"	4.00 "	Jan. 21, 1904

Election Department. —Concluded.

Name	Residence.	Designation.	Compensation	Date of Election or Appointment.
Michael F. McLaughlin	258 Webster st	Assistant Registrar	$4.00 day.	May 11, 1901
Christopher C. Mitchell	49 Wachusett st	"	4.00 "	Sept. 12, 1902
John F. Monahan	32 Dorr st	"	4.00 "	May 18, 1907
Michael F. Morley	239 Parsons st.	"	4.00 "	1882
George H. Norton	1007 Harrison ave	"	4.00 "	July 17, 1903
Henry L. Pelkus	15 Ruthven st	"	4.00 "	Sept. 25, 1900
James Smith	25 Green st	"	4.00 "	June 7, 1878
Charles H. Snow	53 Edgewood st	"	4.00 "	May 11, 1901
Emanuel G. Sterne	179 Walnut ave	"	4.00 "	July 2, 1895
Frank A. Sughrue	73 Howard ave	"	4.00 "	May 11, 1903
Edmund Weber	32 Quincy st	"	4.00 "	18, 1907

Storehouse Employees.

Maurice Murphy	43 Village st	Carpenter	$3.50 day.	Jan. 17, 1902
George W. Knights	17 Howard st	"	3.00 "	" 11, 1902
William H. Hagerty	13 Northfield st	Janitor	2.50 "	" 17, 1902
James J. Ahearn	295 Dorchester st	"	2.50 "	" 17, 1902

Engineering Department.

William Jackson	136 Academy Hill rd	City Engineer	$6,000 yr.	April 21, 1885*
Frank A. McInnes	23 Salcombe st	Assistant City Engineer	3,600 "	June 10, 1887
Edward W. Howe	10 Wayne st	Assistant Engineer	3,150 "	Nov. 10, 1869
Henry Manley	116 Mt. Vernon st., W. R.	"	3,000 "	Feb. 16, 1869
Samuel E. Tinkham	126 Thornton st	"	2,700 "	Oct. 3, 1874
Frederic H. Fay	15 Ashford st	"	2,500 "	Feb. 21, 1895
Christopher J. Carven	34 Centre st., Dor	"	2,400 "	June 18, 1884
Benjamin F. Bates	38 Claybourne st	"	2,000 "	May 18, 1891
Frederic I. Winslow	66 Bloomfield st	"	2,000 "	June 1, 1883*
Sturgis H. Thorndike	The Charlesgate	"	1,800 "	Aug. 14, 1895
Alfred E. Haskell	140 Glenway st	"	1,600 "	May 13, 1891
Louis F. Cutter	Salem, Mass	"	1,500 "	July 12, 1898*
Mayo T. Cook	140 Glenway st	"	6.50 day.	Oct. 14, 1879
Frederic P. Spalding	70 Waltham st	"	6.00 "	May 21, 1880
Harry G. Botsford	40 Ivory st	"	5.00 "	July 27, 1887
Randall D. Gardner	118 Lexington st	"	5.00 "	Oct. 7, 1898
George C. Currier	90 Huntington ave	"	4.50 "	Jan. 19, 1874
Herbert A. Wilson	55 Chestnut Hill ave	"	4.50 "	Feb. 12, 1890*
John E. Carty	106 Harrishof st	"	4.00 "	Oct. 15, 1906*
Roland N. Cutter	186 Park st., W. R	"	4.00 "	May 21, 1891
James J. T. McElligott	27 Bradbury st	"	4.00 "	July 23, 1898
Theodore Parker	9 Carmen st	"	4.00 "	Aug. 18, 1898*
Frederick Porter	32 Rutland sq	"	4.00 "	May 13, 1891
Henry M. Carven	1604 Dorchester ave	"	3.75 "	July 20, 1898
George A. Clough	141 Glenway st	"	3.75 "	Aug. 18, 1898*
Arthur W. Hunt	73 Minot st., Dor	"	3.75 "	Sept. 12, 1895
Samuel L. Leftovith	28 Sherman st	"	3.75 "	April 27, 1896
Patrick J. Malley	246 Park st., Dor	"	3.75 "	Aug. 18, 1898*
James A. McMurry	795 Blue Hill ave	"	3.75 "	July 5, 1896
James M. McNulty	27 Holman st	"	3.75 "	" 6, 1899
Thomas E. Lally	80 Fletcher st	"	3.50 "	June 15, 1896
John S. Lamson	Arlington Heights	Transitman	3.50 "	Aug. 18, 1898*
Alden B. Beal	17 Green st., J. P.	"	3.00 "	June 16, 1898
William F. Sinclair	92 Gainsboro st	"	3.00 "	May 19, 1891
Timothy R. Sullivan	386 W. Fourth st	"	3.00 "	8, 1898
John F. Gorman	27 Vinson st	"	2.75 "	Oct. 15, 1888
Frank McGurn	2 Roseland st	Axeman	2.75 "	Sept. 4, 1871
Ambrose B. Attwood	78 Bellevue st., W. R	Rodman	2.50 "	March 24, 1896
Harry B. Farrell	10 Dartmouth st	"	2.50 "	May 19, 1896
Thomas J. Fitzgerald	6 Hawthorne pl	"	2.50 "	Sept. 5, 1899
Fred W. Jackson	81 Chestnut Hill ave	"	2.50 "	Aug. 18, 1898*
John J. Steele	115 Oakland st., Dor	"	2.50 "	June 15, 1896
August F. Bildt	53 Tuttle st	Draughtsman	4.00 "	Jan. 27, 1902
Frank W. Tucker	Massachusetts Chambers	"	4.00 "	Feb. 24, 1890
Paul S. Yendell	19 Winter st., Dor	"	4.00 "	June 5, 1907
Francis J. Kennedy	150 Blue Hill ave	"	3.50 "	May 14, 1906
Charles S. Parsons	168 Huntington ave	Chief Clerk	2,000 yr.	Jan. 12, 1870
Frank Boyden	15 Samoset st	Clerk	4.00 day.	Aug. 25, 1882
James F. Welch	72 Edgewood st	Messenger	1,100 yr.	June 9, 1890
Matthias J. Horgan	1 Maryland st., Dor	Blueprinter	2.75 day.	Jan. 30, 1908

* Promoted to present position on date given. Previously in the department.

Engineering Department.— Concluded.

Name.	Residence.	Designation.	Compensation.	Date of Election or Appointment.

Inspectors.

Name.	Residence.	Designation.	Compensation.	Date of Election or Appointment.
Ezra K. Garvin	79 Lawrence ave	Inspector	$5.00 day	Sept. 1, 1876
John W. Corbett	76 Keyes st	"	4.00 "	July 5, 1891
Timothy F. Hayes	357 W. Fourth st	"	4.00 "	April 4, 1901
Timothy Fitzmaurice	374 W. Fourth st	"	3.50 "	Sept. 20, 1894
Thomas L. Hayes	320 Warren st	"	3.00 "	Aug. 30, 1902*
John J. Humphrey	27 N. Grove st	"	2.50 "	Oct. 29, 1902
Chester T. Jones	179 Hancock st., Dor	Assistant to Engineer	5.00 "	June 27, 1895*

Surveying Division.

Name.	Residence.	Designation.	Compensation.	Date of Election or Appointment.
Frank O. Whitney †	175 Humboldt ave	Chief of Division	$3,500 yr	June 1, 1899*
Irwin C. Cromack ‡	8 Elm Lawn	Assistant to Chief	2,800 "	" 23, 1899*
Frank M. Miner	17 Parker st., Chsn	Assistant Engineer	2,500 "	April 1, 1868
Charles C. Perkins	422 Columbus ave	"	2,500 "	Feb. 1, 1866
Henry C. Mildram	60 Roslin st	"	2,000 "	Dec. 21, 1908*
Thomas J. Lee	673 Cambridge st., Bri	"	1,600 "	April 11, 1874
William J. C. Semple	665 E. Seventh st	"	1,500 "	Sept. 21, 1871
George B. Smith	74 Glendale st	"	1,450 "	May 30, 1880
William L. Austin	37 Cobden st	"	4.50 day	" 30, 1883
Arthur Howland	15 Congreve st	"	4.50 "	Aug. 6, 1886
Arthur N. Colman	9 Fredericka st	"	4.00 "	" 1, 1892
Edward L. Moulton	29 Idaho st	"	4.00 "	May 10, 1887
Walter H. Bacon	188 Savin Hill ave	"	3.75 "	Sept. 20, 1889
Frederick G. Floyd	325 Park st., W. R	"	3.75 "	" 9, 1885
William H. Macmann	33 Prescott st	Draughtsman	1,300 yr	April 19, 1887
Elwyn L. Russell	9 Sorrento st	"	4.00 day	Aug. 13, 1891
Harrie R. Burrell	35 Myrtle st	Transitman	3.25 "	Nov. 14, 1894
John H. Burroughs	49 Nixon st	"	3.25 "	April 13, 1896
John F. Dacey	11 Wellesley pk	"	3.25 "	July 25, 1892
George F. Haskell	388 Columbia rd	"	3.25 "	Oct. 25, 1895
William J. Sullivan	19 Pinckney st	"	3.25 "	May 13, 1891
George H. Sherman	33 Grampian way	"	3.25 "	July 5, 1898
William G. Joy	26 Royal st	"	3.00 "	May 12, 1891
Richmond P. Souther	691 Adams st., Dor	Rodman	2.50 "	Oct. 27, 1896
John C. Johnson	53 Wrentham st	Messenger	900 yr	Jan. 6, 1896

Fire Department.

Headquarters.

Name.	Residence.	Designation.	Compensation.	Date of Election or Appointment.
Samuel D. Parker	48 Beacon st	Commissioner	$5,000 yr	Feb. 1, 1908
Benjamin F. Underhill	72 Esmond st	Secretary	2,500 "	Sept. 6, 1892
George F. Murphy	294 South st	Clerk	1,650 "	Dec. 1, 1893
James P. Maloney	26 Cordis st	"	1,400 "	Feb. 21, 1895
Daniel J. Quinn	15 Hinckley st	"	1,400 "	March 18, 1898
Edward L. Tierney	39 Robinson st	"	1,000 "	June 21, 1907
Rufus W. Sprague	376 Main st	Medical Examiner	1,300 "	March 9, 1894
Elizabeth C. Greene	4 Derby pl	Janitress	540 "	May 14, 1894

Chief, Deputies and District Chiefs.

Name.	Residence.	Designation.	Compensation.	Date of Election or Appointment.
John A. Mullen	471 E. Fourth st	Chief of Department	$4,000 yr	Feb. 23, 1906
John Grady	72 Bowdoin st	Deputy Chief	2,400 "	" 23, 1906
Peter F. McDonough	36 Winthrop st	Second Deputy Chief	2,220 "	March 9, 1906
John W. Godbold	22 Princeton st	District Chief	2,000 "	Jan. 24, 1908
Charles H. W. Pope	17 Monument ave	"	2,000 "	May 2, 1890
Joseph M. Garrity	37 Hamilton st	"	2,000 "	Feb. 18, 1898
Henry A. Fox	41 Pinckney st	"	2,000 "	March 9, 1906
Daniel F. Sennott	22 Linwood sq	"	2,000 "	May 12, 1905
Edwin A. Perkins	8 Linden st	"	2,000 "	March 21, 1901
Stephen A. Ryder	633 Dorchester ave	"	2,000 "	" 9, 1906
Michael J. Kennedy	6 Dorset st	"	2,000 "	" 9, 1906
John O. Taber	4 Waterlow st	"	2,000 "	" 9, 1906
John F. Ryan	27 Bennett st	"	2,000 "	Feb. 8, 1895
Michael J. Mulligan	7 Lester pl	"	2,000 "	March 9, 1906

* Promoted to present position on date given.   Previously in the department.
† $2,100 paid by Street Laying-Out Department and $1,400 by Engineering Department.
‡ $1,400 paid by Street Laying-Out Department and $1,400 by Engineering Department.

Fire Department.— Continued.

Name.	Residence.	Designation.	Compensation.	Date of Election or Appointment.
Chiefs' Drivers.				
Joseph A. Webber	18 Mason st	Lieut. Aide to Chief	$1,400 yr	March 31, 1905
Thomas F. Callahan	231 Bennington st	Driver	1.75 day	Aug. 7, 1907
William J. Martin	91 River st	"	2.25 "	Feb. 25, 1898
John H. Finnan	29 St. Margaret st	"	2.00 "	Nov. 14, 1902
Thomas J. Stevens	55 Lexington st	"	2.00 "	June 8, 1905
James W. McKenney	9 Shannon st	"	1.75 "	March 9, 1906
Frank L. Jewett	57 White st	"	2.25 "	Oct. 4, 1905
Edward J. Eagan	91 Dix st	"	1.75 "	March 4, 1907
John F. O'Brien	50 Dundee st	"	1.75 "	July 2, 1907
Elias J. Stewart	3270 Washington st	"	1.75 "	Dec. 18, 1907
Thomas W. Devney	17 Hall st	"	2.00 "	Nov. 30, 1906
William H. Lanigan	19 Glenwood st	"	1.75 "	May 11, 1907
Frank D. O'Brien	9 Rosemary st	"	1.75 "	Sept. 27, 1907
Joseph A. Hackett	28 Sudan st	"	1.75 "	" 7, 1906
Engine Company 1.				
William Coulter	779 E. Fourth st	Captain	$1,600 yr	Feb. 18, 1895
John J. Burke	31 Crescent ave	Lieutenant	1,400 "	Sept. 15, 1905
Percy W. Gowen	2 Mercer st	Engineer	1,300 "	Jan. 27, 1899
Winfred C. Bailey	10 Gates st	Assistant Engineer	1,200 "	Dec. 5, 1902
Charles E. Whiting	231 Boston st	Hoseman	1,200 "	June 22, 1892
Ronald J. McDonald	53 Thomas pk	"	1,200 "	Jan. 4, 1895
Edward J. Hartigan	12 Linden st	"	1,200 "	April 17, 1896
Henry A. Woodmancy	530 E. Fourth st	"	1,200 "	Sept. 8, 1904
John J. Lombard	40 Harvest st	"	1,100 "	Dec. 8, 1905
John A. Saunders	15 Harvest st	"	1,000 "	Jan. 21, 1907
Edward J. Donelan	303 Saratoga st	Probationer	900 "	Oct. 20, 1908
Michael F. Quirk	259 E st	"	720 "	Feb. 12, 1909
Engine Company 2.				
Edward Conners	16 Thomas pk	Captain	$1,600 yr	Sept. 1, 1905
Francis McArdle	688 E. Sixth st	Lieutenant	1,400 "	April 18, 1904
Edward R. Stern	740 E. Third st	Engineer	1,300 "	May 18, 1891
Edward J. Twomey	712 E. Sixth st	Assistant Engineer	1,200 "	Oct. 25, 1902
Jeremiah J. Hickey	11 Lark st	Hoseman	1,200 "	Feb. 1, 1896
Patrick H. Boleman	606 E. Fifth st	"	1,200 "	July 1, 1883
James Moroney	389 K st	"	1,200 "	Jan. 7, 1898
James T. Flavin	754 E. Fifth st	"	1,200 "	May 18, 1891
John J. Murphy	302 K st	"	1,200 "	Dec. 4, 1903
Daniel J. Looney	605 E. Seventh st	"	1,200 "	June 30, 1905
Engine Company 3.				
John W. Murphy	761 Columbia rd	Captain	$1,600 yr	Oct. 25, 1902
William F. Field	69 G st	Lieutenant	1,400 "	May 18, 1903
Fred S. Young	19 Wayland st	Engineer	1,300 "	July 29, 1904
Valentine B. Nolan	33 Cohden st	Assistant Engineer	1,200 "	March 31, 1905
George W. Darling	58 Catawba st	Hoseman	1,200 "	Jan. 19, 1900
Thomas J. Feeley	895 Albany st	"	1,200 "	March 23, 1900
Daniel I. Bell	6 Linwood st	"	1,200 "	Jan. 14, 1901
James J. O'Connell	66 Francis st	"	1,200 "	" 10, 1902
Daniel J. Kennedy	442 Harrison ave	"	1,200 "	Oct. 31, 1902
John J. Gately	19 E. Concord st	"	1,100 "	" 27, 1905
Daniel W. O'Leary	34 Winship st	"	1,000 "	Nov. 5, 1906
Anthony E. Nelson	34 Cherokee st	"	1,000 "	Jan. 14, 1907
Engine Company 4.				
William E. Riley	57 Monument ave	Captain	$1,600 yr	March 15, 1907
Avery B. Howard, Jr	57 Elm st	Lieutenant	1,400 "	April 18, 1902
Bernard J. Flaherty	34 Fresno st	Engineer	1,300 "	Dec. 23, 1904
Aloysius A. Hart	453 Saratoga st	Assistant Engineer	1,200 "	June 10, 1903
John J. Kelley	10 Prospect st	Hoseman	1,200 "	March 10, 1899
James J. Connolly	82 Bunker Hill st	"	1,200 "	Feb. 15, 1901
Edward J. Locke	60 Tolman st	"	1,200 "	Sept. 20, 1901
William P. Boudreau	97 Horace st	"	1,200 "	Dec. 5, 1902
William A. Porter	23 Moseley st	"	1,200 "	Oct. 6, 1903
Norman R. Doyle	500 E. Seventh st	"	1,200 "	Jan. 4, 1904
James M. Burke	366 Dorchester st	"	1,200 "	Nov. 4, 1904
Julius H. Cutler	143 Saratoga st	"	1,100 "	Dec. 8, 1905
Arthur W. Helmund	31 Lawrence st	"	1,100 "	June 29, 1906
Daniel E. Murphy	51 Baldwin st	"	1,000 "	May 10, 1907

Fire Department.— Continued.

Name.	Residence.	Designation.	Compensation.	Date of Election or Appointment.

Engine Company 5.

Name.	Residence.	Designation.	Compensation.	Date of Election or Appointment.
Mellen R. Joy	210 Brighton ave	Captain	$1,600 yr	Jan. 5, 1906
Daniel M. Cranitch	214 Princeton st	Engineer	1,300 "	" 11, 1901
Frank H. Laskey	172 Putnam st	Assistant Engineer	1,200 "	March 15, 1895
George B. Atwood	90 Marion st	Hoseman	1,200 "	June 23, 1877
Henry Woodbury	50 Prescott st	"	1,200 "	Dec. 21, 1883
Joseph H. Barry	140 London st	"	1,100 "	May 9, 1906
John J. Katwick	118 Brooks st	"	1,100 "	Dec. 8, 1905
Daniel Crowley	259 Princeton st	"	900 "	April 15, 1908

Engine Company 6.

Name.	Residence.	Designation.	Compensation.	Date of Election or Appointment.
Frank J. Sheeran	32 Oak st	Captain	$1,600 yr	Jan 4, 1907
Dennis J. Dacey	25 Pleasant st	Lieutenant	1,400 "	" 5, 1906
William J. Delany	285 Dudley st	Engineer	1,300 "	Feb. 21, 1908
John F. McDonough	6 N. Meade st	Assistant Engineer	1,200 "	July 15, 1904
George E. Darragh	4 Boyle st	Hoseman	1,200 "	Dec. 24, 1897
Edward S. Humphreys	43 Irving st	"	1,200 "	Sept. 5, 1903
Pellegrino Muolio	55 Hull st	"	1,200 "	Jan. 21, 1905
Thomas W. Roose	28 Green st	"	1,200 "	Oct. 9, 1903
Patrick F. Wall	89 Chelsea st	"	1,200 "	April 17, 1896
Joseph W. Wood	79 Washington st	"	1,200 "	July 8, 1901
Arthur L. Johnson	36 Soley st	"	1,100 "	May 16, 1906
Owen W. Murphy	103 Union Park st	"	1,000 "	July 15, 1907
Sylvester A. Keaney	8 Mystic st	"	900 "	April 15, 1908

Engine Company 7.

Name.	Residence.	Designation.	Compensation.	Date of Election or Appointment.
Jeremiah F. Gillen	56 Saratoga st	Captain	$1,600 yr	April 17, 1903
Michael J. Teehan	67 Ceylon st	Lieutenant	1,400 "	March 15, 1907
John H. Leary	50 Crescent st	Engineer	1,300 "	April 17, 1903
Francis S. Oresteen	7 East st	Assistant Engineer	1,200 "	June 14, 1901
James Agnew	273 Webster st	Hoseman	1,200 "	Oct. 4, 1895
Dennis F. Daly	6 Hecla st	"	1,200 "	March 10, 1902
James J. Hourihan	84 Minden st	"	1,200 "	Nov. 6, 1903
William E. McKeever	604 Massachusetts ave	"	1,200 "	July 17, 1896
Patrick Ryan	269 Sumner st	"	1,200 "	April 2, 1896
Daniel F. Buckley	93 River street	"	1,100 "	Dec. 8, 1905
Thomas F. McFarland	237 Cabot st	"	1,100 "	Nov. 24, 1905
William J. Wiegand	280 Silver st	"	1,100 "	Oct. 27, 1905
William L. Ryan	165 F st	"	1,000 "	July 26, 1907

Engine Company 8.

Name.	Residence.	Designation.	Compensation.	Date of Election or Appointment.
John F. Hines	97 Horace st	Captain	$1,600 yr	Jan. 4, 1907
William J. Lalley	61 Baldwin st	Lieutenant	1,400 "	" 4, 1904
Peter J. Corrigan	38 Harvest st	Engineer	1,300 "	" 19, 1906
William P. Kehoe	24 Mystic st	Assistant Engineer	1,200 "	June 4, 1897
Florence J. Sullivan	7 Prospect st	Hoseman	1,200 "	Feb. 11, 1898
Miles E. Tennihan	5 Cordis st. ave	"	1,200 "	May 7, 1897
Thomas H. Downey	60 Nashua st	"	1,200 "	June 7, 1898
Donald Calder	14 Main st	"	1,200 "	May 18, 1903
Louis C. I. Stickle	66 Blue Hill ave	"	1,200 "	May 8, 1903
John Gibbons	79 London st	"	1,100 "	Dec. 8, 1905
Joseph W. Fix	4 Plymouth ct	"	1,100 "	July 11, 1906
Cornelius J. Sullivan	89 Henley st	"	1,000 "	May 11, 1907
Walter H. Green	34 Myrtle st	"	1,000 "	" 24, 1907

Engine Company 9.

Name.	Residence.	Designation.	Compensation.	Date of Election or Appointment.
Philip A. Grant	26 Monument sq	Captain	$1,600 yr	Jan. 4, 1907
Thomas J. Flynn	75 Wordsworth st	Lieutenant	1,400 "	" 4, 1907
Francis W. Sweeney	301 Lexington st	Engineer	1,300 "	June 19, 1903
Francis H. Boudreau	399 Chelsea st	Assistant Engineer	1,200 "	Feb. 1, 1896
Frank Coyle	18 Dorrance st	Hoseman	1,200 "	Sept. 19, 1893
William J. Dolan	310 Saratoga st	"	1,200 "	April 17, 1896
Thomas F. Flynn, Jr.	178 Lexington st	"	1,200 "	Jan. 29, 1903
John J. Sullivan	2 Lamson st	"	1,100 "	Dec. 8, 1905
Thomas F. Timmins	365 Meridian st	"	1,000 "	May 24, 1907
John J. Blakeley	151 Bennington st	"	900 "	Jan. 22, 1908
Joseph A. Moron	76 Horace st	"	900 "	June 26, 1908
John J. Dunbar	6 Mystic pl	Probationer	720 "	Dec. 8, 1908

Fire Department.— Continued.

Name.	Residence.	Designation.	Compensation.	Date of Election or Appointment.

Engine Company 10.

Name.	Residence.	Designation.	Compensation.	Date of Election or Appointment.
Frank A. Sweeney	35 Mt. Vernon st	Captain	$1,600 yr	Jan. 4, 1907
Cornelius J. Hickey	11 Lark st	Lieutenant	1,400 "	Sept. 1, 1905
Robert Cummings	127 Mt. Vernon st	Engineer	1,300 "	Aug. 11, 1893
John W. S. Crossman	740 E. Sixth st	Assistant Engineer	1,200 "	May 15, 1896
John M. Donovan	30 Oakview ter	Hoseman	1,200 "	Nov. 7, 1902
George F. Doyle	2 Allen pl	"	1,200 "	April 10, 1903
Frank J. Linloff	127 Mt. Vernon st	"	1,200 "	May 16, 1904
Joseph A. Murray	1818 Washington st	"	1,200 "	Aug. 11, 1907
George P. Smith	10 Parker Hill ave	"	1,200 "	May 12, 1899
Joseph F. Burke	15 Bentley st	"	1,100 "	Dec. 8, 1905
George A. West	52 Nashua st	"	1,000 "	May 24, 1907
Austin G. Durham	53 Hano st	"	900 "	" 18, 1908

Engine Company 11.

Name.	Residence.	Designation.	Compensation.	Date of Election or Appointment.
Cornelius H. Leary	82 Havre st	Captain	$1,600 yr	Feb. 16, 1893
Fred W. Battis	336 Meridian st	Lieutenant	1,400 "	March 12, 1907
John B. Sheridan	597 Saratoga st	Engineer	1,300 "	July 30, 1897
Isaac B. Noble	60 Bennington st	Assistant Engineer	1,200 "	Feb. 16, 1882
James B. Akerly	41 Ashley st	Hoseman	1,200 "	July 20, 1895
Andrew R. Hines	656 Bennington st	"	1,200 "	Oct. 11, 1893
William A. McLean	58 Homer st	"	1,200 "	" 26, 1900
William Pease	196 Leyden st	"	1,200 "	Dec. 22, 1893
John H. Callahan	428 Saratoga st	"	1,200 "	Aug. 9, 1900
Joseph Nolan	593 Saratoga st	"	1,200 "	April 26, 1886

Engine Company 12.

Name.	Residence.	Designation.	Compensation.	Date of Election or Appointment.
Albert R. Johnson	327 Dudley st	Captain	$1,600 yr	Feb. 15, 1888
Michael Boyle	4 Thornton st	Lieutenant	1,400 "	" 6, 1903
George W. Woodworth	10 Elmont st	Engineer	1,300 "	July 15, 1904
Samuel Engler	25 Hamilton st	Assistant Engineer	1,200 "	Dec. 24, 1897
John E. Corea	407 Dudley st	Hoseman	1,200 "	March 28, 1890
Mark N. Sibley	11 Fairland st	"	1,200 "	Nov. 20, 1893
Samuel A. Dwight	33 Monument sq	"	1,200 "	May 7, 1897
George R. Hennessy	11 Dean st	"	1,200 "	June 25, 1900
Henry Hartnett	17 Hendry st	"	1,200 "	Nov. 7, 1902
Daniel F. Daley	16 Auburn st	"	1,000 "	Feb. 9, 1907
George Zopf	63 Roseclair st	"	1,100 "	Dec. 8, 1905

Engine Company 13.

Name.	Residence.	Designation.	Compensation.	Date of Election or Appointment.
William J. Gaffey	47 Dale st	Captain	$1,600 yr	Oct. 12, 1896
Thomas E. Conroy	6 Kent st	Lieutenant	1,400 "	Feb. 8, 1901
Charles A. Thompson	18 Auburn st	Engineer	1,300 "	Jan. 7, 1903
George W. Barnard	604 Massachusetts ave	Assistant Engineer	1,200 "	Sept. 7, 1894
William H. Smith	19 Highland Park ave	Hoseman	1,200 "	May 18, 1891
John J. Kelly	53 Olney st	"	1,200 "	April 18, 1899
Tracy O. Littlehale	135 W. Canton st	"	1,200 "	June 25, 1900
Jesse E. Nickerson	40 Lambert st	"	1,200 "	Oct. 4, 1901
John T. Lynch	4 Fellows pl	"	1,200 "	Dec. 6, 1901
Michael H. Devin	113 Winthrop st	"	1,200 "	June 30, 1905
Thomas F. Ryder	40 Blossom st	"	1,100 "	Dec. 8, 1905
William A. F. Hughes	37 Cunard st	"	1,000 "	Jan. 11, 1907

Engine Company 14.

Name.	Residence.	Designation.	Compensation.	Date of Election or Appointment.
George B. Norton	1 Dana pl	Captain	$1,600 yr	May 12, 1905
Dennis Driscoll	76 Regent st	Lieutenant	1,400 "	March 2, 1906
Walter H. Wright	24 Beech Glen st	Engineer	1,300 "	Jan. 1, 1897
James F. Mulhern	2 Huntington ave	Assistant Engineer	1,200 "	Nov. 4, 1894
Walter H. Wells	31 Dorr st	Hoseman	1,200 "	May 12, 1890
Jacob Hyman	16 Parker Hill ave	"	1,200 "	Aug. 27, 1895
George S. Gormley	68 Day st	"	1,200 "	May 4, 1900
David L. Brooks	67 Hillside st	"	1,200 "	Aug. 11, 1899
Richard J. West	96 Vernon st	"	1,200 "	Feb. 1, 1896
John J. Devine	24 Clifton st	"	1,200 "	July 6, 1900
George C. Dowling	27 Centre st	"	1,200 "	March 2, 1892
Thomas E. Cuddihy	9 Anson st	"	1,000 "	Nov. 5, 1906

CITY DOCUMENT No. 105.

Fire Department.—Continued.

Name.	Residence.	Designation.	Compensation.	Date of Election or Appointment.

Engine Company 15.

Name.	Residence.	Designation.	Compensation.	Date of Election or Appointment.
Edwin F. Richardson	18 Romsey st	Captain	$1,600 yr	March 2, 1906
George H. Twiss	623 W. Park st	Lieutenant	1,400 "	Oct. 28, 1904
Harry E. Richardson	30 Roseclair st	Engineer	1,300 "	July 20, 1903
Walter J. Thompson	23 Bellflower st	Assistant Engineer	1,200 "	Aug. 16, 1897
Ernest B. Chittick	69 G st	Hoseman	1,200 "	April 17, 1896
John F. Reynolds	18 Gibson st	"	1,200 "	Jan. 4, 1895
William Hart	9 Newport st	"	1,200 "	May 7, 1897
Alfred D. LeClair	303A W. Third st	"	1,200 "	April 28, 1899
Daniel J. Gearin	825 Dorchester ave	"	1,200 "	" 23, 1900
William I. Johnson	261 E st	"	1,200 "	Nov. 7, 1902
William M. Conners	242 W. Third st	"	1,200 "	Jan. 18, 1904
William O'Connor	95 Decatur st	"	1,200 "	May 26, 1905
Thomas I. Carey	55 Sagamore st	"	1,000 "	July 15, 1907

Engine Company 16.

Name.	Residence.	Designation.	Compensation.	Date of Election or Appointment.
John J. Flanagan	1218 Morton st	Captain	$1,600 yr	Jan. 13, 1899
John Baumeister	2054 Dorchester ave	Lieutenant	1,400 "	Aug. 30, 1903
Thomas A. Andrews	73 River st	Engineer	1,300 "	March 20, 1901
Charles T. Needham	249 Manchester st	Assistant Engineer	1,200 "	May 15, 1896
John K. Wheelock	11 Washington st	Hoseman	1,200 "	" 15, 1896
Francis E. Merrill	62 River st	"	1,200 "	March 2, 1900
Peter J. Donovan	55 Idaho st	"	1,200 "	Aug. 5, 1892
Michael F. Minehan	28 Sturbridge st	"	1,200 "	Jan. 2, 1905
Hugh Mullaney	404 Codman st	"	1,200 "	" 2, 1905
Henry C. Swett	19 Sanford st	Call Substitute	200 "	July 25, 1902
Robert H. Jones	55 Temple st	"	200 "	April 8, 1904

Engine Company 17.

Name.	Residence.	Designation.	Compensation.	Date of Election or Appointment.
Martin F. Mulligan	12 National st	Captain	$1,600 yr	June 26, 1908
John F. Curley	18 Church st	Lieutenant	1,400 "	Nov. 3, 1903
William R. Batchelder	27 Dix st	Engineer	1,300 "	Feb. 10, 1893
Edward I. McLaughlin	49 Hecla st	Assistant Engineer	1,200 "	May 24, 1889
William H. Harkins	126 Neponset ave	Hoseman	1,200 "	Nov. 18, 1899
Charles Ingersoll	263 Dorchester st	"	1,200 "	March 2, 1901
John F. Dowd	38 Hecla st	"	1,200 "	Oct. 9, 1903
James M. Harrington	19 Harvest st	"	1,200 "	May 25, 1903
Joseph F. Coleman	16 Neponset ave	"	1,100 "	Dec. 8, 1905
Adrian R. Grace	13 Grant st	"	1,000 "	Aug. 26, 1907
Peter A. Reilly	105 Brunswick st	"	900 "	April 15, 1908

Engine Company 18.

Name.	Residence.	Designation.	Compensation.	Date of Election or Appointment.
Francis J. Jordan	64 Westville st	Captain	$1,600 yr	March 2, 1906
Thomas J. Muldoon	421 Geneva ave	Lieutenant	1,400 "	June 14, 1901
Joseph M. Holland	93 W. Selden st	Engineer	1,300 "	May 10, 1895
William A. Pickard	143 Bowdoin st	Assistant Engineer	1,200 "	Feb. 14, 1888
George F. Burckhart	463 River st	Hoseman	1,000 "	Aug. 2, 1907
John T. Donahoe	107 Westville st	"	1,200 "	May 15, 1896
Patrick H. Jennings	85 Westville st	"	1,200 "	April 17, 1896
Thomas P. Lohan	26 Chipman st	"	1,000 "	Feb. 6, 1907
James F. Shea	31 Highland st	"	1,000 "	June 14, 1907
John H. Wiemann	12 Hendry st	"	1,200 "	Nov. 7, 1902
Philip T. Smith	8 Cook st	Probationer	720 "	Feb. 12, 1909

Engine Company 19.

Name.	Residence.	Designation.	Compensation.	Date of Election or Appointment.
Maurice Heffernan	15 Hunter st	Captain	$1,600 yr	Jan. 13, 1899
Anthony J. Burns	16 Tokio st	Lieutenant	1,400 "	May 3, 1901
John T. Weston	12 Rosewood st	Engineer	1,300 "	June 10, 1890
Daniel J. Murphy	111 Haven ave	Assistant Engineer	1,200 "	May 30, 1890
Frederick W. Hayes	11 Clarkwood st	Hoseman	1,200 "	June 10, 1879
Edward B. Johnson	25 Sutton st	"	1,200 "	Nov. 10, 1890
Joseph Dooley	562 River st	"	1,200 "	May 18, 1897
James J. Higgins	637 Norfolk st	"	1,200 "	July 6, 1904
Edward G. Chamberlain	586 River st	"	1,000 "	Jan. 25, 1907
David H. Toomey	11 Ferrin st	"	900 "	May 18, 1908

Fire Department.— Continued.

Name.	Residence	Designation	Compensation	Date of Election or Appointment.

Engine Company 20.

Name.	Residence	Designation	Compensation	Date of Election or Appointment.
James M. Littleton	38 Walnut st	Captain	$1,600 yr	Jan. 8, 1889
George H. Bridge	20 Bowman st	Engineer	1,300 "	Sept. 25, 1875
Eugene G. Allen	396 Centre st	Assistant Engineer	1,200 "	Oct. 24, 1890
Andrew J. Burnett	24 Minot st	Hoseman	1,200 "	Dec. 21, 1889
Charles E. Hudson	190 Neponset ave	"	1,200 "	Aug. 31, 1903
Timothy F. Cannon	21 Fort ave	"	1,100 "	June 30, 1905
Timothy J. Costello	333 Adams st	"	1,000 "	Jan. 25, 1907
John A. Killeen	17 Tolman st	"	1,200 "	May 24, 1895
John A. Nicholson	5 Narragansett st	"	1,200 "	" 8, 1903
Arthur W. Warren	5 Ericsson st	"	1,100 "	April 30, 1906

Engine Company 21.

Name.	Residence	Designation	Compensation	Date of Election or Appointment.
Michael Norton	41 Harvest st	Captain	$1,600 yr	Jan. 24, 1908
George H. Hutchings	33 Spring Garden st	Lieutenant	1,400 "	" 18, 1900
Murdock D. McLean	22 Annabel st	Engineer	1,300 "	May 25, 1900
Eben C. Lothrop	755 Columbia rd	"	1,300 "	Sept. 12, 1890
William J. Muir	7 Topliff st	Assistant Engineer	1,200 "	May 24, 1889
Charles F. Macfarlane	7 Glendale st	"	1,200 "	April 2, 1896
George R. Donnelly	17 Hinckley st	Hoseman	1,200 "	July 2, 1882
John B. Hennessy	671 Columbia rd	"	1,200 "	" 3, 1883
Cornelius Donovan	12 Bellflower st	"	1,200 "	Feb. 4, 1887
Daniel J. Murray	11 Sargent st	"	1,200 "	Jan. 20, 1893
James F. Boyle	230 Boston st	"	1,200 "	July 2, 1897
John F. Murphy	68 Sagamore st	"	1,200 "	Nov. 18, 1899
George F. LeFavor	23 Morse st	"	1,200 "	Oct. 12, 1900

Engine Company 22.

Name.	Residence	Designation	Compensation	Date of Election or Appointment.
Fitzgerald M. O'Lalor	24 Wakullah st	Captain	$1,600 yr	March 2, 1906
Harry M. Hebard	736 Norfolk st	Lieutenant	1,400 "	June 29, 1903
Edward G. Hook	66 Whiting st	Engineer	1,300 "	May 10, 1901
John Williams	16 Union Park st	Assistant Engineer	1,200 "	Aug. 27, 1892
John Kippenberger	16 Gardner st	Hoseman	1,200 "	" 23, 1900
Arthur F. Mendall	73 Maywood st	"	1,200 "	April 17, 1896
Daniel F. McDonald	4 Rockview pl	"	1,200 "	March 22, 1900
Joseph W. Shea	19 Shannon st	"	1,200 "	Feb. 6, 1903
Daniel H. Twiss	36 Kempton st	"	1,200 "	Nov. 4, 1902
James P. Gallagher	10 Marmion st	"	1,100 "	Dec. 8, 1905
Thomas A. O'Connell	4 Lawrence pl	"	1,100 "	Oct. 26, 1906
James F. O'Hare	93 Norfolk ave	"	900 "	June 25, 1908

Engine Company 23.

Name.	Residence	Designation	Compensation	Date of Election or Appointment.
Michael Walsh	317 Dudley st	Captain	$1,600 yr	Feb. 10, 1893
John J. McCarthy	150 Quincy st	Lieutenant	1,400 "	Dec. 23, 1904
Henry Heymann	22 Oakview ter	Engineer	1,300 "	July 1, 1886
John J. Burke	24 Fifield st	Hoseman	1,200 "	Aug. 9, 1901
James T. Cunningham	200 Market st	"	1,200 "	June 24, 1901
Cornelius J. Crowley	71 Palmer st	"	1,200 "	Nov. 7, 1902
Fred L. Sargent	11 Dilworth st	"	1,200 "	July 28, 1893
Warren C. Stevens	Waverley House	Assistant Engineer	1,200 "	April 28, 1899
Carl F. Bode	23 Codman pk	Hoseman	1,000 "	March 15, 1907
William A. Ott	21 Sharon st	"	1,000 "	May 22, 1907
Charles S. Lane	19 Burgess st	"	900 "	" 19, 1908
Alfred F. H. Outerbridge	6 Robinson pl	"	900 "	April 15, 1908

Engine Company 24.

Name.	Residence	Designation	Compensation	Date of Election or Appointment.
John X. Lally	15 Hollander st	Captain	$1,600 yr	Feb. 6, 1903
Robert J. Carleton	90 W. Newton st	Lieutenant	1,400 "	Jan. 11, 1901
Richard T. Tuson	88 Waumbeck st	Engineer	1,300 "	" 14, 1891
Michael J. Fallon	6 Auburn st	Assistant Engineer	1,200 "	March 14, 1902
Cornelius J. Doherty	108 Moreland st	Hoseman	1,200 "	Aug. 27, 1895
George N. F. Getchell	45 Intervale st	"	1,200 "	April 11, 1873
William J. Kehoe	52 F st	"	1,200 "	July 15, 1904
William F. Johnson	72 Bennington st	"	1,200 "	Nov. 26, 1894
John I. Quigley	42 Kilton st	"	1,200 "	Sept. 3, 1884
John J. Whalen	88 Regent st	"	1,200 "	Feb. 26, 1904
John J. Rowean	225 Blue Hill ave	"	1,000 "	May 22, 1907

Fire Department.— Continued.

Name.	Residence.	Designation.	Compensation.	Date of Election or Appointment.

Engine Company 25.

Name.	Residence.	Designation.	Compensation.	Date of Election or Appointment.
Cornelius J. O'Brien	50 Chestnut st	Captain	$1,600 yr	Jan. 4, 1897
George A. Carney	6 Wallace ct	Lieutenant	1,400 "	Sept. 2, 1904
John Cullen	5 Lyndeboro st	Engineer	1,300 "	Jan. 11, 1907
Richard J. McLaughlin	26 Auburn st	Assistant Engineer	1,200 "	Oct. 29, 1905
Solomon Aaron	93 Henley st	Hoseman	1,200 "	Jan. 17, 1898
William F. Bryan	60 Allen st	"	1,200 "	Feb. 28, 1902
Coleman E. Clougherty	25 Dorchester st	"	1,200 "	April 23, 1900
Edward J. Coveney	82 Chelsea st	"	1,200 "	Oct. 4, 1904
Michael J. Griffin	61 Havre st	"	1,200 "	Jan. 29, 1903
Ivan P. Mahoney	625 E. Eighth st	"	1,200 "	March 15, 1901
William F. Quigley	1 Fairland st	"	1,200 "	Aug. 31, 1903
Thomas F. Wren	1084 Washington st	"	1,100 "	Jan. 31, 1907
William P. Kelleher	156 Lenox st	"	1,000 "	" 2, 1907

Engine Company 26 and 35.

Name.	Residence.	Designation.	Compensation.	Date of Election or Appointment.
John E. Madison	18 Mason st	Captain	$1,600 yr	March 29, 1901
William Levis	236 Bennington st	Lieutenant	1,400 "	June 26, 1908
Frederick F. Leary	11½ Hillside st	"	1,400 "	" 26, 1908
William S. Abbott	9 Helena st	Engineer	1,300 "	" 7, 1901
William H. Hildreth	87 Washington st	"	1,300 "	Jan. 19, 1906
Patrick J. Ryan	170 Boston st	Assistant Engineer	1,200 "	Dec. 14, 1900
John T. Stewart	813 Tremont st	"	1,200 "	July 10, 1903
Edward E. Williamson	190 Adams st	"	1,100 "	May 11, 1896
Napeen Boutilier	64 Lambert ave	Hoseman	1,200 "	June 3, 1904
Lawrence J. Buchanan	114 Conant st	"	1,100 "	Dec. 8, 1905
Charles H. Cosgrove	42 Union Park st	"	1,200 "	Nov. 15, 1901
Henry J. Enross	720 Harrison ave	"	1,200 "	" 7, 1902
John Griffin	32 Francis st	"	1,200 "	March 31, 1905
James P. Jones	434 Massachusetts ave	"	1,200 "	April 15, 1901
Thomas J. Kennealy	9 Kempton st	"	1,200 "	Feb. 10, 1899
Edward H. Kilday	1037 Tremont st	"	1,200 "	" 12, 1904
John H. Laughlin	52 Green st	"	1,200 "	" 11, 1903
Thomas F. Ryan	306 Bunker Hill st	"	1,200 "	May 26, 1905
James F. Sheehan	112 Murdock st	"	1,200 "	Aug. 4, 1905
Peter F. Towle	10 Galena st	"	1,200 "	July 26, 1901
Edward A. Whalen	51 Vernon st	"	1,200 "	Jan. 7, 1903
Bartholomew J. Dowd	33 Hayden st	"	1,100 "	Oct. 16, 1906
Dennis J. Noonan	194 W. Sixth st	"	1,100 "	April 30, 1906
Joseph M. Donovan	286 E. Sixth st	"	1,000 "	" 12, 1907
Raymond V. Landry	83 Day st	"	1,000 "	" 22, 1907
William O. Cushing	705 E. Fifth st	"	900 "	Nov. 11, 1907
Albert S. Penney	349 Eighth st	Probationer	720 "	Feb. 12, 1909

Engine Company 27.

Name.	Residence.	Designation.	Compensation.	Date of Election or Appointment.
Bartholomew F. Hayes	9 Austin st	Captain	$1,600 yr	Jan. 4, 1907
Timothy J. Heffron	6 Bunker Hill st	Lieutenant	1,400 "	March 2, 1906
James P. Gillogley	23 Trenton st	Engineer	1,300 "	Dec. 5, 1902
Charles F. Elsesser	13 Cook st	Assistant Engineer	1,200 "	April 23, 1896
John C. Holton	36 Decatur st	Hoseman	1,200 "	July 21, 1895
David W. Towle	12 Princeton st	"	1,200 "	Oct. 4, 1895
Dennis F. Quinlan	84 Green st	"	1,200 "	April 28, 1899
Edward McDonough	37 Soley st	"	1,200 "	Feb. 6, 1903
William J. Foster	183 Chelsea st	"	1,200 "	July 8, 1904
Frederick G. Menghi	36 Elm st	"	1,200 "	Aug. 4, 1905
James J. Smith	47 Pearl st	"	1,100 "	Dec. 8, 1905
Francis A. Hoar	47 Pearl st	"	1,100 "	April 30, 1906
Charles F. O'Brien	21 Eden st	"	1,000 "	Feb. 26, 1907

Engine Company 28.

Name.	Residence.	Designation.	Compensation.	Date of Election or Appointment.
David J. O'Connell	14 Spring Park ave	Engineer	$1,300 yr	May 1, 1880
John H. Johnson	15 Goldsmith st	Assistant Engineer	1,200 "	March 23, 1900
Joseph J. Cunningham	105 School st	Hoseman	1,200 "	June 22, 1892
John J. McDonald	74 South st	"	1,200 "	" 30, 1893
John J. McMorrow	97 Hyde Park ave	"	1,100 "	April 30, 1896
Roger T. White	42 Malcolm st	"	900 "	Oct. 23, 1907
James J. Burke	20 Border st	"	1,200 "	April 28, 1899
James F. Cullen	76 S. Huntington ave	"	900 "	Oct. 20, 1908
John F. Good	262 Cabot st	Probationer	720 "	Dec. 18, 1908
Otto P. Faul	cor. Weld and Arthur sts	"	720 "	April 6, 1909

Fire Department.— Continued.

Name.	Residence.	Designation.	Compensation.	Date of Election or Appointment.

Engine Company 29.

Name.	Residence.	Designation.	Compensation.	Date of Election or Appointment.
Joseph M. Gargan	54 Chambers st	Captain	$1,600 yr	May 18, 1891
Thomas E. Kiley	25 Allston st	Lieutenant	1,400 "	Jan. 4, 1907
John Lee	37 Ridgemont st	Engineer	1,300 "	" 18, 1907
Rufus W. Clark	46 Market st	Assistant Engineer	1,200 "	Sept. 21, 1894
Frederick J. Cross	12 Harriet st	Hoseman	1,200 "	Feb. 1, 1896
John L. Crimlisk	2 Taylor st	"	1,200 "	Nov. 8, 1904
Matts C. Porell	295 Market st	"	1,200 "	Jan. 22, 1889
Joseph F. McManus	91 Lake st	"	1,200 "	May 24, 1889
Bernard F. McKinney	32 Etna st	Call Substitute	200 "	March 20, 1896
John A. Welch	20 Academy Hill rd	"	200 "	May 6, 1903
Andrew J. Callahan	555 Washington st	"	200 "	April 20, 1898

Engine Company 30.

Name.	Residence.	Designation.	Compensation.	Date of Election or Appointment.
Thomas M. McLaughlin	83 Gardner st	Captain	$1,600 yr	Dec. 2, 1898
William H. Clay	99 Temple st	Engineer	1,300 "	Oct. 21, 1883
Frederick P. Fullerton	38 Perham st	Assistant Engineer	1,200 "	March 23, 1900
William Condry	145 Bellevue st	Hoseman	1,200 "	Jan. 1, 1874
Patrick J. Dunn	59 Johnson st	"	1,200 "	Aug. 7, 1891
William Chittick	169 Washington st	"	1,200 "	May 2, 1884
Thomas M. Curley	35 Johnson st	"	1,100 "	April 30, 1906
Frank B. Smith	1907 Centre st	Call Man	200 "	Aug. 11, 1890
William J. Noon	1972 Centre st	"	200 "	Oct. 3, 1890
Alvin Spear	511 La Grange st	Call Substitute	200 "	Jan. 8, 1897

Engine Company 32.

Name.	Residence.	Designation.	Compensation.	Date of Election or Appointment.
Thomas H. Ramsey	61 Elm st	Captain	$1,600 yr	March 2, 1906
John E. Redman	15 Princeton st	Lieutenant	1,400 "	April 19, 1904
James H. Meehan	20 Belmont st	Engineer	1,300 "	Dec. 21, 1900
Patrick F. McGough	23 Mill st	Assistant Engineer	1,200 "	Nov. 6, 1903
James A. McGee	86 Bartlett st	Hoseman	1,200 "	Jan. 6, 1888
William F. Thompson	298A Bunker Hill st	"	1,200 "	July 2, 1897
William H. Shute	66 Russell st	"	1,200 "	May 10, 1897
William H. Magner	38 Allston st	"	1,200 "	July 18, 1896
William J. Kelley	10 Prospect st	"	1,200 "	June 10, 1903
Andrew McAuliffe	312 Bunker Hill st	"	1,200 "	July 27, 1903
James Griffin	188 Bunker Hill st	"	1,200 "	March 24, 1898

Engine Company 33.

Name.	Residence.	Designation.	Compensation.	Date of Election or Appointment.
Melvin P. Mitchell	229 L st	Captain	$1,600 yr	Oct. 28, 1904
Michael D. Greene	1629 Tremont st	Lieutenant	1,400 "	" 25, 1902
Jacob H. Desmond	888 Huntington ave	Engineer	1,300 "	March 23, 1894
Thomas F. Cooney	115 Hillside st	Assistant Engineer	1,200 "	April 23, 1900
Thomas F. Frazer	49 Buttonwood st	"	1,200 "	Oct. 10, 1890
Louis H. Boudreau	120 Conant st	Hoseman	1,200 "	Dec. 31, 1897
John M. Cook	45 Woodville st	"	1,200 "	April 15, 1901
Frederick T. Dyer	332 Longwood ave	"	1,200 "	July 20, 1895
John J. Gleason	894 Huntington ave	"	1,200 "	Nov. 2, 1903
Joseph H. McLaughlin	43 Mountfern ave	"	1,100 "	March 9, 1906
Charles C. Shepard	3 Union st	"	1,100 "	Dec. 8, 1905
William H. Gunnan	9 Parker Hill ave	"	1,000 "	Nov. 3, 1906
John J. Sheehan	4 Winship pl	"	1,000 "	Oct. 5, 1907

Engine Company 34.

Name.	Residence.	Designation.	Compensation.	Date of Election or Appointment.
Thomas H. Weltch	8 Reedsdale st	Captain	$1,600 yr	June 23, 1904
Martin F. Conley	25 Harbor View st	Lieutenant	1,400 "	April 16, 1909
Philip Carrigan	74 Antwerp st	Engineer	1,300 "	Oct. 15, 1903
Frank J. Lynch	206 Everett st	Assistant Engineer	1,200 "	" 3, 1890
John J. Driscoll	16 Waverly st	Hoseman	1,200 "	May 26, 1905
John Bowen	7 Delaware pl	"	1,000 "	July 15, 1907
Thomas F. Muldoon	66 Foster st	"	900 "	May 18, 1908
John J. Ryan	54 Lincoln st	"	900 "	April 15, 1908
Edward F. Carroll	13 Lincoln st	"	900 "	June 26, 1908
George W. French	516 Western ave	Call Subtsitute	200 "	March 3, 1896

Fire Department.— Continued.

Name.	Residence.	Designation.	Compensation.	Date of Election or Appointment.

Engine Company 36.

Name.	Residence.	Designation.	Compensation.	Date of Election or Appointment.
Michael J. Lawler	14 Reedsdale st	Captain	$1,600 yr	June 10, 1903
Robert J. Gallagher	282 Bunker Hill st	Engineer	1,300 "	March 17, 1884
Charles M. Griffin	246 Bunker Hill st	Assistant Engineer	1,200 "	" 11, 1895
Frank Turnbull	26 Marion st	Hoseman	1,200 "	May 28, 1890
Henry G. Dwight	38 Monument sq	"	1,200 "	Sept. 1, 1884
John H. Barutio	Revere	"	1,200 "	Oct. 7, 1887
Joseph Murphy	24 Mystic st	"	1,200 "	Feb. 11, 1898
Robert J. McKay	20 School st	"	1,200 "	" 22, 1895
John F. Lawler	95 Keyes st	"	1,200 "	Oct. 27, 1905
William H. Carroll	6 Cordis st	"	1,000 "	Feb. 6, 1907
Joseph L. Ferrari	113 Chelsea st	"	1,100 "	Aug. 11, 1906

Engine Company 37.

Name.	Residence.	Designation.	Compensation.	Date of Election or Appointment.
Charles W. Conway	641 Huntington ave	Captain	$1,600 yr	March 2, 1906
Patrick W. Lynch	318 Longwood ave	Engineer	1,300 "	Oct. 28, 1904
Edward M. Quigley	94 Calumet st	Assistant Engineer	1,200 "	May 12, 1893
Thomas Wyllie	39 St. Alphonsus st	Hoseman	1,200 "	March 10, 1894
George H. Acres	101 Calumet st	"	1,200 "	April 9, 1894
John Whooley	3 Darling st	"	1,200 "	Feb. 14, 1902
Patrick J. Darcy	68 Hillside st	"	1,200 "	Oct. 30, 1902
Aaron A. Tapp	354 Longwood ave	"	1,200 "	Jan. 7, 1903
John Sullivan	52 St. Alphonsus st	"	1,200 "	June 29, 1903
Edward F. Featherston	107 Murdock st	"	1,200 "	Aug. 31, 1903
Thomas Finneran	19 Bartlett st	"	1,200 "	July 15, 1904
Charles F. Hayes	1176 Massachusetts ave	Probationer	720 "	April 6, 1909

Engine Companies 38 and 39.

Name.	Residence.	Designation.	Compensation.	Date of Election or Appointment.
James J. Caine	4 Mt. Vernon st	Captain	$1,600 yr	Jan. 4, 1907
Patrick F. Goggin	22 School st	Lieutenant	1,400 "	Nov. 1, 1901
Peter A. Matthews	773 Columbia rd	"	1,400 "	Jan. 4, 1907
George J. Baumeister	39 Mt. Vernon st	Engineer	1,300 "	June 29, 1903
William F. Crowley	72 Dorchester st	"	1,300 "	May 18, 1891
Eugene H. Alexander	Stoughton	Assistant Engineer	1,200 "	Feb. 28, 1902
Henry S. Marden	23 Newport st	"	1,200 "	June 29, 1903
Thomas F. Roach	25 Pleasant st	"	1,200 "	April 15, 1901
John E. Fleming	279 Highland st	Hoseman	1,200 "	Sept. 5, 1903
George H. Hine	21 Clapp pl	"	1,200 "	Nov. 18, 1899
James A. Higgins	261 E st	"	1,200 "	Oct. 4, 1901
Frank L. Lyons	319 E st	"	1,200 "	Aug. 17, 1900
Edward J. McIntyre	14 Hanson st	"	1,200 "	April 14, 1899
Thomas M. Nary	8 Willard st	"	1,200 "	Nov. 27, 1903
John J. Ryan	33 L st	"	1,200 "	May 17, 1893
Francis C. Shannon	764 E. Fourth st	"	1,200 "	Sept. 7, 1900
John J. Burke	366 Dorchester st	"	1,100 "	April 30, 1906
John P. Griffin	630 Dorchester ave	"	1,100 "	June 28, 1906
William J. Johnson	12 Vale st	"	1,100 "	April 30, 1906
William F. Quinn	114 Hudson st	"	1,000 "	Sept. 7, 1907
James A. Wall	1569B Tremont st	"	900 "	Jan. 22, 1908
William J. Linsky	32 Bay st	"	1,100 "	April 30, 1906

Engine Company 40.

Name.	Residence.	Designation.	Compensation.	Date of Election or Appointment.
Thomas J. Lannary	160 Webster st	Captain	$1,600 yr	April 10, 1903
Philip P. Leahy	247 Saratoga st	Lieutenant	1,400 "	" 10, 1903
John Bickford	320 Saratoga st	Engineer	1,300 "	Jan. 20, 1905
Joseph H. Clemens	211 Maverick st	Assistant Engineer	1,200 "	Feb. 10, 1893
Charles H. Ames	217 Webster st	Hoseman	1,200 "	Aug. 4, 1905
James E. Downey	60 Nashua st	"	1,200 "	July 20, 1895
Peter J. Dunn	136 Webster st	"	1,200 "	April 14, 1902
William F. Heldt	38 Bennington st	"	1,200 "	Feb. 10, 1899
Francis F. Toohig	437 Meridian st	"	1,200 "	May 18, 1891
George F. Moore	76 Williams st	"	1,000 "	April 5, 1907
Frank J. Sullivan	89 Henley st	"	900 "	Jan. 31, 1908

Engine Company 41.

Name.	Residence.	Designation.	Compensation.	Date of Election or Appointment.
Gustavus H. Nichols	16 Olney st	Captain	$1,600 yr	April 9, 1909
John P. Murray	35 St. Germain st	Lieutenant	1,400 "	March 2, 1906
John B. McKay	7 Webster st	Engineer	1,300 "	Aug. 21, 1903

Fire Department.— Continued.

Name.	Residence.	Designation.	Compensation.	Date of Election or Appointment.

Engine Company 41.— Concluded.

Name.	Residence.	Designation.	Compensation.	Date of Election or Appointment.
Joseph M. Ferreira	23 Faneuil ter	Assistant Engineer	$1,200 yr	April 23, 1900
George C. Swift	15 Aldie st	Hoseman	1,200 "	Jan. 13, 1886
Joseph W. Brown	15 Allston sq	"	1,200 "	May 3, 1897
John J. Riley	11 Raymond st	"	1,200 "	3, 1897
Bernard F. McNamara	657 Washington st	"	1,200 "	Oct. 14, 1903
Frederick R. Brophy	27 Shepard st	"	1,200 "	Sept. 19, 1905
Henry B. Heymann	336 Cambridge st	"	1,100 "	May 8, 1906
Francis H. Campbell	57 Hano st	"	1,200 "	Feb. 21, 1898

Engine Company 42.

Name.	Residence.	Designation.	Compensation.	Date of Election or Appointment.
John T. Byron	7 Copley st	Captain	$1,600 yr	Feb. 8, 1895
Charles Windhorn	3136 Washington st	Engineer	1,300 "	10, 1893
Louis J. Howard	108 Byron st	Assistant Engineer	1,200 "	April 5, 1901
Wesley C. Newdick	1937 Columbus ave	Hoseman	1,200 "	Jan. 4, 1889
Daniel W. Mahoney	14 Cliff st	"	1,200 "	May 18, 1891
William F. Donovan	30 Oakview ter	"	1,200 "	March 1, 1900
Thomas J. Lacey	44 Newbern st	"	1,200 "	June 27, 1901
Patrick J. Norton	28 Asticou rd	"	1,200 "	March 12, 1904
William P. Punch	26 Compton st	"	900 "	June 26, 1908
Francis A. Nicholson	1578 Tremont st	Probationer	720 "	Feb. 12, 1909
Leonard Murdock	34 Egleston st	Master Carpenter	1,300 "	Aug. 26, 1904

Engine Company 43.

Name.	Residence.	Designation.	Compensation.	Date of Election or Appointment.
Albert J. Caulfield	14 Atlantic st	Captain	$1,600 yr	June 26, 1908
William M. Lynch	5 Howes st	"	1,600 "	26, 1908
John F. Mooney	74 Idaho st	Lieutenant	1,400 "	April 6, 1907
Edward J. Lynch	379 Dorchester st	Engineer	1,300 "	Jan. 19, 1900
Edward C. Verkampen	252 Dudley st	Assistant Engineer	1,200 "	June 27, 1902
Edward F. Doody	23 Leedsville st	Hoseman	1,200 "	May 15, 1896
Valentine P. McGuire	59 Dustin st	"	1,200 "	July 2, 1897
Francis J. Martin	1081 Dorchester ave	"	1,200 "	Sept. 2, 1904
Thomas A. McLaughlin	494 E. Third st	"	1,200 "	June 15, 1905
Dennis J. Cadigan	1213 Dorchester ave	"	1,100 "	Dec. 8, 1905
Dennis J. Coughlin	230 W. Third st	"	1,060 "	Sept. 7, 1907
Joseph H. Hohmann	142 W. Eighth st	"	1,000 "	June 14, 1907
Michael Ryan	15 Raven st	"	1,000 "	Dec. 14, 1906

Engine Company 44.

Name.	Residence.	Designation.	Compensation.	Date of Election or Appointment.
Robert A. Ritchie	42 Chelsea st	Captain	$1,600 yr	Oct. 16, 1896
Walter S. Eaton	21 Dorset st	Lieutenant	1,400 "	Dec. 14, 1899
Stephen E. O'Brien	527 Medford st	First Engineer	1,400 "	April 12, 1907
Sylvester J. Wynter	442 Saratoga st	Second Engineer	1,300 "	12, 1907
Daniel J. Gibbons	468 Sumner st	Third Engineer	1,200 "	July 22, 1904
Henry D. Marsh	57 Fleet st	Fourth Engineer	1,600 "	April 6, 1907
Charles S. Moran	125 Maverick st	Hoseman	1,200 "	17, 1903
Frank G. Avery	17 Bellflower st	"	1,200 "	Feb. 16, 1903
John F. Murphy	56 Bartlett st	"	1,200 "	April 18, 1904
Herbert E. Smith	88A Falcon st	"	1,200 "	5, 1904
Robert A. Nugent	133 Falcon st	"	1,200 "	June 23, 1905
William S. Slauenwhite	158 Falcon st	"	1,200 "	March 31, 1905
Daniel J. Mahoney	6 Lexington st	"	1,200 "	Oct. 4, 1901
John P. Walsh	182 Webster st	"	1,200 "	May 7, 1897
John W. Smith	158A Falcon st	"	1,000 "	June 19, 1907
William J. Marshall	4 Short st	"	1,100 "	Dec. 8, 1905
Abram H. T. Simpson	1 White st	Shipkeeper	2.00 day	Nov. 23, 1907

Engine Company 45.

Name.	Residence.	Designation.	Compensation.	Date of Election or Appointment.
Roscoe E. Handy	36 Hewlett st	Captain	$1,600 yr	Dec. 22, 1893
Thomas F. Hedrington	47 Cohasset st	Engineer	1,300 "	May 31, 1895
Robert R. Talbot	28 Albano st	Assistant Engineer	1,200 "	12, 1899
Daniel F. Greenlaw	27 Tappan st	Hoseman	1,200 "	Feb. 16, 1888
Frank C. Turner	4294 Washington st	"	1,200 "	22, 1883
John J. Goff	219 Belgrade ave	"	1,200 "	Sept. 3, 1884
Edward A. Burbank	72 Hewlett st	"	1,200 "	Nov. 23, 1888
Robert D. Stewart	19 Heathcote st	"	1,200 "	June 27, 1902
Timothy F. Sullivan	70 Weld Hill st	"	1,200 "	Nov. 7, 1902
Daniel A. White	39 Union st	Probationer	720 "	April 6, 1909

Fire Department.— Continued.

Name.	Residence.	Designation.	Compensation.	Date of Election or Appointment.

Engine Company 46.

Name.	Residence.	Designation.	Compensation.	Date of Election or Appointment.
Walter M. McLean	59 Dracut st	Captain	$1,600 yr	June 3, 1904
James T. Prendergast	47 Dix st	Lieutenant	1,400 "	Jan. 4, 1907
Francis Dolan	36 Newhall ave	Engineer	1,300 "	Oct. 9, 1903
John J. Craddock	411 Neponset ave	Assistant Engineer	1,100 "	May 11, 1906
Patrick J. Cray	6 Wrentham st	Hoseman	1,200 "	June 10, 1903
Ebenezer H. Wheelock	152 Welles ave	"	1,200 "	Jan. 13, 1899
Thomas Brady	62 Hecla st	"	1,200 "	Oct. 25, 1902
Frederick H. Brown	12 Dracut st	"	1,100 "	June 26, 1906
William F. Ruth	21 Dix st	"	1,200 "	Dec. 6, 1901
Timothy J. Sheehan	1112 Dorchester ave	"	900 "	Oct. 20, 1908

Ladder Company 1.

Name.	Residence.	Designation.	Compensation.	Date of Election or Appointment.
Edward J. Shallow	711 E. Fifth st	Captain	$1,600 yr	Feb. 8, 1901
Michael F. Silva	82 Eutaw st	Lieutenant	1,400 "	Jan. 4, 1907
Henry J. Kelly	14 Chapman st	Ladderman	1,200 "	June 21, 1894
Patrick J. Doherty	60 Main st	"	1,200 "	Aug. 10, 1900
Patrick T. Buckley	10 Main st	"	1,200 "	Nov. 15, 1900
Pillsbury C. Fickett	260 Maverick st	"	1,200 "	Jan. 22, 1902
Joseph H. Andreoli	21 Harvard sq	"	1,200 "	Aug. 31, 1903
Charles J. Foley	148 Friend st	"	1,200 "	Dec. 4, 1903
Charles J. Fleming	8 Summer st	"	1,200 "	Jan. 4, 1904
Daniel P. Dacey	38 Pleasant st	"	1,200 "	July 15, 1905
Patrick Curran	32 Lawrence st	"	1,200 "	March 31, 1905
Cornelius I. Meehane	32 Lawrence st	"	1,200 "	June 15, 1905
Garfield R. LaPlante	148 Friend st	"	1,100 "	Dec. 8, 1905

Ladder Company 2.

Name.	Residence.	Designation.	Compensation.	Date of Election or Appointment.
Frank P. Stengel	16 Rill st	Captain	$1,600 yr	April 9, 1909
Patrick F. McLeavey	154 Webster st	Lieutenant	1,400 "	Jan. 4, 1907
John McCarthy	16 London st	Ladderman	1,200 "	Nov. 11, 1892
John J. Sullivan	75 Webster st	"	1,200 "	Feb. 10, 1893
Richard W. Brown	318 Sumner st	"	1,100 "	July 10, 1906
James J. Callahan	280 Maverick st	"	1,100 "	June 1, 1906
Francis P. Walsh	250 Maverick st	"	1,100 "	Sept. 7, 1906
Arthur W. Deleskey	69 W. Eagle st	"	1,000 "	" 27, 1907
Freeman Wagner	41 Condor st	"	1,000 "	June 24, 1907
Cornelius J. Harrington	238 Havre st	"	900 "	May 18, 1908
Robert L. Quilty	358 K st	Probationer	720 "	Feb. 12, 1909

Ladder Company 3.

Name.	Residence.	Designation.	Compensation.	Date of Election or Appointment.
Peter E. Walsh	150 Stanwood st	Captain	$1,600 yr	Nov. 4, 1904
John McCann	246 W. Fifth st	Lieutenant	1,400 "	Jan. 4, 1907
Thomas D. Brown	4 Letterfine ter	Ladderman	1,200 "	May 8, 1903
Charles A. Donohoe	748 Harrison ave	"	1,200 "	" 16, 1893
John J. Earl	46 Dover st	"	1,200 "	Feb. 11, 1903
George L. Evanson	15 Raven st	"	1,000 "	" 20, 1907
John T. Gillen	32 Forest st	"	1,200 "	June 27, 1892
James Gavagan	226 W. Sixth st	"	1,200 "	Aug. 16, 1897
Michael F. Hayes	190 W. Sixth st	"	1,200 "	Feb. 22, 1895
Patrick J. Malone	58 St. James st	"	1,200 "	Aug. 2, 1893
James W. Mahoney	39 Cobden st	"	1,200 "	Dec. 24, 1897
Hugh F. McGaffigan	287 Dudley st	"	1,200 "	April 2, 1896
George A. Waggett	46 Harvard st	"	1,200 "	Oct. 13, 1892

Ladder Company 4.

Name.	Residence.	Designation.	Compensation.	Date of Election or Appointment.
John P. McManus	59 Stanwood st	Captain	$1,600 yr	July 26, 1895
John Hogan	110 Regent st	Lieutenant	1,400 "	March 2, 1906
Thomas F. Boggs	98 W. Canton st	Ladderman	1,200 "	Oct. 15, 1873
Albert M. Laskey	18 Fenelon st	"	1,200 "	June 21, 1889
William H. McDonald	35 Cliff st	"	1,200 "	Jan. 6, 1888
John Prendergast	10 Glendale st	"	1,200 "	July 18, 1882
John J. McKenna	8 Howell st	"	1,100 "	Oct. 16, 1906
John J. Collins	9 Woodville Park st	"	1,000 "	Feb. 22, 1907
Joseph F. Rorke	19 Adams st	"	1,000 "	Oct. 24, 1907
Joseph D. Mitchell	7 Cardington st	"	900 "	Jan. 31, 1908
Harry J. McNealy	8 Brookside ave	"	900 "	Nov. 22, 1907
Edward J. C. Powers	35 Auburn st	"	900 "	Oct. 20, 1908

Fire Department. — Continued.

Name.	Residence.	Designation.	Compensation.	Date of Election or Appointment.

Ladder Company 5.

Name.	Residence.	Designation.	Compensation.	Date of Election or Appointment.
Edward D. Locke	821 E. Fourth st	Captain	$1,600 yr	March 21, 1901
Charles A. Winchester	422 E. Sixth st	Lieutenant	1,400 "	" 20, 1908
Daniel J. Cadden	317 Silva st	Ladderman	1,200 "	Sept. 13, 1888
William A. Baldwin	11 Harbor View st	"	1,200 "	Feb. 10, 1893
Martin J. Flavin	6 Linden st	"	1,200 "	July 10, 1894
Frank P. Chapman	137 W. Eighth st	"	1,200 "	May 15, 1896
James H. Moran	285 W. Fifth st	"	1,200 "	Dec. 5, 1902
Matthew J. Welch	21 Winfield st	"	1,100 "	March 9, 1906
David J. Curran	65 W. Third st	"	1,000 "	April 5, 1907
Guy H. Hendrickson	822 Dorchester ave	"	1,000 "	Jan. 14, 1907
Edward F. Cunniff	801 E. Fifth st	"	900 "	Dec. 20, 1907
Charles H. Hohmann	142 W. Eighth st	"	900 "	June 26, 1908

Ladder Company 6.

Name.	Residence.	Designation.	Compensation.	Date of Election or Appointment.
John A. Noonan	7 Blackwell st	Lieutenant	$1,400 yr	June 25, 1908
George A. Whalen	32 Magdala st	Ladderman	1,200 "	Dec. 13, 1893
John F. Lavelle	271 Codman st	"	1,200 "	Sept. 6, 1901
Andrew J. G. McKee	12 Washington pl	"	1,200 "	Feb. 10, 1893
James M. Elliot	31A Dracut st	"	1,200 "	Oct. 24, 1890
George E. Watson	50 River st	Call Substitute	200 "	May 7, 1897
William E. Leavitt	13 River st	"	200 "	Aug. 11, 1899
Louis E. Weisse	46 Sturbridge st	"	200 "	Jan. 28, 1908
Charles E. Parker	17 Grant st	"	200 "	May 1, 1908

Ladder Company 7.

Name.	Residence.	Designation.	Compensation.	Date of Election or Appointment.
James F. O'Connell	1382 Dorchester ave	Lieutenant	$1,400 yr	Oct. 30, 1908
Cornelius P. Moakley	74 Topliff st	Ladderman	1,200 "	" 18, 1895
Michael B. Mulcahy	12 East st	"	1,200 "	May 24, 1889
William J. Walsh	41 Longfellow st	"	1,200 "	Aug. 15, 1900
William Peterson	94 Barry st	"	1,200 "	May 21, 1897
Patrick J. Norton	45 Hecla st	"	1,200 "	Dec. 14, 1900
Henry F. Brady	11 Ellsworth st	"	1,200 "	Feb. 11, 1898
James L. Tracy	14 Fifield st	"	1,200 "	Sept. 2, 1904
Michael J. O'Donnell	201 Hancock st	"	1,100 "	Dec. 8, 1905
William B. Jennings	14 Folsom st	"	1,200 "	April 28, 1899
John Pendoley	4 Wainwright st	"	1,200 "	Sept. 20, 1876

Ladder Company 8.

Name.	Residence.	Designation.	Compensation.	Date of Election or Appointment.
James F. Ryan	115 Adams st	Captain	$1,600 yr	Jan. 4, 1907
Florence Donahue	11 Vale st	Lieutenant	1,400 "	June 24, 1904
Walter Davey	124 Bennington st	Ladderman	1,200 "	Dec. 24, 1897
James J. Lunny	61 Willowwood st	"	1,200 "	Feb. 11, 1898
Henry J. Power	58 Fairmount st	"	1,200 "	Jan. 12, 1900
John J. Crowley	20 Decatur st	"	1,200 "	Dec. 24, 1897
Michael J. Gilligan	36 Winthrop st	"	1,200 "	Feb. 18, 1902
Thomas L. Darcy	65 Wensley st	"	1,200 "	Oct. 29, 1902
Thomas F. Twomey	31 School st	"	1,200 "	May 4, 1900
James W. Ryan	53 Temple st	"	1,100 "	April 30, 1906
Charles J. Greeley	61 Clarendon st	"	1,100 "	Dec. 8, 1905
Daniel W. Baker	191 High st	"	1,200 "	Feb. 11, 1898
Carl P. Franks	347 Meridian st	"	1,100 "	Dec. 8, 1905
Stephen L. King	76 Crescent ave	"	1,000 "	Feb. 23, 1907

Ladder Company 9.

Name.	Residence.	Designation.	Compensation.	Date of Election or Appointment.
John E. Cassidy	98 Main st	Captain	$1,600 yr	Jan. 4, 1904
William H. Hughes	41 Decatur st	Lieutenant	1,400 "	June 3, 1904
Chauncey R. Delano	61 Elm st	Ladderman	1,200 "	May 21, 1897
William C. Lutz	Somerville	"	1,200 "	March 22, 1902
John J. Reagan	575 Hanover st	"	1,200 "	Jan. 4, 1904
Dennis M. Condon	94 Decatur st	"	1,200 "	June 30, 1905
Thomas M. Carney	148 Chelsea st	"	1,200 "	Oct. 13, 1905
Thomas R. McConologue	16 Polk st	"	1,100 "	April 30, 1906
Alexander McDonald	Somerville	"	1,100 "	" 30, 1906
Patrick F. McDonough	36 Winthrop st	"	1,000 "	June 14, 1907
Henry J. McGonagle	334 Medford st	"	1,000 "	July 15, 1907

Fire Department.— Continued.

Name.	Residence.	Designation.	Compensation.	Date of Election or Appointment.

Ladder Company 10.

Name.	Residence.	Designation.	Compensation.	Date of Election or Appointment.
Thomas B. Flanagan	31 Forbes st	Lieutenant	$1,400 yr	Jan. 7, 1889
Albert A. Bestwick, Jr.	35 Paul Gore st	Ladderman	1,200 "	Feb. 7, 1886
Timothy F. Donovan	13 St. Joseph st	"	1,200 "	May 12, 1903
John D. J. Downey	3764 Washington st	"	1,000 "	June 14, 1907
Leonard F. Griffin	26 Dalrymple st	"	1,200 "	Nov. 7, 1902
John Lynch	9 Keyes st	"	1,200 "	Oct. 8, 1873
Thomas F. Ward	47A Creighton st	"	1,100 "	April 30, 1906

Ladder Company 11.

Name.	Residence.	Designation.	Compensation.	Date of Election or Appointment.
Patrick J. Laffey	51 Lincoln st	Lieutenant	$1,400 yr	Sept. 29, 1905
Michael Cook	39 Goldsmith st	Ladderman	1,200 "	May 1, 1872
William J. Kane	418 Western ave	"	1,200 "	" 16, 1891
Charles A. Fernald	350 Cambridge st	"	1,200 "	Feb. 1, 1896
Joseph L. Bannon	69 Allston st	"	1,100 "	July 12, 1906
James L. McLoughlin	79 Church st	"	1,100 "	Aug. 31, 1906
William P. Dungan	21 Faneuil ter	"	1,000 "	April 30, 1907
Newton Zwicker	57 Dustin st	Call Man	200 "	Dec. 13, 1899
John B. Martin	20 Chestnut Hill ave	Call Substitute	200 "	May 21, 1897
Henry J. Heinlein	49 Bennett st	"	200 "	" 21, 1897
Frank L. Barlow	122 Franklin st	"	200 "	" 21, 1897

Ladder Company 12.

Name.	Residence.	Designation.	Compensation.	Date of Election or Appointment.
Joseph H. Kenney	14 Linwood st	Captain	$1,600 yr	Dec. 6, 1901
Hamilton A. McClay	85 Monroe st	Lieutenant	1,400 "	Jan. 4, 1907
Ernest O. Haines	85 Heath st	Ladderman	1,200 "	June 22, 1894
Patrick H. Kenney	73 Hillside st	"	1,200 "	Sept. 24, 1906
George F. Doyle	171 St. Alphonsus st	"	1,200 "	Aug. 27, 1895
Robert H. Webber	1027 Tremont st	"	1,200 "	Dec. 14, 1900
Dennis J. Crowley	704 Columbus ave	"	1,200 "	Feb. 6, 1903
Walter Hughes	11 Waite st	"	1,200 "	Jan. 14, 1898
Daniel J. O'Leary	689 Parker st	"	1,200 "	June 24, 1904
John L. Glynn	49 Everett st	"	1,100 "	Dec. 8, 1905
James J. Walton	116 Conant st	"	1,100 "	" 8, 1905
Charles Willett	44 E. Brookline st	"	1,100 "	Aug. 24, 1906
Carl S. Bowers	5 Mather st	"	1,000 "	April 5, 1907

Ladder Company 13.

Name.	Residence.	Designation.	Compensation.	Date of Election or Appointment.
Michael J. Nolan	71 Farragut rd	Captain	$1,600 yr	Jan. 4, 1907
DeWitt Lane	38 St. Botolph st	Lieutenant	1,400 "	May 12, 1905
William A. J. Drinan	50 Houghton st	Ladderman	1,200 "	July 15, 1904
Jeremiah A. Feeley	2050 Washington st	"	1,200 "	May 22, 1905
Thomas E. Flanagan	28 Kempton st	"	1,200 "	Oct. 25, 1902
Leroy James	12 Dilworth st	"	1,200 "	March 31, 1905
John P. Olsen	70 Warren ave	"	1,200 "	May 24, 1895
John J. Donohoe	748 Harrison ave	"	900 "	Dec. 20, 1907
John J. Kenney	73 Hillside st	"	900 "	" 20, 1907
Thomas L. Finn	625 E. Second st	Probationer	720 "	April 6, 1909

Ladder Company 14.

Name.	Residence.	Designation.	Compensation.	Date of Election or Appointment.
Patrick W. Lanegan	203 High st	Captain	$1,600 yr	Jan. 4, 1907
Thomas H. Andreoli	3 Fountain Hill st	Ladderman	1,200 "	July 20, 1896
Theodore Gallipeau	19 Lee st	"	1,100 "	April 30, 1906
William R. Boyd	15 Chamberlain st	"	1,100 "	June 29, 1906
Thomas R. O'Brien	41 Decatur st	"	900 "	May 18, 1908

Ladder Company 15.

Name.	Residence.	Designation.	Compensation.	Date of Election or Appointment.
John S. Cleverly	512 Cambridge st	Captain	$1,600 yr	Nov. 12, 1897
Fred I. Adams	2 Kearsarge ter	Lieutenant	1,400 "	March 2, 1906
John J. Baldwin	183 Union st	Ladderman	1,200 "	Dec. 28, 1900
John J. Cremin	127 Moreland st	"	1,200 "	April 14, 1905
Francis J. Dermody	16 Kempton st	"	1,200 "	Nov. 15, 1901
Florence Donoughue	49 Allen st	"	1,200 "	Jan. 14, 1901
William H. Gillis	Medford	"	1,200 "	Nov. 11, 1892
George H. Magwood	Somerville	"	1,200 "	Feb. 11, 1898
William J. Shepard	3 Union st	"	1,200 "	July 15, 1904
Charles A. Wolfe	33 Webster ave	"	1,200 "	Oct. 15, 1901
John L. Chandler	10 Pontiac st	"	1,000 "	Aug. 26, 1907

Fire Department.— Continued.

Name.	Residence.	Designation.	Compensation.	Date of Election or Appointment.

Ladder Company 16.

Name.	Residence.	Designation.	Compensation.	Date of Election or Appointment.
Michael J. Sullivan	32 Tower st	Lieutenant	$1,400 yr	Jan. 4, 1907
William A. Gavin	64 Newberg st	Ladderman	1,200 "	Feb. 12, 1901
Robert Rooney	683 Parker st	"	1,200 "	March 25, 1885
James F. Maguire	32 Worthington st	"	1,200 "	Sept. 13, 1888
Peter F. Gately	480 La Grange st	"	1,200 "	June 21, 1889
Stephen A. Moran	4251 Washington st	"	1,200 "	May 7, 1897

Ladder Company 17.

Name.	Residence.	Designation.	Compensation.	Date of Election or Appointment.
Joseph A. Dolan	112 S Fairview st	Captain	$1,600 yr	March 31, 1905
Henry Krake	235 Webster st	Lieutenant	1,400 "	Jan. 4, 1907
Dennis J. Bailey	92 Calumet st	Ladderman	1,200 "	April 2, 1896
William H. Hawkins	135 Draper st	"	1,200 "	Dec. 22, 1893
Joseph P. Hanton	50 Sumner st	"	1,200 "	Feb. 10, 1899
Dennis J. Hurley	55 Sturbridge st	"	1,200 "	June 24, 1904
James J. Kelleher	156 W. Lenox st	"	1,200 "	Jan. 13, 1905
George T. Magoun	50 Linden Park st	"	1,200 "	July 28, 1904
Morris J. Prendergast	108 Parker Hill ave	"	1,200 "	March 31, 1905
William C. Swan	38 W. Cedar st	"	1,200 "	Feb. 10, 1898
George A. Verkampen	252 Dudley st	"	1,200 "	June 7, 1901
Daniel J. Wallace	44 E. Springfield st	"	1,200 "	Jan. 2, 1905
Daniel B. McAlvin	144 W. Lenox st	"	1,100 "	April 30, 1906

Ladder Company 18.

Name.	Residence.	Designation.	Compensation.	Date of Election or Appointment.
Allan J. McDonald	1 Kearsarge ter	Captain	$1,600 yr	Feb. 6, 1903
William H. McCorkle	18 Nelson st	Lieutenant	1,400 "	Jan. 4, 1907
Patrick T. Burke	430 E. Fifth st	Ladderman	1,200 "	April 28, 1899
Cornelius J. Crowley	7 Lawrence st	"	1,200 "	June 4, 1897
Daniel F. Crowley	777 Columbia rd	"	1,200 "	July 31, 1901
John L. Donovan	610 Broadway	"	1,200 "	March 24, 1902
John F. Haley	626 Freeport st	"	1,200 "	Feb. 6, 1893
Daniel J. Hurley	37 Edson green	"	1,200 "	Oct. 4, 1901
James McTiernan, Jr.	53 Harvest st	"	1,200 "	" 12, 1900
Frederick J. Dobbratz	38 Allston st	"	1,100 "	March 9, 1906
Francis P. Kennedy	10 Vale st	"	1,100 "	Sept. 27, 1906
Daniel J. Leary	14 Thornley st	"	1,100 "	Dec. 8, 1905
Morris Swart	45 Crescent ave	"	1,000 "	May 10, 1907

Ladder Company 19.

Name.	Residence.	Designation.	Compensation.	Date of Election or Appointment.
William C. Greely	70 L st	Lieutenant	$1,400 yr	June 10, 1903
Frank T. Wheeler	745 E. Fifth st	Ladderman	1,200 "	" 16, 1896
John E. Donoghue	188 L st	"	1,200 "	July 5, 1892
Charles P. A. Hurley	3 Bradford st	"	1,200 "	" 15, 1894
Frank J. Hagerty	470 E. Sixth st	"	1,000 "	Feb. 6, 1907
Richard H. Brown	459 W. Fourth st	"	1,000 "	May 31, 1907
George B. S. Kewer	547 E. Seventh st	"	1,000 "	April 5, 1907

Ladder Company 20.

Name.	Residence.	Designation.	Compensation.	Date of Election or Appointment.
Michael J. Dacey	152 Quincy st	Lieutenant	$1,400 yr	March 2, 1906
James F. Bailey	1282 Columbia rd	Ladderman	1,200 "	April 17, 1896
McDarrah Flaherty	22 Leedsville st	"	1,200 "	Feb. 15, 1893
Patrick Hart	23 Harbor View st	"	1,200 "	Nov. 6, 1903
William H. O'Dea	92 Calumet st	"	1,200 "	March 31, 1905
John F. Fitzgerald	30 Crescent ave	"	1,000 "	Nov. 5, 1906
Francis Kehoe	52 F st	"	900 "	June 26, 1906

Ladder Company 21.

Name.	Residence.	Designation.	Compensation.	Date of Election or Appointment.
Edward J. McKendrew	276 Princeton st	Lieutenant	$1,400 yr	March 12, 1897
Frederick L. Carroll	53 Collins st	Ladderman	1,200 "	Aug. 4, 1905
Dennis J. Hedrington	23 Faxon st	"	1,200 "	Sept. 13, 1888
Bernard E. Plunkett	415 Chelsea st	"	1,200 "	Oct. 10, 1890
Joseph T. Smith	328 Chelsea st	"	1,200 "	April 2, 1896
Patrick L. Crowley	20 Decatur st	"	1,100 "	" 30, 1906
Michael L. Dorgan	31 Porter st	Probationer	720 "	" 13, 1909

Fire Department.— Continued.

Name.	Residence.	Designation.	Compensation.	Date of Election or Appointment.

Ladder Company 22.

Daniel L. Cadigan	29 Allston st	Lieutenant	$1,400 yr	Feb. 5, 1907
Philip A. Tague	300A Bunker Hill st	Ladderman	1,200 "	Dec. 20, 1895
John E. F. Griffin	8 Tufts st	"	1,200 "	Nov. 23, 1888
William H. D. Nichols	Somerville	"	1,200 "	Oct. 1, 1895
Owen Tulley	82 Ferrin st	"	1,200 "	May 15, 1896
Philip M. Sullivan	26 Marion st	"	1,200 "	Sept. 6, 1892
Maurice F. Foley	24 Monument sq	"	1,100 "	April 30, 1906
Joseph A. Fierling	Medford	"	1,000 "	Nov. 23, 1906
Richard F. Fleming	30 Everett st	"	1,000 "	March 15, 1907

Ladder Company 23.

John J. Gavin	6 Glenway st	Lieutenant	$1,400 yr	June 10, 1903
Edward J. Berigan	96 Bower st	Ladderman	1,200 "	Oct. 24, 1890
John P. Butler	9 Woodville ave	"	1,200 "	" 4, 1895
Edward W. Fottler	977 Blue Hill ave	"	1,200 "	Aug. 2, 1893
George F. Leary	14 Thornley st	"	1,100 "	Dec. 8, 1905
Thomas F. Lynch	129 Winthrop st	"	1,200 "	" 20, 1901
William J. O'Connell	449 Blue Hill ave	"	1,200 "	July 9, 1892
Charles A. Rodd	1 Cedar ave	"	1,200 "	Feb. 16, 1888

Ladder Company 24.

James F. McMahon	45 Bunker Hill st	Lieutenant	$1,400 yr	Oct. 26, 1900
Thomas J. Cavanagh	35½ Longfellow st	Ladderman	1,200 "	" 17, 1890
Thomas J. Fitzgerald	44 W. Cedar st	"	1,200 "	Jan. 18, 1889
Hugh J. Goodfellow	60 Pearl st	"	1,200 "	Oct. 9, 1903
Michael J. Murphy	16 Burke st	"	1,200 "	June 30, 1905
Frank Patrick	150 W. Canton st	"	1,200 "	March 16, 1900
Michael A. Riley	9 S. Russell st	"	1,200 "	July 2, 1897
Edward McNamara, Jr	657 Washington st	"	1,000 "	Jan. 21, 1907

Ladder Company 25.

Hadwin Sawyer	Holbrook	Lieutenant	$1,400 yr	Feb. 10, 1893
Joseph F. Baumeister	3232 Washington st	Ladderman	1,200 "	Nov. 15, 1901
Joseph H. E. Brown	209 Park st	"	1,200 "	April 13, 1905
William Hall	45 Amherst st	"	1,200 "	" 11, 1894
Harry L. McCartee	123 Anawan ave	"	1,200 "	" 21, 1891
Samuel T. Rutherford	19 Mt. Vernon st	Call Substitute	200 "	" 23, 1900
Edward H. Peters	22 Corinth st	"	200 "	Nov. 21, 1900
Granville H. Wiswell	25 Pleasant st	"	200 "	Sept. 27, 1907

Ladder Company 26.

Patrick J. V. Kelley	1458 Tremont st	Lieutenant	$1,400 yr	April 23, 1900
James J. Doyle	31 Kempton st	Ladderman	1,200 "	Feb. 11, 1898
John M. Fitzgerald	33 Wigglesworth st	"	1,200 "	Sept. 27, 1886
Dennis J. Lane	261 Parker Hill ave	"	1,200 "	May 18, 1891
Frank Meleedy	114 Conant st	"	1,200 "	Aug. 11, 1892
Thomas A. Ring	12 Victoria st	"	1,100 "	Sept. 4, 1906
Charles A. Cardani	90 E. Cottage st	"	1,000 "	Oct. 20, 1908

Ladder Company 27.

John F. Mitchell	8 Minot st	Lieutenant	$1,400 yr	Nov. 15, 1901
Patrick J. Mahan	6 Fairview st	Ladderman	1,200 "	Feb. 1, 1896
Gustav A. Shultz	33 Houghton st	"	1,000 "	July 15, 1907
John Lawson	11 Lorenzo st	"	1,200 "	May 8, 1903
Michael D. Sullivan	4 Chickatawbut st	"	1,200 "	June 16, 1905
John H. Roche	78 Chickatawbut st	"	1,000 "	Dec. 8, 1905

Chemical Company 1.

Victor H. Richer	15 Leroy st	Lieutenant	$1,400 yr	Jan. 24, 1908
Joseph T. Humphreys	3 Wallace ct	Hoseman	1,200 "	Nov. 15, 1901
James F. Trainor	38 Marcella st	"	1,200 "	Jan. 22, 1902
Richard G. Lawless	30 Nashua st	"	900 "	May 19, 1908

Fire Department.— Continued.

Name.	Residence.	Designation.	Compensation.	Date of Election or Appointment.

Chemical Company 2.

Name.	Residence.	Designation.	Compensation.	Date of Election or Appointment.
Charles T. Farren	44 Francis st	Lieutenant	$1,400 yr	Oct. 25, 1902
John F. Watson	12 Hall st	Hoseman	1,200 "	May 7, 1897
James C. Taylor	1098 Washington st	"	1,200 "	Nov. 15, 1901
Edward J. Kelley, Jr	1 Arcadia st	"	1,100 "	Sept. 14, 1906

Chemical Company 3.

Name.	Residence.	Designation.	Compensation.	Date of Election or Appointment.
Thomas F. Quigley	143 Bunker Hill st	Lieutenant	$1,400 yr	March 1, 1907
Frederick H. Gould	Revere	Hoseman	1,200 "	Oct. 10, 1890
William J. Dower	293 Main st	"	1,200 "	May 12, 1890
David Meade	18 Putnam st	"	1,200 "	Oct. 10, 1890
Bernard J. Farren	45 Sullivan st	"	900 "	Nov. 22, 1907

Chemical Company 4.

Name.	Residence.	Designation.	Compensation.	Date of Election or Appointment.
Daniel M. Shaughnessy	75 Edwin st	Lieutenant	$1,400 yr	Dec. 14, 1900
Michael J. F. Brown	4 Letterfine ter	Hoseman	1,100 "	" 8, 1905
James P. Rose	14 Haverford st	"	1,000 "	Feb. 15, 1907
David A. Truesdale	795 Shawmut ave	"	900 "	Jan. 22, 1908

Chemical Company 5.

Name.	Residence.	Designation.	Compensation.	Date of Election or Appointment.
Cornelius F. Driscoll	8 Cobden st	Lieutenant	$1,400 yr	April 17, 1903
William T. McCormack	47 Walk Hill st	Hoseman	1,200 "	March 20, 1896
John H. Murnan	396 Centre st	"	1,200 "	Nov. 23, 1888

Chemical Company 6.

Name.	Residence.	Designation.	Compensation.	Date of Election or Appointment.
Philip G. Flynn	20 Winship st	Lieutenant	$1,400 yr	Aug. 28, 1896
George A. Newhall	25 Aldie st	Hoseman	1,200 "	Sept. 3, 1884
John J. McLane	5 Delaware pl	"	1,200 "	Oct. 4, 1901

Chemical Company 7.

Name.	Residence.	Designation.	Compensation.	Date of Election or Appointment.
Thomas J. Hines	89 Byron st	Lieutenant	$1,400 yr	March 11, 1904
William McCarthy	180 Bennington st	Hoseman	1,200 "	May 24, 1897
William J. Nolan	38 Clifton st	"	900 "	April 15, 1908
Edward J. Crowley	400 Bennington st	Probationer	720 "	Feb. 12, 1909
Frederick L. Hynes	131 Everett st	"	720 "	April 6, 1909

Chemical Company 8.

Name.	Residence.	Designation.	Compensation.	Date of Election or Appointment.
Lorenzo D. Merrill	112 Union Park st	Lieutenant	$1,400 yr	Dec. 5, 1902
David J. Fitzgerald	19 Locust st	Master Painter	1,300 "	Aug. 15, 1902
James H. Stout	259 E st	Hoseman	1,200 "	March 11, 1895
John M. Devine	7 National st	"	1,200 "	Oct. 20, 1893

Chemical Company 9.

Name.	Residence.	Designation.	Compensation.	Date of Election or Appointment.
William J. Toomey	66 Russell st	Lieutenant	$1,400 yr	Jan. 4, 1907
James F. McKirn	43 Pleasant st	Hoseman	1,200 "	Aug. 3, 1892
John J. McDermott	35 Monument sq	"	1,000 "	Jan. 11, 1907

Chemical Company 10.

Name.	Residence.	Designation.	Compensation.	Date of Election or Appointment.
Charles C. Springer	54 Dudley st	Lieutenant	$1,400 yr	April 6, 1900
John F. McBride	100 Vernon st	Hoseman	1,200 "	" 28, 1899
Patrick F. Garrity	12 Reed ter	"	1,200 "	Nov. 26, 1894
Thomas H. Kehoe	52 F st	"	1,000 "	Oct. 23, 1907

Chemical Company 11.

Name.	Residence.	Designation.	Compensation.	Date of Election or Appointment.
Morris L. Galvin	10 Bartlett st	Lieutenant	$1,400 yr	April 14, 1909
William F. Marquardt	22 Dracut st	Hoseman	1,200 "	May 24, 1895
James E. Nolan	203 W. Selden st	"	1,200 "	Dec. 20, 1893
Joseph Smith	7 Dewey st	"	1,200 "	Nov. 7, 1881

Chemical Company 12.

Name.	Residence.	Designation.	Compensation.	Date of Election or Appointment.
Timothy C. O'Neill	51 Mozart st	Hoseman	$1,200 yr	July 16, 1889
William T. Hall	756 Huntington ave	"	1,200 "	May 11, 1904
James J. Doolan	6 Cherokee st	"	900 "	April 15, 1908

Fire Department.— Continued.

Name.	Residence.	Designation.	Com- pensation.	Date of Election or Appointment.

Water Tower 1.

Charles H. Long	15 Prospect st	Lieutenant	$1,400 yr	Dec. 23, 1904
John H. Williams	25 Faneuil ter	Hoseman	1,200 "	Nov. 7, 1902
Thomas F. Lyons	51 Tufts st	Probationer	720 "	Dec. 18, 1908

Water Tower 2.

Martin A. Kenealy	48 Edwin st	Lieutenant	$1,400 yr	Jan. 4, 1907
James J. Hughes	777 Columbia rd	Hoseman	1,200 "	Oct. 1, 1873
Michael T. Barrett	84 W. Rutland sq	"	900 "	May 18, 1908
Charles E. Barry	592 Albany st	"	900 "	Oct. 20, 1908
Jeremiah J. Cronin	90 Hudson st	"	900 "	Jan. 31, 1908

Water Tower 3.

Daniel J. O'Brien	73 Chambers st	Lieutenant	$1,400 yr	Sept. 10, 1906
Patrick F. Dowling	129 River st	Hoseman	1,200 "	June 29, 1905
David F. Sheehan	249 W. Fourth st	"	1,100 "	April 30, 1906
Timothy J. Kelley	113 Warren st	"	900 "	June 26, 1908

Fire-Alarm Branch.

Brown S. Flanders	144 W. Concord st	Superintendent	$3,200 yr	Jan. 1, 1880
Cyrus A. George	150 Warren ave	Assistant Superintendent	2,000 "	" 1, 1880
Richard Donahue	11 Centre ave	Chief Operator	2,000 "	Aug. 10, 1906
Charles M. Chaplin	47 Sever st	Operator	1,600 "	Jan. 1, 1872
John Flavell	24 Stonehurst st	"	1,600 "	Nov. 27, 1896
John Galway	4 Achorn circle	"	1,600 "	Jan. 11, 1907
Peter M. Kendrick	46 Bristol st	"	1,600 "	July 26, 1905
Jonathan M. Morris	54 Harvest st	"	1,600 "	" 13, 1891
Uzziel Putnam	46 Bristol st	"	1,600 "	Jan. 1, 1876
Daniel J. Collins	416 Bowdoin st	Assistant Operator	1,200 "	Nov. 14, 1902
Henry A. Gutermuth	119 Cedar st	"	1,200 "	Jan. 4, 1907
Daniel F. McCarthy	103 Union Park st	"	1,200 "	July 28, 1905
Hiram W. Cherrington	14 Linden st	Foreman of Construction	2,000 "	Dec. 12, 1890
William H. Barker	84 Berkeley st	Asst. Foreman Const	3.75 day	March 15, 1893
Gustav J. H. Gutermuth	14 Linwood st	Expert Machinist	4.25 "	Dec. 3, 1886
Charles E. Randall	57 Samoset st	"	4.00 "	" 4, 1896
Issachar Wells	36 Arundel st	Repairer and Carpenter	3.25 "	Jan. 3, 1885
Robert T. Brown, Jr	478 E. Seventh st	Inside Wireman	3.60 "	" 14, 1907
Edward M. Illingworth	249 Emerson st	"	3.60 "	" 5, 1891
Frank A. Bailey	85 Southern ave	Repairer	3.00 "	Feb. 26, 1907
Dennis J. Burnett	67 Old Harbor st	"	3.00 "	July 2, 1890
Alexander F. Campbell	24 Stanwood st	"	3.00 "	Aug. 27, 1906
John G. Culhane	36 Rochester st	"	3.00 "	June 7, 1894
James Elsworth	283 Cabot st	"	3.00 "	" 4, 1906
John A. Fraser	151 E. Cottage st	"	3.00 "	March 25, 1903
Edward J. Hogan	30 Ball st	"	3.00 "	Oct. 17, 1893
Andrew J. Johnson	217 Paris st	"	3.00 "	Nov. 2, 1896
John J. Larkin	Hotel Bowdoin	"	3.00 "	Sept. 14, 1896
James Mahoney	10 Edson green	"	3.00 "	Dec. 8, 1902
John M. McEwan	62 Torrey st	"	3.00 "	Aug. 27, 1906
Willard R. Pulsifer	5 Haynes pk	"	3.00 "	Dec. 4, 1905
William R. Reid	1436 Columbus ave	"	3.00 "	Nov. 25, 1907
James Tanner	15 Noanet st	"	3.00 "	March 22, 1907
Orlando W. Flynn	46 Chelsea st	"	2.50 "	May 11, 1904
Michael A. Murphy	350 Athens st	Stableman	2.50 "	June 1, 1905
Harry J. Reardon	12 Blackwood st	Clerk and Storekeeper	7.00 yr	Nov. 16, 1908

Repair Shop.

Eugene M. Byington	363 Albany st	Supervisor of Engines	$2,000 yr	April 19, 1906
Christopher F. Curran	44 Shirley st	Foreman H. & H. Shop	1,400 "	March 2, 1906
Vincent B. Buckley	20 Dorr st	Engineer	1,300 "	Dec. 8, 1899
William J. Hurley	291 W. Fifth st	Clerk	900 "	Nov. 1, 1906
Walter L. Finigan	213 Chestnut ave	"	700 "	Feb. 28, 1908
Thomas F. Turner	80 Hamilton st	Painter	3.75 day	June 16, 1876
John L. Gannon	63 Berkeley st	"	3.50 "	Oct. 8, 1906
John F. Haley	259 Meridian st	"	3.50 "	" 8, 1906
Michael J. McGrath	83 Morris st	"	3.50 "	April 15, 1907
Michael Kyle	1294 Dorchester ave	Wheelwright	3.25 "	March 30, 1885
Frederick F. Logan	13 Bodwell st	"	3.25 "	Oct. 11, 1904

Fire Department.— Concluded.

Name.	Residence.	Designation.	Compensation	Date of Election or Appointment.

Repair Shop.— Concluded.

Name.	Residence.	Designation.	Compensation	Date of Election or Appointment.
William H. Baldwin	2436 Washington st	Machinist	$3.25 day.	Nov. 1, 1896
Henry J. Egan	329 Shawmut ave	"	3.25 "	23, 1905
Edward F. Hove	59 Milton ave	"	3.25 "	Dec. 11, 1880
John E. Nolan	44 Grampian way	"	3.25 "	Sept. 1, 1885
Arthur K. Paradise	18 Hartwell st	"	3.25 "	May 4, 1906
John Smith	104 Cowper st	"	3.25 "	Feb. 3, 1903
Thomas Buckley	15 Denny st	Blacksmith	3.50 "	June 27, 1875
John Connell	21 Bloomfield st	"	3.50 "	May 10, 1875
James P. Forde	622 E. Eighth st	"	3.50 "	Oct. 21, 1907
William Bowers	2 Columbia ter	"	3.25 "	May 27, 1875
Thomas J. Collins	15 Vale st	Blacksmith's Helper	2.50 "	Sept. 5, 1906
Frank P. Elliott	549 Harrison ave	"	2.50 "	July 26, 1882
Patrick McLean	51 Bunker Hill st	"	2.50 "	Oct. 30, 1908
Thomas H. Wright	388 Warren st	"	2.50 "	Jan. 24, 1887
Hugh Gallagher	29 Tufts st	Horseshoer	2.50 "	Sept. 5, 1893
Thomas J. Moran	25 Appleton st	Fireman	2.50 "	May 24, 1908
William J. Northway	114 Marcella st	"	2.50 "	Feb. 28, 1908
John F. A. Norton	8 Harlow st	"	2.50 "	Dec. 26, 1895
Ernest R. Matthews	123 Boylston st	"	2.50 "	13, 1908
Jeremiah J. Fitzpatrick	42 Bennett st	Teamster	2.25 "	July 10, 1891
Martin F. Hart	7 Prescott st	"	2.25 "	29, 1901
James M. Reed	39 Telegraph st	"	2.25 "	June 7, 1897
Thomas W. Kennedy	66 Armandine st	Harnessmaker	3.25 "	Oct. 27, 1905
Frank H. Nickerson	48 Temple st	"	2.25 "	April 20, 1898
James Quinn	18 Woodcliff st	Engineer	3.25 "	May 2, 1888
Frank J. Griffin	90 Bunker Hill st	Plumber	4.40 "	Dec. 17, 1908
John H. W. Smith	44 Dundee st	"	4.40 "	17, 1908
Robert A. Finley	19 Rogers st	Carpenter	3.50 "	Jan. 20, 1909
Cornelius McKinnon	9 Lamont st	"	3.50 "	20, 1909
John Thibbitts	7 Smith st	"	3.50 "	20, 1909
Hiram Averhill	13 Tremont st	House Painter	3.16 "	Dec. 4, 1908

Veterinary Hospital.

Name.	Residence.	Designation.	Compensation	Date of Election or Appointment.
George W. Stimpson	717 Massachusetts ave	Veterinary Surgeon	$2,000 yr.	Nov. 28, 1883
James W. Dwyer	193 Eustis st	Lieutenant	1,400 "	June 3, 1904
David Kane	26 Winslow st	Blacksmith	3.00 day.	Sept. 30, 1869
Daniel F. O'Brien	40 Moseley st	Hostler	2.25 "	Aug. 19, 1898
Charles C. Wilfert	46 Palmer st	"	2.25 "	Oct. 9, 1896
Patrick J. Sullivan	96 Hunneman st	"	2.25 "	Dec. 11, 1899

Health Department.

Name.	Residence.	Designation.	Compensation	Date of Election or Appointment.
Samuel H. Durgin, M. D.	65 Chestnut Hill ave	Chairman	$4,500 yr.	Jan. 15, 1873*
Frederick O. North	76 Glendale st	Commissioner	4,000 "	May 12, 1908
John Ritchie, Jr.	14 Whitby ter	"	4,000 "	June 23, 1908
Charles E. Davis, Jr	12 Ruskin st	Secretary and Chief Clerk	3,000 "	Jan. 15, 1873
Francis J. Keany, M. D	73 Marlboro st	Dermatologist	2,000 "	Nov. 24, 1906
Thomas B. Shea, M. D	132 Warren st	Chief Medical Inspector	3,000 "	April 28, 1888
David D. Brough, M. D	15 Charles st	Medical Inspector	2,300 "	Dec. 7, 1896*
William H. Davis, M. D.	23 Beaumont st., Dor	"	2,000 "	April 7, 1908
George A. Sargent, M. D	46 Hereford st	"	500 "	Oct. 19, 1894
Alexander Burr, M. D. V	101 Radcliffe st., Dor	Veterinary Medical Inspector	500 "	Sept. 24, 1894
John MacConnell	6 Greenleaf st	Clerk	1,800 "	April , 1873
Frederick S. Davis	253 Corey st	Bookkeeper	2,000 "	May 1, 1881
James F. Broderick	58 Bartlett st., Chsn	Clerk	1,200 "	Aug. 8, 1898
Stephen L. Maloney	20 Lexington st., Chsn	"	1,000 "	Feb. 1, 1905
Patrick H. Brogan	852 E. Fourth st., S. B	"	12.00 wk.	March 24, 1909
Fidelia Fisk	19 Moreland st	"	16.00 "	Aug. 24, 1900
Mary G. Walkins	93 Munroe st	"	19.00 "	March 30, 1908
Carlisle Reed, M. D	155 Massachusetts ave	"	15.00 "	Jan. 1, 1904
Alice G. Angell	55 Charles st., Dor	"	15.00 "	Feb. 1, 1909
Thomas Jordan	76 Leicester st	Chief Sanitary Inspector	2,500 yr.	June 29, 1891
Carlan A. Brown	33 Bernard st	Sanitary Inspector	1,800 "	April 1, 1885
Thomas A. Crawford	527 Broadway	"	1,800 "	6, 1874
Thomas J. Donnellon	37 Rockland st	"	1,800 "	June 29, 1891

* Promoted to present position on date given. Previously in the department.

Health Department.— Continued.

Name.	Residence.	Designation.	Compensation.	Date of Election or Appointment.
Charles P. Harrington	6 Summer st., Chsn	Sanitary Inspector	$1,800 yr	April 1, 1885
James M. Kilroy	1463 Washington st	"	1,800 "	June 27, 1884
John J. Henry	31 Dunreath st	"	1,700 "	April 1, 1885
Edward A. Kennedy	496 Broadway	"	1,700 "	June 15, 1888
Charles J. Smith	168 Corey st	"	1,700 "	Jan. 7, 1890
Charles H. Filisetti	21 Fletcher st., Ros.	"	1,400 "	Nov. 18, 1896
Joseph M. Harrington	643 Hyde Park ave	"	1,300 "	Dec. 12, 1898
John B. McDonough	15 Bainbridge st	"	1,300 "	" 12, 1898
James A. O'Donnell	627 Shawmut ave	"	1,300 "	March 28, 1899
Albert M. Taylor	120 Glenway st	"	1,100 "	Feb. 2, 1906
James F. Curran	287 C st	"	1,000 "	Aug. 3, 1908*
Henry M. Emmons	428 Centre st., J. P.	"	1,000 "	" 3, 1908
David H. Fitzgerald	36 Liverpool st	"	1,000 "	Nov. 13, 1908
John B. McGrath	31 McLean st	"	1,000 "	Aug. 13, 1908
Francis J. Rowen	12 Irvington st	"	1,000 "	" 3, 1908
Francis H. Spear	14 Empire st	"	1,000 "	" 3, 1908*
William E. Whidden	702 Columbus ave	Inspector of Gas Fixtures	1,200 "	April 13, 1903
John J. Sullivan	128 M st	Constable	1,100 "	Nov. 3, 1906
Aaron A. Downs	50 Auburn st	Chief Disinfector	1,800 "	April 17, 1893
Michael J. Fallon	4 N. Anderson st	Stableman	17.50 wk	Feb. 12, 1902
Patrick Curran	40 Ellery st	"	17.50 "	Nov. 8, 1907
William H. Bourne	45 Forest st., Rox	Disinfector	16.50 "	July 27, 1896
William T. Caffrey	26 Tremont st., Chsn	"	16.50 "	Aug. 1, 1904
William H. Carley	124 N. Harvard st	"	16.50 "	" 10, 1908
James R. Gallivan	39 Gates st	"	16.50 "	Jan. 4, 1901
Joseph W. Haugh	420 Sixth st	"	16.50 "	Nov. 24, 1901
John Kelly	39 Blossom st	"	16.50 "	Sept. 2, 1892
John F. Keilty	67 Brighton st	"	16.50 "	Feb. 13, 1896
John J. Land	25 Wakullah st	"	16.50 "	April 13, 1891
Jeremiah J. Lyons	212 Chambers st	"	16.50 "	March 11, 1905
William G. Maloney	20 Lexington st	"	16.50 "	Oct. 21, 1908*
William J. Murphy	387 Charles st	"	16.50 "	Sept. 2, 1892
Maurice P. Newman	109 Elm st., Chsn	"	16.50 "	Nov. 23, 1901
Martin Norton	49 Dacia st	"	16.50 "	Jan. 29, 1909
John Yore	16 McLean st	"	16.50 "	Aug. 25, 1893
Thomas H. Kingston	18 N. Grove st	Superintendent of Morgue	900 yr	Feb. 8, 1907
Charles E. Bassett	18 N. Grove st	Asst. Supt. of Morgue	750 "	Sept. 9, 1907
John C. Grouse	18 Hartwell st	Inspector of Provisions	1,400 "	July 1, 1895
George W. Roberts	22 Empire st	" "	1,200 "	Sept. 25, 1896
George W. Smith	3 Vernon pl	" "	1,100 "	March 26, 1906
Thomas J. Kelly	60 Waverly st., Bri	Inspector of Animals	1,400 "	June 26, 1893
Eugene A. Dowd	12 Madison st., Rox	Veterinary Inspector	1,200 "	March 26, 1908
John J. McLoughlin	125 Farrington st	Superintendent of Peddlers	1,300 "	Dec. 29, 1893
Jacob Barber	135 Leverett st	Asst. Supt. of Peddlers	3.00 day	Jan. 31, 1896
John F. Fitzgerald, Jr	16 Burney st	Messenger	4.00 wk	Nov. 13, 1909
Anna J. Mulhern	7 Bower st	Telephone Operator	6.00 "	March 9, 1909

Bacteriological Laboratory.

Name.	Residence.	Designation.	Compensation.	Date of Election or Appointment.
Francis H. Slack, M. D.	750 Columbus ave	Director of Laboratory	$2,500 yr	Oct. 14, 1905
Burdett L. Arms, M. D.	29 St. James ave	Asst. Director of Laboratory,	1,400 "	Nov. 6, 1906
E. Marion Wade	40 Francis st	Bacteriologist	1,200 "	Dec. 5, 1908
William M. Campbell	21 Clifton st	Asst. Bacteriologist	1,200 "	Feb. 1, 1907
Nora C. O'Donoghue	25 Cook st., Chsn	Stenographer	15.00 wk	" 6, 1909
John R. Fallon	42 Hano st	Media Man	12.00 "	March 4, 1901
William F. Grady	63 Auburn st	Assistant Media Man	8.00 "	Oct. 14, 1902
Francis A. Berrigan	241 Neponset ave	Media Apprentice	5.00 "	Sept. 12, 1906
Arthur Holston	56 Hano st	Messenger	5.00 "	Nov. 6, 1908

Bureau of Inspection of Milk and Vinegar.

Name.	Residence.	Designation.	Compensation.	Date of Election or Appointment.
James O. Jordan	60 Cushing ave	Inspector	$3,000 yr	Jan. 1, 1905
Frank E. Mott	80 Huntington ave	Chemist	1,500 "	Sept. 1, 1908
William W. Griffin	58 Monument ave	Clerk	1,500 "	June 28, 1895
Patrick H. Cannon	52 Fairbanks st	Collector	3.00 day	Dec. 2, 1901
Edward S. Kelly	197 Eustis st	"	3.00 "	June 28, 1897
John J. Graham	326 Codman st	"	3.00 "	Dec. 28, 1908

Smallpox Hospital (Southampton Street).

Name.	Residence.	Designation.	Compensation.	Date of Election or Appointment.
William E. Jamieson	112 Southampton st	Superintendent	$600 yr	Oct. 13, 1899
Olive Johnson	112 Southampton st	Cook	1.00 day	Aug. 1, 1907

* Promoted to present position on date given.   Previously in the department.

Health Department.— Continued.

Name.	Residence.	Designation	Compensation.	Date of Election or Appointment.

Quarantine Department.

Name.	Residence.	Designation	Compensation.	Date of Election or Appointment.
Paul Carson, M. D.	Deer Island	Port Physician	$1,700 yr.	Oct. 1, 1894
William M. Gay, M. D.	"	Assistant Port Physician	1,000 "	Feb. 15, 1901
Marsalena Saffrino	258 Paris st.	Captain	1,600 "	" 15, 1889
Alonzo W. Buckman	96 Lexington st.	Engineer	1,300 "	Aug. 1, 1887
Egbert A. Oliver	9 Monmouth st.	Assistant Engineer	1,000 "	Sept. 1, 1895
Frederick E. Small	365 Meridian st.	Mate	1,000 "	Dec. 27, 1901
Thomas A. Greenwood	33 White st.	Steward	880 "	Sept. 7, 1894
Antonio W. Francis	260 Paris st.	Deckhand	720 "	Feb. 1, 1897
Joseph T. Rogers, Jr.	215 Lexington st.	Fireman	720 "	Dec. 12, 1901
George Washington	669 Shawmut ave.	"	720 "	Feb. 4, 1909
Albert F. Sherman	Gallop's Island	Overseer	900 "	June 1, 1899
Evelyn E. Sherman	"	Matron	300 "	" 1, 1899
John Roach	"	Farmer	420 "	Nov. 29, 1901
Harry Damon	"	"	560 "	April 28, 1908
James Madden	"	"	360 "	June 16, 1908
Lizzie Roach	"	Cook	300 "	Nov. 6, 1901
Annie Aguiar	"	Laundress	300 "	Oct. 29, 1907

Medical Inspectors of Schools.

Name.	Residence.	Designation	Compensation.	Date of Election or Appointment.
John L. Ames, M. D.	72 Chestnut st.	Medical Inspector	$200 yr.	April 1, 1895
Louis Arkin, M. D.	1 Elm Hill ave.	"	200 "	Oct. 1, 1908
Silas H. Ayer, M. D.	318 Shawmut ave.	"	200 "	Dec. 2, 1895
George S. C. Badger, M. D.	48 Hereford st.	"	200 "	Oct. 1, 1903
Frederick J. Bailey, M. D.	338 Bowdoin st., Dor.	"	200 "	Sept. 1, 1904
Winfred B. Bancroft, M. D.	597 Broadway	"	200 "	Nov. 1, 1894
Frank F. Bishop, M. D.	168 Princeton st.	"	200 "	Dec. 4, 1906
David N. Blakely, M. D.	255 Warren st.	"	200 "	Feb. 1, 1901
William S. Boardman, M. D.	63 Mt. Vernon st.	"	200 "	Nov. 1, 1894
James P. Broderick, M. D.	777 Centre st., J. P.	"	200 "	" 1, 1894
John S. Brownrigg, M. D.	16 Delle ave., Rox.	"	200 "	" 1, 1894
John E. Butler, M. D.	64 Monadnock st.	"	200 "	Feb. 26, 1896
Patrick F. Butler, M. D.	567 Dudley st.	"	200 "	Dec. 4, 1906
John A. Ceconi, M. D.	14 Arcadia st.	"	200 "	" 4, 1906
Arthur B. Coffin, M. D.	10 Rosedale st.	"	200 "	Nov. 22, 1894
Joseph A. Cogan, M. D.	419 Boylston st.	"	200 "	Dec. 4, 1906
Ralph M. Cole, M. D.	456 Broadway	"	200 "	Nov. 1, 1894
John M. Connolly, M. D.	183 Harvard st., Dor.	"	200 "	Jan. 1, 1903
John H. Costello, M. D.	31 Savin Hill ave.	"	200 "	Dec. 4, 1906
William P. Coues, M. D.	261 Beacon st.	"	200 "	Sept. 28, 1906
Michael J. Cronin, M. D.	5 Elm Hill ave.	"	200 "	" 3, 1901
Simon F. Curran, M. D.	102 Norfolk st.	"	200 "	Dec. 10, 1906
James T. Cutler, M. D.	20 Crawford st.	"	200 "	Nov. 27, 1894
John G. Dearborn, M. D.	2 Wood st., Chsn.	"	200 "	Oct. 1, 1899
Edward J. Denning, M. D.	216 W. Broadway	"	200 "	Dec. 4, 1906
John J. Dowling, M. D.	652 Massachusetts ave.	"	200 "	" 4, 1906
David G. Eldridge, M. D.	15 Monadnock st.	"	200 "	Nov. 20, 1894
William H. Ensworth, M. D.	40 Princeton st., E. B.	"	200 "	" 1, 1894
Theodore C. Erb, M. D.	159 St. Botolph st.	"	200 "	Feb. 25, 1898
Arthur W. Fairbanks, M. D.	591 Beacon st.	"	200 "	Sept. 23, 1900
Harry Finkelstein, M. D.	282 Hanover st.	"	200 "	Jan. 17, 1908
Walter T. Fuller, M. D.	36 Harvard st., Dor.	"	200 "	Dec. 4, 1906
James T. Gallagher, M. D.	172 Bunker Hill st.	"	200 "	" 4, 1906
Francis J. Giblin, M. D.	33 Adams st., Dor.	"	200 "	" 4, 1906
William H. Grainger, M. D.	408 Meridian st.	"	200 "	Nov. 1, 1894
Benjamin A. Graves, M. D.	178 Bowdoin st., Dor.	"	200 "	Dec. 10, 1906
James S. Greene, M. D.	1107 Washington st., Dor.	"	200 "	Nov. 1, 1894
William H. Greene, M. D.	322 Warren st., Dor.	"	200 "	Dec. 4, 1906
Henry Harrison, M. D.	153 Huntington ave.	"	200 "	" 4, 1906
David P. Hayes, M. D.	157 Dorchester ave.	"	200 "	" 4, 1906
Louis A. Hermann, M. D.	33 McLean st.	"	200 "	Sept. 12, 1907
John A. Hickey, M. D.	144 Saratoga st.	"	200 "	Dec. 4, 1906
William W. Howell, M. D.	1923 Centre st., W. R.	"	200 "	Sept. 13, 1906
Franklin C. Jillson, M. D.	11 Hastings st., W. R.	"	200 "	Nov. 1, 1894
Herbert J. Keenan, M. D.	254 W. Broadway	"	200 "	Dec. 4, 1906
J. H. H. Kelley, M. D.	7 Dracut st.	"	200 "	" 4, 1906
William D. Kelly, M. D.	57 Hancock st.	"	200 "	" 28, 1904
John S. H. Leard, M. D.	392 Arborway, J. P.	"	200 "	Jan. 13, 1897
Benjamin T. Loring, M. D.	71 Roberts st., Ros.	"	200 "	Aug. 12, 1908

Health Department.— Concluded.

Name.	Residence.	Designation.	Compensation.	Date of Election or Appointment.

Medical Inspectors of Schools.—Concluded.

Name.	Residence.	Designation.	Compensation.	Date of Election or Appointment.
John B. Lyons, M. D.	1 Dexter row	Medical Inspector	$200 yr.	Dec. 4, 1906
Francis Magurn, M. D.	112 Main st.	"	200 "	Nov. 24, 1899
Horace E. Marion, M. D.	5 Sparhawk st.	"	200 "	" 1, 1894
A. A. McCauley, M. D.	3 Mapleton st.	"	200 "	Dec. 4, 1906
Sylvester F. McKeen, M. D.	556 Cambridge st., Allston	"	200 "	Nov. 30, 1906
William J. McNally, M. D.	31 Monument sq.	"	200 "	" 1, 1894
Robert M. Merrick, M. D.	15 Adams st., Dor.	"	200 "	July 10, 1896
John H. Moore, M. D.	419 Boylston st	"	200 "	Dec. 4, 1906
George P. Morris, M. D.	702 Broadway	"	200 "	Nov. 1, 1894
Timothy J. Murphy, M. D.	372 Dudley st	"	200 "	" 1, 1894
John F. O'Brien, M. D.	401 Bunker Hill st.	"	200 "	" 1, 1894
Joseph J. O'Brien, M. D.	2209 Dorchester ave.	"	200 "	Dec. 4, 1906
Walter J. L. O'Brien, M. D.	14½ Hyde Park ave.	"	200 "	" 4, 1906
Edward F. O'Shea, M. D.	5 Chelsea st.	"	200 "	Nov. 1, 1894
Walter H. Parker, M. D.	1773 Dorchester ave.	"	200 "	Jan. 8, 1902
Henry J. Perry, M. D.	636 Beacon st	"	200 "	Sept. 25, 1901
James C. D. Pigeon, M. D.	27 Elm Hill ave	"	200 "	Nov. 1, 1894
Henry L. Plummer, M. D.	728 Saratoga st.	"	200 "	" 1, 1894
James A. Reilly, M. D.	1479 Dorchester ave.	"	200 "	Dec. 4, 1906
Frederick W. Rice, M. D.	16 Elko st.	"	200 "	" 4, 1906
Henry S. Rowen, M. D.	30 Bennett st	"	200 "	June 1, 1895
William J. Sheehan, M. D.	197 Broadway	"	200 "	Dec. 4, 1906
John H. Sherman, M. D.	534 Broadway	"	200 "	Aug. 17, 1895
Frank W. Sleeper, M. D.	748 Dudley st	"	200 "	Dec. 14, 1906
C. Morton Smith, M. D.	437 Marlboro st.	"	200 "	Sept. 12, 1896
Frederick W. Stuart, M. D.	550 Broadway	"	200 "	Nov. 12, 1894
John T. Sullivan, M. D.	129 Beacon st	"	200 "	Dec. 14, 1906
William F. Temple, M. D.	240 Huntington ave	"	200 "	Nov. 1, 1894
Henry F. R. Watts, M. D.	6 Monadnock st.	"	200 "	April 10, 1899
Francis J. Weller, M. D.	580 Broadway	"	200 "	Feb. 1, 1900

Convenience Stations.

Name.	Residence.	Designation.	Compensation.	Date of Election or Appointment.
George W. Boylem.	5 N. Grove st.	Janitor	$2.25 day.	Oct. 23, 1907
John J. Carroll.	94 Bennington st.	"	2.25 "	May 16, 1905
Dennis J. Coleman.	215 Harrison ave.	"	2.25 "	Feb. 28, 1902
William H. Fitzgerald.	40 Monmouth st.	"	2.25 "	Sept. 24, 1903
John Grady.	4 N. Anderson st.	"	2.25 "	July 19, 1900
Michael J. Kane.	54 Southern ave.	"	2.25 "	" 24, 1903
Frank J. McFarland.	14 Noanet st.	"	2.25 "	Feb. 29, 1902
Fergus W. Reilly.	12 Oscar st.	"	2.25 "	Jan. 26, 1900
Frank M. Segall.	14 Allen st.	"	2.25 "	Feb. 15, 1905
Mary E. Devlin.	8 Short-st. pl.	Matron	10.00 wk.	Sept. 27, 1901
Etta A. Harris.	67 Tyler st.	"	10.00 "	Nov. 9, 1899
Annie Kelly.	124 Vernoh st.	"	10.00 "	Sept. 26, 1907*
Ellen F. Leach.	18 Laurel st.	"	10.00 "	Feb. 9, 1900
Mary E. Mosher.	289 Chelsea st.	"	10.00 "	Nov. 29, 1901
Hannah O'Connor.	432 Bunker Hill st.	"	10.00 "	June 29, 1908
Sarah O'Shea.	34 Decatur st., Chsn.	"	10.00 "	Nov. 8, 1899

Hospital Department.

Name.	Residence.	Designation.	Compensation.	Date of Election or Appointment.
Abraham Shuman.	90 Commonwealth ave	President	None	May 1, 1885
Conrad J. Reuter.	61 Burroughs st., J. P.	Trustee	"	Jan. 30, 1896
Francis J. Keany, M. D.	73 Marlboro st.	"	"	May 1, 1897
Edmund D. Codman.	141 Beacon st.	"	"	" 28, 1903
Timothy J. Reardon.	76 Commonwealth ave	"	"	Nov. 28, 1905
John H. McCollom, M. D.	Hospital	Superintendent and Medical Director	$5,000 yr.	Feb. 1, 1909*
Frank H. Holt, M. D.	"	Assistant Superintendent	2,750 "	Jan. 1, 1901*
Arthur J. White, M. D.	"	Executive Assistant	1,200 "	Dec. 2, 1908*
Michael J. Shaughnessy, M.D	"	"	900 "	Feb. 14, 1909*
William J. Brickley, M. D.	"	House Surgeon	None	March 3, 1908
Irving J. Walker, M. D.	"	"	"	" 1, 1908
Walter M. Boothby, M. D.	"	"	"	" 30, 1908
Edward A. Supple, M. D.	"	Gyn. House Surgeon	"	Nov. 1, 1907

* Promoted to present position on date given. Previously in the department.

Hospital Department.— Continued.

Name.	Residence.	Designation.	Compensation	Date of Election or Appointment.
Willis G. Neally, M. D.	Hospital	Ophthalmic and Aural House Surgeon	None	July 6, 1908
James W. Manary, M. D.	"	House Physician	"	March 2, 1908
Fred H. Allen, M. D.	"	"	"	" 2, 1908
Joseph E. Hallisey, M. D.	"	"	"	" 2, 1908
Lucius A. Salisbury, M. D.	"	Senior Interne	"	July 6, 1908
Thomas P. Hennelly, M. D.	"	"	"	" 6, 1908
Henry J. FitzSimmons, M.D.	"	"	"	" 6, 1908
James B. Ayer, Jr., M. D.	"	"	"	" 6, 1908
Edmund H. Sawyer, M. D.	"	"	"	" 6, 1908
Frederick O. West, M. D.	"	"	"	" 6, 1908
Archibald W. Hunter, M. D.	"	Pathological Senior Interne.	"	Oct. 1, 1908
William McFarland, M. D.	"	Gynæcological Senior Interne	"	July 6, 1908
Joseph H. Fay, M. D.	"	Junior Interne	"	Nov. 1, 1908
Halsey B. Loder, M. D.	"	"	"	" 1, 1908
Archibald M. Fraser, M. D.	"	"	"	" 1, 1908
Ralph W. Tuttle, M. D	"	"	"	" 1, 1908
Harold R. C. Mahar, M. D.	"	"	"	" 1, 1908
Edward F. Brennan, M. D.	"	"	"	" 6, 1908
Robert D. Hildreth, M. D.	"	"	"	" 1, 1908
Harry S. Bernstein, M. D.	"	"	"	July 1, 1908
Raymond A. Quigley, M. D.	"	Externe	"	March 1, 1909
James W. J. Marion, M. D	"	"	"	" 1, 1909
Michael A. Dailey, M. D.	"	"	"	" 1, 1909
Frederick A. Coughlin, M. D.	"	"	"	" 1, 1909
Charles F. Gormley, M. D.	"	"	"	" 22, 1909
Wm. T. Miller, Jr., M. D.	"	"	"	" 1, 1909
John J. Curtin, M. D	"	"	"	" 1, 1909
Chester S. Baker, M. D.	"	Ophthalmic and Aural Externe	"	Oct. 1, 1908
Delbert L. Jackson, M. D.	"	Gynæcological Dresser	"	March 1, 1909
Harry A. Clark	9 Brent st	Surgical Dresser	"	April 1, 1909
Edgar C. Steinharter	63 St. Botolph st	"	"	" 1, 1909
Cleon W. Symonds	Waltham	"	"	" 1, 1909
Leonard W. Hassett	West Lynn	"	"	" 1, 1909
Frank B. Mallory, M. D.	Brookline	Asst. Visiting Pathologist	$1,600 yr.	May 7, 1897
Herman M. Adler, M. D.	31 Massachusetts ave	Asst. in Clinical Pathology	500 "	Jan. 29, 1907
Thomas Ordway, M. D.	West Roxbury	First Asst. in Pathology	1,000 "	Aug. 31, 1908
Samuel R. Haythorne, M. D.	Brookline	Second Asst. in Pathology	500 "	Jan. 4, 1909
Hiram McKay	43 Claybourne st., Dor	Steward	1,400 "	Feb. 6, 1880
Howard G. Sawyer	39 Mt. Vernon st	Out-patient Supervisor	900 "	Jan. 3, 1895
Peter J. MacDonald	Hospital	Executive Supervisor	840 "	Sept. 4, 1907*
Cyrus N. Richardson	"	Supervisor	720 "	Nov. 27, 1906*
H. Murray Malcom	"	"	600 "	June 7, 1902*
George E. Chapman	"	"	480 "	Oct. 17, 1905
Henry E. Pond	75 Van Winkle st., Dor	Messenger	520 "	Nov. 2, 1908
Walter W. Holmes	Hospital	Center Orderly	300 "	" 16, 1907
Ralph H. Carleton	"	"	270 "	June 8, 1908
Robert Bustard	"	"	240 "	Aug. 31, 1908
Charles Mehegan	"	"	240 "	March 24, 1909
Herbert J. Emerson	"	Out-patient Orderly	420 "	Jan. 15, 1906*
Arthur E. Leigh	"	"	420 "	Feb. 5, 1908*
Timothy A. O'Brien	"	"	420 "	Oct. 18, 1907
Charles L. Kramer	"	"	360 "	Aug. 25, 1906
Henry J. Kelley	"	"	360 "	Dec. 12, 1906
Nelson M. Inman	"	"	300 "	June 18, 1907
Clarence B. Higgins	"	"	300 "	Jan. 25, 1909
Carlos Grill	"	Orderly	480 "	Dec. 14, 1905*
Harry J. Levy	"	"	480 "	Nov. 3, 1904*
Ralph Chandler	"	"	420 "	March 10, 1908*
Clinton C. Chase	"	"	420 "	Nov. 27, 1907*
Robert E. Hakes	"	"	420 "	Jan. 2, 1908
Daniel R. Higgins	"	"	420 "	" 6, 1908
Walter E. Leighton	"	"	420 "	March 13, 1905*
Robert J. Magee	"	"	420 "	April 15, 1908
James F. Mayall	"	"	420 "	Jan. 31, 1908
Willard B. Fowler	"	"	420 "	April 5, 1909*
Frank J. Ago	"	"	360 "	Oct. 26, 1908
Joseph R. Campbell	"	"	360 "	Aug. 18, 1908
S. George Elkins	"	"	360 "	" 17, 1908
Herbert N. Leigh	"	"	360 "	" 31, 1908*
Dennis F. McCarthy	"	"	360 "	May 11, 1908
George M. Morton	"	"	360 "	Oct. 23, 1908

* Promoted to present position on date given.   Previously in the department.

Hospital Department.— Continued.

Name.	Residence.	Designation.	Compensation.	Date of Election or Appointment.
Herbert H. Parents	Hospital	Orderly	$360 yr	June 15, 1908
William Semple	"	"	360 "	" 8, 1908
Joseph A. Stratton	"	"	360 "	Oct. 15, 1908
Joseph Young	"	"	360 "	" 1, 1908
Patrick Burke	"	"	300 "	Jan. 15, 1909
John L. Concree	"	"	300 "	March 20 1909
Harry Delapierre	"	"	300 "	Feb. 2, 1909
Howard A. Drew	"	"	300 "	March 15, 1909*
William F. Driscoll	"	"	300 "	" 1, 1909
William W. Duncan	"	"	300 "	Dec. 22, 1908
William F. Dunigan	"	"	300 "	Jan. 20, 1909
Ralph O. Emerson	"	"	300 "	" 4, 1909
Bernard L. Foley	"	"	300 "	March 11, 1909
Walter S. Harrub	"	"	300 "	" 1, 1909
Michael T. McGowan	"	"	300 "	Jan. 6, 1909
James McLaughlin	"	"	300 "	Feb. 20, 1909
Floyd Malone	"	"	300 "	Jan. 21, 1909
Frank Rodgers	"	"	300 "	March 17, 1909
Alfred St. Pierre	"	"	300 "	Jan. 24, 1909
Charles Toye	"	"	300 "	March 17, 1909*
Karl Wainwright	"	"	300 "	Jan. 23, 1909
Thomas L. Walsh	"	"	300 "	" 29, 1909
Philip R. Flanders	"	"	300 "	April 4, 1909
Francis G. Hutchins	"	"	300 "	" 6, 1909
Joseph J. Kilcourse	"	"	300 "	" 13, 1909
Harry B. Wood	"	"	300 "	" 15, 1909*
Raymond F. Powers	"	"	300 "	" 14, 1909
William A. Coburn	"	"	300 "	" 15, 1909
Walter G. Chatman	"	"	300 "	" 16, 1909
Frank A. Annis	"	"	300 "	" 19, 1909
Albion White	"	"	300 "	" 8, 1909
Lucy L. Drown	"	"	Matron	1,500 "	Dec. 6, 1881
Ellen Smith	"	"	Assistant Matron	600 "	Jan. 6, 1908*
Frances E. Morley	"	"	1st Asst. Sup'r Nurses	720 "	Aug. 7, 1908*
Ida A. Nutter	"	"	2d Asst. Sup'r Nurses	600 "	Nov. 6, 1908*
Charlotte A. Brown	"	"	Instructor of Nurses (L. A.),	600 "	Dec. 21, 1905
Della M. Currier	"	"	Night Supervisor of Nurses.	540 "	Sept. 8, 1908*
Mary A. Catton	"	"	Head Nurse	540 "	Nov. 1, 1905*
Hannah Crosby	"	"	"	540 "	Oct. 21, 1903*
Annie L. Rand	"	"	"	540 "	March 30, 1904
Annie L. Ray	"	"	"	540 "	May 28, 1908*
Annie M. Hossack	"	"	"	480 "	March 11, 1905
Rose F. Moran	"	"	"	480 "	Aug. 1, 1906*
Mary A. Corrigan	"	"	"	420 "	Oct. 7, 1905
Edith A. Grau	"	"	"	420 "	July 15, 1905
Augusta E. Johnson	"	"	"	420 "	June 22, 1905
Elizabeth A. Lyons	"	"	"	420 "	Nov. 19, 1907*
M. Alice McMahon	"	"	(L. A.)	420 "	March 28, 1905*
Lila E. Stebbins	"	"	"	420 "	" 31, 1909*
Annie S. Borden	"	"	"	420 "	April 2, 1906
May R. Fennelly	"	"	"	420 "	" 1, 1908*
Annie L. Ferguson	"	"	"	420 "	July 3, 1908*
Ina M. Blair	"	"	Nurse	150 "	April 1, 1908*
Bertha Brouse	"	"	"	150 "	Oct. 16, 1908*
Helen G. Churchill	"	"	"	150 "	Feb. 4, 1909*
Margaret M. Coleman	"	"	"	150 "	April 1, 1909*
Mabel T. Cooper	"	"	"	150 "	" 2, 1909*
Eva E. Crockett	"	"	"	150 "	June 19, 1908*
Harriet B. Delamere	"	"	"	150 "	March 10, 1909*
Minnie Fraser	"	"	"	150 "	Nov. 3, 1908*
Martha E. Gilpatrick	"	"	"	150 "	April 22, 1909*
Martha S. Haggerty	"	"	"	150 "	March 3, 1909*
Agatha P. McKenna	"	"	"	150 "	" 3, 1908*
Bertha I. Mills	"	"	"	150 "	Oct. 17, 1908
F. Alberta Page	"	"	"	150 "	April 1, 1908*
Maude M. Russell	"	"	"	150 "	" 1, 1908*
Belinda Scanlan	"	"	"	150 "	Oct. 1, 1908*
Mary T. Simmons	"	"	"	150 "	Jan. 3, 1908*
Carolyn S. True	"	"	"	150 "	July 3, 1908*
M. E. Maude White	"	"	"	150 "	March 3, 1909*
Frances E. Smith	"	"	"	150 "	Oct. 10, 1908*
Lucy D. Adams	"	"	"	100 "	Sept. 2, 1907
Vivian E. Beckwith	"	"	"	100 "	June 3, 1907

* Promoted to present position on date given.   Previously in the department.

Hospital Department.— Continued.

Name.	Residence.	Designation.	Compensation.	Date of Election or Appointment.
Laura B. Bemis	Hospital	Nurse	$100 yr	June 3, 1907
Margaret G. Cairns	"	"	100 "	Sept. 2, 1907
Julia E. Casey	"	"	100 "	June 10, 1907
Mary G. Clancey	"	"	100 "	March 17, 1908*
Helena J. Conroy	"	"	100 "	June 3, 1907
Katherine W. Cramer	"	"	100 "	Sept. 2, 1907
Mary A. Curley	"	"	100 "	Aug. 1, 1907
Edith C. Dalzell	"	"	100 "	March 4, 1907
Effie M. Dewar	"	"	100 "	Sept. 2, 1907
Mary L. Dougherty	"	"	100 "	March 27, 1909*
Ellen E. Dowd	"	"	100 "	June 3, 1907
Etta M. Dwyer	"	"	100 "	March 4, 1907
Pansy B. Hall	"	"	100 "	June 4, 1907
Mary E. Joyce	"	"	100 "	Sept. 9, 1907
Mary Kennedy	"	"	100 "	" 2, 1907
Mary C. Kingston	"	"	100 "	June 3, 1907
Emilie E. La Flamme	"	"	100 "	Sept. 2, 1907
Mabelle E. Linscott	"	"	100 "	June 3, 1907
Daisy E. Milne	"	"	100 "	" 10, 1907*
Eliza M. Morrison	"	"	100 "	Aug. 17, 1908
Julia M. O'Connor	"	"	100 "	June 3, 1907
Sarah O'Meara	"	"	100 "	" 4, 1907
Margaret L. O'Toole	"	"	100 "	" 3, 1907
Annie F. White	"	"	100 "	Sept. 2, 1907
Mabel H. Arnold	"	"	50 "	Dec. 1, 1908
Emma G. Baldwin	"	"	50 "	" 1, 1908
Belle Barbrick	"	"	50 "	" 1, 1908
Annie G. Burns	"	"	50 "	June 1, 1908
Clara G. Calderwood	"	"	50 "	March 4, 1909*
Ella C. Daly	"	"	50 "	June 1, 1908
Emily G. Donovan	"	"	50 "	Dec. 1, 1908
Mabel F. Driscoll	"	"	50 "	" 1, 1908
Nora C. Duncan	"	"	50 "	April 23, 1909*
Ella J. Foley	"	"	50 "	June 1, 1908
Marie L. Giroux	"	"	50 "	Nov. 15, 1908*
Elizabeth M. Holden	"	"	50 "	March 2, 1909*
Bessie S. Huse	"	"	50 "	June 1, 1908
Alice M. Laurie	"	"	50 "	Sept. 1, 1908
Anna M. Lewis	"	"	50 "	" 1, 1908
Stella E. Lorden	"	"	50 "	June 1, 1908
Lillian M. McCabe	"	"	50 "	Sept. 1, 1908
Jessie M. McDonald	"	"	50 "	Dec. 1, 1908
Annie C. O'Brien	"	"	50 "	" 1, 1908
Annie M. O'Connor	"	"	50 "	June 1, 1908
Emma A. Patterson	"	"	50 "	Sept. 1, 1908
Edith A. Sangster	"	"	50 "	June 1, 1908
Mary A. J. O. Sparrow	"	"	50 "	Dec. 10, 1908
Annette L. Sullivan	"	"	50 "	June 1, 1908
Mary C. Sullivan	"	"	50 "	Sept. 7, 1908
Elizabeth A. Townsend	"	"	50 "	" 1, 1908
Florence Wenham	"	"	50 "	" 1, 1908
Margaret Beaton	"	Probationer	None	March 22, 1909
Beatrice M. Bedard	"	"	"	" 1, 1909
Mary E. Carberry	"	"	"	" 23, 1909*
May E. Dongan	"	"	"	" 1, 1909
Margaret M. Fitzpatrick	"	"	"	" 1, 1909
Rose M. Foster	"	"	"	" 1, 1909
Edith F. Gertz	"	"	"	" 1, 1909
Mary T. Grady	"	"	"	" 1, 1909
Kathryn F. Higgins	"	"	"	" 1, 1909
Ruth Hopkins	"	"	"	" 1, 1909
Maude E. Lehman	"	"	"	" 1, 1909
Elizabeth A. McEwen	"	"	"	" 1, 1909
Lucy Power	"	"	"	" 1, 1909
Grace M. Powers	"	"	"	" 1, 1909
Mary H. Silver	"	"	"	" 1, 1909
Mabel C. Willey	"	"	"	" 1, 1909
Fern A. Wing	"	"	"	" 1, 1909
Fannie M. Hamilton	"	"	"	" 1, 1909
Lizzie Harvey	"	Head Laundress	$900 yr	Sept. 5, 1898
William A. Peterson	29 Halleck st	Laundryman	540 "	July 5, 1895
John F. Youngquist	1086 Tremont st	"	420 "	28, 1906
Henry S. Massie	Hospital	"	360 "	Feb. 1, 1909

* Promoted to present position on date given.   Previously in the department.

Hospital Department.— Continued.

Name.	Residence.	Designation.	Compensation.	Date of Election or Appointment.
Adam J. Miller	Hospital	Laundryman	$360 yr.	Nov. 26, 1906
Gowan J. Scott	54 Springfield st.	"	360 "	March 3, 1909
Walter P. Shea	Hospital	"	360 "	July 9, 1908
Walter Woods	"	Gauze Sorter	360 "	Sept. 17, 1907
Anna Ballentyne	"	Laundress	360 "	Oct. 14, 1907*
Annie McDonough	"	"	240 "	Sept. 30, 1907*
Mary Tighe	"	"	240 "	Jan. 28, 1907*
Mollie Bevan	"	"	216 "	Sept. 11, 1905
Cassie Gallagher	"	"	216 "	March 21, 1904*
Hannah McGonigle	"	"	216 "	" 2, 1908*
Margaret Meglio	"	"	216 "	Sept. 11, 1908
Lillie Sheridan	"	"	216 "	July 21, 1906
Lizzie Courtney	"	"	192 "	April 28, 1909
Mary D'Arcy	"	"	192 "	Aug. 31, 1907*
Catherine Diskin	"	"	192 "	July 31, 1908
Clotilda Dwyer	"	"	192 "	Dec. 11, 1906
Mary Hickey	"	"	192 "	May 8, 1907
Sarah McColgan	"	"	192 "	April 19, 1909
Annie Smith	"	"	192 "	March 31, 1908*
Olga Smith	"	"	192 "	May 1, 1908*
Mary DeNigris	"	"	180 "	Aug. 29, 1908
Rose Doherty	"	"	180 "	Sept. 25, 1908
Mary Lally	"	"	180 "	Nov. 16, 1908
Margaret Murray	"	"	180 "	Sept. 3, 1908
Bessie O'Donnell	"	"	180 "	Aug. 26, 1908
Winifred Sampson	"	"	180 "	Nov. 6, 1908
Mary A. Lynch	"	"	168 "	Dec. 30, 1908
Katherine McGrory	"	"	168 "	March 23, 1909
Emma J. Brown		Seamstress	300 "	May 18, 1908
Addie C. Keay	12 Standish st., Dor.	Acting Seamstress	300 "	April 7, 1909
Kathryn Baker	Hospital	Assistant Seamstress	204 "	Nov. 12, 1908
Mary S. Tracy	550 Columbus ave	Assistant Mender	5.00 wk.	Dec. 19, 1908*
S. Helena Batson	Hospital	Assistant Housekeeper	360 yr.	May 18, 1905
Laura H. Willcutt	"		360 "	July 17, 1905
Katie Conlon	972 Harrison ave	Scrubber	5.00 wk.	April 14, 1909
Mary Courtney	8 McLellan st	"	5.00 "	Nov. 2, 1900*
Margaret Dooling	87 Eustis st.	"	5.00 "	Aug. 27, 1903
Mary Dowling	1 McLellan st	"	5.00 "	Nov. 24, 1900*
Margaret Driscoll	8 Washington pl	"	5.00 "	March 25, 1909
Kate Folkel	112 E. Canton st	"	5.00 "	Aug. 2, 1906
Catherine Gallagher	1 Worcester pl	"	5.00 "	July 10, 1905
Emma Gillespie	80 E. Canton st	"	5.00 "	Aug. 20, 1907*
Mary Hayes	828 Albany st	"	5.00 "	May 3, 1907*
Kate Hennessy	3 Hamburg st	"	5.00 "	Sept. 26, 1892
Catherine King	73 W. Lenox st	"	5.00 "	June 6, 1908
Nellie Kingston	1050 Columbus ave	"	5.00 "	March 17, 1909
Delia LaBeau	908 Harrison ave	"	5.00 "	June 9, 1908
Ellen Logan	12 Island st	"	5.00 "	May 22, 1902
Margaret Lynch	74 E. Newton st	"	5.00 "	Sept. 5, 1906
Abbie Marden	1841 Washington st	"	5.00 "	April 14, 1903
Elizabeth Mason	24 Village st	"	5.00 "	Oct. 6, 1904
Mary Mulligan	974 Harrison ave	"	5.00 "	Dec. 22, 1904
May O'Brien	31 E. Springfield st	"	5.00 "	Nov. 8, 1908*
Kate Raphlin	27 Fellows st	"	5.00 "	April 12, 1904
Mary Rigby	51 E. Lenox st	"	5.00 "	Nov. 28, 1908
Mary B. Riley	909 Harrison ave	"	5.00 "	Feb. 5, 1908*
Mary Ring	42 Northampton st	"	5.00 "	Jan. 12, 1903*
Mary Robinson	32 Worcester st	"	5.00 "	" 5, 1909
Sarah Sullivan	93 E. Brookline st	"	5.00 "	Feb. 12, 1901*
Sarah Welsh	599 Harrison ave	"	5.00 "	June 6, 1905
Annie Schaffer	999 Tremont st	"	5.00 "	April 3, 1909
Bridget Foley	83 Norfolk ave	Ward Scrubber	5.00 "	" 3, 1908
Ellen King	659 Harrison ave	Ward Helper	5.00 "	May 6, 1907
Annie M. O'Hare	1013 Harrison ave	"	5.00 "	July 5, 1907*
Sarah Oakes	39 Mechanic st	"	5.00 "	Dec. 1, 1908
Katherine Charlton	Hospital	Ward Maid	144 yr.	March 6, 1907
Mollie Cogan	"	"	144 "	May 29, 1907
Nellie Cox	"	"	144 "	Sept. 29, 1908*
Rose Doherty	"	"	144 "	April 23, 1909
Mary Donegan	"	"	144 "	May 10, 1904*
Anna Downey	"	"	144 "	Jan. 21, 1909
Mary Egan	"	"	144 "	May 15, 1895

* Promoted to present position on date given.   Previously in the department.

Hospital Department. — Continued.

Name.	Residence.	Designation.	Compensation.	Date of Election or Appointment.
Celia Hill	Hospital	Ward Maid	$144 yr	April 17, 1909
Catherine Hughes	"	"	144 "	March 5, 1909
Margaret Kerrigan	"	"	144 "	May 6, 1903
Nellie Lyons	"	"	144 "	Jan. 3, 1908
Jennie McCullough	"	"	144 "	April 13, 1909*
Rose McLaughlin	"	"	144 "	" 7, 1900
May Meehan	"	"	144 "	March 2, 1909
Kate Rafferty	"	"	144 "	Dec. 18, 1908
Mary R. Smith	"	"	144 "	Aug. 8, 1907
Catherine Maguire	"	"	144 "	April 28, 1909
Nellie Stewart	"	Chamber Maid	192 "	Jan. 6, 1901*
Mary Collins	"	"	180 "	Dec. 20, 1906*
Cora Corbett	"	"	180 "	July 11, 1906*
Annie Gallivan	"	"	180 "	June 8, 1905
Annie Horn	"	"	180 "	July 17, 1907
Annie M. Lennon	"	"	180 "	Dec. 21, 1908
Kathryn Lewis	"	"	180 "	Jan. 1, 1909
Ellen Lyons	"	"	180 "	July 24, 1897
Katie Mahoney	"	"	180 "	June 13, 1905*
Delia Walsh	"	"	180 "	Oct. 22, 1907
Julia E. Burke	"	Table Girl (Superintendent)	5.00 wk	Feb. 19, 1909*
Jennie E. Stewart	"	Table Girl	204 yr	Oct. 5, 1900*
Annie Early	"	"	192 "	" 5, 1900*
Nora O'Brien	"	"	192 "	March 7, 1903*
Minnie Peoples	"	"	192 "	Feb. 14, 1907*
Annie Sullivan	"	"	192 "	Sept. 16, 1908
Mary Chisholm	"	"	168 "	" 10, 1908
Mary Kelley	"	"	168 "	Jan. 12, 1904*
Nellie Mack	"	"	168 "	Sept. 26, 1908
Annie Nolan	"	"	168 "	Jan. 23, 1909
Jean Walker	"	"	168 "	May 22, 1908
Agnes Lavin	"	Pantry Girl	168 "	July 2, 1908
Michael A. Kinsella	"	Microtomist	360 "	April 9, 1909
John R. Clendenning	444 Massachusetts ave	Pathological Lab. Diener	360 "	Feb. 9, 1907
Jeremiah Edwards	64 Williams st., Rox	Dispensary Diener	6.00 wk	April 2, 1907
John P. Donnelly	36 Worcester sq	Ward Porter	360 yr	June 10, 1908
William F. King	3 Valentine st	"	360 "	July 20, 1908
John O'Meara	57 Springfield st	"	360 "	Dec. 6, 1906
George B. Welby	1 Waterford st	"	360 "	Feb. 25, 1907*
William J. Robertson	16 Colonial ave., Dor	Porter	360 "	July 10, 1908
Charles Simpson	Hospital	"	360 "	Nov. 30, 1908*
Frank Ogle	"	Head Porter	300 "	Jan. 27, 1909
Hiram Ricker	"	Gate Boy	300 "	July 13, 1908
John J. O'Mara	"	Fruit Porter	300 "	Feb. 3, 1908
John Brosnan	105 Union Park st	House Porter	300 "	March 31, 1909
John C. Donovan	21 Arnold st., Rox	"	300 "	April 15, 1909
Harry V. Hill	290 Centre st., J. P.	"	300 "	July 8, 1908
William Murray	44 E. Springfield st	"	300 "	April 20, 1909
James R. Ogston	Hospital	"	300 "	Feb. 4, 1909
Grace M. Lane	103 Bartlett st., Somerville	Head Bookkeeper (L. A)	15 wk	July 7, 1900
Inez E. Traiton	34 Torrey st., Dor	Secretary	16 "	Aug. 19, 1889
Ella L. Green	639 Saratoga st., E. B.	Head Clerk	14 "	" 1, 1900
Leonie M. Corcoran	39 Delle ave., Rox	Pathological Stenographer	12 "	March 25, 1907
Katherine A. McNulty	30 Pearl st., Chsn	Typewriter	12 "	June 20, 1900*
Elizabeth A. Hunt	Medford	X-Ray Attendant	12 "	March 15, 1909
Helena A. Power	12 Eldora st., Rox	Copyist	12 "	Feb. 21, 1903
Agnes G. Wright	6 Mascoma st., Rox	"	12 "	Sept. 6, 1904*
Joanna E. Sweeney	34 Delle ave., Rox	"	11 "	Feb. 9, 1903
Helen C. Bridge	68 Fowler st., Dor	"	10 "	Oct. 29, 1906
Elizabeth Hinckley	356 Bunker Hill st., Chsn	"	10 "	Sept. 5, 1906
Margaret E. Quinn	191 Highland st., Rox	"	10 "	Nov. 27, 1907
J. Elizabeth Cambridge	Everett	Telephone Operator	10 "	Jan. 13, 1905
Katherine E. Power	415 W. Fourth st	"	10 "	April 23, 1907
James S. Groff	95 St. Botolph st	"	8 "	July 1, 1906*
Thomas Sims	3 Dahlgren st., Dor	Head Chef	1,000 yr	Oct. 3, 1882
William McPherson	Hospital	Assistant Cook	720 "	May 2, 1891
Axel H. Strandberg	"	Butcher	360 "	June 12, 1907
Henry W. Pierce	"	Cook's Assistant	420 "	April 10, 1907*
Thomas D. Sargent	"	Kitchen Man	360 "	March 15, 1908
Samuel J. Wilkinson	"	"	360 "	May 22, 1907
Peter Shilling	"	"	300 "	Aug. 25, 1908
Henry L. Nickerson	"	"	300 "	July 19, 1908

* Promoted to present position on date given. Previously in the department.

Hospital Department.— Continued.

Name.	Residence.	Designation.	Compensation.	Date of Election or Appointment.
Margaret Creedon	Hospital	Kitchen Woman	$192 yr	April 30, 1906
Julia Keegan	"	"	192 "	" 15, 1908
Mary McNamara	"	"	192 "	Dec. 4, 1907
Monica Canavan	"	"	180 "	Jan. 12, 1909
Mary O'Brien	"	"	180 "	March 29, 1909
Julia Regan	"	"	180 "	Feb. 26, 1909
Florence Norton	"	Kitchen Woman (V. H.)	168 "	" 24, 1909*
Robert McLean	1607 Washington st	Kitchen Cleaner	6.00 wk	March 22, 1909*
Lizzie Shanahan	Hospital	Cook (Vose House)	360 yr	May 29, 1901
Hannah Shanahan	"	Assistant Cook (Vose House)	300 "	July 25, 1907
James S. Gill	11 Marble st., Rox	Baker	840 "	Jan. 16, 1889
Karl H. F. Lillie	Hospital	Baker's Assistant	360 "	April 25, 1906
James C. Young	"	"	360 "	" 12, 1907
Catherine Harrington	"	"	192 "	Aug. 22, 1906
John Ferrin	"	Apothecary	900 "	Sept. 25, 1906
Joseph Martin	"	Apothecary's Assistant	480 "	" 30, 1907
Amos P. Wood	"	"	300 "	May 25, 1908
Ernest E. Fewkes	Newton Highlands	Photographer	25.00 wk	June 20, 1898
John J. Burrows	30 Trenton st., E. B.	Photographer's Assistant	10.00 "	April 8, 1907
John L. MacVicar	5 Durham st., E. B.	Engineer	1,560 yr	May 18, 1908
Isaac C. Nelson	30 Mellen st., Dor	Assistant Engineer	25.00 wk	Aug. 13, 1907
Thomas J. McNally	43 Judson st., Dor	"	21.00 "	Oct. 29, 1907
Benjamin Sandiford	35 Worcester st	"	18.00 "	Dec. 15, 1906
Arthur Swanson	35 Worcester st	"	18.00 "	April 15, 1907
William E. Thompson	56 Ceylon st., Dor	Laundry Engineer	18.00 "	Oct. 7, 1890
Richard A. Bawdick	108 W. Springfield st	Electrical Engineer	21.00 "	March 14, 1905
William T. Slater	45 E. Springfield st	Asst. Electrical Engineer	21.00 "	Aug. 26, 1905
John McHale	2493 Washington st	Head Fireman	18.00 "	April 9, 1895
David Bransfield	9 Jenkins st., S. B.	Fireman	17.00 "	Oct. 26, 1907
Edmond Darcy	2495 Washington st	"	17.00 "	Dec. 14, 1907*
John J. Devine	56 Washington st., Chasn.	"	17.00 "	Aug. 8, 1899
Michael Kelley	190 Eustis st., Rox	"	17.00 "	April 13, 1902
Archibald McLachlin	108 W. Springfield st	"	17.00 "	Oct. 16, 1908*
John Norton	10 Dromey av., Rox	"	17.00 "	Nov. 3, 1905
Patrick A. Curran	8 Mulvey ave., Rox	"	15.00 "	April 10, 1907*
John J. Breen	10½ O st.	Coal Passer	12.00 "	Nov. 18, 1908
John D. Long	210 Bennington st., E. B.	Laborer	12.00 "	April 8, 1907
George E. Coburn	19 Worcester sq	"	10.00 "	May 21, 1906
William Lucas	623 Massachusetts ave	Night Porter and Tending Furnace	630 yr	Oct. 1, 1907*
Charles Skory	39 Tolman st., Dor	Electrician	18.00 wk	" 5, 1904*
George Roche	Hospital	Electrician's Helper	240 yr	June 1, 1908*
Frank P. Magee	"	Steamfitter's Helper	180 "	Oct. 1, 1908
Christopher Mullen	"	Plumber's Helper	180 "	May 13, 1908
William J. Robbins	24 Cottage ter., Rox	Jobber	16.00 wk	Feb. 20, 1894
Daniel M. Hurley	96 Hunneman st	"	14.00 "	Dec. 6, 1906*
John Wallace	76 Sterling st	"	420 yr	April 7, 1905
Michael H. Brown	42 Worcester st	"	360 "	" 8, 1907
Henry Hastings	29 E. Concord st	Storekeeper	480 "	May 18, 1893*
James Meehan	45 Springfield st	Storekeeper's Assistant	420 "	July 26, 1895
William Robb	45 Stanwood st., Rox	Gardener	900 "	March 1, 1895
David H. Burns	44 Worcester st	Gardener's Assistant	420 "	April 3, 1907
Lewis A. Pasco	41 Worcester sq	Pathological Diener	900 "	Aug. 17, 1885
George E. Alexander	51 Bloomfield st., Dor	Carpenter	3.00 day	Nov. 12, 1883
Banford G. Leeman	123 Evans st., Dor	"	2.75 "	April 17, 1906*
Frank A. Rutzen	22 Davis st	"	2.75 "	" 16, 1909*
William A. Woodworth	35 Falcon st., E. B.	"	2.75 "	Nov. 9, 1908*
William J. Bean	17 School st., Dor	Painter	3.00 "	March 7, 1894*
Thomas Newsham	9 Grant pl., Allston	"	2.75 "	" 15, 1892
William C. Cunningham	102 Pembroke st	"	2.75 "	Sept. 8, 1908*
William G. Whitney	73 W. Concord st	"	2.75 "	" 11, 1908*
William H. Brown	54 Kendall st	Floor Polisher	1.00 "	June 18, 1902*
Alexander O'Brien	Hospital	Ambulance Foreman	900 yr	March 1, 1893
Michael Daly	"	Asst. Ambulance Foreman	540 "	May 12, 1903
Martin Craven	"	Ambulance Driver	540 "	Feb. 14, 1903
Eugene S. Cronin	"	"	540 "	July 12, 1907*
Thomas Ferris	"	"	540 "	Oct. 12, 1906*
Patrick T. Mahoney	"	"	540 "	May 29, 1907
William Murray	"	"	540 "	March 31, 1908*
Walter J. Camrell	65 Ruggles st., Rox	Elevator Boy	7.00 wk	Oct. 19, 1906
Christopher C. Davenport	2 McLean st., Rox	"	7.00 "	April 20, 1904
James Lee	64 Williams st., Rox	"	7.00 "	Nov. 18, 1907

*Promoted to present position on date given. Previously in the department.

Hospital Department.— Continued.

Name.	Residence.	Designation.	Com pensation.	Date of Election or Appointment.
Nathaniel P. Lee	64 Williams st., Rox	Elevator Boy	$7.00 wk	Sept. 26, 1905
William Patterson	10 Willow pk	"	7.00 "	Nov. 6, 1907*
Ernest E. Shelton	147 Northampton st	"	7.00 "	April 3, 1905
Daniel Smith	93 Camden st	"	7.00 "	May 21, 1907
John M. Johnson	17 Woodbury st	"	7.00 "	April 2, 1909*
G. Herbert Wilder	104 W. Lenox st	House Cleaner	7.00 "	Nov. 9, 1908*
William H. Jewell	7 Greenwich st	"	1.00 day	" 9, 1908
Augustus W. Leoney	77 Middlesex st	"	1.00 "	Dec. 17, 1908
George G. Plano	184 Northampton st	"	1.00 "	" 22, 1908
Fred G. Vassell	184 Northampton st	"	1.00 "	" 22, 1908
Samuel D. Bernard	4 Sawyer st	"	1.00 "	Feb. 4, 1909*
Charles H. Price	87 Northampton st	"	1.00 "	March 10, 1909
John H. Wadsworth	137 Northampton st	"	1.00 "	" 10, 1909*
Percy Cummings	96 Windsor st	"	1.00 "	Nov. 9, 1908*
Moses C. Jones	703 Shawmut ave	"	1.00 "	March 26, 1909
Francis A. Blackman	33 Winchester st	"	1.00 "	" 29, 1909

South Department.

Name.	Residence.	Designation.	Com pensation.	Date of Election or Appointment.
Edwin H. Place, M. D.	South Department	Physician in Chief	$2,000 yr	Dec. 10, 1906
William J. Brown, M. D.	"	Assistant Physician	1,000 "	Sept. 12, 1907
Cadis Phipps, M. D.	"	"	1,000 "	Feb. 1, 1909
William S. Conway	"	House Officer	None	March 16, 1909
Martin J. English, M. D.	"	"	"	" 22, 1909
Edmund W. Wilson, M. D.	"	"	"	" 22, 1909
Ellsworth J. M. Dickson	"	Clinical Clerk	"	" 29, 1909
Arthur H. Mountford	"	"	"	April 1, 1909
Francis J. McMahon	"	"	"	March 26, 1909
Raymond W. Bliss	"	Acting House Officer	"	Nov. 18, 1908
Murray H. Towle, M. D.	"	"	"	April 13, 1909
Emma M. Nichols	"	Matron	$800 yr	May 21, 1907
Ursula C. Noyes	"	Day Supervisor Nurses	600 "	March 7, 1904*
Lillian Reichert	"	Head Nurse	540 "	Jan. 28, 1901*
Marion L. Humphrey	"	Night Supervisor Nurses	480 "	Oct. 23, 1907*
E. Marion Cowie	"	Head Nurse	480 "	Sept. 1, 1908*
Edith M. Grant	"	"	420 "	Oct. 30, 1907
Anna L. Gibson	"	"	420 "	" 10, 1908*
Bessie E. Baldwin	"	Nurse	100 "	Dec. 7, 1908*
Jessie Baldwin	"	"	100 "	" 27, 1908*
Annie M. Burton	"	"	100 "	Oct. 14, 1908*
Dorothy Carruthers	"	"	100 "	Dec. 12, 1908*
Angie B. Coffin	"	"	100 "	March 15, 1909*
Abigail Dewey	"	"	100 "	Nov. 23, 1908*
Helen V. Downing	"	"	100 "	Sept. 28, 1908*
Rose E. Doyle	"	"	100 "	Jan. 7, 1909*
Margaret M. Duncan	"	"	100 "	Oct. 5, 1908
Alice L. Eastman	"	"	100 "	Nov. 2, 1908*
Elizabeth C. Eastwood	"	"	100 "	" 7, 1908*
Margaret J. Fallon	"	"	100 "	Jan. 25, 1909*
Sadie M. Ferrick	"	"	100 "	Feb. 13, 1909*
Gertrude Garren	"	"	100 "	Sept. 30, 1908*
Elizabeth I. Goodrich	"	"	100 "	March 29, 1909*
Emma H. Humble	"	"	100 "	Oct. 5, 1908*
Lucile H. Huntley	"	"	100 "	July 1, 1908*
Minnie Kelly	"	"	100 "	Oct. 17, 1908*
Edna R. Martin	"	"	100 "	Feb. 8, 1909*
Blanche A. MacDonald	"	"	100 "	March 15, 1909*
Melda McDonald	"	"	100 "	Feb. 12, 1909*
Florence A. MacLean	"	"	100 "	Jan. 25, 1909*
Marion Oulton	"	"	100 "	Feb. 1, 1909*
A. Bella O'Brien	"	"	160 "	Nov. 7, 1908*
Viola M. Pollock	"	"	100 "	Jan. 25, 1909*
Elizabeth C. Quinn	"	"	100 "	Nov. 2, 1908*
Mary G. Ramsay	"	"	100 "	Oct. 24, 1908*
Kathryn Reynolds	"	"	100 "	Nov. 28, 1908*
Maude J. Robinson	"	"	100 "	March 15, 1909*
Mabelle H. Still	"	"	100 "	" 8, 1909*
Nellie R. Scanlon	"	"	100 "	Sept. 28, 1908*
Elsie Searles	"	"	100 "	July 5, 1908*
May Stevens	"	"	100 "	March 15, 1909*
Elizabeth R. White	"	"	100 "	Feb. 18, 1909*
Lucy M. Howland	"	"	50 "	" 8, 1909*

* Promoted to present position on date given. Previously in the department.

Hospital Department.— Continued.

Name.	Residence.	Designation.	Compensation.	Date of Election or Appointment.
South Department. —Continued.				
Grace O. E. McLellan	South Department	Nurse	$850 yr	March 23, 1909*
Carolyn E. Gray	"	Clerk	700 "	Aug. 19, 1895
Mary A. Lane	29 Dorr st., Rox.	Copyist	624 "	Sept. 13, 1895*
Helen G. Carolan	35 Preble st., S. B.	"	520 "	March 29, 1909*
Hilda M. Dawson	South Department	Apothecary (L.A.)	600 "	Aug. 29, 1907
Mary L. Dogerty	"	" (supply)	520 "	April 9, 1909
Howard G. Tuttle	"	Apothecary's Assistant	240 "	March 31, 1908
Mary L. Medding	Malden	Telephone Operator (L.A.)	468 "	Feb. 15, 1905*
Edith Medding	Malden	" (temp.)	468 "	April 16, 1909
Fred H. Thorne	572 Massachusetts ave	"	260 "	Sept. 7, 1908*
Ernest F. Cochrane	19 Worcester sq	Assistant Engineer	936 "	Dec. 28, 1906
Thomas J. Kelly	136 Fisher ave., Rox.	Fireman	884 "	March 6, 1908*
Hugh O'Donnell	70 Russell st., Chsn.	"	884 "	Dec. 7, 1907*
Charles F. Field	4 Kittredge ter., Ros.	Carpenter	2.75 day	Sept. 6, 1896*
John Welch	13 Hall st., J. P.	Laborer	624 "	March 6, 1908*
George C. Chapman	Hospital	Jobber (temporary)	540 "	April 16, 1909*
Alexander Ramsay	293 Bennington st., E. B.	Night Watchman	420 "	July 19, 1895*
Daniel Madden	41 Lauriat ave., Dor.	Jobber	420 "	April 27, 1909
Fred C. Way	South Department	Ward Supervisor	540 "	March 9, 1902*
Albert H. Andrews	"	Orderly	420 "	Aug. 24, 1908*
Edward J. Fitzgibbon	"	"	420 "	Jan. 28, 1908*
Chester H. Lampman	"	"	420 "	" 29, 1909*
Delphin Marchand	"	"	420 "	March 26, 1907
Alvin B. Riley	"	"	420 "	Jan. 17, 1909*
Oscar F. Smith	"	"	420 "	" 5, 1909*
William H. Varney	"	Day Lodge Orderly	420 "	Nov. 24, 1896*
Joseph P. Flynn	"	Night Lodge Orderly	360 "	Dec. 14, 1905*
Edward J. Mould	"	Houseman	360 "	April 12, 1907
Edward M. Kenney	"	Center Orderly	300 "	Sept. 13, 1905
Alton W. Howard	"	"	270 "	Aug. 28, 1908
Malcolm Blue	"	Porter	240 "	Jan. 22, 1909*
James Bonner	"	"	240 "	Nov. 13, 1908
John Lawrence	"	"	240 "	Oct. 16, 1908*
Timothy Whooley	"	" (temporary)	240 "	March 12, 1909
Michael A. Malley	"	Window Porter	240 "	Jan. 26, 1909
Albert Beck	"	"	240 "	May 13, 1908
Minnie C. Dunton	"	Seamstress	360 "	July 16, 1904*
Christian A. Thompson	"	Housekeeper	360 "	Sept. 5, 1896*
Nellie Forbes	45 E. Lenox st	Cleaner	260 "	March 3, 1909
Catherine Byrne	698 Massachusetts ave	Scrubber	288 "	May 20, 1907
Eliza Cunningham	35 Newcomb st	"	288 "	Nov. 19, 1908
Frances E. Downs	45 E. Lenox st	"	288 "	Aug. 5, 1908*
Margaret Carten	South Department	"	192 "	Sept. 13, 1905
Dorothy McDonald	"	"	192 "	Jan. 8, 1909*
Catherine McMenamy	"	"	192 "	Oct. 8, 1908
Catherine Williams	"	"	192 "	" 18, 1907
Annie Keenan	"	Supply Woman	180 "	April 22, 1909
Margaret Maloney	"	House Cleaner	168 "	Nov. 24, 1908
Harold Jeffrey	117 Lenox st	"	1.00 day	Jan. 21, 1909
Theodore Armstrong	2987 Washington st	"	1.00 "	April 19, 1909*
Margaret Drummond	19 Washington pl.	Chambermaid	288 yr	Dec. 20, 1908*
Kate Ferguson	South Department	"	192 "	Jan. 6, 1909
Margaret McGinty	"	"	192 "	May 18, 1901*
Daisy Maffey	107 E. Newton st	Waitress	276 "	July 16, 1908
Lizzie Hardy	South Department	"	192 "	Dec. 2, 1908
Katie Murphy	"	"	192 "	June 12, 1908
Grace Dillon	"	"	180 "	April 2, 1909
Margaret McNamara	"	"	180 "	Dec. 16, 1908
Roy E. Smith	"	Head Cook	600 "	May 24, 1907*
Andrew Murray	"	Baker	600 "	Sept. 24, 1897*
Walter Patterson	"	Cook's Assistant	480 "	May 15, 1900
Warner H. Nelson	"	Kitchenman	300 "	April 15, 1907
Mary Monahan	77 W. Dedham st	Kitchenwoman	276 "	" 13, 1909*
Josie Drohan	48 E. Springfield st	Supply Woman	276 "	May 9, 1908*
Jessie Kydd	South Department	Diet Cook	216 "	Nov. 28, 1908
Bridget Mooney	"	Baker's Assistant	180 "	March 31, 1909
John Daly	"	Laundryman	540 "	July 17, 1905*
Margaret Sinclair	"	Head Laundress	420 "	" 27, 1898
Myrtle Jackson	7 Cottage st., S. B.	Laundress	300 "	Oct. 28, 1908
John H. Nolan	South Department	Laundryman	300 "	Aug. 15, 1908
Catherine Gallagher	Cambridge	Laundress	288 "	Feb. 13, 1908

* Promoted to present position on date given.   Previously in the department.

Hospital Department. — Continued.

Name.	Residence.	Designation.	Compensation.	Date of Election or Appointment.

South Department. — Concluded.

Name.	Residence.	Designation.	Compensation.	Date of Election or Appointment.
Mary Carmody	South Department	Laundress	$216 yr.	Feb. 17, 1908
Anna Connor	"	"	216 "	Oct. 17, 1908*
Annie Mooney	"	"	216 "	" 11, 1904
Annie Canning	"	"	192 "	March 25, 1908
Jane B. Ramsay	"	"	192 "	Oct. 14, 1904
Mary Rattray	"	"	192 "	July 22, 1904
Elizabeth G. Ryan	"	"	192 "	Nov. 23, 1908
Julia Sullivan	"	"	192 "	Sept. 20, 1905
Nellie Havey	"	"	180 "	Feb. 15, 1909
Mary A. Mooney	"	"	180 "	Oct. 16, 1908
Anna Bohlin	"	Ward Attendant	260 "	" 21, 1907*
Christine Endresen	"	"	260 "	Feb. 3, 1909*
Jessie Falconer	"	"	260 "	Oct. 22, 1908*
Marie Hansen	"	"	260 "	" 6, 1908*
Henrietta Gundersen	"	"	260 "	April 13, 1909*
Dorothy Henriksen	"	"	260 "	Oct. 6, 1908*
Pauline Panewicz	"	"	260 "	April 10, 1908
Caroline Robertson	"	"	260 "	June 9, 1908
Sarah Spiers	"	"	260 "	April 15, 1909*
Annie Sragsudie	"	"	260 "	" 23, 1908
Margaret Austin	"	Ward Maid	180 "	Feb. 27, 1909
Annie Dean	"	"	180 "	June 6, 1907*
Mamie Hickey	"	"	180 "	March 2, 1909
Alice O'Brien	"	"	180 "	Feb. 11, 1908
Mary Rowe	"	"	180 "	Nov. 10, 1908
Mary Tobin	"	"	180 "	Sept. 17, 1908
John J. Connorton	Hospital	Ambulance Driver	540 "	March 29, 1909*
Michael S. Ryan	"	Stableman	540 "	April 26, 1906*

Convalescent Home.

Name.	Residence.	Designation.	Compensation.	Date of Election or Appointment.
Elizabeth C. Fairbank	Convalescent Home	Matron	$720 yr.	June 22, 1900*
Martha S. Barr	"	Head Nurse	420 "	Oct. 9, 1908*
Elizabeth Melley	"	Cook	420 "	" 5, 1908
Annie Riley	"	Laundress	260 "	Mar. 5, 1909
Lizzie Buchter	"	Chambermaid	208 "	April 12, 1903*
Mary Armstrong	"	"	208 "	" 3, 1909
Esther Collins	"	Housemaid	156 "	" 29, 1909
Monica Fitzpatrick	"	House Cleaner	260 "	" 12, 1909
Herbert E. Russell	"	Farmer	360 "	Oct. 12, 1908*

East Boston Relief Station.

Name.	Residence.	Designation.	Compensation.	Date of Election or Appointment.
George F. Keenan, M. D.	East Boston Relief Station	Resident Surgeon	$1,000 yr.	Oct. 9, 1908*
Daniel F. Maguire, M. D.	"	Asst. Resident Surgeon	800 "	" 12, 1908*
Josephine Higgins	"	Matron	600 "	April 26, 1909*
Bertha V. Connors	"	Nurse	150 "	March 16, 1909*
Margaret M. Hughes	"	"	150 "	Jan. 2, 1909*
Isabel M. Nash	"	"	150 "	Dec. 29, 1908*
Daniel J. Sullivan	"	Supervisor	480 "	Oct. 12, 1908*
Frank A. Burdick	"	Orderly	420 "	" 13, 1908*
Carl H. K. Tucker	"	"	420 "	" 16, 1908*
Ernest Holland	"	Desk Orderly	300 "	" 12, 1908*
Delia McManus	"	Cook	360 "	" 8, 1908
Mary McGinn	"	Kitchenwoman	5.00 wk.	Feb. 26, 1909
Catherine McDonough	"	Chambermaid	180 yr.	Oct. 12, 1908*
Carrie Sampson	Hospital	Laundress	216 "	Nov. 27, 1908*
Mary A. Ahern	214 Havre st., E. B.	Scrubber	5.00 wk.	Sept. 28, 1908
Mary Moran	211 Havre st., E. B.	"	5.00 "	March 12, 1909
Patrick Joyce	40 Moulton st., Chsn.	Night Porter and Tender of Furnace	630 yr.	" 17, 1909*
Michael M. Fitzgerald	303 Saratoga St., E. B.	Day Porter and Tender of Furnace	630 "	Oct. 16, 1908

Haymarket Square Relief Station.

Name.	Residence.	Designation.	Compensation.	Date of Election or Appointment.
Loring B. Packard, M. D.	Haym'kt Sq. Relief Station	Resident Surgeon	$1,500 yr.	July 18, 1905*
Edwin L. Drowne, M. D.	"	"	1,000 "	" 19, 1906*
George H. Jonah	Somerville	Supervisor	720 "	Jan. 17, 1902*
Frank H. Monahan	Haym'kt Sq. Relief Station	Head Orderly	420 "	Dec. 12, 1906*

* Promoted to present position on date given. Previously in the department.

Hospital Department.—Concluded.

Name.	Residence.	Designation.	Compensation.	Date of Election or Appointment.
Haymarket Square Relief Station.—Concluded.				
Francis L. Norman	Hospital	Desk Orderly	$420 yr	Aug. 3, 1906*
Michael J. Walsh	"	Night Orderly	420 "	July 21, 1907*
Paul Baxter	Haym'kt Sq. Relief Station	Orderly	360 "	Oct. 17, 1908*
John J. Dugan	"	"	300 "	Feb. 20, 1909*
John T. Wheeler	"	Desk Orderly	420 "	June 17, 1906*
George J. Macdonald	"	"	300 "	Sept. 27, 1907*
Lucretia S. Smart	"	Matron	720 "	July 2, 1907*
Effie M. Palmer	"	Head Nurse	420 "	Nov. 3, 1907*
Hattie Chapman	"	Nurse	150 "	Jan. 12, 1909*
Rheta C. MacDonald	"	"	150 "	March 2, 1909*
Elsie F. Smith	"	"	150 "	" 1, 1909*
Mary L. Cheever	"	Cook	360 "	Nov. 30, 1908
Norah O'Leary	"	Kitchenwoman	180 "	April 17, 1909
Annie Shannon	"	Chambermaid	180 "	Jan. 21, 1907
Ada E. Hodnett	"	"	180 "	July 17, 1908
Margaret Sharkey	336 Medford st., Chsn	Scrubber	192 "	Jan. 4, 1903
Mary Hurley	21 Medford st., Chsn	"	192 "	March 3, 1907
Mary Brennan	Haym'kt Sq. Relief Station	Ward Maid	180 "	May 3, 1904*
Margaret Bartlett	229 London st., E. B	Ward Helper	260 "	April 17, 1907
Alberta F. Drury	Haym'kt Sq. Relief Station	Waitress	180 "	Oct. 8, 1908
Bridget McLaughlin	Hospital	Laundress	216 "	" 9, 1908*
May Holmes	"	"	204 "	" 27, 1905*
Nora Burke	"	"	192 "	May 15, 1908*
Annie M. Scott	"	"	180 "	Oct. 9, 1908*
John Monaghan	"	Laundryman	420 "	May 1, 1908*
Thomas Clark	Haym'kt Sq. Relief Station	Ambulance Foreman	600 "	July 7, 1904*
William Tumulty	"	Ambulance Driver	540 "	March 28, 1902*
Patrick Connors	"	"	540 "	Feb. 4, 1902*
John Anderson	Hospital	"	540 "	April 13, 1909*
William J. Cooney	Cambridge	Day Porter	630 "	Oct. 2, 1908*
Edward G. Reed	Everett	Night Porter	630 "	May 14, 1908
James Kelsick	6 Rollins pl	Elevator Boy	7.00 wk	Aug. 25, 1905
George Bryan	36 Irving st	House Boy	6.00 "	May 9, 1907
Seth F. Arnold, M. D	94 Worcester st	House Officer	None	March 1, 1909*
Fred A. Bartlett, M. D	Haym'kt Sq. Relief Station	"	"	" 1, 1909
Adelbert S. Merrill, M. D		"	"	" 1, 1909
George H. Jardine, M. D	682 Tremont st	Surgical Dresser	"	April 14, 1909*

Institutions Registration Department.

Name.	Residence.	Designation.	Compensation.	Date of Election or Appointment.
William P. Fowler	275 Newbury st	Institutions Registrar	None	April 27, 1908
John Koren	784 Beacon st	Statistician	$3,000 yr	June 15, 1899
Charles F. Gaynor	59 Bernard st., Dor	Chief Clerk	2,200 "	April 1, 1901
F. W. A. Sachs	59 Minden st., Rox	Clerk	1,300 "	" 8, 1901
William P. Costello	19 Cross st., Chsn	"	800 "	Jan. 16, 1906
Dudley L. Philbrick	285 Emerson st., S. B	Visitor	1,300 "	March 8, 1893
Edward L. Ahern	38 Homes ave., Dor	"	1,200 "	Feb. 1, 1898
Lucy M. Bosworth	25 Pearl st., Chsn	Stenographer	850 "	Sept. 7, 1897
Mary G. Hart	220 Lexington st., E. B	Typewriter	600 "	" 16, 1904
Mary J. Prescott	66 Revere st	Matron	850 "	May, 1887
Walter Barry	30 Nazing st., Rox	Carriage Driver	1,500 "	" 10, 1886
John H. Burke	72 Bromley st., Rox	Ambulance Driver	1,200 "	Nov. 10, 1895
George J. Uriot †	190 Harrison ave	"	900 "	Sept. 1, 1906

Law Department.

Name.	Residence.	Designation.	Compensation.	Date of Election or Appointment.
Thomas M. Babson	138 St. Botolph st	Corporation Counsel	$9,000 yr	July 1, 1904*
John D. McLaughlin	155 Bellevue st	Asst. Corporation Counsel	6,000 "	" 1, 1904
Arthur L. Spring	58 Selkirk rd	" "	5,000 "	Sept. 15, 1900
George A. Flynn	104 Norway st	" "	3,000 "	July 15, 1904
David D. Leahy	25 E. Springfield st	" "	2,200 "	Aug. 1, 1906
Karl Adams	352 Walnut ave	" "	2,500 "	March 1, 1908

* Promoted to present position on date given.   Previously in the department.
† See, also, Boston Infirmary Department and Children's Institutions Department.

Law Department.— Concluded.

Name.	Residence.	Designation.	Compensation.	Date of Election or Appointment.
Joseph A. Campbell	33 Athelwold st	Asst. Corporation Counsel.	$2,200 yr.	March 1, 1909
Charles F. Day	483 Beacon st	Conveyancer	3,750 "	July 3, 1880
Roscoe P. Owen	146 Massachusetts ave	"	3,750 "	" 4, 1881
Elizabeth M. Taylor	99 Newbury st	"	1,800 "	" 1, 1900
Fisher Ames	6 Mt. Vernon pl	Secretary	2,000 "	May 16, 1866
Nina F. Bachelor	Garrison Hall	Stenographer	960 "	Oct. 22, 1906
Daniel B. Carmody	15 Wyoming st	Messenger	600 "	April, 1894
James McGoldrick	38 Monument st	Telephone Boy	240 "	May 4, 1908
Joseph H. Robishow	17 Hamburg st	"	184 "	Oct. 3, 1908

Library Department.

Name.	Residence.	Designation.	Compensation.	Date of Election or Appointment.
Josiah H. Benton	265 Newbury st	President	None	May 29, 1894
Thomas F. Boyle	879 Beacon st	Vice President	"	" 6, 1902
Samuel Carr	403 Commonwealth ave	Trustee	"	" 1, 1908
William F. Kenney	1287 Commonwealth ave	"	"	Dec. 30, 1907
Alexander Mann	233 Clarendon st	"	"	May 25, 1908

Executive Department.

Name.	Residence.	Designation.	Compensation.	Date of Election or Appointment.
Horace G. Wadlin	Reading	Librarian	$6,000 yr.	Feb. 1, 1903
Otto Fleischner	8 Melton rd	Assistant Librarian	3,000 "	Jan. 12, 1900*
Della Jean Deery	Trinity ct	Assistant Grade B, Special and Clerk of Corporation	1,000 "	Nov. 9, 1900*
George V. Mooney	6 Minot pl	Assistant Grade B Special	1,000 "	Aug. 20, 1894*
Marion H. Shumway	32 Mather st	Assistant Grade B	15.00 wk.	Oct. 9, 1906*
William A. McGowan †	18 Smith st	Assistant Grade E	8.00 "	March 12, 1909*
Timothy J. Mackin †	12 Longwood ave	" " E	7.00 "	July 11, 1906*
William E. Clegg †	5 Bismarck st	" " E	4.75 "	April 23, 1909*
Adelaide A. Nichols	16 Pleasant st., Dor.	Auditor	1,500 yr.	Nov. 1, 1874*
Mary A. C. Berran †	140 Mt. Vernon st	Auditor's First Assistant	15.00 wk.	April 6, 1906*
Katharine M. Doyle	67 Beacon st	Auditor's Second Assistant	10.50 "	" 13, 1908

Catalogue Department.

Name.	Residence.	Designation.	Compensation.	Date of Election or Appointment.
Samuel A. Chevalier †	3 Linden st	Chief	$2,500 yr.	Feb. 23, 1906*
Lindsay Swift †	388 Park st., W. R.	Editor	35.00 wk.	" 7, 1896*
John Murdoch †	Cambridge	First Assistant	27.50 "	" 23, 1906*
William M. Arnolt	3 Linden st	Cataloguer	22.50 "	April 26, 1907*
Mary A. Tenney	Hotel Eliot	"	19.50 "	Oct. 22, 1905*
Lucien E. Taylor	9 Haviland st	"	17.50 "	" 9, 1903
Mary R. Bartlett	7 Concord sq.	"	15.00 "	July 1, 1897
Dora L. Cutler	29 Hartford st	"	15.00 "	Jan. 17, 1887
Frances N. A. Whitman	Newton	"	15.00 "	Feb. 1, 1905*
Elsie W. Coolidge	Watertown	"	13.00 "	Nov. 3, 1903
Flora N. Lilienthal	Brookline	"	12.00 "	Sept. 28, 1906*
E. Carolyn Merrill	104 Belvidere st	"	12.00 "	Oct. 8, 1906
M. Theresa Campbell ‡	47 Vine st	Assistant Cataloguer	12.00 "	July 20, 1903*
Anna E. Monahan	2 Howland st	"	12.00 "	Jan. 22, 1909*
Edwin F. Rice	45 Concord sq.	Curator Public Catalogue	17.50 "	" 1892*
Ida W. Gould	226 Massachusetts ave	Curator Official Catalogue	15.00 "	Oct. 8, 1901*
Thomas F. Brennan †	10 Crescent ave	Assistant Curator Official Catalogue	15.00 "	Feb. 1, 1901*
Lucius A. Blinn †	296 Dudley st	Assistant Grade E	5.50 "	July 1, 1907
Mary H. Rollins	74½ Pinckney st	Extra Special Cataloguer	26.25 "	June 6, 1907*

Shelf Department.

Name.	Residence.	Designation.	Compensation.	Date of Election or Appointment.
William G. T. Roffe †	148 Harvard st	First Assistant	$22.50 wk.	Jan. 1, 1897*
John F. Locke	3 Elmont st	Classifier	17.50 "	Dec., 1894
George H. Connor †	212 Chambers st	Assistant Grade C, Special	15.00 "	April 2, 1895*
John H. Reardon †	15 Sunnyside st	" "	15.00 "	Dec. 15, 1896*
John Eberhart	84 Walker st	" "	14.25 "	Sept. 17, 1894
Michael McCarthy, Jr. †	22 Humphreys st	" "	14.25 "	July 5, 1892
Joseph W. Ward †	24 Church st	" "	14.25 "	June 8, 1900*
Katherine J. Gorham	118 W. Sixth st	Assistant Grade C	12.00 "	Sept. 1, 1904*

* Promoted to present position on date given.   Previously in the department.
† Also in the Sunday and evening service, Central Library.
‡ Also in the Sunday and evening service at the branches.

Library Department.— Continued.

Name.	Residence.	Designation.	Compensation.	Date of Election or Appointment.

Shelf Department.—Concluded.

Name.	Residence.	Designation.	Compensation.	Date of Election or Appointment.
John J. Horgan †	14 Emerald st	Assistant Grade E	$9.00 wk	Jan. 15, 1909*
Anna G. Doonan ‡	12 Gay Head st	" " E	8.00 "	Sept. 1, 1904*
Alice M. Hennessy	590 Broadway	" " E	8.00 "	" 1, 1904*
James L. Sullivan †	80 Williams st	" " E	8.00 "	Jan. 15, 1909*
Abraham Snyder	1213 Tremont st	" " E	4.75 "	Oct. 2, 1908

Ordering Department.

Name.	Residence.	Designation.	Compensation.	Date of Election or Appointment.
Theodosia E. Macurdy	Watertown	Chief	$1,500 yr	June 1, 1893*
Emily O. Frinsdorff	10 Ware st	First Assistant	1,000 "	March 17, 1905*
Helen G. Cushing	Trinity ct	Second Assistant	16.00 wk	" 17, 1905
William C. Maiers, Jr. †	7 Gay Head st	Assistant Grade B, Special	17.50 "	May 11, 1906*
Frances H. Goddard	Trinity ct	Assistant Grade B	14.00 "	April 11, 1892
Margaret F. Collins	179 Walnut ave	" " C	14.00 "	Oct. 26, 1903*
Nellie L. Cunniff	174 Forest Hills st	" " C	14.00 "	March 23, 1903*
Mary J. Minton	13 Sargent st	" " C	10.00 "	July 31, 1908
Gertrude Boyle	23 Highgate st	" " E	10.00 "	Oct. 11, 1906
Lillian A. Tortorella	17 Oneida st	" " E	6.25 "	May 14, 1906
Daniel W. Travers	4 Germania st	" " E	4.00 "	March 29, 1909

Statistical Department.

Name.	Residence.	Designation.	Compensation.	Date of Election or Appointment.
James L. Whitney	Cambridge	Chief	$2,000 yr	Feb. 1, 1903*
Horace L. Wheeler †	42 Rutland sq	First Assistant	17.50 wk	July 23, 1900
Morris J. Rosenberg †	128 Stanwood st	Assistant Grade C	12.00 "	Oct. 26, 1903*

Bates Hall (Catalogue and Reference).

Name.	Residence.	Designation.	Compensation.	Date of Election or Appointment.
Oscar A. Bierstadt	10 W. Cedar st	Custodian	$3,000 yr	Feb. 1, 1899
Agnes C. Doyle	36 Hillside st	First Assistant	1,000 "	April 1, 1895*
Walter G. Forsyth †	Hemenway Chambers	Second Assistant	16.00 wk	Jan. 1, 1905
George H. Hughes †	East Cambridge	Assistant Grade E	7.00 "	Oct. 16, 1905

Bates Hall (Center Desk), Patent and Newspaper Departments.

Name.	Residence.	Designation.	Compensation.	Date of Election or Appointment.
Pierce E. Buckley †	6 National st	Custodian	$25.50 wk	Jan. 1, 1905*
Michael J. Conroy †	393 Broadway	Assistant Center Desk	12.00 "	Nov. 5, 1903*
Alphild Olson	99 Lauriat st	"	9.50 "	Sept. 29, 1905*
William A. Connolly †	14 Devon st	" " Grade E	4.00 "	April 22, 1909
Arthur R. Maier	131 Boylston st., J. P.	" " "	4.75 "	Oct. 12, 1908
William J. Mulloney †	2 Highland pk	First Asst. Patent Room	13.50 "	Nov. 7, 1905*
William G. Corbett †	9 Parker Hill ave	Asst. Grade E	7.00 "	April 14, 1908*
Charles V. Gillis	509 E. Sixth st	" " "	4.75 "	June 16, 1908
Frederic Serex †	16 Woodside ave	First Assistant News Room	14.00 "	Feb. 14, 1896*
William J. Ennis †	36 Chadwick st	Second " "	10.00 "	Oct. 6, 1902*

Periodical Room.

Name.	Residence.	Designation.	Compensation.	Date of Election or Appointment.
Frederika Wendte	101 Pinckney st	First Assistant	$14.00 wk	April 20, 1897*
Frank J. Hannigan †	29 Eastman st	Second Assistant	12.00 "	March 12, 1909*
William C. Wallace †	115 W. Third st	Assistant Grade E	7.00 "	July 3, 1905

Special Libraries.

Name.	Residence.	Designation.	Compensation.	Date of Election or Appointment.
Garrick M. Borden	23 St. Botolph st	Custodian	$20.00 wk	Nov. 11, 1907
Florence A. Westcott	71 Gainsboro st	First Assistant	12.00 "	April 20, 1909
Alice H. O'Neill	265 N. Beacon st	Assistant Barton Library	14.00 "	Oct. 20, 1905
Barbara Duncan	15 Gleason st	Assistant Music Room	12.00 "	Dec. 2, 1907*
Margaret L. Cassidy †	1395 Blue Hill ave	Assistant Grade C, Special	12.00 "	Nov. 5, 1895*
Annie G. Murphy	11 Grant st	" " C	12.00 "	Sept. 29, 1905*
James L. Doyle †	71 E. Brookline st	" " C	10.00 "	" 21, 1906*
John G. Downey †	117 Longwood ave	" " E	7.00 "	Dec. 7, 1906*
Clement T. Hayes †	3 Echo st	" " E	7.00 "	Feb. 15, 1909*
Joseph A. Crowley	24 Lark st	" " E	4.00 "	April 23, 1909*
Walter T. Hanna †	28 Burmah st	" " E	4.75 "	Sept. 1, 1908
Jeremiah J. O'Meara	14 Oregon st	Extra Assistant	4.84 "	Dec. 1, 1908*

* Promoted to present position on date given.   Previously in the department.
† Also in the Sunday and evening service, Central Library.
‡ Also in the Sunday and evening service at the branches.

Library Department.— Continued.

Name.	Residence.	Designation.	Compensation	Date of Election or Appointment.

Registration Department.

Name.	Residence.	Designation.	Compensation	Date of Election or Appointment.
John J. Keenan †	378 Columbus ave	Chief	$1,000 yr.	Aug. 20, 1894*
Margaret M. Barry	145 Bowdoin st	First Assistant	10.50 wk.	June 28, 1905*
Robert F. X. Dixon †	43 W. Concord st	Assistant Grade C	10.50 "	March 12, 1909*
Anna F. Rogers ‡	139 Centre st	" E	7.50 "	Nov. 3, 1905*
Anna M. Moran ‡	346 K st	" E	7.00 "	Jan. 19, 1906*

Issue Department.

Name.	Residence.	Designation.	Compensation	Date of Election or Appointment.
Frank C. Blaisdell †	67 St. Botolph st	Chief	$1,500 yr.	Jan. 1, 1905*
Mary C. Sheridan	6 Waterlow st	First Assistant	1,000 "	Feb. 1, 1902*
M. Florence Cufflin	20 Faneuil st	Assistant Grade C, Special	14.50 wk.	Oct. 18, 1895*
Mary A. Reynolds	3 Harding ct	" C	12.00 "	" 28, 1907*
S. Jennie Dowling	318 Warren st	" C	11.00 "	" 9, 1906*
Jean M. Bryce †	571 Washington st., Bri	" C	10.50 "	" 28, 1907*
Florence F. Richards ‡	23 Fayette st	" C	10.50 "	" 28, 1907*
Grace Williams ‡	76 Adams st	" C	11.00 "	" 26, 1900*
Mary E. Hagerty †	27 Brook ave	" C	10.00 "	" 9, 1906*
Mary A. Shaughnessy ‡	60 Withington st	" C	9.00 "	June 21, 1907*
Josephine A. Day ‡	16 Worthington st	" E	7.50 "	Sept. 4, 1908*
Mary M. Burke ‡	23 Auburn st	" E	7.00 "	June 29, 1904*
Gertrude M. Concree	29 Elmo st	" E	5.50 "	July 8, 1907
Agnes J. Daley ‡	7 Dallas pl	" E	7.00 "	Oct. 9, 1905
Bessie L. Doherty	7 Gay Head st	" E	7.00 "	June 14, 1905
Alice A. Downing ‡	29 Phillips st	" E	7.00 "	" 14, 1905
Maizie E. Doyle	71 E. Brookline st	" E	5.50 "	Oct. 28, 1907
Flora A. Ennis	36 Chadwick st	" E	7.00 "	" 14, 1904
Olive V. Greenlaw	27 Tappan st	" E	4.75 "	Nov. 4, 1907
James P. Haverty	7 Pine st	" E	4.00 "	Jan. 15, 1909
Elsie M. Holden	119 Massachusetts ave	" E	5.50 "	Oct. 4, 1907
William T. Lipshutz †	13 Jess st	" E	6.25 "	Sept. 5, 1906
Susan Maguire	935 Parker st	" E	7.00 "	Aug. 7, 1905
Annie E. Mantle	4 Elmwood pl	" E	7.00 "	Oct. 9, 1905
Mary E. Mulvaney ‡	1 Rena st	" E	7.00 "	June 21, 1907*
Ella T. Shea	75 Carver st	" E	7.00 "	Sept. 13, 1905
Katharine G. Sullivan	13 Hartford st	" E	7.00 "	Feb. 9, 1906
Mary G. Wall	6 Melbourne st	" E	4.75 "	Aug. 19, 1908
Julia R. Zaugg	253 Ruggles st	" E	7.00 "	Nov. 3, 1905*

Children's Department.

Name.	Residence.	Designation.	Compensation	Date of Election or Appointment.
Alice M. Jordan	142 Hemenway st	Custodian	$1,000 yr.	May 1, 1902*
Mildred E. Grush	35 Everton st	First Assistant	10.50 wk.	April 18, 1907*
Mary C. Toy	67 Beacon st	Assistant Grade C	9.00 "	Oct. 2, 1905*
Eleanor M. Williams † ‡	76 Adams st	" E	7.50 "	" 9, 1905*

Engineer and Janitor Department.

Name.	Residence.	Designation.	Compensation	Date of Election or Appointment.
Henry Niederauer	7 Intervale st	Chief	$1,700 yr.	Sept. 13, 1894
John P. Malone	38 Dennis st	First Engineer	21.09 wk.	Aug. 29, 1904*
George Zittel, Jr.	Durant st., Ros	"	21.09 "	April 19, 1895*
Nils J. Herland	48 Brush Hill rd	Second Engineer	21.00 "	March 10, 1895
Alexander McCready	57 Fort ave	"	21.00 "	Feb. 1, 1904*
Charles W. Karlson	21 Selwyn st	Electrician	21.00 "	Sept. 1, 1896
John A. Lawrence	7 Carmen st	Carpenter	21.00 "	May 26, 1899*
Alexander D. McGee	12 Upton st	Painter	21.00 "	April 15, 1896
Garrett Lacey	143 Union st., Bri	Fireman	17.50 "	Aug. 29, 1904
Timothy J. Quirk	760 Eighth st	"	17.50 "	July 16, 1906
William T. Hanna	28 Burmah st	Marble Polisher	16.00 "	Feb. 28, 1895
Daniel T. Kelly	452 E. Seventh st	Watchman	15.75 "	March 31, 1906
Dennis McCarty	359 Cambridge st	"	15.75 "	May 21, 1888
John L. Williams	2 Weldon st	Janitor	18.00 "	April 19, 1895*
Edward Berran	15 Mt. Hope st	"	15.50 "	March 2, 1903
Henry W. Frye	1 St. James pl	"	15.50 "	Oct. 31, 1898
James J. Kelley	466 Parker st	"	15.50 "	April 23, 1900
Charles W. Murphy	34 Chambers st	"	15.00 "	Sept. 6, 1904
William E. Cole	40 Hammond st	Elevator Attendant	10.00 "	March 7, 1898
Patrick A. Kennedy	73 Village st	"	10.00 "	June 19, 1906

* Promoted to present position on date given.   Previously in the department.
† Also in Sunday and evening service, Central Library.
‡ Also in Sunday and evening service at the branches.

Library Department. — Continued.

Name.	Residence.	Designation.	Compensation.	Date of Election or Appointment.

Engineer and Janitor Department.—Concluded.

Name.	Residence.	Designation.	Compensation.	Date of Election or Appointment.
Charles Webster	16 Davenport st	Elevator Attendant	$10.00 wk	Jan. 13, 1906
Mary F. Mullen	130 Huntington ave	Matron	12.00 "	June 16, 1905
Esther Corcoran †	27 Fayette st	Cleaning	12.20 "	Oct. 22, 1899
Julia Connors †	5 Edgerly pl	"	5.40 "	Jan. 9, 1909
Bridget Day †	677 Harrison ave	"	5.40 "	Nov. 16, 1904
Bridget Donohue †	75 Cabot street	"	6.60 "	Oct. 7, 1906
Hannah Evans †	12 Flagg st	"	4.80 "	March, 1890
Hannah Foley †	3 Sheridan pl	"	5.40 "	Nov. 11, 1907
Mary Foley †	77 E. Dedham st	"	5.40 "	Oct. 12, 1907
Mary Frazer †	599 Shawmut ave	"	4.80 "	Nov. 11, 1905
Bridget Healy †	82 W. Canton st	"	5.40 "	March 17, 1906
Margaret Hurley †	5 Roach st	"	4.80 "	Oct. 13, 1904
Mary Johnson †	24 Woodbury st	"	4.80 "	March 2, 1907
Ellen Kennedy †	73 Village st	"	3.60 "	April, 1895
Mary Kennedy †	581 Shawmut ave	"	5.40 "	June 23, 1905
Hannah Lydon †	85 Baxter st	"	6.00 "	Oct. 17, 1907
Bridget Lydon †	10 Gold st	"	5.40 "	Sept. 28, 1909
Annie Murray †	13 Newland st	"	5.60 "	July 31, 1905
Minnie Otto †	193 Camden st	"	5.40 "	Sept., 1897
Mary Saunders †	24 W. Dedham st	"	5.40 "	May 31, 1908
Norah Sullivan †	108 Union Park st	"	4.80 "	April 6, 1909
Elizabeth Weidner †	6 Wellington st	"	4.80 "	Aug. 3, 1900

Printing Department.

Name.	Residence.	Designation.	Compensation.	Date of Election or Appointment.
Francis W. Lee‡	Technology Chambers	Chief	$42.00 wk	Nov. 22, 1895*
Willfried H. Geyer	87 Appleton st	Pressman	21.60 "	Jan. 6, 1896
Charles J. O'Keefe	13 Elmore st	Job Pressman	19.00 "	June 10, 1899
Mary T. M. Boyle	4 Marcella st	Linotype Operator	17.47 "	April 13, 1903
Annie F. Land	Cambridge	"	17.47 "	" 15, 1896
Minnie A. Munson	20 Joy st	"	17.47 "	Feb. 4, 1902
Thomas Bowen	28 Riverdale st	Assistant	6.00 "	March 10, 1908

Bindery.

Name.	Residence.	Designation.	Compensation.	Date of Election or Appointment.
Frank Ryder	141 Westville st	Chief	$1,800 yr	March 17, 1890*
Dennis J. Collins	347 W. Fourth st	Finisher	23.00 wk	Dec. 27, 1887
Konrad E. Löfström	70 Tower st	"	20.00 "	Aug. 22, 1892
Frank H. Callahan	823 Dorchester ave	Forwarder	19.17 "	Oct. 8, 1906
Theodore W. Cellarius	100 Poplar st	"	19.17 "	Feb. 3, 1905*
William Connell	4 Everett sq	"	19.17 "	Oct. 17, 1904
Fred J. Drew	95 Quincy st	"	19.17 "	March 3, 1909
Michael J. Doyle	52 Montfern ave	"	19.17 "	July 21, 1902
Maximilian L. Eichorn	171 I st	"	19.17 "	June 15, 1904
William P. Hemstedt ‡	18 Johnston rd	"	19.17 "	April 14, 1883
George Hoeffner	3150 Washington st., J. P.	"	19.17 "	Sept. 8, 1891
John F. Murphy	74 Waltham st	"	19.17 "	April 7, 1885
J. Henry Sullivan	35 Bayard st	"	19.17 "	Aug. 15, 1898
John H. Watson	444 Beech st	"	19.17 "	July 29, 1902
John J. O'Brien	31 Newman st	Apprentice Forwarder	17.00 "	April 15, 1904*
Therese A. Masterson	1 Danforth pl	General Assistant Grade C	12.00 "	Jan. 8, 1907
Alice M. Abely	276 Sumner st	Sewer	9.00 "	July 16, 1906
Elizabeth F. Cooney	43 Hillside st	"	10.00 "	Aug. 13, 1906
Ellen A. Coullahan	260 Temple st., J. P.	"	10.00 "	Sept. 29, 1905
Ida G. Denney ‡	670 Columbia rd	"	10.00 "	July 21, 1902
Joanna Doiron	50 Bickerstaff st	"	10.00 "	June 9, 1896
Mary E. Fitzgerald	69 Fort ave	"	9.00 "	Feb. 4, 1907
Annie T. Flynn	151 Bowdoin st	"	9.00 "	Aug. 20, 1907
Mary A. Glancy	284 Quincy st	"	9.00 "	July 16, 1906
Mary T. McElaney	42 Chestnut st., Chsn	"	10.00 "	" 21, 1902
Ellen F. Potts	23 Parsons st	"	10.00 "	Sept. 6, 1892
Lucy E. Soule	17 Farrington ave	"	10.00 "	Jan. 7, 1891
George W. Gallagher ‡	22 E. Cottage st	General Assistant Grade E	7.00 "	May 29, 1907*
Catherine T. Donnelly	167 Chestnut st., J. P.	Extra Sewer	9.00 "	June 15, 1908

* Promoted to present position on date given.   Previously in the department.
† Paid 20 cents per hour.
‡ Also in Sunday and evening service, Central Library.

Library Department. — Continued.

Name.	Residence.	Designation.	Compensation.	Date of Election or Appointment.

Branch Department.

Name.	Residence.	Designation.	Compensation.	Date of Election or Appointment.
Langdon L. Ward	13 Garrison st	Supervisor of Branches and Stations	$1,800 yr	July 1, 1898*
Alice V. Stevens	Wellesley	First Assistant	17.50 wk	" 3, 1899
Cecilia W. Kueffner	99 Newbury st	Cataloguer	14.00 "	June 1, 1898
Amy W. Adams	Melrose	Second Assistant	13.50 "	Sept. 21, 1903*
Maud M. Morse †	134 W. Newton st	Assistant Grade C	13.50 "	Feb. 27, 1893*
Marion A. McCarthy	359 Cambridge st	" " C	13.00 "	April, 1897*
Mary G. Cunniff	174 Forest Hills st	" " C	9.00 "	Aug. 28, 1908*
Joseph A. Maier †	123 Minden st	" " C	10.00 "	March 29, 1895*
Chester A. S. Fazakas †	908 Harrison ave	" " E	8.00 "	July 5, 1903*
Charles J. Mackin	12 Longwood ave	" " E	4.75 "	Sept. 14, 1908
Otto A. Heimann †	8 Enfield st	" " C, Special	15.00 "	Dec. 12, 1890
Richard Brown †	9 Oakman st	" " E	9.00 "	" 5, 1898

Brighton Branch.

Name.	Residence.	Designation.	Compensation.	Date of Election or Appointment.
Louise Prouty	Gardner st., Bri	Custodian	$17.50 wk	Oct. 27, 1905*
Ellen F. Conley	55 Bennett st	First Assistant	12.00 "	July 30, 1891*
Geneva Watson	149 Foster st	Second Assistant	10.50 "	Jan. 18, 1904*
Eleanor R. Mohan	30 Gordon st	General Assistant	7.00 "	July 8, 1907*
Thomas J. O'Neil	12 Bennett st	Janitor	18.00 "	Oct. 3, 1908
Francis P. Devlin	39 Surrey st	Extra Assistant	.30 "	Sept. 27, 1908
John Sullivan	35 Bayard st	"	1.20 "	" 24, 1908
Michael O'Brien	381 Chestnut Hill ave	"	.80 "	July, 1907
Marion W. Brackett ‡	10 Princeton st., E. B	Sunday Assistant §	2.45 "	Dec., 1908
Mary E. Mulvaney ‡	1 Rena st	" §	1.75 "	" 1908

NOTE. — John P. O'Hara alternates with Marion W. Brackett, and Mary M. Burke with Mary E. Mulvaney in the Sunday service.

Charlestown Branch.

Name.	Residence.	Designation.	Compensation.	Date of Election or Appointment.
Elizabeth F. Cartee	50 Commonwealth ave	Custodian	$17.50 wk	Feb. 1, 1886
Katherine S. Rogan	33 Monument ave	First Assistant	12.00 "	Jan. 19, 1906*
Ellen L. Sullivan	119 High st	Second Assistant	10.50 "	July 14, 1905*
		Sunday Service §	2.45 "	Nov., 1905
Annie M. Donovan	85 Ferrin st	General Assistant	7.00 "	April 28, 1899*
Clara L. Jones	254 Massachusetts ave	"	7.00 "	July 14, 1905*
		Sunday Service §	2.45 "	Nov., 1907
Alice F. Carroll	611 E. Seventh st	General Assistant	6.00 "	Feb. 6, 1909
William McNamee	4 Sever st	Janitor	6.00 "	June 1, 1908
		Sunday Service §	2.00 "	Dec., 1908
Timothy A. O'Neil	83 Washington st	Extra Assistant	1.80 "	April, 1908
William S. Townsend	69 Chapman st	"	1.20 "	Sept. 21, 1908

NOTE.— Annie M. Donovan alternates with Ellen L. Sullivan, and Helen J. L. Kennelly with Clara Jones in the Sunday service.

Dorchester Branch.

Name.	Residence.	Designation.	Compensation.	Date of Election or Appointment.
Elizabeth T. Reed	34 Arcadia st	Custodian	$17.50 wk	Nov. 16, 1891*
		Sunday Service §	2.45 "	Dec., 1908
Mary G. Donovan	6 Paisley pk	First Assistant	12.00 "	Oct. 4, 1907*
Margaret H. Reid	Somerville	Second Assistant	10.50 "	" 4, 1907*
Grace M. Connell	208 Dudley st	General Assistant	7.00 "	" 4, 1907*
		Sunday Service §	2.45 "	Dec., 1908
Anna G. Lynch	348 Geneva ave	General Assistant	7.00 "	Oct. 4, 1907*
John F. Halligan	365 Quincy st	Janitor	7.75 "	Feb. 12, 1902
Wilfred A. J. Curran	38 Topliff st	Extra Assistant	2.60 "	June 18, 1908

NOTE.— Mary G. Donovan and Margaret H. Reid alternate with Elizabeth T. Reed, and Anna G. Lynch with Grace M. Connell in the Sunday service.

* Promoted to present position on date given.   Previously in the department.
† Also in Sunday and evening service, Central Library.
‡ Also in regular service.
§ Sunday service at branches, November to May each year.

Library Department.— Continued.

Name.	Residence	Designation.	Compensation.	Date of Election or Appointment.

East Boston Branch.

Name.	Residence	Designation.	Compensation.	Date of Election or Appointment.
Ellen O. Walkley	420 Meridian st.	Custodian	$17.50 wk.	July 1, 1897
Alice M. Wing	40 Princeton st.	First Assistant.	12.00 "	1875*
Marion W. Brackett	40 Princeton st.	Second Assistant.	10.50 "	April 2, 1897
Lillian A. Bickford	320 Saratoga st.	General Assistant	9.00 "	Aug. 31, 1891
		Sunday Service †	2.45 "	Nov., 1903
Florence M. Bethune	32 Princeton st.	General Assistant	7.00 "	Oct. 5, 1903*
Everett F. Matthews	37 Prescott st.	Janitor (also Station Z)	11.75 "	April 28, 1890
		Sunday Service †	2.45 "	Nov., 1903
James J. Donnelly	45 Lamson st.	Assistant Janitor	3.00 "	Oct. 1, 1904
		Sunday Service †	2.00 "	Nov., 1904
Joseph H. Driscoll	585 Bennington st.	Extra Assistant	1.70 "	April, 1908
		Sunday Service †	.35 "	Nov., 1907
Ethel E. Knowles	7 Stanley st.	Extra Assistant	.90 "	March 4, 1909
Elizabeth McLaughlin	226 Princeton st.	"	.80 "	Sept. 16, 1907
Helen L. Murphy	50 Falcon st.	"	.90 "	Oct. 9, 1907
John A. Murphy	50 Falcon st.	"	.70 "	" 12, 1908

NOTE.— Florence M. Bethune alternates with Lillian A. Bickford, and Helen B. Shannon with Everett F. Matthews in the Sunday service.

Jamaica Plain Branch.

Name.	Residence	Designation.	Compensation.	Date of Election or Appointment.
Mary P. Swain	30 Grovenor rd.	Custodian	$17.50 wk.	Dec. 5, 1892*
Nellie F. Riley	30 Grovenor rd	First Assistant	12.00 "	1889*
Alice B. Orcutt	440 E. Sixth st.	Second Assistant	10.50 "	Oct. 5, 1906*
Elizabeth M. Kelley	107 St. Alphonsus st.	General Assistant	7.00 "	June 8, 1906*
		Sunday Service †	2.45 "	Nov., 1906
Alice McEttrick ‡	453 Dudley st.	" †	2.45 "	" 1904
John F. Houston, Jr.	51 Call st.	Extra Assistant	1.35 "	April 20, 1909

NOTE.— Nellie F. Riley alternates with Alice McEttrick, and Anna G. Doonan with Elizabeth M. Kelley in the Sunday service.

Roxbury Branch.

Name.	Residence	Designation.	Compensation.	Date of Election or Appointment.
Helen M. Bell	Hotel Park, Dale st.	Custodian	$17.50 wk.	Aug. 1, 1886*
Katie F. Albert	13 Bromley pk.	First Assistant	12.00 "	Oct. 5, 1906*
Martha L. C. Berry	8 Hazel pk.	Second Assistant	11.50 "	Aug. 1, 1886*
		Sunday Service †	2.45 "	Nov., 1902
Sarah W. Griggs	12 Circuit st.	General Assistant	9.75 "	Aug. 1, 1886
Gertrude L. Connell	208 Dudley st.	"	8.50 "	Dec. 2, 1904*
		Sunday Service †	2.45 "	Nov., 1905
Louise B. Bell	1 Dabney pl.	General Assistant	7.00 "	Oct. 5, 1906*
William B. Nugent	46 Millmont st.	Janitor	13.50 "	May 11, 1906
		Sunday Service †	2.00 "	Nov., 1907
Mary F. Baker	27 Woodbine st.	Extra Assistant	2.40 "	Oct. 9, 1899
Florence F. Richards ‡	23 Fayette st.	Sunday Service †	1.75 "	Nov., 1907
Gertrude Wentworth	36 Dunlow st.	Extra Assistant	.20 "	Oct. 1, 1907
Eulalia S. Masterson	27 Lambert ave	"	1.15 "	" 6, 1908

NOTE.— K. F. Albert alternates with Martha L. C. Berry, Sarah W. Griggs with Gertrude L. Connell and Agnes L. Murphy with Florence F. Richards in the Sunday service.

South Boston Branch.

Name.	Residence	Designation.	Compensation.	Date of Election or Appointment.
Alice M. Robinson	Cambridge	Custodian	$17.50 wk.	March 31, 1902
Ellen A. Eaton	412 E. Fifth st.	First Assistant	12.00 "	1883*
Idalene L. Sampson	675 E. Sixth st.	Second Assistant	11.50 "	June 1, 1885*
Annie C. McQuarrie	290 Athens st.	General Assistant	9.00 "	Nov. 2, 1896*
Catherine F. Kiley	Fargo st.	"	7.00 "	Jan, 4, 1907*
Joseph Baker	253 W. Broadway	Janitor	11.75 "	April 30, 1872
		Sunday Service †	2.45 "	Nov., 1897
Alice B. Orcutt ‡	440 E. Sixth st.	" †	2.45 "	" 1897
Thomas Sanders	393 E. Fifth st.	Sunday Janitor †	2.00 "	" 1897
William J. Gross	6 Dixfield st.	Extra Assistant	1.80 "	Sept. 14, 1908
Charles H. Ryan	580 E. Eighth st.	"	.50 "	" 30, 1903
Mary F. Thornton	517 Fifth st.	"	3.30 "	Oct., 1904

* Promoted to present position on date given.   Previously in the department.
† Sunday service at branches, November to May each year.
‡ Also in regular service.

Library Department. — Continued.

Name.	Residence.	Designation.	Compensation.	Date of Election or Appointment.

South End Branch.

Name.	Residence.	Designation.	Compensation.	Date.
Margaret A. Sheridan	6 Waterlow st	Custodian	$17.50 wk	July 1, 1887*
Alice McEttrick	453 Dudley st	First Assistant	12.00 "	Feb. 12, 1906*
Emma F. Lynch	14 School st., Dor	Second Assistant	11.50 "	1890*
Amelia F. McGrath	36 Union pk	General Assistant	11.50 "	March 1, 1905*
Katherine E. Walsh	45 Burrell st	"	7.00 "	Oct. 2, 1905*
William L. Harris	Malden	"	7.00 "	March 18, 1907
John I. VanTassel	8 School street pl.	Janitor	17.00 "	Dec. 24, 1908
Théophile J. Bernhardt	133 Centre st	Extra Assistant	2.00 "	Sept. 20, 1907
William R. Meroth	25 E. Springfield st	"	3.00 "	28, 1908
Katherine S. Rogan ‡	33 Monument ave	Sunday Service †	2.45 "	Nov., 1904
Eleanor M. Williams	76 Adams st	" †	2.45 "	1907
Marguerite Coydevant	89 Union Park st	" †	1.75 "	1905
Frederick A. Garth	74 E. Brookline st	" †	1.75 "	Feb. 28, 1905

NOTE.— Emma F. Lynch alternates with Katherine S. Rogan, Amelia F. McGrath with Eleanor Williams, and Loren N. Downes with Frederick A. Garth in the Sunday service.

Upham's Corner Branch.

Name.	Residence.	Designation.	Compensation.	Date.
Mary L. Brick	124 Brook ave	Custodian	$14.00 wk	Sept. 1, 1904*
Mary F. Curley	10 Holborn pl	First Assistant	8.00 "	May 4, 1906*
Margaret A. Murphy	16 Hancock st	Second Assistant	7.00 "	March 6, 1905
Olive M. Neilson	9 Cortes st	General Assistant	6.25 "	Oct. 4, 1907
Caroline Curtis	22 Clifton st	Extra Assistant	3.60 "	Nov. 7, 1907
Ida G. Denney ‡	670 Columbia rd	"	1.50 "	Sept. 25, 1906
Alice A. Downing ‡	29 Phillips st	"	1.00 "	July, 1907
Katherine F. McEttrick	453 Dudley st	"	2.15 "	Dec. 17, 1906
Mary E. Hagerty ‡	27 Brook ave	Sunday Service †	2.45 "	Nov., 1905
Katherine E. Walsh ‡	45 Burrell st	" †	1.75 "	1906

NOTE.— Margaret A. Murphy alternates with Mary E. Hagerty, and Ida G. Denney with Katherine E. Walsh in the Sunday service.

West End Branch.

Name.	Residence.	Designation.	Compensation.	Date.
Eliza R. Davis	53 Dale st	Custodian	$17.50 wk	Feb. 1, 1896*
Margaret S. Barton	17 Walnut pk	First Assistant	12.00 "	Nov. 25, 1896*
George W. Forbes	10 Dundee st	Reference Assistant	12.00 "	Jan. 6, 1896
		Extra Service	5.00 "	1896
Mary E. Kiley	49 Allen st	Second Assistant	10.50 "	Aug. 21, 1896*
Rebecca Millmeister	238 Chambers st	General Assistant	10.50 "	May 8, 1905*
Mary E. Riley	397 Charles st	"	9.00 "	Nov. 18, 1895*
Catherine M. McMullen	35 Moreland st	"	7.00 "	July 8, 1907*
Eugene Cardarelli	1 Allen pl	"	7.00 "	Oct. 16, 1905*
Naaman Menaker	Cambridge	"	7.00 "	9, 1903
Daniel J. Sullivan	Beacon Chambers	Janitor	17.25 "	Nov. 17, 1898
James E. McKenna	127 Charles st	Extra Assistant	4.65 "	Oct. 16, 1905

West Roxbury Branch.

Name.	Residence.	Designation.	Compensation.	Date.
Carrie L. Morse	113 Corey st	Custodian	$14.00 wk	Oct. 1, 1890
Rebecca S. Willis	Lorette st	Assistant	7.00 "	5, 1903*
Edward Schwartz	1907 Centre st	Janitor	5.00 "	Nov. 18, 1904
Mary G. Enos	370 La Grange st	Extra Assistant	1.60 "	April 3, 1907
Mattie C. Martin	82 Montello st	(also Station B)	.75 "	Dec. 12, 1900

Station A.

Name.	Residence.	Designation.	Compensation.	Date.
M. Addie Hill	123 Richmond st	Custodian	$40.00 wk	June 7, 1875
Ruth E. Spargo	63 Temple st., Dor	Substitute	.50 "	1898

Station B.

Name.	Residence.	Designation.	Compensation.	Date.
Grace L. Murray	259 Park st., Ros	Custodian	$12.00 wk	Dec. 10, 1900*
Alice M. Regan	133 Florence st	Assistant	7.00 "	Oct. 5, 1903*
Mattie C. Martin	82 Montello st	Substitute (also West Roxbury Branch)	1.00 "	Oct. 31, 1907

* Promoted to present position on date given. Previously in the department.
† Sunday service at branches, November to May each year.
‡ Also in regular service.

Library Department.— Continued.

Name.	Residence.	Designation.	Compensation.	Date of Election or Appointment.

Station D.

| Emma G. Capewell | 733 Norfolk st | Custodian | $10.00 wk | Aug. 15, 1892 |
| Edith Baker | 461 River st | Substitute | .80 " | 1895 |

Station E.

| Mary M. Sullivan | 13 Hartford st | Custodian | $9.00 wk | June 21, 1907* |
| Beatrice M. Flanagan | 64 Newhall ave | Extra Assistant | 4.00 " | July 27, 1907 |

Station F.

Elizabeth G. Fairbrother	43 Rossiter st	Custodian	$10.00 wk	Jan. 1, 1887
Isabel E. Wetherald	20 Old rd	Assistant	7.00 "	Oct. 17, 1902*
Ruth B. Sather	35 Selden st	Extra Assistant	.85 "	Aug. 19, 1907

Station G.

Katharine F. Muldoon	29 Maple ave	Custodian	$10.00 wk	April 17, 1905*
Margaret V. Rooney	8 Kingsley st	Extra Assistant	3.60 "	March, 1906
Anna M. Moran ‡	346 K st	Sunday Service †	2.10 "	Dec., 1908

NOTE.— Margaret V. Rooney alternates with Anna M. Moran in the Sunday service.

Station J.

Gertrude M. Harkins	Brookline	Custodian	$12.00 wk	Feb. 7, 1905
Abbie E. Sargent	51 Ashland st	Assistant	7.00 "	" 12, 1906
Katrina M. Sather	35 Selden st	Extra Assistant	4.20 "	Dec. 29, 1905
William A. Bailey	15 Kerwin st	Sunday Service †	2.45 "	Nov., 1907
Charles White	11½ Whitman st	" †	1.75 "	" 1907

Station N.

| Anna M. Witherell | 20 Woodville st | Custodian | $10.00 wk | Aug. 4, 1900 |
| Agnes J. Daley ‡ | 7 Dallas pl | Substitute | .50 " | July, 1908 |

Station P.

Cora L. Stewart	22 Dix pl	Custodian	$12.00 wk	Oct. 28, 1898
		Sunday Service †	2.10 "	Nov., 1907
Mary Linda	6 Asylum st	Assistant	7.00 "	Aug. 28, 1908*

Station R.

Mary L. Kelly	361 Charles st	Custodian	$10.00 wk	April 18, 1907*
Edith F. Pendleton	2 Tupelo st	Extra Assistant	5.40 "	Oct. 22, 1906
Frederick H. Busby	468 Shawmut ave	Sunday Service †	2.10 "	Nov., 1907

Station S.

Laura M. Cross	14 Upton st	Custodian	$10.00 wk	May 29, 1905*
Rosella F. McKay	1 Buchanan pl	Extra Assistant	2.70 "	March 10, 1909
Katherine E. Kelly	39 Calumet st	"	.50 "	Oct. 12, 1908
Mary A. Shaughnessy ‡	60 Withington st	Sunday Service †	2.10 "	Nov., 1905

NOTE.— M. Theresa Campbell alternates with Mary A. Shaughnessy in the Sunday service.

Station T.

Elizabeth P. Ross	415 Seaver st	Custodian	$10.00 wk	May 29, 1905*
Edith R. Nickerson	63 Wyman st	Extra Assistant	3.00 "	Dec. 28, 1908
Agnes J. Daley ‡	7 Dallas pl	Sunday Service †	2.10 "	" 1908
Anna F. Rogers ‡	139 Centre st	Substitute	.50 "	Nov., 1907

NOTE.— Anna F. Rogers alternates with Agnes J. Daley in the Sunday service.

* Promoted to present position on date given.   Previously in the department.
† Sunday service at the branches, November to May each year.
‡ Also in the regular service.

Library Department.— Continued

Name.	Residence.	Designation.	Compensation.	Date of Election or Appointment.

Station Z.

Helen M. McDougall	34 Central sq	Custodian	$8.00 wk	June 1, 1901
E. Belle Battis	9 Gladstone st	Substitute	.50 "	Aug., 1903
Everett F. Matthews	37 Prescott st	Janitor (also E. B. Branch)	2.50 "	June 14, 1901

Station 22.

| Iside Boggiano | 41 Endicott st | Custodian | $8.00 wk | Oct. 2, 1903 |
| Theresa V. Arato | 7 Henchman st | Substitute | .75 " | Aug., 1904 |

Station 23.

Josephine E. Kenney	46 Faneuil st	Custodian	$9.00 wk	July 8, 1907*
Sylvia Donegan	134 M st	Extra Assistant	2.00 "	Sept. 3, 1908
Grace V. Meehan	556 E. Sixth st	"	3.53 "	July 25, 1906
Grace Williams ‡	76 Adams st	Substitute	.50 "	1906
Annie C. McQuarrie ‡	290 Athens st	Sunday Service †	2.10 "	Dec., 1908
Ruth L. McQuarrie	290 Athens st		1.50 "	1908

NOTE.— Grace Williams alternates with Annie C. McQuarrie, and Josephine Day with Ruth McQuarrie in the Sunday service.

Station 24.

Mary F. Kelley	16 Worthington st	Custodian	$10.00 wk	July 8, 1907*
		Sunday Service †	2.10 "	Nov., 1907
Margaret F. Meehan	556 E. Sixth st	Extra Assistant	4.95 "	Sept. 24, 1906
		Sunday Service †	1.50 "	Nov., 1907
Alice A. Downing ‡	29 Phillips st	Extra Assistant	.50 "	1908

NOTE.— Margaret S. Barton alternates with Mary F. Kelley, and Alice A. Downing with Margaret F. Meehan in the Sunday service.

Sunday and Evening Service, Central Library. §

John W. Athridge	6 Bartlett ter	Assistant Grade E	$4.70 wk	Sept. 16, 1905
Edward J. Berran	15 Mt. Hope st	" E	2.10 "	May 7, 1905
Mary A. C. Berran ‡	140 Mt. Vernon st	" C	1.20 "	Nov. 12, 1904
Clarence Bissett	260 Clarendon st	" E	1.20 "	April 18, 1908
Frank C. Blaisdell ‡	67 St. Botolph st	In charge of service	16.40 "	March 17, 1895*
Lucius Blinn ‡	296 Dudley st	Assistant Grade E	.60 "	Jan. 20, 1908
Frank A. Bourne	130 Mt. Vernon st	" B	5.36 "	Aug. 11, 1896
Thomas F. Brennan ‡	10 Crescent ave	" C	5.68 "	March 17, 1895
Walter M. Broderick	31 Yarmouth st	" E	2.00 "	1903
Richard Brown ‡	9 Oakman st	" E	5.20 "	" 17, 1900
Edward E. Bruce	Cambridge st	" E	1.00 "	Oct. 19, 1900
Jean M. Bryce ‡	571 Washington st., Bri	" C	3.50 "	Sept. 26, 1906
Pierce E. Buckley ‡	6 National st	" B	12.80 "	Nov. 22, 1895
Frederick H. Busby	368 Shawmut ave	" E	1.20 "	Oct. 26, 1908
Margaret L. Cassidy ‡	1395 Blue Hill ave	" C	2.68 "	April 1, 1909
Samuel A. Chevalier ‡	3 Linden st	" B	8.80 "	March 17, 1895*
William E. Clegg ‡	5 Bismarck st	" E	.75 "	Dec. 1, 1908
James J. Coady	68 E. Canton st	" E	1.20 "	Jan. 29, 1908
Charles C. Concannon	Cambridge	" E	3.00 "	Sept. 16, 1905
William A. Connolly ‡	14 Devon st	" E	1.20 "	Aug. 18, 1908
George H. Connor ‡	212 Chambers st	" B	9.54 "	March 17, 1895
Michael J. Conroy ‡	293 Broadway	" C	8.00 "	Sept. 6, 1898
William J. Corbett ‡	9 Parker Hill ave	" E	1.50 "	Jan. 29, 1909
Alexander A. Courtney	7 Dorset st	" E	1.80 "	March 23, 1909
Francis X. Courtney	7 Dorset st	" E	2.80 "	Jan. 8, 1907
Arthur E. Cufflin	199 Market st	" E	3.00 "	Oct. 28, 1902
Francis P. Devlin	39 Surrey st	" E	1.20 "	Aug. 18, 1908
Robert F. Dixon ‡	43 E. Concord st	" C	4.40 "	Oct. 28, 1902
Wendell P. Dodge	50 St. Germain st	" E	.60 "	March 23, 1909

* Promoted to present position on date given. Previously in the department.
† Sunday service at the branches, November to May each year.
‡ Also in the regular service.
§ Paid by the hour, as follows:
   Grade E.— 20, 25 and 30 cents.
   Grade C.— 35, 40 and 50 cents.
   Grade B.— 67, 80 and $1.10.

Library Department.— Continued.

Sunday and Evening Service, Central Library.†— Continued.

Name.	Residence.	Designation.	Compensation.	Date of Election or Appointment.
Charles W. Dolan	1428 Tremont st	Assistant Grade C	$6.00 wk	March 3, 1904
John G. Downey ‡	117 Longwood ave	" " E	1.00 "	Oct. 1, 1905
John G. Downing	8 National st	" " E	2.60 "	May 19, 1906
Loren N. Downs, Jr.	33 Clarendon st	" " E	3.00 "	June 1, 1905
James L. Doyle ‡	71 E. Brookine st	" " C	5.40 "	Sept. 28, 1901
William J. Ennis ‡	36 Chadwick st	" " C	4.80 "	Dec. 1, 1901
Chester A. S. Fazakas ‡	908 Harrison ave	" " E	1.40 "	" 1, 1905
Thomas J. Fitzgerald	15 Sargent st	" " E	1.20 "	Jan. 20, 1908
Frank V. Flanagan	20 Maxwell st	" " E	.60 "	Sept. 26, 1906
John Fleming	130 W. Brookline st	" " E	1.20 "	March 23, 1909
Walter G. Forsyth ‡	Hemenway Chambers	" " B	5.36 "	Feb. 1, 1904
George W. Gallagher ‡	22 E. Cottage st	" " E	1.20 "	Oct. 1, 1907
Charles V. Gillis ‡	509 E. Sixth st	" " E	.60 "	Jan. 29, 1909
Thomas H. Gillis	509 E. Sixth st	" " E	1.00 "	Oct. 1, 1903
Thomas G. Goodwin	238 South st	" " E	2.40 "	Sept. 21, 1902
Charles A. Gordon	70 E. Newton st	" " E	1.20 "	Jan. 29, 1909
Terrance Gordon	70 E. Newton st	" " E	3.15 "	March 12, 1906
Stanton Gorman	112 Berkeley st	" " E	1.20 "	Sept. 26, 1906
Leo J. Grady	8 Oswald st	" " E	1.40 "	March 12, 1906
Cornelius Guiney	79 E. Brookline st	" " E	2.70 "	Sept. 26, 1906
Carville Hands	19 Dwight st	" " E	1.40 "	March 23, 1909
Walter T. Hanna	28 Burnah st	" " E	2.60 "	Jan. 29, 1909
Frank J. Hannigan ‡	29 Eastman st	" " B	8.00 "	March 17, 1895
Walter T. Hannigan	29 Eastman st	" " C	9.60 "	" 17, 1895
Clement T. Hayes	3 Echo st	" " E	5.50 "	Dec. 7, 1907
Otto A. Heimann ‡	8 Enfield st	" " C	3.90 "	April 15, 1895
William P. Hemstedt ‡	18 Johnston rd	" " C	2.80 "	" 14, 1895
Charles E. Herekson	8 Eaton st	" " E	2.65 "	April 14, 1906
John J. Horgan ‡	14 Emerald st	" " C	4.80 "	Oct. 1, 1903
Fernald Hutchins	Dedham	" " C	1.40 "	" 1, 1901
Bradley Jones	254 Massachusetts ave	" " E	3.00 "	" 1, 1903
John J. Keenan ‡	378 Columbus ave	" " B	9.54 "	March 24, 1895
William H. J. Kennedy	16 Northfield st	" " E	2.88 "	Sept. 16, 1905
John A. Lahive	498 Southampton st	" " E	5.75 "	April 21, 1908
Charles O. Lee	7 Field st	" " E	4.90 "	Oct. 1, 1907
Francis W. Lee ‡	Technology Chambers	" " B	13.40 "	March 24, 1895
William T. Lipshutz ‡	13 Jess st	" " E	1.35 "	Feb. 28, 1908
Michael McCarthy, Jr.‡	22 Humphreys st	" " C	8.90 "	April 16, 1895
Peter V. McFarland	5 Sachem st	" " E	3.90 "	March 20, 1897
William A. McGowan ‡	18 Smith st	" " E	3.90 "	" 3, 1904
Constantine McGuire	103 Appleton st	" " E	5.60 "	Sept. 26, 1906
Timothy J. Mackin ‡	12 Longwood ave	" " E	2.40 "	March 3, 1904
Joseph F. McLean	145 Geneva ave	" " E	1.20 "	April 21, 1908
Charles McNamee	52 Forest st	" " E	2.60 "	March 23, 1909
Joseph A. Maier ‡	123 Minden st	" " E	7.10 "	Dec. 1, 1898
William C. Maiers, Jr.	7 Gay Head st	" " B	3.90 "	June 1, 1899
Francis B. Masterson	27 Lambert ave	" " E	2.20 "	Aug. 18, 1908
Harry F. Mayer	26 Green st	" " E	2.80 "	June 1, 1899
Maud M. Morse ‡	134 W. Newton st	" " C	2.40 "	Oct. 1, 1901
William J. Mulloney ‡	2 Highland pk	" " C	4.80 "	March 11, 1901
John Murdoch ‡	Cambridge	" " B	6.41 "	Dec. 30, 1900
Max H. Newman	24 Davis st	" " E	2.60 "	May 20, 1901
Robert R. O'Keefe	29 St. Rose st	" " E	1.20 "	July 3, 1908
Jeremiah J. O'Meara ‡	14 Oregon st	" " E	3.15 "	Sept. 26, 1906
Albert J. Plunkett	421 W. Fourth st	" " C	3.20 "	April 15, 1895
John H. Reardon ‡	15 Sunnyside st	" " B	12.28 "	March 17, 1895
William G. T. Roffe ‡	148 Harvard st	" " B	6.03 "	" 17, 1895*
Morris J. Rosenberg ‡	128 Stanwood st	" " C	7.60 "	" 17, 1900
Walter Rowlands	Needham	" " B	10.72 "	Dec. 1, 1901
Frederic Serex ‡	16 Woodside ave	" " B	8.04 "	Sept. 24, 1896
Paul Serex, Jr.	118 Chestnut ave., J. P.	" " E	2.60 "	April 21, 1908
Albert Shaughnessy	21 Cypress st	" " E	1.40 "	Jan. 29, 1909
Mary A. Shaughnessy ‡	60 Wirhington st	" " C	1.20 "	Sept. 26, 1906
Richard T. Shea	72 Walter st	" " E	2.80 "	Oct. 28, 1908
Isidor Singer	112 Walter st	" " E	3.95 "	Sept. 16, 1905

* Promoted to present position on date given.   Previously in the department.
† Paid by the hour, as follows:
    Grade E.— 20, 25 and 30 cents.
    Grade C.— 35, 40 and 50 cents.
    Grade B.— 67, 80 and $1.10.
‡ Also in regular service.

Library Department. — Concluded.

Name.	Residence.	Designation	Compensation.	Date of Election or Appointment.

Sunday and Evening Service.‡ — Concluded.

Name.	Residence.	Designation	Compensation.	Date
Irving Stark	11 Fairview st	Assistant Grade E	$3.60 wk.	Aug. 18, 1908
Daniel J. Sullivan	29 Mt. Vernon st	" " E	1.20 "	Jan. 29, 1909
James L. Sullivan †	80 Williams st	" " E	6.40 "	March 17, 1903
John F. Sullivan	35 Bayard st	" * " E	1.40 "	Aug. 18, 1908
Lindsey Swift †	388 Park st., W. R.	" " B	8.80 "	April 15, 1895
Frederick H. Toye	55 Angell st	" " E	1.75 "	Oct. 1, 1903
William C. Wallace †	115 W. Third st	" " E	2.25 "	Sept. 26, 1906
Joseph W. Ward †	24 Church st	" " C	3.90 "	March 17, 1895
Horace L. Wheeler †	42 Rutland sq	" " B	13.40 "	Dec. 1, 1901
Charles J. White	11½ Whitman st	" " E	1.20 "	Jan. 29, 1909
David L. Williams	59 Dover st	" " B	14.07 "	March 17, 1895
Eleanor M. Williams †	76 Adams st	" " C	2.40 "	Aug. 17, 1908
William E. Cole †	40 Hammond st	Coat Room (Evenings)	2.00 "	March 7, 1898
Patrick A. Kennedy †	73 Village st	" "	2.00 "	June 19, 1906
Charles Webster †	16 Davenport st	"	2.00 "	April 1906
N. J. Herland †	48 Brush Hill rd	Engineer (Evenings)	.75 "	April 25, 1908
Timothy J. Quirk †	766 Eighth st	Fireman (Evenings)	.62 "	" 25, 1908

Licensing Board.

Commissioners.

Name	Residence	Designation	Compensation	Date
Ezra H. Baker	88 Commonwealth ave	Chairman	$4,000 yr	June 1, 1906
Fred A. Emery	2 Thornton st	Commissioner	3,500 "	" 1, 1906
Samuel H. Hudson	423 Marlboro st	"	3,500 "	" 1, 1906

Secretary.

Name	Residence	Designation	Compensation	Date
Louis Epple	22 Chilton rd	Secretary	$2,500 yr	July 1, 1906

Clerks.

Name	Residence	Designation	Compensation	Date
William H. Barter	Winthrop	Clerk	$1,800 yr	July 19, 1906
Mary F. Gould	15 St. James ave	"	1,500 "	" 19, 1906
Harriet L. Rea	68 Brent st	"	1,500 "	" 19, 1906
John D. Fogarty, Jr.	14 Savin st	"	1,200 "	" 19, 1906
Helen C. Smith	Winthrop	Stenographer	1,200 "	Nov. 26, 1906
Maximilian A. J. Barlow	732 E. Sixth st	"	900 "	Jan. 18, 1909
Timothy F. Ahern	33 Neponset ave	Messenger	780 "	July 19, 1906

Temporary Clerks.

Name	Residence	Designation	Compensation	Date
Emma A. L. Fielding	109 Brookline ave	Clerk	$50.00 mo.	Jan. 28, 1908
Maud MacLachlan	3563 Washington st	"	50.00 "	" 29, 1908

Janitress.

Name	Residence	Designation	Compensation	Date
Annie A. Hicks	29 Pemberton sq	Janitress	$1,700 yr	July 19, 1906

Market Department.

Name	Residence	Designation	Compensation	Date
George E. McKay	8 Wayne st	Superintendent of Markets	$3,000 yr	April 1, 1877
Charles H. Webster	43 Vernon st	Deputy Supt. of Markets	1,500 "	July 1, 1895*
William D. Fay	82 Arlington st	Weigher, City Scales	900 "	Nov. 11, 1906
Charles A. Lurten	106 Sherwood st	Watchman	1,000 "	July 20, 1904
Israel N. Young	211 Brighton ave	"	1,000 "	May 13, 1907
Thomas F. O'Brien	40 Dewey st	Messenger	800 "	Aug. 14, 1892
Patrick Powers	4 Springer st	Janitor at Convenience sta.	3.00 day	May 3, 1905

* Promoted to present position on date given. Previously in the department.
† Also in regular service.
‡ Paid by the hour, as follows:
   Grade E. — 20, 25, and 30 cents.
   Grade C. — 35, 40, and 50 cents.
   Grade B. — 67, 80, and $1.10.

Music Department.

Name.	Residence.	Designation.	Compensation.	Date of Election or Appointment.
John A. O'Shea	20 Wales st., Dor	Chairman Trustees	None	May 9, 1898
Alfred P. DeVoto	50 Winthrop st., Rox	Music Trustee	"	" 9, 1898
Edwin A. Franklin	71 Litchfield st.,Allston	"	"	Nov. 27, 1905
Daniel P. Shedd	42 Columbia rd	"	"	July 16, 1906
William C. Brooks	7 Waldorf st	"	"	May 1, 1908
William A. Leahy	523 Fourth st	Secretary	$1,200 yr	Jan. 23, 1902
Agnes G. Lawless	110 Smith st	Clerk	1.33 day	April 7, 1904

Overseeing of the Poor Department.

Name.	Residence.	Designation.	Compensation.	Date of Election or Appointment.
John Brant	315 Paris st	Overseer of Poor	None	May 1, 1903
Frederick P. Cabot	72 Chestnut st	" "	"	" 1, 1908
John H. Colby	1 Wellington st	" "	"	" 1, 1908
Thomas Downey	362 Park rd	" "	"	" 1, 1902
Martha W. Folsom	15 Marlboro st	" "	"	Nov. 1, 1900
William P. Fowler	275 Newbury st	" "	"	April 1, 1889
Margaret J. Gookin	356 Seaver st	" "	"	May 1, 1908
Patrick J. Greene	350 Hanover st	" "	"	Nov. 1, 1900
Simon E. Hecht	16 Keswick st	" "	"	May 1, 1908
Matthew J. Mullen	650 E. Broadway	" "	"	" 1, 1906
Thomas Sproules	31 Hillside st	" "	"	April 1, 1883
Joseph A. Turnbull	531 Main st	" "	"	Oct. 1, 1906
Richard C. Humphreys	49 Humphreys st	Treasurer	$1,000 yr	Nov. 2, 1898
Benjamin Pettee	33 Lawrence ave	Secretary	3,500 "	" 2, 1874
William H. Hardy	14 Bullard st	Settlement Visitor	2,000 "	Aug. 2, 1899*
Frederick L. Gillooly	10 Belmore ter	Bookkeeper	1,800 "	Jan. 6, 1904*
Frederic L. Kelley	54 Hollander st	Clerk	900 "	Aug. 13, 1907
Henry F. Lyons	25 Hartford st	"	800 "	Sept. 27, 1908
Arthur L. Curry†	106 Cedar st	"	700 "	July 1, 1908
John F. Cleary	33 Hillside st	Visitor	1,600 "	May 7, 1894
Timothy J. Good	35 Woodbine st	"	1,600 "	Nov. 3, 1886
Marcus Kallmann	5 Howe st	"	1,600 "	Sept. 3, 1884
John J. Kelley	104 Brooks st	"	1,600 "	May 22, 1901
Edward F. Kenney	7 Thetford st	"	1,600 "	April 6, 1904*
Bernard McNellis	12 Sackville st	"	1,600 "	" 20, 1884
Horatio W. Nelson	3 Mather st	"	1,100 "	Sept. 15, 1908*
Charles A. Stoddard	133 Olney st	"	1,600 "	Oct. 6, 1899
Charles W. Twombly	69 Perham st	"	1,600 "	Feb. 6, 1901
Walter E. Butler	76 W. Rutland sq	Visitor at Hospital	1,400 "	June 6, 1906*
Bartholomew J. Bresnahan	21 Mackin st	Clerk at Hospital	1,000 "	Aug. 7, 1908*
Louis A. DuBois	573 Massachusetts ave	"	900 "	July 24, 1907
Thomas A. Regan	4 Mt. Pleasant pl	"	700 "	Oct. 23, 1908
James Gallagher	205 Falcon st	Engineer	900 "	March 29, 1909
James P. Quinn	43 Hawkins st	Janitor	1,000 "	June 12, 1905
John D. Reed	81 Waldeck st	Storekeeper	1,400 "	May 15, 1878
Isaiah L. Hinckley	21 Arundel st	Assistant Storekeeper	18.00 wk	" 8, 1899
John J. Bench	140 Elmo st	"	15.00 "	March 1, 1899
Walter F. McLeod	16 Harris st	"	12.00 "	Jan. 28, 1906
Edward Riley	274 Bunker Hill st	Superintendent of Lodge	1,400 yr	Sept. 1, 1879
Thomas H. Devlin	33 Bernard st	Night Steward	25.00 wk	May 14, 1903
Richard T. Pope	207 Hemenway st	Clerk	1,000 yr	Sept. 18, 1901
Robert E. Harney	90 Lauriat ave	Medical Inspector	14.00 wk	Oct. 4, 1908
Anna A. Johnson	Chardon st	Matron Temporary Home	50.00 mo	Sept. 7, 1904
Mary A. White	Chardon st	Assistant Matron	40.00 "	April 12, 1904
Maria E. Kilduff	Chardon st	Night Matron	30.00 "	Oct. 5, 1898
Emma L. McDowell	49 Union pk	Matron's Assistant	30.00 "	Feb. 3, 1897
Sarah McGrath	Chardon st	Cook	300 yr	Aug. 21, 1905

Park Department.

Name.	Residence.	Designation.	Compensation.	Date of Election or Appointment.
Robert S. Peabody	22 Fenway	Chairman	None	April 12, 1909
James M. Prendergast	135 Bay State rd	Commissioner	"	May 8, 1899
Daniel H. Coakley	52 Parsons st	"	"	" 17, 1906
John A. Pettigrew	Franklin Park	Superintendent	$4,200 yr	Jan. 1, 1897

* Promoted to present position on date given. Previously in the department.
† Transferred May 1, 1909, to Assessing Department.

Park Department.— Continued.

Name.	Residence.	Designation.	Compensation.	Date of Election or Appointment.
James B. Shea	319 Perkins st	Assistant Superintendent	$2,025 yr	June 28, 1901
John W. Duncan	40 Farrington st	"	1,800 "	April 1, 1901
George F. Clarke	1 Autumn st	Secretary and Clerk	3,000 "	Oct. 6, 1875
Charles G. Lawrence	11 Pond st	Accountant	2,250 "	Nov. 16, 1883
Emma W. Bumstead	70 Mora st	Stenographer	900 "	Oct. 2, 1893
Bessie I. Towne	11 E. Newton st		785 "	July 16, 1907
Arthur E. Ogden	5 P st	Clerk	3.00 day	Dec. 29, 1898
Charles A. Hogan	4 Hammett st	"	2.50 "	Sept. 27, 1906
Joseph P. Howe	3742 Washington st	Gardener and Greenkeeper	2.25 "	May 1, 1908
Charles E. Putnam	137 Hutchins st	Engineer	2,500 yr	Aug. 31, 1888
Charles E. Houghton	33 Cheshire st	Transitman	3.50 day	April 29, 1887
James E. Bean	9 Atherton st	Foreman	4.50 "	Dec. 5, 1881
William H. Allen	178 Millet st	"	3.25 "	March 29, 1909
James D. Edgeworth	5 Glen rd	Sub-foreman	3.75 "	Sept. 29, 1884
John P. Kelly	12 Mystic st	"	3.25 "	Aug. 25, 1887
Michael McNulty	32 Tower st	"	3.25 "	July 11, 1901
William L. Tuttle	33 Monadnock st	"	3.25 "	May 7, 1887
Julius Weidner	582 E. Seventh st	"	3.25 "	June 10, 1887
Patrick McKenzie	282 Lamartine st	Powderman and Gardener	3.25 "	Oct. 9, 1908
Peter Barker	722 Centre st	Gardener	3.00 "	April 11, 1904
John T. Conboy	44 Creighton st	"	3.00 "	July 13, 1906
Patrick Donoghue	1466 Washington st	"	3.00 "	March 9, 1906
Frank Drewett	269 Lamartine st	"	3.00 "	Dec. 11, 1907
Kenneth Finlayson	63 Paul Gore st	"	3.00 "	May 9, 1904
William E. Fischer	16 Union ter	"	3.00 "	8, 1893
James J. Hodgens	39 Gould st	"	3.00 "	Dec. 1884
Peter M. McManus	4½ Sheldon st	"	3.00 "	April, 1885
Charles Walters	101 Florence st	"	3.00 "	June 3, 1901
Robert Coulsey	3266 Washington st	"	2.75 "	" 27, 1902
Edward T. Bean	784 Canterbury st	"	2.50 "	June 12, 1901
Thomas J. Murphy	Williams Farm	"	2.50 "	March 27, 1906
James F. Hannon	244 Hancock st	"	2.25 "	Aug. 2, 1887
John Travers	72 Neponset ave	"	2.25 "	Oct. 17, 1884
Anton Volk	30 Longwood ave	Tree Pruner	2.50 "	Nov. 3, 1887
William Knight	54 Dakota st	Blacksmith	3.00 "	April 5, 1909
Bartholomew M. Ryan	64 Jewett st	Assistant Blacksmith	3.00 "	June 19, 1900
John McGreil	52 Elmwood st	Blacksmith's Helper	2.25 "	Aug. 24, 1906
Michael J. Burke	21 Moseley st	Wagonmaker	3.50 "	Nov. 5, 1903
David H. Nugent	72 Clifton st	Carpenter	3.50 "	Oct. 9, 1908
Owen J. Phinn	6 Gore st	"	3.50 "	Sept. 15, 1897
Thomas F. Quirk	17 Cable st	"	3.50 "	July 16, 1906
Michael Slowe	50 Ward st	"	3.50 "	Sept. 18, 1903
Patrick J. Sullivan	21 Moseley st	"	3.50 "	" 13, 1897
Thomas M. Walsh	3802 Broadway	"	3.50 "	July 23, 1906
Joseph Batts	578 Dorchester ave	"	3.00 "	Aug. 24, 1906
Peter Coleman	9 Plainfield st	"	3.00 "	July 31, 1884
John McNeill	398 Amory st	"	3.00 "	Sept. 20, 1899
James C. Dunn	83 Spencer st	Carpenter's Helper	2.25 "	Oct. 9, 1908
Daniel J. Hurley	94 Brookside ave	Plumber	3.00 "	April 30, 1903
John E. Johnson	167 Walnut st	Mason	3.00 "	May 16, 1906
Arthur S. Allen	217 W. Fourth st	Machinist	3.00 "	April 2, 1909
Bernard J. Conley	10 Orchardale st	"	3.00 "	May 31, 1907
William F. Conklin	75 Day st	"	3.00 "	March 30, 1909
William H. Taylor	150 Canterbury st	"	3.00 "	July 20, 1906
John Glennon	52 Brook rd	Machinist's Helper	2.50 "	" 20, 1906
George H. Conner	47 Keyes st	"	2.25 "	Oct. 9, 1908
Benjamin F. Gleason	128 Huntington ave	"	2.25 "	" 9, 1908
William H. Carter	59 Newman st	Steam-roller Engineer	3.00 "	March 29, 1909
George A. Field	135 Centre st	"	3.00 "	" 30, 1909
Edward J. Moriarty	140 Leyden st	" "	3.00 "	June 18, 1892
William H. Smith	42 Sheppard st	" "	3.00 "	May 2, 1904
Michael V. Dailey	33 Malden st	Painter	3.50 "	April 17, 1903
John J. Brooks	2 Merton pl	"	2.75 "	March 5, 1907
Thomas Kelly	97 St. Alphonsus st	"	2.75 "	" 19, 1907
Henry G. Farrington	90 Jamaica st	"	2.50 "	Aug. 24, 1906
Richard T. Norton	rear 64 Whitney st	"	2.25 "	Oct. 9, 1908
Gilman J. Raymond	14 Dartmouth st	Ironworker	2.75 "	Sept. 9, 1904
Malachi Kenney	12A Adams st	"	2.50 "	Oct. 9, 1908
John Monahan	31 Bennett st	Pipefitter	3.00 "	July 26, 1907
Martin Feeley	55 Jamaica st	"	2.75 "	Sept. 9, 1904
James H. Kelley	21 Danforth st	Janitor	2.50 "	March 30, 1897
Joseph S. Perry	20 Greenwood ave	"	2.50 "	May 1, 1891
William Scanlan	20 Grant st	Harnessmaker	3.00 "	Dec. 8, 1902
John Younie	12 Trenton st	Watchman	2.50 "	April 26, 1907

Park Department.— Continued.

Name.	Residence.	Designation.	Compensation.	Date of Election or Appointment.
Joseph N. Tierney	rear 70 N. Market st	Instructor	$1.97 day	July 12, 1907
Ann I. Loftus	601 E. Seventh st	"	1.97 "	April 15, 1907
Margaret Mulhern	243 Cambridge st	Matron	1.50 "	May 15, 1903
Mrs. Willie Campbell	92 Erie st	"	1.50 "	Dec. 17, 1904
Lizzie V. Wallace	100 Tyler st	"	1.50 "	June 5, 1908
Mary Baker	7 Hyde Park ave	"	$1.42\frac{6}{7}$ "	April 1, 1904
Ellen Burke	131 Neptune ave	"	$1.42\frac{6}{7}$ "	" 8, 1897
Mrs. Bartholomew Brennan	22 Thwing st	"	$1.42\frac{6}{7}$ "	May 21, 1906
Ellen Donahue	36 St. Martin st	"	$1.42\frac{6}{7}$ "	June 16, 1895
Catherine Dwyer	27 Riverdale st	"	$1.42\frac{6}{7}$ "	April 27, 1908
Jane Lynch	86 Putnam st	"	$1.42\frac{6}{7}$ "	Dec. 11, 1908
Mary A. McLaughlin	329 Perkins st	"	$1.42\frac{6}{7}$ "	May 23, 1908
Jane Maguire	14 Jess st	"	$1.42\frac{6}{7}$ "	June 7, 1895
Winfred V. Redding	342 Amory st	"	$1.42\frac{6}{7}$ "	April 1, 1904
Ann Turcotte	169 Bennington st	"	$1.42\frac{6}{7}$ "	Jan. 8, 1904
Helen J. L. Kennelly	147 Harrishof st	Librarian	$1.33\frac{1}{3}$ "	Feb. 1, 1909
Thomas Dillon	311 Lamartine st	Driver	2.25 "	" 22, 1902
George W. H. Timson	9 Fallon st	Timekeeper	2.50 "	March 1, 1904
Fred A. Plyer	2 Water st	Barnboss	$2.71\frac{3}{7}$ "	April 1898
John Carlin	138 Spencer st	Teamster	$2.11\frac{3}{7}$ "	March 28, 1902
John Coughlin	504 Parker st	"	$2.11\frac{3}{7}$ "	May 19, 1900
John Dargin	63 Union st	"	$2.11\frac{3}{7}$ "	April 16, 1898
James T. Donley	539 Hyde Park ave	"	$2.11\frac{3}{7}$ "	May 22, 1901
Joseph Doyle	47 Marshfield st	"	$2.11\frac{3}{7}$ "	Dec. 2, 1904
Cornelius Downey	1326 Dorchester ave	"	$2.11\frac{3}{7}$ "	June 21, 1907
Patrick J. Gleason	32 Lee st	"	$2.11\frac{3}{7}$ "	Sept. 18, 1908
Thomas Keenan	138 Athens st	"	$2.11\frac{3}{7}$ "	Feb. 21, 1908
James Kelly, 1st	121 Rawson st	"	$2.11\frac{3}{7}$ "	April 10, 1908
James J. O'Brien	47 Perkins st	"	$2.11\frac{3}{7}$ "	" 5, 1907
James J. O'Neill	3387 Washington st	"	$2.11\frac{3}{7}$ "	Aug. 10, 1909
John J. Quigley	202 Keyes st	"	$2.11\frac{3}{7}$ "	June 21, 1898
Patrick J. Callanan	29 Leon st	"	$2.19\frac{4}{7}$ "	April 1, 1903
John F. Coakley	630 Canterbury st	"	$2.19\frac{4}{7}$ "	May 20, 1898
Michael H. Condrey	22 Anson st	"	$2.19\frac{4}{7}$ "	Feb. 14, 1908
Thomas Connell	9 Posen st	"	$2.19\frac{4}{7}$ "	June 27, 1902
Jeremiah Cronin, 2d	57 Shannon st	"	$2.19\frac{4}{7}$ "	March 2, 1899
Patrick Daley	cor. Columbia rd. & Preble st.	"	$2.19\frac{4}{7}$ "	Sept. 1, 1899
Dennis Daly	97 Call st	"	$2.19\frac{4}{7}$ "	June 21, 1907
Thomas J. Delaney	531 Adams st	"	$2.19\frac{4}{7}$ "	" 28, 1901
William J. Donely	135 Spencer st	"	$2.19\frac{4}{7}$ "	June 21, 1898
Bernard J. Fay	3389 Washington st	"	$2.19\frac{4}{7}$ "	April 6, 1909
Michael Glynn	10 Plainfield st	"	$2.19\frac{4}{7}$ "	" 19, 1901
James J. Melynn	56 Alpine st	"	$2.19\frac{4}{7}$ "	Jan. 18, 1901
John Morrissey	2 Roxbury ter	"	$2.19\frac{4}{7}$ "	May 19, 1899
Thomas H. Mulvey	80 Terrace st	"	$2.19\frac{4}{7}$ "	June 26, 1899
Patrick Sheehan	51 Bromley pk	"	$2.19\frac{4}{7}$ "	Aug. 15, 1902
Thomas Carroll	260 Highland st	Skilled Laborer	2.25 "	March 1, 1904
Jeremiah J. Downey	26 Hecla st	"	2.25 "	May 4, 1906
Michael O'Brien	381 Chestnut Hill ave	Park Keeper and Skilled Laborer	2.50 "	Oct. 9, 1908
Michael O'Neill	40 Erie st	Park Keeper and Skilled Laborer	2.25 "	" 9, 1908
James Sweeney	Franklin Field	Shepherd	2.25 "	Sept. 18, 1884
Henry H. Adolph	50 E. Springfield st	Boy	1.00 "	Aug. 15, 1907
John J. Regan	41 Lee st	"	$1.28\frac{4}{7}$ "	Dec. 13, 1907
John J. Abbott	489 E. Third st	Laborer	2.25 "	June 28, 1882
Thomas Ahern	42 Bartlett st	"	2.25 "	April 1, 1884
Martin P. Barrett	116 Keyes st	"	2.25 "	May 10, 1907
Patrick Barry	73 High st	"	2.25 "	March 29, 1906
Alexander Boyd	10 Hanover ave	"	2.25 "	May, 1882
John Brennan	197 Endicott st	"	2.25 "	July 27, 1898
Thomas J. Breslin	Walker st	"	2.25 "	May 21, 1898
James Broderick	414 Broadway	"	2.25 "	" 4, 1898
Cornelius L. Buckley	481 Broadway	"	2.25 "	Aug. 15, 1887
Andrew Buttomer	248 W. First st	"	2.25 "	April 27, 1897
John J. Cady	731 Parker st	"	2.25 "	" 17, 1906
John Cahill	707 Broadway	"	2.25 "	March 3, 1887
Thomas A. Callahan	3 Murray ave	"	2.50 "	Feb. 21, 1908
Robert F. Carter	443 Lubec st	"	2.25 "	March 29, 1906
Patrick J. Clinton	87 Smith st	"	2.25 "	May 10, 1907
Michael F. Cody	244 Blue Hill ave	"	2.25 "	April 17, 1909
Thomas Conley	441 Chelsea st	"	2.25 "	July 31, 1901
William E. Connell	3302 Washington st	"	2.25 "	April 17, 1909
Patrick Connelly, 1st	447 E. Seventh st	"	2.25 "	July 15, 1898

Park Department.— Continued.

Name.	Residence.	Designation.	Compensation.	Date of Election or Appointment.
Michael Connely	11 Perkins st	Laborer	$2.25 day	Sept. 6, 1887
John J. Connolly	2 Norfolk ave	"	2.25 "	May 10, 1907
Patrick Connolly, 2d	168 Green st	"	2.25 "	April 16, 1906
John Conner	48 Arklow st	"	2.25 "	Nov. 3, 1887
Martin Corcoran	52 Weld Hill st	"	2.25 "	June 11, 1897
John Corliss	224 Blue Hill ave	"	2.25 "	May 3, 1898
Martin Cosgrove	21 Ballard st	"	2.25 "	May 13, 1907
Matthias Costello	49 Parkman st	"	2.25 "	June 21, 1898
Patrick Costello	26 Whalen st	"	2.25 "	Aug. 1, 1897
Moses A. Coulter	3411 Washington st	"	2.25 "	" 25, 1887
James Cowan	59 Copeland st	"	2.25 "	July 27, 1898
John Crimlisk	18 Mt. Vernon st	"	2.25 "	" 30, 1901
Patrick F. Crosby	49½ Yeoman st	"	2.25 "	June 14, 1897
Cornelius M. Crowley	145 Rutherford ave	"	2.25 "	March 14, 1906
George T. Cunning	221 Bennington st	"	2.25 "	June 15, 1906
Thomas F. Curtin	59 Wadsworth st	"	2.25 "	March 14, 1906
Pasquale D'Elia	160 Salem st	"	2.25 "	July 30, 1901
John E. Daley	287 Bunker Hill st	"	2.25 "	Nov. 7, 1887
John T. Daley	47 Jamaica st	"	2.25 "	May 7, 1887
John Dean	19 Everett st	"	2.25 "	Sept. 30, 1889
Timothy Devine	308 Codman st	"	2.25 "	Oct. 25, 1887
James Divver	193 Kilton st	"	2.25 "	July 30, 1901
Patrick J. Doherty	127 Milton st	"	2.25 "	April 5, 1906
Robert Doherty	4 Poplar ave	"	2.25 "	March 24, 1884
John J. Dolan	41 West Walnut pk	"	2.25 "	May 10, 1907
Peter F. Dolan	116 Child st	"	2.25 "	Dec. 29, 1897
Thomas F. Dolan, 1st	12 Jewett st	"	2.25 "	March 23, 1906
Thomas F. Dolan, 2d	62 Neponset ave	"	2.25 "	April 9, 1906
Daniel Donovan	40 Terrace st	"	2.25 "	" 7, 1884
John J. Donovan	155 Athens st	"	2.25 "	July 23, 1891
Michael Dooley	86 Call st	"	2.25 "	" 14, 1897
Michael Downes	58 Adams st	"	2.25 "	" 27, 1891
Maurice Downey	6 Ellsworth st	"	2.25 "	May 10, 1907
William Dunbar	6 Mystic pl	"	2.25 "	Oct. 1, 1889
Martin Duran	243 E st	"	2.25 "	Aug. 15, 1887
Martin Earley	1274 Tremont st	"	2.25 "	Sept. 20, 1889
Joseph Fallon	6 Cedar ave	"	2.25 "	June 9, 1898
William Fallon	42 Carolina ave	"	2.25 "	Nov. 30, 1906
William Fanning	44 Winship st	"	2.25 "	May 27, 1904
James Farrell	29 Mt. Vernon st	"	2.25 "	April 6, 1906
Michael Farren	11 Ingleside st	"	2.25 "	July 8, 1897
John W. Finn	75 Bower st	"	2.25 "	Aug. 15, 1887
Martin Finnegan	49 Shannon st	"	2.25 "	March 29, 1906
Hugh Fitzgerald	103 Sixth st	"	2.25 "	" 28, 1906
Daniel J. Flynn	319 Dorchester st	"	2.25 "	" 14, 1906
Patrick Flynn	29 Goldsmith st	"	2.25 "	July 22, 1891
Edward Foley	310 Adams st	"	2.25 "	Aug. 25, 1887
Michael Foley	5 Marcella st	"	2.25 "	April 16, 1898
James Galvin	22 Jackson pl	"	2.25 "	May 20, 1887
Thomas Ganley	17 Linden st	"	2.25 "	June 5, 1887
Thomas Garvin	45 Speedwell st	"	2.25 "	Aug. 15, 1887
Patrick T. Gilligan	1429 Dorchester ave	"	2.25 "	May 10, 1907
Patrick Glennon, 1st	128 Terrace st	"	2.25 "	March 24, 1884
Patrick Glennon, 2d	3554 Washington st	"	2.25 "	June 26, 1899
Michael Gorman	11 Lauriat ave	"	2.25 "	" 1897
Peter Gorman	1280 Tremont st	"	2.25 "	Aug. 12, 1887
Michael J. Grady	29 Geneva ave	"	2.25 "	May 20, 1898
Terrence N. Griffin	63 Crescent ave	"	2.25 "	June 9, 1898
Timothy Hagan	15 Downing st	"	2.25 "	Jan. 18, 1892
Russell Hale	90 Erie st	"	2.25 "	July 22, 1891
Patrick Halligan	19 Conant st	"	2.25 "	" 31, 1901
James Hanlon	68 Clifford st	"	2.25 "	" 27, 1891
Michael Hartigan	173A Cabot st	"	2.25 "	May 4, 1898
John Hartin	222 Gold st	"	2.25 "	July 17, 1906
Jeremiah Hayes	64 Monument st	"	2.25 "	Aug. 5, 1901
Richard Healey	5 Copeland pl	"	2.25 "	May 3, 1887
Dennis J. Healy	140 M st	"	2.25 "	April 20, 1909
Thomas Heavey	1344 Dorchester ave	"	2.25 "	May 10, 1907
Edward Henneberry	18 Greenleaf st	"	2.25 "	Sept. 23, 1883
James P. Hennessey	8 Draper st	"	2.25 "	May 5, 1898
John Hennessey	592 East Fourth st	"	2.25 "	June 28, 1882
John Higgins, 2d	60 Heela st	"	2.25 "	Aug. 2, 1901
Matthew Horgan	10 Duncan st	"	2.25 "	May 20, 1898
Peter Houghton	13 Mindoro st	"	2.25 "	March 22, 1884
James F. Hurley	56 Tolman st	"	2.25 "	July 7, 1897

Park Department.— Continued.

Name.	Residence.	Designation.	Compensation.	Date of Election or Appointment.
John Hurley	Willis st	Laborer	$2.25 day	May 1883
Michael Hurley	130 Howard ave	"	2.25 "	June 21, 1898
Daniel Keenan	1287 Columbus ave	"	2.25 "	May 4, 1898
Charles J. Kelly	101 Marcella st	"	2.25 "	April 3, 1897
Patrick Kelly, 1st	25 Ball st	"	2.25 "	June 6, 1887
James M. Kennedy	247 Washington st	"	2.25 "	Dec. 6, 1907
Patrick J. Kielty	11 Orchardale st	"	2.25 "	Oct. 27, 1899
Lawrence F. Kilroy	67 Call st	"	2.25 "	May 8, 1903
James H. Kissick	880 Columbus ave	"	2.25 "	July 5, 1887
Martin Lally*	1 Grosvenor pl	"	2.25 "	" 22, 1891
Michael Lally	520 Saratoga st	"	2.25 "	March 28, 1906
John J. Leary	83 Orleans st	"	2.25 "	April 5, 1907
Patrick Lee	rear 324 Washington st	"	2.25 "	July 14, 1906
Charles Lennon	65 Paine st	"	2.25 "	Sept. 7, 1887
Andrew Linahan	6 Spring ter	"	2.25 "	May 10, 1907
William Locke	663 Parker st	"	2.25 "	April 2, 1885
Michael Lordan	384 Amory st	"	2.25 "	June 21, 1887
Owen Lynch	54 F st	"	2.25 "	Aug. 13, 1891
Patrick F. Lynch	5 Oriental ct	"	2.25 "	May 10, 1907
Martin Lyons	174 Centre st	"	2.25 "	Aug. 2, 1897
Daniel McCarthy	Grover st	"	2.25 "	" 12, 1887
Lawrence McCarthy	38 Phillips st	"	2.25 "	May 1883
Stephen H. McCarthy	177½ Green st	"	2.25 "	" 20, 1898
John McConn	24 Creighton st	"	2.25 "	" 23, 1887
John McDonald	110 Call st	"	2.25 "	Aug. 25, 1887
Thomas McDowell	105 Lamartine st	"	2.25 "	April 22, 1897
John McEleney	82 E. Lenox st	"	2.25 "	March 21, 1906
Hugh McGinnis	221 New Keyes st	"	2.25 "	June 21, 1898
Phillip F. McGinn	20 Adams pl	"	2.25 "	May 10, 1907
William McGowan	3 School st pl	"	2.25 "	March 25, 1884
John F. McKernan	2 Brookside ave	"	2.25 "	" 28, 1906
John A. McLaughlin	39 Field st	"	2.25 "	May 12, 1887
Neil McLaughlin	18 Cross st	"	2.25 "	Oct. 20, 1887
Patrick F. McNamara	6 Bromley pk	"	2.25 "	June 21, 1887
Bernard T. McNulty	4014 Washington st	"	2.25 "	April 4, 1884
Daniel McQuarrie	290 Athens st	"	2.25 "	May 11, 1887
Jeremiah Mackey	217 West 4th st	"	2.25 "	April 5, 1906
John F. Maguire	22 Thwing st	"	2.25 "	" 17, 1909
Patrick Malia	11 Perkins st	"	2.25 "	June 26, 1899
Michael A. Martin	4 Blanchard st	"	2.25 "	Jan. 13, 1897
John Matchett	1345 Dorchester ave	"	2.25 "	May 10, 1907
John J. Meekin	945 Parker st	"	2.25 "	July 7, 1897
John Morgan	1392 Columbus ave	"	2.25 "	May 4, 1898
Samuel J. Moran	100 E. Canton st	"	2.25 "	April 17, 1907
James Morrissey	59 Rockland st	"	2.25 "	May 3, 1898
Edward L. Morse	3 Murray ave	"	2.25 "	Aug. 9, 1907
Thomas Mulcahy	8 Eastburn pl	"	2.25 "	April 16, 1898
Michael Mullen	206 Ninth st	"	2.25 "	Aug. 25, 1887
Peter J. Mullen	20 Frederick st	"	2.25 "	June 10, 1887
Bartholomew Murphy	121 Lenox st	"	2.25 "	July 30, 1901
Edmond Murphy	37 Greenwich pl	"	2.25 "	May, 1883
Edward A. Murphy	79 Concord sq	"	2.25 "	March 8, 1909
John Murphy, 1st	7 Ascot st	"	2.25 "	Aug. 12, 1887
John F. Murphy	1625 Tremont st	"	2.25 "	April 15, 1901
John J. Murphy	30 Whitney st	"	2.25 "	May, 1882
Michael Murphy	1153 Dorchester ave	"	2.25 "	" 20, 1898
Michael H. Murray	7 Linden ave	"	2.25 "	June 21, 1898
Thomas Murray	226 Highland st	"	2.25 "	March 28, 1906
John Myers	604 Sixth st	"	2.25 "	Sept. 6, 1887
James Noonan	64 Northfield st	"	2.25 "	July 24, 1891
Jeremiah Noonan	12 Magdala st	"	2.25 "	April 7, 1897
James E. Norton	314 Amory st	"	2.25 "	March 27, 1906
John O'Brien, 1st	10 Nassau st	"	2.25 "	July 5, 1887
Patrick O'Connell	40 Kirkland st	"	2.25 "	June 20, 1899
Patrick O'Rourke	8 Mindoro st	"	2.25 "	May 20, 1898
Michael O'Toole	52 Perkins st	"	2.25 "	June 18, 1897
Reuben Overton	55 Sawyer st	"	2.25 "	April 17, 1909
Patrick J. Owens	264 Maverick st	"	2.25 "	Sept. 20, 1889
John Parlon	19 Union ave	"	2.25 "	May 16, 1887
James F. Pendergast	cor. Seaver & Humbolt ave	"	2.25 "	" 13, 1907
James Powers	3516 Washington st	"	2.25 "	April 23, 1887
Peter Powers	18 Julian st	"	2.25 "	March 23, 1906
James Quinn	24 Conant st	"	2.25 "	" 29, 1906
Michael T. Quinn	1077 Tremont st	"	2.25 "	April 9, 1906
Redmond Quirk	199 New Keyes st	"	2.25 "	July 7, 1897

*Veteran. Absent 2 yrs. Infirm.

Park Department.— Concluded.

Name.	Residence.	Designation.	Compensation.	Date of Election or Appointment.
Daniel Regan	442 W. Fourth st	Laborer	$2.25 day	April 23, 1904
Nicholas Roache	376 Chelsea st	"	2.25 "	June 21, 1898
Thomas Roche	48 Hall st	"	2.25 "	Aug. 25, 1887
Bernard Rogan	143 Ruggles st	"	2.25 "	May 20, 1898
Andrew Rourke	4 Dimock st	"	2.25 "	June 2, 1887
Bernard Rourke	293 Highland st	"	2.25 "	Sept. 23, 1889
James Scannell	4 St. Alphonsus ave	"	2.25 "	June 14, 1897
Michael Scannell	3 Oriental ct	"	2.25 "	May 13, 1907
Michael Shanney	7 Jamaica pl	"	2.25 "	June 9, 1884
John Shea	100 Kneeland st	"	2.25 "	Oct. 6, 1897
Patrick Shea, 2d	27 Shepard st	"	2.25 "	Aug. 12, 1887
Martin Shiel	6 Dove st	"	2.25 "	June 8, 1887
Cornelius J. Shields	227 Keyes st	"	2.25 "	March 14, 1906
Patrick J. Shields	Plainfield st	"	2.25 "	July 13, 1897
John J. Stapleton	10 Academy Hill rd	"	2.25 "	April 16, 1898
William H. Stewart	10 Reno st	"	2.25 "	May 24, 1898
Thomas F. Stokes	26 Jenkins st	"	2.25 "	April 20, 1904
John F. Swank	299 Grove st	"	2.25 "	July 25, 1887
John J. Tatten, jr	365 Market st	"	2.25 "	April 5, 1906
Thomas Thornton	35 East st	"	2.25 "	June 29, 1898
Dennis Toland	81 Border st	"	2.25 "	Oct. 1, 1884
John Toland	6 Schiller st	"	2.25 "	July 13, 1897
Festis Wallace	210 Ninth st	"	2.25 "	March 28, 1906
Dennis Walsh*	2002 Washington st	"	2.25 "	May 3, 1887
Michael Walsh, 1st	303 Bolton st	"	2.25 "	June 18, 1897
Michel Walsh	12 School st	"	2.25 "	" 21, 1898
John Welsh	466 Parker st	"	2.25 "	April, 1883
Charles H. Witham	2 Bay View pl	"	2.25 "	Jan. 3, 1885
Cornelius Wren	117 Child st	"	2.25 "	Sept. 20, 1889
Mary T. Kelly	21 Ellingwood st	Scrub woman	1.50 "	March 10, 1900

Penal Institutions Department.
See County of Suffolk.

Police Department.

Name.	Residence.	Designation.	Compensation.	Date of Election or Appointment.
Stephen O'Meara	585 Beacon st	Police Commissioner	$6,000 yr	June 4, 1906
Leo A. Rogers	20 Robinwood ave	Secretary	3,000 "	July 17, 1906
Thomas Ryan	107 Blue Hill ave	Captain and Chief Clerk	2,500 "	May 23, 1906

Superintendent's Office.

Name.	Residence.	Designation.	Compensation.	Date of Election or Appointment.
William H. Pierce	55 Dale st	Superintendent	$4,025 yr	June 1, 1901
George E. Savory	80 Gainsboro st	Captain	2,500 "	May 20, 1895
William H. Dyer	25 Monadnock st	"	2,500 "	Oct. 3, 1895
Dennis Donovan	57 Crawford st	"	2,500 "	July 10, 1894
James O'Neill	115 Dale st	"	2,500 "	May 31, 1906
George A. Hall	132 Rosseter st	"	2,500 "	Feb. 8, 1908
James F. Driscoll	5 Belmore ter	"	2,500 "	" 8, 1908
William L. Devitt	480 Columbus ave	Lieutenant	1,600 "	Sept. 3, 1901
Hugh J. Lee	33 Mercer st	"	1,600 "	Jan. 30, 1905
Timothy J. Murphy	26 Bailey st	"	1,600 "	March 16, 1903
George E. Saxton	6 Sargent st	"	1,600 "	Aug. 24, 1903
Charles W. Searles	9 Irving pl	"	1,600 "	Jan. 30, 1905
George C. Garland	6 Westerly st	"	1,600 "	June 26, 1893
Daniel A. Doherty	69 Clarkson st	Sergeant	1,400 "	Nov. 11, 1907
Horatio J. Homer	686 Massachusetts ave	"	1,400 "	Sept. 23, 1895
Edwin W. Abbott	75 Dakota st	Patrolman	1,200 "	April 20, 1875
Thomas M. Carty	126 Eustis st	"	1,200 "	June 27, 1870
Fred P. Colby	155 Bunker Hill st	"	1,200 "	July 6, 1888
Jeremiah J. Downey	9 Harold st	"	1,200 "	May 8, 1875
Frank E. Dudley	511 Massachusetts ave	"	1,200 "	Jan. 10, 1881
Frank Fitzpatrick	46 Woodward ave	"	1,200 "	Dec. 21, 1882
Charles L. Howell	190 Lauriat ave	"	1,200 "	Nov. 6, 1890
Thomas W. Kenefick	48 Baldwin st	"	1,200 "	June 14, 1890
John W. Pyne	79 W. Cottage st	"	1,200 "	Oct. 12, 1895
Herman Schiel	54 Erie st	"	1,200 "	Aug. 7, 1901
Harry S. Phipps	219 Trenton st	Telephone Operator	18.00 wk	July 20, 1899
Marcia O. Milliken	382 Warren st	"	15.00 "	Sept. 2, 1906
Elizabeth V. Pierce	32 Holbrook st	"	15.00 "	" 2, 1906

*Veteran. Absent 6 mos. Infirm.

Police Department.—Continued.

Name.	Residence.	Designation.	Compensation.	Date of Election or Appointment.

Bureau of Criminal Investigation.

Name.	Residence.	Designation.	Compensation.	Date
William B. Watts	67 Homestead st	Chief Inspector	$2,800 yr	Oct. 25, 1894
Joseph Dugan	118 Chestnut ave	Captain	2,500 "	Dec. 24, 1895
Walter A. Abbott	8 Hancock st	Inspector	1,600 "	May 20, 1895
Ainsley C. Armstrong	144 Foster st	"	1,600 "	Jan. 1, 1904
Levi W. Burr	3 Wallace ct	"	1,600 "	Feb. 26, 1907
James G. Collins	403 Massachusetts ave	"	1,600 "	" 27, 1893
James D. Conboy	12 Beethoven st	"	1,600 "	May 5, 1905
Edward T. Conway	133 Cedar st	"	1,600 "	Jan. 1, 1904
Michael H. Cronin	91 Roseclair st	"	1,600 "	" 1, 1904
James A. Dennessey	28 Leyland st	"	1,600 "	Oct. 5, 1907
Alfred N. Douglas	49 Norfolk st	"	1,600 "	Jan. 7, 1898
Patrick J. Gaddis	13 Batchelder st	"	1,600 "	May 2, 1898
Gustaf Gustafson	11 Wachusett st	"	1,600 "	Jan. 1, 1904
John H. Harris	814 Blue Hill ave	"	1,600 "	May 2, 1898
Daniel W. Hart	75 Homer st	"	1,600 "	Jan. 1, 1904
Joseph H. Knox	64 Perkins st	"	1,600 "	Dec. 24, 1884
Thomas H. Lynch	722 Morton st	"	1,600 "	Feb. 26, 1907
Francis J. McCauley	145 Falcon st	"	1,600 "	Jan. 1, 1908
John R. McGarr	188 Chestnut ave	"	1,600 "	" 7, 1898
Michael J. Morrissey	58 Baldwin st	"	1,600 "	Dec. 24, 1900
Walter M. Murphy	154 Stanwood st	"	1,600 "	Feb. 8, 1908
Thomas J. Norton	91 Dix st	"	1,600 "	Dec. 16, 1908
George W. Patterson	96 Hancock st	"	1,600 "	Jan. 1, 1904
William H. Pelton	212 Columbus ave	"	1,600 "	Dec. 16, 1908
Henry M. Pierce	55 Dale st	"	1,600 "	Jan. 1, 1904
George F. Pinkerton	14 Howland st	"	1,600 "	May 20, 1895
George M. Robinson	14 Everett st	"	1,600 "	Feb. 27, 1893
William J. Rooney	14 Paris st	"	1,625 "	Jan. 1, 1904
Thomas A. Sheehan	59 Bowdoin st	"	1,600 "	" 4, 1902
Michael C. Shields	99 Regent st	"	1,600 "	" 14, 1896
Walker A. Smith	61 Hancock st	"	1,600 "	Feb. 26, 1907
Silas F. Waite	56 Forbes st	"	1,600 "	" 8, 1908
Oliver J. Wise	3 Oxford ter	"	1,600 "	Jan. 7, 1898
Morris Wolf	43 Humboldt ave	"	1,600 "	Dec. 24, 1900
Gilbert H. Angell	15 Forrest st	Sergeant	1,400 "	Sept. 17, 1908
Joseph F. Loughlin	23 Gates st	"	1,400 "	Dec. 16, 1908
Owen Farley	220 Saratoga st	Patrolman	1,200 "	Jan. 9, 1891
George J. Farrell	10 Eulita ter	"	1,200 "	May 14, 1898
Thomas F. Gleavey	3 Richfield st	"	1,200 "	Aug. 7, 1891
Frank E. Hall	39 Paul Gore st	"	1,200 "	Dec. 24, 1877
John F. Linton	65 Sagamore st	"	1,200 "	Oct. 12, 1895
William A. Sayward	71 Aldie st	"	1,200 "	Dec. 1, 1897

City Prison.

Name.	Residence.	Designation.	Compensation.	Date
George A. Wyman	33 Thetford ave., Dor	Captain	$2,500 yr	June 24, 1893
George F. Howe	15 Madison st	Sergeant	1,400 "	Sept. 10, 1888
John H. Morse	347 Centre st., J. P	"	1,400 "	Jan. 12, 1889
William G. Blazo	55 Chestnut st., Chsn	"	1,400 "	Feb. 8, 1908
Jacob G. Ruby	9 W. Tremlett st., Dor	Patrolman	1,200 "	July 6, 1875
Gershom S. Files	33 Holborn st., Rox	"	1,200 "	Oct. 18, 1878
Thomas R. Clark	493 Columbia rd	"	1,200 "	Jan. 19, 1881
George W. Watts	20 Shafter st., Dor	"	1,200 "	Dec. 21, 1882
James A. Langley	40 Lynde st	Janitor	2.00 day	May 11, 1891
Merritt A. Coates	175 Bunker Hill st., Chsn	Assistant Janitor	2.00 "	Dec. 10, 1908

House of Detention.

Name.	Residence.	Designation.	Compensation.	Date
Amelia B. White	1 Allston st	Chief Matron	$1,000 yr	Feb. 1, 1901
Ida E. Hall	115 Dale st., Rox	Assistant Chief Matron	800 "	March 5, 1905
Mary Kenney	345 Washington st., J. P	Assistant Matron	600 "	June 1, 1905
Genevieve Barretta	48 Winthrop st., Chsn	"	600 "	Oct. 27, 1905
Mary E. Smith	9 Park st., Dor	"	600 "	Feb. 4, 1907
Frank H. Pease	97 Bowdoin st., Dor	Van Driver	3.00 day	Aug. 10, 1891
Joseph A. Hoey	47 Auckland st., Dor	"	3.00 "	June 1, 1893
Frances M. Mahoney	169 M st., S. B	Janitress	2.00 "	March 12, 1908

Clerk's Office.

Name.	Residence.	Designation.	Compensation.	Date
John P. J. Ronan	6 Glendale st	Clerk	$1,500 yr	Jan. 27, 1899
Elizabeth A. MacLaughlin	29 Leyland st	Stenographer	1,500 "	May 20, 1903
Thomas S. Gill	8 Adams st., Chsn	Clerk	1,400 "	Jan. 26, 1898

Police Department.— Continued.

Name.	Residence.	Designation.	Compensation.	Date of Election or Appointment.

Clerk's Office.—Concluded.

Name.	Residence.	Designation.	Comp.	Date
Elwin H. Hauver	42 Partridge st., W. R.	Stenographer	$1,400 yr.	March 16, 1903
William M. Gaddis	20 Church st., Dor.	Clerk	1,350 "	Oct. 20, 1899
Mary A. Magrath	117 Myrtle st.	"	1,200 "	March 9, 1881
Fannie L. Stowell	63 Harvard st., Newtonville	"	1,200 "	May 28, 1889
John J. Baxter	173 Townsend st., Rox	"	1,200 "	Sept. 7, 1896
Edward J. Sherlock	32 G st., S. B.	"	1,200 "	Dec. 14, 1896
Timothy F. Manning	118 F st., S. B.	"	1,000 "	Sept. 14, 1900
Catherine C. Sullivan	847 E. Fifth st., S. B.	"	900 "	Aug. 1, 1904
William F. A. O'Brien	46 Babcock st., Brookline	"	790 "	Oct. 13, 1898
William J. Healey	10 Langdon st., Rox	"	16.00 wk.	Aug. 4, 1902
John F. Woods	25 Woodward ave	"	10.00 "	Dec. 21, 1908
Elizabeth M. Hunt	519 Dudley st.	"	6.00 "	Oct. 25, 1907
John L. McCoy	Williams pk., Dor.	Messenger	5.00 "	" 25, 1907
Thomas D. Sullivan	144 Minden st., Rox	"	5.00 "	April 3, 1908

Division 1.

Name.	Residence.	Designation.	Comp.	Date
Otis F. Kimball	78 Kenwood st	Captain	$2,500 yr.	Sept. 3, 1901
William H. Allen	102 Falcon st	Lieutenant	1,625 "	March 3, 1905
Matthew J. Dailey	4 Arcadia ter	"	1,600 "	Sept. 11, 1907
John J. Rooney	55 Dewey st	Sergeant	1,400 "	Jan. 30, 1905
Jeremiah F. Gallivan	57 Dix st	"	1,400 "	April 14, 1906
John S. Ridlon	38 Auckland st	"	1,400 "	" 25, 1907
James McDevitt	1 Puritan ave	"	1,400 "	June 1, 1907
Cornelius H. Donovan	10 Ophir st	"	1,400 "	Feb. 8, 1908
Allen W. Alger	25 Warren ave	Patrolman	1,200 "	Nov. 1, 1901
Carl R. Ammelin	5 Trent st	"	1,200 "	Dec. 1, 1897
Joseph H. Battos	74 Pearl st	"	1,100 "	Jan. 7, 1908
Fred H. Bean	47 Princeton st	"	1,200 "	April 8, 1895
Malcolm D. Blue	20 Longfellow st	"	1,200 "	Sept. 19, 1900
Cornelius Brennan	40 Hewlett st	"	1,200 "	April 13, 1906
Henry J. Boutlier	664 Bennington st	"	1,200 "	Nov. 10, 1898
Napoleon P. Boutilier	114 Byron st	"	1,200 "	Jan. 5, 1893
Michael Bowlen	135 Lauriat ave	"	1,200 "	March 16, 1901
James J. Bray	156 Calumet st	"	1,100 "	Dec. 9, 1907
Joseph F. Buckley	122 Camden st	"	1,200 "	Nov. 25, 1903
James J. Burns	11 Valentine st	"	1,200 "	March 21, 1880
Thomas Byrne	52 Chambers st	"	1,200 "	Nov. 10, 1905
Ewen S. Cameron	63 Maple ave	"	1,200 "	Jan. 30, 1905
Joseph L. A. Cavagnaro	6 Mechanic ct	"	1,200 "	June 12, 1905
John N. Chaisson	48 Baldwin st	"	1,000 "	Nov. 5, 1908
William J. Cogan	88 W. Sixth st	"	1,000 "	Sept. 17, 1908
William R. Connolly	17 Newport st	"	1,200 "	March 29, 1904
Frederick H. Cotser	115 Chandler st	"	1,200 "	Jan. 1, 1904
James Costello	468 E. Sixth st	"	1,100 "	" 7, 1908
William F. Crawford	39 London st	"	1,200 "	Oct. 29, 1906
Dennis J. Cronan	25 Knoll st	"	1,200 "	Sept. 17, 1903
John F. Desmond	10 Danube st	"	1,200 "	Nov. 8, 1895
Daniel Dineen	302 Bunker Hill st	"	1,200 "	April 25, 1907
John J. Donovan	4½ Centre st	"	1,200 "	Dec. 26, 1901
Jeremiah J. Driscoll	726 Columbia rd	"	1,200 "	Sept. 1, 1888
John B. Durham	24 Mt. Pleasant ave	"	1,200 "	July 11, 1904
John F. Fitzpatrick	116 Brooks st	"	1,200 "	April 27, 1901
Michael F. Flanagan	172 St. Alphonsus st	"	1,200 "	Oct. 16, 1902
John R. Flynn	92 Green st	"	1,200 "	June 9, 1888
William J. Flynn	440 Saratoga st	"	1,200 "	Jan. 28, 1894
Walter M. French	50 Maywood st	"	1,200 "	March 29, 1904
Daniel J. Gavin	23 Adams st	"	1,200 "	Sept. 19, 1900
Joseph P. Glancy	154 Stanwood st	"	1,200 "	March 28, 1885
Wesley A. Gordon	3 Hancock st	"	1,100 "	Oct. 3, 1907
William H. Gordon	247 Princeton st	"	1,225 "	July 28, 1891
Charles K. Hilton	8 Allston pl	"	1,200 "	June 8, 1888
Jacob H. Jacobson	166 W. Springfield st	"	1,200 "	May 18, 1903
Elmer W. Jones	4 Nantasket st	"	1,200 "	Jan. 6, 1892
Walter Kavanagh	34 Highland st	"	1,200 "	Nov. 25, 1903
James B. Keiran	26 Sydney st	"	1,200 "	Dec. 14, 1885
John J. Kelleher	74 Day st	"	1,100 "	Nov. 7, 1907
John D. Kelliher	34 Fisher ave	"	1,200 "	May 24, 1901
Charles B. Kelly	187 Lexington st	"	1,225 "	Jan. 5, 1893
William Kelly	113 Warren st	"	1,000 "	" 14, 1909
Patrick J. Kenneally	87 Dacia st	"	1,200 "	April 25, 1907
Ephraim M. Kennedy	49 Homestead st	"	1,200 "	March 14, 1898
Charles M. Lamb	16 Lawrence st	"	1,200 "	April 8, 1895

Police Department.— Continued.

Name.	Residence.	Designation.	Compensation.	Date of Election or Appointment.

Division 1.— Concluded.

Name.	Residence.	Designation.	Compensation.	Date
Martin Leonard	78 Hillside st	Patrolman	$1,200 yr	March 16, 1901
James W. Lewis	2 Sumner st	"	1,000 "	Dec. 7, 1908
John Lynch	41 Maple ave	"	1,200 "	July 11, 1904
Daniel T. Mayo	144A Broadway	"	1,200 "	March 11, 1907
Joseph M. McCabe	211 L st	"	1,200 "	Oct. 20, 1904
George H. McCaffrey	185 Thornton st	"	1,200 "	April 8, 1895
George S. McCard	171 Coleridge st	"	1,200 "	Nov. 1, 1900
John D. McDonald	26 Auburn st	"	1,100 "	Jan. 7, 1908
William McDonald	53 Custer st	"	1,200 "	April 13, 1906
Angus V. McEachern	16 Bigelow st	"	1,200 "	Aug. 7, 1906
Harry W. McGarr	92 W. Springfield st	"	1,000 "	Jan. 14, 1909
Donald A. McGillivray	302 Washington st	"	1,200 "	July 11, 1904
Robert C. Mooney	49 Lawn st	"	1,000 "	Jan. 14, 1909
James A. Murphy	36 Condor st	"	1,200 "	June 27, 1895
John G. Murphy	93 Erie st	"	1,200 "	April 25, 1907
Arthur W. Nickerson	8 Allston pl	"	1,200 "	July 31, 1896
Allen V. Nixon	2161 Washington st	"	1,200 "	Nov. 6, 1895
Frank T. O'Brien	9 Parker st	"	1,000 "	Feb. 4, 1909
Thomas W. O'Donnell	10 Savin Hill ave	"	1,200 "	Aug. 10, 1904
John O'Neill	23 London st	"	1,200 "	Sept. 19, 1900
John H. Patterson	372 Main st	"	1,200 "	Aug. 10, 1895
John J. Phelan	15 Rosemary st	"	1,200 "	March 28, 1885
Charles S. Richardson	26 Marion st	"	1,200 "	April 4, 1891
George L. Richardson	499 Columbia rd	"	1,200 "	Dec. 15, 1889
John T. Sheehan	63 Chestnut st	"	1,200 "	Oct. 11, 1881
Frederick W. Sonnemann	481 Blue Hill ave	"	1,200 "	April 21, 1899
Thomas H. Soutter	28 Tremont st	"	1,000 "	Sept. 17, 1908
Granville B. Spinney	119 Park st	"	1,200 "	Oct. 29, 1906
Francis Spring	19 Plain st	"	1,200 "	April 8, 1895
Usher St. George	41 Worcester sq	"	1,000 "	June 22, 1908
Maurice Sullivan	610 Bennington st	"	1,200 "	" 14, 1890
Samuel J. Sweetland	219 Saratoga st	"	1,200 "	May 18, 1903
Michael T. Walsh	128 Chandler st	"	1,100 "	Oct. 3, 1907
William E. Walsh	276 E. Cottage st	"	1,000 "	June 22, 1908
Andrew J. Widdup	15 Pleasant ter	"	1,200 "	Oct. 29, 1906
William Wilson	57 Wensley st	"	1,100 "	Jan. 7, 1908
James F. Costello	15 Whitney st	Reserve Officer	2.25 day	April 29, 1908
Charles E. Deininger	11 Arcola st	"	2.25 "	" 29, 1908
John F. J. Dolan	145 Falcon st	"	2.00 "	Nov. 16, 1908
Gustave C. Falk	79 Auckland st	"	2.25 "	April 29, 1908
John R. Fitzgerald	50 Ellery st	"	2.25 "	" 29, 1908
John J. Flavin	61 P st	"	2.25 "	" 29, 1908
James Hanlon	291 Havre st	"	2.00 "	Jan. 18, 1909
Jeremiah J. Mahoney	18 E. Brookline st	"	2.25 "	April 29, 1908
John D. McLaughlin	146 N st	"	2.25 "	" 29, 1908
Francis R. McManus	16 Eulita ter	"	2.25 "	" 29, 1908
Timothy F. Murphy	26 Bailey st	"	2.25 "	" 29, 1908
Joseph A. Verkampen	252 Dudley st	"	2.00 "	Nov. 16, 1908
Carl M. Wilson	21 Marshfield st	"	2.25 "	April 29, 1908
Albert F. Winslow	65 Lexington st	"	2.00 "	Oct. 12, 1908
James F. Pierce	187 Webster st	Janitor	15.00 wk	Jan. 15, 1905
Robert F. Pierce	47 Lawrence st	"	14.00 "	" 15, 1905

Division 2.

Name.	Residence.	Designation.	Compensation.	Date
Edward F. Gaskin	55 Dale st	Captain	$2,500 yr	May 4, 1889
Frederick J. Smith	175 Union st., Bri	Lieutenant	1,600 "	March 20, 1899
William J. Hyland	555 Bennington st	"	1,600 "	Aug. 24, 1903
Philip E. O'Neil	46 Francis st	Sergeant	1,400 "	Jan. 30, 1905
Charles T. Reardon	45 Stonehurst st	"	1,400 "	June 1, 1907
John F. Ahearn	18 Foster st., Bri	"	1,400 "	Feb. 8, 1908
Bradley C. Mason	39 Allston st., Bri	"	1,400 "	" 8, 1908
Walter G. Horton	37 Thetford ave	"	1,425 "	" 8, 1908
Walter J. Andrews	65 Lexington st	Patrolman	1,100 "	Jan. 16, 1908
August H. Barthel	27 Webber st	"	1,200 "	April 15, 1902
Edward M. Bates	34 Colberg ave	"	1,200 "	Aug. 10, 1880
John H. Bohling	37 Train st	"	1,200 "	Oct. 21, 1884
George C. Brennan	162 Webster st., E. B	"	1,200 "	May 26, 1880
Michael C. Bresnehan	93 Munroe st	"	1,200 "	April 8, 1895
Thomas F. Brown	88 Baldwin st., Chsn	"	1,200 "	" 19, 1889
George A. Buchanan	87 1 st	"	1,000 "	May 18, 1908
Dennis P. Buckley	664A E. Eighth st	"	1,000 "	Jan. 14, 1909

Police Department.—Continued.

Division 2.— Continued.

Name.	Residence.	Designation.	Compensation.	Date of Election or Appointment.
Michael J. Burke	7 Lawrence pl	Patrolman	$1,200 yr.	April 15, 1902
Daniel P. Cameron	54 W. Newton st	"	1,200 "	March 16, 1901
William J. Carey	55 Sagamore st	"	1,100 "	Jan. 7, 1908
Dennis J. Casey	346 Geneva ave	"	1,200 "	April 18, 1895
Alba E. Chamberlin	164 Dorchester st	"	1,200 "	Feb. 11, 1879
Horatio C. Chase	Ashland ter., J. P.	"	1,200 "	March 5, 1903
Duncan G. Chisholm	72 Day st	"	1,200 "	Sept. 2, 1902
Frank J. Christie	78 Parsons st., Bri	"	1,200 "	July 1, 1895
Thomas F. Connolly	11 Primrose st	"	1,225 "	March 16, 1901
Wilson Cordiner	2 Faulkner circle	"	1,200 "	May 19, 1898
Patrick J. Cunningham	88 Fisher ave	"	1,200 "	Sept. 17, 1903
John F. Curran	92 Milton ave	"	1,200 "	April 27, 1901
Joseph V. Daly	31 Rexhame st	"	1,200 "	Aug. 7, 1906
Almon L. Daniels	84 Tower st	"	1,200 "	July 20, 1900
Thomas S. F. Devine	34 Parkman st	"	1,200 "	May 26, 1901
John Doyle	8 Wallace pk	"	1,100 "	June 28, 1907
Daniel F. Driscoll	32 Academy Hill rd	"	1,200 "	" 18, 1892
Daniel J. Driscoll	209 Parsons st	"	1,200 "	Sept. 1, 1903
Maurice Driscoll	669 Second st	"	1,200 "	Dec. 24, 1901
Francis S. Duffin	640 E. Ninth st	"	1,200 "	March 29, 1904
Andrew W. Duncan	96 Wadsworth st	"	1,200 "	April 29, 1901
Timothy S. L. Ellis	122 Armandine st	"	1,200 "	Aug. 30, 1901
Hollis W. Engley	133 South st., J. P.	"	1,200 "	June 15, 1882
Thomas D. Feeney	167 King st	"	1,200 "	Nov. 22, 1897
Robert Ferris	31 Foster st., Bri	"	1,200 "	Dec. 27, 1900
Dana W. Fisher	26 Walk Hill st	"	1,200 "	May 26, 1901
John Fitzgerald	39 Chestnut st., Chsn	"	1,200 "	July 1, 1895
John V. Foley	82 Magnolia st	"	1,200 "	Jan. 1, 1898
John P. Fox	53 Elmo st	"	1,000 "	Feb. 4, 1909
John Gallagher	19 Winship st	"	1,200 "	Oct. 14, 1889
Richard J. Gallivan	29 Wrentham st	"	1,200 "	April 25, 1907
James A. Gately	434 Dudley st	"	1,200 "	Dec. 27, 1872
Thomas S. Graham	26 Creighton st	"	1,225 "	April 8, 1895
Francis P. Haggerty	27 Brook ave	"	1,000 "	Jan. 14, 1909
John N. Harkins	8 Monument st	"	1,200 "	Dec. 19, 1891
Daniel J. Hart	36 Florence st	"	1,200 "	Nov. 9, 1898
Alfred H. Hildreth	30 Colberg ave	"	1,200 "	April 19, 1889
Matthew B. Hopkins	787 Columbia rd	"	1,200 "	Nov. 1, 1900
Daniel F. Houghton	19 Kingston st., Chsn	"	1,200 "	May 20, 1880
Edward F. Hyland	6 Harvard ave	"	1,200 "	Jan. 5, 1893
Edmund J. Ivers	155 Leyden st	"	1,200 "	" 10, 1901
Fred J. Jacobus	170 Gardner st	"	1,200 "	April 8, 1895
Charles E. Johnquist	72 Tuttle st	"	1,200 "	March 30, 1903
Patrick Keane	140 Calumet st	"	1,200 "	April 27, 1901
John B. Kennedy	18 Bulfinch st	"	1,200 "	Mar. 12, 1907
Patrick J. Kennedy	145 W. Concord st	"	1,200 "	Nov. 2, 1895
Timothy Kenney	23 Stratton st	"	1,200 "	Aug. 7, 1901
Charles A. Kihlgren	2761 Washington st	"	1,200 "	Nov. 1, 1900
Martin H. King	49 Hancock st., Dor	"	1,200 "	April 15, 1902
Patrick J. Lahey	76 Allen st	"	1,200 "	Oct. 8, 1889
Thomas F. Lane	17 Harbor View st	"	1,100 "	Feb. 13, 1908
Peter C. Lawson	268 Minot st	"	1,200 "	Oct. 20, 1904
John T. Leary	786 Parker st	"	1,200 "	June 9, 1888
Cornelius J. Lee	46 Barry st	"	1,200 "	May 20, 1880
Alexander Lindsay	832 Dorchester ave	"	1,200 "	Dec. 8, 1899
John J. Mathony	31 Telegraph st	"	1,200 "	Oct. 20, 1904
John J. McCarthy	50 Everdean st	"	1,200 "	Nov. 22, 1897
Patrick McGahey	74 Mapleton st	"	1,200 "	Dec. 29, 1879
John F. McGillicuddy	35 Temple st	"	1,200 "	March 6, 1903
Edward McHugh	11 Charlotte st	"	1,200 "	May 5, 1873
John F. McInnes	191 L st	"	1,000 "	Nov. 5, 1908
Wilbur L. Melvin	289 Poplar st	"	1,200 "	Sept. 19, 1900
Edson T. Miner	76 Dudley st	"	1,200 "	Jan. 30, 1904
George Murray	37 Romsey st	"	1,200 "	May 26, 1901
William J. Nealon	32 Fountain st	"	1,200 "	Jan. 30, 1904
Elijah L. Nickerson	56 Chickatawbut st	"	1,200 "	Sept. 20, 1900
Frederick H. Norcross	623 Park st	"	1,200 "	April 27, 1901
William A. Norton	5 Tupelo st	"	1,200 "	Nov. 27, 1878
Emerson H. Nye	16 Kensington st	"	1,200 "	Jan. 6, 1894
Francis P. O'Bryan	17 Sumner st	"	1,200 "	April 4, 1894
James G. Peters	424 Seaver st	"	1,100 "	Jan. 6, 1908
Arthur J. Putnam	48 Hillside st	"	1,200 "	April 18, 1895

Police Department.— Continued.

Name.	Residence.	Designation.	Compensation.	Date of Election or Appointment.

Division 2.— Concluded.

Name.	Residence.	Designation.	Compensation.	Date of Election or Appointment.
Joseph Rankin	9 Common st	Patrolman	$1,200 yr	July 6, 1875
William Ready	675 Washington st, Bri	"	1,200 "	April 11, 1887
Edwin H. Rich	728 E. Third st	"	1,200 "	Dec. 29, 1879
Lawrence L. Riley	316 Saratoga st	"	1,200 "	Oct. 12, 1895
William H. Robinson	569 E. Eighth st	"	1,200 "	July 6, 1894
Edgar E. Rowell	9 Rockville pk	"	1,200 "	May 1, 1895
Thomas E. Ryan	720 E. Fourth st	"	1,200 "	April 27, 1873
Frank E. Small	27 Longfellow st	"	1,200 "	Dec. 15, 1896
Michael Sullivan	40 Dudley st	"	1,100 "	Jan. 7, 1908
Peter Sullivan	575 E. Eighth st	"	1,000 "	June 22, 1908
Charles M. Tighe	139 Mt. Pleasant ave	"	1,200 "	Dec. 9, 1899
James A. Toomey	8 Gates st	"	1,200 "	Nov. 10, 1904
Michael T. Travers	2 Auburn pl	"	1,000 "	Jan. 14, 1909
Clarence E. Wharff	6 Savin st	"	1,200 "	Nov. 27, 1878
Joseph S. Whitehead	22 Barry st	"	1,200 "	Jan. 30, 1905
Martin F. Connolly	114 W. Seventh st	Reserve Officer	2.00 day	July 20, 1908
William P. Dolan	18 Parker Hill ave	"	2.00 "	June 22, 1908
John P. Farrell	29 Romsey st	"	2.00 "	July 20, 1908
Edward J. Ford	28 Arcadia st	"	2.25 "	April 29, 1908
Patrick A. Hanley	21 Dorchester st	"	2.25 "	" 29, 1908
Thomas J. Mahoney	48 Crescent ave	"	2.00 "	July 20, 1908
John J. Manning	12 Story st	"	2.25 "	April 29, 1908
Augustine J. Marks	1043 Dorchester ave	"	2.00 "	July 20, 1908
John F. McCarthy	12 Folsom st	"	2.25 "	April 29, 1908
Charles A. Steppe	60 Maxwell st	"	2.00 "	July 20, 1908
John G. Murray	17 Newark st	Janitor	14.00 wk	April 27, 1905
Mary E. Tatten	3 Hull row	Janitress	12.70 "	June 9, 1908

Division 3.

Name.	Residence.	Designation.	Compensation.	Date of Election or Appointment.
Irving A. H. Peabody	15 Nottingham st	Captain	$2,500 yr	Sept. 3, 1901
John A. O'Rourke	11 Rill st	Lieutenant	1,600 "	" 11, 1899
James P. Sullivan	8 Dennison st	"	1,600 "	Oct. 24, 1894
James W. Brooks	17 Hendry st	Sergeant	1,400 "	Feb. 8, 1908
Harry P. Burns	30 Batavia st	"	1,400 "	" 8, 1908
Michael H. Crowley	11 Dracut st	"	1,400 "	April 25, 1907
Francis J. Mulligan	20 Grafton st	"	1,400 "	Feb. 8, 1908
Alpheus W. Parker	42 Norton st	"	1,400 "	" 8, 1908
William J. Ahern	142 Princeton	Patrolman	1,200 "	March, 1886
Henry J. Barry	603 Bennington st	"	1,200 "	Jan. 30, 1905
John Campbell	5 Linden st	"	1,200 "	Feb. 4, 1907
Charles E. Carbee	10 Auckland st	"	1,200 "	" 27, 1893
Michael Casey	90 Fisher ave	"	1,200 "	Aug. 14, 1899
Patrick J. Chambers	552 E. Broadway	"	1,200 "	Nov. 9, 1898
William H. Cobb	9 Morley st	"	1,200 "	Dec. 22, 1903
Patrick H. Connerny	25 Eden st	"	1,200 "	June, 1888
Andrew B. Cuneo	187 Amory st	"	1,100 "	Jan. 7, 1908
William F. Cunningham	55 Clarkson st	"	1,200 "	Dec. 22, 1903
Eugene F. Dagle	177 Belgrade ave	"	1,200 "	" 31, 1903
Thomas Delahunt	27 Maryland st	"	1,200 "	Aug. 24, 1899
Francis A. Dudley	22 Edison green	"	1,200 "	" 7, 1901
Patrick J. Duke	420 Saratoga st	"	1,200 "	April 8, 1895
Samuel Dunlap	25 Allen st	"	1,200 "	May 24, 1901
Patrick J. Fay	37 Norton st	"	1,200 "	Sept. 2, 1902
Thomas F. Fay	235 Highland st	"	1,200 "	July 11, 1904
Richard A. Fisher	29 Burgess st	"	1,200 "	March 16, 1901
Daniel E. Fitzgerald	68 W. Cottage st	"	1,200 "	Oct. 11, 1881
Thomas F. Fitzpatrick	26 W. Dedham st	"	1,000 "	Dec. 16, 1908
John B. Glawson	63 McLellan st	"	1,200 "	Oct. 8, 1889
Lorin S. Gray	10 Auckland st	"	1,200 "	" 8, 1889
John J. Griffin	23 Faxon st	"	1,000 "	June 22, 1908
William C. Hankey	17 Danforth st	"	1,200 "	Sept. 2, 1902
Henry C. Herman	8 Oak st	"	1,100 "	" 11, 1907
Michael J. Horrigan	791 Huntington ave	"	1,200 "	April 13, 1906
Timothy W. Hurley	1 Everett ave	"	1,000 "	June 22, 1908
Thomas M. Igoe	2948 Washington st	"	1,100 "	April 30, 1908
William J. Joyce	21 Roberts ave	"	1,200 "	July 11, 1904
Henry F. Koerber, Jr	118½ Dorchester st	"	1,200 "	March 11, 1907
Orlando B. Lailer	15 Moultrie st	"	1,200 "	Jan. 21, 1889
Thomas F. Lane	2 S. Walter st	"	1,200 "	May 24, 1901
John K. Lewis	3 Charles st	"	1,200 "	July 11, 1904
Richard H. Lombard	50 Harvard st	"	1,200 "	Nov. 4, 1885

Police Department.— Continued.

Name.	Residence.	Designation.	Compensation.	Date of Election or Appointment.

Division 3.— Concluded.

Name.	Residence.	Designation.	Compensation.	Date of Election or Appointment.
John J. Lordan	15 Bellflower st	Patrolman	$1,200 yr.	April 25, 1907
Louis E. Lutz	1880 Dorchester ave	"	1,200 "	July 30, 1896
Augustus V. F. Mangene	362 Tremont st	"	1,200 "	Dec. 21, 1906
Frank L. Merritt	149 Bennington st	"	1,200 "	April 25, 1899
Charles W. McAdams	18 Elmore st	"	1,200 "	Aug. 7, 1901
Patrick J. McAuliffe	7 Oakview ter	"	1,200 "	Sept. 20, 1900
Felix McCarthy	6 Downer ct	"	1,100 "	Oct. 8, 1907
John J. McDonald	86 E. Cottage st	"	1,000 "	Sept. 17, 1908
William F. McDonald	86 E. Cottage st	"	1,000 "	Jan. 14, 1909
Patrick J. McDonough	74 Roseclair st	"	1,200 "	Nov. 9, 1898
John McGrath	64 Hancock st	"	1,200 "	Sept. 2, 1902
Hugh P. McGuire	9 Cottage pk	"	1,200 "	Nov. 9, 1898
Elam W. Morgan	40 Bigelow st	"	1,200 "	May 18, 1903
John P. Morrisey	6 Brookford st	"	1,100 "	Jan. 16, 1908
Jonathan J. Murphy	555 Adams st	"	1,200 "	April 9, 1895
James E. Nickerson	51 Dewey st	"	1,200 "	May 19, 1903
Jeremiah O'Keeffe	101 Russell st	"	1,200 "	Aug. 24, 1899
John H. O'Neil	129 Harold st	"	1,200 "	March 15, 1884
Joseph F. O'Neill	261 Parker Hill ave	"	1,000 "	Jan. 14, 1909
Hugh O'Neill	163 Revere st	"	1,200 "	Oct. 12, 1904
Otis D. Parmenter	77 Bowdoin ave	"	1,200 "	Sept. 19, 1900
Albert R. Peterson	7 Fenner st	"	1,100 "	Jan. 7, 1908
Norman S. Ramsay	343 Warren st	"	1,100 "	Nov. 14, 1907
Frederick Sullivan	876 Fourth st	"	1,200 "	Dec. 22, 1903
Thomas F. Supple	4 Shepard st	"	1,200 "	Oct. 10, 1890
Arthur J. Thompson	1 Bulfinch st	"	1,200 "	Nov. 11, 1896
Perley G. Tilton	25 Sudan st	"	1,100 "	June 1, 1907
Jonathan Tomlinson	28 Church st	"	1,200 "	April 27, 1901
George L. Twombly	6 Prospect st	"	1,200 "	July 30, 1896
George Walker	623 Columbus ave	"	1,200 "	April 27, 1901
Winfield S. Wallace	120 Cedar st	"	1,200 "	Oct. 4, 1890
James A. J. Walsh	667 E. Seventh st	"	1,200 "	Feb. 9, 1905
Peter S. Walsh	25 Curtis st	"	1,000 "	" 4, 1909
Alvy P. Williamson	16 Bayswater st	"	1,200 "	Jan. 10, 1889
John P. M. Wolfe	12 Emerald st	"	1,000 "	Nov. 4, 1908
Arthur W. Wyman	36 Hampstead rd	"	1,200 "	Jan. 9, 1881
Benjamin Alexander	690 Shawmut ave	Reserve Officer	2.00 day.	April 20, 1909
Charles R. Brennan	41 Tyler st	"	2.00 "	July 20, 1908
James L. Butler	37 Story st	"	2.00 "	Oct. 12, 1908
Joseph J. Cadigan	12 Bennett st	"	2.00 "	Nov. 16, 1908
Thomas Foley	77 Marcella st	"	2.25 "	April 29, 1908
John L. Gallagher	46 Myrtle st	"	2.00 "	July 20, 1908
Arthur F. Marston	6 Thornton st	"	2.00 "	" 20, 1908
David A. Nash	46 Myrtle st	"	2.00 "	" 20, 1908
Michael Noonan	254 Lincoln st	"	2.00 "	Nov. 16, 1908
Maurice W. Sullivan	616 E. Third st	"	2.25 "	April 29, 1908
Joseph P. Trainor	51 Baldwin st	"	2.25 "	" 29, 1908
John Lydon	16 Poplar st	Janitor	14.00 wk.	June 12, 1905
Abbie K. Jackson	63 Hancock st	Janitress	12.70 "	April 15, 1874

Division 4.

Name.	Residence.	Designation.	Compensation.	Date of Election or Appointment.
Laurence Cain	22 Warnbeck st	Captain	$2,500 yr.	Feb. 16, 1888
James P. Canney	9 Claybourne st	Lieutenant	1,600 "	Aug. 2, 1906
Herbert W. Goodwin	619 Walk Hill st	"	1,600 "	Feb. 8, 1908
Sumner S. Foster	88 Oak ave	Sergeant	1,400 "	Dec. 17, 1908
George H. Guard	372 Cornell st	"	1,400 "	Oct. 25, 1899
James Laffey	51 Lincoln st	"	1,400 "	Feb. 7, 1908
Arthur B. McConnell	88 Garden st	"	1,400 "	Jan. 30, 1905
Jeremiah N. Mosher	141 Foster st	"	1,400 "	Feb. 7, 1908
John M. L. Anderson	4 Dahlgren st	Patrolman	1,200 "	Dec. 22, 1903
George Brooks	35 Dudley ave	"	1,200 "	May 12, 1894
William J. Brown	5 Arcadia ter	"	1,200 "	Dec. 24, 1901
Charles H. Bullock	53 Bakersfield st	"	1,200 "	Jan. 10, 1889
Oscar W. Burgess	8 Hewins st	"	1,200 "	Sept. 20, 1900
Edward L. Butters	43 Tower st	"	1,200 "	Jan. 5, 1903
Alden S. Calder	32 O st	"	1,200 "	July 20, 1900
Fred L. Chase	40 Lambert st	"	1,200 "	Nov. 14, 1883
John A. Connare	46 Dustin st	"	1,200 "	Oct. 12, 1905
Timothy F. Donovan	62 Heela st	"	1,200 "	May 18, 1903
John J. Downey	77 Bower st	"	1,200 "	June 7, 1897
Richard H. Evans	1 Haynes pk	"	1,200 "	" 9, 1888

Police Department.— Continued.

Name.	Residence.	Designation.	Compensation.	Date of Election or Appointment.

Division 4.— Continued.

Name.	Residence.	Designation.	Compensation.	Date of Election or Appointment.
William W. Fay	132 Park st	Patrolman	$1,200 yr	March 3, 1905
George H. Foley	60 Bartlett st	"	1,200 "	Oct. 12, 1895
James J. Gallagher	1079 Dorchester ave	"	1,200 "	July 19, 1897
George G. Gallop	25 Ditson st	"	1,200 "	April 27, 1901
Thomas H. Galligan	53 Wenham st	"	1,200 "	May 20, 1898
James J. Gillen	91 Maxwell st	"	1,200 "	Oct. 16, 1893
Daniel H. Gould	3 Richfield pk	"	1,200 "	Nov. 9, 1898
Harry T. Grace	5 Herman st	"	1,200 "	Feb. 4, 1907
William G. Graham	77 Savin st	"	1,200 "	Oct. 21, 1884
James Hanlon	18 Calder st	"	1,200 "	Sept. 21, 1900
John J. Hanrahan	5 Codman Hill st	"	1,200 "	July 11, 1904
John J. Harney	112 Hillside st	"	1,200 "	Jan. 1, 1904
Dennis Harrington	106 Dustin st	"	1,200 "	Oct. 12, 1904
William Hartigan	29 East st	"	1,200 "	April 24, 1901
Peter A. Hayes	28 Mead st	"	1,225 "	June 14, 1886
Thomas P. Healy	59 Chambers st	"	1,200 "	Aug. 7, 1906
Bernard J. Hoppe	353 Norfolk st	"	1,200 "	March 16, 1901
Frederick S. Howell	9 Hamlet st	"	1,200 "	Dec. 24, 1901
Frank W. Huckins	44 Copeland st	"	1,200 "	Jan. 10, 1889
James J. Hughes	20 Parker Hill ave	"	1,200 "	May 18, 1903
Thomas F. Kennedy	46 Dustin st	"	1,200 "	June 9, 1888
Mark V. Kilroy	1463 Washington st	"	1,200 "	March 5, 1903
Linwood S. Leavitt	5 May st	"	1,200 "	Sept. 21, 1900
William Lewis	31 Lawrence ave	"	1,200 "	July 30, 1896
Woodbury L. Lewis	15 Bidwell st	"	1,200 "	Jan. 6, 1893
Dexter Littlefield	6 Victor st	"	1,200 "	" 30, 1904
Arthur Lovejoy	36 Rockford st	"	1,200 "	April 18, 1895
John H. Lynch	77 Topliff st	"	1,200 "	March 7, 1892
James J. Macksey	105 W. Eighth st	"	1,200 "	April 25, 1907
Patrick J. Mahoney	61 Ferrin st	"	1,200 "	Jan. 30, 1905
Hugh F. Marston	29 Chambers st	"	1,200 "	April 27, 1901
John McCarron	72 Calumet st	"	1,200 "	Oct. 16, 1902
Daniel W. McCarthy	15 Homes ave	"	1,200 "	May 19, 1898
Timothy A. McCarthy	66 Julian st	"	1,200 "	Nov. 22, 1897
James McCready	33 East st	"	1,200 "	June 12, 1905
Patrick J. McLaughlin	54 Edwin st	"	1,200 "	Oct. 31, 1900
Thomas McTigue	18 Harvard st	"	1,200 "	Sept. 20, 1900
Charles W. Miller	1118 Bennington st	"	1,200 "	April 13, 1906
John F. Mitchell	314 Bunker Hill st	"	1,200 "	Aug. 28, 1894
Thomas F. Moore	24 Middlesex st	"	1,200 "	Oct. 21, 1884
William F. Moore	373A Warren st	"	1,200 "	" 23, 1886
Patrick J. Murphy	35 Union st	"	1,200 "	" 29, 1906
Joseph H. Neal	33 Monument sq	"	1,200 "	Dec. 9, 1893
James S. Orr	352 Centre st	"	1,200 "	" 24, 1884
Thomas W. Rae	4 Dahlgren st	"	1,200 "	April 8, 1895
John H. Reagan	60 Wheatland ave	"	1,200 "	Oct. 15, 1881
Jeremiah J. Riordan	148 Westville st	"	1,200 "	Sept. 21, 1900
Winfield A. Studley	2996 Washington st	"	1,200 "	July 11, 1904
James J. Sullivan	772 Columbus ave	"	1,200 "	Oct. 16, 1902
Michael J. Sullivan	106 Moreland st	"	1,225 "	March 5, 1903
John H. Sweeney	40 Monument sq	"	1,200 "	April 25, 1899
Frank Tays	5 Burroughs pl	"	1,200 "	" 8, 1895
Thomas A. Thompson	517A Dudley st	"	1,200 "	Sept. 21, 1900
John F. Walsh	4 Gates st	"	1,200 "	July 10, 1875
William D. Walsh	16 Saxton st	"	1,200 "	Oct. 16, 1902
Dana J. Walton	10 Columbus sq	"	1,200 "	Sept. 21, 1900
John J. Welch	76 Parsons st	"	1,200 "	Nov. 6, 1895
George Wilson	1051 Saratoga st	"	1,200 "	" 10, 1905
Herbert L. Wingate	2440 Washington st	"	1,200 "	March 16, 1901
Michael C. P. Bresnahan	50 Charles st	"	1,100 "	April 30, 1908
Harry R. Butler	47 Maverick st	"	1,100 "	Nov. 7, 1907
William J. Chapman	96 Bunker Hill st	"	1,100 "	July 20, 1907
George F. DeLeskey	211 E. Eagle st	"	1,100 "	Jan. 16, 1908
Frederick M. Forde	43 Bainbridge st	"	1,100 "	Feb. 13, 1908
John J. Moran	5 Rogers ave	"	1,100 "	June 1, 1907
Timothy C. Murphy	38 Milford st	"	1,100 "	Jan. 7, 1908
Thomas O. O'Neil	5 O st	"	1,100 "	May 18, 1907
John F. Rooney	24 Everett ave	"	1,100 "	Nov. 7, 1907
Harris T. Smith	100 W. Newton st	"	1,100 "	Sept. 11, 1907
William H. Carnes	11 Estey st	"	1,000 "	" 17, 1908
William G. Cleminson	448 W. Fourth st	"	1,000 "	Jan. 14, 1909
Michael L. Daly	136 Bellevue st	"	1,000 "	" 14, 1909
Thomas A. Foley	24 Vinton st	"	1,000 "	Nov. 5, 1908

Police Department.— Continued.

Name.	Residence.	Designation.	Compensation.	Date of Election or Appointment.

Division 4. — Concluded.

Name.	Residence.	Designation.	Compensation.	Date of Election or Appointment.
Gustave A. Sandberg	258 Massachusetts ave	Patrolman	$1,000 yr	Feb. 4, 1909
Michael J. Welch	6 Sumner st	"	1,000 "	Dec. 17, 1908
Joseph M. Balk	16 Winfield st	Reserve Officer	2.25 day	April 29, 1908
Edward F. Brennan	3 Norfolk st	"	2.25 "	" 29, 1908
David Buckley	54 Pinckney st	"	2.25 "	" 29, 1908
David E. Mulcahy	7 Ascot st	"	2.25 "	" 29, 1908
James W. Caffrey	94 Decatur st	"	2.00 "	June 25, 1908
Patrick Capstick	9 Parsons st	"	2.00 "	Jan. 18, 1909
Joseph F. Crotty	84 Day st	"	2.00 "	June 22, 1908
Frank C. Durgin	29 Elmore st	"	2.00 "	" 22, 1908
Grant H. Farwell	21 Greenwich pk	"	2.00 "	July 20, 1908
John P. McNealy	21 Albion st	"	2.00 "	June 22, 1908
John F. Sheehan	15 Hancock st	"	2.00 "	Jan. 18, 1909
Charles D. Wildes	18 Calder st	"	2.00 "	July 20, 1908
Francis E. Kennedy	13 Kent st	Janitor	14.00 wk	May 1, 1905
Joseph Ernst	224 Lamartine st	"	14.00 "	July 17, 1907

Division 5.

Name.	Residence.	Designation.	Compensation.	Date of Election or Appointment.
Daniel A. Ritter	70 Wellington Hill st	Captain	$2,500 yr	Feb. 8, 1908
John E. Driscoll	12 Fulda st	Lieutenant	1,600 "	" 8, 1908
Clinton E. Bowley	3 Parker st	"	1,600 "	" 8, 1908
Edward H. Mullen	7 Lincoln st	Sergeant	1,425 "	" 8, 1908
Michael J. Goff	39 Mystic st	"	1,400 "	April 5, 1895
Murray Munro	8 Primrose st	"	1,400 "	" 25, 1907
Joseph F. Hurley	34 Evergreen st	"	1,400 "	Feb. 8, 1908
Charles B. McCloskey	123 Faneuil st	"	1,400 "	May 27, 1908
Joseph M. Connor	56 Blue Hill ave	Patrolman	1,225 "	" 16, 1904
William G. Hill	74 Hamilton st	"	1,225 "	Feb. 13, 1902
Sherman W. Augusta	56 Quincy st	"	1,200 "	July 21, 1905
Edward F. Buckley	58 Austin st	"	1,200 "	Dec. 24, 1901
Archibald F. Campbell	37 Cobden st	"	1,200 "	May 24, 1901
Samuel B. Chick	71 Centre st	"	1,200 "	Jan. 14, 1881
John T. Clifford	9 Dorset st	"	1,200 "	Feb. 4, 1893
James E. Conant	332 Eighth st	"	1,200 "	May 18, 1903
John T. Corcoran	6 Oswald st	"	1,200 "	" 21, 1901
George H. Cushing	10 Ballou st	"	1,200 "	July 21, 1905
George W. A. Dawson	44 Mark st	"	1,200 "	March 6, 1903
Dennis F. Desmond	31 Stanley st	"	1,200 "	June 9, 1888
Thomas J. Donohue	157 N st	"	1,200 "	Oct. 30, 1906
Charles M. Eaton	126 St. Botolph st	"	1,200 "	May 18, 1903
Patrick F. Flaherty	147 Bowdoin st	"	1,200 "	Feb. 14, 1907
William P. Gaffney	434 Bowdoin st	"	1,200 "	May 18, 1903
Norman F. Garland	28 W. Walnut pk	"	1,200 "	Nov. 9, 1898
John E. Geary	128 Calumet st	"	1,200 "	May 18, 1903
Charles W. Gillette	28 Park View st	"	1,200 "	" 8, 1875
Vinal W. Harmon	12 Saxon st	"	1,200 "	Oct. 12, 1899
Michael F. Harrington	162 Walter st	"	1,200 "	March 29, 1904
Wilbur F. Harris	11 Brown ave	"	1,200 "	Oct. 30, 1900
William Hazlett	87 Lonsdale st	"	1,200 "	" 16, 1902
William J. Irwin	14 Rutland sq	"	1,200 "	Dec. 24, 1901
John M. Jackson	2 Ferdinand st	"	1,200 "	May 24, 1901
Lincoln H. Jones	4A Milford st	"	1,200 "	Aug. 7, 1901
Timothy F. Keane	172 W. Canton st	"	1,200 "	March 15, 1884
Frank J. Kelley	8 Ray st	"	1,200 "	" 5, 1903
John Lane	40 Robinson st	"	1,200 "	May 3, 1899
Ralph H. P. Langlan	30A Spring Park ave	"	1,200 "	March 2, 1905
Daniel J. Leary	718 E. Sixth st	"	1,200 "	Jan. 30, 1904
William F. Lewis	4 Allston st	"	1,200 "	Oct. 18, 1878
Ashley S. Littlefield	19 Vine st	"	1,200 "	Jan. 30, 1904
William W. Livingston	85 W. Brookline st	"	1,200 "	Dec. 24, 1901
William Macbeth	548 Tremont st	"	1,200 "	Sept. 19, 1900
Frank M. Magee	21 Forest Hills st	"	1,200 "	March 16, 1901
Dennis Mahoney	94 Mt. Pleasant ave	"	1,200 "	June 14, 1877
Andrew H. McCarthy	104 Warren st	"	1,200 "	March 19, 1883
Daniel A. McGillivray	136 Stanwood st	"	1,200 "	" 29, 1904
John P. V. McKee	41 Mozart st	"	1,200 "	Dec. 26, 1902
Bernard J. McNally	716 E. Fourth st	"	1,200 "	Nov. 9, 1898
Patrick J. Morrissey	3 Oswald st	"	1,200 "	May 24, 1901
Martin F. Mullen	751 E. Fifth st	"	1,200 "	Jan. 1, 1904
James F. Murphy	5 Sharon st	"	1,200 "	May 24, 1901
Thomas H. Murphy	8 Fifield st	"	1,200 "	March 29, 1904
James M. Nelson	307 Maverick st	"	1,200 "	Aug. 28, 1894

Police Department.— Continued.

Name.	Residence.	Designation.	Compensation.	Date of Election or Appointment.

Division 5.— Concluded.

Name.	Residence.	Designation.	Compensation.	Date of Election or Appointment.
Ward E. Neily	28 E. Brookline st	Patrolman	$1,200 yr	Dec. 8, 1899
Charles A. Newell	23 Margaret st	"	1,200 "	April 4, 1891
Peter J. Norton	28 Church st	"	1,200 "	Dec. 22, 1899
Charles A. Ochs	10 Glendale st	"	1,200 "	May 24, 1901
George I. O'Bryan	8 Marlowe st	"	1,200 "	March 5, 1903
Robert W. Pierce	35 Clifford st	"	1,200 "	" 14, 1898
Joseph H. Porter	38 Wellington rd	"	1,200 "	Feb. 13, 1902
Aldred W. Readmon	42 Knoll st	"	1,200 "	Oct. 31, 1900
Edward A. Ryan	14 Thetford st	"	1,200 "	Sept. 19, 1900
Jeremiah B. Sheehan	912 E. Broadway	"	1,200 "	" 17, 1903
Nicholas P. Tangney	53 Wensley st	"	1,200 "	" 19, 1900
William J. Trainor	31 Union st	"	1,200 "	Oct. 12, 1904
Louis L. Twomey	67 Chelsea st	"	1,200 "	Feb. 14, 1907
Walter H. Underhill	100 Parker Hill ave	"	1,200 "	April 8, 1902
Thomas H. Vincent	80 St. Botolph st	"	1,200 "	March 5, 1903
Guy E. V. Whitman	114 Erie st	"	1,200 "	" 29, 1904
James F. Concannon	424 Bowdoin st	"	1,100 "	Jan. 4, 1908
Stephen H. Delosh	33 Hayden st	"	1,100 "	Oct. 9, 1907
Patrick F. Grant	828 E. Second st	"	1,100 "	April 30, 1908
James J. McCurey	66 Gardner st	"	1,100 "	" 30, 1908
George W. McKenzie	27 Circuit st	"	1,100 "	Jan. 16, 1908
Andrew W. Ryan	603 E. Fourth st	"	1,100 "	" 7, 1908
Robert A. Stewart	58 Highland st	"	1,100 "	" 16, 1908
Daniel F. Sullivan	111 St. Alphonsus st	"	1,100 "	June 29, 1907
Robert M. P. Chalmers	37 Howell st	"	1,000 "	Jan. 14, 1909
Martin S. Cosgrove	26 Leroy st	"	1,000 "	" 14, 1909
Daniel J. Fraser	40 Brookford st	"	1,000 "	Nov. 5, 1908
James W. Kennedy	242 La Grange st	"	1,000 "	Dec. 17, 1908
Emerson P. Marsh	174 Spring Park ave	"	1,000 "	Sept. 17, 1908
Frederick I. Morrill	93 Birch st	"	1,000 "	Dec. 17, 1908
James F. Sullivan	7 Keyes st	"	1,000 "	Feb. 4, 1909
Edward McGarr	17 Gayland st	Reserve Officer	2.25 day	April 29, 1908
Max B. F. Thormer	47 Savin Hill ave	"	2.25 "	" 29, 1908
Timothy Carroll	67 Roseclaire st	"	2.00 "	July 20, 1908
Robert T. Dale	220 N. Harvard st	"	2.00 "	Jan. 18, 1909
Michael McD. Foley	33 Woodcliff st	"	2.00 "	April 20, 1909
James Lynch	149 Boston st	"	2.00 "	June 22, 1908
Joseph A. Sullivan	327 E. Eighth st	"	2.00 "	Oct. 12, 1908
Thomas B. Lafayette	391 Bunker Hill st	Janitor	14.00 wk	April 16, 1904
James Walsh	41 Highland Park ave	"	14.00 "	July 14, 1907

Division 6.

Name.	Residence.	Designation.	Compensation.	Date of Election or Appointment.
Forrest F. Hall	2 Allen rd	Captain	$2,500 yr	Feb. 8, 1908
Henry J. Walkins	22 Angell st	Lieutenant	1,600 "	May 31, 1907
William F. Manning	725 E. Third st	"	1,600 "	Feb. 8, 1908
Henry Hazlett	87 Lonsdale st	Sergeant	1,400 "	Nov. 22, 1899
Thomas Keane	52 McLellan st	"	1,400 "	Jan. 30, 1905
James P. Smith	46 Greenwood ave	"	1,400 "	March 3, 1905
Dennis F. Murphy	26 Norton st	"	1,400 "	Feb. 8, 1908
William T. Blair	7 Edison green	Patrolman	1,100 "	Jan. 4, 1908
James M. Breen	106 I st	"	1,200 "	Sept. 19, 1900
Michael J. Brennick	35 Mt. Ida rd	"	1,200 "	Oct. 11, 1881
John Buckley	727 E. Fourth st	"	1,200 "	" 8, 1889
Dennis Callaghan	161 Pleasant st	"	1,200 "	Dec. 22, 1903
John J. Callahan	657 E. Broadway	"	1,200 "	May 12, 1894
John Carroll	44 Tolman st	"	1,100 "	Jan. 16, 1908
Patrick H. Coffey	30 Cunningham st	"	1,200 "	April 4, 1891
William F. Cogan	891 E. Fourth st	"	1,200 "	" 19, 1889
Dennis J. Collins	592 E. Fourth st	"	1,200 "	Oct. 21, 1882
Michael J. Connors	4 Phillips st	"	1,000 "	Feb. 4, 1909
Jeremiah J. DeYone	52 Newport st	"	1,200 "	Jan. 30, 1904
William A. Donahoe	26 Everett st	"	1,200 "	May 12, 1894
John J. Donovan	32 Blaine st	"	1,000 "	June 22, 1908
Norman A. Eaton	200 Emerson st	"	1,200 "	Sept. 19, 1900
Irving Elder	27 Pearl st	"	1,200 "	July 20, 1900
Thomas J. Fallon	47 Creighton st	"	1,200 "	Oct. 11, 1881
Levi P. Fernald	30 Concord sq	"	1,200 "	May 20, 1880
James S. Fox	122 F st	"	1,200 "	April 23, 1896
James W. Gammon	269 W. Fifth st	"	1,200 "	Aug. 8, 1888
George M. Gould	849 E. First st	"	1,100 "	Nov. 14, 1907
John O. Greg	103 Harvard st	"	1,200 "	March 3, 1905
William G. J. Hanrahan	58 Belfort st	"	1,100 "	Oct. 9, 1907

Police Department.— Continued.

Name.	Residence.	Designation.	Compensation.	Date of Election or Appointment.

Division 6.— Concluded.

Name.	Residence.	Designation.	Compensation.	Date of Election or Appointment.
Martin Haverty	15 Harvest st	Patrolman	$1,000 yr.	Jan. 14, 1909
John H. Hill	16 Cameron st	"	1,200 "	Oct. 20, 1904
John E. Hughes	33 G st	"	1,200 "	Jan. 10, 1889
Olof Johnson	45 Mattapan st	"	1,200 "	Oct. 16, 1902
William J. Kinsman	189 Dorchester st	"	1,200 "	June 1, 1893
James P. Kirley	2 Louise pk	"	1,200 "	March 5, 1893
Henry J. Lampe	1026 Dorchester ave	"	1,200 "	Oct. 31, 1900
William H. Linton	727 E. Fourth st	"	1,200 "	July 12, 1891
Daniel J. Lynch	34 Hecla st	"	1,200 "	Oct. 12, 1904
Patrick J. Magner	152 Chelsea st	"	1,100 "	April 30, 1908
Thomas L. Maxon	40 Silver st	"	1,200 "	May 18, 1903
Murdo McDonald	696 Massachusetts ave	"	1,100 "	Jan. 7, 1908
Athanasius McGillivray	50 Mt. Vernon st	"	1,200 "	July 11, 1904
George H. Mitchell	110 Draper st	"	1,200 "	Oct. 12, 1895
Jeremiah Monahan	11 Walnut ct	"	1,100 "	June 29, 1907
Edward A. Moore	23 Maywood st	"	1,200 "	Sept. 19, 1900
Henry M. Nash	297 W. Broadway	"	1,200 "	Dec. 14, 1885
John T. O'Dea	793 Columbia rd	"	1,200 "	March 3, 1905
John E. Powers	751 E. Broadway	"	1,200 "	July 13, 1894
John J. Reilly	87 O st	"	1,200 "	Jan. 4, 1886
Charles C. Ridlon	205 Washington st	"	1,100 "	June 29, 1907
Ernest W. Robertson	10 Hatch st	"	1,200 "	April 24, 1905
John T. Scott	98 Wyman st	"	1,200 "	Jan. 30, 1905
Weston Shorey	843 E. Fifth st	"	1,200 "	Dec. 24, 1901
Charles L. Skelton	7 Grant st	"	1,200 "	April 1, 1882
Edmund M. Smith	854 E. Broadway	"	1,200 "	" 8, 1895
Mellen L. Stickney, Jr	150 Welles ave	"	1,200 "	Feb. 13, 1902
Peter P. F. Toner	24 Bunker Hill st	"	1,000 "	Jan. 14, 1909
Patrick J. Trimlet	210 L st	"	1,000 "	" 14, 1909
Edwin A. Waldron	77 Milton ave	"	1,200 "	Oct. 21, 1884
John P. Walsh	786 Washington st	"	1,200 "	Sept. 19, 1900
Richard J. Buckley	33 Cordis st	Reserve Officer	2.00 day	Nov. 16, 1908
Thomas H. Dowling	153 Richmond st	"	2.00 "	" 16, 1908
Robert J. Eberts	164 Boston st	"	2.25 "	April 29, 1908
Daniel J. Hurley	26 Charles st	"	2.25 "	" 29, 1908
Michael Lynch	750 E. Third st	"	2.00 "	Nov. 16, 1908
James A. McCormack	24 Minot st	"	2.00 "	April 20, 1909
David W. McDonald	20 Ball st	"	2.25 "	" 29, 1908
John H. O'Donnell	54 North st	"	2.00 "	" 20, 1909
Jeremiah O'Neil	343 Maverick st	"	2.25 "	" 29, 1908
John J. Reardon	69 Telegraph st	"	2.00 "	July 20, 1908
Olvin Saunders	268 E. Cottage st	"	2.25 "	April 29, 1908
Norman F. Sherman	282 Columbus ave	"	2.25 "	" 29, 1908
Albert A. Sullivan	60 Rockwell st	"	2.00 "	Nov. 16, 1908
William J. Knauber	45 Allen st	Janitor	14.00 wk	May 4, 1905
Timothy Connolley	250 Silver st	"	14.00 "	" 12, 1901

Division 7.

Name.	Residence.	Designation.	Compensation.	Date of Election or Appointment.
John A. Brickley	10 Mystic st., Chsn	Captain	$2,500 yr.	Feb. 8, 1908
Millard M. Frohock	1065 Saratoga st., E. B.	Lieutenant	1,600 "	Aug. 30, 1894
John P. Clark	18 Chestnut st., Chsn	"	1,600 "	Sept. 3, 1901
George A. Rohrer, Jr	6 Ashmont pk	Sergeant	1,425 "	Dec. 24, 1895
James L. Hines	91 Horace st	"	1,400 "	Sept. 26, 1898
William F. Aubens	760 E. Fourth st	"	1,425 "	" 3, 1901
Daniel J. Sweeney	316 Saratoga st	"	1,400 "	Dec. 21, 1901
James H. Adams	17 Oakley st	Patrolman	1,200 "	Nov. 14, 1870
John L. Ahern	871 Saratoga st	"	1,200 "	" 4, 1891
Edwin N. Anderson	8 Pope st	"	1,200 "	" 25, 1903
Milton E. Bailey	105 Lexington st	"	1,200 "	June 19, 1893
William E. Brown	87 Homer st	"	1,200 "	May 26, 1878
John F. Burke	20 Border st	"	1,200 "	Nov. 8, 1895
George W. Bussey	1088 Bennington st	"	1,200 "	" 21, 1895
Michael J. Christopher	124 Bayswater st	"	1,200 "	" 9, 1898
Ashton D. Clark	65 Gladstone st	"	1,200 "	July 6, 1892
William J. Conway	18 Prospect st	"	1,000 "	Sept. 17, 1908
Thomas H. Donahoe	174 Webster st	"	1,200 "	April 27, 1901
Florence J. Driscoll	179 London st	"	1,200 "	March 5, 1903
James J. Driscoll	328 Bunker Hill st	"	1,100 "	Jan. 16, 1908
Stoddard C. Erskine	134 Newberg st	"	1,200 "	Oct. 21, 1882
Patrick J. Fitzgerald	1 Webster ct., Chsn	"	1,225 "	April 8, 1895
Edward F. Flanigan	76 Byron st	"	1,200 "	Oct. 1, 1877

Police Department.— Continued.

Name.	Residence.	Designation.	Com. pensation.	Date of Election or Appointment.

Division 7.— Concluded.

Thomas H. Flaherty	82 Homer st	Patrolman	$1,200 yr	April 19, 1899
James E. Flynn	1126 Bennington st	"	1,200 "	" 4, 1891
Michael Goodman	46 Quincy st	"	1,000 "	Jan. 14, 1909
John J. Greene	190 Eustis st	"	1,000 "	Feb. 4, 1909
George H. Greer	863 Saratoga st	"	1,200 "	June 12, 1905
Michael Hafey	6 Union ct	"	1,100 "	Feb. 13, 1908
Michael J. Hankard	553 Bennington st	"	1,225 "	April 8, 1895
Bernard Harte	17 Mt. Vernon st., Chsn.	"	1,000 "	Feb. 4, 1909
Michael Healy	173 Princeton st	"	1,200 "	July 10, 1899
William J. Healy	207 Falcon st	"	1,200 "	April 8, 1895
James Herdman	784 Saratoga st	"	1,200 "	Jan. 4, 1897
Charles F. Hooper	120 Falcon st	"	1,200 "	Dec. 24, 1884
James H. Jacobs	254 E. Eagle st	"	1,200 "	Sept. 19, 1900
Edward F. Kelley	10 Prospect st., Chsn.	"	1,200 "	March 3, 1905
William D. Kerr	60 Putnam st	"	1,200 "	Dec. 24, 1884
Stephen J. Kline	5 Garden st., Chsn	"	1,200 "	April 8, 1895
John E. McCarthy	603 Bennington st	"	1,100 "	June 1, 1907
James A. McKenna	64 Paris st	"	1,200 "	May 24, 1901
James McKenzie	167 Leyden st	"	1,200 "	March 30, 1892
James J. Moran	105 Homer st	"	1,200 "	Oct. 24, 1896
William M. Morse	114 Byron st	"	1,200 "	Jan. 5, 1893
Edward F. Murphy	9 Albion st	"	1,100 "	" 16, 1908
Hugh E. O'Donnell	81 Horace st	"	1,200 "	April 19, 1889
Patrick J. O'Neill	273 Webster st	"	1,200 "	July 27, 1896
Dennis L. Reagan	871 Saratoga st	"	1,200 "	Aug. 27, 1892
Charles W. Rollins	48 Princeton st	"	1,200 "	Jan. 16, 1890
Hugh A. Rourke	286 Lexington st	"	1,225 "	Nov. 8, 1895
George A. Scott	34 Falcon st	"	1,200 "	Oct. 18, 1878
Bernard J. Sloan	168 London st	"	1,200 "	May 20, 1880
William J. Spillane	154 Bennington st	"	1,200 "	April 26, 1896
Eward W. Sprague	262 E. Eagle st	"	1,200 "	Jan. 10, 1889
John A. Stewart	7 Butler ave	"	1,200 "	Nov. 9, 1898
John J. Sweeney	90 P st	"	1,200 "	Jan. 30, 1905
Frederick G. Trask	1 Farrington st	"	1,200 "	Nov. 25, 1891
Alfred Tryder	273 Lexington st	"	1,200 "	Oct. 11, 1881
George R. Weatherby	423 Meridian st	"	1,200 "	June 3, 1897
Thomas York	619 Saratoga st	"	1,200 "	May 24, 1901
Michael Alesi	10 Bridge ct	Reserve Officer	2.00 day	July 20, 1908
Patrick Hickey	5 Delaware pl	"	2.25 "	April 29, 1908
James H. McNamara	6 Blackwell st	"	2.00 "	Oct. 12, 1908
Michael F. Scully	5 Edge Hill st	"	2.00 "	" 12, 1908
George C. Stevens	929 E. Broadway	"	2.00 "	" 12, 1908
John A. Tyo	7 Oakland ave	"	2.00 "	" 12, 1908
Jane A. Sheridan	374 Border st	Janitress	12.70 wk	Feb. 7, 1908
Jane A. Sheridan	374 Border st	Matron	3.84 "	" 7, 1908

Division 8.

Edward A. Pease	16 Marion st., E. B	Captain	$2,500 yr	Feb. 8, 1908
George H. Adams	60 Rosseter st., Dor	Lieutenant	1,600 "	" 5, 1903
Charles H. Tighe	28 Lawrence Ave., Rox	Sergeant	1,400 "	Oct. 31, 1883
George F. McCausland	95 Waldeck st., Dor	"	1,400 "	Feb. 13, 1884
William T. Maguire	18 Pomeroy st., Bri	"	1,400 "	Aug. 24, 1903
Ibri W. H. Curtis	5 Cleaver st., W. Rox	"	1,400 "	Jan. 30, 1905
Francis J. Bird	29 Charles st., Dor	"	1,400 "	March 3, 1905
Ross A. Perry	222 Neponset ave., Dor	"	1,400 "	Feb. 8, 1908
Charles Carlson	83 Lonsdale st., Dor	Patrolman	1,200 "	Nov. 25, 1897
Thomas Connor	630 East Third st., S. B.	"	1,200 "	March 15, 1884
Herbert L. Cross	41 Holiday st., Dor	"	1,200 "	April 8, 1895
Peter C. Eldridge	33 Border st., E. B.	"	1,200 "	March 27, 1886
Gorham H. Everbeck	270 Princeton st., E. B.	"	1,200 "	April 20, 1874
John J. Freeman	68 Bellevue st., Dor	"	1,200 "	Oct. 12, 1904
John H. Lidl	524 East Broadway, S. B.	"	1,200 "	April 8, 1895
Emil F. Liermann	428 Saratoga st., E. B	"	1,200 "	" 8, 1895
John J. McCarthy	46 Monmouth st., E. B.	"	1,200 "	Nov. 4, 1885
James Nannery	28 London st., E. B	"	1,200 "	Feb. 6, 1879
John F. O'Connor	439 Meridian st., E. B.	"	1,200 "	Dec. 24, 1884
William J. Shea	537 East Seventh st., S. B.	"	1,200 "	Nov. 8, 1895
Peter K. Smith	28 Gaylord st., Dor	"	1,200 "	May 20, 1880
Frederic J. Swendeman	30 Gibson st., Dor	"	1,200 "	July 11, 1904
Nicholas C. Tallon	83 Orleans st., E. B.	"	1,200 "	Oct. 11, 1881
Leslie Kierstead	6 Woodward Park st., Dor	Asst. Engineer	1,200 "	July 10, 1899
William Currie	167 Coleridge st., E. B	Fireman	3.00 day	June 10, 1900

Police Department.—Continued.

Name.	Residence.	Designation.	Compensation.	Date of Election or Appointment.

Division 8.—Concluded.

Name.	Residence.	Designation.	Compensation.	Date of Election or Appointment.
Michael Gannon	23 Morris st., E. B.	Fireman	$3.00 day	May 30, 1900
Robert S. Holmes	23 Chelsea st., E. B.	"	3.00 "	June 7, 1884
Joseph Kelly	12 Moulton st., Chsn.	"	3.00 "	Jan. 1, 1894
Johan P. Mattson	112 Falcon st., E. B.	"	3.00 "	April 10, 1908
Walter M. Miller	221 Saratoga st., E. B.	"	3.00 "	" 28, 1889
Duncan Miller	173 Coleridge st., E. B.	"	3.00 "	Oct. 12, 1892
Judah Crowell	27 Saratoga st., E. B.	Janitor	12.70 wk	June 14, 1894
George B. Blinn	53 Falcon st., E. B.	Fireman (temporary)	3.00 day	April 4, 1909

Division 9.

Name.	Residence.	Designation.	Compensation.	Date of Election or Appointment.
Thomas C. Evans	4 Windermere rd.	Captain	$2,525 yr	May 6, 1895
Charles H. Denton	4 Greenheys st.	Lieutenant	1,600 "	Jan. 4, 1902
William F. Perry	63 Minot st.	"	1,600 "	April 11, 1900
Charles F. Bannister	23 Concord sq.	Sergeant	1,400 "	Aug. 2, 1906
Wesley W. Chandler	27 Alaska st.	"	1,425 "	Sept. 11, 1907
Richard Fitzgerald	50 Elmira st.	"	1,400 "	March 28, 1908
James F. Hickey	144 Saratoga st.	"	1,400 "	Nov. 12, 1899
James E. Aherin	46 Sawyer ave.	Patrolman	1,200 "	Oct. 3, 1892
Wylie H. Benjamin	26 Thetford ave.	"	1,200 "	" 8, 1889
Tuffil Bostwick	85 Cushing ave.	"	1,200 "	June 1, 1892
Adolph F. Butterman	151 Stanwood st.	"	1,200 "	Nov. 8, 1895
Andrew Brauer	5 Metcalf st.	"	1,200 "	Dec. 24, 1901
John W. Carroll	37 Lyon st.	"	1,200 "	Jan. 1, 1904
Thomas Casey	3 Stanwood ter.	"	1,100 "	April 30, 1908
John J. Cashman	7 Tebroc st.	"	1,200 "	" 13, 1906
John J. Coffey	312 Washington st.	"	1,200 "	Nov. 6, 1891
Robert H. Connor	132 E. Cottage st.	"	1,200 "	April 4, 1891
Edward A. Dever	118 Eustis st.	"	1,200 "	Dec. 29, 1879
John W. Doherty	17 Rutherford ave.	"	1,200 "	July 30, 1896
John J. Donahue	33 Harold st.	"	1,200 "	" 11, 1904
George N. Durkee	rear 11A Forest st.	"	1,200 "	May 25, 1887
Michael J. Fitzgerald	12 Copps Hill ter.	"	1,200 "	Oct. 12, 1895
John T. Flatley	7 Mt. Vernon st.	"	1,200 "	Jan. 1, 1904
William A. Fraser	31 Bromley pk.	"	1,000 "	Dec. 17, 1908
Stephen J. Gillis	548 E. Fifth st.	"	1,100 "	March 30, 1908
Christopher Grant	170 Winthrop st.	"	1,000 "	Dec. 17, 1908
Timothy F. Graham	58 Glenway st.	"	1,200 "	Jan. 10, 1881
Albert S. Hendry	101 Princeton st.	"	1,000 "	Dec. 17, 1908
Frederick G. Higgins	46 Richfield st.	"	1,200 "	Sept. 21, 1900
Daniel J. Hines	5 Saco st.	"	1,200 "	Oct. 12, 1895
Charles W. Hoisington	689 Walk Hill st.	"	1,200 "	" 8, 1889
Michael F. Hunt	15 Holiday st.	"	1,200 "	" 12, 1895
Michael R. Hurley	58 Tolman st.	"	1,200 "	April 8, 1895
Samuel C. Hutchins	67 Walnut ave.	"	1,200 "	July 30, 1896
Timothy F. Killard	74 Roseclair st.	"	1,200 "	Nov. 8, 1895
Howard P. Kempton	11 Adams st.	"	1,200 "	Sept. 9, 1900
Willis M. Kempton	23 Thetford ave.	"	1,200 "	April 18, 1895
John F. Kenny	121 Dale st.	"	1,200 "	Nov. 21, 1895
Dennis Kerrigan	116 Howard ave.	"	1,200 "	" 8, 1895
Philip A. Keveney	21 Speedwell st.	"	1,200 "	July 11, 1904
Michael S. King	1 Harvest ter.	"	1,100 "	Jan. 7, 1908
Charles S. Kingsley	9 Morley st.	"	1,200 "	Aug. 7, 1901
Silas F. Kingsley	87 Bird st.	"	1,200 "	May 24, 1901
William H. Leonard	76 Hamilton st.	"	1,200 "	Aug. 8, 1888
David T. Long	90 Harrishof st.	"	1,200 "	Jan. 10, 1881
Bernard F. Lynch	97 Birch st.	"	1,200 "	Oct. 12, 1904
Martin J. Lyons	100 Arundel st.	"	1,200 "	March 2, 1905
George A. Mahoney	663 Columbia rd.	"	1,200 "	Dec. 24, 1901
John H. McCullough	19 Lyons st.	"	1,200 "	" 24, 1901
Daniel McDonald	14 East st.	"	1,200 "	Jan. 1, 1904
James McFarland	32 Howard ave.	"	1,200 "	Dec. 19, 1881
Edward McMahon	722 Dudley st.	"	1,200 "	April 15, 1906
Peter A. McNeil	231 Dudley st.	"	1,200 "	Feb. 13, 1902
Joseph H. Metcalf	330 Centre st.	"	1,200 "	June 2, 1887
James H. Mitchell	589 Dudley st.	"	1,200 "	Oct. 8, 1889
Albert Moran	49 Union Park st.	"	1,200 "	" 8, 1889
John Moran	82 Hamilton st.	"	1,200 "	March 19, 1883,
Charles H. Morse	95 Elmo st.	"	1,000 "	Dec. 17, 1908
John J. Mullen	339 Bowdoin st.	"	1,200 "	Aug. 7, 1901
James F. Mullins	47 E. Cottage st.	"	1,200 "	June 14, 1890
Thomas F. Mulrey	818 Canterbury st.	"	1,100 "	Feb. 13, 1908
Joseph F. Murphy	29 Worcester st.	"	1,200 "	July 11, 1891

Police Department.— Continued.

Name.	Residence.	Designation.	Compensation.	Date of Election or Appointment.

Division 9.— Concluded.

Name.	Residence.	Designation.	Compensation.	Date of Election or Appointment.
John E. Nowland	25 East st	Patrolman	$1,200 yr	March 23, 1899
Joseph C. Reiser	2 Mechanic st	"	1,000 "	Nov. 5, 1908
Cornelius J. Ring	159 Western ave	"	1,000 "	Jan. 14, 1909
Frank Rooney	94 Maywood st	"	1,200 "	April 24, 1905
James S. Ryan	20 East st	"	1,200 "	July 11, 1904
Thomas Ryan	8 Dorset st	"	1,000 "	Feb. 4, 1909
William J. Ryan	73 Delle ave	"	1,000 "	June 22, 1908
William H. Rymes	74 Tuttle st	"	1,200 "	Aug. 7, 1901
George S. Shattuck	61 Moreland st	"	1,200 "	Nov. 9, 1898
Thomas E. Smith	42 A st	"	1,200 "	Feb. 13, 1902
John J. Smith	37 Dewey st	"	1,200 "	Jan. 10, 1889
Joseph W. Smith	7 Brookford st	"	1,200 "	April 8, 1895
Frederick E. Stafford	36 Burgess st	"	1,200 "	" 8, 1895
William W. Steward	356 Dorchester st	"	1,200 "	Nov. 25, 1903
Thomas Sullivan	1 La Grange pl	"	1,200 "	Feb. 4, 1905
Henry C. Tanck	13 Rockland ave	"	1,200 "	April 19, 1889
Frederick J. Thorn	289 Dudley st	"	1,200 "	Sept. 19, 1900
Thomas M. Towle	30 Mead st	"	1,200 "	" 20, 1900
Andrew J. Walsh	44 W. Cedar st	"	1,200 "	March 28, 1904
John C. Williams	6 Josephine st	"	1,200 "	Aug. 7, 1906
James F. Wright	36 Church st	"	1,200 "	Oct. 8, 1889
Thomas E. Young	23 Folsom st	"	1,200 "	May 24, 1901
Maurice Zeeman	400 Centre st	"	1,100 "	Feb. 13, 1908
Francis P. Cronin	10 Everett st	Reserve Officer	2.00 day	Jan. 18, 1909
Ambrose M. Donahue	2 Mt. Washington pl	"	2.00 "	April 20, 1909
Michael Finnegan	16 Brighton st	"	2.00 "	Jan. 18, 1909
George A. Hughes	273 Broadway	"	2.25 "	April 29, 1908
George J. McNulty	46 Robinson st	"	2.00 "	Jan. 18, 1909
William A. Moore	2 Champney st	"	2.25 "	April 29, 1908
Israel Solomon	9 Michigan ave	"	2.00 "	" 20, 1909
Charles C. Taylor	61 Howard ave	"	2.00 "	Oct. 12, 1908
Charles E. Arris	4 Lewis pl	Janitor	14.00 wk	Dec. 22, 1905
Mary A. Lloyd	30 Vine st	Matron	7.98 "	" 25, 1886

Division 10.

Name.	Residence.	Designation.	Compensation.	Date of Election or Appointment.
John J. Hanley	7 Abbotsford st	Captain	$2,500 yr	Oct. 18, 1878
Rufus G. Fessenden	5 Hopestill st	Lieutenant	1,600 "	March 15, 1884
Albert F. Lovell	95 Blue Hill ave	"	1,600 "	April 6, 1886
William J. Sheehan	49 Homestead st	Sergeant	1,400 "	June 15, 1882
Joseph A. Cassidy	24 Newberg st	"	1,400 "	" 15, 1882
Charles B. Brazir	7 Browning ave	"	1,400 "	Oct. 23, 1886
Patrick J. O'Neil	92 Coleman st	"	1,400 "	Aug. 21, 1893
Delbert R. Augusta	121 Hill st	Patrolman	1,200 "	July 1, 1890
Arthur Bostwick	7 Glendale st	Reserve Officer	2.25 day	April 29, 1908
Harrison P. Bourie	79 Hunneman st	Patrolman	1,100 yr	March 11, 1907
John W. Boutilier	96 Day st	"	1,200 "	Jan. 14, 1904
Charles A. Bowers	48 Francis st	"	1,200 "	Aug. 4, 1896
William H. Burgess	75 Savin Hill ave	"	1,000 "	Oct. 14, 1907
Charles D. Burke	893 South st	"	1,200 "	March 28, 1885
Edward F. Byrne	21 Wyman st	"	1,200 "	" 30, 1903
Patrick Cassidy	6 Carmel st	"	1,200 "	Nov. 6, 1895
William F. Cassidy	147 Ashland st	"	1,200 "	" 10, 1898
Patrick J. Carr	282 Fourth st	Reserve Officer	2.00 day	April 20, 1909
James M. Carroll	52 Julian st	"	2.25 "	" 29, 1908
Walter Chalmers	7 Duncan st	"	2.25 "	" 29, 1908
Thomas F. Clarke	16 Eulita ter	"	2.00 "	June 22, 1908
William V. Chisholm	37 Cobden st	Patrolman	1,200 yr	Aug. 4, 1896
James Colbert	8 Wigglesworth st	"	1,200 "	Dec. 24, 1884
Robert M. Coughlin	64 Humboldt ave	"	1,200 "	Feb. 15, 1904
Arthur J. Creighton	16 Egleston st	"	1,200 "	July 11, 1904
Alfred H. Daniels	23A Highland st	"	1,200 "	Oct. 21, 1895
Gardner H. Davis	56 Northfield st	"	1,200 "	July 1, 1890
John B. Dolliver	13 Fairview st	"	1,200 "	March 26, 1900
Daniel J. F. Donovan	56 Johnson st	"	1,000 "	July 24, 1907
Dennis F. Driscoll	46 Norton st	Reserve Officer	2.00 day	Nov. 16, 1908
Joseph F. Eberlein	21 Tokio st	"	2.25 "	April 29, 1908
John F. Egan	39 E. Canton st	Patrolman	1,200 yr	Oct. 21, 1895
Andrew Fay	34 Creighton st	"	1,200 "	Jan. 18, 1893
Patrick Fitzmaurice	10 Gore st	"	1,200 "	July 24, 1905
Frank E. Gilman	102 Poplar st	"	1,100 "	May 9, 1906
Peter F. Grady	21 Atwood sq	Reserve Officer	2.00 day	April 20, 1909
Alfred W. Gray	21 Lambert ave	Patrolman	1,200 yr	March 7, 1903

Police Department.— Continued.

Name.	Residence.	Designation.	Compensation.	Date of Election or Appointment.

Division 10.— Concluded.

Name.	Residence.	Designation.	Compensation.	Date of Election or Appointment.
Michael J. Hartnett	131 W. Eighth st	Patrolman	$1,200 yr	May 29, 1898
Jeremiah S. Healey	3 Oswald st	"	1,200 "	Jan. 12, 1900
Warren D. Hewett	20 Rosemary st	"	1,200 "	Aug. 19, 1903
James Hickey	1624 Tremont st	Reserve Officer	2.25 day	April 29, 1908
Peter J. Hurley	514 Massachusetts ave	"	2.00 "	Nov. 16, 1908
William A. C. Hulbig	44 Loretto st	Patrolman	1,200 yr	" 27, 1903
Charles H. Jackson	49 Blue Hill ave	"	1,000 "	" 18, 1907
George A. Johnson	10 Howland st	Reserve Officer	2.25 day	April 29, 1908
Roy F. Jordan	38 Aldrich st	Patrolman	1,200 yr	Nov. 26, 1901
William W. Jordan	7 Morley st	"	1,200 "	July 9, 1891
Michael A. Kelley	55 Circuit st	"	1,200 "	Jan. 18, 1893
George M. Kelley	4 Cathedral st	Reserve Officer	2.00 day	" 18, 1909
John W. Kilday	14 Linwood sq	Patrolman	1,200 "	June 1, 1893
Matthew Killen	53 Creighton st	"	1,200 "	Dec. 14, 1898
Patrick H. Kirley	93 Quincy st	"	1,200 "	Aug. 4, 1896
James Knowles	60 Wyman st	"	1,200 "	March 19, 1883
Alfred F. Leavitt	5 May st	"	1,200 "	" 7, 1903
George E. Lewis	53 Adams st	"	1,200 "	Nov. 4, 1885
Thomas F. Lyons	21 Elmore st	"	1,200 "	Jan. 30, 1904
Timothy F. McCarthy	17 Rosemary st	"	1,200 "	Nov. 10, 1904
Bernard P. McGarry	15 Spaulding st	"	1,200 "	April 11, 1895
Joseph J. McGillivray	151 Hillside st	"	1,200 "	Dec. 1, 1897
James L. McGovern	53 Hillside st	"	1,200 "	" 29, 1879
Thomas F. J. McGrade	20 Alexander st	Reserve Officer	2.00 day	Nov. 16, 1908
Daniel R. McLean	15 Kilton st	Patrolman	1,000 yr	" 18, 1907
James H. McLean	46 Guild st	"	1,200 "	Jan. 18, 1893
Dennis L. Murphy	13 Sachem st	"	1,200 "	Aug. 4, 1899
William H. Murphy	47 Hillside st	"	1,200 "	June 14, 1886
Edward H. Murtagh	15 Santuit st	"	1,200 "	Feb. 28, 1901
Edward T. Norton	12 Grover ave	"	1,200 "	Nov. 21, 1905
Michael J. Nugent	23 Dorr st	"	1,200 "	June 5, 1877
Richard J. O'Day	7 Bellflower st	"	1,200 "	March 29, 1886
Alexander D. O'Handley	156 Hillside st	"	1,200 "	April 27, 1900
Daniel P. O'Neill	5 Carson st	"	1,100 "	July 24, 1905
Henry A. Petit	10 Creighton st	"	1,000 "	" 22, 1907
George E. Plummer	24 Day st	"	1,200 "	April 11, 1895
Benjamin L. Powers	9 Hillside st	"	1,200 "	March 7, 1903
Michael J. Reardon	33 Howell st	"	1,200 "	" 30, 1903
Donald J. Reynolds	55 Spring Park ave	"	1,200 "	Feb. 1, 1881
Charles J. Riley	7 Linwood sq	"	1,200 "	Oct. 5, 1900
Frederick M. Rooney	11 Elmore st	"	1,200 "	Nov. 10, 1898
Gustave Rosenfeld	59 Bartlett st	"	1,200 "	March 28, 1885
Martin J. Rush	13 Mark st	"	1,200 "	Aug. 7, 1901
Clifford E. Smith	36 Burgess st	"	1,200 "	March 7, 1903
Arthur R. Smith	328 Lincoln st	Reserve Officer	2.00 day	June 22, 1908
Daniel F. Sullivan	1142 Dorchester ave	Patrolman	1,200 yr	May 1, 1895
Frank V. Sullivan	57 Eustis st	"	1,100 "	Nov. 12, 1906
John J. Sullivan	6 Beach st	"	1,100 "	Feb. 9, 1905
Michael Sullivan	125 Hillside st	"	1,200 "	Nov. 26, 1901
Daniel Thompson	23 Wigglesworth st	"	1,200 "	Aug. 4, 1896
Patrick J. Trainor	54 Savin st	"	1,000 "	Dec. 9, 1907
William H. Turner	14 Dorr st	"	1,200 "	Nov. 6, 1895
Ulysses G. Varney	6 Romar ter	"	1,200 "	Aug. 4, 1896
Charles J. Wallace	19 Dracut st	"	1,200 "	May 19, 1905
Bartholomew D. Winn	43 Mt. Vernon st	Reserve Officer	2.00 day	Nov. 16, 1908
William E. Wiseman	86 Humboldt ave	Patrolman	1,200 yr	March 20, 1893
John A. Wragg	62 Shepton st	"	1,200 "	Nov. 12, 1892
Martin Feltis	8 Bicknell ave	Janitor	15.25 wk	Oct. 10, 1898
Catherine E. Regan	221 Cabot st	Matron	7.98 "	" 17, 1907

Division 11.

Name.	Residence.	Designation.	Compensation.	Date of Election or Appointment.
Clarence A. Swan	42 Rosseter st	Captain	$2,500 yr	March 3, 1905
Oscar H. Peare	6 Windermere rd	Lieutenant	1,600 "	Jan. 5, 1893
James E. Sanford	16 Linden st., S. B	"	1,000 "	Feb. 8, 1908
Harrison B. Vinal	715 Walk Hill st	Sergeant	1,400 "	March 23, 1881
John J. Keefe	27 Mt. Vernon st., Chsn	"	1,400 "	Jan. 5, 1893
James E. Pendergast	64 Auckland st	"	1,400 "	Oct. 21, 1893
Charles Maynes	16 Folsom st	"	1,400 "	Dec. 24, 1895
Frederick Schlehuber	9 Vinson st	"	1,400 "	Feb. 8, 1905
John T. O'Hearn	18 Holiday st	"	1,400 "	" 8, 1908
Edgar F. Palmer	170 Dudley st	"	1,400 "	Dec. 17, 1908

Police Department.— Continued.

Name.	Residence.	Designation.	Com-pensation.	Date of Election or Appointment.

Division 11.—Continued.

Name.	Residence.	Designation.	Com-pensation.	Date of Election or Appointment.
Amasa E. Augusta	1543 Dorchester ave	Patrolman	$1,225 yr	July 30, 1896
William Balch	85 Capen st	"	1,200 "	Nov. 25, 1895
John E. Bride	129 Draper st	"	1,200 "	April 18, 1895
John H. Brown	77 Harbor View st	"	1,200 "	" 15, 1895
George A. Burrill	61A Bailey st	"	1,200 "	Oct. 29, 1906
Everett E. Chandler	393 Adams st	"	1,200 "	April 8, 1895
Thomas W. Chisholm	51 Speedwell st	"	1,200 "	Dec. 24, 1901
Lyman H. Clark	15 Minot pl	"	1,200 "	" 29, 1892
John C. E. Clarke	107 Maxwell st	"	1,200 "	Oct. 31, 1901
William S. Cumings	12 Draper st	"	1,200 "	Dec. 21, 1882
John Coffey	75 Glenway st	"	1,200 "	July 20, 1900
James G. Curtis	68 Dix st	"	1,200 "	Oct. 8, 1889
John M. Devine	19 Sagamore st	"	1,200 "	Dec. 24, 1901
Benjamin F. Danforth	34 Sagamore st	"	1,200 "	Oct. 8, 1908
Michael J. Devin	73 Moseley st	"	1,200 "	Sept. 2, 1902
Thomas J. Dillon	17 Temple st	"	1,200 "	March 28, 1885
Leroy W. Dinsmore	15 Centre st	"	1,200 "	Aug. 10, 1880
Bernard Doherty	230 Boston st	"	1,200 "	July 30, 1896
Charles H. Doherty	12 Elmore st., Rox	"	1,200 "	Jan. 18, 1881
William J. Doherty	438 Fourth st., S. B.	"	1,200 "	Nov. 8, 1895
John S. Donahue	68 Draper st	"	1,200 "	April 4, 1891
Daniel F. Dunn	98 Richmond st	"	1,200 "	June 30, 1894
George A. Durgin	84 Alexander st	"	1,200 "	July 1, 1895
Edward J. Eustace	43 Clarkson st	"	1,200 "	Nov. 9, 1898
George L. Fenderson	30 Saxton st	"	1,200 "	July 30, 1896
James H. Flood	16 Champney pl., Rox	"	1,200 "	April 8, 1895
Thomas Gallagher	83 Norton st	"	1,200 "	June 15, 1893
Charles W. Gardner	699 E. Sixth st., S. B.	"	1,200 "	Oct. 21, 1884
Thomas A. Gibbs	40 Westville st	"	1,200 "	Jan. 30, 1905
Edward C. Goode	29 Carson st	"	1,200 "	May 24, 1901
Albert F. Gould	124 Glenway st	"	1,200 "	June 19, 1888
Charles W. Gray	10 Hunter st	"	1,200 "	April 8, 1895
James E. Halligan	45 Shirley st., Rox	"	1,200 "	" 8, 1895
William A. Harrington	15 Idaho st	"	1,200 "	" 8, 1895
Charles J. Haskins	12 Downer ct	"	1,200 "	Nov. 25, 1901
George E. Hawthorne	1164 Adams st	"	1,200 "	April 8, 1895
Walter F. Higgins	24 Perrin st	"	1,200 "	Nov. 21, 1895
Charles Hill	160 Hillside st	"	1,200 "	Jan. 10, 1899
Duncan Hunter	86 Milton st	"	1,200 "	Nov. 9, 1895
James W. Kelley	421 Blue Hill ave	"	1,200 "	Dec. 24, 1884
George D. Kennedy	46 Oak ave	"	1,200 "	April 24, 1901
Richard H. Leary	41 L st., S. B.	"	1,200 "	March 29, 1886
William T. Lewis	85½ High st., Chsn.	"	1,200 "	Oct. 15, 1881
John F. Lindsay	Cor. Highland and East sts.	"	1,200 "	" 12, 1895
John J. Lynch	384 Geneva ave	"	1,200 "	April 28, 1873
Edward C. Maguire	2767 Washington st	"	1,200 "	" 4, 1891
George B. Maxim	60 Rockville st	"	1,200 "	Dec. 29, 1879
William J. McDermott	78 Edson st	"	1,200 "	April 27, 1894
Patrick J. McNealy	21 Albion st	"	1,200 "	" 18, 1895
Henry S. Meyers	699 Walk Hill st	"	1,200 "	Jan. 5, 1893
John C. Miller	162 Bowdoin st	"	1,200 "	" 5, 1893
George H. Munier	74 Astoria st	"	1,200 "	Oct. 8, 1889
William A. Murdoch	2187 Dorchester ave	"	1,200 "	" 11, 1895
James J. Murrin	120 Milton st	"	1,200 "	March 16, 1901
William H. Noble	303 Freeport st	"	1,200 "	Oct. 29, 1906
Nathan W. Nutting	180 Adams st	"	1,200 "	Nov. 9, 1898
Bartholomew A. O'Brien	7 Copeland st	"	1,200 "	Aug. 28, 1894
Charles B. Patten	29 Dorset st	"	1,200 "	May 9, 1906
Edwin Piper	26 Grosvenor rd	"	1,200 "	April 23, 1873
Michael J. Quirk	30 Speedwell st	"	1,200 "	March 22, 1900
Stephen J. Rafferty	36 Holiday st	"	1,200 "	April 8, 1895
Wiswall W. Randolph	94 Harvard st	"	1,200 "	Nov. 21, 1895
Cornelius J. Reardon	31 Greenwich st	"	1,200 "	Feb. 26, 1899
James A. Rogers	45 Woodcliff st	"	1,200 "	April 8, 1895
Peter H. Rogers	19 Adams st	"	1,200 "	Dec. 8, 1899
Frank J. Sanders	4 Conrad st	"	1,200 "	Oct. 25, 1894
Fred W. Seavey	253 Westville st	"	1,200 "	April 23, 1883
Peter J. Sheehan	47 Clarkson st	"	1,200 "	" 29, 1899
Lewis G. Smith	78 Fowler st	"	1,200 "	" 8, 1894
Thomas J. F. Smith	72 Milton ave	"	1,200 "	Oct. 31, 1900
Fred C. Spargo	53 Mallet st	"	1,200 "	April 23, 1896
Herbert E. Stevens	32 Saxton st	"	1,200 "	Sept. 21, 1900
William L. Stinson	268 Neponset ave	"	1,200 "	Dec. 30, 1889

Police Department.— Continued.

Name.	Residence.	Designation.	Compensation.	Date of Election or Appointment.
Division 11.— Concluded.				
James H. Waldron	36 Howell st	Patrolman	$1,200 yr	Feb. 26, 1899
William B. Walker	11 Victoria st	"	1,200 "	Oct. 8, 1889
Freeman C. Webber	25 Edison green	"	1,200 "	Sept. 12, 1900
Patrick J. Williams	9 Vaughn st	"	1,200 "	April 8, 1895
Arthur C. Cooper	103 Templeton st	"	1,000 "	Nov. 5, 1908
Frederick D. Donovan	30 Oakview ter	"	1,000 "	Dec. 17, 1908
Thomas J. Hagan	2654 Washington st	"	1,000 "	June 23, 1908
Daniel F. McLaughlin	23 Arcadia pk	"	1,000 "	Sept. 17, 1908
William C. Norton	16 Wensley st	"	1,000 "	Dec. 17, 1908
Michael O'Neil	19 Buckman st	"	1,000 "	Jan. 14, 1909
Michael J. O'Rourke	53 Marcella st	"	1,000 "	Nov. 5, 1908
Frederick A. Sullivan	150A Blue Hill ave	"	1,000 "	June 22, 1908
Alfred Boucher	5 Kenney st	Reserve Officer	2.25 day	April 29, 1908
Joseph Cohen	207 Blue Hill ave	"	2.25 "	" 29, 1908
Angus W. Dakin	11 Copeland st	"	2.00 "	Oct. 12, 1908
George H. Delaney	rear 3886 Washington st	"	2.00 "	Jan. 18, 1909
John T. Edwards	96 Marcella st	"	2.00 "	Nov. 16, 1908
William F. Foley	432 W. Second st	"	2.00 "	" 16, 1908
John J. Gale	15 Dorset st	"	2.25 "	April 29, 1908
James F. McInnis	27 O st	"	2.25 "	" 29, 1908
John J. Ridge	660 Eighth st	"	2.00 "	" 20, 1909
Richard F. Warren	23 Hamlet st	"	2.00 "	Jan. 18, 1909
William S. Workman	10 James st	"	2.00 "	" 18, 1909
Walter J. Hickey	705 Washington st	Hostler	14.00 wk	April 4, 1902
John J. Sullivan	66 Leonard st	"	14.00 "	July, 1898
Mary Welch	76 Granger st	Janitress	12.70 "	Feb., 1894
Elizabeth Nash	280 Hancock st	"	7.25 "	May, 1904
Addie Short	18 Oakland st	"	7.25 "	May 2, 1887
Harriet C. McIntire	14 Charles st	Matron	3.84 "	Feb., 1888
Division 12.				
William J. Lowery	36 Pratt st	Captain	$2,500 yr	Aug. 24, 1903
Hiram H. Rich	98 Crawford st	Lieutenant	1,600 "	July 14, 1888
Daniel F. Eagan	20 Wigglesworth st	"	1,600 "	April 25, 1907
James J. Walkins	93 Munroe st	Sergeant	1,400 "	June 23, 1894
William J. Allison	297 Bennington st	"	1,400 "	May 2, 1905
James J. Cratty	136 Kittredge st	"	1,400 "	" 5, 1905
Frederick N. Wheeler	52 Story st	"	1,400 "	Feb. 8, 1908
John Armstrong	60 Allen st	Patrolman	1,200 "	Aug. 7, 1901
Frederick E. Bostwick	163 Devon st	"	1,200 "	Nov. 4, 1890
William E. Brace	30 Dorset st	"	1,200 "	Oct. 21, 1882
William H. Caswell	227 Westville st	"	1,200 "	June 15, 1882
Patrick Corbett	10 I st	"	1,200 "	May 20, 1880
Wilson F. Crane	12 Bird st	"	1,200 "	Sept. 11, 1900
Michael J. Cronin	125 W. Sixth st	"	1,200 "	Nov. 4, 1885
Harry G. Dow	15 Hendry st	"	1,000 "	Jan. 14, 1909
Denis J. Dowd	510 E. Sixth st	"	1,200 "	Oct. 21, 1882
Edward J. Drew	913 E. Second st	"	1,200 "	" 11, 1890
Clarence M. Dunbar	8 Doris st	"	1,200 "	April 9, 1889
Perry W. Eaton	rear 553 Sixth st	"	1,200 "	Aug. 27, 1906
William J. Farrell	326 K st	"	1,200 "	" 7, 1900
John H. Ferguson	198 W. Selden st	"	1,200 "	July 30, 1896
John Flynn	36 Maywood st	"	1,200 "	" 30, 1896
Hugh F. Garrity	317 Norfolk ave	"	1,100 "	Feb. 13, 1908
Charles W. Glynn	887 E. Fourth st	"	1,200 "	May 8, 1875
Peter P. Golden	8 Concord st	"	1,000 "	Sept. 17, 1908
Patrick A. Grady	606 Broadway	"	1,000 "	Dec. 17, 1908
Michael J. Greeley	868 E. Fifth st	"	1,200 "	April 9, 1887
William E. Hagan	93 Old Harbor st	"	1,200 "	Oct. 20, 1904
Frank G. Hale	1021 Dorchester ave	"	1,200 "	April 29, 1904
Andrew J. Hurley	11 Monument sq	"	1,000 "	Jan. 14, 1909
William H. Innis	9 Charles st	"	1,200 "	Oct. 18, 1878
James S. Keating	140 Trenton st	"	1,000 "	Dec. 17, 1908
Thomas M. Keenan	40 Middle st	"	1,200 "	April 8, 1895
Nahum J. Kidder	476 E. Fourth st	"	1,200 "	Dec. 24, 1884
Henry W. Laskey	312 Bremen st	"	1,000 "	Feb. 4, 1909
Edward H. Mahoney	235 Saratoga st	"	1,200 "	March 19, 1883
John C. McDonald	400 Centre st	"	1,200 "	July 11, 1904
Joseph W. F. McDonough	287 C st	"	1,200 "	April 25, 1907
John McLean	614 E. Sixth st	"	1,200 "	Nov. 21, 1895
Kenneth McLeod	59 Barry st	"	1,200 "	July 11, 1893
John M. Mernin	38 High st	"	1,200 "	Nov. 1, 1900

Police Department.— Continued.

Name.	Residence.	Designation.	Com-pensation.	Date of Election or Appointment.

Division 12.— Concluded.

Name.	Residence.	Designation.	Com-pensation.	Date of Election or Appointment.
William J. Moore	653 E. Sixth st.	Patrolman	$1,200 yr.	Nov. 3, 1893
Patrick A. Moynihan	3 Phillips st.	"	1,200 "	July 21, 1905
Thomas F. Ryan	7 Dewey st.	"	1,200 "	Oct. 29, 1906
William H. Ryan	106 Northampton st.	"	1,200 "	April 25, 1905
George V. Scanlan	131 Falcon st.	"	1,100 "	" 29, 1908
Peter J. Schricker	56 Millwood st.	"	1,200 "	Jan. 14, 1904
Philip B. Smith	20 Darling st.	"	1,200 "	April 25, 1905
John H. Spratt	773 E. Fourth st.	"	1,200 "	May 25, 1894
Charles A. Stickney	97 P st.	"	1,200 "	June 4, 1897
Orrington Waugh	1786 Washington st.	"	1,200 "	" 12, 1905
Emmons F. Winslow	17 Pleasant ter.	"	1,100 "	Nov. 7, 1907
John J. Carew	82 E. Newton st.	Reserve Officer	2.00 day	June 22, 1908
Thomas J. Crocker	88 Russell st.	"	2.25 "	April 29, 1908
John A. Dorsey	11A Pine Hill ave.	"	2.00 "	June 22, 1908
John J. Ford	94 Milton st.	"	2.25 "	April 29, 1908
Charles S. Gordon	515 Geneva ave.	"	2.00 "	" 20, 1909
William J. Hayes	15 Shannon st.	"	2.25 "	" 29, 1908
Frank J. Kuhlman	276 Prescott st.	"	2.00 "	June 22, 1908
Patrick J. Lydon	16 Roach st.	"	2.25 "	April 29, 1908
William S. McKendry	8 Princeton st.	"	2.00 "	June 22, 1908
Elmer F. Rider	60 Rockwell st.	"	2.25 "	April 29, 1908
James A. Tahaney	67 Chambers st.	"	2.00 "	Jan. 18, 1909
James A. Wallace	288 Chelsea st.	"	2.00 "	June 22, 1908
Catherine E. Hurley	532 E. Fifth st.	Janitress	12.70 wk.	July 11, 1898
Susan L. Finn	101 D st.	Matron	7.98 "	June 1, 1900

Division 13.

Name.	Residence.	Designation.	Com-pensation.	Date of Election or Appointment.
George W. Wescott	59 Bainbridge st., Rox.	Captain	$2,500 yr.	Nov. 13, 1893
Herman B. Bodenschatz	86 Temple st., W. Rox.	Lieutenant	1,600 "	March 20, 1899
William Fottler	72 Dudley st., Rox.	"	1,600 "	Jan. 5, 1893
Frank Arnold	1 Clarendon pk., Ros.	Sergeant	1,400 "	" 8, 1902
Thomas F. Busby	111 Sheridan st., J. P.	"	1,400 "	Feb. 16, 1899
Henry Fetridge	48 Humboldt ave., Rox.	"	1,400 "	March 3, 1905
Charles A. Gilman	17 Cohasset st., Ros.	"	1,400 "	July 1, 1895
John J. Good	31 Newbern st., Rox.	"	1,400 "	Feb. 8, 1908
William J. Hennessey	17 Holborn st., Rox.	"	1,400 "	Oct. 25, 1899
William H. Rideout	21 Aldrich st., Ros.	"	1,400 "	April 16, 1891
Frank H. Thompson	111 Wheaton ave., Dor.	"	1,400 "	" 25, 1907
George W. Bacher	82 Nelson st., Dor.	Patrolman	1,200 "	Nov. 8, 1895
John D. Becker	44 Bradford ave., Ros.	"	1,200 "	May 18, 1903
Francis H. Bertrand	61 South st., J. P.	"	1,200 "	Feb. 13, 1902
Frederick G. Brauer	85 Dudley ave., Ros.	"	1,200 "	Oct. 30, 1900
Frank Brock	1991 Centre st., W. R.	"	1,200 "	June 14, 1882
Louis Brown, Jr.	4191 Washington st., Ros.	"	1,200 "	Aug. 15, 1899
Seymour C. Butler	40 Holborn st., Rox.	"	1,200 "	" 7, 1906
Watson W. H. Cook	2 Willis ter., Rox.	"	1,200 "	Nov. 1, 1900
David Coburn	21 Seaverns ave., J. P.	"	1,200 "	June 2, 1874
James A. Cullen	29 Marcella st., Rox.	"	1,200 "	April 25, 1907
Thomas F. Dolan	30 Keyes st., J. P.	"	1,200 "	March 17, 1901
Joseph A. Delaney	3886 Washington st.	"	1,200 "	May 4, 1891
William O. Dupee	134 Walter st., Ros.	"	1,200 "	April 20, 1895
James H. Egan	141 Chestnut ave., J. P.	"	1,200 "	Oct. 29, 1906
John W. Forbes	16 Millmont st., Rox.	"	1,200 "	May 24, 1901
Herbert S. Ford	20 Metcalf st., Ros.	"	1,200 "	Jan. 10, 1881
William R. Forde	218 Wren st., W. R.	"	1,200 "	Dec. 19, 1891
William M. Frank	13 Lester pl., J. P.	"	1,200 "	May 27, 1893
Andrew J. Gemmel	32 Tappan st., Ros.	"	1,200 "	Nov. 8, 1895
Timothy F. Gleason	211 South st., J. P.	"	1,200 "	" 10, 1905
Jeremiah Hayes	3 Kingsbury st., Rox.	"	1,200 "	Oct. 31, 1881
Thomas Hensey	35 Green st., J. P.	"	1,200 "	Dec. 29, 1879
Nicholas Herthel, Jr.	51 Boylston st., J. P.	"	1,200 "	July 30, 1896
Gustav F. Hollstein	69 Albano st., Ros.	"	1,200 "	Oct. 20, 1904
Joseph O. Hodgkins	17 Rosemary st., J. P.	"	1,200 "	April 8, 1895
James A. Howes	2 Herbert st., Dor.	"	1,200 "	" 8, 1895
Edmund R. Inglis	95 Brown ave., Ros.	"	1,200 "	Aug. 7, 1906
Lawrence T. Kane	2163 Centre st., W. R.	"	1,200 "	Nov. 14, 1883
Charles E. Keith	6 Erie pl., J. P.	"	1,200 "	Oct. 25, 1899
John T. Kelly	7 New Heath st., Rox.	"	1,200 "	April 4, 1891
George E. Keyes	85 Dudley ave., Ros.	"	1,200 "	Oct. 16, 1902
William T. Kirley	33 Ashfield st., Ros.	"	1,200 "	April 23, 1896
William N. H. Knight	29 Green st., J. P.	"	1,200 "	Nov. 4, 1885

Police Department. — Continued.

Name.	Residence	Designation.	Compensation.	Date of Election or Appointment.

Division 13. — Concluded.

Name.	Residence	Designation.	Compensation.	Date
William A. Lyons	34 Keyes st., J. P.	Patrolman	$1,200 yr.	March 6, 1903
Reuben Marsh	11 Goldsmith st., J. P.	"	1,200 "	May 8, 1875
John McAdams	71 Hyde Park ave	"	1,200 "	Nov. 8, 1895
John J. McCarthy	122 Brown ave., Ros	"	1,200 "	" 1, 1894
John H. McDonald	20 Rosemary st., J. P.	"	1,200 "	June 4, 1897
John F. McLain	26 Pleasant st., W. Rox	"	1,200 "	Jan. 1, 1904
Frederick W. Miller	43 Peter Parley rd., J. P.	"	1,200 "	July 1, 1895
James T. Monahan	3578 Washington st., J. P.	"	1,200 "	April 24, 1907
William H. Morris	11 Tappan st., Ros	"	1,200 "	Jan. 30, 1905
Lewis R. Morrison	176 Bowdoin st., Dor	"	1,200 "	Aug. 10, 1892
Robert A. F. Morse	96 Montebello rd., J. P.	"	1,200 "	April 19, 1889
James J. Mullin	5 Clarendon pk	"	1,200 "	July 20, 1901
Edward J. Murphy	1525 Centre st., W. R	"	1,200 "	Jan. 5, 1893
Herbert Murray	11 Germania st., J. P.	"	1,200 "	July 16, 1903
Isaac T. Myers	8 Enfield st., J. P.	"	1,200 "	May 18, 1903
William J. Noonan	21 Fletcher st., Ros	"	1,200 "	July 30, 1896
William P. O'Brien	19 Rosemary st., J. P.	"	1,200 "	Dec. 9, 1899
James M. O'Sullivan	73 Jamaica st., J. P.	"	1,200 "	Feb. 9, 1905
Fred A. Pulsifer	17 Thomas st., J. P.	"	1,200 "	July 30, 1896
Frank J. Rich	20 Congreve st., Ros	"	1,200 "	Aug. 13, 1887
James Riley	24 Dalrymple st., J. P.	"	1,200 "	July 1, 1895
George Riley	2041 Columbus ave	"	1,200 "	" 1, 1895
Charles B. Ryan	112 Brown ave., Ros	"	1,200 "	" 30, 1896
Andrew Shannon	59 Farrington st., W. R	"	1,200 "	Feb. 27, 1879
Joseph L. Snow	15 Brown ave., Ros	"	1,200 "	May 18, 1903
Ira W. Stevens	40 Sherwood st., Ros	"	1,200 "	" 25, 1874
Patrick J. Sullivan	15 Alaric st., W. Rox	"	1,200 "	" 20, 1880
William C. M. Tilton	31 Garden st., W. Rox	"	1,200 "	April 8, 1895
William H. Wallace	13 Prospect ave., Ros	"	1,200 "	Nov. 6, 1895
Edward F. Welsh	57 Sycamore st., Ros	"	1,200 "	Aug. 10, 1904
Harvey T. Wood	283 Chestnut ave., J. P.	"	1,200 "	Feb. 11, 1879
Dennis J. Buckley	5 Clarendon pk., Ros	"	1,100 "	Sept. 11, 1907
John H. McCabe	1567A Tremont st., Rox	"	1,100 "	July 20, 1907
Patrick McGuckian	rear 23 Anawan ave., Ros	"	1,100 "	June 1, 1907
George R. Hilton	2 Romar ter	"	1,100 "	Oct. 9, 1907
John J. Brearton	781 Shawmut ave	"	1,000 "	Jan. 14, 1909
James Greer	24 Clifton st., Rox	"	1,000 "	" 14, 1909
Dennis T. Lordan	1451 Tremont st	"	1,000 "	Dec. 17, 1908
Daniel F. L. McLaughlin	39 Folsom st	"	1,000 "	Feb. 4, 1909
Albert J. Nott	186 Neponset ave., Dor	"	1,000 "	Nov. 5, 1908
John P. O'Neil	56 Calumet st	"	1,000 "	Feb. 4, 1909
Thomas P. Thompson	24 Mountain ave., Dor	"	1,000 "	Sept. 17, 1908
Jeremiah F. Buckley	1 Wise st	Reserve Officer	2.25 day	April 29, 1908
Frederick W. Copithorn	72 Lexington st., Chsn	"	2.25 "	" 29, 1908
Joseph N. Flanagan	23 Glenwood st., Rox	"	2.25 "	" 29, 1908
James Goode	1346 Tremont st	"	2.25 "	" 29, 1908
Richard O'Hern	482 Geneva ave., Dor	"	2.25 "	" 29, 1908
Leonard M. Pike	6 Harrison pk., Dor	"	2.25 "	" 29, 1908
Joseph F. Quilty	58 Carolina ave., J. P.	"	2.25 "	" 29, 1908
Thomas N. Trainor	50 Monument sq., Chsn	"	2.25 "	" 29, 1908
Walter F. Welsh	37 Sackville st., Chsn	"	2.25 "	" 29, 1908
William J. Barrett	38 Shannon st., Bri	"	2.00 "	" 20, 1909
Patrick Cullen	9 Sachem st., Rox	"	2.00 "	Jan. 18, 1909
Owen A. Katon	15 Warren pl., Rox	"	2.00 "	Nov. 16, 1908
Michael F. Kennedy	43 Longwood ave., Rox	"	2.00 "	June 22, 1908
Walter B. King	16 Taber st., Rox	"	2.00 "	Nov. 16, 1908
Henry A. Lueth	93 Bragdon st., Rox	"	2.00 "	" 16, 1908
John V. Marena	86 Eustis st., Rox	"	2.00 "	April 20, 1909
Richard Murphy	2806 Washington st	"	2.00 "	Nov. 16, 1908
Francis Scanlan	47 Roxbury st., Rox	"	2.00 "	April 20, 1909
John W. Shone	111 Dale st., Rox	"	2.00 "	Oct. 12, 1908
Dominick F. Spellman	62 New Heath st., Rox	"	2.00 "	Nov. 16, 1908
Wallace W. Brown	31 Green st., J. P.	Hostler	17.00 wk.	April 29, 1895
Patrick F. Toland	146 Chelsea st., Chsn	"	14.00 "	Dec. 11, 1904
William J. Fleming	185 W. Seventh st	Janitor	14.00 "	Nov. 16, 1908
Nora A. Hurley	90 Call st., J. P.	Janitress	12.70 "	Dec. 24, 1901
Lizzie C. Hurley	90 Call st., J. P.	Matron	3.84 "	Feb., 1886

Division 14.

Name	Residence	Designation	Compensation	Date
Philemon D. Warren	733 Cambridge st., Bri	Captain	$2,500 yr.	May 18, 1874
Michael O'Neil	24 Oakley st., Dor	Lieutenant	1,600 "	Dec. 20, 1899
John F. Dobbyn	70 Pearl st., Chsn	"	1,600 "	Feb. 8, 1905

Police Department.— Continued.

Name.	Residence.	Designation.	Compensation.	Date of Election or Appointment.

Division 14.— Concluded.

Thomas M. Mullen	20 Bentley st., Bri.	Sergeant	$1,400 yr	Oct. 23, 1894
Patrick Byrne	60 Allen st., city	"	1,400 "	May 2, 1903
Ernest R. Taylor	59 Fairbanks st., Bri.	"	1,400 "	Aug. 24, 1903
Harry C. Berry	16 Seaver st., Chsn	"	1,425 "	April 4, 1908
Frederick A. Acorn	5 Everett sq., Bri.	Patrolman	1,200 "	Nov. 25, 1903
Albert N. Bates	39 Pratt st., Bri.	"	1,200 "	July 6, 1875
Augustine E. Beliveau	30 Chestnut st., Chsn	"	1,000 "	Jan. 14, 1909
Michael F. Blewitt	164 Putnam st., E. B.	"	1,000 "	Dec. 17, 1908
Edwin F. Briggs	35 Allston st., Bri.	"	1,200 "	Jan. 4, 1894
Willie H. Burns	26 Arlington st., Bri.	"	1,200 "	July 1, 1895
Carl Carlstein	19 Norway st.	"	1,200 "	Nov. 21, 1895
Cornelius J. Coakley	Harriet st., Bri.	"	1,200 "	April 23, 1896
Francis W. Curry	67 Surrey st., Bri.	"	1,200 "	Aug. 21, 1878
John T. Dolan	161 Union st., Bri.	"	1,200 "	Jan. 5, 1893
Kieran Duffy	11 Hunnewell st., Bri.	"	1,200 "	April 27, 1901
John T. Foynes	56 Winship st., Bri.	"	1,200 "	Nov. 6, 1895
John B. Gildea	110 Murdock st., Bri.	"	1,200 "	June 12, 1905
John A. Gleeson	175 Union st., Bri.	"	1,200 "	Dec. 21, 1882
Francis A. Gorman	76 Paris st., E. B.	"	1,000 "	Feb. 4, 1909
Thomas E. Hamilton	605 Bennington st., E. B.	"	1,000 "	Sept. 17, 1908
Thomas P. Higgins	24 Wexford st., Bri.	"	1,200 "	April 13, 1906
Asa G. Howland	35 Pratt st., Bri.	"	1,200 "	Sept. 19, 1900
Morgan F. Kelleher	30 Mead st., Chsn	"	1,000 "	Feb. 4, 1909
William E. Lowell	50 Fairbanks st., Bri.	"	1,200 "	Oct. 4, 1891
Patrick Malley	51 Montfern ave., Bri.	"	1,200 "	" 8, 1889
Bartholomew Merchant	42 Waverley st., Bri.	"	1,200 "	Sept. 20, 1900
Michael J. Muldoon	77 Arlington st., Bri.	"	1,200 "	April 6, 1895
Frank W. Osborn	179 Foster st., Bri.	"	1,200 "	Nov. 5, 1881
Chester E. Pierce	121 Parsons st., Bri.	"	1,200 "	Oct. 12, 1895
Thomas J. Quinan	50 Winship st., Bri.	"	1,200 "	April 14, 1906
William B. Quinan	114 Murdock st., Bri.	"	1,200 "	March 3, 1905
Maurice P. Ryan	74 Spring st., Bri.	"	1,200 "	Dec. 24, 1906
Sumner F. Starbird	141 Foster st., Bri.	"	1,200 "	" 21, 1889
Daniel F. Sullivan	52 Dustin st., Bri.	"	1,200 "	Nov. 6, 1895
Frank J. Shaughnessy	21 Etna st., Bri.	"	1,100 "	Feb. 13, 1908
William Scott	22 Eulita ter., Bri.	"	1,200 "	Nov. 9, 1898
Daniel F. Sugrue	20 Dell ave., Rox.	"	1,200 "	Feb. 13, 1902
Louis H. Stewart	449 Bennington st., E. B.	"	1,000 "	Dec. 17, 1908
Hobert W. Turner	407 Washington st., Bri.	"	1,100 "	Jan. 4, 1908
Edward J. White	53 Bennett st., Bri.	"	1,200 "	April 19, 1889
Charles C. Woodman	29 Bigelow st., Bri.	"	1,200 "	Jan. 5, 1893
Calvin S. Wyer	409 Washington st., Bri.	"	1,200 "	April 7, 1894
Fred A. Willis	34 Gordon st., Bri.	"	1,200 "	Nov. 1, 1894
Hugh Wyllie	465 Washington st., Bri.	"	1,200 "	Oct. 16, 1902
William P. Wills	107 Murdock st., Bri.	"	1,200 "	April 14, 1906
Nicholas R. Bowe	20 Havre st., E. B.	Reserve Officer	2.00 day.	" 20, 1909
Ambrose S. Cosgrove	16 Eulita ter., Bri.	"	2.00 "	Jan. 18, 1909
William F. Frost	776 Cambridge st., Bri.	"	2.25 "	April 29, 1908
Joseph P. Murray	16 Sprague st., Chsn.	"	2.25 "	" 29, 1908
Joseph Mattey	16 Eulita ter., Bri.	"	2.25 "	" 29, 1908
Michael Sullivan	16 Eulita ter., Bri.	"	2.25 "	" 29, 1908
Caspar Tochterman	1 Monument pl., Chsn.	"	2.00 "	" 20, 1909
Jonathan McCannell	23 Foster st., Bri.	Hostler	17.00 wk.	June 17, 1889
John O'Donnell	7 Delaware pl., Bri.	"	14.00 "	April 13, 1900
Mary C. Nyman	347 Market st., Bri.	Janitress	12.70 "	Dec. 24, 1898

Division 15.

George D. Yeaton	52 Haynes st.	Captain	$2,500 yr	Feb. 8, 1908
Hayden J. Ringer	16A Eden st.	Lieutenant	1,600 "	" 8, 1908
Joseph Harriman	97 Bowdoin st.	"	1,600 "	March 28, 1908
John W. Riordan	444 Hyde Park ave.	Sergeant	1,400 "	Nov. 27, 1901
Ernest A. Webster	443 Saratoga st.	"	1,400 "	Jan. 1, 1903
Abraham L. Killam	288 Meridian st.	"	1,400 "	Feb. 8, 1908
Daniel F. Toomey	460 Saratoga st.	"	1,400 "	" 8, 1908
Martin J. Allen	7 Prospect st.	Patrolman	1,200 "	June 27, 1895
William O. Bailey	8 Irving pl.	"	1,200 "	April 9, 1887
Arthur H. Barker	4 Cordis st.	"	1,200 "	May 19, 1898
Frank A. Barthelness	26 Parker st.	"	1,200 "	July 30, 1896
Stanley C. Blenus	19 Margaret st.	"	1,200 "	April 27, 1901
John F. Brady	63 Decatur st.	"	1,200 "	" 8, 1895
John J. Buckley	36 Moseley st.	"	1,200 "	Oct. 23, 1902
Bartholomew Connolly	23 Savoy st.	"	1,100 "	" 9, 1907

Police Department.— Continued.

Name.	Residence.	Designation.	Compensation.	Date of Election or Appointment.

Division 15.— Concluded.

Name.	Residence.	Designation.	Compensation.	Date of Election or Appointment.
Thomas S. Comorton	32 Chestnut st	Patrolman	$1,200 yr	Oct. 20, 1895
Charles T. Corey	47 High st	"	1,200 "	April 8, 1895
Walter F. Corwin	45 Sever st	"	1,200 "	Oct. 8, 1895
Walter S. Crockett	20 Michigan ave	"	1,200 "	Sept. 20, 1900
Jeremiah J. Crowley	61 Elm st	"	1,200 "	April 8, 1895
Augustus F. Cunio	49 Austin st	"	1,200 "	Jan. 1, 1904
George H. Dickinson	88 Bartlett st	"	1,200 "	Oct. 31, 1900
Edward Doherty	77 Monument st	"	1,200 "	Jan. 10, 1881
Thomas J. Donahue	12 Guilford st	"	1,200 "	2, 1894
Michael J. Feeley	13 Mystic st	"	1,200 "	Sept. 10, 1901
Anthony Fitzpatrick	19 Vale st	"	1,100 "	Feb. 13, 1908
Albert R. Foster	14 Whittemore ter	"	1,200 "	Dec. 8, 1899
Jeremiah J. Haggerty	28 St. Martin st	"	1,200 "	July 30, 1896
William M. Hanscom	15 Quincefield st	"	1,200 "	Oct. 21, 1884
Thomas H. Hoadley	286 Lexington st	"	1,200 "	Nov. 25, 1903
James J. Hoy	78 Green st	"	1,200 "	" 9, 1898
John Horgan	50 Auburn st	"	1,100 "	June 7, 1907
Lyman Johnson	55 Mendum st	"	1,200 "	May 18, 1903
Perley C. Kneeland	69 Highland st	"	1,200 "	Sept. 7, 1903
John H. Laughlin	20 Monument st	"	1,200 "	Oct. 10, 1881
Dennis Leary	328 Bunker Hill st	"	1,100 "	Jan. 16, 1908
John C. J. Loughlin	28 Broadway, S. B.	"	1,000 "	Dec. 17, 1908
Michael J. Lynch	42 Hollingsworth st	"	1,100 "	Feb. 13, 1908
Edward G. McAllister	328 Bunker Hill st	"	1,100 "	April 29, 1908
Michael J. McDonough	18 Sprague st	"	1,200 "	24, 1899
Thomas McTiernan	3 Bartlett st	"	1,200 "	July 30, 1896
Richard Meehan	30 Laurel st	"	1,200 "	Oct. 29, 1906
Joseph E. Moisan	34 Tremont st	"	1,200 "	21, 1901
John F. Montague	17 Fayette st	"	1,100 "	June 7, 1907
Charles M. Montgomery	38 Harvard st	"	1,200 "	April 8, 1895
Everett A. Nash	8 Adams st	"	1,200 "	Dec. 24, 1901
James P. Norton	127 Westville st	"	1,200 "	March 18, 1903
Jeremiah O'Brien	30 Allston st	"	1,200 "	19, 1883
Jeffrey J. O'Connell	302A Bunker Hill st	"	1,200 "	May 21, 1893
Edward R. Olds	25 Harvard sq	"	1,225 "	Jan. 10, 1889
Harry Quirk	199 Market st	"	1,200 "	March 31, 1905
John T. Riordan	9½ Hancock st	"	1,200 "	April 27, 1902
John Ross	31 Prescott st	"	1,200 "	Oct. 16, 1893
Dennis A. Shea	246 Fifth st	"	1,200 "	Nov. 6, 1896
Michael J. Shea	17 Rutherford ave	"	1,000 "	5, 1905
Michael M. Shea	43 High st	"	1,100 "	April 29, 1908
George F. Small, jr	89 Lexington st	"	1,200 "	May 24, 1901
John W. Shaw	19 Essex st	"	1,200 "	Nov. 27, 1878
Coleman Sullivan	37 O st	"	1,100 "	Feb. 13, 1908
Dennis F. Sweeney	108 Bennington st	"	1,100 "	Nov. 7, 1907
Wayland F. Tripp	33 Bigelow st	"	1,100 "	Jan. 4, 1908
Henry C. Wadleigh	8 Essex st	"	1,200 "	Sept. 19, 1900
Bertrand F. Webb	33 Monument sq	"	1,200 "	April 16, 1897
Charles F. Bartick	299 Ninth st	Reserve Officer	2.25 day	29, 1908
Frederick L. Clauss	186 I st	"	2.25 "	29, 1908
James P. Doyle	22 Halleck st	"	2.00 "	Nov. 16, 1908
John J. Fahey	122 Falcon st	"	2.00 "	June 22, 1908
John J. Fitzgerald	94 Bennington st	"	2.25 "	April 29, 1908
Charles A. Griffin	304 Chelsea st	"	2.00 "	July 20, 1908
Thomas P. Landrigan	75 Gates st	"	2.00 "	Nov. 16, 1908
John T. O'Brien	718 E. Sixth st	"	2.00 "	" 16, 1908
Jeremiah T. Sullivan	91 Calumet st	"	2.00 "	16, 1908
Thomas A. Sullivan	280 Maverick st	"	2.00 "	July 20, 1908
Thomas H. J. Waldron	44 Newman st	"	2.00 "	Nov. 16, 1908
John J. Walsh	163 Charles st	"	2.00 "	Jan. 18, 1909
Elizabeth Holm	17 Rutherford ave	Janitress	12.70 wk	July 1, 1886
Elizabeth Holm	17 Rutherford ave	Matron	7.98 "	Nov. 30, 1887

Division 16.

Name.	Residence.	Designation.	Compensation.	Date of Election or Appointment.
Frank I. Jones	39 Dustin st	Captain	$2,500 yr	Feb. 8, 1908
James E. Sargent	10 Chester st	Lieutenant	1,600 "	Aug. 29, 1888
Patrick F. King	306 Beech st	"	1,600 "	Feb. 8, 1908
Thomas F. Goode, jr	95 Calumet st	Sergeant	1,400 "	May 2, 1903
Daniel G. Murphy	90 Hamilton st	"	1,400 "	April 25, 1907
Terrence McNeil	111 Dale st	"	1,400 "	Nov. 11, 1907
Henry F. Barry	99 Quincy st	"	1,425 "	Feb. 8, 1908
Perley S. Skillings	55 Seaverns ave	"	1,400 "	" 8, 1908

Police Department.— Continued.

Name.	Residence.	Designation.	Compensation.	Date of Election or Appointment.

Division 16.—Continued.

Name.	Residence.	Designation.	Compensation.	Date of Election or Appointment.
John H. Becker	526 Dudley st	Patrolman	$1,200 yr	April 25, 1907
Edward C. Blake	98 Hewlett st	"	1,200 "	Aug. 7, 1906
George H. Boothby	326 Shawmut ave	"	1,200 "	Oct. 8, 1889
Martin Brock	21 Rosemary st	"	1,200 "	Sept. 19, 1900
Walter Brown	127 Nonantum st	"	1,200 "	Jan. 30, 1905
Edmund J. Burke	35 Bower st	"	1,100 "	June 16, 1907
Michael J. Cadigan	12 Bennett st	"	1,200 "	April 19, 1889
Thomas D. Carmichael	52 Hopedale st	"	1,200 "	June 4, 1897
Edward B. Carthy	11 Olney	"	1,000 "	Nov. 5, 1908
Fremont Chase	88 Tuttle st	"	1,200 "	Jan. 5, 1893
James E. Collins	124 Amherst st	"	1,200 "	Nov. 21, 1895
Joseph W. Comerford	11 Eastburn st	"	1,000 "	Dec. 17, 1908
John J. Coughlin	684 Ninth st	"	1,200 "	Aug. 30, 1896
William H. Crowley	21 Aldie st	"	1,200 "	Sept. 2, 1902
Owen M. Cunningham	200 Market st	"	1,200 "	May 18, 1903
John J. Delaney	30 Julian st	"	1,000 "	June 22, 1908
Harry N. Dickinson	26 Greenwood st	"	1,000 "	Sept. 17, 1908
Thomas F. Donohue	55 Dustin st	"	1,200 "	April 8, 1895
William W. Dunn	165 Massachusetts ave	"	1,200 "	March 5, 1903
Timothy M. Ferris	97 Parker Hill ave	"	1,200 "	Nov. 21, 1895
Charles T. Florentine	26 Lynde st	"	1,200 "	" 25, 1903
Edward L. Foley	556 E. Second	"	1,100 "	April 30, 1908
Thomas E. Green	23 Evergreen st	"	1,200 "	Oct. 9, 1889
Stillman B. H. Hall	42 Bigelow st	"	1,200 "	July 31, 1896
Frank N. Harrington	49 Pratt st	"	1,200 "	April 8, 1895
Timothy F. Harrington	190 London st	"	1,000 "	Feb. 4, 1909
Stephen K. Higgins	5 Dracut st	"	1,200 "	March 29, 1904
Joseph W. Hobbs	3 Parker Hill ter	"	1,200 "	Sept. 2, 1902
Patrick E. Holleran	9 Heathcote st	"	1,200 "	March 5, 1903
Patrick W. Horan	105 N st	"	1,000 "	June 22, 1908
George J. Horgan	85 P st	"	1,000 "	Jan. 14, 1909
Edward G. Kennedy	51 Mendum st	"	1,200 "	Sept. 17, 1903
William G. Johnson	21 Woodward ave	"	1,000 "	June 22, 1908
George E. Lewis	89 Easton st	"	1,200 "	Nov. 27, 1878
Joseph H. Loran	166 W. Springfield st	"	1,200 "	" 26, 1906
John W. Lothrop	3 Hollis pl	"	1,200 "	" 9, 1898
Daniel J. Lynch	118 Aldrich st	"	1,200 "	March 29, 1886
William M. Lynn	17 Durham st	"	1,200 "	Feb. 13, 1889
John F. Lyons	260 L st	"	1,200 "	March 5, 1903
John J. Maguire	87 Etna st	"	1,200 "	July 20, 1900
Joseph J. Maguire	75 Elmira st	"	1,200 "	Nov. 25, 1903
David L. Martin	275 Dudley st	"	1,200 "	July 11, 1904
John A. McGillivray	219 Parsons st	"	1,200 "	April 24, 1905
Francis J. McGovern	158 Howard ave	"	1,100 "	Jan. 7, 1908
Joseph McKinnon	21A Bennett st	"	1,200 "	Sept. 17, 1903
Patrick J. Monahan	37 Harbor View st	"	1,200 "	Nov. 8, 1895
Edwin L. Montgomery	10 Allston sq	"	1,200 "	April 29, 1899
Matthew Mullen	17 Belvidere st	"	1,200 "	" 8, 1895
John C. Murphy	74 Dalton st	"	1,200 "	Sept. 17, 1903
John F. Murphy	749 Dorchester ave	"	1,200 "	April 8, 1895
Patrick Murphy	125 Walter st	"	1,200 "	Nov. 1, 1900
Herbert I. Nickerson	293 Poplar st	"	1,200 "	April 13, 1889
John B. O'Neill	1 Parker Hill ter	"	1,200 "	" 8, 1895
Perley C. Palmer	8 Holden st	"	1,200 "	Sept. 17, 1903
John F. Peers	29 Foster st	"	1,200 "	April 17, 1899
Charles B. Piper	17 Pond st	"	1,200 "	Nov. 1, 1900
Francis T. Power	6 Woodcliff st	"	1,200 "	Oct. 31, 1881
Thomas J. Shaw	3 Grafton st	"	1,200 "	" 21, 1884
Arthur J. Smith	34 King st	"	1,200 "	April 15, 1902
John J. Smith	58 Hopedale st	"	1,225 "	July 18, 1896
Johan F. Sternberg	5 Iroquois st	"	1,200 "	May 18, 1903
George Stewart	72 Forbes st	"	1,200 "	April 25, 1907
Patrick W. Toland	21 Bainbridge st	"	1,200 "	" 23, 1896
Michael J. Trainor	10 Akron st	"	1,200 "	Oct. 31, 1900
Thomas F. Welsh	8 Everett	"	1,200 "	March 29, 1904
James F. Blaney	446 E. Third st	Reserve Officer	2.25 day	April 29, 1908
John R. Brett	199 Blue Hill ave	"	2.25 "	" 29, 1908
James A. Burns	885 E. Fourth st	"	2.00 "	Oct. 12, 1908
Robert L. Boyd	1 Stanmore pl	"	2.00 "	June 22, 1908
Michael E. Conway	4 Spring st	"	2.00 "	" 22, 1908
Daniel J. Cronin	27 W. Fifth st	"	2.00 "	Oct. 12, 1908
Arthur T. Dolan	179 Paris st	"	2.25 "	April 29, 1908
Stephen J. Flaherty	361 Mercer st	"	2.25 "	" 29, 1908

Police Department.— Concluded.

Name.	Residence.	Designation.	Compensation.	Date of Election or Appointment.

Division 16.— Concluded.

Name.	Residence.	Designation.	Compensation.	Date of Election or Appointment.
John J. Gorman	263 W. Fifth st	Reserve Officer	$2.00 day	Nov. 16, 1908
James J. Graney	3 Orchard pk	"	2.00 "	April 20, 1909
James W. Gray	173 Roxbury st	"	2.00 "	Nov. 16, 1908
Arthur G. Hamilton	6 Bearse ave	"	2.25 "	April 29, 1908
Robert C. Huddy	1 Sumner pl	"	2.25 "	" 29, 1908
Thomas S. J. Kavanagh	52 Mercer st	"	2.00 "	Nov. 16, 1908
William R. Leary	112 Marcella st	"	2.25 "	April 29, 1908
Maurice F. Lee	15 Sumner st	"	2.00 "	Nov. 16, 1908
Daniel J. Linehan	4 Vernon pl	"	2.25 "	April 28, 1908
Joseph A. Lorenz	36 Mozart st	"	2.00 "	" 20, 1909
Albert Morris	85 Florence st	"	2.00 "	July 20, 1908
Bartholomew J. Mulhern	285 Cabot st	"	2.25 "	April 29, 1908
Francis J. O'Neil	420 E. Sixth st	"	2.00 "	July 20, 1908
David J. Redmond	30 Telegraph st	"	2.00 "	Oct. 12, 1908
David T. Ryan	15 Dickens st	"	2.00 "	" 12, 1908
Edward J. Sullivan	778 Parker st	"	2.25 "	April 29, 1908
John J. Elbery	55 Litchfield st	Janitor	14.00 wk	" 14, 1905
Sarah E. Homer	1 Hope pl	Janitress	12.70 "	Dec. 21, 1888
Michael J. McCarthy	29 Leon st	Hostler	14.00 "	" 29, 1901
Daniel McWilliams	99 Cowper st	"	14.00 "	May 16, 1903
James J. Newton	291 Highland st	"	14.00 "	Dec. 29, 1901
James Kelly	176 Northampton st	"	14.00 "	April 1, 1909

Police Signal Service.

Name.	Residence.	Designation.	Compensation.	Date of Election or Appointment.
John Weigel	82 Humboldt ave., Rox	Director	$2,500 yr	Aug. 20, 1888
Frank A. Richardson	17 Webster st., Alls	Assistant Director	2,000 "	" 20, 1888
Edwin P. Cochran	23 Wait st., Rox	Signalman	1,300 "	Sept. 19, 1900
G. William Goodwin	31 Georgia st., Rox	"	1,300 "	Nov. 1, 1888
Dudley W. Hook	1046 Bennington st., E. B	"	1,300 "	Oct. 1, 1893
Louis F. Nevert	317A Washington st., Dor	"	1,300 "	March 14, 1895
Henry L. Roberts	70 Athol st., All	"	1,300 "	May 10, 1900
Walter R. Sweet	67 Spring Park ave., J. P.	"	1,300 "	Nov. 25, 1889
Walter A. Capron	100 Savin Hill ave., Dor	Machinist	1,500 "	April 1, 1896
James E. Goodale	37 Laurel st., Dor	"	1,300 "	March 3, 1904
James F. Aylward	591 Seventh st., S. B	Foreman	25.00 wk	Oct. 1892
Michael F. Birmingham	283 Washington st., Bri	Lineman	3.00 day	Nov. 11, 1907
George N. Embree	38 Cobden st	"	3.00 "	Sept. 1899
Jeremiah Mackey	58 Custer st., J. P.	"	3.00 "	Dec. 1895
Michael Murphy	20 Sheridan st., J. P	"	3.00 "	May 1895
C. Chester Carter	42 Joy st	"	3.00 "	Feb. 5, 1906
Duncan MacDonald	10 Humphrey st	"	3.00 "	Jan. 24, 1908
Ernest W. Outhet	328 Washington st., Bri	"	3.00 "	" 24, 1908
John B. Burke	29 S. Russell st	Painter and Groundman	1,000 yr	June 1897
J. Frank Chase	36 Holton st., Alls	Driver	1,000 "	Oct. 1893
William E. Keen	40 Joy st	Foreman, stable	21.00 wk	Sept. 1, 1899
Thomas B. Green	406 Bunker Hill st., Chsn	Hostler	14.00 "	March 23, 1900
John Barry	125 Warren st., Rox	"	14.00 "	Sept. 28, 1908
Cornelius Driscoll	162 Silver st., S. B	"	7.00 "	July 3, 1905

Printing Department.

Name.	Residence.	Designation.	Compensation.	Date of Election or Appointment.
James H. Smyth	57 Donnybrook rd	Superintendent	$3,000 yr	Feb. 17, 1908
Ella C. Richards	290 Geneva ave	Bookkeeper	30.00 wk	March 19, 1907
Agnes G. Kenney	791 Columbia rd	Clerk	21.00 "	June 10, 1897
Frances G. Lambert	155 Dorchester st	"	18.00 "	Sept. 25, 1903
Ida S. R. Goldberg	47 Chambers st	Stenographer	15.00 "	Feb. 1, 1909
William J. Casey	48 Elton st	General Foreman	40.00 "	March 6, 1897
Daniel F. Pierce	43 Stillman st	Stockman	21.00 "	April 11, 1893
John J. Dolan	45 Maywood st	Foreman	30.00 "	July 5, 1898
Frederick Zeigler	17 Peabody st	"	30.00 "	March 18, 1897
Edward J. Stanton	112 Berkeley st	Proofreader	20.00 "	" 15, 1897
Julia G. Tobin	798 Center st	"	20.00 "	Jan. 18, 1909
Charles G. Wilkins	223 South st	"	20.00 "	March 28, 1897
Harriet M. Wood	rear 717 Centre st	"	20.00 "	Nov. 9, 1908
Harriet A. Fairchild	676 Tremont st	Copyholder	18.00 "	March 5, 1906
Fannie M. Fraser	24 Richfield st	"	18.00 "	May 22, 1908
Anna C. O'Malley	624 Third st	"	18.00 "	July 9, 1908
Catherine Crowley	13 Southwood st	Operator	18.00 "	May 16, 1908

Printing Department.—Continued.

Name.	Residence.	Designation.	Compensation.	Date of Election or Appointment.
Mary E. Cronin	42 Francis st	Operator	$18.00 wk	April 21, 1908
Mary L. Knight	Everett	"	18.00 "	June 6, 1908
Rose Lee	120 Conant st	"	18.00 "	" 15, 1897
Margaret Rose	1 Paul Gore ter	"	23.00 "	July 10, 1908
Alice L. Raymond	684 Massachusetts ave	"	21.00 "	Feb. 15, 1909
Francis J. Sullivan	4 Bunker Hill ct	"	18.00 "	May 3, 1903
Marion Trainor	15 Wendover st	"	18.00 "	April 16, 1908
Mary F. Hurley	21 Sumner st., Dor	Apprentice Operator	12.00 "	March 29, 1909
Rose V. Mellen	23 Medford st	"	15.00 "	" 19, 1906
Edwin J. Paulsrud	40 Clarence st	Caster	30.00 "	April 13, 1908
Herman Blum	14 Lowell st	"	15.00 "	" 14, 1908
Cornelius E. Collins	35 E. Concord st	Apprentice Caster	12.00 "	Nov. 9, 1897
Harold D. Hurwitch	33 Rose st	"	10.00 "	Feb. 18, 1908
George S. Betts	1323 Washington st	Compositor	18.00 "	March 27, 1897
Renforth C. Bleakney	208 Shawmut ave	"	20.00 "	" 25, 1899
Margaret Blizard	4 Atherton st	"	18.00 "	" 19, 1909
Paul M. Crowley	23 Wales st	"	18.00 "	" 4, 1897
George F. Coulter	98 Day st	"	18.00 "	" 24, 1909
John F. Delaney	265 Bunker Hill st	"	18.00 "	" 1, 1897
Cornelius Driscoll	5 Jefferson ave	"	20.00 "	June 4, 1900
Charles H. Fayle	30 Oakdale st	"	18.00 "	Feb. 26, 1906
Charles P. Florentine	9 S. Russell st	"	18.00 "	March 24, 1909
Frank W. Brault	29 Doris st	Caster	24.00 "	April 2, 1909
Edward F. Ford	9 Van Winkle st	Compositor	18.00 "	May 23, 1904
Daniel J. Gill	20 East st	"	18.00 "	March 22, 1897
Elizabeth F. Grant	35 E. Newton st	"	18.00 "	July 28, 1902
William J. Hancock	34 Condor st., E. B	"	18.00 "	Aug. 5, 1897
Mary E. Herrick	84 Baldwin st	"	18.00 "	May 6, 1898
Thomas J. Hurley	606 Freeport st	"	20.00 "	March 25, 1901
Richard E. Keyes	595 E. Fifth st	"	18.00 "	June 2, 1902
William E. Kenefick	9 Bradbury st	"	18.00 "	" 2, 1905
Charles S. Lawler	9 King st	"	18.00 "	May 22, 1905
Peter J. Mulvee	23 Webber st	"	18.00 "	" 17, 1897
Timothy J. Murphy	899 Washington st	"	18.00 "	March 9, 1897
Felix McManus	35 McLellan st	"	20.00 "	" 5, 1907
John J. McNeil	49 Hecla st	"	18.00 "	May 21, 1908
Edmund F. O'Connell	90 Lexington st	"	18.00 "	Feb. 26, 1902
John O'Connor	90 W. Newton st	"	18.00 "	Jan. 24, 1897
Arthur A. O'Leary	50 Roseclair st	"	18.00 "	March 1, 1897
Patrick H. O'Leary	13 G st	"	18.00 "	Feb. 8, 1909
Charles W. Pasco	31 Bowdoin st	"	18.00 "	April 26, 1909
Annie G. Reardon	145 Bunker Hill st	"	18.00 "	Feb. 24, 1897
Patrick J. Sullivan	33 Alpine st	"	18.00 "	May 21, 1906
Richard L. Tweed	207 Endicott st	"	18.00 "	July 15, 1901
John F. Ward	98 Ashmont st	"	18.00 "	Aug. 13, 1902
Helen E. Walsh	786 Washington st	"	18.00 "	May 25, 1904
William F. Hayes	500 Sumner st	Stoneman	21.00 "	March 25, 1897
Joseph DeCastro	25 Charter st	Apprentice	12.00 "	Sept. 28, 1908
Elizabeth M. Leary	131 Havre st., E. B	"	10.00 "	June 19, 1908
Frank M. Toomey	244 Fifth st	"	6.00 "	Feb. 18, 1908
John R. Cadogan	39 Standish st	Assistant Foreman	25.00 "	March 17, 1897
Henry P. Barry	379 Savin Hill ave	Pressman	21.00 "	" 5, 1906
Eugene T. Brazzell	272 E st	"	21.00 "	July 22, 1907
John J. Cosgrove	15 Beckler ave	"	18.00 "	April 6, 1897
Frederick M. McCarthy	76 Revere st	"	21.00 "	May 23, 1908
James T. Roche	84 High st	"	21.00 "	March 29, 1897
Thomas J. Gately	19 Winslow st	Press Feeder	14.00 "	Sept. 19, 1906
John H. Murphy	792 Fourth st	"	14.00 "	March 24, 1902
Harvey J. Malouson	1 Seaver pl	"	14.00 "	Feb. 26, 1909
Joseph F. McGiveran	37 Maywood st	"	14.00 "	March 10, 1897
Thomas H. Ryan	11 Boynton st	"	14.00 "	" 19, 1902
John J. Reynolds	153 Everett st	"	14.00 "	Jan 4, 1903
William A. Ryan	289 E. Eighth st	"	14.00 "	April 14, 1900
Frank W. Crowley	16 Barry st	Job Pressman	16.50 "	Feb. 19, 1902
Edmund J. Connolly	16 Barry st	"	16.50 "	May 22, 1900
Charles W. Clayton	40 Bennington st	"	16.50 "	Feb. 14, 1900
Moses P. Doyle	38 Nashua st	"	16.50 "	March 30, 1905
William F. Driscoll	43 Gove st., E. B	"	16.50 "	May 15, 1897
James J. Donovan	132 Pleasant st	"	16.50 "	" 1, 1897
William J. McCarthy	11 Monument sq	"	21.00 "	March 8, 1897
Asa N. Church	16 Clarendon st	Apprentice	10.00 "	July 10, 1908
Thomas M. Donnelly	37 Chambers st	"	8.00 "	Oct. 19, 1905
Peter J. McCullough	229 Third st	"	15.00 "	Feb. 26, 1906
William J. Looney	37 Chambers st	Cutter	20.00 "	April 24, 1897
John F. Birch	256 E. Ninth st	Helper	14.00 "	" 13, 1897

Printing Department.— Concluded.

Name.	Residence.	Designation.	Compensation.	Date of Election or Appointment.
Henry McQuade	60 Chambers st	Shipper	$15.00 wk	Sept. 29, 1897
Richard J. Wren	154 H st	Metalman	16.00 "	Feb. 2, 1906
Thomas J. Farley	186 Bowen st	Errand Boy	6.00 "	May 5, 1908
Simon Goodman	977 Washington st		6.00 "	April 16, 1908
Frank Hurley	9½ Hancock st	"	6.00 "	" 3, 1908
Charles D. Martin	199 W. Fifth st	"	6.00 "	Feb. 14, 1908
Frank E. Schayer	201 D st	"	6.00 "	May 11, 1908

Public Buildings Department.

Name.	Residence.	Designation.	Compensation.	Date of Election or Appointment.
George W. Morrison	35 St. James st	Superintendent	$3,600 yr	Jan. 28, 1908
William P. Van Tassel	4 Dalrymple st	Executive Clerk	2,000 "	Feb. 23, 1898
Frederick C. Ward	28 Lexington st., Chsn	Clerk	1,300 "	Jan. 3, 1902
William A. Dannahy	7 Spencer st	Clerk and Messenger	800 "	June 22, 1905
Thomas J. Vaughan	90 Tremont st., Chsn	Foreman Steamfitter	1,500 "	July 7, 1902
Jeremiah W. O'Brien	340 Centre st., J. P.	Superintendent of Janitors	1,200 "	Feb. 4, 1902
Patrick J. Curley	60 St. James st	Carpenter	3.50 day	Dec. 31, 1907
Thomas W. Fitzgerald	58 Gove st., E. B	Electrician	3.60 "	Oct. 23, 1906
John F. Swift	48 Elmwood st	Electrician and Dynamo Tender	3.60 "	March 24, 1905
Edward F. X. McCarthy	720 Harrison ave	Sheet Iron Worker	3.60 "	Oct. 8, 1907
Samuel W. Washington	176 Northampton st	Locksmith	2.25 "	Aug. 22, 1900

City Hall.

Name.	Residence.	Designation.	Compensation.	Date of Election or Appointment.
Collinwood C. Millar	151 Trenton st	Chief Engineer	$28.00 wk	May 17, 1907
John Sheridan	58 Joy st	Assistant Engineer	1,100 yr	April 5, 1906*
George A. Betters	94 Waltham st	Fireman	17.00 wk	Jan. 24, 1903
Robert J. Brady	5 St. Margaret st	"	17.00 "	Feb. 21, 1902
James Campbell	44 Cooper st	"	17.00 "	Aug. 10, 1906
John Reynolds	240 Maverick st	"	17.00 "	April 26, 1896
Philip McDermott	28 E. Canton	Janitor and Storekeeper	2.50 day	Feb. 7, 1902

Old Court House.

Name.	Residence.	Designation.	Compensation.	Date of Election or Appointment.
John E. Fleming	19 Norway st	Elevatorman	$2.50 day	Nov. 21, 1902
Thomas J. Barry	186 L st	Janitor	2.50 "	Feb. 21, 1902
John J. Fogarty	11 Ward st	"	2.50 "	April 8, 1904
David J. Hagerty	651 E. Fourth st	"	2.50 "	Feb. 11, 1902
Edward Mulhearn	172 Harrison ave	"	2.50 "	" 28, 1902
James J. Porter	70 W. Cedar st	"	2.50 "	" 11, 1902
Daniel J. Fitzpatrick†	170 Winthrop st	Watchman	2.50 "	" 11, 1902
Annie Edwards	474 Shawmut ave	Cleaning	.20 hour	Jan. 27, 1905
Margaret Fitzgerald	135 Winthrop st	"	.20 "	April 14, 1906
Helena Gaffney‡	30 Newman st	"	.20 "	June 27, 1902
Annie Hutchins	162 L st	"	.20 "	Jan. 27, 1905
Mary Kane	30 Salutation st	"	.20 "	March 23, 1906
Ellen F. Kelleher	480 W. Eighth st	"	.20 "	April 21, 1905
Bridget A. Lyons	943 Washington st	"	.20 "	Aug. 3, 1906
Mary McElroy	9 Mark st	"	.20 "	April 1, 1902
Matilda Newby	654 E. Second st	"	.20 "	Jan. 27, 1905
Mary E. Welch	10 Rockingham pl	"	1.50 day	Dec. 16, 1899
Sarah E. Shipsey	6 Forest pl	Janitress	360 yr	Jan. 24, 1884
Elizabeth Bennett	44 Hudson st	Washing Towels	.25 doz	March 30, 1906
Mary A. Donovan	313 W. Third st	"	.25 "	" 30, 1906
Nellie Gage	779 E. Sixth st	"	.25 "	July 5, 1900
Maria Geehan	235 W. Third st	"	.25 "	March 30, 1906
Nellie McCool	711 Broadway	"	.25 "	" 30, 1906

28 Court Square and 30 and 32 Tremont Street.

Name.	Residence.	Designation.	Compensation.	Date of Election or Appointment.
Edward Fitzwilliam	27 Windom st	Chief Janitor	$1,000 yr	Feb. 4, 1902
Max Stone†	78 Brighton st	Watchman	2.50 day	March 26, 1901
Timothy J. Donoghue	164 W. Third st	Janitor	2.50 "	Feb. 21, 1902
John Hagerty	36 Sharon st	"	2.50 "	" 21, 1902
James F. Malone	62 Allen st	"	2.50 "	April 1, 1895

* Promoted to present position on date given. Previously in the department.
† Watchman at Old Court House, 28 Court square and 30 and 32 Tremont street.
‡ See County Buildings.

Public Buildings Department.— Continued.

Name.	Residence.	Designation.	Compensation.	Date of Election or Appointment.

28 Court Square and 30 and 32 Tremont Street.—Concluded.

Name	Residence	Designation	Compensation	Date
Jacob L. Whiteman	237 W. Canton st	Janitor	$2.50 day	Feb. 11, 1902
Sarah J. Balden	42 Revere st	Cleaning	.20 hour	Dec. 4, 1908
Julia Churchill	65 Phillips st	"	.20 "	July 27, 1906
Cynthia Gilmore	4 Belknap pl	"	.20 " "	27, 1906
Mary May	24 Emerson st	"	.20 "	Nov. 21, 1902
Rose Riley	16 Tennyson st	"	.20 "	Jan. 27, 1905
Caroline Ross	16 Tennyson st	"	.20 "	Nov. 30, 1906
Margaret Hoar	1207 Massachusetts ave	Washing Towels	.25 doz.	" 21, 1899
Mary A. Hughes	7 Malden st	"	.25 "	Jan. 18, 1907

11 Wareham Street.

Name	Residence	Designation	Compensation	Date
Thomas J. Callahan	315 Paris st	Janitor	$2.50 day	April 18, 1907
Peter Glancy	2 Codman Hill st	"	2.50 "	Feb. 11, 1902
Dorothy Davidson	2 Harvest ter	Cleaning	416 yr	Dec. 28, 1900
Mary Stuart	88 Hudson st	"	416 "	Jan. 17, 1907

Ward 16 Municipal Building.

Name	Residence	Designation	Compensation	Date
James J. Dolan	18 Wayland st	Custodian	$1,000 yr	Dec. 1, 1904
Harry J. Foster	1 Jerome st	Janitor	2.50 day	Nov. 20, 1903
Ferdinand W. Webber	114 Hamilton st	"	2.50 "	Feb. 21, 1902
Bartholomew O'Brien	835 Columbia rd	Engineer	900 yr	Oct. 14, 1904
Michael O'Riordan	22 Brookford st	"	900 "	Sept. 30, 1904
Margaret Canning	102 Buttonwood st	Cleaning	.20 hr	April 25, 1904
Mary Gill	rear 94 Quincy st	"	.20 "	Jan. 27, 1905
Mary Hennessey	103 Alexander st	"	.20 "	Oct. 13, 1905
Mary Lyons	15 Dacia st	"	.20 "	Jan. 27, 1905
Hannah Murphy	21 Howell st	"	.20 "	Feb. 1, 1900
Mary A. Sullivan	102 Fellows st	"	.20 "	Jan. 5, 1905
Margaret F. Sullivan	895 E. Fourth st	Janitress	2.00 day	" 8, 1908

64 Pemberton Square.

Name	Residence	Designation	Compensation	Date
Patrick A. Murphy	36 Cherokee st	Janitor	$2.25 day	June 3, 1898
Annie Flaherty	149 W. Third st	Cleaning	.20 hr	June 24, 1904
Annie Kerrigan	2 Prospect ave., Chsn	Washing Towels	.25 doz.	Nov. 23, 1906

Ambulance Station.

Name	Residence	Designation	Compensation	Date
Benjamin D. Drohan	5 Cross st., Ros	Janitor	$2.50 day	Nov. 30, 1896
John L. Devereaux	539 E. Seventh st	Driver	15.00 wk	May 21, 1900
Nathan Prescott	628 E. Eighth st	"	15.00 "	Feb. 21, 1902
James H. Quigley	20 Lark st	"	15.00 "	June 1, 1905
Uranus Young	120 Dorchester st	"	15.00 "	Aug. 30, 1900
Bridget McNulty	35 Old Harbor st	Cleaning	5.00 "	May 21, 1900

Faneuil Hall.

Name	Residence	Designation	Compensation	Date
William A. McLaughlin	6 Sawyer ave	Custodian	$1,200 yr	Jan. 17, 1903
John Cannon	191 W. Seventh st	Janitor	2.50 day	July 10, 1903
Mary Cavanaugh	41 Ottawa st	Cleaning	.20 hr	Dec. 4, 1901
Catherine Murray	1476 Washington st	"	.20 "	April 17, 1903

Old State House.

Name	Residence	Designation	Compensation	Date
John T. Callahan	31 Washington st., Chsn	Janitor	$1,000 yr	April 1, 1906*
Alice F. Hook	484 Tremont st	Cleaning	234 "	March 1, 1905
Mary Phillips	17 Wharf st	"	.20 hr	April 24, 1907

Old City Hall, Charlestown.

Name	Residence	Designation	Compensation	Date
Joseph H. Butt	172 Cowper st	Engineer	$17.00 wk	Dec. 27, 1906
William McNamee†	4 Seaver st	Janitor	1.50 day	Feb. 12, 1902
Catherine Bagley	75 Decatur st., Chsn	Cleaning	.20 hr	March 29, 1907

Milk Inspectors' Division, Huntington Chambers.

Name	Residence	Designation	Compensation	Date
Catherine McLaughlin	12 Hamlet st	Cleaning	$7.00 wk	July 20, 1907

* Promoted to present position on date given.   Previously in the department.
† See Library Department.

Public Buildings Department.— Concluded.

Name.	Residence.	Designation.	Compensation.	Date of Election or Appointment.

Charity Bureau.

Minnie Esdaile	25 Sheridan st	Cleaning	$10.00 wk.	Oct. 4, 1907
Catherine Bradley	63 Whitney st	"	.20 hr.	Feb. 1, 1905

City Building, Washington and Norfolk Streets, Dorchester.

James F. Conboy	67 Armandine st	Custodian	$1,000 yr.	May 22, 1905
Nellie M. Cahill	8 Bloomington st	Cleaning	.20 hr.	Dec. 1, 1904

Curtis Hall.

Thomas H. Kenney	24 John A. Andrew st	Janitor	$900 yr.	Feb. 7, 1902

Ward Rooms.

James H. Pridham	49 Condor st	Janitor, Ward 2	$300 yr.	Oct. 9, 1908
James A. Carroll	31 Lexington st., Chsn.	" 3	336 "	Nov. 15, 1902*
John J. Mullally	327 Charles st	" 8	300 "	May 29, 1902
Emery W. Frost †	5 Hawthorne pl	" 9	370 "	Dec. 1, 1901
Abraham Curby	20 St. James st	" 17	300 "	March 1, 1908
William S. Arnaud ‡	325 Washington st., Bri	" 25	48 "	Dec. 31, 1901
Jennie A. O'Connell ‡	19 Union st., Bri	Cleaning, Ward 25	.20 hr.	May 2, 1908

Public Grounds Department.

D. Henry Sullivan	93 Howland st	Superintendent	$4,000 yr.	Nov. 19, 1906
Mary R. Roche	46 Vine st	Clerk	1,200 "	Oct. 22, 1883
Katherine M. FitzGerald	825 Third st	"	3.00 day	Jan. 14, 1907
Edwin A. Baldwin	312 K st	Machinist	3.00 "	Sept. 21, 1894
William Barry	149 Eighth st	Tree climber	2.25 "	March 13, 1902
William A. Black	196 Blue Hill ave	Gardener	2.75 "	April 24, 1906
Neal Boyle	48 W. Tremlett st	"	2.25 "	" 7, 1905
William Burns	41 Mall st	Moth Destroyer	2.25 "	Oct. 22, 1906
Timothy F. Callahan	44 Stonehurst st	Messenger	2.50 "	March 29, 1893
August Carlson	9 Drayton ave	Nurseryman	3.00 "	May 8, 1901
Valentine Carroll	13 Hull st	Sodder	2.25 "	April 26, 1897
George W. Chapman	Alexander st	Gardener	2.50 "	" 21, 1900
John F. Costello	47 Thorndike st	"	3.00 "	" 3, 1894
Cornelius Collins	143 Cabot st	Moth Destroyer	2.25 "	Oct. 24, 1906
Joseph H. Collins	223 Eustis st	"	2.25 "	March 27, 1906
Charles H. Cooke	10 Cottage pk	Gardener	3.00 "	Feb. 16, 1905
James J. Coughlin	123 F st	"	2.50 "	May 2, 1899
Jeremiah Crowley	211 E. Cottage st	Sodder	2.50 "	April 16, 1889
Jane Cullen	21 Leyland st	Plant Cleaner	2.25 "	Dec. 27, 1903
Thomas Cox	2 Pope's Hill	Gardener	3.00 "	May 4, 1891
Thomas Cunningham	5 Lark st	Moth Destroyer	2.25 "	Feb. 5, 1907
Dominick Dagosta	3 Salem st	"	2.25 "	Oct. 22, 1906
Mary Deering	35 Garden st	Office Cleaner	1.50 "	Nov., 1908
John H. Dillon	57 Columbia rd	Gardener	3.50 "	Jan. 8, 1892
John Doherty	132 Whitfield st	Moth Destroyer	2.25 "	March 26, 1907
William Dowling	73 Wenham st	Foreman	3.50 "	May 15, 1883
Luke J. Doogue	21 Mt. Ida rd	Clerk	1,200 yr.	Nov. 5, 1886
James J. Doogue	28 Fayette st	Watchman	2.50 day	April 11, 1890
Edward Dever	127 Fifth st	Moth Destroyer	2.25 "	Feb. 13, 1907
Michael H. Dooley	1 Stirling st	Sodder and Grader	2.25 "	April 26, 1906
Samuel D. Dickson	19½ Centre st	Gardener	3.00 "	" 29, 1901
James A. Dixon	62 Everett st	"	3.00 "	" 9, 1900
John C. Dolan	92 Dedham st	Moth Destroyer	2.25 "	March 27, 1905
William Driscoll	119 Union Park st	"	2.25 "	Oct. 23, 1906
William H. Erskine	4 E. Cottage st	Painter	3.00 "	May 13, 1896
Martin Finaghty	71 Harbor View st	Gardener	3.00 "	Dec. 1, 1903
William Flatley	64 Terrace st	Sodder	2.75 "	May 7, 1888
James W. Follen	4 Fields ct	Clerk	2.50 "	Feb. 26, 1906
Patrick Fitzgerald	2 Gore st	Sodder and Grader	3.00 "	April 24, 1891
Thomas Farrell	7 Parsons st	Sodder	2.25 "	March 27, 1905

* Only employed during winter season.
† Paid at rate of $10 per week during winter season and $10 per month in summer.
‡ See County Buildings.

Public Grounds Department.— Continued.

Name	Residence.	Designation.	Compensation.	Date of Election or Appointment.
William E. Fay	5 Auburn st	Moth Destroyer	$2.50 day	March 18, 1904
Michael Flaherty	64 Tremont st	Gardener	2.50 "	" 19, 1900
Thomas F. Flanagan	39 Forbes st	Moth Destroyer	2.50 "	May 27, 1905
Joseph P. Germaine	22 Copley st	Nurseryman	3.00 "	April 9, 1900
William H. Gavin	39 Humphreys st	Farmer	2.75 "	March 27, 1905
Timothy J. Guiney	142 D st	Tree Climber	2.25 "	April 27, 1905
Jere Gibbons	201 Boylston st	Moth Destroyer	2.25 "	Jan. 12, 1907
James H. Grant	54 Bromley st	Gardener	3.00 "	May 5, 1901
Richard J. Hayden	732 Dudley st		3.50 "	Feb. 17, 1904
Charles Hayes	88 Village st	Sodder and Grader	2.50 "	April 3, 1903
Frank Hill	2 Mt. Vernon ave	Tree Expert	3.00 "	Dec. 12, 1885
James J. Hines	36 Goldsmith st	Sodder and Grader	2.25 "	April 25, 1906
William J. Hartnett	15 Knox st	Moth Destroyer	3.00 "	Jan. 19, 1907
Elbridge G. Hicks	80 Chestnut ave	Farmer	2.50 "	March 16, 1905
Charles F. Hicks	35 Abbottsford st	Painter	3.00 "	April 16, 1900
Daniel Hourihan	19 Worthington st	Tree Climber	3.00 "	March 7, 1902
Walter Halloran	79 Corbet st	Moth Destroyer	2.75 "	Jan. 10, 1907
Frank J. Jefferson	167 Ninth st		2.25 "	March 11, 1904
John A. Johnson	22 Fenwick st	Sodder and Grader	3.00 "	April 10, 1900
Luke Kilduff	34 Kent st	Gardener	2.50 "	" 23, 1900
John F. Kyle	50 Harvard st	Moth Destroyer	2.25 "	Oct., 1906
Matthew T. J. Keenan	963 Parker st	Laborer	2.50 "	Dec. 24, 1906
George E. Keenan	26 Shirley st	Moth Destroyer	2.25 "	Jan. 11, 1907
Joseph P. Kilday	27 Kenney st	Tree Climber	2.25 "	April 16, 1906
John P. Lane	40 Thomas pk	Caretaker	2.25 "	March 18, 1907
Peter Laverty	229 Eustis st	Tree Climber	2.25 "	Jan. 5, 1906
Patrick H. Long	371 E st	Sodder and Grader	2.50 "	April 25, 1906
William P. Long	55 Weld Hill st	Foreman	1.200 yr	Jan. 7, 1889
Laurence Lally	25 G st	Moth Destroyer	2.25 day	" 8, 1906
Thomas F. Manning	18 Hamlet st	"	2.50 "	March 17, 1904
Michael Maguire	17 Roach st	"	2.25 "	Oct. 20, 1906
Thomas Mealey	946 Parker st	Sodder	2.50 "	April 24, 1904
Peter Minton	278 E. Cottage st	Gardener	3.00 "	May 2, 1892
Warren S. Marden	19 Cornell st	Master Mechanic	1.200 yr	April 15, 1878
Walter T. Meroth	14 Burrell st	Moth Destroyer	2.50 day	" 6, 1898
Philip A. Monahan	16 Shirley st	"	2.50 "	Jan. 11, 1907
John Mullen	12 Jewett st	Sodder and Grader	2.25 "	May 1, 1906
James F. Morgan	621 Hyde Park ave	Moth Destroyer	2.25 "	Oct. 19, 1906
Thomas F. Mealey	946 Parker st	"	2.25 "	Jan. 3, 1906
James J. Murphy	264 Norfolk ave	"	2.25 "	Oct. 17, 1906
John B. Murphy	410 Bowdoin st	"	2.50 "	March 24, 1905
John J. Murphy	41 Malden st	Teamster	2.25 "	April 18, 1900
Hugh McGoldrick	91 High st	Moth Destroyer	2.50 "	Jan. 12, 1907
John J. McDermott	17 Kearsarge ave	"	2.25 "	Oct. 17, 1906
William McGowan	49 Smith st	"	2.25 "	Feb. 14, 1907
John J. McManus	3 Parnell st	"	2.50 "	" 3, 1905
Patrick McQuiggan	32 Summit ave	Laborer	2.25 "	July 27, 1896
Nathan McConn	31 Vaughan ave	Moth Destroyer	2.25 "	Oct. 22, 1906
John T. Neary	182 Cabot st	"	2.25 "	Feb. 20, 1905
James J. O'Brien	12 Pontiac st	Tree Climber	2.25 "	Oct. 16, 1906
William F. Ochs	9 Wendover st	Sodder	3.00 "	April 26, 1894
Michael O'Malley	143 Seventh st	Steamfitter's Helper	2.25 "	July 4, 1900
Dennis O'Connell	12 N. Mead st	Mason's Tender	2.50 "	April 14, 1900
John P. O'Connell	284 Park st	Foreman	1.200 yr	May 27, 1895
Daniel J. O'Keeffe	30 Stonehurst st	Clerk	2.50 day	Sept. 18, 1907
James A. O'Rourke	167 Broadway	Tree Climber	2.25 "	Oct. 22, 1906
Aaron Parker	71 Dacia st		2.50 "	March 14, 1902
Robert J. Powers	38 Dearborn st	Gardener	3.00 "	April 6, 1901
Michael Prior	6 Orchard Park st	Moth Destroyer	2.50 "	Jan. 11, 1907
James B. Quinn	13 Stafford st	General Work	3.00 "	March 30, 1885
Frank M. Ryan	251 Kilton st	Gardener	2.75 "	April 9, 1906
John C. Rooney	141 Eustis st	Moth Destroyer	2.25 "	March 18, 1904
Augustus J. Rasmusen	312 Endicott st	Moth Inspector	3.00 "	April 16, 1900
Michael J. Reardon	210 Washington st	Gardener	2.75 "	" 30, 1906
Joseph P. Rosatta	9 Monument st	Sodder	2.50 "	" 16, 1900
William H. Rumney	112 Trenton st	Carpenter	3.00 "	Jan. 25, 1907
Nellie Skehan	157 Marion st	Plant Cleaner	1.66 "	Oct. 8, 1907
James J. Sullivan	88 Marcella st	Sodder	2.25 "	June 18, 1906
Ignatius F. Sheerin	360 Walnut ave	"	2.50 "	May 10, 1904
Peter Sweeney	34 Dale ave	Steamfitter's Helper	2.25 "	April 14, 1900
Harry Shaw	115 Warren ave	Gardener	3.50 "	" 24, 1886
Richard Skeffington	154 Terrace st	Moth Destroyer	2.25 "	March 27, 1906
Patrick F. Taylor	489 Sixth st	Tree Climber	2.50 "	" 14, 1902
Richard Tyler	70 Revere st	Sodder	3.00 "	May 3, 1890

Public Grounds Department.— Concluded.

Name.	Residence.	Designation.	Compensation	Date of Election or Appointment.
John Toole	41 W. Fifth st	Moth Destroyer	$2.25 day	Nov. 1, 1906
Thomas F. Walsh	20 Alexander st	Driver	3.00 "	Sept. 30, 1896
Richard Welch	76 Clarkson st	Moth Destroyer	2.50 "	Jan. 10, 1907
John J. Walsh	266 E. Cottage st	"	2.50 "	May 2, 1901
Mathild Zaun	229 Metropolitan ave	Plant Cleaner	2.25 "	April 1, 1907

Registry Department.

Name.	Residence.	Designation.	Compensation	Date of Election or Appointment.
Edward W. McGlenen	145 Ashmont st	Registrar	$4,000 yr	July 25, 1900*
James O. Fallon	2767 Washington st	Assistant Registrar	1,700 "	" 24, 1894*
John M. Ludden	55 Guernsey st		1,700 "	Dec. 1901*
Herbert M. Manks	95 King st	Ancient Record and Statistic Clerk	1,500 "	Oct. 6, 1900
Jeremiah J. Leary	131 Havre st	Death Return Clerk	1,500 "	Jan. 1, 1902*
John J. Browne	123 M st	Clerk and Bookkeeper	1,200 "	March 12, 1901
John H. L. Noyes	37 London st	Clerk	1,000 "	Jan. 18, 1908
Darwin M. Cressey	24 Nightingale st	Messenger	1,100 "	Aug. 21, 1901
Timothy J. Callahan	11 Elder st	Constable	1,200 "	July 17, 1906
Florence White	38 Laurel st	Birth Record Clerk	799 "	" 1892
Isabelle C. O'Brien	175 Boston st	Marriage Record Clerk	775 "	Nov. 1887
Agnes J. Murray	878 Fourth st	Death Record Clerk	775 "	Oct. 28, 1899
Mary J. McGuigan	32 Summit ave	State Death Clerk	700 "	July, 1895
Charlotte F. McKenney	2 Murdock pk	State Marriage Clerk	675 "	Feb. 27, 1897
Margaret M. Foley	61 Murdock st	Marriage Return Clerk	800 "	Dec. 31, 1897
Nora E. Kendricken	117 Bowdoin st	Clerk	675 "	July 6, 1896
Grace E. Bliss	146 Massachusetts ave	"	12.00 wk	June 27, 1904
Katherine I. Corbett	682 Columbia rd	"	12.00 "	Dec. 1, 1906
Mary L. Costello	11½ Belvidere st	"	12.00 "	Feb. 16, 1899
Mary E. J. Hanley	26 Wendover st	"	12.00 "	Dec. 4, 1903
Elizabeth F. Hurley	15 Bennett st	"	12.00 "	May 1, 1902
Sarah J. McBrien	6 Ware st	"	12.00 "	July 5, 1902
Anna T. McCormick	96 Bower st	"	12.00 "	May 16, 1904
E. Louise McVey	33 Robinson st	"	12.00 "	Dec. 11, 1901
Bessie E. Tilden	175 Boston st	"	12.00 "	May 4, 1900
Helena C. Mahony	5 Normandy st	"	10.00 "	Jan. 7, 1907
Sarah F. McMurry	795 Blue Hill ave	"	10.00 "	Oct. 28, 1907

Schoolhouse Department.

Name.	Residence.	Designation.	Compensation	Date of Election or Appointment.
R. Clipston Sturgis	153 Beacon st	Chairman	$4,000 yr	May 1, 1902
James B. Noyes	186 Bay State rd	Commissioner	3,500 "	March 18, 1908
Tilton S. Bell	11 Gleason st	"	3,500 "	June 15, 1908
Horace B. Fisher	19 Orkney rd	Assistant Secretary	2,000 "	" 24, 1901
Daniel A. Casey	17 Potosi st	Executive Clerk	2,000 "	Jan. 1, 1902
Augusta L. Sheehan	15 Holden st	Clerk	860 "	April 10, 1908
Henry M. Curry	383 Fourth st	"	420 "	Oct. 15, 1908
Gertrude C. Bayley	175 Walnut ave	Stenographer	1,000 "	June 9, 1902
Edythe M. Mahony	90 G st	"	2.00 day	" 15, 1908
Eva A. Duplessis	71 Rutland st	"	624 yr	Nov. 12, 1908
Thomas D. Madden	644 Seventh st	Messenger	3.00 wk	" 21, 1908
Joseph P. Bulter	4 Linden st	Inspector	1,800 yr	June 24, 1901
Michael J. Donovan	5 Haynes pk	"	1,800 "	Jan. 1, 1908
Thomas P. Glynn	34 Hillside st	"	1,800 "	June 4, 1908
George H. Grueby	70 W. Rutland st	"	1,800 "	" 24, 1901
Charles E. Cadigan	29 Alliston st	"	1,500 "	April 15, 1909
William P. O'Toole	557 Massachusetts ave	"	2,000 "	June 24, 1901
Henry C. Pickering	23 Ormond st	"	1,800 "	Jan. 2, 1902
Everard W. Pinkham	34 Catawba st	"	6.00 day	April 26, 1909
Joshua B. Blair	54 Olney st	Architect	2,500 yr	" 26, 1909
John J. Driscoll	48 M st	Draughtsman	1,400 "	Jan. 1, 1902
William J. Ivers, Jr.	649 E. Broadway	"	840 "	May 6, 1907
Henry H. Austin	8 Ashford st	Civil Engineer	2,000 "	Feb. 1, 1902
Herbert L. Patterson	24 Oak ave	Transitman	1,200 "	May 1, 1907
Daniel A. Murphy	19 Dewey st	Rodman	620 "	April 29, 1907
Charles F. Eveleth	9 Chestnut st	Domestic Engineer	2,500 "	March 1, 1907

* Promoted to present position on date given. Previously in the department.

Schoolhouse Department.— Concluded.

Name.	Residence.	Designation.	Compensation.	Date of Election or Appointment.
Joseph L. Hern	56 East st	Superintendent	$1,500 yr	May 13, 1907
James J. Mahar	68 L st	Draughtsman	1,300 "	Nov. 15, 1902
Lewis B. Jones	1485 Washington st	Supt. Heating Control	1,200 "	March 15, 1909
John S. Webb	1 Myrtle st	Draughtsman	730 "	Aug. 1, 1908
Benjamin B. Hatch	11 Sawyer ave	Electrical Engineer	2,500 "	Oct. 10, 1906
George C. Glidden	26 Saxton st	Draughtsman	1,650 "	July 15, 1907
Clyde M. Durgin	1588 Centre st	"	3.00 day	Dec. 21, 1908
Herbert A. Dallas	4 Fort ave	Electrician	1,280 yr	Oct. 10, 1906
Theodore Gould	17 Wigglesworth st	"	1,280 "	April 10, 1908
Jere A. Desmond	56 Crescent ave	"	3.60 day	Jan. 27, 1909
Myer Cobe	27 Larchmont st	Messenger	1,000 yr	June 24, 1901
Nellie E. Aldrich	9 Common st	Department Janitress	420 "	July 3, 1901
Patrick Hanlon	37 A st	Storehouse Janitor	480 "	" 15, 1902
Edward A. Moore	10 Rodman st		120 "	Feb. 4, 1909
Walter P. Moulton	19 Grant pl	Clerk of Works, Longfellow Addition	1,800 "	" 15, 1904
Owen J. McLaughlin	406 Codman st	Clerk of Works, Dudley Elementary School	5.00 day	Dec. 12, 1908
William H. Haddock	12 Edson st	Clerk of Works, Blackinton Elementary School	4.00 "	April 1, 1909
Gilbert H. Smith	178 Humboldt ave	Clerk of Works, Edward Everett School	4.00 "	" 15, 1909

School Department.

School Committee.

David A. Ellis	12 Keswick st	Chairman	None	Jan. 7, 1907
James P. Magenis	190 Harvard st	"	"	" 6, 1908
David D. Scannell, M. D.	366 Commonwealth ave	"	"	" 6, 1908
George E. Brock	68 Surrey st., Bri	"	"	" 4, 1909
Joseph Lee	96 Mt. Vernon st	"	"	" 4, 1909

Officers and Assistants.

Stratton D. Brooks	96 Kilsyth rd., Bri	Superintendent	$6,000 yr	March 21, 1906
Jeremiah E. Burke	60 Alban st	Assistant Superintendent	4,500 "	May 16, 1904
Robert E. Burke	156 M st	"	4,500 "	Jan. 14, 1907
Walter S. Parker	Reading	"	4,500 "	Sept. 1, 1904
Augustus L. Rafter	41 Bradlee st	"	4,500 "	" 28, 1904
Ellor E. C. Ripley	1247 Commonwealth ave	"	4,500 "	May 1, 1902
Maurice P. White	Wallingford rd., Bri	"	4,500 "	Sept. 10, 1902
Thornton D. Apollonio	244 Massachusetts ave	Secretary	3,780 "	" 1, 1896
William J. Porter	34 Wenonah st	Auditor	3,780 "	July 8, 1879
William T. Keough	326 Saratoga st	Business Agent	3,780 "	Dec. 15, 1907
Elizabeth A. Clayton	47 Pratt st., Alls	Superintendent's Assistant	660 "	Nov. 5, 1907
Marion L. Foster	85 Worcester st	"	660 "	Jan. 1, 1908
Mary A. Fisher	10 Thane st	"	600 "	" 29, 1909
Louise Kane	64 Brooks st	"	600 "	Oct. 1, 1908
Helena W. McMahon	43 Baldwin st	"	720 "	Nov. 6, 1906
Stella L. Sherman	8 Joy st	"	840 "	Dec. 26, 1902
Alice G. Walsh	18 Gates st	"	600 "	Oct. 1, 1908
Marie T. Corkery	W. Medford	Secretary's Assistant	660 "	Sept. 25, 1907
Nellie M. Cronin	22 Everett ave	"	1,008 "	Jan. 10, 1908
Agnes R. Hurley	523 Fourth st	"	660 "	Sept. 16, 1907
Mary L. Morris	61 Maywood st	"	660 "	July 1, 1907
Alice Stevens	49 Copeland st	"	840 "	Feb. 12, 1906
Rose A. McBrien	6 Ware st	Auditor's Copyist	1,008 "	Nov. 16, 1896
Mary G. Walsh	70 Brown ave	" Assistant	840 "	Jan. 1, 1905
Almira S. Johnson*	18 Pond st., J. P	Business Agent's Assistant	660 "	Oct. 1, 1879
Lillie F. M. Bluemer	11 Dewey st	" "	600 "	Jan. 1, 1909
Margaret M. Brady	26 Rosemary st., J. P	" "	600 "	April 15, 1909
Annie M. Burke	119 Webster st	" "	840 "	May 8, 1901
Annie V. Hillis	23 Liverpool st	" "	660 "	Feb. 17, 1908
Alexander M. Sullivan	46 Clarence st	" "	600 "	" 1, 1909
Margaret Flynn	400 Norfolk st	Superintendent's and Business Agent's Assistant	660 "	April 1, 1908
J. Frederick Sayer	15 Johnston rd	Messenger	1,200 "	Feb. 21, 1872
Claude H. Bates	35 Mt. Pleasant ave	"	630 "	May 1, 1895

* Year's leave of absence on half pay, resignation to take effect April 8, 1910.

School Department. — Continued.

Name.	Residence.	Designation.	Compensation.	Date of Election or Appointment.

Officers and Assistants.—Concluded.

Name.	Residence.	Designation.	Compensation.	Date of Election or Appointment.
William F. Butler	298 W. Fifth st.	Messenger	$300 yr.	Aug. 19, 1907
James E. Gannon	24 Monument sq.	"	540 "	Oct. 1, 1908
William L. Reardon	210 Washington st.	"	840 "	May 1, 1896
Walter T. Walsh	65 Story st.	"	300 "	Feb., 1909
Charles H. Slattery*	520 E. Broadway	Teachers' Retirement Fund Custodian	1,000 "	May 1, 1906
Mark B. Mulvey	169 Stratford st., W. R	Schoolhouse Custodian	2,004 "	Sept. 12, 1905
Marie E. Nolan	19 Paul Gore st.	Schoolhouse Custodian's Clerk	720 "	April 1, 1908
Amos M. Kierstead	210 Hamilton st.	Asst. Supply Department, including two horses, two wagons and extra man.	3,000 "	July. 1, 1884
Fred L. Wetherbee	259 Webster st.	Assistant Supply Dept.	1,200 "	Aug. 1, 1882
Frank L. Kelliher	44 W. Newton st.	" "	900 "	25, 1890
Ellen T. Ryan	30 Monument st.	" "	840 "	Feb. 1, 1904
Charles A. Neuert	Winthrop	Janitor	33.62 wk†.	Dec., 1876
Gustave E. Kingsbury	11 Clement pk.	Janitor's Assistant	18.46 "	Feb., 1876
John T. Randolph	36 Bradford st.	"	6.92 "	March 1, 1897
Frank D. Mardin‡	Everett	Janitor	3.46 "	4, 1909
Joseph Brown	Melrose Highlands	Doorkeeper	9.23 "	Oct. 1, 1902

Normal School.

Name.	Residence.	Designation.	Compensation.	Date of Election or Appointment.
Wallace C. Boyden	Newtonville	Head Master	$3,780 yr.	March 14, 1900
Leonard O. Packard	31 Bullard st.	Master, Head of Dept.	2,484 "	Sept. 11, 1907
Charles M. Lamprey§	53 Donnybrook rd., Bri	"	2,628 "	March 1, 1908
Colin A. Scott	Cambridge	Master	3,204 "	Oct. 15, 1902
Katharine H. Shute	331 Walnut ave	First Asst., Head of Dept.	1,764 "	Dec. 17, 1907
Gertrude E. Bigelow	12 Cumberland st.	Supervisor of Practice	1,764 "	17, 1907
Rose A. Carrigan	53 Sydney st.	Assistant	1,620 "	March 14, 1900
Fannie E. Coe	4 Brewer st., J. P.	"	1,620 "	Jan. 2, 1894
Alice M. Dickey	32 Rockview st., J. P	"	1,620 "	May 1, 1893
Sarah A. Lyons	Dedham	"	1,380 "	Sept. 13, 1905
Laura S. Plummer	12 Cumberland st.	"	1,620 "	16, 1891
Mary C. Shute	531 Walnut ave	"	1,620 "	Dec. 1, 1902
Lillian M. Towne	89 Surrey st., Bri	"	1,620 "	Oct. 1, 1896
Gertrude Weeks	Cambridge	"	1,320 "	Sept. 13, 1905
Dora Williams	74 Mt. Vernon st.	"	1,620 "	5, 1888
Henry Warren Poor	Medford	Instructor in Drawing	2,508 "	Oct. 13, 1891
Mary E. Carney	17 Schuyler st.	Clerical Assistant	660 "	22, 1907
Nellie I. Simpson	23 Franklin st.	Substitute	4.00 day	April 12, 1909
Michael J. Crowley	310 Centre st., J. P	Janitor	135.29 wk‖	Oct. 14, 1907
Margaret Donovan	174 H st.	Attendant in Gymnasium	5.77 "	Jan. 25, 1909

Public Latin School.

Name.	Residence.	Designation.	Compensation.	Date of Election or Appointment.
Arthur I. Fiske	17 Montrose st.	Head Master	$3,780 yr.	Jan. 6, 1902
Patrick T. Campbell	Winthrop	Master, Head of Dept.	3,204 "	March 15, 1908
William T. Campbell	Cambridge	" "	3,204 "	15, 1907
Byron Grace	4 Schuyler st	" "	3,204 "	15, 1907
William P. Henderson	27 Johnston rd.	" "	3,270 "	15, 1907
Henry Pennypacker	Cambridge	" "	3,204 "	15, 1907
John K. Richardson	Wellesley Hills	" "	3,204 "	15, 1908
Charles J. Capen	Dedham	Master	3,060 "	July 10, 1852
Francis DeM. Dunn	Needham	"	3,060 "	Dec. 8, 1886
Selah Howell	9 Kirk st., W. R.	"	3,060 "	May 1, 1894
Henry C. Jones	Cambridge	"	3,060 "	Sept. 8, 1884
William R. Morse	112 Warren ave	"	3,060 "	Jan. 9, 1893
William K. Norton	30 Meredith st., W. R.	"	3,060 "	Sept. 12, 1900
Walter A. Robinson	Arlington	"	3,060 "	27, 1894
Alaric Stone	Newton Centre	"	3,060 "	Dec. 1, 1896
Louis W. Arnold	Waban	Junior Master	1,908 "	Sept. 13, 1905
Joseph L. Powers	Arlington	"	1,908 "	25, 1905
William F. Rice	178 School st	"	2,052 "	14, 1904
Herbert T. Rich	Hyde Park	"	2,916 "	12, 1898
Charles F. Winslow	188 School st	"	2,052 "	May 1, 1905

* See Treasury Department, Sinking Funds Department and County of Suffolk.
† Includes attendance and assistance at Board meetings.
‡ Janitor at 168 Tremont street.
§ Also master of Martin School and director of Model School.
‖ Includes Girls' Latin School and High School of Commerce.

School Department.— Continued.

Name.	Residence.	Designation.	Compensation.	Date of Election or Appointment.

Public Latin School.-- Concluded.

Stacy B. Southworth	18 Avalon rd., W. R	Instructor	$2,040 yr	Sept. 16, 1907
George F. Burt	Swampscott	Assistant Instructor	900 "	Nov. 17, 1908
Henry R. Gardner	Somerville	"	900 "	Sept. 9, 1908
Leon O. Glover	8 Vandyke st	"	900 "	" 9, 1908
Ethel A. Owen	251 Princeton st	Clerical Assistant	660 "	Oct. 1, 1908
Matthew R. Walsh	4 Dabney pl	Janitor	36.92 wk	Dec. 27, 1880

Girls' Latin School.

John Tetlow	Brookline	Head Master	$3,780 yr	Jan. 22, 1878
Edward H. Atherton	82 Ruthven st	Master, Head of Dept	3,204 "	March 15, 1907
Ernest G. Hapgood	Newton Highlands	"	2,340 "	Sept. 9, 1908
Fred H. Cowan	307 Chestnut ave., J. P.	Junior Master	1,764 "	Oct. 8, 1906
Florence Dix	42 Crafts rd., Bri	First Asst., Head of Dept.	1,764 "	March 15, 1908
Mary C. C. Goddard*	Cambridge	" "	882 "	" 15, 1908
Abby C. Howes	68 Charles st	" "	1,764 "	" 15, 1908
Helen A. Stuart	180 Huntington ave	" "	1,764 "	" 15, 1908
Rosalie Y. Abbot	108 Pembroke st	Assistant	1,116 "	Oct. 1, 1906
Sybil B. Aldrich	45 Walnut ave	"	1,620 "	Sept. 20, 1897
Mary D. Davenport	28 Newbury st	"	1,620 "	Oct. 21, 1895
Mary J. Foley	9 St. James ave	"	1,620 "	Sept. 12, 1888
Matilda A. Fraser	Garrison Hall., Garrison st.	"	1,620 "	" 15, 1897
Julia K. Ordway	71 Glen rd., J. P.	"	1,548 "	" 17, 1900
Adeline G. Simmons	319 Marlboro st	"	1,260 "	Jan. 16, 1905
Alice M. Smith	24 Mapleton st., Bri	"	972 "	Oct. 9, 1907
Mary R. Stark	97 Pembroke st	"	972 "	Dec. 1, 1908
Cora B. Mudge	Chestnut pl., J. P.	Assistant Instructor	972 "	Sept. 9, 1908
Eva Z. Prichard	240 Newbury st	"	900 "	" 9, 1908
Jacob Lehmann	Melrose Highlands	Special Instructor	1,920 "	June 8, 1908
M. Eloise Talbot	The Buckminster, Beacon st.	"	1,116 "	Sept. 1, 1906
Clara A. Hawthorne	93 Gainsboro st	Clerical Assistant	720 "	Nov. 12, 1906
Grace T. Pratt	Cambridge	Temporary Teacher	4.00 day	March 23, 1909
Helen E. Fries	2 Wabon st	Substitute	4.00 "	April 12, 1909
Michael J. Crowley	310 Centre st., J. P.	Janitor	†	Oct. 14, 1907

Brighton High School.

Frederic A. Tupper	7 Menlo st., Bri	Head Master	$3,780 yr	April 10, 1899
Sidney Peterson	Watertown	Master, Head of Dept	2,628 "	March 15, 1907
Ernest V. Page	74 Montello st., W. R	" "	2,340 "	Sept. 12, 1908
Marian A. Hawes	90 Bay State rd	Assistant Principal	1,836 "	Jan. 16, 1905
Mariette F. Allen	Somerville	First Asst., Head of Dept.	1,764 "	March 15, 1908
Eunice A. Critchett	Watertown	Assistant	1,620 "	Sept. 4, 1895
Ida M. Curtis	25 Kinross rd	"	1,620 "	Oct. 5, 1885
Laura M. Kendrick	Newton Highlands	"	1,620 "	Sept 14, 1897
Elvira B. Smith	29 Murdock st., Bri	"	1,620 "	" 29, 1896
Cornelia H. Stone	Chelsea	"	1,260 "	" 14, 1904
Lucy W. Warren	66 Westland ave	"	1,620 "	Dec. 1, 1897
Franklin E. Sullivan	26 Monmouth st	Assistant Instructor	900 "	Jan. 2, 1908
George F. Hatch	125 Corey st	Special Instructor	1,560 "	Sept. 11, 1907
Sara L. Shaw	56 Parsons st., Bri	"	1,116 "	Jan. 25, 1905
Annie E. Goodman	38 Linden st., Allston	Special Assistant Instructor.	900 "	Sept. 9, 1908
Mabel S. Blackman	Cambridge	Special Assistant	600 "	Oct. 6, 1908
Grace A. Reed‡	89 Pinckney st	Assistant	888 "	Sept. 22, 1902
Jennette A. Moulton	20 Hancock st	Substitute	4.00 day	Oct. 19, 1908
Charles H. Kelly	1 Foster st., Bri	Janitor	34.48 wk	Aug. 15, 1896

Charlestown High School.

George W. Evans	17 Everett ave	Headmaster	$3,780 yr	Sept. 1, 1905
Lotta A. Clark	Beachmont	First Asst., Head of Dept.	1,764 "	Mar. 15, 1908
Abby M. Thompson	39 Huntington ave	" "	1,692 "	Dec. 1, 1908
Margaret T. Wise	25 Batavia st	" "	1,692 "	" 1, 1908
Philip Goodrich	Malden	Junior Master	1,620 "	Nov. 4, 1907
Carleton E. Preston	11 Danville st., W. R	"	1,620 "	Sept. 9, 1908
John W. Regan	49 Winchester st	"	1,476 "	" 9, 1908
Grace Hooper	40 Huntington ave	Assistant	1,620 "	Oct. 1, 1891
Harriet E. Hutchinson	25 Batavia st	"	1,620 "	Sept. 7, 1897
Abbie T. Nye	94 Gainsboro st	"	1,620 "	Oct. 1, 1884

* Year's leave of absence on half pay, resignation to take effect September 1, 1908.
† See Normal School.   ‡ Temporarily transferred from the Prescott School.

School Department.—Continued.

Name.	Residence.	Designation.	Compensation.	Date of Election or Appointment.

Charlestown High School. — Concluded.

Name.	Residence.	Designation.	Compensation.	Date
Clio M. Chilcott	152 Huntington ave	Assistant Instructor	$900 yr	Sept. 9, 1908
Maud M. Cunningham	Somerville	"	900 "	" 9, 1908
Katherine E. Leonard	28 Prospect st	"	972 "	" 9, 1908
John H. Moore	26 Glenarm st	Special Instructor	2,160 "	" 12, 1900
Miriam Harris	12 Carlisle st	"	900 "	Dec. 8, 1908
Bernadette M. White	8 Cedar st	Special Assistant Instructor	972 "	Sept. 11, 1907
Clara J. A. Smith	19 Worcester sq	Clerical Assistant	660 "	Oct. 22, 1907
Charles J. Hurlbert	Charlestown High School	Janitor	17.25 wk	May 15, 1907

Dorchester High School.

Name.	Residence.	Designation.	Compensation.	Date
Charles J. Lincoln	11 Mountfort st	Head Master	$3,780 yr	Sept. 7, 1885
Albert S. Perkins	70 Lyndhurst st	Master, Head of Dept	3,204 "	March 15, 1907
Milford S. Power	2 Melville ave	"	3,204 "	" 15, 1907
Anna M. Fries	2 Carlisle st	First Asst. Head of Dept	1,764 "	" 15, 1908
Louisa E. Humphrey	Weymouth Heights	"	1,764 "	" 15, 1908
Katherine K. Marlow	63 Murdock st., Bri	"	1,764 "	" 15, 1908
Laura E. Hovey	86 Centre st	Assistant Principal	1,836 "	May 11, 1904
Henry W. B. Arnold	57 Ocean st	Junior Master	2,196 "	Jan. 4, 1904
Harold Bisbee	11 Hudson st., Dor	"	2,196 "	" 4, 1904
John Haynes	25 Mellen st	"	2,916 "	Sept. 6, 1898
Frederick G. Jackson	6 Seaborn st	"	2,916 "	Dec. 6, 1898
Charles T. Wentworth	8 Carruth st	"	2,484 "	Sept. 11, 1901
Jessie L. Adams	31 Kenwood st	Assistant	1,476 "	" 11, 1901
Margaret Cunningham	319 Marlboro st	"	1,620 "	" 24, 1894
Edith S. Cushing	N. Cambridge	"	1,620 "	" 9, 1889
Lucy A. Frost	70 Montello st	"	1,620 "	Oct. 3, 1892
Carolyn M. Gerrish	319 Marlboro st	"	1,188 "	Nov. 15, 1905
Jane E. Gormley	1 Worthington st	"	1,188 "	Sept. 26, 1905
Maud A. Hartwell	253 Norfolk st	"	1,332 "	Nov. 2, 1903
Mary A. Leavens	32 Rockview st	"	1,476 "	Sept. 16, 1901
Martha P. Luther	3 Nixon st	"	1,332 "	Nov. 2, 1903
Lilian G. Marr	653 Dorchester ave	"	1,188 "	Oct. 2, 1905
Edith A. Mayberry	Brookline	"	1,188 "	" 2, 1905
Catharine M. McGinley	58 Alpine st	"	1,332 "	" 21, 1903
Sarah L. O'Toole	Garrison Hall, Garrison st	"	1,044 "	Dec. 8, 1908
Mable M. Taylor	510 Washington st	"	1,620 "	Sept. 11, 1901
Elizabeth M. Wood	6 Lyndhurst st	"	1,044 "	Dec. 8, 1908
Frances Zirngiebel	61 Bower st	"	1,116 "	" 31, 1906
Henri Morand	103 Walnut ave	Instructor	1,920 "	Sept. 15, 1875
Harriet V. Elliott	Malden	Assistant Instructor	900 "	Oct. 20, 1908
Lena A. Glover	Danvers	"	900 "	Sept. 9, 1908
Florence M. Homer	56 Parsons st., Bri	"	900 "	April 12, 1909
William L. Anderson	17 Moultrie st	Special Instructor	2,286 "	Oct. 3, 1899
Joseph H. Hawes	40 Fairmount st	"	1,980 "	March 1, 1905
Mable S. Morse	31 Bicknell st	"	1,200 "	Sept. 11, 1901
Lucy G. Annable	2 Colonial ave	Special Assistant Instructor	900 "	" 9, 1908
Adalena R. Farmer	30 J. A. Andrew st., J. P	"	1,404 "	" 19, 1899
Rebekah C. Riley	77 Rockview st., J. P	"	1,116 "	" 25, 1906
Bessie A. Roberts	1644 Dorchester ave	"	1,332 "	Oct. 27, 1902
Mary F. Stratton	4 Gardner st., Alls	"	900 "	" 15, 1903
Nina E. Titus	92 Gainsboro st	"	1,260 "	Nov. 11, 1903
Mary A. C. Ward	10 Howes pl	Special Assistant	744 "	Dec. 10, 1906
Arthur E. Baker *	3 Chauncey pl., J. P	Temporary Teacher	1,620 "	Jan. 18, 1909
Joseph F. Carter †	353 Sumner st	"	996 "	Sept. 14, 1909
Grace I. Scott	Chicopee Falls	"	3.00 day	Feb. 8, 1909
Helen G. Dolan	32 Centre pl., J. P	Substitute	4.00 "	Sept. 21, 1908
Elizabeth H. Norman	74 Fuller st	"	4.00 "	Jan. 2, 1908
Albert Siebert‡	31 Kenwood st	"	50.00 mo	Feb., 1909
John McCloskey	14 Ashmont st	Janitor	73.92 wk	May 2, 1901
Elizabeth F. Hunter	104 Lonsdale st	Matron	10.38 "	Sept., 1901

East Boston High School.

Name.	Residence.	Designation.	Compensation.	Date
John F. Eliot	Hyde Park	Head Master	$3,780 yr	Sept. 11, 1889
George D. Bussey	Winthrop	Master, Head of Dept	3,060 "	March 15, 1907
Charles W. Gerould	Cambridge	"	3,204 "	" 15, 1907

* Temporarily transferred from the Bowditch District.
† Temporarily transferred from the Department of Drawing and Manual Training.
‡ Visiting Prussian teacher.

School Department.— Continued.

Name.	Residence.	Designation.	Compensation.	Date of Election or Appointment.

East Boston High School. — Concluded.

Name.	Residence.	Designation.	Compensation.	Date of Election or Appointment.
Alfred M. Butler	Brookline	Junior Master	$1,476 yr	Sept. 9. 1908
Lucy R. Beadle	24 Princeton st	First Asst. Head of Dept	1,764 "	March 15, 1908
Gracia E. Read	17 Greenwich pk	" "	1,764 "	" 15, 1908
Alma F. Silsby	Cambridge	" "	1,620 "	" 15, 1908
Lucretia E. Berry	Somerville	Assistant	1,044 "	Oct. 14, 1907
Kate W. Cushing	Cambridge	"	1,620 "	" 17, 1882
Maud G. Leadbetter	867 South st., Ros	"	1,620 "	" 5, 1896
Anna M. Linscott	136 W. Newton st	"	1,332 "	Sept. 10, 1903
M. Ursula Magrath	11 E. Newton st	"	1,188 "	" 15, 1905
Lucia R. Peabody	9 St. James st	"	1,620 "	" 14, 1896
Almira W. Bates	Cambridge	Assistant Instructor	900 "	April 12, 1909
Edith Rose	86 Arlington st., Bri	"	972 "	Oct. 16, 1907
Marjorie Bouvé	Brookline	Special Instructor	900 "	Sept. 9, 1908
Augustus F. Rose	Cambridge	"	1,680 "	Dec. 31, 1906
Charles E. Simpson	Winthrop	"	2,040 "	Sept. 30, 1901
Lizzie F. Fitzgerald	30 Vaughan st	Special Asst. Instructor	1,548 "	Nov. 1, 1899
Amy H. Jones	87 Mt. Vernon st., W. R.	Clerical Assistant	600 "	Oct. 5, 1908
Charlotte H. Lovell	Harding	Substitute	4.00 day	April 1, 1909
James A. Howe	211 Princeton st	Janitor	49.38 wk	Sept. 24, 1908

English High School.

Name.	Residence.	Designation.	Compensation.	Date of Election or Appointment.
John F. Casey	166 W. Canton st	Head Master	$3,780 yr	Sept. 11, 1901
Frank O. Carpenter	86 Gainsboro st	Master, Head of Dept	3,204 "	March 15, 1907
S. Curtis Smith	Newton	" "	3,204 "	" 15, 1907
William B. Snow	Stoneham	" "	3,204 "	" 15, 1907
James E. Thomas	166 W. Canton st	" "	3,204 "	" 15, 1907
Samuel F. Tower	W. Newton	" "	3,204 "	" 15, 1907
Henry M. Wright	Quincy	" "	3,204 "	" 15, 1907
James A. Beatley	11 Wabon st	Master	3,060 "	Nov. 8, 1886
Edward H. Cobb	Cambridge	"	3,060 "	Sept. 17, 1894
Peter F. Gartland	9 Merlin st	"	3,060 "	" 8, 1896
Frederic B. Hall	54 Brunswick st	"	3,060 "	" 4, 1895
Charles P. Lebon	42 Waumbeck st	"	3,060 "	" 7, 1887
Frank E. Poole	116 Englewood ave, Bri	"	3,060 "	" 13, 1889
William T. Strong	424 Newbury st	"	3,060 "	" 8, 1890
William H. Sylvester	Newtonville	"	3,060 "	" 3, 1883
Charles B. Travis	51 Chestnut Hill ave., Bri	"	3,060 "	" 12, 1868
Rufus P. Williams	Cambridge	"	3,060 "	" 18, 1883
Malcolm D. Barrows	Melrose	Junior Master	2,772 "	Dec. 11, 1899
Edwin F. A. Benson	25 Congreve st., Ros	"	1,908 "	Sept. 25, 1905
John J. Cadigan	18 Armadine st	"	2,196 "	" 9, 1903
Francis J. Conlin	Winthrop	"	1,764 "	Dec. 4, 1906
John A. Marsh	112 Brooks st	"	1,908 "	Sept. 13, 1905
Fred R. Miller	Newton Highlands	"	2,916 "	" 6, 1898
Edward P. O'Hara	47 E. Concord st	"	2,052 "	" 26, 1904
John E. Denham	30 Mapleton st., Bri	Instructor	1,440 "	Oct. 8, 1906
William W. Gallagher	Braintree	"	1,200 "	Sept. 9, 1908
John E. J. Kelley	13 Winter st	"	1,200 "	" 9, 1908
Frank E. Lakey	26 Royal st., Alls	"	1,320 "	Oct. 8, 1907
Bertram C. Richardson	3 Gaylor st	"	2,040 "	Sept. 21, 1908
Harry E. Bryant	19 Worcester st	Assistant Instructor	900 "	" 14, 1908
Joseph P. Cady	106 Geneva ave	"	972 "	" 11, 1907
Thomas E. Winston	199 Marion st	"	900 "	" 9, 1908
Edward R. Kingsbury	18A Rockville pk	Special Instructor	2,508 "	" 13, 1899
James W. Mace	26 Glenarm st	"	1,920 "	" 15, 1902
Carrie L. Tewksbury	7 Dalrymple st., J. P	Clerical Assistant	600 "	Dec. 1, 1908
Frederick W. Doring	Cambridge	Substitute	5.00 day	Sept. 9, 1908
Patrick W. Tighe	72 Alexander st	Janitor	80.77 wk	Dec. 27, 1880*

Girls' High School.

Name.	Residence.	Designation.	Compensation.	Date of Election or Appointment.
Albert P. Walker	Newtonville	Head Master	$3,492 yr	Sept. 1, 1907
Thomas H. H. Knight	Melrose Highlands	Master, Head of Dept	3,060 "	March 15, 1907
Parnell S. Murray	2 Akron pl., Rox	First Asst., Head of Dept	1,764 "	" 15, 1908
Emma G. Shaw	7 Alveston st., J. P	" "	1,764 "	" 15, 1908
S. Annie Shorey	194 Park st., W. Rox	" "	1,764 "	" 15, 1908
Laura B. White	29 Wallingford rd., Bri	" "	1,764 "	" 15, 1908
Samuel Thurber	13 Westminster ave., Rox	Master	3,060 "	Sept. 5, 1887
Francis A. Smith	26 Conway st., Ros	Junior Master	1,620 "	" 11, 1907
Abby N. Arnold	North Abington	Assistant	1,620 "	Oct. 24, 1899

* Also engineer for Public Latin School.

School Department.— Continued.

Name.	Residence.	Designation.	Compensation.	Date of Election or Appointment.

Girls' High School.— Concluded.

Name.	Residence.	Designation.	Compensation.	Date of Election or Appointment.
Gertrude P. Davis	182 Park st., W. Rox	Assistant	$1,332 yr	Sept. 9, 1903
Louise M. Endicott	Canton	"	1,332 "	" 21, 1903
Mabel A. Fitz	Somerville	"	1,116 "	Oct. 8, 1906
Alla W. Foster	Hotel Eliot	"	1,620 "	Sept. 10, 1883
Emma M. George	13 Haviland st	"	1,260 "	" 19, 1904
Isabel P. George	82 Myrtle st	"	1,620 "	" 12, 1888
Elizabeth E. Hough	74 Mt. Vernon st	"	1,620 "	Nov. 2, 1891
Frances H. Manny	18 St. James ave	"	1,332 "	Sept. 9, 1903
Sarah J. C. Needham	Hotel Eliot	"	1,620 "	" 22, 1884
Emerette O. Patch	Lexington	"	1,620 "	Oct. 1, 1870
Sarah E. Potter	45 Walnut ave	"	1,620 "	Sept. 15, 1897
Elizabeth M. Richardson	331 Walnut ave	"	1,620 "	" 8, 1896
Laura E. Richardson	331 Walnut ave	"	1,620 "	Nov. 14, 1894
Esther L. Sanborn	63 Maple st., W. Rox	"	1,332 "	Sept. 21, 1903
May M. Smith	Newton Centre	"	1,620 "	" 6, 1895
Elizabeth J. Strongman	58 Hewlett st., Ros	"	1,188 "	Jan. 2, 1906
Ellen I. Tryon	Cambridge	"	1,332 "	Sept. 9, 1903
Alice M. Twigg	665 Columbia rd	"	1,116 "	" 24, 1906
Mary E. Wynne	11 Oakwood st	"	1,620 "	" 21, 1896
Bertha A. Bonart	Melrose	Assistant Instructor	900 "	" 9, 1908
Katherine E. Cufflin	20 Faneuil st., Bri	"	900 "	Jan. 4, 1909
Marie A. Goddard	Wellesley Hills	"	900 "	Sept. 14, 1908
Mary A. M. Papineau	14 Spring Park ave., J. P	"	1,044 "	" 30, 1907
Jennie E. Wier	335 Seaver st., Dor	"	900 "	" 28, 1908
C. Ross Appler	Melrose	Special Instructor	1,200 "	Oct. 1, 1908
Edith T. Sears	Marshfield	"	1,200 "	Sept. 12, 1900
Margaret C. Brawley	6 Sachem st	Special Asst. Instructor	1,044 "	" 5, 1877
Helen F. Church	118 Mt. Vernon st	" "	900 "	" 9, 1908
Clara H. Hanks	23 Westville st	" "	1,476 "	" 20, 1900
Mabel S. Hastings	Lynnfield Centre	" "	900 "	" 9, 1908
Margaret J. Patterson	Arlington Heights	" "	1,548 "	" 11, 1907
Helen Torrey	25 Concord sq	" "	1,548 "	Nov. 1, 1899
Julia D. Buck	25 Wolcott st	Clerical Assistant	600 "	Oct. 1, 1908
Lucy F. Hunter	65 Chestnut st., Chsn	Temporary Teacher	3.00 day	Jan. 5, 1909
Jennie E. Bailey*	West Newton	"	936 yr	Sept. 9, 1908
Harriet D. Buckingham	Lexington	Substitute	4.00 day	" 9, 1908
Emily A. Daniell	40 Crawford st	"	4.00 "	Dec. 11, 1908
Isabella H. Howe	Cambridge	"	4.00 "	Sept. 9, 1908
Isabel S. Kelley	North Easton	"	3.00 "	" 9, 1908
John Murphy	149 Howard ave	Janitor	63.33 wk	Jan. 27, 1887

High School of Commerce.

Name.	Residence.	Designation.	Compensation.	Date of Election or Appointment.
Frank V. Thompson	84 Brooks st., Bri	Head Master	$3,780 yr	April 9, 1906
James E. Downey	677 Dudley st	Master, Head of Dept	2,484 "	Sept. 11, 1907
David T. Edwards	Cambridge	" "	2,484 "	" 11, 1907
Oscar C. Gallagher	14 Park lane	" "	2,484 "	" 11, 1907
Joel Hatheway	Cambridge	" "	2,484 "	" 11, 1907
Raymond G. Laird	22 Rockview st., J. P	" "	2,484 "	" 11, 1907
Owen D. Evans	55 Brookdale rd	" "	2,484 "	" 11, 1907
Lyman G. Smith	Cambridge	Master	3,060 "	Nov. 1, 1897
Edward F. Holden	Melrose	"	3,060 "	March 31, 1888
Newton D. Clarke	65 Oak sq. ave., Bri	Junior Master	1,476 "	Sept. 9, 1908
Adolph C. Ely	Watertown	"	1,620 "	" 11, 1907
Francis E. Mason	48 Oak sq. ave., Bri	"	1,476 "	" 9, 1908
Leonard B. Moulton	Beverly	"	1,476 "	" 9, 1908
Edward Bergé-Soler	92 Charles st	Instructor	1,200 "	" 9, 1908
Winthrop Tirrell	Cambridge	"	1,200 "	" 9, 1908
Oscar H. Peters	Cambridge	Assistant Instructor	972 "	Oct. 18, 1907
F. Edwin Walter	Canton	Special Instructor	1,320 "	April 29, 1907
Rollin H. Fisher	19 Norfolk st	Special Asst. Instructor	962 "	Sept. 11, 1907
Samuel B. Trumbull	72 Hunt ave	" "	900 "	" 9, 1908
Arthur J. Fotch	863½ Broadway	Special Assistant	744 "	Dec. 10, 1906
Johannes Adler	Cambridge	Visiting Prussian Teacher	50.00 mo	Oct. 5, 1908
Elizabeth M. Brennan	87 Old Harbor st	Clerical Assistant	660 yr	" 18, 1908
Michael J. Crowley	310 Centre st., J. P	Janitor	†	" 14, 1907

High School of Practical Arts.

Name.	Residence.	Designation.	Compensation.	Date of Election or Appointment.
Herbert S. Weaver	32 High Rock way, Alls	Head Master	$3,492 yr	Sept. 1, 1907
W. Hollis Godfrey	West Medford	Master, Head of Dept	2,628 "	" 11, 1907

* Temporarily transferred from Lawrence District.   † See Normal School.

School Department. — Continued.

Name.	Residence.	Designation.	Compensation.	Date of Election or Appointment.
High School of Practical Arts.—Concluded.				
Annie L. Bennett	33 Montrose st	First Asst. Head of Dept	$1,764 yr	March 15, 1908
Josephine Hammond	11 Saxton st	" "	1,620 "	Sept. 11, 1907
Grace G. Starbird	561 Dudley st	" "	1,764 "	March 15, 1908
Elizabeth Goldsmith	152 Huntington ave	Assistant Instructor	900 "	Sept. 9, 1908
Katherine S. Nash	75 Mayfield st		972 "	" 9, 1908
R. Deverd Parker	15 Cushing ave	Special Asst. Instructor	900 "	" 9, 1908
Ellen A. Whalen	46 E. Newton st		612 "	" 9, 1908
Mary H. Brown	279 Walnut ave	Industrial Instructor	1,020 "	" 9, 1908
Clara S. Gay	9 Newbury st	"	1,020 "	" 9, 1908
Ruth B. Gibson	33 Highland st	"	1,020 "	" 9, 1908
Margaret L. Ryan	592 E. Fourth st	Clerical Assistant	660 "	Oct. 1, 1908
Patrick H. Breanan*	25 Rill st	Janitor	38.06 wk	Sept. 9, 1907
Mechanic Arts High School.				
Charles W. Parmenter	Cambridge	Head Master	$3,780 yr	Sept. 5, 1894
William Fuller	Newton	Master, Head of Dept	3,204 "	March 15, 1907
Charles L. Hanson	Cambridge	" "	3,060 "	" 15, 1907
Roswell Parish	Brookline	" "	3,204 "	" 15, 1907
Charles S. Reed	54 Riverview rd., Bri	" "	3,060 "	Sept. 11, 1907
Harriet E. Bird	Cambridge	First Asst. Head of Dept	1,764 "	" 11, 1907
Thomas G. Rees	51 Orchard st., J. P	Master	3,060 "	" 18, 1899
Herbert M. Woodward	56 Ridgemont st., Alls	"	3,060 "	" 14, 1904
Frederick C. Adams	Natick	Junior Master	2,196 "	Feb. 10, 1904
Kenneth Beal	Newton	"	1,476 "	Sept. 9, 1908
Jonathan I. Buck	Lexington	"	2,340 "	Feb. 1, 1909
William B. Carpenter	54 Brooksdale rd., Bri	"	2,628 "	Sept. 17, 1900
Frederick G. Getchell	Somerville	"	1,476 "	" 9, 1908
Adelbert H. Morrison	Brookline	"	2,052 "	" 14, 1904
Ambrose B. Warren	128 Olney st	"	1,476 "	" 9, 1908
Roy Davis	Cambridge	Instructor	1,200 "	" 9, 1908
Benjamin F. Eddy	West Newton	"	2,340 "	July 1, 1893
Edwin F. Field	Somerville	"	1,200 "	Sept. 9, 1908
Ludwig Frank †	42 Webster st., Alls	"	2,340 "	" 6, 1893
David H. Fulton	Somerville	"	1,200 "	" 9, 1908
Samuel W. Hoyt	Cambridge	"	1,200 "	" 9, 1908
John W. Raymond	Beverly	"	2,340 "	Jan. 2, 1895
Allan K. Sweet	Cambridge	"	2,580 "	Sept. 4, 1895
Frederick W. Turner	Cambridge	"	1,980 "	" 14, 1904
Louis R. Wells	Cambridge	"	1,320 "	Nov. 11, 1907
Josephine D. Brooks	Wellesley	Assistant Instructor	972 "	Sept. 11, 1907
Gertrude M. Hall	Winchester	"	900 "	April 30, 1909
Mary A. Harriman	Framingham	"	1,320 "	Dec. 16, 1903
Ralph H. Knapp	139 Newburg st., W. R	"	1,476 "	Sept. 11, 1901
Henry C. Short	45 Stanton st	"	1,260 "	" 14, 1904
Francis J. Emery	71 Cedar st	Special Asst. Instructor	900 "	" 9, 1908
Eunice J. Weston	Wakefield	Clerical Assistant	720 "	Oct. 1, 1908
Sadie H. Roberts	109 Oak ave	Temp. Clerical Assistant	600 "	" 19, 1908
Joseph H. Allen	47 Falmouth st	Special Assistant	2.00 day	Sept. 9, 1908
Robert C. Buttrick	919 Blue Hill ave	"	1.50 "	" 9, 1908
Raymond P. Gilman	1 Oakville ave	"	1.50 "	" 9, 1908
Hugo F. Rehling	22 Dalrymple st., J. P	"	1.50 "	" 9, 1908
Allen R. Seaver	63 Aldrich st., Ros	"	1.50 "	Jan. 4, 1909
Charles M. Toole	68 Weld Hill st., W. R	"	1.50 "	Feb. 17, 1909
Joseph A. Tosi	Revere	"	2.00 "	Sept. 9, 1908
J. Franklin Warren, Jr	80 Rockview st., J. P	"	2.00 "	" 9, 1908
Edward H. Temple	W. Somerville	Temporary Teacher	4.00 "	Feb. 1, 1909
George W. Fogg	16 Claybourne st	Janitor	52.00 wk	April 1, 1894
Charles S. Drew	34 Houghton st	Engineer	60.00 "	Feb. 1, 1896
George F. Barker	27 Clement pk	Regular Substitute Janitor	11.54 "	Dec. 16, 1908
Roxbury High School.				
Charles M. Clay	The Warren	Head Master	$3,780 yr	Oct. 15, 1883
Henry C. Shaw	Hemenway Chambers	Master, Head of Dept	3,204 "	March 15, 1907
Irving H. Upton	20 Park View st	" "	3,204 "	" 15, 1907
Persis P. Drake	3 Holbrook st., J. P	First Asst., Head of Dept	1,764 "	" 15, 1908
Mary T. Loughlin	16 Thornley st	" "	1,404 "	" 15, 1908
Edith A. Parkhurst	Somerville	" "	1,764 "	" 15, 1908
Jennie I. Ware	South Framingham	Assistant Principal	1,836 "	Jan. 1, 1897

* See Mather District.
† Leave of absence without pay from February 3, 1909, to February 3, 1910.

School Department.— Continued.

Name.	Residence.	Designation.	Compensation.	Date of Election or Appointment.

Roxbury High School.— Concluded.

Name.	Residence.	Designation.	Compensation.	Date of Election or Appointment.
Myron W. Richardson	67 Brooksdale rd., Bri	Master	$3,060 yr	Sept. 11, 1901
Elsie M. Blake	Franklin Square House	Assistant	1,620 "	27, 1899
Helen A. Bragg*	28 Greenville st	"	810 "	5, 1888
Marion W. Clark	Franklin Square House	"	1,260 "	28, 1904
Mary F. Gould	Everett	"	1,044 " Oct.	21, 1907
Florence E. Leadbetter	867 South st., Ros	"	1,620 " Dec.	1, 1897
Charlotte W. Montgomery	1 Burr Oak pk	"	1,476 " Jan.	13, 1902
Celia F. Stacy	116 Perham st., W. R	"	1,404 " Oct.	8, 1906
Prudence E. Thomas	28 Glenarm st	"	1,404 " Sept.	10, 1902
Mabel L. Warner	10 Conway st., Ros	"	1,620 " Oct.	5, 1891
Myrtle C. Dickson	22 Greenville st	Assistant Instructor	900 " April	12, 1909
Margaret F. Keenan	1329 Blue Hill ave	"	900 " Sept.	9, 1908
K. Isabel Mann	Weymouth	"	900 " "	9, 1908
Roy E. Mooar	South Weymouth	"	1,116 " "	15, 1902
Harriet C. Taylor	Weston	"	972 " "	23, 1907
Daniel Foley	61 Murdock st., Bri	Special Instructor	1,560 " Oct.	2, 1905
Mary Hubbard	The Warren	"	1,200 " Sept.	4, 1895
Helen J. McShane	15 Chestnut Hill ave., Bri	Special Assistant Instructor	1,260 " "	1, 1908
Alice C. Riordan	Rockland	" "	900 " "	9, 1908
Bessie J. Sanger	144 Hemenway st	" "	1,404 " Dec.	20, 1900
Florence L. Carter	Watertown	" "	900 " "	4, 1899
Winifred K. Feeney	169 St. Botolph st	Clerical Assistant	660 " Oct.	6, 1908
Alice E. Dacy †	28 Ward st	Temporary Teacher	936 " Feb.	3, 1896
Olga A. F. Stegelmann ‡	434 Norfolk st., Mattapan	"	936 " Oct.	5, 1896
E. Marion Williams	41 Bay State rd	Substitute	4.00 day April	12, 1909
Frank W. Turner	3 Sherman st	Janitor	51.62 wk "	15, 1898

South Boston High School.

Name.	Residence.	Designation.	Compensation.	Date of Election or Appointment.
Augustus D. Small	67 Ashford st., Alls	Head Master	$3,780 yr April	9, 1901
William I. Corthell	39 Walnut pk	Master, Head of Dept	2,628 " March	15, 1907
James Mahoney	72 G st	"	3,204 " April	1, 1907
Susan L. Mara	Hotel Denmark, Dudley st	Assistant Principal	1,836 " Feb.	1, 1905
Arthur F. Campbell	58 Bloomfield st	Junior Master	1,908 " April	9, 1906
Clara W. Barnes	191 Trenton st	First Asst., Head of Dept	1,548 " March	15, 1908
Lillian J. MacRae	103 Rosseter st	" "	1,548 " "	15, 1908
Annie M. Mulcahy	924 E. Fourth st	" "	1,548 " "	15, 1908
Lillian A. Bragdon	5 Falcon st	Assistant	1,476 " Feb.	17, 1902
Minnie L. Butland	665 Columbia rd	"	1,404 " Oct.	1, 1902
Mary L. Green	16 Marcella st	"	1,404 " "	1, 1902
Grace V. Lynch	10 Batavia st	"	1,188 " May	1, 1905
Mary T. O'Donnell	Cambridge	"	1,188 " Oct.	1, 1905
Marie A. Solano	165 Hemenway st	"	1,476 " Sept.	11, 1901
Elisabeth G. Tracy	8 Penhallow st	"	1,476 " "	11, 1901
Bertha Vogel	120 Pembroke st	"	1,476 " "	11, 1901
Priscilla Whiton	11 Albemarle Chambers	Assistant Instructor	1,332 " "	21, 1908
Blanche A. Bemis	Swampscott	Special Instructor	1,200 " "	11, 1901
Helen G. Davis	66 Westland ave	Special Assistant Instructor	1,044 " "	12, 1906
Henriette Goldstein	2737 Washington st	" "	1,260 " "	1, 1908
Christina M. McCarthy	253 Emerson st	" "	900 " "	9, 1908
Annie G. Merrill	404 Columbus ave	" "	1,404 " Nov.	13, 1901
Mary C. Rice	3 National st	Clerical Assistant	600 " Sept.	9, 1908
Caroline R. Pulsifer§	9 Payson ave	Temporary Teacher	792 " Dec.	5, 1903
Stephen J. Murdock	39 Monument ave	Substitute	4.00 day Sept.	9, 1908
Ellen A. Whalen	46 E. Newton st	Assistant Special Instructor, 2½ days a week	‖ "	9, 1908
George F. Barry	15 Mt. Vernon st	Janitor	61.02 wk "	11, 1901
Mary G. Devine	3 National st	Matron	10.38 " Dec.	21, 1903

West Roxbury High School.

Name.	Residence.	Designation.	Compensation.	Date of Election or Appointment.
George C. Mann	2 Greenough ave., J. P	Head Master	$3,780 yr Jan.	1, 1898
George A. Cowen	22 Holbrook st., J. P	Master, Head of Dept	2,772 " March	15, 1907
George F. Partridge	48 St. John st., J. P	"	3,204 " "	15, 1907
Mary I. Adams	15 Eliot st., J. P	First Asst., Head of Dept	1,764 " "	15, 1908
Caroline W. Trask	7 Alveston st., J. P	"	1,764 " "	15, 1908

* Year's leave of absence on half pay.   Resignation to take effect September 1, 1909.
† Temporarily transferred from the John A. Andrew District.
‡ Temporarily transferred from John A. Andrew District. Leave of absence without pay from February 1 to September 1, 1909.
§ Temporarily transferred from the Washington District.   ‖ See High School of Practical Arts.

School Department.— Continued.

Name.	Residence.	Designation.	Compensation	Date of Election or Appointment.

West Roxbury High School.— Concluded.

Name.	Residence.	Designation.	Compensation	Date of Election or Appointment.
Blanche G. Wetherbee	18 Harris ave., J. P.	First Asst., Head of Dept.	$1,764 yr.	March 15, 1908
Frances B. Wilson	134 Huntington ave	"	1,692 "	Oct. 6, 1908
Annie N. Bunker	25 Aldworth st., J. P.	Assistant	1,620 "	Nov. 1, 1900
M. Alice Jackson	1 Maple st., W. R.	"	1,044 "	Oct. 1, 1907
Rebecca Kite	66 Mt. Vernon st	"	1,620 "	Dec. 1, 1898
Mabel O. Mills	Winter Hill	"	1,404 "	Sept. 22, 1902
Emma F. Simmons	51 Gardner st., Alls.	"	1,332 "	Oct. 2, 1905
Mary K. Tibbits	25 Greenough ave., J. P.	"	1,548 "	Sept. 14, 1904
Mildred K. Bentley	Brookline	Assistant Instructor	900 "	" 9, 1908
Bertha E. Dennis	3 Carlisle st	"	972 "	" 16, 1908
Leon C. Colman	Quincy House	Special Instructor	1,560 "	Nov. 15, 1905
Catharine L. Bigelow	Norwood	"	1,200 "	Sept. 11, 1901
Ellen F. G. O'Connor	42 Highland ave	Special Assistant Instructor.	1,332 "	" 10, 1902
Mabel E. Woodworth	8 Alveston st., J. P.	Special Assistant	744 "	Nov. 20, 1906
Mary O'Connell*	14 Spring Park ave., J. P.	Temporary Teacher	936 "	Oct. 26, 1908
Jane I. Gannett	South Hanover	Substitute	4.00 day	April 1, 1909
Ella M. Parker	181 Huntington ave	Temporary Spec. Asst. Inst.	3.00 "	Feb. 1, 1909
John H. Kelley	Nathaniel Weld pl., J. P.	Janitor	49.19 wk.	Oct. 1, 1900
Mary E. McDonough	59 Monadnock st	Matron	10.38 "	Sept. 1, 1901

Adams District.

Name.	Residence.	Designation.	Compensation	Date of Election or Appointment.
Frank F. Preble	Melrose	Master	$3,180 yr.	Oct. 1, 1875
Joel C. Bolan	Brookline	Sub-Master	2,340 "	Sept. 3, 1883
Charlotte L. Voigt	54 Worcester st	Master's Assistant	1,260 "	May 14, 1902
Adiline H. Cook	8 Cazenove st	First Assistant, Grammar.	1,116 "	Nov. 1, 1905
Fanny M. Morris	183 Webster st	First Assistant in Charge	1,164 "	April 10, 1905
Annice A. Anderson	189 Webster st	Assistant	696 "	" 9, 1906
Eleanor C. Butler	424 Columbus ave	"	936 "	Sept. 8, 1898
Lydia A. Buxton	Everett	"	936 "	" 13, 1897
Caroline G. Chard	Chelsea	"	648 "	Nov. 6, 1906
M. Luetta Choate	36 Princeton st	"	936 "	Feb. 4, 1884
Ethel M. Coe	12 Myrtle st., J. P.	"	696 "	Sept. 13, 1905
Helen L. Dennison	Chelsea	"	936 "	" 8, 1896
Agnes R. Driscoll	45 M st	"	552 "	Jan. 4, 1909
Ruth M. Haynes	6 Ainsley st	"	552 "	March 16, 1909
Mary H. Healey	140 Lamartine st., J. P.	"	552 "	Nov. 17, 1908
Josephine M. Hodgkinson	86 E. Newton st	"	552 "	Feb. 17, 1908
Anna E. Keaney	110 Boston st	"	792 "	Jan. 18, 1904
Annie F. Keating	Natick	"	840 "	Nov. 6, 1905
Blanche F. Kingsley	207 Newbury st	"	936 "	" 1, 1900
Laura M. Lane	1574 Tremont st	"	552 "	" 3, 1908
Florence E. Marshall	38 Rockview st., J. P.	"	936 "	Feb. 1, 1900
Jennie A. Mayer	Norfolk	"	936 "	Oct. 15, 1887
Martha F. McElvoy	4 Worthington st	"	552 "	Dec. 8, 1908
Eleanor L. McGourty	104 Calumet st	"	600 "	April 8, 1907
Ellen E. Melleney	14 Elmore st	"	840 "	Jan. 16, 1905
Mary J. Monahan	24 St. Germain st	"	888 "	Sept. 30, 1901
Ellen L. Moran	1 Dunford st	"	888 "	March 2, 1903
Elizabeth J. Murphy	57 Saratoga st	"	552 "	Jan. 7, 1908
Mary A. Palmer	20 Payson ave	"	936 "	Oct. 1, 1879
Ellenette Pillsbury	19 Princeton st	"	936 "	Dec. 21, 1864
May H. Sears	61 Westland ave	"	840 "	Nov. 24, 1905
Harriet Sturtevant	56 Trenton st	"	936 "	March 1, 1870
Rosella V. Sweeney	47 Union pk	"	744 "	Jan. 23, 1905
Mary E. Towne	12 Moultrie st	"	888 "	" 16, 1905
Clara M. White	Beachmont	"	936 "	Sept. 17, 1900
Cora E. Bigelow	Newton	First Asst., Kindergarten.	792 "	" 7, 1892
Mabel J. Houlahan	Waverley	"	792 "	April 8, 1901
Catherine P. Bishop	45 Westland ave	Assistant	624 "	Jan. 4, 1904
Mary E. Kennedy	Braintree	"	624 "	Sept. 9, 1903
Alice L. Kelley	East Boston	Substitute	2.00 day	" 9, 1908
Sarah G. Stowers	Somerville	"	2.00 "	April 13, 1909
Mary Moore	346 Sumner st., E. B.	Attendant	.50 "	" 16, 1909
Mary L. Clark	221 Everett st., E. B.	"	.50 "	March 9, 1909
Francis P. Linnehan	89 Clarkson st., Dor.	Janitor	21.47 wk.	May 1, 1908
John H. Crafts	301 Maverick st., E. B.	"	31.39 "	April 1, 1897

Agassiz District.

Name.	Residence.	Designation.	Compensation	Date of Election or Appointment.
John T. Gibson	17 Myrtle st., J. P.	Master	$3,180 yr.	Sept. 20, 1872
Joshua Q. Litchfield	Quincy	Sub-Master	2,340 "	Nov. 9, 1896

* Temporarily transferred from the Bowditch District.

School Department.— Continued.

Name.	Residence.	Designation	Compensation.	Date of Election or Appointment.

Agassiz District. — Concluded.

Name.	Residence.	Designation	Compensation.	Date
Caroline N. Poole	108 Corey st., W. R.	Master's Assistant	$1,068 yr.	Oct. 1, 1906
Caroline D. Putnam	20 St. John st., J. P.	First Assistant in charge	1,116 "	Nov. 2, 1896
Annie E. Bancroft	Woburn	Assistant	936 "	April 15, 1889
Clara E. Bertsch	68 Paul Gore st., J. P.	"	888 "	Jan. 7, 1902
Elvera M. Bloom	Hyde Park	"	840 "	Sept. 13, 1905
Mabel A. Campbell	18 Holbrook st., J. P.	"	600 "	Nov. 5, 1907
Alice G. Cleaveland	152 Brown ave., Ros.	"	888 "	" 3, 1902
Mary A. Cooke	286 Chestnut ave., J. P.	"	936 "	Sept. 14, 1891
Mary J. Haggerty	167 Sydney st., Dor.	"	744 "	May 16, 1904
Julia A. Mahan	Natick	"	552 "	Sept. 14, 1908
Mary H. McCready	Milton	"	936 "	Jan. 2, 1894
Clara I. Metcalf	21 Beech Glen st	"	936 "	Oct. 26, 1880
Sarah A. Moody	92 Gainsboro st	"	936 "	Feb. 1, 1897
Clara J. Reynolds	29 Seaverns ave., J. P.	"	936 "	Sept. 1, 1873
Ethelyn A. Townsend	Cambridge	"	888 "	" 11, 1901
May E. Ward	15 Blagden st	"	936 "	Nov. 1, 1897
Emma F. West	Cambridge	"	936 "	" 3, 1902
Isabelle H. Earnshaw	108 Corey st., W. R.	First Asst., Kindergarten	792 "	May 16, 1904
Helen B. Foster	5 Agassiz pk., J. P.	Assistant	624 "	Dec. 1, 1896
Mary V. O'Regan	616 Massachusetts ave	Temporary Teacher	2.00 day	Oct. 1, 1908
Margaret M. F. Conley	56 Lexington st	Substitute	2.00 "	April 12, 1909
Frances E. Kelly	31 Pembroke st	"	2.00 "	Sept. 9, 1908
Edna K. Lane	5 Prescott st., E. B.	"	1.50 "	Feb. 1, 1909
William A. Reed	146 Massachusetts ave.	"	2.43 "	April 12, 1909
Eleanor M. Brohm	66 Call st., J. P.	Attendant	.50 "	Sept. 9, 1908
George A. Cottrell	22 Thomas st., J. P.	Janitor	37.28 wk.	Jan. 1, 1894

Bennett District.

Name.	Residence.	Designation	Compensation.	Date
Henry L. Sawyer	16 Sparhawk st., Bri.	Master	$3,180 yr.	Dec. 1, 1886
James H. Burdett	Dedham	Sub-Master	2,340 "	Oct. 19, 1896
Isabel M. Wier	335 Seaver st	Master's Assistant	1,308 "	Sept. 10, 1902
Maude E. Rice	15A Linden st., Alls.	First Assistant in Charge	972 "	Jan. 4, 1909
Margaret J. Scollans	89 Foster st., Bri.	"	1,116 "	Dec. 1, 1903
Rena I. Black	Newton	Assistant	552 "	Nov. 17, 1908
Elizabeth R. Bradbury	84 Astor st	"	936 "	Sept. 6, 1898
Vesta E. Chadwick	Everett	"	696 "	Nov. 3, 1908
Jennie M. Chandler	41 St. Botolph st	"	888 "	June 1, 1904
Frances W. Currier	12 Surrey st., Bri.	"	936 "	May 30, 1870
Jennie M. Good	53A Dale st	"	840 "	Sept. 10, 1902
Clara L. Harrington	407 Washington st., Bri.	"	936 "	Oct. 1, 1880
E. May Hastings	87 Dunboy st., Bri.	"	936 "	Nov. 2, 1896
Rose S. Havey	770 Dudley st	"	936 "	June 2, 1890
Leslie D. Hooper	41 Ashford st., Alls.	"	936 "	Jan. 3, 1888
Katharine R. McManus	Natick	"	600 "	Sept. 11, 1907
Mary E. A. McPherson	34 Peter Parley rd., J. P.	"	552 "	March 3, 1908
Anne Neville	52 Winship st., Bri.	"	936 "	Oct. 10, 1892
Mary R. Quinn	21 Circuit st	"	600 "	Nov. 19, 1907
Gertrude B. Sanderson	25 Leicester st., Bri.	"	792 "	Sept. 9, 1903
Helena D. Smith	93 Surrey st., Bri.	"	936 "	" 13, 1899
Margaret A. Sullivan	Newton	"	552 "	Nov. 17, 1908
Katherine F. Wood	48 Parsons st., Bri.	"	936 "	Oct. 1, 1900
Jennie L. Worth	9 Newton st., Bri.	"	936 "	" 1, 1900
Helen L. Arnold	Braintree	First Asst., Kindergarten	792 "	May 11, 1904
Margaret T. McCabe	66 Murdock st., Bri.	"	792 "	Feb. 1, 1899
Helen S. Eaton	1 Wadsworth st., Alls.	Assistant	624 "	Jan. 16, 1905
Julia M. Fitzpatrick	111 Hutchins st	Temporary Teacher	2.00 day	Oct. 19, 1908
Edith F. Russell	85 Chestnut ave., J. P.	Special Assistant	1.50 "	Jan. 4, 1909
Alma G. Crossman	40 Newton st., Bri.	Attendant	.50 "	Sept. 17, 1908
Walter H. Bickford	9 Parsons st., Bri.	Janitor	23.89 wk.	June 2, 1902
Joseph A. Crossman	40 Newton st., Bri.	"	11.88 "	April 1, 1885
William H. Lyman	38 Newton st., Bri.	"	10.59 "	Sept. 1, 1903
Samuel H. Mitchell	1 Baldwin pl., Bri.	"	10.32 "	May 1, 1902
John W. Remmonds	14 Wadsworth st., Alls.	"	28.05 "	Sept. 6, 1882

Bigelow District.

Name.	Residence.	Designation	Compensation.	Date
J. Gardner Bassett	Bridgewater	Master	$3,180 yr.	Dec. 1, 1896
Thomas J. Barry	31 Mt. Vernon st	Sub-Master	1,740 "	Sept. 25, 1901
Theobald A. Lynch	71 Farragut rd	"	1,500 "	Nov. 3, 1908
Amelia B. Coe	West Newton	Master's Assistant	1,308 "	Sept., 1875
Ellen Coe	West Newton	First Assistant, Grammar	1,212 "	" 7, 1897

School Department.— Continued.

Name.	Residence.	Designation.	Compensation.	Date of Election or Appointment.

Bigelow District.— Concluded.

Name.	Residence.	Designation.	Compensation.	Date of Election or Appointment.
Annie S. McKissick	11 Elton st	First Assistant in Charge	$1,116 yr	Jan. 6, 1902
Annie T. Burke	56 N st	Assistant	936 "	Nov. 3, 1902
Annie G. Casey	East Cambridge	"	882 "	Dec. 1, 1902
Geraldine I. Donoghue	139 L st	"	648 "	" 31, 1906
Helen M. Donohue	122 Mt. Pleasant ave	"	552 "	Feb. 3, 1908
Ella F. Fitzgerald	30 Vaughan st	"	936 "	" 2, 1880
Clara M. French	36 Magnolia st	"	1,032 "	Oct. 2, 1905
Martha A. Goodrich	525 Fourth st	"	936 "	Sept. 9, 1891
Katharine P. Kelly	15 Gates st	"	936 "	Oct. 10, 1898
Louise C. Keyes	595 Fifth st	"	600 "	" 22, 1907
Susan H. Lynch	616 Broadway	"	744 "	Sept. 14, 1904
Mary G. McDermott	23 Old Harbor st	"	792 "	" 14, 1904
Annie C. MacDonald	793 Columbia rd	"	744 "	Oct. 18, 1905
Katharine C. McDonnell	27 Mercer st	"	792 "	Sept. 9, 1903
Sarah D. McKissick	11 Elton st	"	936 "	Oct. 16, 1882
Ellen A. McMahon	223 Gold st	"	936 "	June 1, 1891
Angeline S. Morse	212 Dorchester st	"	936 "	Jan. 11, 1886
Alice M. Mulrey	Cambridge	"	840 "	Oct. 5, 1903
Cora L. Mulrey	Cambridge	"	552 "	" 1, 1908
Alice M. Robinson	572 Broadway	"	936 "	Dec. 7, 1907
Emma J. Ross	Somerville	"	936 "	" 1, 1902
Julia A. Rourke	515 Warren st	"	936 "	Nov. 11, 1892
Laura S. Russell	13 Woodville pk	"	936 "	May 16, 1882
Florence L. Spear	59 Bakersfield st	"	936 "	Sept. 20, 1892
Henrietta L. Stumpf	652 Broadway	"	744 "	" 14, 1904
Mary G. Sullivan	44 Templeton st	"	696 "	" 22, 1905
Sabina G. Sweeney	718 Columbia rd	"	936 "	" 7, 1885
Alice E. Thornton	58 Shepton st	"	936 "	Jan. 6, 1902
Cecelia V. Mara	35 Clayton st	Substitute	2.00 day	April 30, 1909
Charles H. Carr	66 Westville st., Dor	Janitor	*41.56 wk	March 26, 1902
John B. Dooley	204 Eighth st., S. B.	"	17.10 "	July 1, 1907

Blackinton District.

Name.	Residence.	Designation.	Compensation.	Date of Election or Appointment.
Herbert L. Morse	35 St. Botolph st	Master	$3,060 yr	Sept. 1, 1904
Everett L. Getchell	23 Allston st	Sub-Master	1,620 "	Feb. 5, 1907
Bremen E. Sinclair	37 Forest Hills st., J. P.	"	2,340 "	Jan. 2, 1899
Catherine E. McCarthy	7 Hawes ave	Master's Assistant	1,164 "	Sept. 14, 1904
Mabel A. C. Anderson	617 Hyde Park ave., Ros	Assistant	600 "	" 11, 1907
Ellen S. Bloomfield	Winthrop	"	936 "	" 26, 1888
Hazel N. Boice	384 Boylston st	"	552 "	Nov. 3, 1908
Helen A. Burke	119 Webster st	"	936 "	" 1, 1897
Florence G. Erskine	134 Newburg st., W. R	"	936 "	" 1, 1900
Minnie Goldsmith	72 Devon st	"	888 "	Sept. 11, 1901
Eliza D. Graham	191 Trenton st	"	936 "	Oct. 2, 1899
Margaret E. Gray	29 Bennington st	"	936 "	Nov. 1, 1895
Elizabeth Hiscock	22 Mellen st	"	696 "	" 3, 1908
Helen M. Horton	191 Lexington st	"	840 "	April 11, 1904
Harriet G. Jones	93 St. Botolph st	"	936 "	Nov. 11, 1903
Annie C. Lamb	69 Regent st	"	888 "	Jan. 16, 1905
Margaret T. Leahy	186 Leyden st	"	840 "	" 16, 1903
Sara F. Littlefield	72 W. Eagle st	"	936 "	Feb. 1, 1894
Alice M. Macdonald	34 Wenonah st	"	936 "	Sept. 6, 1898
Annie F. McGillicuddy	21 Wharf st	"	936 "	" 4, 1895
Kate E. McMullin	31 Princeton st	"	696 "	" 13, 1905
Caroline E. Nutter	260 Lexington st	"	936 "	" 6, 1886
Lucy A. O'Brien	Arlington	"	840 "	Oct. 1, 1903
Abigail F. Sullivan	57 Charlotte st	"	888 "	Jan. 6, 1902
Mabel E. Vaughan	424 Massachusetts ave	"	696 "	March 2, 1908
Nellie S. Morris	97 Bellevue, W. R	First Asst., Kindergarten	624 "	Oct. 23, 1901
Eliza L. Osgood	Peabody	" "	744 "	Sept. 12, 1906
Ruth Perry	3 Monadnock st	" "	792 "	" 14, 1904
Margaret Chandler	161 Saratoga st	Assistant	576 "	" 13, 1905
Gertrude A. Fuller	29 St. James ave	"	432 "	Oct. 12, 1908
Hortense J. Parker	120 Dartmouth st	Special Assistant	1.75 day	Sept. 9, 1908
Esther Fenocetti	191 Gladstone st	Attendant	.50 "	" 9, 1908
Frances Beadle	Saratoga and Butler ave	Janitor	22.04 wk	Oct. 1, 1902
Walter L. McLean	87 Horace st	"	22.02 "	" 1, 1904

* Includes $252 for care of baths.

School Department.— Continued.

Name.	Residence.	Designation.	Compensation.	Date of Election or Appointment.

Bowditch District.

Name.	Residence.	Designation.	Compensation.	Date of Election or Appointment.
Edward W. Schuerch	Corey st., W. R	Master	$3,180 yr	Dec. 3, 1894
Amy Hutchins	Cambridge	Master's Assistant	1,308 "	Feb. 1, 1879
Elizabeth G. Melcher	486 Massachusetts ave	First Assistant, Grammar	1,212 "	Sept. 6, 1886
Lena L. Carpenter	204 W. Springfield st	First Assistant in Charge	1,020 "	Dec. 3, 1907
Margaret E. Winton	Beverly	"	1,116 "	Nov. 2, 1896
Viola M. Allen	27A Lindsey st	Assistant	936 "	April 1, 1898
Eliza D. Bean	286 Chestnut ave., J. P.	"	744 "	Oct. 1, 1907
Sarah P. Blackburn	34 Oakdale st., J. P.	"	936 "	March 6, 1871
Lucy M. Burln	100 Paul Gore st., J. P.	"	936 "	Sept. 8, 1896
Mary J. Capen	41 Huntington ave	"	936 "	March 6, 1871
Tabitha Fitz Gerald	22 Kent st	"	792 "	Sept. 20, 1898
Helen J. Gormley	17 Eliot st., J. P.	"	936 "	" 9, 1903
Alice Greene	274 Chestnut ave., J. P.	"	936 "	Nov. 16, 1893
Annie M. Johnson	1092 Bennington st	"	936 "	Jan. 10, 1901
Ella F. Jordan	517 South st., Ros.	"	936 "	April 14, 1902
Nellie I. Lapham	47 Mt. Vernon st., W. R	"	936 "	Feb. 1, 1893
Annie E. Lees	Wellesley Hills	"	936 "	Jan. 10, 1901
Mary E. McDonald	19 Maywood st	"	936 "	Dec. 1, 1887
Gertrude A. Poor	2 Greenough ave., J. P	"	624 "	Nov. 1, 1906
Agnes E. Regan	31 Howell st	"	552 "	" 3, 1908
Isabel P. Reagh	39 Maple st., W. R	"	936 "	" 1, 1900
Annie C. Shea	196 Green st., J. P.	"	552 "	Jan. 4, 1909
Alice B. Stephenson	236 Chestnut ave., J. P.	"	936 "	Sept. 1873
Elizabeth L. Stodder	436 Columbus ave	"	936 "	" 7, 1887
Anna K. Vackert	84 Wyman st., J. P.	"	936 "	Jan. 24, 1900
Olive A. Wallis	22 Union ter., J. P.	"	936 "	Sept. 5, 1894
Margaret G. Wilder	Newton	"	600 "	" 11, 1907
Anna E. Marble	Brookline	First Asst., Kindergarten	792 "	" 5, 1888
Lillian B. Poor *	2047 Columbus ave	"	792 "	" 10, 1894
Florence J. Ferguson	Winthrop Centre	Assistant	624 "	" 10, 1902
Edna F. Hawes	Winchester	"	528 "	Oct. 1, 1906
Adelaide G. Nelson	616 Massachusetts ave	Temporary Teacher	2.00 day	" 26, 1908
Florence Herbsman	44 Lynde st	Substitute	2.00 "	April 12, 1909
Jessie B. Smith	6 Floyd st	Special Assistant	1.75 "	Oct. 20, 1908
Edna L. Black	111 Warren st	Substitute	1.75 "	March 1, 1909
Christine W. MacLachlan	3563 Washington st., J. P.	"	2.00 "	Sept. 9, 1908
Louis N. Marison	283 Chestnut ave., J. P.	Janitor	12.71 wk.	Oct. 7, 1907
Samuel S. Marison	327 Lamartine st., J. P.	"	23.77 "	Sept. 23, 1873
Edward Sealer	128 Green st., J. P.	"	9.05 "	July 20, 1905
Charles F. Travis	51 Chestnut Hill ave., Bri.	"	14.17 "	May 5, 1906

Bowdoin District.

Name.	Residence.	Designation.	Compensation.	Date of Election or Appointment.
Alonzo Meserve	87 Linden st., Alls	Master	$3,180 yr	Sept. 6, 1886
Sarah R. Smith	Beverly	Master's Assistant	1,308 "	Nov. 3, 1879
Martha S. O'Hea	Brookline	First Assistant, Grammar	1,212 "	Jan. 6, 1902
Sarah E. Brown	67 Pinckney st	First Assistant in Charge	972 "	Nov. 17, 1908
Annetta F. Armes	Nashua, N. H	Assistant	936 "	Sept. 8, 1896
Hattie H. Batson	46 Maxwell st	"	600 "	April 22, 1907
Mabel Carling	33 Hawthorne st	"	552 "	Nov. 3, 1908
Edith L. Caverly	Chelsea	"	936 "	Feb. 1, 1900
Catherine M. Dolan	50 W. Cedar st	"	936 "	Oct. 1, 1897
Susan S. Faden	90 Rockview st., J. P.	"	648 "	Nov. 1, 1906
Mary W. French †	33 Mt. Vernon st	"	936 "	March 16, 1898
Florence M. Halligan	41 Fairview st., Ros.	"	936 "	" 14, 1900
Margaret G. Hatch	46 Tuttle st	"	552 "	Dec. 8, 1908
Julia F. Holland	Winchester	"	936 "	" 5, 1889
Marion F. Kiely	24 Brighton st	"	552 "	April 30, 1909
Mary A. Long	20 Allcott st., Alls	"	888 "	Nov. 13, 1901
Ella L. Macomber	53 Mt. Vernon st	"	936 "	Dec. 15, 1878
Julia G. L. Morse	Somerville	"	936 "	" 4, 1889
Mary F. Murphy	23 Wellesley pk	"	936 "	March 1, 1900
Gertrude G. O'Brien	Sharon	"	936 "	Sept. 18, 1895
Serena F. Perry	55 Pinckney st	"	936 "	March 2, 1868
Eudora E. W. Pitcher	50 Hereford st	"	936 "	Sept. 1, 1873
Ethel G. Ross	1463 Blue Hill ave	"	744 "	" 14, 1905
Harriet L. Smith	75 Brent st	"	936 "	March 22, 1889
Eliza A. Thomas	89 Gainsboro st	"	936 "	Oct. 16, 1894
May A. Treen	95 Mt. Vernon st	"	936 "	Nov. 26, 1902

* Leave of absence without pay, Feb. 1, 1909, to June 1, 1909. † Retired on pension from April 30, 1909.

School Department. — Continued.

Name.	Residence.	Designation.	Compensation.	Date of Election or Appointment.

Bowdoin District. — Concluded.

Name.	Residence.	Designation.	Compensation.	Date of Election or Appointment.
Mabel West	64 Mt. Vernon st.	Assistant	$936 yr.	Feb., 1873
Serena J. Frye	Brookline	First Asst., Kindergarten.	792 "	Nov. 14, 1888
Sarah E. Kilmer	Brookline	"	792 "	Oct. 5, 1902
Carolyn M. Fletcher	22 Huntington ave.	Assistant	624 "	Dec. 11, 1899
Maude A. Lynch	45 Hereford st.	"	576 "	Oct. 2, 1905
Alma M. Nilson	66 Romsey st.	Special Assistant	1.75 day.	Feb. 23, 1909
Mary T. Sherry	146 Dorchester st.	Substitute	2.00 "	Nov. 16, 1908
Matilda Block	199 Chambers st.	Attendant	.50 "	Oct. 21, 1908
Elizabeth Kuskin	39 Revere st.	"	.50 "	Sept. 9, 1908
Denis J. Wilson	86 Buttonwood st.	Janitor	26.57 wk.	Feb. 22, 1908
John J. Murphy	106 Myrtle st.	"	11.45 "	Oct. 23, 1907

Brimmer District.

Name.	Residence.	Designation.	Compensation.	Date of Election or Appointment.
George W. Ransom	Cambridge	Master	$2,820 yr.	Oct. 1, 1906
John J. Maloney	66 Webster st.	Sub-Master	1,620 "	Dec. 17, 1907
John A. Russell	18 Huntington ave.	"	2,340 "	Feb. 12, 1902
Nellie A. Manning	76 Calumet st.	Master's Assistant	1,164 "	Jan. 16, 1905
Margaret L. Eaton	49 Rockland st.	First Assistant in Charge	1,068 "	Nov. 10, 1906
Sarah E. Adams	515 Massachusetts ave.	Assistant	936 "	Feb. 3, 1879
Alma Boodro	265 Gold st.	"	552 "	March 16, 1909
Margaret E. Brennan	12 Oscar st.	"	600 "	Feb. 4, 1907
Elizabeth G. Cahill	Cambridge	"	936 "	Sept. 15, 1886
Mary A. Carney	277 Everett ave., Alls.	"	936 "	Nov. 29, 1880
Mary E. Collins	384 Boylston st.	"	936 "	" 1, 1881
Frances A. Curtis	Cambridge	"	840 "	Sept. 9, 1903
Grace F. Gardner	West Hanover	"	936 "	March 30, 1903
Mary E. W. Hagerty	39 E. Brookline st.	"	936 "	Oct. 7, 1885
Ellen G. Hayden	Methuen	"	936 "	" 15, 1902
Catherine G. Kelleher	18 Mt. Vernon st., Dor.	"	552 "	Nov. 3, 1908
Mary M. McLaughlin	4 Harvest ter.	"	600 "	Sept. 11, 1907
Grace W. Mitchell	East Weymouth	"	936 "	Dec. 1, 1902
Anna T. O'Brien	806 Parker st.	"	600 "	Nov. 5, 1907
Theresa G. O'Brien	24 Freeman st.	"	744 "	Jan. 16, 1905
Josephine A. Power	9 Union st.	"	600 "	April 8, 1907
Frances A. Putnam	55 W. Cedar st.	"	936 "	Dec. 10, 1902
Mary E. Tiernay	4 Crawford st.	"	936 "	Sept. 4, 1874
Etta D. Morse	348 Walnut st.	First Asst., Kindergarten.	792 "	Jan. 2, 1894
Hope Davison	101 Pinckney st.	Assistant	480 "	Dec. 3, 1907
Daisy Slocomb	83 Clifton st.	Attendant	.50 day.	Feb. 15, 1909
Michael Cunningham	76 E. Newton st.	Janitor	10.10 wk.	April 5, 1904
James Latrobe	6½ Nassau st.	"	16.51 "	" 1, 1894
John J. Norton	153 D st.	"	14.70 "	Oct. 23, 1907

Bunker Hill District.

Name.	Residence.	Designation.	Compensation.	Date of Election or Appointment.
Frank L. Keith	72 Gardner st., Alls.	Master	$2,820 yr.	Sept. 12, 1906
Joseph F. Gould	Somerville	Sub-Master	1,500 "	" 9, 1908
Henry F. Sears*	Melrose	"	1,170 "	" 1, 1868
Harriet H. Norcross	Watertown	Master's Assistant	1,308 "	" 8, 1890
Abby P. Josselyn*	Winthrop	First Assistant, Grammar.	696 "	" 1, 1879
Elizabeth B. Norton	Malden	First Assistant in Charge	1,116 "	Nov. 2, 1896
Kate T. Brooks	18 Oak st., Chsn.	Assistant	936 "	Sept. 4, 1889
Clara B. Brown*	Pittsfield, N. H.	"	468 "	April 1, 1885
Charlotte Z. Church	32 Greenville st.	"	936 "	Oct. 1, 1900
Helen F. Davol	Somerville	"	744 "	Jan. 2, 1905
Elizabeth F. Doherty	249 Bunker Hill st.	"	552 "	Nov. 3, 1908
Cora V. Enwright	Medford	"	936 "	Sept. 12, 1900
Mary E. Flanders	Newton	"	936 "	" 1, 1873
Anna P. Hannon	Somerville	"	936 "	Nov. 17, 1892
Annie B. Hunter	Somerville	"	936 "	Jan. 3, 1881
Catherine M. McHugh	123 M st.	"	552 "	April 30, 1909
Anastasia F. Murphy	364 Bunker Hill st.	"	840 "	Oct. 1, 1902
Nellie E. Powers	22 Monument sq.	"	936 "	Jan. 2, 1908
Anna M. Prescott	51 High st.	"	936 "	Nov., 1870
Charlotte E. Seavey	Melrose	"	936 "	Sept. 4, 1882
Augusta S. Tavender	5 Bertram st.	"	552 "	Nov. 3, 1908
Katherine Thompson	Medford	"	936 "	March 6, 1871
Grace A. Tully	86 Washington st.	"	552 "	Nov. 17, 1908
Jennie F. White	27 Essex st.	"	936 "	March 12, 1883

* Year's leave of absence on half pay.   Resignation to take effect September 1, 1909.

School Department.— Continued.

Name.	Residence.	Designation.	Compensation.	Date of Election or Appointment.

Bunker Hill District.— Concluded.

Name.	Residence.	Designation.	Compensation.	Date of Election or Appointment.
Adah F. Whitney	Somerville	Assistant	$936 yr	Jan. 4, 1897
Gertrude F. Chamberlain	Somerville	First Asst., Kindergarten	792 "	Oct. 24, 1892
Jacqueline Carroll	30 Saunders st., Alls	Assistant	528 "	Nov. 13, 1906
Catherine A. Hogan	Medford	Special Assistant	1.75 day	" 3, 1908
Annie J. Murphy	9 Carter st	Attendant	.50 "	Sept. 10, 1908
Gustavus F. Gibbs	52 High st	Janitor	28.55 wk	Aug. 1, 1889
Francis L. O'Connor	14 Frederick st	"	13.25 "	March 1, 1909

Chapman District.

Name.	Residence.	Designation.	Compensation.	Date of Election or Appointment.
Tilson A. Mead	181 Walnut ave	Master	$3,180 yr	March 1, 1894
William L. Bates	14 Park View st	Sub-Master	2,340 "	Sept. 6, 1893
Lucy W. Eaton	156 Newbury st	Master's Assistant	1,308 "	" 6, 1893
Jane F. Reid	212 Princeton st	First Assistant, Grammar	1,212 "	April 1, 1879
Marietta Duncan	106 White st	First Assistant in Charge	1,116 "	Nov. 2, 1896
Clara H. Allen	Winthrop	Assistant	744 "	Jan. 16, 1905
Catharine F. Atwood	173 Lexington st	"	936 "	March 11, 1895
Margaret D. Barr	124 Coleridge st	"	936 "	Feb. 1, 1893
Clara A. Brown	34 Collins st	"	936 "	" 1, 1888
Annie C. Deering	334 Meridian st	"	840 "	Sept. 9, 1903
Grace E. Fogg	135 Brooks st	"	744 "	April 9, 1906
Frances A. Gallagher	285 Walnut ave	"	936 "	Oct. 1, 1900
Gertrude L. Gardner	420 Meridian st	"	936 "	Jan. 24, 1898
Florence M. Glover	112 Putnam st	"	936 "	Oct. 1, 1896
Marion P. McPhee	169 Princeton st	"	696 "	Sept. 13, 1905
Gertrude W. Merrill	Winthrop	"	936 "	March 15, 1898
Katharine L. Niland	202 Byron st	"	936 "	" 28, 1888
Clara A. Otis	128 Lexington st	"	936 "	Oct. 15, 1873
Imogene L. Owen	39 Kenwood st	"	792 "	" 19, 1903
Mary E. Sheridan	Wellesley Hills	"	936 "	Sept. 8, 1896
Mariannie H. Simmons	169 Brooks st	"	888 "	Jan. 9, 1908
Jessie C. Skinner	41 Bennington st	"	936 "	Sept. 9, 1903
S. Catherine Smith	466 Sumner st	"	888 "	" 10, 1902
Beatrice E. Strong	329 Paris st	"	744 "	Nov. 14, 1905
Grace M. Strong	428 Meridian st	"	936 "	Sept. 7, 1892
Caroline Swift	24 Marion st	"	936 "	Oct. 14, 1903
Frances R. Wilson	Cambridge	"	552 "	March 16, 1909
Lucy E. Woodwell	47 Monmouth st	"	936 "	Sept. 1, 1872
H. Maud Marshall	28 Worcester sq	First Asst., Kindergarten	696 "	Feb. 4, 1908
Helen M. Paine	11 Albermarle Chambers	"	792 "	May 14, 1900
Adelaide M. Clarke	3 Meridian st	Assistant	624 "	Sept. 9, 1903
Grace G. Daly	14 Sparhawk st., Bri	"	624 "	Jan. 16, 1905
Helen L. Leahy	186 Leyden st	Substitute	2.00 day	April 1, 1909
Alice F. Hughes	663 Saratoga st	Attendant	.50 "	Sept. 9, 1908
Estelle E. Wallace	112 Falcon st	"	.50 "	" 9, 1908
Bradford H. Blinn	288 Meridian st	Janitor	13.47 wk	Feb., 1894
Arthur Mooney	299 Lexington st	"	38.91 "	Oct. 16, 1905

Charles Sumner District.

Name.	Residence.	Designation.	Compensation.	Date of Election or Appointment.
Loca P. Howard	Hyde Park	Master	$3,180 yr	Sept. 7, 1897
Irving M. Norcross	42 Esmond st	Sub-Master	2,340 "	Dec. 18, 1899
Charlotte B. Hall	15 Montview st., W. R	Master's Assistant	1,308 "	Oct. 21, 1896
Angeline P. Nutter	52 Corey st., W. R	First Assistant, Grammar	1,212 "	April 11, 1893
Katharine M. Coulahan	802 Parker st	First Assistant in Charge	1,116 "	Nov. 2, 1896
Anna M. Leach	18 Laurel st	"	1,116 "	" 2, 1896
Alice M. Barton	1841 Centre st., W. R	Assistant	936 "	Dec. 2, 1895
Louise M. Cottle	13 Copley st	"	936 "	Sept. 8, 1896
Esther M. Davies	Hollbrook	"	936 "	" 4, 1895
Ida M. Dyer	197 St. Botolph st	"	936 "	Oct. 19, 1896
Josie E. Evans	38 Mechanic st	"	936 "	Sept. 4, 1895
Martha W. Hanley	175 Walnut st	"	936 "	Nov. 4, 1889
Maude C. Hartnett	54 Creighton st	"	936 "	Oct. 5, 1896
Alice J. Jewett	2 Brown ter., J. P	"	936 "	Feb. 1, 1900
Mary G. Kelley	Alaric st., W. R	"	936 "	" 8, 1895
Ellen J. Kiggen	Hyde Park	"	936 "	April 22, 1884
Dora M. Leonard	Sharon	"	936 "	Sept. 15, 1881
Emma C. Lincoln	4380 Washington st	"	936 "	Oct. 14, 1891
Mary E. Lynch	92 Hyde Park ave	"	936 "	Dec. 22, 1884
Margaret F. Marden	196 St. Botolph st	"	936 "	May 12, 1891
Bertha L. Palmer	807 South st., Ros	"	936 "	Dec. 1, 1900

School Department.— Continued.

Name.	Residence.	Designation.	Compensation.	Date of Election or Appointment.

Charles Sumner District.— Concluded.

Name.	Residence.	Designation.	Compensation.	Date of Election or Appointment.
Katharine Macdonald	23 S. Fairview st	First Asst., Kindergarten	$792 yr	Sept. 11, 1901
Marion L. Weston	24 Farquhar st	" "	792 "	March 1, 1901
Margaret F. Hilliard	221 Corey st., W. R.	Assistant	432 "	Nov. 3, 1908
Pauline F. Smith	3 Congreve st., Ros		480 "	Sept. 11, 1907
Violet E. Barry	26 Regent st	Special Assistant	1.75 day	Jan. 4, 1909
Lillie M. Redfern	28 Dalrymple st	Substitute	2.00 "	April 20, 1909
Callahan T. Hogan	45 Rockland st	Janitor	12.77 wk	June 1, 1908
William L. Lovejoy	41 Florence st., Ros	"	19.13 "	Feb. 1, 1897
Carl F. Meyer	24 Roslindale ave	"	14.04 "	April 1, 1902

Christopher Gibson District.

Name.	Residence.	Designation.	Compensation.	Date of Election or Appointment.
William E. C. Rich	99 Moreland st	Master	$3,180 yr	March 10, 1891
Joseph T. F. Burrell	30 Rosedale st	Sub-Master	2,340 "	Jan. 2, 1900
Catherine F. Byrne	125 Zeigler st	Master's Assistant	1,212 "	Dec. 7, 1903
Rose E. A. Redding	19 Akron st	First Assistant in Charge	1,068 "	Nov. 1, 1906
Corinna Barry	5 Bowdoin ave	Assistant	936 "	Sept. 13, 1899
Flora E. Billings	Canton	"	936 "	" 8, 1896
Josephine E. Clark	Medford	"	936 "	Nov. 20, 1901
Lucy B. Conner	538 Massachusetts ave	"	936 "	Dec. 16, 1901
Florence A. Dunbar	Canton	"	936 "	Sept. 4, 1895
Emily A. Evans	17 Everett ave	"	936 "	Nov. 17, 1890
Mabel B. Fuller	95 Alexander st	"	696 "	Oct. 16, 1905
Bessie C. Jones	268 Normandy st	"	936 "	" 1, 1890
Marion E. Killion	52 Forbes st., J. P.	"	552 "	April 12, 1909
Katharine T. Lyons	9 Cottage side	"	888 "	March 2, 1903
Deborah A. McColl	95 Harvard st	"	936 "	Nov. 3, 1902
Mary P. McIsaac	5 Homes ave	"	648 "	" 20, 1906
Annie H. Pitts	23 Alaska st	"	936 "	Dec. 2, 1889
Rosemary Purcell	275 Heath st	"	600 "	Sept. 11, 1907
Florence I. Reddy	24 Elm Hill pk	"	936 "	Oct. 2, 1893
Edith M. Sandsberry	33 Abbotsford st	"	936 "	Nov. 1, 1898
Florence A. Stone	9 Mt. Bowdoin ter	"	936 "	Sept. 12, 1900
Agnes G. Strong	329 Paris st., E. B.	"	648 "	Nov. 1, 1906
A. Gertrude Powker	46 Port Norfolk st	First Asst., Kindergarten	792 "	Sept. 14, 1904
Elizabeth A. Hickey	Holbrook	Assistant	432 "	Nov. 17, 1908
Mary F. O'Meara	135 Kilton st	"	624 "	Jan. 16, 1905
Thomas Buckley	273 Columbia rd	Janitor	13.95 wk	Sept. 9, 1907
Charles J. Carlson	26 Cunningham st	"	32.60 "	July 20, 1905

Comins District.

Name.	Residence.	Designation.	Compensation.	Date of Election or Appointment.
William H. Martin	Sharon	Master	$3,180 yr	Sept. 12, 1894
Thomas J. Sheahan	129 Minden st	Sub-Master	1,620 "	" 11, 1907
Margaret T. Dooley	804 Parker st	Master's Assistant	1,212 "	Nov. 11, 1903
Lillian E. Cronin	72 Wachusett st., J. P.	First Assistant, Grammar	1,164 "	Jan. 16, 1905
Anna R. McDonald	25 Woodbine st	First Assistant in Charge	1,116 "	Nov. 2, 1896
May Bradford	17 Hillside st	Assistant	936 "	April 11, 1898
Elizabeth P. Brewer	8 Cazenove st	"	936 "	Sept. 9, 1872
Linna E. Clark	40 Clarkwood st., Mattapan	"	888 "	May 13, 1901
Ellen M. Cronin	72 Wachusett st., J. P.	"	840 "	Dec. 10, 1902
Rosanna M. Dowd	53 Stratford st., W. R.	"	552 "	March 3, 1908
Sabina Egan	29 Terrace st	"	936 "	April 1, 1879
Grace M. Goodrich	10 Larchmont st	"	648 "	Nov. 1, 1906
Anna J. Griffin	53 Fenwood rd	"	888 "	April 11, 1904
Helena R. Guiney	62 Troy st	"	552 "	" 30, 1909
A. Harriet Haley	6 Pacific st	"	888 "	Sept. 10, 1902
Katherine F. Hartnett	120 W. Lenox st	"	744 "	Feb. 1, 1906
Caroline M. Hauck	52 Idaho st	"	600 "	Dec. 3, 1907
Martha T. Howes*	2043 Columbus ave	"	936 "	Jan. 4, 1897
Elizabeth T. Lavey	86 Thornton st	"	840 "	Oct. 16, 1903
Margaret S. Lunt	118 Hutchings st	"	696 "	Feb. 1, 1906
Lucy A. MacKenzie	48 Wait st	"	744 "	March 28, 1905
Mary A. Mahoney	28 Binney st	"	744 "	Sept. 13, 1905
Theresa C. Murray	18 Thwing st	"	552 "	Dec. 8, 1908
Mary E. O'Donnell	16 Bromley pk	"	696 "	Sept. 13, 1905
Elizabeth M. Quigley	58 Monument ave	"	552 "	March 3, 1908
Mary G. L. Quinlan	Brookline	"	600 "	Oct. 22, 1907
Alice L. Reed	Sharon	"	936 "	Jan. 21, 1901

* Leave of absence without pay to September 1, 1909.

School Department. — Continued.

Name.	Residence.	Designation.	Compensation	Date of Election or Appointment.

Comins District. — Concluded.

Name.	Residence.	Designation.	Compensation	Date of Election or Appointment.
Mary A. Rourke	515 Warren st	Assistant	$936 yr	May 9, 1900
Margaret F. Sullivan	31 St. Botolph st	"	936 "	Sept. 27, 1897
Claire F. Sullivan	13 Hartford st	"	552 "	Nov. 17, 1908
Annie S. Burpee	22 W. Walnut pk	First Asst., Kindergarten	792 "	Oct. 17, 1892
Clara G. Dennis	3 Carlisle st	"	792 "	Nov. 24, 1902
Mary M. Oswald	406 Centre st., J. P.	Assistant	624 "	" 11, 1903
Ellen M. Pinkham	28 Charlotte st	First Asst., Kindergarten	792 "	" 12, 1900
Marion R. Stevens	Needham	Assistant	576 "	Sept. 13, 1905
Lilian A. Smith	37 W. Cedar st	Special Assistant	1.50 day	Oct. 8, 1908
Samuel A. Dodds	124 Fisher ave	Janitor	19.87 wk	Jan. 6, 1908
Thomas F. Whalen	6 Dove st	"	19.23 "	Aug. 20, 1879
John Cole	8 Bickford ave	"	7.50 "	Jan. 6, 1908
Carl I. Priest	643 Huntington ave	"	2.31 "	Feb. 7, 1909
Mary E. Boyd	34 Elmwood st	Attendant	.50 day	Jan. 6, 1909
Helen F. Dalton	63 Smith st	"	.50 "	Sept. 9, 1908
Anna L. Feeley	5 Terry st	"	.50 "	March 29, 1909

Dearborn District.

Name.	Residence.	Designation.	Compensation	Date of Election or Appointment.
Charles F. King	107 Elm Hill ave	Master	$3,180 yr	Sept. 7, 1887
Alanson H. Mayers	104 Geneva ave	Sub Master	2,340 "	" 7, 1887
Lily B. Atherton	Medford	Master's Assistant	1,308 "	Oct. 10, 1887
Lillian A. Wiswell	18 St. Stephen st	First Asst. Grammar	1,116 "	May 1, 1905
Mary A. P. Cross	567 Massachusetts ave	First Asst. in Charge	1,116 "	Nov. 2, 1896
Katharine O'Brien	30 Mall st	"	1,116 "	Sept. 13, 1905
Abbie G. Abbott	66 Westville st	Assistant	936 "	" 16, 1895
Helen R. Campbell	34 Vine st	"	888 "	April 1, 1902
Mattie M. Clough	88 Waltham st	"	936 "	Sept. 11, 1901
Annie L. Coffey	Weymouth	"	936 "	" 13, 1899
C. Agnes Dailey	44 E. Dedham st	"	840 "	Jan. 5, 1903
Florence M. DeMerritt	2033 Columbus ave	"	936 "	May 13, 1896
Helen Doherty	17 Pearl st	"	936 "	Nov. 3, 1890
Michael J. Downey	10 Fenwick st	"	696 "	Feb. 1, 1906
Sarah A. Driscoll	283 Walnut ave	"	936 "	Nov. 1, 1893
Amanda C. Ellison	16 Hewins st	"	936 "	April 13, 1899
Mary G. Finnegan	27 Coolidge rd., Alls	"	840 "	Sept. 9, 1903
Abby E. Flagg	5 Mt. Pleasant ter	"	936 "	Oct. 16, 1896
Emma Frye	Somerville	"	936 "	Sept. 12, 1900
Mary L. Gaylord	Brookline	"	936 "	Nov. 30, 1896
Lucy A. Hamlin	152 Quincy st	"	936 "	Sept. 12, 1900
Mary C. Harrington	11 Camden pl	"	936 "	Oct. 1, 1900
Teresa C. Hoye	1016 Washington st	"	552 "	Dec. 8, 1908
Mary L. Kelly	70 Bloomfield st	"	600 "	Nov. 19, 1907
Mary G. Kenney	79 Glenway st	"	600 "	Dec. 3, 1907
Lucy H. Littlefield	102 Talbot ave	"	936 "	Sept. 10, 1902
Mary A. Lynch	70 Julian st	"	936 "	Oct. 10, 1900
Elizabeth B. McKeon	E. Dedham	"	936 "	Sept. 6, 1898
Emma L. Merrill	The Warren	"	936 "	Feb. 16, 1889
Mary L. Moran	39 G st	"	552 "	April 30, 1909
M. Agnes Murphy	856 Columbus ave	"	936 "	May 16, 1879
Katherine R. Murphy	124 Eustis st	"	552 "	Nov. 3, 1908
Kate A. Nason	Hotel Nightingale	"	936 "	Sept. 1, 1873
Elizabeth W. O'Connell	14 Spring Park ave., J. P.	"	744 "	Oct. 3, 1904
Ellen M. Oliver	6 Pevear pl	"	936 "	March, 1866
Katherine T. O'Sullivan	Dedham	"	744 "	Sept. 13, 1905
Katharine A. Regan	49 Winchester st	"	936 "	May 1, 1896
Josephine A. Simonton	30 Greenville st	"	936 "	Dec. 5, 1895
Anna M. Stevens	12 Hewins st	"	888 "	Oct. 14, 1901
Abby W. Sullivan	23 Winthrop st	"	936 "	" 21, 1885
Eloise B. Walcott	447 Massachusetts ave	"	936 "	Feb. 5, 1872
Mary F. Walsh	19 E. Springfield st	"	936 "	March, 1871
Carrie M. Wellington	Somerville	"	792 "	Jan. 16, 1905
Mary T. Hale	Brookline	First Asst., Kindergarten	792 "	Sept. 8, 1896
Amy E. Lang	25 Rowen st	Assistant	624 "	Feb. 1, 1900
Mary J. O'Neil	196 W. Fourth st	Special Assistant	1.75 day	March 2, 1909
Natalie Irving	221 Corey st., W. R	"	1.50 "	Sept. 9, 1908
Bertha T. Hucksam	22 Reading st	Attendant	.50 "	" 9, 1908
William H. Bowman	2139 Dorchester ave	Janitor	24.71 wk	April 1, 1896
John J. Dignon	51 Taber st	"	6.18 "	Sept. 1, 1894
Michael Glasheen	203 K st	"	14.30 "	April 17, 1908
Edward A. Moore	288A Dudley st	"	37.90 "	July 15, 1905

School Department.— Continued

Name.	Residence.	Designation	Com-pensation.	Date of Election or Appointment.

Dillaway District.

Emma S. Gulliver	Hotel Eliot	Master	$2,700 yr	May 7, 1907
Elizabeth M. Blackburn	108 Thornton st	Master's Assistant	1,308 "	Sept. 9, 1891
Helen C. Mills	108 Thornton st	First Assistant, Grammar	1,212 "	" 24, 1900
Anna M. Balch	Brookline	First Assistant in Charge	1,116 "	Nov. 2, 1896
Annie E. Mahan	109 Warwick st	"	1,068 "	" 1, 1906
Mary L. Shepard	Wakefield	" "	1,116 "	" 2, 1896
Abby M. Clark	13 Rockville pk	Assistant	936 "	Sept., 1860
M. Edith Cole	Watertown	"	936 "	Nov. 1, 1899
Katherine A. Cunniff	Natick	"	936 "	April 13, 1903
F. Louise Dacey	196 Walnut ave	"	552 "	Nov. 3, 1908
Julia E. Dickson	22 Greenville st	"	936 "	April 10, 1899
Ada L. Donkin	386 Newbury st	"	936 "	Sept. 6, 1898
Ella M. Donkin	386 Newbury st	"	936 "	Jan. 3, 1898
Lucia A. Ferguson	92 Moreland st	"	936 "	Feb. 15, 1893
Elizabeth M. Finneran	6 Abbotsford st	"	888 "	Sept. 11, 1901
Theresa B. Finneran	6 Abbotsford st	"	936 "	Jan. 2, 1896
Mabel L. Harrington	28 Circuit st	"	744 "	" 2, 1905
Katherine Keenan	115 Warwick st	"	792 "	Sept. 14, 1904
Sarah B. C. Lane	30 Harvard st., Chsn	"	744 "	" 14, 1904
Eleanor A. Larivee	51 Tuttle st	"	552 "	Nov. 3, 1908
Lena Lee	12 Humboldt ave	"	792 "	Jan. 4, 1904
Annie E. McCormick	108 Highland st	"	888 "	April 1, 1902
Susan H. McKenna	196 St. Botolph st	"	936 "	Dec. 4, 1893
Elizabeth A. O'Neil	115 Vernon st	"	936 "	Jan. 2, 1894
Marion L. Owen	12 Humboldt ave	"	936 "	Sept. 24, 1900
Elizabeth Palmer	4 Peter Parley rd., J. P.	"	936 "	Oct. 13, 1879
Elizabeth G. Phelps	Cambridge	"	936 "	Jan. 2, 1894
Carolena C. Richards	5 Lambert ave	"	936 "	Oct. 1, 1895
Edith Rose	19 Chauncy pl., J. P.	"	936 "	Jan. 16, 1894
Ellen A. Scollin	494 Parker st	"	936 "	Sept. 13, 1892
Cordelia G. Torrey	23 Winthrop st	"	936 "	Oct. 1, 1886
Agnes A. Watson	103 Highland st	"	936 "	Nov. 15, 1888
Annie L. Wood	Wellesley	"	936 "	Oct. 10, 1900
Elizabeth C. Barry	25 Alpine st	First Asst., Kindergarten	792 "	" 1, 1894
Florence A. Fitzsimmons	16 Cedar st	"	792 "	" 1, 1895
Ida G. Beverly	111 Lexington st	Assistant	624 "	Jan. 16, 1905
Flora M. Hoyt	3 Duncan st	"	432 "	Nov. 3, 1908
Margaret C. Regan	27 Stratton st	Special Assistant	1.75 day	Dec. 8, 1908
Mary E. Brazil	41 Whitney st	Attendant	.50 "	Sept. 9, 1908
Jessie F. McLean	22 Sarsfield st	"	.50 "	" 9, 1908
John J. Kearns	11 Moseley st	Janitor	12.63 wk	Oct. 15, 1906
William M. Kendricken	117 Bowdoin st	"	21.95 "	April 25, 1898
Albert C. Litchfield	15 Warren ave	"	6.03 "	Feb. 1, 1903
John Schromm	1 Cedar pk	"	21.96 "	April 23, 1904

Dudley District.

Abram T. Smith	Sharon	Master	$3,180 yr	Jan. 1, 1901
William L. Phinney	Sharon	Sub-Master	2,340 "	Oct. 8, 1894
Edward F. O'Dowd	15 Whitby ter	"	2,100 "	Jan. 4, 1904
Alice M. Crowell	67 Bartlett st	Master's Assistant	1,020 "	April 21, 1908
Charles E. Harris	188 West Brookline st	First Assistant, Grammar	1,116 "	Oct. 13, 1905
Helen P. Hall	The Warren	First Assistant in Charge	1,116 "	Nov. 2, 1896
Alice L. Williams	224 Dudley st	"	1,116 "	" 2, 1896
Mary A. Brennan	59 Calumet st	Assistant	936 "	May 21, 1888
Lucy G. M. Card	34 Regent st	"	936 "	Jan. 3, 1888
Mary H. Cashman	215 Harvard st	"	936 "	Oct., 1867
Mary I. Chamberlin	21 Grosvenor st	"	936 "	May 1, 1878
L. Adelaide Colligan	1040 Adams st	"	936 "	Jan. 1, 1874
Katherine L. Connell	127 Zeigler st	"	936 "	March 1, 1901
Alice M. Duston	1 Conrad st	"	552 "	Nov. 3, 1908
Helena M. Follen	11 East Newton st	"	792 "	" 6, 1905
Antoinette M. Getchell	6 Windermere rd	"	936 "	Oct. 15, 1900
Ella M. Hersey	9 Dyer st	"	936 "	Sept. 5, 1894
Elizabeth F. Johnson	19 Laurel st	"	936 "	Oct. 29, 1867
Emma V. Kennedy	16 Northfield st	"	888 "	" 7, 1901
Delia T. Killion	1 Alleghany st	"	936 "	" 1, 1875
Hattie A. Littlefield	6 Cleveland st	"	936 "	April 1, 1880
Mary L. Logan	2 Longmeadow st	"	840 "	Jan. 5, 1903
Mary L. Long	Hotel Dale Annex, Regent st	"	936 "	Oct. 17, 1900
Harriet E. Lyman	57 Rutland sq	Assistant, Special Class	1,032 "	Dec. 13, 1899
Jennie G. Maguire	14 Jess st., J. P.	Assistant	552 "	April 21, 1908

School Department.— Continued.

Name.	Residence.	Designation.	Compensation.	Date of Election or Appointment.

Dudley District.— Concluded.

Name.	Residence.	Designation.	Compensation.	Date of Election or Appointment.
Viola R. Marsh	11 Ocean st	Assistant	$888 yr	Sept. 25, 1901
Josephine Marston	147 Appleton st	"	696 "	Nov. 3, 1908
Hugh J. McElaney	77 Hillside st	"	600 "	Oct. 22, 1907
Helen S. Murphy	12 Judson st	"	888 "	Sept. 25, 1901
Olivia C. Penell	Natick	"	552 "	April 28, 1909
Sarah E. Rumrill	74 Dale st	"	936 "	May 1, 1883
Ella M. Seaverns	2 Kenilworth st	"	936 "	Sept. 5, 1864
Hannah E. Tobin	7 Copeland st	"	936 "	Oct. 1, 1902
Mary L. Veazie	71 Tonawanda st	"	600 "	Dec. 17, 1907
Maria F. Wood	36 Kenwood st	"	936 "	Oct. 16, 1882
Ellen M. Fiske	48 Rutland sq	First Asst., Kindergarten	792 "	Jan. 2, 1895
Sarah H. Williams	278 Walnut st, Brookline	"	792 "	April 21, 1898
Mabelle L. Boyer	Cambridge	Assistant, Kindergarten	624 "	Dec. 23, 1903
Edna Long	41 Charles st	Substitute	2.00 day	April 1, 1909
Eleanor M. Osterberg	53 Hillside st	Special Assistant	1.75 "	Sept. 9, 1908
Mary Fitzgerald	22 Kent st	Substitute	2.00 "	April 29, 1909
Mary E. Coveney	115 Walnut ave	"	2.00 "	" 29, 1909
Joseph P. Fleming	69 Fort ave	Janitor	31.88 wk	Feb. 15, 1901
Perez H. Knight	26 Linden Park st	"	20.82 "	Oct. 20, 1897
Frank W. Munroe	65 Brighton ave., Alls	"	16.49 "	Sept. 1, 1898

Dwight District.

Name.	Residence.	Designation.	Compensation.	Date of Election or Appointment.
Jason L. Curtis	Hyde Park	Master	$3,060 yr	Sept. 1, 1904
Carroll M. Austin	Stoughton	Sub-Master	2,340 "	Jan. 4, 1897
Elmer E. Sherman	118 Highland st	"	1,980 "	Oct. 17, 1904
Ruth G. Rich	31 Windermere rd	Master's Assistant	1,308 "	" 23, 1874
Emma F. Gallagher	61 E. Concord st	First Assistant in Charge	1,116 "	March 26, 1897
Miriam Sterne	179 Walnut ave	"	1,116 "	Sept. 12, 1909
Margaret L. Carolan	35 Preble st	Assistant	792 "	March 20, 1906
E. Adelaide Child	446 Massachusetts ave	"	936 "	Oct. 15, 1899
Georgie M. Clarke	30 Greenville st	"	936 "	March 7, 1892
Grace G. Colman	42 Edwin st	"	552 "	Feb. 1, 1909
Grace E. Coyne	Medford	"	840 "	Jan. 16, 1905
Sarah C. Fales	46 Rutland st	"	936 "	Feb. 3, 1873
Mary H. Fruean	393 Norfolk st	"	936 "	Nov. 14, 1901
Mary V. Gormley*	1 Worthington st	"	936 "	Sept. 6, 1893
Teresa A. Hurley	Dedham	"	552 "	Jan. 4, 1909
Mary Kelly	189 W. Springfield st	"	744 "	March 1, 1905
Mabel E. Latta	19 Randolph rd	"	936 "	Sept. 8, 1896
Georgina E. MacBride	12 Wabon st	"	936 "	May 1, 1893
Anna M. Meyer	70 Farquhar st., Ros	"	552 "	Jan. 4, 1909
Sara Mock	458 Shawmut ave	"	936 "	Nov. 1, 1889
Agnes T. Nolan	65 Dorchester st	"	552 "	Dec. 8, 1908
Minnie A. Noyes	38 St. Botolph st	"	936 "	Nov. 22, 1897
Anna J. O'Brien	105 Howland st	"	936 "	Sept. 9, 1891
Mary Ranney	3 Round Hill st	"	936 "	March 19, 1900
Mary C. R. Towle	8 Athelwold st	"	936 "	" 5, 1863
Delia L. Viles	57 Rutland sq	"	936 "	Sept. 29, 1885
Clara P. Wardwell	Salem	"	936 "	Oct. 14, 1889
Cora E. Wood	171 W. Brookline st	"	1,032 "	Nov. 14, 1900
Ella T. Burgess	1285 Commonwealth ave	First Asst., Kindergarten	792 "	Oct. 17, 1892
Eleanor P. Gay	15 Greenwich pk	"	792 "	Sept. 4, 1889
Lillian M. Bonelli	165 Hemenway st	Assistant	480 "	May 1, 1907
Mina Guyton	468 Massachusetts ave	"	624 "	Feb. 2, 1903
Annie E. Dennis	Milton	Temporary Teacher	2.00 day	" 15, 1909
Bessie C. MacBrine	Medford	"	2.00 "	March 22, 1909
A. Grace Emery	34 Dean st	Substitute	2.00 "	April 27, 1909
Frances E. Woods	19 Union st., Bri	"	2.00 "	" 20, 1909
Helen F. Dalton	63 Smith st	Attendant	.50 "	Sept. 9, 1908
May Douglass	3 Cumston st	"	.50 "	April 27, 1909
Marion Morrison	14 Upton st	"	.50 "	Oct. 26, 1908
Michael Dundon	42 Mystic st	Janitor	19.90 wk	" 1, 1900
Charles O. Newell	12 Clifton pl	"	19.74 "	Jan. 9, 1904
John J. Timmins	79 Waverly st., Bri	"	10.79 "	March 1, 1909
Pauline E. Taylor	85 W. Brookline st	Attendant	.50 day	Sept. 9, 1908

Edward Everett District.

Name.	Residence.	Designation.	Compensation.	Date of Election or Appointment.
Henry B. Miner	Hyde Park	Master	$3,180 yr	Sept. 10, 1872
Leonard M. Patton	61 McClellan st	Sub-Master	1,860 "	" 13, 1905

* Leave of absence, no pay to September 1, 1909.

School Department.— Continued.

Name.	Residence.	Designation.	Compensation.	Date of Election or Appointment.

Edward Everett District.— Concluded.

Name.	Residence.	Designation.	Compensation.	Date of Election or Appointment.
Mary F. Thompson	15 Pearl st	Master's Assistant	$1,308 yr	Oct. 1, 1877
Henrietta A. Hill	49 Hartford st	First Asst., Grammar	1,212 "	Jan. 1, 1892
Florence N. Sloane	3 Hartford st	First Assistant in Charge	1,116 "	Nov. 2, 1896
Alice E. Aldrich	9 S. Munroe st	Assistant	936 "	Dec. 4, 1893
Josephine M. Barrett	84 W. Rutland st	"	840 "	March 2, 1903
Maud J. Bray	57 Cushing ave	"	744 "	Dec. 31, 1906
Mae H. Bromley	121 Stoughton st	"	936 "	Nov. 9, 1903
C. Margaret Brown	28 Downer ave	"	936 "	Jan. 4, 1892
Rosa M. Bumstead	15 Peverell st	"	888 "	Sept. 19, 1904
Marion E. Buswell	30 Wendover st	"	936 "	" 12, 1902
Ella M. Clarke	35 Rockwell st	"	936 "	March 28, 1900
Harriet A. Darling	113 Cushing ave	"	936 "	" 10, 1879
Elizabeth G. Diman	40 Spencer st	"	840 "	Feb. 6, 1906
Emma F. Ditchett	5 Sagamore st	"	552 "	Jan. 4, 1909
Mary E. Donovan	152 W. Concord st	"	792 "	Sept. 13, 1905
Margaret R. Dwyer	42 Fuller st	"	648 "	Oct. 1, 1906
Bessie M. Elliot	11 Morse st	"	840 "	Nov. 20, 1902
Hildegard Fick	109 Warren ave	"	936 "	Dec. 3, 1894
Sally T. Fletcher	25 Athelwold st	"	936 "	Nov. 16, 1897
Lucy G. Flusk	4 Montello st	"	936 "	March 16, 1888
Florence A. Goodfellow	61 Sagamore st	"	936 "	Oct. 2, 1893
Rose D. Hoye	1116 Washington st	"	648 "	Nov. 6, 1906
L. Cora Morse	20 Montrose st	"	936 "	Sept. 8, 1884
Charlotte Rafter	41 Bradlee st	"	696 "	Dec. 4, 1905
Etta C. Rochefort	74 Pleasant st	"	696 "	Jan. 15, 1907
Emma M. Savil	Quincy	"	936 "	Dec. 1, 1874
Ellen R. Scott	96 Thornton st	"	600 "	Nov. 5, 1907
Alice H. Shaw	6 Windermere rd	"	888 "	Sept. 26, 1904
Catherine J. Sullivan	423 Fourth st	"	552 "	April 30, 1909
A. Gertrude Malloch	51 Waldeck st	First Asst., Kindergarten	792 "	May 1, 1900
Alice E. Leavens	32 Rockview st	Assistant	576 "	Nov. 22, 1905
Cecilia H. O'Brien	24 Freeman st	Substitute	2.00 day	April 1, 1909
George L. Chessman	75 Tuttle st	Janitor	34.56 wk	Sept. 6, 1903
Laura Reed	281 Hancock st	"	11.13 "	May 1, 1899

Eliot District.

Name.	Residence.	Designation.	Compensation.	Date of Election or Appointment.
John F. McGrath	Natick	Master	$2,820 yr	Sept. 12, 1906
Paul V. Donovan	Rockland	Sub-Master	1,740 "	Nov. 20, 1906
John J. Sheehan	225 Savin Hill ave	"	2,340 "	" 19, 1888
Alvin P. Wagg	30 Claremont pk	"	1,500 "	Jan. 2, 1908
Mary E. Hanney	154 Chelsea st	Master's Assistant	1,308 "	Dec. 27, 1904
Rosa M. E. Reggio	Everett	First Assistant in Charge	1,116 "	Nov. 2, 1896
Carrie A. Waugh	64 Dudley st	" "	1,116 "	" 2, 1896
B. Louise Hagerty	39 E. Brookline st	First Assistant, Primary	1,080 "	Dec. 27, 1904
Martha J. Ambrose	23 Batavia st	Assistant	936 "	Jan. 5, 1897
Theresa V. Arato	7 Heachman st	"	744 "	Sept. 28, 1904
Ellen G. Bird	11 Chestnut st	"	936 "	" 8, 1896
Bridget T. Boyle	Cambridge	"	696 "	Jan. 2, 1908
Lura A. Chase	86 Draper st	"	792 "	Sept. 9, 1903
Josephine A. Coulahan	802 Parker st	"	744 "	Feb. 6, 1905
James A. Crowley	512 Fourth st	"	600 "	Sept. 11, 1907
Catherine J. Cunningham	North Cambridge	"	936 "	April 1, 1891
Mary V. Cunningham	North Cambridge	"	936 "	Oct. 14, 1885
Theresa Currie	25 Rosemary st., J. P.	"	936 "	Feb. 14, 1900
Louise M. De Voto	50 Winthrop st	"	600 "	Jan. 16, 1907
Marcella E. Donegan	60 Richfield st	"	936 "	Sept. 3, 1877
Etta C. Ernst	2 Silvia st., J. P.	"	792 "	" 9, 1903
Anna L. Foster	5 Mt. Pleasant ter	"	936 "	Oct. 1, 1898
Annie M. H. Gillespie	19 E. Springfield st	"	936 "	Sept. 1, 1875
Mary E. Hartnett	109 M st	"	936 "	Nov. 26, 1900
Isabel R. Haskins	118 Mt. Vernon st	"	936 "	Oct. 25, 1875
Mary E. Hughes	122 Englewood ave	"	936 "	May 22, 1899
S. Frances Jordan	22 Follen st	"	936 "	Jan. 4, 1897
Sophia E. Krey	56 Virginia st	"	936 "	Oct. 14, 1884
Celia V. Leen	2 Dexter row	"	936 "	April 1, 1892
Ida E. Malaney	22 Myrtle st	"	792 "	Sept. 9, 1903
Mary E. McCormick	108 Highland st	"	744 "	Oct. 11, 1905
M. Elizabeth McGinley	90 Pinckney st	"	936 "	Nov. 1, 1888
Agnes L. McMahan	392 Fourth st	"	888 "	Sept. 10, 1902
Frances A. McMahan	392 Fourth st	"	600 "	Oct. 1, 1907
Mary M. McNeil	10 Putnam st	"	696 "	Nov. 13, 1905
Mary T. Melia	13 Bainbridge st	"	840 "	Jan. 28, 1903

School Department. — Continued.

Name.	Residence.	Designation.	Compensation.	Date of Election or Appointment.

Eliot District. — Concluded.

Name.	Residence.	Designation.	Compensation.	Date of Election or Appointment.
Agnes C. Moore	36 E. Brookline st	Assistant	$936 yr	Feb. 27, 1888
George B. Moran	Natick	"	552 "	Nov. 3, 1908
Alice M. Murray	Woburn	"	600 "	Oct. 1, 1907
Katherine G. O'Donnell	48 Pinckney st	"	792 "	Jan. 2, 1905
Linda C. O'Dowd	6 Adams st	"	552 "	April 27, 1909
Annie E. Regan	Cambridge	"	840 "	Sept. 9, 1903
E. Idella Seldis	22 Batavia st	"	936 "	March 28, 1894
Anna M. T. Sheehan	23 Bernard st	"	936 "	May 23, 1900
Mary L. Sullivan	Winter Hill	"	792 "	Sept. 14, 1904
Katherine G. Sutliff	101 King st	"	936 "	9, 1891
M. Persis Taylor	108 Mt. Vernon st	"	936 "	Oct. 14, 1885
Harriet White	11 Aberdeen st	"	600 "	Dec. 17, 1907
Ellen M. Murphy	West Somerville	First Asst., Kindergarten	792 "	April 1, 1898
Margaret V. Quinlan	29 Mill st	"	648 "	Dec. 17, 1907
Mary A. Cahill	Cambridge	Assistant	624 "	Sept. 24, 1903
Mildred M. Hood	Cambridge	"	480 "	Dec. 17, 1907
Mary J. O'Neil	15 Edgeworth st	Special Assistant	1.75 day	Nov. 19, 1908
Katherine E. Hurley	542 E. Fifth st	"	1.75 "	April 15, 1909
Elizabeth L. Prendergast	108 Parker Hill ave	"	1.75 "	Feb. 1, 1909
Gertrude P. Tobin	368 Washington st	"	1.75 "	April 15, 1909
Elinor G. Cowan	9 Greenheys st	Substitute	2.00 "	12, 1909
Louisa Garibotto	40 N. Bennett st	Attendant	.50 "	Sept. 9, 1908
Celia Pote	Chelsea	"	.50 "	9, 1908
Frank J. Connolly	73 South st., J. P.	Janitor	41.69 wk.	20, 1904
William Swansey	7 Joiner st	"	26.22 "	April, 1877

Emerson District.

Name.	Residence.	Designation.	Compensation.	Date of Election or Appointment.
J. Willard Brown	Stoneham	Master	$3,180 yr	Feb. 24, 1891
James H. Leary	67 Peter Parley rd	Sub-Master	2,340 "	Jan. 4, 1901
Mary R. Thomas	89 Gainsboro st	Master's Assistant	1,260 "	April 22, 1907
Mary A. Ford	Greenbush	First Assistant, Grammar	1,212 "	March 18, 1878
Mary E. Plummer	12 Cumberland st	First Assistant in Charge	1,116 "	Nov. 2, 1896
Gertrude A. A'Hearn	34 Covington st	Assistant	552 "	Dec. 8, 1908
Anna A. Aronie	117 Devon st	"	648 "	Nov. 6, 1906
Sarah A. Atwood	North Cambridge	"	936 "	Oct. 1, 1891
Grace Bourne	274 Lexington st	"	888 "	Sept. 20, 1901
Esther M. Buchan	East Watertown	"	552 "	Nov. 3, 1908
Marion Chesley	192 Huntington ave	"	552 "	3, 1908
H. Elizabeth Cutter	Hyde Park	"	936 "	Dec. 1, 1865
Edith A. Duclos	9 Haley st	"	648 "	Nov. 20, 1906
Julia V. Guiney	62 Troy st	"	552 "	April 21, 1908
Ida E. Halliday	212 Lexington st	"	936 "	Jan. 3, 1881
Emma J. Irving	Winchester	"	936 "	Oct. 1, 1889
Mabel L. Josselyn	5 Monmouth st	"	840 "	Nov. 3, 1902
Avis A. Kingston	267 Corey rd, Alls	"	600 "	Oct. 9, 1907
Harriet E. Litchfield	Malden	"	936 "	April 15, 1873
Sarah B. McGinn	15 Concord st., Chsn	"	792 "	Sept. 14, 1904
Sarah E. McNeill	194 Leyden st., O. H.	"	792 "	14, 1904
Lizzie M. Morrissey	175 Princeton st	"	936 "	10, 1879
Eliza J. Murphy	Beverly	"	936 "	Dec. 3, 1900
Ella F. Murray	11 Sargent st	"	552 "	Jan. 4, 1909
Ona I. Nolan	South Weymouth	"	744 "	Dec. 4, 1905
Charlotte G. Ray	247 Lexington st	"	936 "	Sept. 8, 1890
Isabella J. Ray	204 Lexington st	"	936 "	4, 1895
Lena A. Sherwood	11 E. Newton st	"	648 "	Nov. 1, 1906
Susan A. Slavin	18 Vaughan st	"	936 "	Feb. 19, 1877
Emma L. Steves	18 Hanson st	"	552 "	April 30, 1909
Mary L. Sweeney	Newton Highlands	"	936 "	Dec. 15, 1883
Flora S. McLean	119 Princeton st	First Asst., Kindergarten	792 "	Sept. 9, 1891
Christine G. Long	2 Corey st., Chsn	Assistant, Kindergarten	624 "	Feb. 16, 1903
Mary L. Murphy	233 Bennington st	Attendant	.50 day	Sept. 9, 1908
Edward C. Chessman	50 Prescott st	Janitor	29.58 wk	Dec. 5, 1871
William A. McManus	14 Mercer st., S. B.	"	18.78 "	Jan. 1, 1907

Everett District.

Name.	Residence.	Designation.	Compensation.	Date of Election or Appointment.
Myron T Pritchard	125 School st	Master	$3,180 yr	Sept. 6, 1886
Eliza M. Evert	Newton Centre	Master's Assistant	1,308 "	4, 1882
Evelyn E. Morse	5 Dale st	First Assistant	1,164 "	14, 1904
Louise Robinson	77 Bushnell st., Ash	First Assistant in Charge	1,116 "	Oct. 25, 1899
Susan E. Abbot	108 Pembroke st	Assistant	936 "	March 9, 1899
Sarah L. Adams	70 W. Newton st	"	936 "	Oct. 7, 1875

School Department.— Continued.

Name.	Residence.	Designation.	Compensation.	Date of Election or Appointment.

Everett District.— Concluded.

Name.	Residence.	Designation.	Compensation.	Date of Election or Appointment.
Susan S. Foster	2029 Columbus ave	Assistant	$936 yr	Sept. 16, 1869
Annie H. Gardner	5 Sumner st	"	936 "	" 5, 1885
Grace D. Hall	95 Gainsboro st	"	696 "	Nov. 20, 1905
Ida B. Henderson	27 Clarkson st	"	936 "	Dec. 4, 1893
Emily T. Kelleher	35 Wenonah st	"	936 "	" 4, 1893
Sarah C. Linscott	9 Ruthven st	"	936 "	" 1, 1898
Bertha L. Mulloney	Cambridge	"	936 "	" 1, 1897
Florence A. Perry	14 Albion st	"	936 "	Sept. 25, 1879
Emma F. Porter	248 Warren st	"	936 "	April 1, 1880
Annie J. Reed	15 Blagdon st	"	936 "	Oct. 2, 1893
Dora W. Rohlsen	Newton Centre	"	936 "	Sept. 4, 1895
Ethel M. Rowland	Brookline	"	744 "	Feb. 16, 1905
Josephine C. Scholtes	259 Park st	"	840 "	Oct. 8, 1902
Helen J. Scott	Cambridge	"	744 "	Jan. 16, 1905
Alice E. Stevens	16 Durham st	"	936 "	" 19, 1883
Minnie T. Varney	Sharon	"	936 "	April 11, 1898
Catherine T. Whalen	46 E. Newton st	"	696 "	Jan. 30, 1906
Estelle M. Williams	Holliston	"	936 "	Feb. 17, 1896
Caroline S. Winslow	23 Wellington st	"	840 "	Oct. 8, 1902
Clara L. Hunting	99 Bowdoin ave	First Asst., Kindergarten	792 "	Sept. 9, 1891
Margaret Stedman	77 Bushnell st., Ash	Assistant, Kindergarten	432 "	April 21, 1908
Leila E. Boles	62 Sidney st	Special Assistant	1.75 day	Jan. 11, 1909
Ella G. Finn	41 Linwood st	"	1.75 "	Nov. 20, 1908
Florence M. Fogarty	110 Brook ave	Substitute	2.00 "	Sept. 9, 1908
Mary F. Martin	64 Warwick st	Attendant	.50 "	" 9, 1908
Henry F. Beverstock	525 Columbus ave	Janitor	20.02 wk	Jan. 17, 1906
Florence J. Nugent	456 Shawmut ave	"	15.41 "	Oct. 16, 1905

Francis Parkman District.

Name.	Residence.	Designation.	Compensation.	Date of Election or Appointment.
Arthur Stanley	Hyde Park	Master	$2,580 yr	Sept. 1, 1908
Edward J. Muldoon	18 Bellflower st	Sub-Master	1,500 "	Feb. 16, 1909
F. Maude Joy	21 Gardner st., Alls	Master's Assistant	972 "	Sept. 9, 1908
Margaret M. Burton	11 Chauncey pl., J. P.	Assistant	936 "	" 12, 1900
Josephine Crockett	430 Centre st., J. P.	"	936 "	Feb. 6, 1895
Frances M. Flanagan	77 Ashland st., Ros.	"	552 "	Jan. 4, 1909
Elizabeth Kiggen	Hyde Park	"	936 "	" 30, 1882
Lucinda R. Kinsley	11 Euclid st	"	936 "	March 13, 1901
Mabelle E. Lounsbury	66 Montclair ave., Ros.	"	936 "	Nov. 16, 1900
Annie V. Lynch	92 Hyde Park ave	"	936 "	Jan. 4, 1892
May C. O'Brien	South Framingham	"	696 "	Oct. 7, 1907
Mary A. O'Neil	129 Harold st	"	792 "	Sept. 14, 1904
Mary E. Roome	68 Day st., J. P.	"	936 "	Oct. 1, 1885
Josephine A. Slayton	16 Cohasset st., Ros.	"	936 "	" 3, 1889
Helen K. Somers	Mansfield	"	648 "	Nov. 1, 1906
Juliette Billings	15 Pond st., J. P.	First Asst., Kindergarten	792 "	Dec. 2, 1901
Olivia B. Hazelton (Mrs.)	Wellesley Hills	" "	624 "	Oct. 13, 1902
Leslie H. Somes	132 Hyde Park ave	Attendant	.50 day	Sept. 4, 1908
Henry T. Allchin	49 Oakview ter., J. P.	Janitor	24.99 wk	May 1, 1905
Patrick M. Connelly *	75 South st., J. P.	"		
Ellen Norton	49 Paine st	Janitor	6.62 wk	Nov. 1878

Franklin District.

Name.	Residence.	Designation.	Compensation.	Date of Election or Appointment.
Seth Sears	Cambridge	Master	$3,180 yr	Feb. 12, 1902
Jennie S. Tower †	44 Rutland sq	Master's Assistant	654 "	Oct. 1, 1870
Emma F. Jenkins	89 Gainsboro st	"	972 "	Sept. 9, 1908
Margaret J. Crosby	W. Medford	First Assistant, Grammar	1,212 "	" 10, 1902
Elizabeth F. Dorn	113 Maple st., W. R	First Assistant in Charge	1,116 "	Oct. 2, 1905
Etta M. Smith	144 Worcester st	" "	1,116 "	Jan. 16, 1905
Gabrielle Abbot	108 Pembroke st	Assistant	936 "	May 1, 1896
Emma E. Allin	1 Hanson st	"	936 "	Dec. 1, 1874
M. Josephine Blaisdell	1467 Dorchester ave	"	936 "	Feb. 1, 1901
Katherine E. Cotter	22 Wellington st	"	840 "	" 1, 1906
Eva M. Cotton	106 Warren st., Bri	"	552 "	" 16, 1909
Octavia L. Cram	Brookline	"	936 "	Oct. 19, 1891
Margaret C. Donovan	Randolph	"	744 "	May 1, 1905
Ella F. Erskine	134 Newbury st	"	888 "	Sept. 11, 1901
Agnes G. R. Fitzsimmons	35 Woodward st	"	600 "	April 8, 1907
Kate R. Gookin	Brookline	"	936 "	Sept. 27, 1875

* Leave of absence without pay for nine months from Sept. 10, 1908.
† Leave of absence on half pay to Sept. 1, 1909.

School Department.— Continued.

Name.	Residence.	Designation.	Compensation.	Date of Election or Appointment.

Franklin District.— Concluded.

Name.	Residence.	Designation.	Compensation.	Date of Election or Appointment.
Carrie M. Goulding	1 Kalada pk	Assistant	$888 yr	Oct. 23, 1901
Elizabeth Greenman	28 Rockland st	"	648 "	Dec. 14, 1906
Kate R. Hale	Brookline	"	936 "	Nov. 1, 1880
Abby A. Hayward	10 Berwick pk	"	936 "	Dec. 1, 1890
Ruth C. Higbee	Brookline	"	936 "	Sept. 13, 1899
Frances S. Jordan	63 Tonawanda st	"	792 "	" 9, 1903
Helen E. MacFarlane	627 Walk Hill st	"	552 "	Nov. 17, 1908
Violet M. Nevins	Melrose	"	648 "	" 6, 1906
Rose A. Plunkett	Medford	"	936 "	Oct. 29, 1902
Mary J. Rogers	20 Robinwood ave., J. P.	"	552 "	Nov. 3, 1908
Charlotte E. Romer	95 Orange st	"	840 "	Oct. 1, 1903
Alice M. Russell	85 Chestnut ave., J. P.	"	552 "	Nov. 3, 1908
Anna Sansiper	36 McLean st	"	552 "	March 3, 1908
Mary M. Simpson	Dedham	"	840 "	" 16, 1904
Florence M. Stephens	11 E. Newton st	"	888 "	Dec. 11, 1901
Ruth D. Stevens	Cliftondale	"	936 "	Oct. 15, 1902
Alice M. Sweeney	35 Bennington st	"	552 "	Nov. 3, 1908
Teresa A. Tehan	44 Linden st., Alls	"	600 "	" 19, 1907
Lillian Tishler	111 Waumbeck st	"	936 "	Sept. 23, 1892
Isabel H. Wilson	134 Huntington ave	"	936 "	Feb. 4, 1884
Martha L. Eaton	Brookline	First Asst., Kindergarten	696 "	Sept. 11, 1907
Mary T. Mears	11 Joy st	"	792 "	" 5, 1888
Elsie A. Burrage	Chestnut Hill	Assistant	480 "	March 18, 1907
Sara E. L'Orage	123 W. Concord st	"	480 "	Sept. 11, 1907
Anna A. Cassidy	24 Newburg st., Ros	Special Assistant	1.75 day	" 15, 1908
Gertrude P. Stephen	104 Brook ave	"	1.75 "	April 13, 1909
Dorothy A. Busby	386 Shawmut ave	Substitute	2.00 "	" 15, 1909
Marguerite F. Lally	73 Fletcher st., Ros	"	2.00 "	" 13, 1909
Mary J. Mimeri	80 Shawmut ave	Attendant	.50 "	Jan. 4, 1909
Margaret E. Ring	274A Shawmut ave	Janitor	14.75 wk	April 16, 1903
John F. Tolan	46 Erie st	"	24.78 "	July 20, 1905
Thomas Brennan	20 Tufts st	Substitute Janitor	1.28 day	April 30, 1909

Frederic W. Lincoln District.

Name.	Residence.	Designation.	Compensation.	Date of Election or Appointment.
William E. Perry	Brookline	Master	$3,180 yr	Sept. 10, 1902
Charles S. Davis	Cambridge	Sub-Master	2,220 "	Nov. 21, 1902
Charles I. Gates	19 Bentham rd	"	1,500 "	Feb. 16, 1909
Martha F. Wright	Newton	Master's Assistant	1,308 "	Dec. 4, 1889
Laura L. Newhall	534 Broadway	First Assistant in Charge	1,116 "	Nov. 2, 1896
Mary E. Bunton	Franklin Square House	Assistant	696 "	Oct. 1, 1908
Helen M. Canning	Dedham	"	936 "	Dec. 2, 1895
Gertrude P. Cole	Albemarle Chambers	"	744 "	" 31, 1906
Vodesa J. Comey	168 W. Newton st	"	936 "	Sept. 14, 1869
Kate A. Coolidge	65 G st	"	936 "	April 1, 1882
Frances W. Dalrymple	170 W. Brookline st	"	744 "	Nov. 1, 1907
Helen A. Emery	557 Fifth st	"	936 "	May 1, 1894
M. Jeannette Grady	164 Baker st., W. R	"	888 "	Nov. 1, 1907
Edna F. Henderson	27 Clarkson st	"	696 "	Sept. 13, 1905
Lillian K. Lewis	78 Huntington ave	"	936 "	" 6, 1893
E. Cecilia Mackin	844 Broadway	"	552 "	April 1, 1908
Alice F. Moore	Albemarle Chambers	"	648 "	Dec. 31, 1906
Agnes G. Nash	75 Mayfield st	"	936 "	Sept. 17, 1900
Harriet E. Sargent	Quincy	"	936 "	Dec. 5, 1895
Stella F. Thomas	12 Humphrey pl	"	744 "	" 3, 1907
Rachael W. Washburn	Lincoln	"	936 "	Nov. 1, 1898
Daisy E. Welch	13 Westville st	"	936 "	March 1, 1893
Gertrude L. Wright	Brookline	"	936 "	Oct. 14, 1901
Annie E. Pousland	Salem	First Asst., Kindergarten	792 "	" 7, 1901
Mary E. McCarthy	64 Peter Farley rd, J. P.	Assistant	528 "	Nov. 13, 1906
Gertrude A. Sullivan	147 Mt. Vernon st	Special Assistant	1.75 day	Sept. 15, 1908
Alice L. Lynch	622 Third st	Attendant	.50 "	" 9, 1908
George L. Dacey	28 Ward st	Janitor	15.95 wk	Oct. 4, 1894
Joseph S. Luther	414 Fifth st	"	23.18 "	Jan. 24, 1890

Frothingham District.

Name.	Residence.	Designation.	Compensation.	Date of Election or Appointment.
William B. Atwood	Malden	Master	$3,180 yr	Sept. 1, 1887
Charles E. Quirk	53 Farragut rd	Sub-Master	1,980 "	Jan. 16, 1905
Charlotte E. Camp	Medford	Master's Assistant	1,308 "	" 5, 1874
Margaret J. O'Hea	Brookline	First Assistant, Grammar	1,212 "	Feb. 3, 1902

School Department.— Continued.

Name.	Residence.	Designation.	Compensation.	Date of Election or Appointment.

Frothingham District.— Concluded.

Name.	Residence.	Designation.	Compensation.	Date of Election or Appointment.
Fannie M. Lamson	51 High st	First Assistant in Charge	$1,116 yr	Nov. 2, 1896
Florence O. Brock	63 Elm st	Assistant	936 "	Sept. 12, 1900
Nellie L. Cullis	43 High st	"	936 "	Oct. 16, 1882
Mabel A. Collins	West Somerville	"	744 "	" 2, 1905
Mary Colesworthy	Chelsea	"	936 "	Sept. 8, 1890
Mary E. Corbett	14 Monument sq	"	936 "	" 5, 1881
Etta G. Clarke	Cambridge	"	936 "	Oct. 1, 1900
Bertha F. Dodge	58 Walker st	"	600 "	Feb. 17, 1908
Mary J. Driscoll	73 Walter st	"	552 "	Nov. 3, 1908
Mary E. Delaney	112 Armandine st	"	936 "	Feb. 5, 1877
Madeline A. Foppiano	Chelsea	"	936 "	Jan. 2, 1900
Theresa E. Hayes	15 Monument sq	"	936 "	Oct. 3, 1892
Anna F. Kingston	9 Monument sq	"	888 "	May 16, 1901
Esther L. McNellis	12 Sackville st	"	552 "	Dec. 8, 1908
Mary L. Murphy	419 Fourth st	"	552 "	Jan. 4, 1909
Margaret A. Mernin	38 High st	"	936 "	Feb. 1, 1897
Abbie C. McAuliffe	17 Chestnut st	"	936 "	Sept. 1, 1878
Elizabeth L. McCarthy	7 Marion st	"	840 "	June 2, 1902
Frances L. Nickerson	Newtonville	"	744 "	March 20, 1906
Sara H. Nowell	406 Massachusetts ave	"	936 "	Jan. 5, 1874
Mary A. Quirk	West Somerville	"	936 "	June 7, 1898
Jennie L. Quirk	West Somerville	"	792 "	Sept. 14, 1904
Helen G. Stark	815 Beacon st	"	936 "	Oct. 1, 1895
Persis M. Whittemore	8 Cross st	"	936 "	Jan. 5, 1874
Martha Yeaton	Somerville	"	936 "	" 5, 1874
Phebe A. De Lande	26 Monument sq	First Asst., Kindergarten	792 "	Sept. 4, 1895
Angeline K. Mudge	1200 Commonwealth ave	Assistant	624 "	Feb. 1, 1904
Margaret M. O'Connor	32 Prospect st	Special Assistant	1.75 day	Sept. 9, 1908
Mary E. Briggs	44 Holborn st	Substitute	2.00 "	" 9, 1908
Josephine A. Hurley	24 Monument ave	"	1.75 "	April 27, 1909
Mary J. Hughes	140 Chelsea st	Attendant	.50 "	Sept. 9, 1908
George A. King	84 School st	Janitor	26.56 wk	Oct. 1, 1903
Jeremiah F. Horrigan	34 Bunker Hill st	"	17.22 "	April 16, 1895
Mary Watson	21 Decatur st	"	2.31 "	May 15, 1905
Margaret Walsh	48 Rutherford ave	"	6.77 "	Sept. 18, 1900

Gaston District.

Name.	Residence.	Designation.	Compensation.	Date of Election or Appointment.
Thomas H. Barnes	773 Broadway	Master	$3,180 yr	Sept. 6, 1869
Juliette R. Hayward	Malden	Master's Assistant	1,308 "	" 6, 1880
Sarah C. Winn	Cambridge	First Assistant, Grammar	1,212 "	Feb. 19, 1872
Ellen V. Courtney	745 Broadway	First Asst. in Charge	1,116 "	Oct. 1, 1903
Edith M. Allen	3 Highland pk	Assistant	840 "	" 8, 1902
Mary B. Barry	118 M st	"	936 "	Sept. 5, 1881
Elizabeth M. T. Bartlett	528 Broadway	"	792 "	Oct. 2, 1905
A. Josephine Bogan	7 Gaylord st	"	888 "	April 25, 1905
Florence E. Bryan	94 Brunswick st	"	936 "	March 28, 1900
Elizabeth G. Burke	99 Brunswick st	"	936 "	Nov. 6, 1901
Jennie G. Carmichael	Braintree	"	936 "	Sept. 10, 1890
Emily M. Desmond	Medford	"	552 "	April 12, 1909
Mary A. Dorgan	632 Third st	"	648 "	Nov. 1, 1906
Eleanor F. Elton	105 King st	"	936 "	June 1, 1893
Carrie A. Harlow	587 Eighth st	"	936 "	Nov. 3, 1879
M. Isabel Harrington	Brookline	"	936 "	" 1, 1889
Lila Huckins	115 Dale st	"	936 "	Sept. 7, 1874
Caroline M. Kingman	108 Mt. Vernon st	"	936 "	March 1, 1889
Mary S. Laughton	284 K st	"	936 "	Sept. 8, 1890
Margaret M. Lannon	86 South st., J. P.	"	552 "	Nov. 3, 1908
Mary F. Lindsey	71 Edwin st	"	936 "	Sept. 8, 1896
Hannah L. Manson	Winthrop Beach	"	936 "	Oct. 27, 1884
Josephine A. Powers	758 Broadway	"	936 "	Sept. 2, 1878
Clara A. Sharp	528 Broadway	"	936 "	" 2, 1878
Emma M. Sibley	Newtonville	"	936 "	" 3, 1883
Anna E. Somes	217 K st	"	936 "	" 3, 1883
Irene M. Walsh	317 Dudley st	"	600 "	Nov. 19, 1907
Alice L. Williams	10 Kingsdale st	"	600 "	Oct. 14, 1907
Ellen R. Wyman	636 Dudley st	"	936 "	March 5, 1862
Grace L. Sanger	144 Hemenway st	First Asst., Kindergarten	792 "	April 8, 1901
Maud L. Richardson	South Weymouth	Assistant	576 "	Oct. 2, 1905
Alice G. Coughlin	Broadway	Attendant	.50 day	Nov. 30, 1908
John McLeod	645 Sixth st	Janitor	31.02 wk	Aug. 16, 1903
Nicholas J. Innis	30 Dustin st., Bri.	"	16.42 "	Jan. 20, 1908

School Department.— Continued.

Name.	Residence.	Designation.	Compensation	Date of Election or Appointment.

George Putnam District.

Name.	Residence.	Designation.	Compensation	Date of Election or Appointment.
Henry L. Clapp	70 West Cottage st	Master	$3,180 yr	Sept. 1, 1882
Joseph A. Reddy	24 Elm Hill pk	Sub-Master	2,340 "	Oct. 9, 1899
Katharine W. Huston	71 Montebello rd	Master's Assistant	1,308 "	Feb. 28, 1887
Julia H. Cram	Brookline	First Asst. in Charge	1,116 "	April 14, 1904
Ella J. Brown	1 Wabon st	Assistant	936 "	Nov. 5, 1895
Mabel L. Brown	151 Worcester st	"	936 "	8, 1892
Carrie A. Colton	165 Roxbury st	"	936 "	Dec. 1, 1896
Mary L. Crowe	East Braintree	"	936 "	1, 1897
Charlotte E. Dogherty	8 Cobden st	"	600 "	Sept. 16, 1907
Annie G. Ellis	17 Cleaver st	"	936 "	" 6, 1886
Amoritta E. Esilman	66 School st	"	936 "	" 4, 1882
Minnie E. Farnsworth	177 Warren st	"	936 "	Oct. 19, 1903
Mary M. French	135 School st	"	648 "	Nov. 20, 1906
Lura B. Galbraith	8 Cobden st	"	888 "	April 10, 1905
Anna L. Gormley	81 School st	"	552 "	Nov. 3, 1908
Mary A. Gove	19 Dixwell st	"	936 "	Sept. 8, 1896
Ellen E. Leach	28 Dartmouth st	"	936 "	20, 1858
Anna H. O'Connell	14 Spring Park ave	"	744 "	May 1, 1905
Louisa Prescott	19 Dixwell st	"	888 "	Jan. 16, 1905
Helen M. Richardson	92 Ruthven st	"	552 "	Nov. 3, 1908
Isabel J. Ross	13 Linwood sq	"	744 "	May 11, 1905
Annie C. Simmons	28 Templeton st	"	744 "	Jan. 16, 1905
Mary L. Sullivan	39 Bainbridge st	"	936 "	May 1, 1900
Eileen R. Tewksbury	23 Thornton pk	"	552 "	Nov. 3, 1908
Ede F. Travis	51 Chestnut Hill	"	936 "	Oct. 26, 1891
Elizabeth A. Wood	25 Burr st	"	600 "	Feb. 4, 1907
Anita F. Weston	146 Mass. ave	First Asst., Kindergarten	792 "	Oct. 18, 1897
M. Alice Costello	Newton Lower Falls	Assistant	576 "	Nov. 1, 1905
Florence R. LeBlanc	47 Prentiss st	Special Assistant	1.75 day	Oct. 14, 1908
William N. Carr	20 Burr st	Janitor	21.14 wk	Sept. 26, 1906
Luke Kelley	193 Boylston st	"	32.44 "	May 1, 1887

Gilbert Stuart District.

Name.	Residence.	Designation.	Compensation	Date of Election or Appointment.
Edward M. Lancaster	803 Shawmut ave	Master	$3,180 yr	June 1, 1885
Edwin F. Kimball	107 Greenbrier st	Sub-Master	2,340 "	Nov. 21, 1887
Caroline F. Melville	Brookline	Master's Assistant	1,308 "	April 1, 1902
Carrie M. Weis	50 River st	First Assistant in Charge	1,116 "	Oct. 1, 1903
A. Maude Briggs	Atlantic	Assistant	888 "	Sept. 11, 1901
Cornelia M. Collamore	36 Walton st	"	936 "	Jan. 3, 1887
Mary M. Dacey	17 Wood st	"	936 "	May 15, 1894
Lucy D. Ellis	17 Cleaves st	"	840 "	Sept. 10, 1902
Ella M. B. Hayes	19 Linden st	"	648 "	Nov. 6, 1906
Mary M. Hoye	1016 Washington st	"	936 "	Sept. 13, 1899
Lydia D. Johnson	58 River st	"	936 "	" 13, 1899
Anna M. McMahon	Randolph	"	936 "	" 9, 1891
Verna G. Pitt	19 Evelyn st	"	600 "	" 11, 1907
Hazel E. Poole	Milton	"	648 "	Nov. 1, 1906
Della Prescott	4 Atherstone st	"	936 "	May 1, 1902
John C. Riley	7 Lonsdale st	"	600 "	Oct. 22, 1907
Edith A. Scanlon	11 Castlegate rd	"	936 "	Feb. 1, 1897
H. Adelaide Sullivan	70 River st	"	936 "	Nov. 1, 1889
Mary E. Walsh	314 Codman st	"	792 "	Sept. 10, 1903
Elizabeth B. Wetherbee	2 Holden pl	"	936 "	8, 1896
Julia E. Hall	115 Richmond st	First Asst., Kindergarten	792 "	March 1, 1901
Ellen W. Porter	34 Port Norfolk st	"	696 "	Dec. 3, 1907
Grace L. White	5 Houghton st	Assistant	528 "	Nov. 6, 1906
Elizabeth F. Lee	15 St. James st	Special Asst., Kindergarten	1.50 day	Jan. 4, 1909
Asa C. Hawes	46 River st	Janitor	37.55 wk	Nov. 1, 1892
Henry Keenan	625 Norfolk st	"	8.99 "	March 9, 1908

Hancock District.

Name.	Residence.	Designation.	Compensation	Date of Election or Appointment.
Ellen C. Sawtelle	Newton Highlands	Master	$3,180 yr	March 1, 1904
Honora T. O'Dowd	96 Ruthven st	Master's Assistant	1,308 "	Sept. 4, 1895
Ella A. Curtis	Newton Upper Falls	First Assistant, Grammar	1,020 "	Feb. 3, 1908
Teresa M. Gargan	316 Longwood ave	First Assistant in Charge	1,116 "	Nov. 2, 1896
Margaret D. Mitchell	61 Monument ave	"	1,116 "	March 1, 1899
Annie M. Niland	202 Byron st	First Assistant, Primary	1,080 "	Sept. 28, 1904
Ida E. Ansley	73 Glendale st	Assistant	792 "	Oct. 19, 1903
Matilda F. Bibbey	21 Wales st	"	936 "	1, 1889
F. Maud Briggs	6 Westland ave	"	936 "	Sept. 12, 1909

School Department.— Continued.

Name.	Residence.	Designation.	Compensation.	Date of Election or Appointment.

Hancock District. — Concluded.

Name.	Residence.	Designation.	Compensation.	Date of Election or Appointment.
Mary C. Brine	85 Chandler st	Assistant	$888 yr	April 1, 1902
Teresa L. Carlin	524 East Broadway	"	888 "	Oct. 1, 1902
Annie G. Colbert	52 Quincy st	"	936 "	Sept. 12, 1900
Eleanor M. Colleton	59 Beech Glen st	"	936 "	Dec. 5, 1894
Geraldine F. Corbett	866 East Fifth st	"	696 "	Sept. 13, 1905
Jessie C. Davidson	12 Nixon st	"	552 "	Dec. 8, 1908
Mary L. Desmond	445 Washington st., Dor	"	936 "	" 10, 1872
Anna T. Dinand	59 Bowdoin ave	"	840 "	Sept. 9, 1903
Marian A. Dogherty	Cambridge	"	936 "	Dec. 1, 1897
Katherine F. Doherty	69 Howland st	"	936 "	Sept. 8, 1896
Catherine W. Fraser	73 Walnut ave	"	936 "	May 16, 1891
Harriet M. Fraser	73 Walnut ave	"	936 "	Sept. 12, 1871
Hattie L. Gates	470 Warren st	"	936 "	Oct. 1, 1900
Katherine E. Gillespie	19 E. Springfield st	"	936 "	Sept. 6, 1886
Marcella C. Halliday	139 Worcester st	"	936 "	Nov. 1, 1867
Emily J. Hare	Brockton	"	936 "	Oct. 21, 1901
Mary A. Kirby	Marlboro	"	888 "	Jan. 6, 1903
Susan E. Mace	Waverley House	"	936 "	" 7, 1871
Mary G. Mahar	68 L st	"	936 "	Dec. 1, 1896
Margaret Mais	12 Paul Gore, J. P.	"	936 "	" 1, 1897
Mary E. Meaney	Brookline	"	936 "	March 1, 1900
Mary F. Montrose	14 Evergreen st., J. P.	"	840 "	Jan. 4, 1904
Lucy M. A. Moore	36 E. Brookline st	"	936 "	" 2, 1884
Margaret Mulligan	Winchester	"	936 "	Sept. 8, 1896
Mary J. Murray	25 Sharon st	"	936 "	May 16, 1891
Anna E. Neal	75 Norton st	"	936 "	Sept. 12, 1900
Catherine C. O'Connell	Somerville	"	936 "	" 8, 1896
Mary E. O'Hare	21 Bartlett st	"	936 "	May 1, 1899
Evelyn M. Pearce	26 Thwing st	"	936 "	Dec. 1, 1897
Lena M. Rendall	Medford	"	936 "	Nov. 2, 1891
Fanny L. Rogers	310 Warren st	"	936 "	May 17, 1897
Mary G. Ruxton	5 Tupelo st	"	936 "	Dec. 1, 1880
Mary J. Ryan	60 McLellan st	"	936 "	" 1, 1897
Elsie M. Sawyer	18 Tremont st	"	936 "	Nov. 15, 1900
Emma L. Spratt	West Somerville	"	792 "	Jan. 16, 1905
Katherine M. Sullivan	6 Willis st	"	888 "	Sept. 10, 1902
Sophia G. Whalen	14 Edison green	"	936 "	Dec. 17, 1894
Bertha M. Druley	9 Gainsboro st	First Asst., Kindergarten	796 "	Jan. 5, 1903
Julia E. Keith	25 Folsom st	" "	648 "	Sept. 9, 1908
Esther F. McDermott	6 St. Martin st	" "	792 "	Feb. 1, 1894
Margaret V. Meade	Brookline	" "	792 "	Oct. 1, 1903
Minnie A. Prescott	11 Rutledge st	" "	792 "	April 10, 1905
Anna E. Fiske	1 Lester pl., J. P.	Assistant	432 "	Feb. 16, 1909
Bertha V. Martin	212 Webster st	"	480 "	April 8, 1907
Ethel S. Murkland	Lynn	"	528 "	Nov. 1, 1906
Agnes G. Ryan	Danvers	"	576 "	Jan. 2, 1906
Hetty B. Schriftgeisser	427 Geneva ave	"	432 "	April 21, 1908
Linda C. O'Dowd	131 Bunker Hill st	Special Assistant	1.75 day	Sept. 9, 1908
Mary A. Ford	988 Tremont st., Rox.	"	1.75 "	March 29, 1909
Margaret D. Sawyer	16 Tremont st	"	1.75 "	" 10, 1909
Laura Cataldo	88 Cottage st	Attendant	.50 "	Sept. 9, 1908
Jennie Gavonie	11 Unity st	"	.50 "	" 9, 1908
Raphaella Langone	19 Unity st	"	.50 "	" 9, 1908
Jennie Strollo	195 Salem st	"	.50 "	" 9, 1908
Mary Strollo	195 Salem st	"	.50 "	" 9, 1908
Edward P. Clark	439 Fourth st	Janitor	24.81 wk	Feb. 15, 1901
John S. Keller	217 Brighton ave., Alls.	"	19.08 "	Dec. 13, 1898
Humphrey C. Mahoney	27 Thornley st	"	*40.93 "	Jan. 1, 1899
Mary McDermott †	82 Devens st	"	2.93 "	Aug. 1, 1878
Honora Hanson	8 Vernon pl	Matron	10.38 "	Feb. 27, 1899

Harvard District.

Name.	Residence.	Designation.	Compensation.	Date of Election or Appointment.
Henry C. Parker	Reading	Master	$3,180 yr	Nov. 1, 1903
Philo G. Noon	Somerville	Sub-Master	1,620 "	Sept. 11, 1907
Sarah E. Leonard	30 High st	Master's Assistant	1,308 "	" 1, 1885
Abbie M. Libby	Chelsea	First Assistant, Grammar	1,212 "	" 13, 1899
Catherine G. Foley	86 Mt. Pleasant ave	First Assistant in Charge	972 "	Oct. 1, 1908
Agnes A. Herlihy	32 Winthrop st	" "	1,116 "	Nov. 2, 1896

* Includes $432 for supervision of baths.
† Year's leave of absence on half pay. Resignation to take effect December 31, 1909.

School Department.— Continued.

Name.	Residence.	Designation.	Compensation	Date of Election or Appointment.

Harvard District.— Concluded.

Name.	Residence.	Designation.	Compensation	Date
Georgiana Benjamin	Malden	Assistant	$936 yr	Feb. 18, 1884
Grace M. Broaders	51 Elm st	"	936 "	Sept. 12, 1900
Genevieve Costello	Auburndale	"	552 "	April 12, 1909
Elizabeth G. Desmond	36 Harvard st	"	936 "	Sept. 4, 1889
Sarah R. Dodge *	Somerville	"	936 "	Jan. 1, 1892
Mabel P. Foster	94 Rockview st., J. P.	"	936 "	Nov. 1, 1893
Pauline M. Garey	Cambridge	"	600 "	Sept. 11, 1907
Caroline E. Gary	Chelsea	"	936 "	1, 1879
S. Janet Jameson	18 Tremont st., Chsn.	"	936 "	Oct. 6, 1892
Fanny E. Jennison	Somerville	"	936 "	1, 1902
Mary C. Leonard	28 Prospect st	"	792 "	May 25, 1904
Sarah V. Porter	37 Winthrop st	"	936 "	Dec. 3, 1900
Alice G. Ryan	106 Sheridan st., J. P.	"	552 "	Feb. 16, 1909
Isabel A. Smith	Somerville	"	936 "	Sept. 17, 1900
Laura F. Wentworth	Dedham	"	648 "	Oct. 1, 1906
Louisa A. Whitman	Medford	"	936 "	1, 1873
Lucy C. Wiig	2 Concord st	"	696 "	Sept. 13, 1905
Lana J. Wood	Lynn	"	936 "	6, 1880
Sarah J. Worcester	43 Green st	"	936 "	March 1, 1873
Sallie Bush	108 Mt. Vernon st	First Asst., Kindergarten	792 "	Nov. 5, 1888
Eliza A. Maguire	51 Monument ave	"	792 "	March 1, 1905
Hattie F. Mason	9 Oak st	Assistant	624 "	Jan. 16, 1905
Alice C. Ringer	16A Eden st	"	576 "	Dec. 4, 1905
Margaret D. Sawyer	16 Tremont st., Chsn.	Special Assistant	1.75 day	March 10, 1909
Nora L. Downey	31 Winthrop st	Attendant	.50 "	Sept. 9, 1908
Eden E. Fox	11 Gray st	"	.50 "	9, 1908
William A. Kingsley	107 Bartlett st	Janitor	9.18 wk	Dec. 16, 1908
Thomas F. Powell †	56 Delle ave	"	9.46 "	March 1, 1909
Walter I. Sprague	187 Bunker Hill st	"	21.82 "	Sept. 1, 1896

Henry L. Pierce District.

Name.	Residence.	Designation.	Compensation	Date
Horace W. Warren	57 Ocean st	Master	$3,180 yr	May 1, 1892
William W. Howe	106 Howland st	Sub-Master	2,340 "	April 24, 1901
M. Ella Mann	15 Westville st	Master's Assistant	1,308 "	1, 1892
Clara B. Cutler	56 Rutland sq	First Assistant, Grammar	1,164 "	Jan. 16, 1905
Keziah J. Anslow	32 Wellington Hill st	First Assistant in Charge	1,068 "	Nov. 1, 1906
Anna B. Badlam	64 Bowdoin st	"	1,116 "	Jan. 2, 1901
Lilian S. Bourne	1112 Adams st	Assistant	936 "	Dec. 1, 1890
Elizabeth R. Brady	110 Canterbury st	"	936 "	Sept. 12, 1900
Helen F. Burgess	72 Fuller st	"	936 "	1, 1881
Ella F. Carr	2 Allston st	"	936 "	Nov. 18, 1895
Mary J. Collingwood	828 Blue Hill ave	"	936 "	Jan. 2, 1901
Anne M. Coveney	Somerville	"	600 "	Oct. 20, 1908
Lucina Dunbar	Hyde Park	"	936 "	Nov. 1, 1886
Frances L. Eager	28 River st	"	600 "	Oct. 22, 1907
Laura D. Fisher	21 Rockwell st	"	936 "	Nov. 1, 1900
Mary A. Fruean	393 Norfolk st	"	936 "	1, 1897
Hannah Greenberg	127 Myrtle st	"	552 "	3, 1908
Alice G. Haggerty	49 Dale st	"	600 "	Oct. 22, 1907
Elizabeth E. Haggerty	12 Port Norfolk st	"	744 "	Jan. 16, 1905
Ethel M. Haynes	6 Ainsley st	"	696 "	May 1, 1905
Annie I. Heffernan	65 Farragut rd	"	600 "	Sept. 11, 1907
Gertrude L. McCormick	3090 Washington st	"	552 "	Jan. 7, 1908
Marie L. Mahoney	112 Ocean st	"	552 "	Nov. 3, 1908
M. Louise Merrick	671 Washington st	"	936 "	March 28, 1892
Catherine J. Norton	19 Olney st	"	696 "	Nov. 14, 1905
Pauline F. Rafter	41 Bradlee st	"	552 "	3, 1908
Mary A. Watson	29 Vaughan ave	"	744 "	Jan. 16, 1905
Flora C. Woodman	52 Alexander st	"	936 "	Sept. 6, 1893
Gertrude F. Briggs	44 Holborn st	First Asst., Kindergarten	744 "	March 18, 1907
Blanche E. Thayer	Hotel Oxford, Hunt'gton ave	"	792 "	Feb. 12, 1902
Ethel M. Coleman	25 Gaylord st	Assistant	528 "	Nov. 12, 1906
Eleanor L. Rand	100 Hutchings st	"	432 "	April 21, 1908
Adeline J. Oswald	406 Centre st., J. P.	Special Assistant	1.75 day	Sept. 9, 1908
Timothy Donahoe	29 Withington st	Janitor	29.96 wk	March 10, 1892
John A. Downey	21 Buttonwood st	"	14.26 "	Nov. 16, 1908
John J. Smith	47 Withington st	"	17.77 "	July 1, 1905

* Leave of absence without pay from April 1 to September 1, 1909.
† Regular substitute janitor.

School Department.— Continued.

Name.	Residence.	Designation.	Compensation.	Date of Election or Appointment.

Horace Mann School for the Deaf.

Name.	Residence.	Designation.	Compensation.	Date of Election or Appointment.
Sarah Fuller	Newton Lower Falls	Principal	$3,180 yr.	Sept. 21, 1869
Ella C. Jordan	Newton Lower Falls	Assistant Principal	1,512 "	April 12, 1893
Ida H. Adams	102 Brook rd., Mat.	Assistant	1,284 "	Sept. 7, 1887
Mabel E. Adams	38 Percival st.	"	1,284 "	March 1, 1891
Mary B. Adams	102 Brook rd., Mat.	"	1,212 "	Sept. 15, 1902
Mary F. Bigelow	14 Warren sq., J. P.	"	1,284 "	May 1, 1873
Josephine L. Goddard	27 Conway st., Ros.	"	1,284 "	Feb. 6, 1895
Jennie M. Henderson	57 Birch st., Ros.	"	996 "	Jan. 25, 1909
Elsa L. Hobart	52 Rutland sq.	"	1,284 "	April 1, 1886
Kate F. Hobart	52 Rutland sq.	"	1,284 "	Nov. 4, 1889
Sadie W. Jenkins	Ashland	"	996 "	Feb. 8, 1909
Sarah A. J. Monro	North Andover	"	1,284 "	Nov. 1, 1880
Amy M. Pleadwell	89 Pinckney st.	"	996 "	Sept. 13, 1905
Mary Helen Thompson	50 Rutland sq.	"	1,284 "	Oct. 23, 1901
Sally B. Tripp	Newton Upper Falls	"	1,284 "	" 3, 1887
Stella E. Weaver	18 Claxton st.	"	1,284 "	Sept. 7, 1897
Kate D. Williams	Dedham	"	1,284 "	" 2, 1872
Aloyse M. Owen	251 Princeton st.	Special Assistant	1.75 day.	" 9, 1908
George F. Wheeler	57 N. Beacon st., Alls.	Janitor	15.31 wk.	April 17, 1908
Flora H. Frizzell	1577 Blue Hill ave., Mat.	Matron	8.08 "	Oct. 1, 1904
Annie L. Gaunou	West Newton	"	5.77 "	" 1, 1904

Hugh O'Brien District.

Name.	Residence.	Designation.	Compensation.	Date of Election or Appointment.
John R. Morse	31 Bicknell st.	Master	$3,180 yr.	Oct. 16, 1890
George E. Murphy	467 Columbia rd.	Sub-Master	2,340 "	Feb. 15, 1899
Edwin I. Beal	Quincy	"	1,740 "	Sept. 12, 1906
Myra E. Wilson	209 Dudley st.	Master's Assistant	1,164 "	Jan. 2, 1905
Margaret Holmes	Winthrop	First Assistant, Grammar	1,212 "	March 19, 1888
Emily M. Pevear	209 Dudley st.	First Assistant in Charge	1,116 "	Oct. 10, 1892
Elinore G. Lynch	28 Rockland st.	First Assistant, Primary	1,080 "	Sept. 15, 1903
Deborah F. Barry	147 Charles st.	Assistant	552 "	March 16, 1909
Mary P. Barry	307 Lexington st.	"	696 "	Oct. 25, 1905
Helen L. Bradford	389 Seaver st.	"	936 "	Feb. 14, 1899
Amy L. Burbank	Waverly	"	936 "	Sept. 11, 1901
Alice Church	2 Rockland st.	"	840 "	Oct. 2, 1905
Anna W. Clark	573 Dudley st.	"	936 "	" 3, 1892
Evangeline Clark	573 Dudley st.	"	936 "	Nov. 1, 1893
Viola M. I. Clark	47 Clarkwood st.	"	936 "	" 1, 1900
Elizabeth Cushing	44 W. Cottage st.	"	936 "	Feb. 11, 1901
Isabella M. Duguid	11 E. Newton st.	"	936 "	Sept. 23, 1901
Sarah J. Fallon	32 Hewins st.	"	888 "	Nov. 18, 1901
Ellen M. Greany	691 Columbia rd.	"	840 "	Sept. 9, 1903
Ellen F. A. Hagerty	92 Chandler st.	"	936 "	Feb. 1, 1887
Thomas E. Kelley	27 Worcester sq.	"	600 "	April 8, 1907
Margaret M. A. Kennedy*	12 Brown ave., Ros.	"	792 "	Oct. 14, 1903
Mary F. MacGoldrick	19 Homes ave.	"	600 "	Sept. 11, 1907
Mary E. Mahan	Natick	"	936 "	March 31, 1904
Grace M. Maher	138 Cushing ave.	"	936 "	Dec. 18, 1899
Mary J. Mohan	42 Carson st.	"	936 "	Sept. 8, 1884
Abbie S. Oliver	9 Pevear pl.	"	936 "	Oct. 1, 1878
Florence W. Parry	28 Mt. Pleasant ave.	"	888 "	Nov. 18, 1901
Julia E. Phalen	7 Mystic st.	"	840 "	Dec. 1, 1902
Elizabeth F. Pinkham	28 Charlotte st.	"	936 "	" 1, 1892
Alice G. Russell	57 Clifton st.	"	936 "	April 14, 1896
Bridget F. Scanlon	3 Hartford st.	"	936 "	Oct. 1, 1878
Cora F. Taylor	Methuen	"	936 "	Nov. 11, 1901
Louise Townsend	41 Union pk.	"	840 "	Jan. 2, 1906
Helen M. West	17 Ashmont st.	"	552 "	Dec. 8, 1908
Hilda Williamson	30 Rockland st.	"	936 "	Feb. 5, 1901
M. Gertrude Breckenridge	64 Clifton st.	First Asst., Kindergarten	792 "	Sept. 9, 1903
Clara Ransom	12 Harlow st.	" "	744 "	" 13, 1905
Anna Harris	6 Burr st., J. P.	Assistant	576 "	Feb. 1, 1906
Anna L. Smith	18 Howe st.	"	528 "	Nov. 1, 1906
Bessie G. Russell	57 Clifton st.	Temporary Teacher	2.00 day.	April 20, 1909
Catherine Parks	Dunmore st.	Attendant	.50 "	Sept. 9, 1908
Mary McNamara	130 Hampden st.	"	.50 "	" 9, 1908
Thomas J. Gill	9 North ave.	Janitor	33.05 wk.	March 12, 1887
Michael J. Lally	30 Woodward ave.	"	19.99 "	July 15, 1905
William H. Bowman †	30 Faulkner st.	"		April 1, 1896

* Leave of absence without pay from September 1, 1908, to September 1, 1909.
† See Dearborn District.

School Department.— Continued.

Name.	Residence.	Designation.	Compensation.	Date of Election or Appointment.

Hyde District.

Name.	Residence.	Designation.	Compensation.	Date of Election or Appointment.
Silas C. Stone	51 Mt. Vernon st., W. R.	Master	$3,180 yr.	Jan. 1, 1871
Susan J. Ginn	12 Westminster ave	Master's Assistant	1,020 "	Dec. 3, 1907
Jane Reid	22 Thornley st	First Assistant, Grammar	1,164 "	Jan. 2, 1905
Delia E. Cunningham	33 Woodbine st	First Assistant in Charge	1,116 "	Oct. 9, 1901
Celia Bamber	6 Marshall ter., Alls	Assistant	936 "	Sept. 9, 1891
Ellen J. Brosnahan	100 I st	"	600 "	May 1, 1907
Grace M. Clark	69 St. James st	"	936 "	April 16, 1890
Anna F. Cotter	11 Langdon st	"	744 "	March 1, 1905
Mary W. Currier	5 Henshaw ter., W. R.	"	936 "	Sept. 6, 1886
Annie G. Flaherty	11 Ashland st	"	840 "	May 1, 1902
Elvira T. Harvey	Newton Highlands	"	840 "	Dec. 1, 1902
Jane Hay	5 Holiday st	"	552 "	April 12, 1909
Mary A. Higgins	51 Norfolk st	"	936 "	Oct. 1, 1891
Louise A. Kelley	53 Forest st.	"	936 "	Jan. 2, 1878
Alice G. Mace	11 Ashland st	"	792 "	Sept. 9, 1903
Mary A. McKinlay	8 Amherst st	"	888 "	10, 1902
Caroline K. Nickerson	285 Columbus ave	"	936 "	" 1860
A. Gertrude O'Bryan	9 Telegraph st	"	840 "	Feb. 2, 1903
Helen Perry	14 Albion st.	"	936 "	March 1, 1886
Edith M. Snow	291 Lamartine st., J. P.	"	600 "	Nov. 5, 1907
Ellen J. Stuart	10 Holl orn st	"	792 "	Dec. 4, 1905
Frances M. Supple	1513 Washington st	"	936 "	Sept. 1, 1869
Mary B. Tenney *	32 Melville ave	"	936 "	Oct. 15, 1896
Zelpha L. Thayer	Reading	"	744 "	Feb. 4, 1907
Jessie E. B. Thompson	Brookline.	"	936 "	Sept. 10, 1902
Augusta M. Wood	80 Winthrop st	"	888 "	Nov. 2, 1903
Etta Yerdon	44 Pinckney st	"	936 "	Sept. 7, 1887
Ada M. Fitts	183 Massachusetts ave	Assistant, Special Class	1,032 "	Nov. 10, 1902
Edna W. Marsh	95 Munroe st	First Asst., Kindergarten	792 "	Sept. 11, 1901
Mary R. Crane	Cambridge	Assistant	624 "	Jan. 16, 1905
Caroline G. Tunis	Cambridge	Temporary Teacher	2.00 day.	Nov. 30, 1908
Emma L. Harris	18 Windsor st., Rox.	Attendant	.50 "	Oct. 19, 1908
Patrick F. Higgins	51 Norfolk st., Rox.	Janitor	28.97 wk.	May 1, 1897
Jeremiah Shaw	649 Washington st., Bri		17.61 "	April 16, 1903

Jefferson District.

Name.	Residence.	Designation.	Compensation.	Date of Election or Appointment.
Edward P. Sherburne	46 Brent st	Master	$3,180 yr.	Dec. 23, 1896
John W. Lillis	Everett	Sub-Master	1,860 "	Sept. 13, 1905
Elinor W. Leavitt	34 Akron st	Master's Assistant	1,308 "	Dec. 1, 1895
Edith E. Cox	3 Sunnyside st	Assistant	792 "	Sept. 14, 1904
Annie B. Dooley	804 Parker st	"	936 "	Oct. 27, 1897
Vincent A. Keenan	477 Dudley st	"	744 "	Nov. 15, 1905
Helen C. Laughlin	446 Massachusetts ave	"	936 "	Sept. 5, 1888
Mary A. Leary	Sharon	"	936 "	Nov. 3, 1902
Annie W. Leonard	64 Colberg ave	"	936 "	Sept. 26, 1894
Ellen C. McDermott	30 Francis st	"	936 "	Oct. 4, 1880
Mary E. Murphy	124 Eustis st	"	936 "	Nov. 1, 1897
Susan H. Nugent	23 Dorr st	"	936 "	Oct. 27, 1897
Mary M. Phelan	18 New Heath st	"	744 "	April 10, 1905
Mary V. Prendergast	108 Parker Hill ave	"	936 "	Oct. 27, 1897
Eleanor F. Somerby	2 Mt. Pleasant ter	"	936 "	" 27, 1897
Mary J. Stark	258 Athens st	"	888 "	Nov. 18, 1901
Margaret L. Toole	128 Boylston st	"	792 "	Sept. 21, 1904
Helen E. Wray	20 Brent st	"	552 "	March 3, 1908
Catharine L. Gately	796 Parker st	First Asst., Kindergarten	696 "	Dec. 3, 1907
Ida E. McElwain	Brookline	"	792 "	April 13, 1896
Christine E. Glynn	257 Heath st	Assistant	480 "	May 1, 1907
Mary G. Murray	6 Wadsworth st	"	576 "	" 1, 1905
Alice L. McCormick	108 Highland st	Special Assistant	1.75 day.	Oct. 6, 1908
Patrick J. Riordan	317 Blue Hill ave	Janitor	28.36 wk.	" 14, 1907
Nellie G. Watson	2 Lawn st		6.30 "	Aug. 1, 1903

John A. Andrew District.

Name.	Residence.	Designation.	Compensation.	Date of Election or Appointment.
Joshua M. Dill	Newton Centre	Master	$3,180 yr.	Nov. 21, 1881
Edgar L. Raub	9 Windermere rd	Sub-Master	2,340 "	June 12, 1889
Emma M. Cleary	109 Dorchester st	Master's Assistant	1,308 "	Jan. 31, 1891
Bertha E. Miller	10 Virginia st	First Assistant, Grammar	1,116 "	Sept. 13, 1905
Mary A. Jenkins	Wellesley Hills	First Assistant in Charge	1,116 "	Nov. 2, 1896

* Leave of absence without pay to September 1, 1909.

School Department.— Continued.

Name.	Residence.	Designation.	Compensation.	Date of Election or Appointment.

John A. Andrew District.— Concluded.

Mary E. Bernhard	502 Fourth st	Assistant	$936 yr	March 17, 1891
Ethel A. Borden	180 Mt. Vernon st	"	933 "	Dec. 17, 1900
Agnes M. Cochran	570 Broadway	"	936 "	Feb. 1, 1886
Ellen M. Collins	502 Fourth st	"	936 "	Jan. 2, 1901
Alice T. Cornish	12 Mellen st	"	936 "	Sept. 4, 1889
A. Elizabeth Crowell	483 Massachusetts ave	"	936 "	March 28, 1904
Alice E. Dacy	(See Roxbury High)			
Annie M. Driscoll	38 Homestead st	"	936 "	Dec. 1, 1890
Anna M. Edmands	61 Quincy st	"	936 "	Feb. 1, 1895
Mary L. Fitzgerald	176 Humboldt ave	"	936 "	" 3, 1879
Mary C. Gartland	20 Roslin st	"	936 "	Oct. 1, 1900
Charlotte C. Hamblin	63 Coolidge rd	"	936 "	" 29, 1900
Mabel A. Hebb	20 Cross st., Ros	"	600 "	Dec. 17, 1907
Emily F. Hodsdon	96 St. Botolph st	"	936 "	Sept. 3, 1883
Grace E. Holbrook	72 King st	"	936 "	April 15, 1890
Alice P. Howard	203 Brunswick st	"	936 "	" 29, 1878
Mary E. Keohan	Weymouth	"	936 "	Sept. 29, 1902
Alice L. Littlefield	31 G st	"	936 "	Nov. 10, 1874
Maude E. McClure	313 Huntington ave	"	744 "	Jan. 15, 1906
Gertrude E. Puffer	113 Stanwood st	"	840 "	Dec. 2, 1902
Olga A. F. Stegelmann *	(See Roxbury High)			
Margaret D. Stone	Waban	"	936 "	March 13, 1901
Helen E. Waterman	39 Kenwood st	"	792 "	Nov. 2, 1903
Sarah E. Welch	61 Linden st	"	936 "	Sept. 9, 1881
Annie M. Zbrosky	10 Dorset st	"	936 "	" 12, 1900
Isabel B. Trainer	21 Crawford st	First Asst., Kindergarten	792 "	Nov. 1, 1895
Mabel G. Finlay	230 E. Eagle st	Assistant	528 "	" 13, 1906
Eleanor F. Morris	66 Tudor st	Temporary Teacher	2.00 day	Dec. 9, 1908
Katherine G. O'Brion	34 Savin st	"	2.00 "	Sept. 11, 1907
Mary A. Mullin	Canton Junction	Special Assistant	1.75 "	April 30, 1909
Catherine J. Sullivan	423 Fourth st	"	1.75 "	Sept. 21, 1908
Kathryn E. G. Barry	147 Charles st	Substitute	2.00 "	April 12, 1909
Gertrude A. Le Blanc	64 Tremont st	"	2.00 "	" 27, 1909
Mary F. Dunphy	224 Almont st	Attendant	.50 "	Sept. 9, 1908
Thomas Buckner	644 Columbia rd	Janitor	24.72 wk	March 27, 1878
James H. Dickie	23 Howell st	"	19.77 "	Oct. 8, 1906

Lawrence District.

Amos M Leonard	United States Hotel	Master	$3,180 yr	Sept. 1, 1872
Edwin C. Howard	Wollaston	Sub-Master	1,740 "	Dec. 31, 1906
Clara G. Hinds	Hotel Monadnock	Master's Assistant	1,260 "	May 14, 1902
Maud F. Crosby	787 Fourth st	First Assistant in Charge	1,116 "	Sept. 9, 1903
Martha S. Damon	47 Ocean ave	" "	1,116 "	Nov. 23, 1897
Elizabeth J. Andrews	6 Wellington ct	Assistant	936 "	Sept. 9, 1891
Jennie E. Bailey	(See Girls' High School)			
Emma Britt	510 Broadway	"	936 "	March 1, 1882
Margaret M. Burns	105 M st	"	936 "	Nov. 9, 1885
Edward J. Carroll	202 Seventh st	"	552 "	March 2, 1909
Isabella F. Crapo	562 Broadway	"	936 "	Sept. 2, 1878
Lena J. Crosby	787 Fourth st	"	936 "	June 7, 1882
Marcella F. Dowd	Winchester	"	840 "	Oct. 23, 1903
Florence R. Faxon	Quincy	"	936 "	" 16, 1903
Mary F. Flynn	29 Claxton st	"	936 "	Dec. 1, 1879
Annie E. George	134 Huntington ave	"	936 "	Sept. 9, 1903
Catherine E. Halligan	387A Broadway	"	792 "	" 13, 1905
Katherine Haushalter	Medford	"	936 "	Nov. 1, 1884
Sabina F. Kelly	182 Bowdoin st., Dor	"	936 "	Jan. 2, 1895
Lucy E. Killea	77 Baxter st	"	744 "	March 16, 1905
Martha J. Krey	56 Virginia st	"	936 "	May 17, 1897
Eva C. Morris	503 Broadway	"	936 "	Jan. 2, 1895
Henrietta Nichols	250 Warren st	"	936 "	Feb. 1, 1882
Mary F. O'Brien	463A Broadway	"	936 "	" 1, 1895
John A. O'Keefe, Jr	Lynn	"	648 "	Sept. 24, 1906
Margaret J. Schenck	69 Hancock st	"	936 "	Oct. 1, 1896
Bertha M. Arnold	Braintree	First Asst., Kindergarten	792 "	Nov. 1, 1900
Helen L. Holmes	Wollaston	"	792 "	" 11, 1901
Blanche G. F. Horner	10 Sumner st	Assistant	624 "	" 12, 1903
Florence J. Crawford	527 Broadway	"	576 "	Sept. 13, 1905
Margaret M. Sullivan	5 Kerwin st	Temporary Teacher	2.00 day	Oct. 9, 1908

* On leave of absence without pay, from February 1 to September 1, 1909.

School Department. — Continued.

Name.	Residence.	Designation.	Compensation.	Date of Election or Appointment.

Lawrence District. — Concluded.

Name.	Residence.	Designation.	Compensation.	Date of Election or Appointment.
Marguerite V. Brickley	10 Mystic st	Special Assistant	$1.75 day	Feb. 8, 1909
Anna C. Adams	88 Seventh st	Attendant	.50 "	Sept. 9, 1908
Florence Nuttall	6 First st		.50 "	" 9, 1908
William F. Griffin	394 Fourth st	Janitor	19.41 wk	Dec. 27, 1880
Cornelius A. Kenneally	170 Sixth st	"	15.24 "	Aug. 16, 1903
Edward J. Powers	105 Lauriat ave	"	12.77 "	April 30, 1909

Lewis District.

Name.	Residence.	Designation.	Compensation.	Date of Election or Appointment.
Charles C. Haines	515 Talbot ave	Master	$3,180 yr	April 10, 1901
Allan L. Selley	62 Bloomfield st	Sub-Master	2,340 "	Jan. 3, 1898
W. Stanwood Field	76 Hutchins st		2,220 "	Oct. 29, 1902
Alice O'Neil	11 McClellan st	Master's Assistant	1,308 "	Sept. 5, 1888
Anna A. von Groll	486 Warren st	First Assistant in Charge	1,116 "	April 1, 1900
Marguerite G. Brett	7 Laurel st	First Assistant, Primary	1,080 "	Jan. 15, 1906
Anna F. Bayley	175 Walnut ave	Assistant	936 "	Oct. 18, 1886
Emily I. Boardman	257 Warren st	"	936 "	" 10, 1899
Grace C. Boyden	17 Dale st	"	936 "	Sept. 13, 1899
Miriam J. Bronski	34 Berwick pk	"	600 "	Oct. 22, 1907
Mary H. Burgess	794 Norfolk st	"	936 "	" 1, 1896
Alice D. Burke	119 Webster st	"	744 "	Jan. 16, 1905
Dorothy M. Carney	98 Howard ave	"	552 "	" 4, 1909
Delia B. Condron	20 Clifford	"	888 "	" 16, 1905
Grace A. Cunningham	24 Harlem st	"	936 "	Sept. 10, 1902
Mary E. Deane	Arlington Heights	"	936 "	Feb. 5, 1877
James T. Donovan	101 Old Harbor st	"	552 "	April 21, 1908
Madeline B. Driscoll	7 Michigan ave	"	840 "	Dec. 20, 1902
Anna V. Fallon	211 M st	"	696 "	Sept. 13, 1905
Alice H. Fogarty	1 Pickering ave	"	552 "	Nov. 3, 1908
May M. Gormley	81 School st	"	696 "	Sept. 13, 1905
Emma R. Gragg	44 Rutland sq	"	936 "	" 18, 1877
Beatrice L. Hadcock	2702 Washington st	"	936 "	" 24, 1900
Arvilla T. Harvey	Newton Highlands	Assistant, Disciplinary Class	1,032 "	Feb. 8, 1892
Mary E. Howard	Hotel Park, Dale st	Assistant	936 "	Dec. 3, 1888
M. Genevieve Kiely	395 Bunker Hill st	"	792 "	Sept. 9, 1903
Gertrude H. Lakin	4 Carlisle st	"	936 "	Oct. 1, 1894
Marguerite L. Lillis	Natick	"	936 "	Sept. 5, 1894
Katherine V. McBreen	291 Walnut ave	"	744 "	" 14, 1904
C. Isabel Mention	30 Orchard st	"	744 "	" 14, 1904
Mary L. Murphy	12 Judson st	"	936 "	" 24, 1900
Desire E. Nickels	Franklin Square House	"	888 "	Jan. 16, 1905
Mary A. Nolan	800 Parker st	"	888 "	Feb. 17, 1902
Elizabeth B. Richardson	50 St. Germain st	"	936 "	Sept. 12, 1900
Rachel Rosnosky	29 Richfield st	"	888 "	Nov. 11, 1901
Abigail A. Scannell	741 Norfolk st	"	936 "	Oct. 1, 1896
Alice M. Sibley	86 Winthrop st	"	936 "	April 14, 1886
James F. Tyrrell	83 Medford st	"	552 "	March 2, 1909
Edith A. Willey	88 Charles st	"	936 "	" 1, 1892
Mabel G. Berry	Cambridge	First Asst., Kindergarten	744 "	Jan. 2, 1906
Agnes R. Elliott	2 Cortes st	"	792 "	" 5, 1903
Esther Babcock	7 Haynes pk	Assistant	480 "	April 15, 1907
Ethel Hutchinson	7 Fairfax st	"	432 "	Nov. 3, 1908
Grace M. Rayner	247 Harvard st	"	576 "	Sept. 13, 1905
Agnes G. Gunning	46 Mellen st	Special Assistant	1.75 day	" 29, 1908
Hazel L. Barker	28 Robinhood ave	Attendant	.50 "	Nov. 20, 1908
Frank P. Bartlett	19 Clement pk	Janitor	22.79 wk	Oct. 15, 1908
Patrick J. Downey	405 E. Seventh st	"	30.82 "	Dec. 28, 1905
James McNabb	38 Sherman st	"	19.51 "	Aug. 1, 1901

Longfellow District.

Name.	Residence.	Designation.	Compensation.	Date of Election or Appointment.
Frederic H. Ripley	1247 Commonwealth ave	Master	$3,180 yr	April 10, 1889
John Carroll	Brockton	Sub-Master	1,500 "	Jan. 21, 1908
Elizabeth M. Mann	Cambridge	Master's Assistant	1,308 "	Sept. 7, 1897
Jennie A. Owens	Quincy	First Assistant, Grammar	1,212 "	Feb. 1, 1898
Emma Burrows	480 Centre st., J. P	Assistant	936 "	April 10, 1893
Mary D. Chadwick	415 Massachusetts ave	"	936 "	Sept. 10, 1902
Emma L. Dahl	243 Metropolitan ave., Ros.	"	840 "	" 15, 1902
Lila C. Fisher	46 Stratford st., W. R	"	936 "	Oct. 16, 1902
Helen M. Fogarty	14 Savin st	"	648 "	" 1, 1906
Leila R. Haynes	6 Cedar pk	"	936 "	May 8, 1900
Mabel A. Hebb	20 Cross st., Ros	"	600 "	Dec. 17, 1907

School Department.— Continued.

Name.	Residence.	Designation.	Compensation.	Date of Election or Appointment.

Longfellow District.— Concluded.

Name.	Residence.	Designation.	Compensation.	Date of Election or Appointment.
Edith Irving	162 Carey st., W. R.	Assistant	$888 yr.	Oct. 14, 1901
Henrietta F. Johnson	279 Poplar st., Ros.	"	936 "	April 8, 1901
Lydia W. Jones	44 St. Stephens st	"	936 "	Dec. 1, 1897
Elizabeth A. Keenan	109 Warwick st	"	552 "	Jan. 2, 1908
Theresa D. Lewis	11 E. Newton st	"	936 "	Nov. 17, 1902
Mary A. McCarthy	77 Walter st., Ros.	"	936 "	Sept. 7, 1897
Ethel L. Sawyer	16 Sparhawk st., Bri.	"	840 "	Oct. 8, 1902
Elnora O. C. Standish	4350 Washington st., Ros.	"	744 "	April 23, 1906
Mary M. A. Twombly	59 Perham st., W. R.	"	936 "	Sept. 8, 1896
Hilda G. Watkins	87 Poplar st., Ros.	"	888 "	" 10, 1902
Jennie H. Haxton	3 Revere st., J. P.	First Asst., Kindergarten	744 "	" 13, 1905
Katherine A. Daly	107 Academy Hill rd., Bri.	Assistant	480 "	Dec. 17, 1907
Mary E. Shea	742 Centre st., J. P.	Special Assistant	1.75 day.	" 18, 1908
Annie H. FitzGerald	825 E. Third st	Substitute	2.00 "	April 12, 1909
Elsie M. Oberacker	337 Cornell st., Ros.	Attendant	.50 "	Dec. 8, 1908
Patrick A. O'Brien	8 Burnett st., J. P.	Janitor	27.54 wk.	Sept. 6, 1897
John D. Devine	68 Cohasset st., Ros.	"	13.20 "	Jan. 1, 1909
Patrick M. Devine	655 South st., Ros.	"	2.31 "	Dec. 1. 1904

Lowell District.

Name.	Residence.	Designation.	Compensation.	Date of Election or Appointment.
E. Emmons Grover	61 Hastings st	Master	$3,060 yr.	Sept. 1, 1904
Edward J. Cox	Newtonville	Sub-Master	2,340 "	Jan. 4, 1897
Mary E. G. Collagan	Wollaston	Master's Assistant	972 "	Sept. 9, 1908
Flora J. Perry	29 Vine st	First Assistant in Charge	1,116 "	Nov. 2, 1896
Carolin F. Cutler	77 South st	" "	1,116 "	" 2, 1896
Alice A. Bachelor	66 W. Rutland sq	Assistant	936 "	Jan. 4, 1897
Susan E. Chapman	50 Elmore st	"	936 "	Sept. 14, 1877
Mary E. Clapp	26 Beaufort rd	"	936 "	" 4, 1895
Rebecca Coulter	5 Belmore ter.	"	936 "	Jan. 2, 1878
Mary Crompton	8 Fremont ave.	"	600 "	Sept. 11, 1907
Mary C. Crowley	63 Rutland st	"	936 "	Nov. 1, 1892
Mary F. Cummings	519 Beacon st.	"	936 "	Sept. 6, 1875
Louise Graham	Brookline	"	600 "	Dec. 17, 1907
Ethelyn C. Dallstrom	11 Whitford st	"	744 "	Feb. 12, 1906
Jessie K. Hampton	43 Oakview ter.	"	936 "	Jan. 2, 1896
Georgia L. Hilton	11 Sunnyside st	"	936 "	Sept. 7, 1892
Lillian S. Hilton	11 Sunnyside st	"	936 "	March 1, 1889
Elsie D. Keniston	16 Cohasset st	"	888 "	Nov. 11, 1901
Mary G. Lyons	23 Sedgewick st	"	936 "	" 1, 1900
Emma L. MacDonald	19 Maywood st	"	936 "	Oct. 1, 1897
Marguerite J. Martin	155 Humboldt ave.	"	888 "	Jan. 3, 1905
Mary E. Moran	1 Dunford st.	"	936 "	Sept. 11, 1896
Mary E. Morse	22 Rockville pk	"	936 "	Nov. 2, 1885
Katherine E. McEnroe	East Weymouth	"	552 "	April 12, 1909
Catherine T. Sullivan	20 Clarkwood st	"	936 "	Sept. 8, 1896
Amelia W. Watkins	Braintree.	"	936 "	March 1, 1897
Jane J. Wood	98 Waumbeck st	"	936 "	Oct. 1, 1890
R. Genevieve McMorrow	171 South st.	First Asst., Kindergarten	792 "	" 1,.1901
Beatrice H. Gunn	10 Castleton st	" "	792 "	" 1, 1903
Sarah H. Pratt	Andover.	Assistant	432 "	Sept. 11, 1907
Ruth Dasey	17 Ocean st.	"	432 "	" 11, 1907
Marguerite McKenna	Winthrop.	Special Assistant	1.75 day.	" 15, 1908
Catherine L. Levins	251 Fourth st.	Substitute	2.00 "	April 30, 1909
Louisa Janusen	9 Bromley st.	Attendant	.50 "	Sept. 9, 1908
Anna P. Kohler	49 Mozart st.	"	.50 "	Nov. 13, 1908
Frank L. Harris	337 Centre st	Janitor	28.28 wk.	April 20, 1874
John Riordan	63 Etna st.	"	15.95 "	Nov. 21, 1907
Robert S. Scott	15 Gay Head st	"	15.96 "	Jan. 8, 1908

Lyman District.

Name.	Residence.	Designation.	Compensation.	Date of Election or Appointment.
Augustus H. Kelley	57 Montview st., W. R.	Master	$3,180 yr.	Sept. 5, 1888
George A. Tyzzer	1529 Centre st., Ros.	Sub-Master	2,340 "	April 10, 1899
Frank E. Hobart	Malden	"	1,980 "	Jan. 16, 1905
Emma B. Harvey	44 Saratoga st	Master's Assistant	1,380 "	Oct. 1, 1900
Nellie M. Porter	144 Trenton st	First Assistant, Grammar.	1,212 "	April 1, 1897
Lucy M. Goodwin	112 Evans st	First Assistant in Charge	1,116 "	Nov. 1, 1905
Annie M. Wilcox	117 Trenton st	" "	1,116 "	Oct. 2, 1899
Mary E. Williams	60 Princeton st	" "	1,116 "	Sept. 7, 1897
Julia A. Logan	111 Trenton st	Assistant	936 "	March 1, 1894
Myrtie A. Adams	149 Lexington st	"	552 "	Jan. 4, 1909
Alvira M. Bartlett	44 Byron st	"	936 "	Nov. 1, 1897

School Department. — Continued.

Name.	Residence.	Designation.	Compensation.	Date of Election or Appointment.

Lyman District.— Concluded.

Name.	Residence.	Designation.	Compensation.	Date
Mary C. Burns	205 Ruggles st	Assistant	$552 yr	Feb. 1, 1909
Mary C. Carr	1183 Bennington st	"	600 "	Dec. 17, 1907
Margaret A. Cronin	56 P st	"	696 "	Sept. 13, 1905
Harriet L. Dahl	25 Walnut pk	"	552 "	Dec. 8, 1908
Frances E. Donovan	776 Huntington ave	"	744 "	Oct. 21, 1907
Gazelle Eaton	197 Stratford st	"	936 "	March 5, 1901
Mary E. Fennelly	101 Warren st	"	552 "	April 21, 1908
Josephine Fitz Gerald	79 Maverick st	"	936 "	Oct. 1, 1900
Katharine L. Fitzpatrick	161 Leyden st	"	936 "	" 1, 1900
Margaret R. Flanagan	66 London st	"	552 "	April 27, 1909
Clara G. George	West Newton	"	936 "	Oct. 5, 1874
M. Gertrude Godwin	11 Carolina ave., J. P.	"	792 "	Jan. 16, 1905
May Harty	376 Bowdoin st	"	552 "	Nov. 3, 1908
Helen Harvie	Cambridge	"	936 "	Oct. 22, 1896
Harriet L. Jewell	73 Montgomery st	"	744 "	Nov. 19, 1907
Agnes J. Kenney	Somerville	"	888 "	Sept. 11, 1901
Mildred R. Kimball	40 Green st	"	600 "	Oct. 22, 1907
Agnes M. Mahoney	235 Saratoga st	"	600 "	" 11, 1907
Gertrude E. Mayo	6 Park Lane st., J. P.	"	648 "	Dec. 3, 1906
Lillian A. McCall	102 Murdock st., Bri.	"	744 "	Jan. 16, 1905
Mary E. McCormack	Cambridge	"	888 "	" 16, 1905
Rose E. McEnaney	460 Sumner st	"	792 "	Sept. 11, 1904
Helena McGinnis	56 Bartlett st	"	552 "	Nov. 17, 1908
Eva L. Morley	439 Meridian st	"	936 "	April 8, 1895
Alice D. Murley	89 Bennington st	"	552 "	Jan. 7, 1908
Sarah C. Needham	225 Brooks st	"	792 "	Sept. 14, 1904
Grace R. Neeley	42 Rutland sq	"	936 "	Dec. 1, 1903
Grace O. Peterson	16 Princeton st	"	936 "	Sept. 8, 1896
Grace M. Plummer	Melrose Highlands	"	888 "	Oct. 1, 1901
Berenice E. Reardon	Cambridge	"	744 "	Jan. 16, 1905
Mary A. Ryan	17 Prospect st	"	888 "	March 2, 1903
Leonora E. Scolley	439 Meridian st	"	936 "	" 1, 1897
Alice E. Steer	Chelsea	"	744 "	Oct. 1, 1907
Mary A. Stillman	233 Webster st	Assistant, Special Class	1,032 "	Sept. 22, 1902
Loretta Sullivan	Winthrop	"	936 "	Nov. 1, 1897
Louise G. Sullivan	Winthrop	"	840 "	Feb. 2, 1903
Lena E. Synette	192 Brooks st	"	936 "	Nov. 1, 1887
Annie E. Theisinger	87 Hewlett st., Ros.	"	600 "	April 22, 1907
Mary B. Waldstein	54 Billerica st	"	552 "	30, 1909
Hattie Browne	28 Downer ave	First Asst., Kindergarten	744 "	Nov. 1, 1905
Marion R. Fenno	212 Princeton st	"	648 "	" 3, 1908
Grace S. Mansfield	305 Havre st	" "	792 "	April 13, 1896
Alice L. McLauthlin	54 Eutaw st	"	792 "	Nov. 1, 1894
Bernice A. Hill	8 Crawford st	Assistant	576 "	" 27, 1905
Clara B. Cochran	171 Lexington st	"	624 "	" 18, 1905
Sibylla R. Crawford	37 Rutland sq	"	432 "	Jan. 4, 1909
Maud Sprague	169 Meridian st	"	576 "	Nov. 1, 1905
Jennie A. Tyrrell	83 Medford st	Special Assistant	1.75 day	Sept. 16, 1908
Elizabeth J. Mahoney	235 Saratoga st	Substitute	1.75 "	April 21, 1909
Mary B. Lane	58 Bennington st	Attendant	.50 "	Sept. 9, 1908
Mary L. Moran	233 Bennington st	"	.50 "	1908
Dora Standel	5 Morris st	"	.50 "	1908
David Falconer	128 Trenton st	Janitor	22.06 wk	April 19, 1906
Edward H. Gilday	39 Dewey st	"	20.42 "	July 15, 1905
Timothy D. Murphy	851 Saratoga st	"	23.76 "	April 11, 1906
Oliver E. Wood	51 Eutaw st	"	20.72 "	Oct. 1, 1904

Martin District.

Name.	Residence.	Designation.	Compensation.	Date
Arthur L. Gould	36 Sherman st	Sub-Master	$1,980 yr	Sept. 12, 1906
Emma E. Lawrence	51 St. Stephen st	Master's Assistant	1,404 "	Oct. 1, 1901
Nellie G. Kelley	Dedham	First Assistant in Charge	1,212 "	Sept. 14, 1904
Ellen Carver	18 Hawthorn st	Assistant	1,032 "	Oct. 27, 1897
Margaret E. Collins	162 Harold st	"	1,032 "	Sept. 11, 1901
Annie A. Doran	Cambridge	"	1,032 "	" 7, 1897
Teresa R. Flaherty	46 Leicester st	"	1,032 "	Feb. 18, 1901
Julia L. Frank	29 Cushing ave	"	984 "	Sept. 14, 1904
Mary E. Harris	29 Cushing ave	"	1,032 "	" 12, 1900
Margaret E. Hart	51 Hillside st	"	984 "	" 30, 1901
Olive A. Kee	423 Meridian st	"	936 "	Oct. 1, 1903
Annie T. McCloskey	55 Minot st	"	1,032 "	Sept. 10, 1900
Mary A. I. O'Brien	10 Edison green	"	936 "	" 10, 1902
Elizabeth W. O'Connor	16A Mt. Vernon st	"	1,032 "	" 12, 1900

School Department.— Continued.

Name.	Residence.	Designation.	Compensation.	Date of Election or Appointment.

Martin District. — Concluded.

Name.	Residence.	Designation.	Compensation.	Date of Election or Appointment.
Mary C. Rogers	11 Seaverns ave., J. P.	Assistant	$792 yr	Dec. 4, 1905
Nellie L. Shaw	Brookline	"	1,032 "	Nov. 17, 1876
Marion R. Weymouth	242 Newbury st	"	888 "	Jan. 2, 1905
Clara S. Ziersch	2 Eliot pl., J. P.	"	792 "	Dec. 4, 1905
Lucy Kummer	West Medford	First Asst., Kindergarten	888 "	Jan. 28, 1889
Alice L. Brummett	49 Holborn st	Assistant	624 "	Nov. 1, 1906
Veronica E. Doyle	123 Pinckney st	Special Assistant	1.75 day	April 12, 1909
Mary M. Fitzgerald	33 Wigglesworth st	"	1.75 "	Nov. 3, 1908
Louise M. Fitzpatrick	287 Walnut ave	"	1.75 "	Sept. 9, 1908
Helen H. Goulter	37 W. Cedar st	"	1.75 "	" 22, 1908
John J. Mulligan	9 Conant street pl.	Janitor	25.60 wk	July 15, 1905
Charles H. Priest	643 Huntington ave	"	25.66 "	Dec. 16, 1905

Mary Hemenway District.

Name.	Residence.	Designation.	Compensation.	Date of Election or Appointment.
N. Hosea Whittemore	28 Mather st	Master	$3,180 yr	March 1, 1881
Harlan P. Ford	22 Mellen st	Sub-Master	2,100 "	Sept. 23, 1903
Frederic L. Owen	7 Bowdoin ave	"	2,340 "	Nov. 10, 1890
L. Gertrude Howes	96 Winthrop st	Master's Assistant	1,308 "	Sept. 6, 1893
Mary Polk	12 Florida st	First Assistant, Grammar	1,212 "	May 1, 1900
Ida K. McGiffert	32 Waldeck st	First Assistant in Charge	1,116 "	March 14, 1898
Susan J. Berigan	3 Clarkson st	Assistant	936 "	April 20, 1897
Bertha F. Cudworth	94 Centre st	"	936 "	Dec. 5, 1888
Annie B. Drowne	16 Remington st	"	936 "	Feb. 23, 1886
Annie S. Hagarty	1 Centre ave	"	552 "	Nov. 3, 1908
Gertrude E. Kendall	91 Melville ave	"	840 "	Sept. 13, 1905
Martha E. Lang	25 Rowena st	"	936 "	" 12, 1900
Anna E. Leahy	207 Eighth st	"	936 "	Oct. 1, 1896
Alice G. Maher	138 Cushing ave	"	888 "	Jan. 6, 1902
Mary E. Warren	105 Bowdoin st	"	600 "	Sept. 11, 1907
Evelyn G. McGinley	58 Alpine st	"	792 "	Dec. 31, 1906
Annie L. McGrory	South Weymouth	"	552 "	Nov. 3, 1908
Mary F. McMorrow	4 Sumner st	"	936 "	April 8, 1895
Annie L. McMurry	795 Blue Hill ave	"	552 "	Dec. 8, 1908
Ellen G. McTernan	305 Adams st	"	792 "	Jan. 16, 1905
Jessie L. Nolte	88 Minot st	"	840 "	Sept. 14, 1903
Lillian G. Pattinson	Arlington	"	552 "	March 2, 1908
Alice B. Poor	2047 Columbus ave	"	936 "	Sept. 10, 1902
Florence M. Robinson	14 E. Cottage st	"	840 "	Dec. 1, 1902
Ellen L. Roche	South Weymouth	"	600 "	Oct. 23, 1907
Fanny L. Short	502 Talbot ave	"	936 "	" 17, 1898
Emily F. Small	67 Ashford st	"	936 "	May 1, 1900
Mary J. H. Taylor	103 Brook rd	"	888 "	Dec. 9, 1901
Martha E. Tracy	25 Freeman st	"	792 "	April 10, 1905
Mary Waterman	7 Sayward st	"	936 "	Sept. 10, 1884
Ellen Welin	89 Minot st	"	936 "	Feb. 4, 1901
Mary E. Wilbar	96 Winthrop st	"	936 "	Oct. 17, 1893
Cora I. Young	Quincy	"	936 "	Sept 6, 1886
Annie M. Smith	1653 Dorchester ave	First Asst., Kindergarten	792 "	" 13, 1905
Anna M. White	5 Houghton st	"	792 "	Nov. 15, 1905
Clara A. Perkins	1122 Adams st	Assistant	576 "	" 20, 1905
A. Olive Wigley	55 Mather st	"	432 "	" 3, 1908
Eileen V. Driscoll	1161 Massachusetts ave	Special Assistant	1.75 day	April 14, 1909
John L. Galway	165 Welles ave	Janitor	18.28 wk	Jan. 17, 1909
Thomas J. Hatch	29 Adams st	"	16.92 "	Sept., 1870
Conrad J. Hermann	241 Centre st	"	13.73 "	Aug. 16, 1903
Wallace Kenney	9 Euclid st	"	26.45 "	Jan. 7, 1898

Mather District.

Name.	Residence.	Designation.	Compensation.	Date of Election or Appointment.
Edward Southworth	Quincy	Master	$3,180 yr	Sept. 2, 1878
George A. Smith	19 Winter st	Sub-Master	2,340 "	Oct. 1, 1895
Arthur A. Lincoln	29 Percival st	"	2,340 "	Jan. 4, 1897
J. Annie Bense	7 Bowdoin ave	Master's Assistant	1,260 "	Sept. 16, 1878
Marietta S. Murch	75 Howard ave	First Assistant, Grammar	1,212 "	Jan. 1, 1892
Clara A. Jordan	677 Dudley st	First Assistant in Charge	1,116 "	Nov. 2, 1896
Elizabeth Donaldson	19 Monadnock st	"	1,116 "	Jan. 3, 1898
Grace O. Allen	Trinity Court	Assistant	936 "	April 9, 1894
Lillian B. Blackmer	13 Sayward st	"	936 "	" 17, 1893
Elizabeth C. Bonney	47 Norton st	"	936 "	Oct. 2, 1899
Alice M. Cahill	502 Shawmut ave	"	792 "	Nov. 25, 1903
Mary G. Cahill	66 Pleasant st	"	936 "	Dec. 3, 1900
Viola S. Churchill	7 Oakman st	"	936 "	Nov. 1, 1897

School Department.— Continued.

Name.	Residence	Designation	Compensation.	Date of Election or Appointment.

Mather District.— Concluded.

Name.	Residence	Designation	Compensation.	Date of Election or Appointment.
Grace R. Clark	573 Dudley st	Assistant	$936 yr	Dec. 3, 1900
Elizabeth V. Cloney	46 Tonawanda st	"	840 "	Sept. 10, 1902
Mary B. Carr	80 Magnolia st	"	936 "	Oct. 4, 1881
Ella J. Costello	Cambridge	"	936 "	Jan. 3, 1898
Loretta J. Curran	38 Topliff st	"	744 "	" 16, 1905
Minnie A. Day	19 Roslin st	"	696 "	" 7, 1908
Mary A. Dunican	1113 Dorchester ave	"	696 "	May 1, 1905
Lucy J. Dunnels	Newtonville	"	936 "	Feb., 1869
Frances Forsaith	30 Magnolia st	"	936 "	Sept. 7, 1897
M. Ellen Forsaith	30 Magnolia st	"	936 "	Oct. 1, 1901
Helen M. French	36 Magnolia st	"	936 "	" 1, 1900
Elizabeth M. Grant	3 Holborn ter	"	936 "	Sept. 7, 1892
Gertrude A. Hastings	Lynnfield Centre	"	936 "	Nov. 1, 1901
Ella L. Howe	114 Park st	"	936 "	Sept., 1867
Louise C. Howes	119 Townsend st	"	936 "	Oct. 1, 1900
Mary H. Knight	75 Howard ave	"	936 "	Dec. 1, 1892
Rena Lewis	31 Lawrence ave	"	552 "	Nov. 3, 1908
Grace E. Lingham	19 Monadnock st	"	936 "	May 14, 1902
Annie Mackenzie	12 Fox st	"	936 "	Feb. 11, 1903
Bessie MacBride *	12 Wabon st	"	936 "	Oct. 26, 1897
Lucy D. Macarthy	17 Rockland ave	"	840 "	March 2, 1903
Mary L. McCollough	96 Gainsboro st	"	936 "	Nov. 1, 1900
Martha A. Norton	19 Olney st	"	696 "	" 27, 1905
Mary E. O'Kane	40 Blakeville st	"	936 "	March 1, 1901
Caroline Pendleton	12 Mellen st	"	936 "	Oct. 1, 1901
Carrie F. Parker	178 Columbia rd	"	936 "	Sept. 5, 1894
Alice M. Packard	57 Cushing ave	"	936 "	Oct. 8, 1903
Jennie E. Phinney	15 Peverell st	"	936 "	Sept. 17, 1894
M. Cecilia Power	58 Wales pl	"	600 "	Dec. 17, 1907
Mary Smith	178 Humboldt ave	"	744 "	Jan. 16, 1905
Mary R. Stapleton	27 Old Harbor st	"	552 "	April 21, 1908
Mary A. Starkey	94 Calumet st	"	552 "	Jan. 4, 1909
Mary E. Vogel	32 Anawan ave	"	648 "	Nov. 1, 1906
Eleanor G. Hutchinson	12 Bradlee st	First Asst., Kindergarten	792 "	Sept. 25, 1905
Ada Cushing	South Hingham	"	648 "	Oct. 20, 1908
Mary I. F. Montgomery	8 Sunnyside st	Assistant	528 "	Nov. 1, 1906
Grace R. Hallet	22 Thornley st	"	432 "	" 3, 1908
Frances G. Dixon	4 Davidson ave	Temporary Teacher	2.00 day	Jan. 4, 1909
Rebecca F. Silbert	28 Devon st	Substitute	2.00 "	" 4, 1909
Olive E. Barry	23 Monument sq	"	2.00 "	" 4, 1909
Michael H. Murphy	39 Samoset st	Janitor	53.85 wk	Feb. 10, 1905
Patrick H. Brennan	121 Shirley st	"	38.06 "	April 11, 1906
Joel Sargent	2 Saxton st	"	7.51 "	Dec. 21, 1907
Thomas Kinsley	11 Euclid st	"	15.89 "	Feb. 6, 1908

Minot District.

Name.	Residence	Designation	Compensation.	Date of Election or Appointment.
F. Morton King	23 Bushnell st	Master	$3,180 yr	Sept. 8, 1896
Edson L. Ford	39 Eldon st	Sub-Master	2,100 "	Dec. 9, 1903
Mary E. Palmer	4 Montello st	Master's Assistant	1,164 "	Jan. 16, 1905
Celia A. Scribner	476 Massachusetts ave	First Assistant in Charge	1,116 "	Oct. 12, 1898
Katherine M. Adams	7 Silloway st	Assistant	936 "	June 1, 1886
Anna E. Burke	24 Mayfield st	"	552 "	Dec. 22, 1908
Grace E. Feeney	169 St. Botolph st	"	600 "	Nov. 3, 1908
Alice B. Fuller	North Weymouth	"	936 "	Sept. 5, 1894
Evelyn A. Gammons	74 Seaverns ave	"	600 "	" 25, 1907
Katherine R. Haley	626 Freeport st	"	840 "	Feb. 13, 1903
Mabel A. Jepson	47 Humphreys st	"	936 "	Nov. 1, 1900
Elizabeth L. Keefe	63 Palmer st	"	552 "	March 2, 1909
Fannie D. Lane †		"	468 "	April 11, 1881
A. Isabelle Macarthy	17 Rockland ave	"	936 "	Sept. 4, 1895
Amy K. Pickett	10 Stanton st	"	936 "	" 4, 1895
Lillian A. Richardson	Hyde Park	"	936 "	Feb. 25, 1903
Lillian A. Simmons	84 Waltham st	"	936 "	Oct. 12, 1899
Ida F. Wall	81 Browne ave	"	552 "	April 21, 1908
Mary B. Johnson	16 Dover st	First Asst., Kindergarten	792 "	Sept. 7, 1892
Mary E. Flynn	25 Greenwich pl	Special Assistant	1.75 day	" 9, 1908
Isabel E. Clark	40 Clarkwood st	Substitute	2.00 "	Jan. 2, 1909
John Walsh	73 Gibson	Janitor	20.38 wk	Oct. 15, 1908
Robert J. Walsh	5 Pope's Hill st	"	12.32 "	Dec. 1, 1908

* Leave of absence without pay to September 1, 1909.
† Year's leave of absence on half pay. Resignation to take effect September 1, 1909.

School Department.— Continued.

Name.	Residence.	Designation.	Compensation.	Date of Election or Appointment.

Norcross District.

Name.	Residence.	Designation.	Compensation.	Date of Election or Appointment.
Fred O. Ellis	Braintree	Master	$3,180 yr	Nov. 1, 1882
Mary R. Roberts	75 G st	Master's Assistant	1,308 "	Sept. 7, 1897
Emma L. Eaton	412 E. Fifth st	First Assistant, Grammar	1,212 "	10, 1902
Eleanor J. Cashman	415 Harvard st	First Assistant in Charge	1,116 "	Nov. 2, 1896
Ann E. Newell	518 Broadway	" "	1,116 "	" 2, 1896
Estelle C. Chase	86 Draper st	Assistant	600 "	" 6, 1906
Mary E. Downing	870 E. Sixth st	"	936 "	May 1, 1873
Kate E. Fitzgerald	218 Athens st	"	936 "	Feb. 1, 1883
Alice M. Flanagan	77 Ashland st., Ros.	"	552 "	Dec. 22, 1908
Anna F. Gorman	726 Eighth st	"	600 "	" 17, 1907
Jennie M. Gray	57 G st	"	552 "	Jan. 2, 1908
Agnes J. Hallahan	208 W. Canton st	"	936 "	Feb. 14, 1900
Fannie W. Hussey	12 Ward st	"	936 "	Sept. 4, 1872
Bessie E. Kennedy	12 Thomas pk.	"	744 "	Feb. 1, 1905
Katherine J. Kincade	309 Huntington ave	"	600 "	Dec. 3, 1907
Josephine J. Mahoney	185 Seventh st	"	936 "	Jan. 5, 1898
Jennie A. Mullaly	61 Harvest st	"	936 "	Sept. 2, 1878
Abbie C. Nickerson	524 Broadway	"	936 "	March 19, 1869
Ellen T. Noonan	1516 Columbia rd.	"	936 "	" 1, 1874
Elsie M. Paul	799 Broadway	"	936 "	" 1, 1900
Ethel N. Pope	45 Julian st	"	936 "	" 18, 1901
Harriet L. Rayne	Cambridgeport	"	936 "	Oct. 1, 1868
Alice B. Stebbins	170 Sydney st	"	552 "	March 16, 1909
Eva Steele	16 Pleasant st	"	936 "	Oct. 15, 1902
Carrie A. Whitaker	Chelsea	"	936 "	" 3, 1902
Louise M. Davis	31 Humboldt ave	First Asst., Kindergarten	792 "	Sept. 4, 1895
Mary M. Loughlin	917 Broadway	Assistant	624 "	Jan. 16, 1905
Margaret M. Kenney	22 Tremont st., Chsn.	Special Assistant	1.75 day	Sept. 9, 1908
Catherine F. Shinnick	79 W. Seventh st	Attendant	.50 "	" 9, 1908
James J. Bulman	38 Boston st	Janitor	14.79 wk	Dec. 20, 1904
Robert A. Butler	4 Linden st	"	21.45 "	Jan. 1, 1909
Margaret M. Gilligan	531 Second st	"	10.54 "	June 1, 1906

Oliver Hazard Perry District.

Name.	Residence.	Designation.	Compensation.	Date of Election or Appointment.
Charles N. Bentley	Cambridge	Master	$3,060 yr	Feb, 1, 1905
Stanley A. Starratt	558 Warren st	Sub-Master	1,860 "	Nov. 20, 1905
Louise A. Pieper	849 Fourth st	Master's Assistant	1,164 "	Feb. 1, 1905
Julia A. Noonan	Waban	First Assistant, Grammar.	1,116 "	Dec. 4, 1905
Ella R. Johnson	Hotel Eaton	First Assistant in Charge	1,116 "	Nov. 2, 1896
Agnes E. Barry	246 W. Sixth st	Assistant	840 "	Sept. 13, 1905
Anna M. Cogan	88 W. Sixth st	"	696 "	" 13, 1905
Jennie G. J. Cox	46 N st	"	744 "	Jan. 16, 1905
Mary E. Dee	104 G st	"	936 "	Sept. 8, 1885
Elizabeth A. Freeto	Marblehead	"	840 "	Nov. 2, 1903
Carrie W. Hayden	Hotel Eaton	"	936 "	March 20, 1875
Lelia R. Hayden	Braintree	"	936 "	Sept. 2, 1878
Margaret L. Higgins	141 L st	"	840 "	Feb. 16, 1903
Minnie A. Kennedy	12 Thomas Park	"	744 "	Jan. 16, 1905
Helen F. Kenney	551 E. Fifth st	"	840 "	Sept. 10, 1902
Frances G. Keyes	595 E. Fifth st	"	888 "	Dec. 2, 1901
Julia G. Leary	936 Broadway	"	936 "	March 9, 1891
K. Gertrude Marden	7 Greenbrier st	"	792 "	Nov. 2, 1903
Katharine J. McMahan	392 W. Fourth st	"	936 "	" 1, 1895
Margaret A. Murphy	645 E. Fifth st	"	744 "	May 2, 1904
Isabella J. Murray	42 Longfellow st	"	936 "	Oct. 10, 1888
Elizabeth A. Nash	75 Mayfield st	"	744 "	Jan. 16, 1905
Maria L. Nelson	1792 Columbia Road	"	936 "	Feb. 5, 1877
Mary E. Nicolson	27 Concord sq	"	888 "	Oct. 3, 1904
Edith M. Robertson	Dean way	"	648 "	Dec. 31, 1906
Nellie B. Vinal	589 Dudley st	"	552 "	April 27, 1908
Margaret R. Kenneally	27 Oakley st	Substitute	2.00 day	" 1, 1909
Willena E. Browne	4 Oxford ter	First Asst., Kindergarten	696 yr	" 13, 1908
Elsie M. Gannon	49 Kenwood rd.	Assistant	576 "	Dec. 4, 1905
Ethel J. Hillier	132 P st	Attendant	.50 day	Nov. 16, 1908
Thomas M. Hogan	118 G st	Janitor	30.24 wk	Dec. 20, 1904
David F. Sennott	53 Savin Hill ave	"	18.34 "	April 1, 1908

Oliver Wendell Holmes District.

Name.	Residence.	Designation.	Compensation.	Date of Election or Appointment.
Michael E. Fitzgerald	South Weymouth	Master	$3,180 yr	Sept. 9, 1903
Frederick W. Shattuck	39 Algonquin st	Sub-Master	2,340 "	April 13, 1897
John J. Cummings	52 Mapleton st., Bri	"	1,500 "	Nov. 3, 1908

School Department. — Continued.

Name.	Residence.	Designation.	Compensation.	Date of Election or Appointment.

Oliver Wendell Holmes District. — Concluded.

Name.	Residence.	Designation.	Compensation.	Date of Election or Appointment.
E. Gertrude Dudley	10 Spencer st	Master's Assistant	$1,116 yr	Sept. 13, 1905
Anna A. Maguire	34 Sherman st	First Assistant, Grammar	1,116 "	" 13, 1905
Katherine J. Daily	16 Wellington st	First Assistant in Charge	972 "	Jan. 4, 1909
Alicia F. McDonald	25 Woodbine st	"	1,116 "	" 4, 1904
Frances M. Bell	Hotel Eaton, Emerson st	Assistant	552 "	Nov. 17, 1908
Mary H. Brick	147 Draper st	"	936 "	Dec. 3, 1894
Ellen A. Brown	42 Rutland sq	"	936 "	April 11, 1884
Mary A. Cussen	57 Bowdoin st	"	936 "	Sept. 8, 1896
Marietta H. Delaney	3 Larchmont st	"	696 "	" 13, 1905
Genevieve R. Dore	10 Howland st	"	552 "	April 21, 1908
Rose M. Driscoll	14 Sagamore st	"	552 "	Nov. 17, 1908
Ellen K. Eichorn	263 Fuller st	"	840 "	May 1, 1902
Harriet E. Ells	160 Magnolia st	"	936 "	Dec. 4, 1900
Blanche E. Fallon	32 Hewins st	"	888 "	May 15, 1901
Feroline W. Fox	255 Fuller st	"	936 "	Sept. 4, 1895
C. Angela Gartland	20 Roslin st	"	696 "	" 13, 1905
Isabel M. Horsford	10 Bird st	"	936 "	Dec. 4, 1899
Clara C. Howland	40 Spencer st	"	936 "	Sept. 12, 1900
Joanna G. Keenan	126 Crawford st	"	936 "	Feb. 1, 1893
Evelyn E. Kelley	13 Winter st	"	936 "	Nov. 1, 1899
Katharine C. Kelley	77 Bowdoin ave	"	840 "	March 23, 1904
Agnes T. Kelly	70 Bloomfield st	"	936 "	Nov. 1, 1899
Annie L. Knight	575 Washington st	"	936 "	" 2, 1899
Carolyn I. Lynch	60 Alban st	"	792 "	March 1, 1905
Susie J. McCloskey	55 Minot st	"	552 "	Nov. 3, 1908
Mary T. McColl	95 Harvard st	"	936 "	Dec. 2, 1901
Mary A. McNaught	186 Harvard st	"	888 "	Oct. 1, 1903
Helen M. Mead	35 Norway st	"	936 "	Sept. 11, 1901
Josephine A. Merrick	671 Washington st., Dor.	"	552 "	Feb. 1, 1909
Eleanor J. Murphy	114 Bowdoin st	"	936 "	May 16, 1900
Clara E. Nixon	8 Kingsdale st	"	600 "	Sept. 18, 1907
Areminta V. Paasche	19 Roslin st	"	936 "	Nov. 1, 1901
Angela M. Pearce	20 Thwing st	"	600 "	Sept. 11, 1907
Elizabeth R. Phelan	20 McLellan st	"	840 "	March 1, 1905
E. Leora Pratt	4 Holborn ter	"	936 "	Sept. 8, 1896
Mary C. Sinnott	70 Bernard st	"	744 "	" 14, 1904
Katharine G. Sheehan	23 Bernard st	"	744 "	Nov. 1, 1905
Josephine C. Sullivan	114 Melville ave	"	744 "	Jan. 16, 1905
Helen F. Tarpey	39 Oakview ter., J. P.	"	936 "	Dec. 4, 1899
Aloyse B. Tierney	743 Huntington ave	"	936 "	April 9, 1900
Grace V. Walsh	65 Story st	"	600 "	Nov. 19, 1907
Alice M. Williams	6 Hopestill st	"	936 "	" 1, 1900
Edith L. Phelan	589 Park st., Dor.	First Asst., Kindergarten	792 "	Oct. 2, 1899
Margaret C. Seaver	Belmont	"	648 "	April 13, 1908
Grace E. Brett	285 Centre st	Assistant	432 "	Nov. 3, 1908
Helen L. Brown	126 Bird st	"	432 "	" 3, 1908
Helen G. Gormley	81 School st	"	480 "	" 1, 1906
May M. Gordon	66 Centre st	Special Assistant	1.75 day	Jan. 11, 1909
Regina E. Rolfe	1648 Washington st	"	1.75 "	" 7, 1909
Mary E. Mullen	508 Main st., Chsn	"	1.75 "	March 23, 1909
Loretta W. Dinn	42 Howland st	"	1.50 "	" 23, 1909
Gertrude M. Glynn	122 Radcliffe st	"	1.50 "	" 1, 1909
Charles L. Glidden	26 Vaughan st	Janitor	17.21 wk	" 14, 1906
Frank M. Murphy	148 Westville st	"	21.58 "	June 1, 1907
Winthrop B. Robinson	126 Rosseter st	"	50.83 "	July 1, 1905

Phillips Brooks District.

Name.	Residence.	Designation.	Compensation.	Date of Election or Appointment.
Henry B. Hall	156 Pleasant st	Master	$3,180 yr	Sept. 12, 1900
James H. Gormley	1 Worthington st	Sub-Master	2,340 "	" 12, 1900
James A. Treanor	30 Bloomfield st	"	1,860 "	" 13, 1905
Alice G. Maguire	34 Sherman st	Master's Assistant	1,308 "	" 12, 1900
Julia S. Dolan	537 Talbot ave	First Assistant, Grammar	1,164 "	Oct. 3, 1904
Matilda Mitchell	5 Howland st	First Assistant in Charge	1,116 "	Nov. 1, 1902
Elizabeth R. Wallis	102 Mt. Pleasant ave	"	1,116 "	" 2, 1896
Fannie E. Barnett	79 Savin st	Assistant	696 "	" 13, 1905
Isabella L. Bissett	12 Folsom st	"	936 "	April 16, 1890
Alice A. Brophy	1133 Washington st	"	840 "	Feb. 2, 1903
Adelaide E. Burke	6 Rockland ave	"	888 "	Sept. 11, 1901
Florence Cahill	3 Monadnock st	"	936 "	" 7, 1896
Minnie B. Conant	Cambridge	"	648 "	Nov. 6, 1906
Elleanor P. Cox	78 Alexander st	"	600 "	Oct. 22, 1907

School Department.— Continued.

Name.	Residence.	Designation.	Compensation.	Date of Election or Appointment.

Phillips Brooks District.— Concluded.

Name.	Residence.	Designation.	Compensation.	Date of Election or Appointment.
Emma F. Crane	25 Castlegate rd	Assistant	$936 yr	Dec. 1, 1877
Helen Crombie	507 Warren st	"	936 "	Oct., 1869
Frances E. Dailey	44 Winthrop st	"	648 "	Dec. 31, 1906
Jane K. Daly	10 Bloomington st	"	696 "	Oct. 30, 1905
Mary L. Fogarty	1 Pickering ave	"	552 "	Nov. 3, 1908
Clara E. Glover	22 Brown ave	"	792 "	" 9, 1903
Josephine F. Hannon	298 Ashmont st	"	936 "	" 2, 1896
Grace M. Hart	64 Homestead st	"	744 "	" 13, 1905
Eunice C. Hearn	31 Harvard st	"	648 "	" 6, 1906
Constance Horsford	10 Bird st	"	600 "	Jan. 21, 1907
Mary E. Kelleher	398 Centre st., J. P	"	840 "	Sept. 9, 1903
Katherine E. Lahey	The Gladstone, Dudley st	"	936 "	Feb. 28, 1898
Lavinia M. MacLean	22 Annabel st	"	648 "	Nov. 26, 1906
Elizabeth H. Mahar	68 L st	"	552 "	Dec. 8, 1908
Mary C. Maloy	24 Duke st	"	936 "	Sept. 25, 1900
Etta A. Manning	914 Fourth st	"	888 "	Nov. 21, 1901
Dora E. McCarty	897 Albany st	"	744 "	Sept. 13, 1905
Mary E. McCarty	897 Albany st	"	936 "	" 5, 1894
Mary F. McDonald	49 Brent st	"	936 "	May 2, 1892
Katherine A. McMurry	795 Blue Hill ave	"	744 "	Jan. 16, 1905
Mary J. Moore	3 Monadnock st	"	936 "	Sept. 20, 1894
Mary F. O'Brien	78 Blue Hill ave	"	936 "	Jan. 21, 1901
Blanche L. Ormsby	32 Mall st	"	936 "	Sept. 5, 1888
Blanche V. Smith	45 Clifford st	"	792 "	Nov. 9, 1903
Gertrude Stahl	169 Massachusetts ave	"	552 "	March 17, 1908
Catherine J. Sullivan	39 Bainbridge st	"	744 "	Oct. 23, 1905
Henrietta L. Wallburg	54 Dale st	"	552 "	Dec. 8, 1908
Madeline M. Waxer	3 Way pl	"	552 "	Nov. 3, 1908
Helen S. S. Wilkinson	23 W. Cottage st	"	696 "	" 13, 1905
Emma F. Wilson	209 Dudley st	"	936 "	May 1, 1897
Mary A. Daly	107 Academy Hill rd	First Asst., Kindergarten	792 "	Oct. 1, 1903
Alice J. Sughrue	73 Howard ave	"	792 "	March 2, 1903
Gertrude L. Gavin	346 Dudley st	Assistant	624 "	" 2, 1903
Frances L. O'Connell	14 Spring pk ave., J. P	"	624 "	April 10, 1905
Jessie M. Wilkinson	23 W. Cottage st	"	528 "	Nov. 1, 1906
Edward L. Curran	City Club	Temporary Sub-Master	3.75 day	Feb. 12, 1909
Martha L. Ireland	132 Hudson st	Special Assistant	1.75 "	Oct. 12, 1908
Mary J. Hynes	41 Batchelder st	"	1.75 "	Feb. 15, 1909
M. Agnes McClennan	103 Brook ave	Attendant	.50 "	Sept. 9, 1908
Julia Nixon	38 Dacia st	"	.50 "	" 9, 1908
Charles F. Hartson	54 Julian st	Janitor	32.47 wk	" 20, 1900
Henry C. Hunneman	8 Wabon st	"	17.26 "	April 25, 1895
Samuel T. McClennan	103 Brook ave	"	28.83 "	May 4, 1906

Prescott District.

Name.	Residence.	Designation.	Compensation.	Date of Election or Appointment.
W. Lawrence Murphy	33 Bicknell st	Master	$3,060 yr	Nov. 1, 1904
Melzar H. Jackson	19 White st	Sub-Master	2,340 "	Oct. 7, 1896
Mary E. Keyes	49 Monmouth st	Master's Assistant	1,308 "	Feb. 2, 1902
Mary E. Franklin	Cambridge	First Assistant in Charge	1,116 "	Nov. 2, 1906
Helen I. Bridge	17 Sydney st	Assistant	648 "	" 6, 1906
Alice F. Connell	Braintree	"	888 "	March 17, 1905
Elizabeth J. Doherty	Melrose Highlands	"	936 "	Sept. 21, 1885
Agnes C. Flynn	55 Baldwin st	"	744 "	" 14, 1904
Mary R. Fitzgerald	41 Mt. Vernon st	"	840 "	Oct. 1, 1902
Ellen G. Garraghan	98 Blue Hill ave	"	888 "	Sept. 11, 1901
Lydia E. Hapenny	81 Russell st	"	936 "	" 1, 1878
Elizabeth V. Mahoney	Belmont	"	648 "	Nov. 1, 1906
Florence A. McDonough	36 Winthrop st	"	888 "	May 1, 1901
Katherine F. O'Brien	7 Fiske ter	"	936 "	Sept. 24, 1900
Julia F. Sawyer	215 Bunker Hill st	"	936 "	Dec. 1, 1872
Alice Simpson	23 Franklin st	"	936 "	" 1, 1881
Lizzie Simpson	23 Franklin st	"	936 "	Oct. 3, 1887
Esther F. Sullivan	254 Bunker Hill st	"	840 "	Sept. 9, 1903
Hattie L. Todd	59 Monument ave	"	936 "	Oct. 1, 1878
Agnes M. Turnbull	47 Corey st	"	936 "	Jan. 2, 1900
Margaret M. Whalen	294 Bunker Hill st	"	936 "	Nov. 1, 1893
Daisy G. Dame	Medford	First Asst., Kindergarten	792 "	Sept. 7, 1892
Rose B. Sullivan	22 Blakeville st	Assistant	624 "	May 11, 1904
Elizabeth V. Doherty	Somerville	Temporary Teacher	2.00 day	Sept. 9, 1908
Gertrude E. Welch	48 Haverhill st	Special Assistant	1.75 "	Jan. 4, 1909

School Department. — Continued.

Name.	Residence.	Designation.	Compensation	Date of Election or Appointment.

Prescott District.— Concluded.

Name.	Residence.	Designation.	Compensation	Date of Election or Appointment.
Grace T. Garrity	119 Elm st	Attendant	80.50 day	Jan. 9, 1908
Edward Sullivan	18 Oak st	Janitor	16.50 wk	April 12, 1909
Michael B. Sliney	102 Pearl st	"	19.68 "	Oct. 1, 1903

Prince District.

Name.	Residence.	Designation.	Compensation	Date of Election or Appointment.
E. Bentley Young	104 Appleton st	Master	$3,180 yr	Sept. 1, 1876
Charles G. Wetherbee	Newton Highlands	Sub-Master	2,340 "	Feb. 17, 1902
Lillian F. Sheldon	Hotel Oxford	Master's Assistant	1,308 "	Oct. 2, 1899
Laura K. Hayward	Malden	First Assistant in Charge	1,116 "	Nov. 2, 1896
E. Isabelle Bense	7 Bowdoin ave	Assistant	936 "	Dec. 15, 1887
Luthera W. Bird	104 Appleton st	"	936 "	March 7, 1864
Nellie E. Boyd	Chelsea	"	936 "	Dec. 12, 1898
Katherine L. Campbell	Brookline	"	936 "	Jan. 6, 1890
Anna C. Consens	21 St. Botolph st	"	936 "	Sept. 12, 1900
Laura A. Ells	132 Devon st	"	936 "	Dec. 1, 1897
Amy E. Emery	1 Holborn ter	"	936 "	March 28, 1900
Mabel C. Friend	Brookline	"	936 "	Nov. 4, 1901
Sarah A. Ginn	12 Westminster ave	"	888 "	Dec. 2, 1901
Annie A. Horton	Mansfield	"	936 "	" 1, 1903
Inez A. Hunt	8 Garrison st	"	936 "	Sept. 18, 1903
Anna C. Murdock	136 Huntington ave	"	936 "	Oct. 1, 1884
Manetta W. Penney	Cambridge	"	936 "	Nov. 2, 1891
Mary A. Perkins	Cambridge	"	936 "	Oct. 7, 1901
Katherine A. Raycroft	Quincy	"	936 "	" 1, 1884
Eva G. Reed	Quincy	"	936 "	Sept. 15, 1897
Harriet M. Simpson	Cambridge	"	888 "	Oct. 6, 1902
Abbie E. Wilson	277 Dartmouth st	"	936 "	Jan. 5, 1885
Ellen G. Wiseman	Cambridge	"	648 "	Sept. 24, 1906
Ellen Gray	Brookline	First Asst., Kindergarten	792 "	" 5, 1888
Helen M. Cobb	33 St. James ave	Assistant	480 "	" 11, 1907
Mary A. Molloy	Randolph	Substitute	2.00 day	" 9, 1908
Bernard L. Donnelly	55 E. Newton st	Janitor	21.31 wk	" 1, 1895
James A. Hanlon	1438 Dorchester ave	"	6.95 "	Jan. 16, 1909

Quincy District.

Name.	Residence.	Designation.	Compensation	Date of Election or Appointment.
Alfred Bunker	29 Juniper st	Master	$3,180 yr	Sept. 8, 1884
George G. Edwards	Cambridge	Sub-Master	2,340 "	" 8, 1896
Frederick W. Swan	59 Wren st	"	2,340 "	Oct. 8, 1901
Angie C. Damon	29 Upton st	Master's Assistant	1,308 "	Jan. 20, 1896
Annie F. Merriam	657 Tremont st	First Assistant in Charge	1,116 "	Nov. 2, 1896
Abbie E. Batchelder	24 Waumbeck st	Assistant	936 "	March 3, 1890
Harriet M. Bolman	41 Perrin st	"	936 "	Oct. 2, 1865
Mary Burkhardt	14 Highland st	"	840 "	Sept. 9, 1903
Maria A. Callanan	100 Harrison st	"	936 "	April 28, 1875
Margaret E. Carey	Auburndale	"	936 "	Sept. 4, 1889
Ellen L. Collins	124 Mt. Vernon st	"	936 "	" 1866
Mary E. Conley	39 E. Canton st	"	936 "	Oct. 15, 1877
Marion L. Dally	2 Shafter st	"	936 "	Nov. 20, 1899
Ida H. Davis	Malden	"	936 "	Oct. 2, 1882
A. Teresa Fennelly	104 Warren st	"	600 "	Nov. 19, 1907
Bridget A. Foley	43 E. Newton st	"	936 "	Sept., 1873
Marion G. Fottler	68 Canterbury st	"	552 "	Feb. 4, 1908
Lavina M. Grimes	423 Massachusetts ave	"	552 "	Nov. 3, 1908
Roberta J. Hardie	Needham	"	936 "	Oct. 3, 1898
Emily E. Maynard	40 Mather st	"	936 "	Sept., 1867
Theresa A. Mullen	Cambridge	"	936 "	Feb. 1, 1896
Lillian D. Peirce	19 Clifford st	"	696 "	Sept. 13, 1905
Elva A. Price	West Somerville	"	840 "	" 13, 1905
Alice M. Roche	224 Northampton st	"	600 "	Feb. 4, 1907
Grace H. Smith	Somerville	"	840 "	Jan. 4, 1904
Lillian M. Watts	863 Boylston st	"	600 "	May 1, 1907
Katherine L. Wilson	134 Huntington ave	"	936 "	Feb. 14, 1881
Caroline M. Burke	Cambridge	First Asst., Kindergarten	792 "	" 3, 1896
Mary E. Denehy	8 Cambridge ter	"	792 "	Nov. 10, 1902
Edith F. Barker	Wollaston	Assistant	624 "	Jan. 23, 1905
Edith C. Johnson	919 Blue Hill ave	"	624 "	Sept. 24, 1902
Frances E. Woods	19 Union st., Bri	Special Assistant	1.75 day	March 8, 1909
Azniv Beshgeturian	12 Harvard ave	"	1.75 "	Sept. 9, 1908
Mary A. Haverty	48 Regent st	"	1.75 "	" 9, 1908

School Department.— Continued.

Name.	Residence.	Designation.	Compensation.	Date of Election or Appointment.

Quincy District.— Concluded

Name.	Residence.	Designation.	Compensation.	Date of Election or Appointment.
John H. Graham	64 Dudley st	Substitute	$3.75 day	Jan. 14, 1909
Margaret A. Cronin	32 Oneida st	Attendant	.50 "	Sept. 9, 1908
Mary E. O'Brien	114 Hudson st	"	.50 "	" 11, 1908
George F. Chessman	299 Albany st	Janitor	17.92 wk	" 1896
Jane A. Daly	11 Vine st	"	20.94 "	June, 1894
Alexander Nelson	823 E. Sixth st	"	8.85 "	March 22, 1908

Rice District.

Name.	Residence.	Designation.	Compensation.	Date of Election or Appointment.
Lincoln Owen	53 Montview st., W. R.	Master	$3,180 yr	Sept. 12, 1893
Joseph L. Caverly	Newton	Sub-Master	2,340 "	" 1, 1879
Archer M. Nickerson	169 Willow st., W. R.	"	1,500 "	Jan. 19, 1909
Mary E. Mailman	1 Circuit sq	Master's Assistant	1,308 "	Dec. 1, 1896
Margaret A. Nichols	68 Glendale st	First Assistant, Grammar	1,212 "	March 23, 1904
Mabel I. Emerson	13 Sherman st	First Assistant in Charge	1,116 "	April 13, 1898
Sarah E. Bowers	163 Washington st	Assistant	936 "	Oct. 3, 1872
Katherine C. Brady	7 Fenton pl	"	552 "	March 17, 1908
Dora Brown	17 Greenwich pk	"	936 "	Nov. 10, 1870
Helen M. Connelly	102 Myrtle st	"	600 "	" 19, 1907
Clara C. Dunn	Hotel Eliot, Rox	"	936 "	Oct. 13, 1879
Adalyn P. Henderson	122 Huntington ave	"	936 "	Feb. 1, 1898
Mattie H. Jackson	West Newton	"	936 "	June 22, 1877
Alice J. F. Kane	109 Pembroke st	"	552 "	Nov. 3, 1908
Eleanor F. Lang	14 St. James st	"	936 "	" 2, 1885
Elinor Maher	139 Blue Hill ave	"	648 "	" 12, 1906
Alice M. May	Cambridge	"	936 "	March 1, 1874
F. Helen Mayo	87 Mt. Vernon st., W. R.	"	936 "	Jan. 14, 1907
Edith F. Parry	15 Greenwich pk	"	936 "	Sept., 1882
J. Vida Spear	406 Massachusetts ave	"	696 "	Oct. 23, 1907
Emma L. Wyman	Woburn	"	936 "	Sept. 1, 1872
Evelyn L. Barrows	45 Boutwell st	First Asst., Kindergarten	648 "	" 9, 1908
Mary E. Keenan	914 Dorchester ave	Special Assistant	1.75 day	Jan. 18, 1909
Anna M. Doherty	69 Howland st	"	1.50 "	Nov. 2, 1908
Marguerite F. Lally	73 Fletcher st., Rox	"	1.75 "	Feb. 1, 1909
Thomas F. Durkin	128 Bunker Hill st	Janitor	25.10 wk	Sept. 1, 1894
Edward L. Menz	31½ Rand st	"	17.00 "	March, 1909

Robert G. Shaw District.

Name.	Residence.	Designation.	Compensation.	Date of Election or Appointment.
Francis A. Morse	55 Hastings st., W. R.	Master	$3,180 yr	Sept. 7, 1885
Gardner P. Balch	16 Montview st., W. R.	Sub-Master	2,340 "	" 6, 1898
Alice E. Farrington	16 Hastings st., W. R.	Master's Assistant	1,308 "	Feb. 20, 1893
Frances R. Newcomb	21 Lambert ave	First Assistant, Grammar	1,212 "	Oct. 1, 1902
Rita G. Baker	72 Huntington ave	Assistant	600 "	Nov. 5, 1907
Mary Butler	64 Monadnock st	"	936 "	May 1, 1889
F. Mabel Cassidy	Glendale rd., W. R.	"	936 "	Nov. 13, 1899
Blanche J. Conner	538 Massachusetts ave	"	936 "	June 3, 1901
Julia F. Coombs	16 Montview st., W. R.	"	936 "	Sept. 7, 1897
Josephine Garland	250 Corey st., W. R.	"	936 "	Feb. 1, 1886
Frances A. Griffin	71 Montview st., W. R.	"	936 "	Sept. 5, 1894
Helen S. Henry	34 Montclair st., Ros.	"	936 "	Oct. 3, 1887
Mary G. Hudson	Carnauba st., Ros.	"	936 "	April 11, 1889
Martha B. Johnson	279 Poplar st., Ros.	"	648 "	Nov. 13, 1906
Anna L. Maguire	3811 Washington st	"	792 "	Sept. 9, 1903
Mary C. Moller	59 School st	"	936 "	Jan. 2, 1889
Mary C. Richards	1977 Centre st., W. R.	"	936 "	Oct. 18, 1886
Ellen G. Earnshaw	108 Corey st., W. R.	First Asst., Kindergarten	792 "	May 1, 1900
Lelia A. Flagg	19 Ruskin st., W. R.	"	792 "	Feb. 1, 1894
Stella W. Seymour	Cambridge	Assistant	480 "	April 30, 1907
Mary C. Aikern	98 Revere st	Special Assistant	1.75 day	Sept. 29, 1908
Mary I. Foley	10 Gayland ave., Dor	"	1.75 "	Nov. 16, 1908
Lulu M. Godfrey	83 Arundel st., Ros	"	1.75 "	Oct. 6, 1908
Alice E. McMurrough	7 Rosemary st., J. P.	"	1.75 "	Sept. 14, 1908
Eileene A. Sweeney	321 Athens st	Substitute	2.00 "	Oct. 12, 1908
Gertrude L. Lambert	1744 Centre st., W. R.	Attendant	.50 "	Sept. 9, 1908
Alice G. Kane	2163 Centre st., W. R.	"	.50 "	" 14, 1908
Minnie K. Brodbeck	5254 Washington st	Janitor	6.32 wk	April 23, 1896
Patrick F. Devney	260 Temple st., W. R.	"	15.92 "	" 1, 1902
George J. Hurley	20 Garfield st., J. P.	"	13.03 "	Jan. 4, 1909
Wendell P. Getchell	88 Maple st., W. R	"	21.45 "	Oct. 1, 1904

School Department.— Continued.

Name.	Residence.	Designation.	Compensation	Date of Election or Appointment.

Roger Wolcott District.

Hiram M. George	694 Walk Hill st	Master	$3,180 yr	Jan. 1, 1897
Orris L. Beverage	24 Nixon st	Sub-Master	2,340 "	Feb. 23, 1897
Henry E. Loring	Hingham	"	2,340 "	Sept. 6, 1898
Ida T. Weeks	14 Wales st	Master's Assistant	1,308 "	Feb. 1, 1897
Louisa W. Burgess	72 Fuller st	First Assistant in Charge	1,116 "	April 11, 1904
Mary E. Nichols	64 Bowdoin st	"	1,116 "	Feb. 1, 1897
Mary W. Baker	29 Wildwood st	Assistant	936 "	Sept. 9, 1903
Elizabeth C. Banker	19 Cottage side	"	936 "	Nov. 1, 1898
Nellie E. Briggs	Somerville	"	744 "	April 8, 1907
Louise L. Carr	13 Everett st	"	936 "	Oct. 1, 1889
Violet C. Coates	183 Centre st	"	840 "	April 11, 1904
Irene A. Dooley	804 Parker st	"	600 "	" 8, 1907
Blanche I. Evans	Somerville	"	936 "	Oct. 13, 1902
Helen F. Farrell	Somerville	"	696 "	Jan. 7, 1908
Alicia G. Frawley	55 Evelyn st	"	744 "	" 16, 1905
Mary E. Garrity	Quincy	"	936 "	Oct. 1, 1901
Harriet M. Gould	27 Paisley pk	"	936 "	Jan. 2, 1895
Mary E. Jenkins	Waverley House	"	600 "	Dec. 3, 1907
Sigrid T. Larson	15 Mascot st	"	600 "	" 17, 1907
Anna F. Maybury	138 W. Selden st	"	696 "	Oct. 2, 1905
Margaret C. McCloskey	14 Ashmont st	"	696 "	Sept. 13, 1905
Alice G. Meade	615 Adams st	"	888 "	" 10, 1902
Katharine C. Merrick	671 Washington st	"	936 "	Jan. 2, 1896
Mary G. Morton	106 Maple st	"	936 "	Sept. 13, 1899
Florence M. Murphy	12 Judson st	"	600 "	Oct. 22, 1907
Julia R. O'Brien	Norwood	"	696 "	Jan. 2, 1908
Josephine L. Pickett	10 Stanton st	"	792 "	" 16, 1905
Florence J. Preston	Everett	"	600 "	Oct. 22, 1907
Bertha C. Quinnan	47 Mattapan st	"	600 "	Nov. 19, 1907
Agatha P. Razoux	5 Union pk	"	936 "	" 1, 1897
Katharine V. Rowe	100 Houghton st	"	840 "	Sept. 28, 1903
Alice M. Ryan	502 Columbus ave	"	936 "	Nov. 2, 1896
Emma L. Samuels	Hyde Park	"	936 "	June 10, 1895
Annie G. Shay	108 Capen st	"	840 "	Oct. 15, 1902
Anna L. Sullivan	87 W. Selden st	"	600 "	Dec. 17, 1907
F. Mable Sykes	51 McLellan st	"	936 "	Nov. 1, 1899
Mary G. Woodman	15 Blagden st	"	936 "	March 31, 1902
Anina L. Fitzsimmons	16 Cedar st	First Asst., Kindergarten	792 "	Sept. 10, 1902
Lucy E. Low	30 Dunreath st	"	648 "	Nov. 3, 1908
Katharine H. Perry	3 Monadnock st	"	792 "	May 1, 1900
Marguerite C. McDermott	23 Old Harbor st	Assistant	576 "	Sept. 13, 1905
Helen V. Peck	369 Talbot ave	"	624 "	Jan. 16, 1905
Margaret F. Cummings	16 Bellflower st	Special Assistant	1.75 day	Feb. 16, 1909
Mary L. Walsh	20 Nazing st	"	1.50 "	Sept. 23, 1908
Helen L. Irons	3 Weldon st	Substitute	2.00 "	Jan. 25, 1909
Mabel V. Mulrey	42 Olney st	"	1.75 "	Sept. 14, 1908
William H. Cook	20 Fremont pl	Janitor	16.84 wk	Nov. 1, 1905
Cornelius O'Sullivan	336 E st	"	16.28 "	March 1, 1909
Henry E. Meyer	59 Woolson st	"	31.73 "	Dec. 10, 1901
Patrick F. Powers	105 Lauriat ave	"	16.46 "	April 25, 1906

Sherwin District.

Edward P. Shute	78 Gainsboro st	Master	$2,940 yr	Oct. 2, 1905
Casper Isham	40 Charlotte st	Sub-Master	2,340 "	" 1, 1897
John F. Suckling	8 Pinckney rd	"	2,340 "	Jan. 2, 1895
Elizabeth B. Walton	Wakefield	Master's Assistant	1,308 "	Sept. 7, 1885
Nellie H. Crowell	18 Durham st	First Assistant in Charge	1,116 "	" 11, 1901
Emma L. Peterson	9 Schuyler st	First Assistant, Primary	1,080 "	Nov. 2, 1896
Sara M. Baker	759 Fremont st	Assistant	936 "	Sept. 7, 1897
Adella L. Baldwin	21 Worcester sq	"	936 "	" 4, 1895
Athelston Brandt	7 Laurel st	"	888 "	Nov. 1, 1901
Isabel M. Brown	314 Saratoga st	"	744 "	Jan. 16, 1905
Laura L. Brown	11 Fairland st	"	936 "	May 1, 1897
Rebecca E. Carson	55 Roxbury st	"	552 "	Nov. 3, 1908
Rose E. Conaty	103 Hampshire st	"	936 "	June 1, 1888
Alice M. Colleton	59 Beech Glen st	"	840 "	Dec. 1, 1903
Sarah E. Gould	8 Bullard st	"	936 "	Sept. 1, 1874
Mary E. T. Healy	112 Cedar st	"	936 "	Oct. 12, 1886
Rose L. Hurvitz	146 Webster st	"	696 "	Sept. 13, 1905
Minnie A. Perry	Hyde Park	"	936 "	Dec. 20, 1880
Oria J. Perry	Hyde Park	"	936 "	Oct. 1, 1885

School Department.— Continued.

Name.	Residence.	Designation.	Com-pensation.	Date of Election or Appointment.

Sherwin District.— Concluded.

Name.	Residence.	Designation.	Com-pensation.	Date of Election or Appointment.
Mary M. Regan	49 Winchester st	Assistant	$936 yr	Nov. 1, 1892
Florence Rice	135 Savin Hill ave	"	552 "	April 21, 1908
Mary F. Roome	Hyde Park	"	936 "	Dec. 3, 1888
Amy W. Shaw*	42 Woodbine st	"	936 "	Sept. 14, 1904
Catherine G. Sheahan	129 Minden st	"	744 "	" 13, 1905
Mary F. Sullivan	22 Intervale st	"	936 "	June 3, 1901
Elizabeth F. Todd	29 Woodbine st	"	936 "	Feb. 6, 1871
Isabella F. Wallace	35 Spring Park ave., J. P.	First Asst., Kindergarten	792 "	Sept. 11, 1901
Beulah S. Cone	61 Trenton st	"	648 "	Oct. 20, 1908
Frances A. English	20 Spring Park ave	Assistant	432 "	Nov. 3, 1908
Catherine E. Hurley	24 Monument ave	Temporary Teacher	2.00 day	Oct. 5, 1908
M. Gertrude Rebholz	36 Saunders st., Alls	Special Assistant	1.75 "	Sept. 9, 1908
Margaret E. McMahon	Brookline	"	1.75 "	Jan. 4, 1909
Mary F. Powers	64 Elm ave., J. P.	"	1.50 "	April 13, 1908
Grace M. Welch	13 Robin Hood st	"	1.50 "	Sept. 9, 1908
Annie M. Trundy	Hotel Oxford	Substitute	2.00 "	April 20, 1909
Margaret M. O'Brien	806 Parker st	"	2.00 "	" 29, 1909
Annie Lehman	5 Whittier pl	Attendant	.50 "	Sept. 9, 1908
Ellen G. Hart	214 Ruggles st	Janitor	9.24 wk	" 16, 1901
Frederick V. Howe	401 Warren st	"	26.48 "	Aug. 16, 1903
Hilary J. Johnson	9 Carmel st	"	16.94 "	Nov. 11, 1903

Shurtleff District.

Name.	Residence.	Designation.	Com-pensation.	Date of Election or Appointment.
Agnes G. Gilfether	772 Fourth st	Principal	$3,060 yr	Jan. 2, 1905
Mary M. Clapp	18 Atlantic st	Master's Assistant	1,164 "	" 2, 1905
Winnifred C. Folan	1015 Dorchester ave	First Assistant, Grammar	1,164 "	" 2, 1905
Alice G. Dolbeare	427 Sixth st	First Assistant in Charge	1,116 "	Nov. 25, 1901
Jane M. Bullard	478 Columbia rd	Assistant	936 "	Sept. 8, 1863
Marguerite S. Clapp	24 Salcombe st	"	936 "	" 10, 1894
Mary J. Cullen	297 Bunker Hill st	"	840 "	Jan. 5, 1905
Ella G. Fitzgerald	218 Athens st	"	936 "	Sept. 5, 1894
Annie E. Flood	63 Farragut rd	"	600 "	Oct. 22, 1907
Florence G. Frazer	182 Seventh st	"	936 "	March 8, 1898
Lillian M. Hall	532 Fourth st	"	936 "	Nov. 1, 1892
Abbie S. Mendell	142 Dorchester st	"	936 "	Sept. 14, 1903
Mary E. Morse	212 Dorchester st	"	936 "	March 1, 1870
Anna E. Murphy	84 P st	"	600 "	Dec. 17, 1907
Margaret L. Nolan	65 Dorchester st	"	936 "	March 1, 1896
Mary L. O'Neill	16 Almont st	"	696 "	Sept. 3, 1905
Alice M. Riley	172 I st	"	552 "	Nov. 17, 1908
Marion W. Rundlett	756 Broadway	"	936 "	Dec. 14, 1865
Alice C. Ryan	578 Broadway	"	936 "	Sept. 20, 1875
Anna L. Scallan	604 Seventh st	"	936 "	March 1, 1885
Mary Taylor	682 Blue Hill ave	"	888 "	Jan. 6, 1902
Florence H. Murray	Cambridge	First Asst., Kindergarten	792 "	Sept. 10, 1902
Ida G. Thurston	30 Johnston rd	"	792 "	Nov. 2, 1903
Katherine S. Haskell	480 Fourth st	Assistant	624 "	Sept. 9, 1903
Mary M. Glennon	65 Regent st	Substitute	2.00 day	March 26, 1908
Gertrude Craigen	200 F st	Attendant	.50 "	Sept. 9, 1908
Lucy F. Thurston	30 Johnston rd	"	.50 "	" 9, 1908
Andrew J. Dole	247 Eighth st	Janitor	15.52 wk	Feb. 6, 1908
Georgianna Griffin	151 Dorchester st	"	5.77 "	Oct. 1, 1906
Michael T. Reagan	31 Howell st	"	24.53 "	Jan. 1, 1909

Thomas Gardner District.

Name.	Residence.	Designation.	Com-pensation.	Date of Election or Appointment.
Charles F. Merrick	55 Ashford st	Master	$2,940 yr	Sept. 1, 1905
Alexander Pearson	19 Linden st	Sub-Master	2,340 "	" 5, 1888
Herbert F. Sylvester	Newtonville	"	1,740 "	Nov. 20, 1906
Marion Keith	16 Ashford st	Master's Assistant	1,308 "	Sept. 5, 1888
Lillian S. Allen	27 Lindsey st	Assistant	936 "	May 1, 1895
Agnes A. Aubin	49 Gardner st	"	936 "	" 1, 1890
Elva E. Buck	Cambridge	"	840 "	Oct. 1, 1902
Margaret T. Casey	11A Bayard st	"	744 "	" 10, 1904
Ella L. Chittendon	56 Parsons st	"	936 "	Dec. 13, 1875
Imogene J. M. Conland	2 Batavia st	"	552 "	April 12, 1909
Mary E. Cosgrove	28 Hancock st	"	648 "	Sept. 17, 1906
Bertha E. Davis	24 Dustin st	"	600 "	Oct. 22, 1907
Mary A. Duston	1 Conrad	"	936 "	May 16, 1900

* On leave of absence without pay until September 1, 1909.

School Department.— Continued.

Name.	Residence.	Designation.	Compensation.	Date of Election or Appointment

Thomas Gardner District.— Concluded.

Name.	Residence.	Designation.	Compensation.	Date of Election or Appointment
Edna C. Farrington	17 Pratt st	Assistant	$600 yr.	Oct. 22, 1907
Margaret A. Foley	62 Linden st	"	936 "	Nov. 1, 1898
Annie C. Forbes	15 Calder st	"	648 "	" 1, 1906
Julia B. Harvell	10 Holborn st	"	744 "	Oct. 2, 1905
Ruby A. Johnson	455 Massachusetts ave	"	936 "	March 25, 1895
Grace A. Kelleher	11 Maywood st	"	744 "	Jan. 16, 1905
Mabel J. Neil	34 Brentwood st	"	744 "	" 16, 1905
Eva M. Neth	5 Parker Hill ter	"	552 "	Nov. 17, 1908
Mary E. O'Neill	Cambridge	"	936 "	Sept. 6, 1893
Blanche A. Russell	424 Massachusetts ave	"	888 "	Feb. 13, 1905
M. Grace Seymour	Cambridge	"	840 "	Nov. 3, 1902
Leona J. Sheehan	W. Newton	"	936 "	Jan. 2, 1896
Ida F. Taylor	69 Franklin st	"	936 "	Sept. 17, 1889
Elsie L. Travis	51 Chestnut Hill ave	"	936 "	Jan. 2, 1896
Mizpeh B. Zewicker	14 Berwick park	"	888 "	March 11, 1902
Annie L. Ziersch	2 Eliot pl	"	888 "	Sept. 11, 1901
Alice R. Eliot	Brookline	First Asst., Kindergarten	792 "	Oct. 23, 1905
Annie L. McCarty	Brookline	"	792 "	Sept. 10, 1902
Dorothy Hill	20 Webster st	Assistant	528 "	Nov. 6, 1906
Carolyn B. Shattuck	Newton	"	624 "	Oct. 3, 1904
Jessie L. Sweet	1 Webster ave	"	480 "	Jan. 7, 1907
Mary G. Coyle	39 Bayard st	Special Assistant	1.75 day	Oct. 6, 1908
Faith M. Ellis	3 Wadsworth st	Attendant	.50 "	Sept. 9, 1908
Margaret E. Finnegan	40 Holton st	"	.50 "	" 2, 1908
Bartholomew J. Dooley	15 Elko st	Janitor	33.17 wk.	July 1, 1905
Margaret Kelley	36 Raymond st	"	7.10 "	Jan. 1, 1896
Charles McLaughlin	2 Appian way	"	*	Oct., 1887
Dennis J. O'Regan	3 Ascot st	"	24.13 "	July 1, 1905

Thomas N. Hart District.

Name.	Residence.	Designation.	Compensation.	Date of Election or Appointment
John F. Dwight	24 Algonquin st	Master	$3,180 yr.	Sept. 9, 1895
Robert S. Atkins	3 Alexander st	Sub-Master	2,220 "	Jan. 5, 1903
Chester H. Wilbar	Chelsea	"	1,980 "	Feb. 20, 1905
Margaret J. Stewart	184 W. Canton st	Master's Assistant	1,308 "	Jan. 1, 1876
Mary E. Perkins	144 Hemenway st	First Asst. in Charge	1,116 "	" 5, 1903
S. Louella Sweeney	718 Columbia rd	"	1,116 "	Sept. 9, 1903
Emma J. Channell	171 Newbury st	Assistant	936 "	Oct. 22, 1883
M. Edna Cherrington	Hyde Park	"	936 "	June 1, 1897
Evelyn M. Condon	496 Broadway	"	936 "	Oct. 13, 1890
Alice M. Desmond	53 G st	"	840 "	Dec. 10, 1902
Mary E. Donnelly	37 G. st	"	936 "	Sept. 12, 1900
Mary E. Farrell	18 Mt. Vernon st	"	936 "	Jan. 29, 1900
Laura J. Gerry	750 Fourth st	"	936 "	Sept. 7, 1857
Jennie P. Grose	87 Brighton ave., Alls	"	840 "	" 9, 1902
Florence Harlow	587 Eighth st	"	936 "	" 9, 1891
Anastasia G. Hyde	764 Columbia rd	"	936 "	Nov. 21, 1887
Anna T. Maher	68 L st	"	936 "	" 1, 1898
Jennie F. McKissick	11 Elton st	"	936 "	Feb. 2, 1880
Lillian G. Norris	128 Fourth st	"	600 "	Nov. 19, 1907
Joseph A. F. O'Neil	45 Sixth st	"	552 "	" 3, 1908
Fannie G. Patten	7 Hotel Eaton	"	936 "	Sept. 6, 1875
Bertha Peirce	65 G st	"	936 "	Feb. 4, 1889
Laura M. Power	583 Broadway	"	936 "	Oct. 1, 1889
Mary B. Powers	758 Broadway	"	936 "	Feb. 2, 1880
Carrie L. Prescott	Milton	"	936 "	Sept. 9, 1895
Maude C. Tinkham	Weymouth	"	936 "	Jan. 2, 1899
Ella M. Warner	757 Broadway	"	936 "	Sept. 2, 1872
Mary I. Hamilton	7 Hawes ave	First Asst., Kindergarten	792 "	Jan. 3, 1898
Emily E. Willett	Needham	"	648 "	Oct. 5, 1908
Elizabeth S. Tash	18 Atlantic st	Assistant	624 "	Jan. 16, 1905
Dorothy Fairbanks	7 Stanmore pl	"	480 "	April 21, 1908
Bessie M. Manary	173 Emerson st	Special Assistant	1.75 day	Sept. 9, 1908
Marie B. Crowley	690 Fifth st	Attendant	.50 "	" 21, 1908
Nathan Gray	57 G st	Janitor	23.66 wk.	Dec. 1, 1889
Mary A. Walsh	65 Story st	"	14.15 "	" 1, 1899
Carrie Sargent	2 Saxton st	"	13.32 "	July 15, 1905

* See Washington Allston District.

School Department.— Continued.

Name.	Residence.	Designation.	Compensation.	Date of Election or Appointment.

Warren District.

Name.	Residence.	Designation.	Compensation.	Date of Election or Appointment.
Edward Stickney	Chelsea	Master	$3,180 yr	April 25, 1893
Walter J. Phelan	Waverley House	Sub-Master	2,100 "	Nov. 11, 1903
Anna D. Dalton	Somerville	Master's Assistant	1,308 "	Jan. 2, 1894
Caroline E. Morse	33 St. James ave	First Assistant in Charge	1,116 "	Sept. 14, 1904
Abbie M. Mott	Swampscott	First Assistant, Grammar	1,212 "	Nov. 1, 1897
Helen T. Carmody	Brookline	Assistant	552 "	" 17, 1908
Rose M. Cole	28 Wenham st	"	936 "	Oct. 9, 1893
Mary M. Crane	57 Olney st	"	840 "	" 16, 1902
Alice Hall	West Somerville	"	936 "	Sept., 1867
Mary T. Laughlin	52 Green st	"	888 "	Oct. 23, 1901
Caroline A. Meade	Brookline	"	936 "	Sept. 5, 1894
Annie A. F. Mellish	2 Albemarle Chambers	"	936 "	" 11, 1901
Ellen M. O'Connor	Waverley House	"	936 "	May 25, 1898
Georgietta Sawyer	Somerville	"	936 "	" 1, 1895
Katharine A. Sweeney	Somerville	"	936 "	Oct. 3, 1887
Sarah J. Taff	Hooper Estate	"	936 "	March 16, 1893
Anna H. Cullen	29 Marcella st	Assistant	696 "	Nov. 1, 1905
Carrie F. Gammell	Medford	"	936 "	Sept. 8, 1884
Caroline E. Osgood	Everett	"	936 "	" 2, 1872
Fannie L. Osgood	Somerville	"	936 "	" 6, 1886
Jessie G. Paine	Cambridge	"	936 "	" 9, 1891
M. Josephine Smith	11 Sullivan st	"	936 "	" 7, 1860
Cora A. Wiley	Everett	"	936 "	" 3, 1877
Elizabeth J. Turnbull	47 Corey st	Special Assistant	1.75 day	Nov. 17, 1908
Katharine L. Roche	29 Charlotte st	First Asst., Kindergarten	792 yr	Oct. 16, 1901
Alice V. Tuttle	Everett	"	792 "	" 1, 1903
Marie A. Robbins	West Newton	Assistant	432 "	Nov. 3, 1908
Dora Weisman	Malden	"	432 "	" 3, 1908
Alice Phalan	27 Auburn st	Attendant	.50 day	Sept. 9, 1908
Ellen L. Devaney	288 Bunker Hill st	Janitor	16.55 wk	" 1, 1901
Margaret M. O'Neil	64 Decatur st	"	7.59 "	March 19, 1909
John P. Swift	37 School st	"	19.85 "	Sept. 1, 1881
Annie L. Doyle	6 Edgeworth st	Matron	10.38 "	" 1, 1901

Washington District.

Name.	Residence.	Designation.	Compensation.	Date of Election or Appointment.
Benjamin J. Hinds	Stoneham	Master	$2,820 yr	May 21, 1906
Joseph B. Egan	Cambridge	Sub-Master	1,980 "	Sept. 14, 1904
Theresa E. Fraser	73 Walnut ave	Master's Assistant	1,308 "	" 14, 1904
James M. Murdock	33 Monument ave	First Assistant, Grammar	1,164 "	" 14, 1904
Eleanor B. Jamison	128 Birch st., Ros.	First Assistant in Charge	972 "	Nov. 3, 1908
Katherine L. King	19 Copley st	First Assistant, Primary	1,080 "	Sept. 14, 1904
Mabel M. Anderson	28 Akron st	Assistant	936 "	Oct. 18, 1897
Angie P. S. Andrews	617 Shawmut ave	"	936 "	Jan. 16, 1891
Helena R. Baldrey	106 Topliff st	"	552 "	Nov. 3, 1908
Mary L. Bibbey	21 Wales st	"	936 "	Jan. 23, 1883
Frances Burnce	76 Allen st	"	648 "	Nov. 6, 1906
Idabel F. Butler	Quincy	"	792 "	March 14, 1905
Josephine T. Collagan	Wollaston	"	696 "	Nov. 5, 1907
M. Claire Cooper	827 Third st	"	552 "	April 12, 1909
Mary V. Cronin	117 Dale st	"	648 "	Nov. 20, 1906
Annie L. Curly	117 Nonantum st., Bri	"	792 "	Feb. 16, 1904
Emily M. Curtis	21 Linwood st	"	552 "	Nov. 3, 1908
Theresa A. Dacey	8 Lexington st	"	936 "	" 5, 1900
Alice A. Doherty	30 Soley st	"	888 "	Jan. 16, 1905
Katherine L. Driscoll	283 Walnut ave	"	600 "	Feb. 19, 1907
Mary F. Driscoll	644 Third st	"	552 "	Dec. 8, 1908
Mary E. Durgin	Cambridge	"	840 "	Oct. 16, 1902
Mary E. Gately	250 Park st	"	888 "	March 2, 1905
Matilda J. Graumann	169 Boylston st., J. P.	"	552 "	Nov. 17, 1908
Anna E. Haley	Salem	"	840 "	Jan. 2, 1905
Mary J. Jenkins	Waverley House	"	936 "	May 16, 1898
Elizabeth M. Keefe	109 Dustin st., Bri.	"	840 "	Oct. 16, 1902
Frances C. Lamb	125 Warren st	"	552 "	Dec. 8, 1908
Mary H. Leavey	20 Mansur st	"	552 "	Nov. 3, 1908
Mary C. Locke	222 Neponset ave	"	648 "	" 6, 1906
Mary T. Lynch	75 Marcella st	"	552 "	March 16, 1909
Alice E. Mackusick	West Somerville	"	648 "	Nov. 20, 1906
Anna F. Moran	39 G st	"	744 "	Feb. 20, 1905
Adeline M. Murphy	20 Stephen st	"	936 "	Dec. 1, 1902
Margaret F. Murphy	49 Prospect st., W. R.	"	936 "	Feb. 16, 1903
Alice Neilan	West Medford	"	792 "	Jan. 16, 1905
Alice H. O'Connell	14 Spring Park ave., J. P.	"	552 "	Nov. 3, 1908

School Department. — Continued.

Name.	Residence.	Designation.	Compensation.	Date of Election or Appointment.

Washington District.— Concluded.

Name.	Residence.	Designation.	Compensation.	Date of Election or Appointment.
Johanna J. O'Neill	74 Green st., Chsn	Assistant	$840 yr	Oct. 16, 1903
Gertrude O. Oppenheim	Cambridge	"	744 "	Jan. 16, 1905
Myra K. Parker	Reading	"	600 "	Oct. 14, 1907
Minnie D. Penzanski	76 Allen st	"	552 "	Jan. 7, 1908
Katie Roud	85 Fowler st	"	552 "	March 16, 1909
Josephine Smith	43 Grampian way	"	936 "	Sept. 9, 1903
Gertrude F. Sullivan	Somerville	"	744 "	Jan. 2, 1905
Gertrude H. Sullivan	Watertown	"	696 "	May 1, 1905
Mary V. Sullivan	Cambridge	"	600 "	Oct. 14, 1907
Leonora E. Taft	5 Albemarle st	"	936 "	Sept. 13, 1899
Mary A. L. Timony	720 Harrison ave	"	744 "	March 14, 1905
Charlotte R. Weild	5 Salem st, ave	"	648 "	Nov. 1, 1906
Anna M. Mullins	11 Elm Hill pk	First Asst., Kindergarten	792 "	Jan. 2, 1905
Ida A. Noyes	52 Pinckney st	"	792 "	Sept. 5, 1888
Elizabeth A. Lyons	23 Sedgwick st., J. P.	Assistant	576 "	" 13, 1905
Amy A. Snelling	143 Mt. Vernon st., W. R.	"	624 "	Oct. 16, 1903
Esther L. Kimball	26 Vinson st	Temporary Teacher	2.00 day	March 29, 1909
Emma A. Brust	1199 Tremont st	Substitute	2.00 "	April 27, 1909
Mary F. Lynch	10 Pinckney st	"	2.00 "	" 27, 1909
Mary M. Macdonald	13 Malden st	"	2.00 "	" 27, 1909
Mary E. Smith	113 Brookline ave	"	2.00 "	" 29, 1909
Theresa M. Cotter	5 Allston st	"	1.75 "	" 27, 1909
Mary Castanza	27 Lyman st	Attendant	.50 "	Sept. 9, 1908
Julia F. Cody	48 Soley st	"	.50 "	" 9, 1908
John F. Harrington	24 Chambers st	Janitor	56.22 wk	Oct. 27, 1904
William Sennott	15 Kenney st., J. P.	"	9.24 "	Nov. 16, 1908
William Swansey	7 Joiner st	"		1884
Abigail J. Riley	397 Charles st	Matron	10.38 wk	Sept. 20, 1904

Washington Allston District.

Name.	Residence.	Designation.	Compensation.	Date of Election or Appointment.
William C. Crawford	596 Cambridge st., Alls	Master	$3,180 yr	Dec. 7, 1903
Louis P. Nash	9 Mansfield st., Alls	Sub-Master	1,860 "	Nov. 1, 1905
Jessie W. Kelly	110 Academy Hill rd., Bri	Master's Assistant	1,020 "	Oct. 17, 1907
Alice A. Swett	186 Brighton ave., Alls	First Assistant, Grammar	1,212 "	May 1, 1889
Emma F. Martin	53 Chestnut Hill ave., Bri	First Assistant in Charge	1,116 "	Dec. 4, 1899
Sarah F. Boynton†	348 N. Harvard st., Alls	Assistant	468 "	Feb., 1872
Anna N. Brock	1577 Commonwealth ave., Alls	"	936 "	Nov. 1, 1882
Elizabeth L. Bush	24 Gardner st., Alls	"	888 "	Sept. 29, 1904
Lina K. Eaton	1 Wadsworth st., Alls	"	888 "	Oct. 9, 1904
Marion E. Hood	Cambridge	"	792 "	Sept. 9, 1903
Edith J. Jones	116 Brighton ave., Alls	"	936 "	Dec. 1, 1903
Louise A. Keeler	116 Adams st	"	936 "	Oct. 10, 1900
Elizabeth C. Muldoon	2 Fern st., Alls	"	936 "	April 16, 1888
Annie P. O'Hara	Winthrop	"	744 "	Feb. 20, 1905
Helen E. Raymond	Lynn	"	936 "	Sept. 8, 1896
Fannie B. Sanderson	25 Leicester st., Bri	"	936 "	" 17, 1900
Frances M. Spooner	596 Cambridge st., Alls	"	936 "	" 1, 1902
Eleanor L. Sullivan	717 Massachusetts ave	"	936 "	March 16, 1900
Annabelle L. Troupe	776 Huntington ave	"	744 "	Nov. 5, 1907
Helen L. Duncklee	59 Chestnut Hill ave., Bri	First Asst., Kindergarten	792 "	Feb. 1, 1897
Jessie A. Adams	65 Chestnut Hill ave., Bri	Assistant	576 "	Jan. 2, 1906
Mary A. J. Brady	43 Telegraph st	Special Assistant	1.75 day	Nov. 2, 1908
Alice T. McNamara	9 St. James st	Substitute	2.00 "	Sept. 9, 1908
Rose Hanratty	Riverdale st., Alls	Attendant	.50 "	" 9, 1908
Charles McLaughlin	2 Appian way, Alls	Janitor	36.62 wk	May 16, 1880
Augustus Robinson	16 Gordon st	"	16.31 "	Jan. 1, 1907

Wells District.

Name.	Residence.	Designation.	Compensation.	Date of Election or Appointment.
Orlendo W. Dimick	Watertown	Master	$3,180 yr	Sept. 1, 1882
Elizabeth Campbell	Everett	Master's Assistant	972 "	Oct. 6, 1908
Emeline E. Durgin	Somerville	First Assistant, Grammar	1,212 "	March 1, 1881
Georgia D. Barstow	31 Mt. Vernon st	First Assistant in Charge	1,116 "	Feb. 16, 1898
Sarah G. Fogarty	Watertown	"	1,116 "	Nov. 2, 1896
Mary F. Gargan	316 Longwood ave	" "	1,116 "	" 2, 1896
Adelaide E. Badger	127 Newbury st	Assistant	936 "	Sept. 3, 1877
Agnes L. Berry	Malden	"	936 "	March 3, 1902
Selina A. Black	Somerville	"	936 "	Sept. 12, 1893

* See Eliot District.
† Year's leave of absence on half pay. Resignation to take effect September 1, 1909.

School Department.— Continued.

Name.	Residence.	Designation.	Com- pensation.	Date of Election or Appointment.

Wells District.—Concluded.

Name.	Residence.	Designation.	Com- pensation.	Date of Election or Appointment.
Lilian C. Burbank	Lowell	Assistant	$840 yr	Sept. 9, 1903
Jennie L. Carter	Wakefield	"	936 "	March 21, 1904
Carrie M. Cogswell	12 Bloomfield st	"	936 "	Feb. 5, 1896
Hannah E. Collins	445 Washington st	"	936 "	Oct. 3, 1892
Alicia I. Collison	104 Harrishof st	"	936 "	Sept. 1, 1879
Alice M. Conley	9 DeWolf st	"	552 "	Jan. 7, 1908
Laura W. Cook	Newton	"	696 "	Sept. 13, 1905
Anna F. Daly	8 Zamora st., J. P	"	936 "	May 2, 1893
Gertrude M. Dimick	Watertown	"	936 "	April 12, 1897
Nellie M. Durgin	Somerville	"	936 "	March 24, 1890
Alice Dunn	Quincy	"	936 "	Sept. 8, 1896
Mary F. Finneran	205 Heath st	"	936 "	Nov. 4, 1891
Annie E. Flanagan	East Dedham	"	936 "	Sept. 5, 1894
Mary F. Flanagan	East Dedham	"	936 "	Nov. 1, 1893
Susan R. Gifford	75 Pinckney st	"	936 "	Feb. 8, 1876
Hazel P. Gore	Cambridge	"	600 "	Oct. 22, 1907
Helen M. Graves	58 Temple st	"	936 "	May 1, 1883
Alice M. Hagerty	15 Gardner ave	"	936 "	Dec. 16, 1898
Lula A. L. Hill	37 Pinckney st	"	936 "	Sept. 3, 1883
Eleanore E. Hubbard	36 Holmes ave., Alls	"	648 "	Nov. 20, 1906
Ellen F. Jones	Somerville	"	936 "	April 8, 1878
Ellen F. Joyce	60 Weld Hill st., J. P	"	888 "	Feb. 16, 1903
Katherine A. Kiggen	Hyde Park	"	936 "	Nov. 16, 1885
Amy V. Kingston	267 Corey rd., Alls	"	648 "	" 20, 1906
Mary Lillis	Natick	"	936 "	Feb. 6, 1896
Alice G. Lincoln	4380 Washington st., Ros	"	936 "	Nov. 18, 1901
Dora L. Lourie	30 Allen st	"	600 "	Dec. 17, 1907
Agnes McCloskey	14 Ashmont st	"	552 "	Nov. 3, 1908
Emma C. McNamara	Cambridge	"	648 "	" 1, 1906
Mary R. McNamara	35 Roslin st	"	888 "	Sept. 15, 1902
Margaret G. Melia	13 Bainbridge st	"	936 "	Oct. 16, 1899
Jeanette A. Nelson	154 Willow st., W. R	"	936 "	Sept. 7, 1897
Mary F. O'Neil	24 Oakley st	"	552 "	Dec. 8, 1908
Lillian W. Prescott	Somerville	"	936 "	June 1, 1886
Lena H. Romberg	114 Union Park st	"	600 "	Nov. 19, 1907
Ambrosine Salsbury	65 St. Botolph st	Assistant, Special Class	984 "	Sept. 11, 1907
Clara B. Shaw	Lexington	Assistant	936 "	Oct. 17, 1898
Caroline A. Shay	69 Pinckney st	"	888 "	" 16, 1901
Eleanora A. Smith	20 Worthington st	"	936 "	Dec. 18, 1899
Lizzie F. Stevens	Everett	"	936 "	Feb. 5, 1877
Alice D. Strong	329 Paris st	"	888 "	Dec. 2, 1901
Hattie A. Watson	23 Batavia st	"	936 "	" 4, 1871
Frances W. Weeks	532 Adams st	"	600 "	" 17, 1907
Kate Wilson	71 Paul Gore st., J. P	"	936 "	" 1, 1877
Maizie E. Wilson	Malden	"	600 "	Feb. 1, 1907
Josephine H. Calef	Malden	First Asst., Kindergarten	792 "	Oct. 21, 1901
Mary P. Corrigan	57 Fort ave	" "	744 "	" 1, 1906
Ada C. Williamson	118 Mt. Vernon st	" "	792 "	Jan. 2, 1894
Dora L. Adler	Somerville	" "	480 "	May 1, 1907
Frances M. Gueth	36 Decatur st	" "	528 "	Nov. 1, 1906
Helen T. O'Reilly	Wollaston	" "	432 "	" 17, 1908
Ella M. Dolben	3 Prescott st	Special Assistant	1.50 day	Dec. 1, 1908
Harriet E. Kingsbury	12 Oswald st	Substitute	2.00 "	Oct. 19, 1908
Mary E. Nugent	3 Call st., J. P	"	2.00 "	Feb. 1, 1909
Minnie Herrick	153 Chelsea st	Attendant	.50 "	Sept. 9, 1908
Rose A. Levi	14 Ashland st	"	.50 "	Jan. 11, 1909
Ellen F. McNeil	16 Allen st	"	.50 "	Sept. 9, 1908
Michael E. Colleary	70 Oak st	Janitor	11.34 wk	June 3, 1908
Christopher P. Curtis	19 Highland st	"	25.76 "	Feb. 5, 1898
Charles D. Gallagher	63 W. Cedar st	"	24.13 "	Oct. 1, 1899
Jeremiah O'Connor	359 Cambridge st	"	21.54 "	Nov. 15, 1885

Wendell Phillips District.

Name.	Residence.	Designation.	Com- pensation.	Date of Election or Appointment.
Elias H. Marston	Somerville	Master	$3,180 yr	Sept. 1, 1882
Cyrus B. Collins	Rockland	Sub-Master	2,340 "	Jan. 2, 1894
Edgar E. Hulse	25 Congreve st., Ros	"	1,860 "	Oct. 11, 1905
Joel W. Reynolds	Marblehead	"	1,740 "	Nov. 13, 1906
Nellie M. Whitney	590 Columbus ave	Master's Assistant	1,308 "	Sept. 8, 1884
Katharine A. Burns	Newton	First Assistant in Charge	1,116 "	June 1, 1901
Ella J. Boyle	Cambridge	Assistant	936 "	Oct. 16, 1901
Katharine J. Burke	61 E. Concord st	"	936 "	March 1, 1899
Katherine C. Coveney	Somerville	"	936 "	Oct. 1, 1897

School Department.— Continued.

Name.	Residence.	Designation.	Compensation.	Date of Election or Appointment.

Wendell Phillips District. – Concluded.

Name.	Residence.	Designation.	Compensation.	Date of Election or Appointment.
Agnes B. Doyle	31 Moore st., E. B.	Assistant	$696 yr	Nov. 23, 1905
Mary E. Doyle	123 Pinckney st	"	936 "	Sept. 26, 1899
Henrietta L. Dwyer	Brookline	"	936 "	" 25, 1866
Effie L. Evans	91 Dale st	"	552 "	Nov. 17, 1908
Nellie M. Foley	4 Brimmer st	"	936 "	Sept. 10, 1902
Elizabeth G. Hutchison	Cambridge	"	936 "	Oct. 2, 1899
Margaret E. Kelleher	41 Laurel st	"	552 "	Feb. 3, 1908
Mary R. Kennedy	Somerville	"	936 "	April 15, 1901
Winifred L. Kinsley	Cambridge	"	696 "	Nov. 17, 1908
Martha A. Knowles	3 Eliot st	"	936 "	Sept. 1, 1872
Ellen J. MacMahon	Cambridge	"	936 "	Jan. 16, 1902
Susan A. McKenna	50 Thomas pk	"	840 "	Feb. 16, 1906
William T. Miller	16 Leicester st., Bri	"	648 "	Nov. 1, 1906
Leila M. Nicholl	23 Aldie st., Alls	"	888 "	" 18, 1901
Annie G. Scollard	East Braintree	"	936 "	Oct. 4, 1897
Elizabeth M. Shine	Cambridge	"	936 "	March 1, 1899
Harriet F. Smith	134 Franklin st., Alls	"	888 "	Jan. 30, 1905
Mary E. Smith	4 Logan st	"	600 "	Dec. 17, 1907
Julia E. Sullivan	9 Marion st., Chsn	"	936 "	March 1, 1897
Agnes G. Tarpey	39 Oakview ter., J. P.	"	936 "	" 16, 1898
Mary E. Towle	8 Prospect st., Chsn	"	936 "	Nov. 15, 1878
Laura J. Wescott	Wakefield	"	648 "	Sept. 9, 1908
Jeremiah W. Murphy	106 Myrtle st	Janitor	19.00 wk	Jan. 20, 1885
Annie J. Butler	375 Charles st	"	11.59 "	Dec. 1, 1891
Francis L. Butler	375 Charles st	"	8.15 "	May 16, 1908

William E. Russell District.

Name.	Residence.	Designation.	Compensation.	Date of Election or Appointment.
Edwin T. Horne	11 Tileston pl	Master	$3,180 yr	Jan. 1, 1870
Murray H. Ballou	71 Stanley st	Sub-Master	2,340 "	Oct. 16, 1896
Nellie J. Breed †	31 Mather st	Master's Assistant	1,308 "	" 22, 1896
Jessie D. Stoddard	7 Hawes ave	First Assistant, Grammar	1,212 "	Sept. 10, 1902
Minnie E. G. Price	220 Dorchester ave	First Assistant in Charge	1,116 "	Oct. 26, 1903
Williamina Boise	Quincy	Assistant	936 "	" 16, 1896
Kate L. Brown	163 Massachusetts ave	"	936 "	Sept. 13, 1897
Maud I. Carter	6 Windermere rd	"	888 "	Feb. 16, 1905
Grace M. Cavanagh	59 Olney st	"	552 "	Nov. 17, 1908
Stella M. Coates	183 Centre st	"	744 "	Sept. 13, 1905
Mary K. Corbett	866 E. Fifth st	"	648 "	Nov. 1, 1906
Sarah T. Driscoll *	72 Columbia rd	"	936 "	Oct. 16, 1896
Mary G. Ellis	43 Bellevue st	"	936 "	Sept. 6, 1893
Winifred Emerson	48 Astor st	"	936 "	Feb. 2, 1898
Cora L. Etheridge	8 Bruce st	"	936 "	Jan. 1, 1870
Julia J. Ford	Quincy	"	936 "	" 16, 1901
Katherine G. Garrity	77 Gainsboro st	"	936 "	Sept. 8, 1896
Mary E. Griffin	3 Dayton ave	"	888 "	" 10, 1902
Josephine M. Haney	119 Pinckney st	"	552 "	Dec. 8, 1908
Alice B. Hennessey	8 Draper st	"	936 "	Jan. 4, 1897
Katharine T. A. Hogan	118 G st	"	792 "	" 16, 1905
Charlotte K. Holmes	104 Magnolia st	"	936 "	Sept. 23, 1893
Lillie M. M. Loughlin	917 Broadway	"	936 "	June 1, 1900
Josephine A. Martin	11 Homes ave	"	936 "	Oct. 16, 1896
Sarah E. C. McMahan	265 Dorchester st	"	600 "	Nov. 27, 1906
Gertrude E. Merrill	70 Auckland st	"	840 "	Jan. 16, 1905
Annie R. Mohan	42 Carson st	"	936 "	Oct. 18, 1897
Margaret T. Morse	129 Devon st	"	936 "	Dec. 3, 1900
Frances A. Nolan	800 Parker st	"	888 "	" 16, 1901
Freda Salisberg	49 Hancock st	"	840 "	Jan. 4, 1904
Gertrude W. Simpson	782 Dudley st	"	888 "	" 13, 1902
Mary C. Sullivan	63 Old Harbor st	"	600 "	April 8, 1907
Caroline J. Trommer	42 Lauriat ave	"	648 "	Nov. 6, 1906
Mabel A. Woodward	Somerville	"	936 "	Sept. 10, 1902
Mabel F. Kemp	Brookline	First Asst., Kindergarten	792 "	Jan. 11, 1904
Elizabeth E. Curley	332 Amory st., J. P.	Assistant	624 "	" 11, 1904
Rose A. Conry	49 Milton ave	Substitute	2.00 day	Sept. 9, 1908
Margaret A. F. Cotter	4 Leeds st	"	2.00 "	March 8, 1909
Vera G. Briggs	33 Milton ave	Attendant	.50 "	Oct. 12, 1908
Joseph W. Batchelder	89 Tuttle st	Janitor	24.69 wk	Nov. 1, 1896
Albion Elwell	23 Willis st	"	35.61 "	Aug. 16, 1903
Nellie A. Phelan	28 Crescent ave	"	11.66 "	Oct. 1, 1906

* Year's leave of absence without pay until March 8, 1910.
† Year's leave of absence on half pay until August 31, 1909.

School Department.— Continued.

Name.	Residence.	Designation.	Compensation.	Date of Election or Appointment.

Winthrop District.

Name.	Residence.	Designation.	Com.	Date
Emily F. Carpenter	486 Massachusetts ave	Master	$3,180 yr	Sept. 10, 1902
Helen L. Hilton	12 Folsom st	Master's Assistant	1,308 "	" 12, 1900
Mary A. Murphy	60 Mapleton st., Bri	First Assistant, Grammar	1,212 "	Jan. 5, 1903
Mary E. Noonan	23 Hillside st	First Assistant in Charge	1,116 "	Oct. 1, 1895
Effie E. Beal	39 Upton st	Assistant	840 "	Dec. 11, 1905
Marguerite C. Cronan	8 Louise pk	"	744 "	Sept. 14, 1904
Mabel A. Grogan	Cambridge	"	648 "	Oct. 11, 1906
Ethel F. Grove	56 F st	"	744 "	Jan. 16, 1905
Mary L. Hennessy	24 Melrose st	"	936 "	March 15, 1893
Edith M. Holway	14 Tyler st	"	840 "	Sept. 17, 1902
Grace E. Maloney	31 Highland st	"	552 "	Nov. 3, 1908
Elizabeth M. McDermott	116 Franklin st., Alls	"	600 "	" 19, 1907
Winnifred E. McKay	Malden	"	936 "	Jan. 5, 1903
Carrie Merrill	Canton	"	936 "	Sept. 7, 1885
Anna M. Murray	106 Magnolia st	"	600 "	April 29, 1907
Jane M. O'Brien	5 Murdock pk., Bri	"	936 "	Oct. 27, 1897
Dorothy A. O'Reilly	E. Dedham	"	936 "	Nov. 12, 1900
Emily H. Osborne	Somerville	"	936 "	" 20, 1899
Mary A. Reardon	9 Half Moon st	"	936 "	Oct. 3, 1888
Mary L. B. Reynolds	Stoughton	"	936 "	" 25, 1899
Schassa G. Row	427 Geneva ave	Assistant, Special Class	1,032 "	March 31, 1903
Josephine L. Smith	77 Hamilton st	Assistant	936 "	Sept. 19, 1894
Theresa M. Staek	51 McClellan st	"	552 "	March 16, 1909
Minnie E. Sutherland	72 Robinwood ave., J. P	"	936 "	Sept. 26, 1900
Mary B. Thompson *	84 Brooks st., Bri	"	696 "	" 13, 1905
Ellen M. Underwood	Cambridge	"	936 "	Dec. 21, 1874
Elizabeth A. Welsh	30 Batavia st	"	744 "	Jan. 21, 1907
Helen Wilson	Reading	"	936 "	March 30, 1903
Sara C. Bullard	502 Talbot ave	First Asst., Kindergarten	744 "	Jan. 26, 1905
Mary A. G. Jones	Winthrop	Temporary Teacher	2.00 day	Nov. 23, 1908
Mary L. Barry	49 Paul st	Special Assistant	1.75 "	Dec. 22, 1908
Angela M. L. Brown	87 Homer st	"	1.50 "	Sept. 21, 1908
Anna S. Olson	128 Huntington ave	Substitute	2.00 "	Oct. 5, 1908
John J. Holthaus	153 D st	Janitor	9.92 wk.	Dec. 16, 1908
John J. Norton	153 D st	"	†	Oct. 8, 1906
Joseph T. Whitehouse	56 Telegraph st	"	16.78 "	Sept. 6, 1893

Department of Drawing and Manual Training.

Name.	Residence.	Designation.	Com.	Date
Walter Sargent	North Scituate	Director	$3,000 yr	Dec. 1, 1906
Frank M. Leavitt	32 Akron st	Assistant Director	2,628 "	Feb. 1, 1893
John C. Brodhead	38 Montclair ave	Asst. in Manual Training	1,740 "	Sept. 1, 1906
Helen E. Cleaves	Medford	Assistant in Drawing	1,284 "	" 11, 1907
Grace E. Hackett	134 Franklin st	" "	1,212 "	Feb. 16, 1909
Estelle E. Potter	127 Newbury st	" "	1,500 "	April 26, 1899
Lucy D. Taylor	85 Rockview st	" "	1,212 "	Jan. 2, 1908
Amy R. Whittier	76 Gainsboro st	" "	1,500 "	Dec. 31, 1906
Frank Carter	North Woburn	Inst. in Manual Training	1,200 "	Sept. 14, 1904
Sigrid Cederroth	12 Westland ave	" "	1,104 "	Jan. 21, 1908
James C. Clarke	West Somerville	" "	1,200 "	Sept. 22, 1904
Grace J. Freeman	39 Montclair ave	" "	1,200 "	" 14, 1904
Celia B. Hallstrom	11 Whitford st	" "	1,200 "	" 10, 1902
Olive I. Harris	78 Huntington ave	" "	1,200 "	Jan. 8, 1907
I. Virginia Lyons	Lynnfield Centre	" "	1,200 "	Feb. 1, 1907
Margaret A. Mahoney	9 Walnut st	" "	1,056 "	March 1, 1909
Mary J. Marlow	63 Murdock st	" "	1,200 "	Sept. 13, 1905
Mary E. Pierce	32 Waldeck st	" "	1,200 "	" 10, 1902
Anna M. Pond	Auburndale	" "	1,200 "	" 14, 1904
Helen I. Whittemore	Garrison st	" "	1,200 "	" 14, 1904
Sarah M. Aldrich	22 Batavia st	Asst.Inst., Manual Training	996 "	" 14, 1904
Edna L. Allen	10 Woodbine st	" "	996 "	Oct. 3, 1904
Mary T. Baker	76 Monument st	" "	804 "	April 21, 1908
Mary C. Barstow	67 Bartlett st	" "	996 "	Oct. 17, 1904
Florence O. Bean	6 Westland ave	" "	996 "	Sept. 12, 1906
Lillian M. Beckwith	8 May st	" "	996 "	" 29, 1902
Sheba E. Berry	Somerville	" "	996 "	Feb. 10, 1908
Louise H. Billings	49 Hemenway st	" "	996 "	Oct. 29, 1900
Ella L. Bresnehen	21 Mackin st	" "	852 "	Feb. 1, 1907
Alice S. Bryant	30 Vaughn st	" "	900 "	Sept. 12, 1906
Cornelia D. Burbank	17 Concord sq	" "	996 "	Jan. 15, 1900

* Leave of absence without pay from September 1, 1908, to September 1, 1909.
† See Brimmer District.

School Department.—Continued.

Name.	Residence.	Designation.	Compensation.	Date of Election or Appointment.

Department of Drawing and Manual Training.—Concluded.

Name.	Residence.	Designation.	Compensation.	Date of Election or Appointment.
Jessie L. Burns	12 Ashford st	Asst. Inst. Manual Training	$996 yr	Oct. 10, 1904
Katherine L. Colbert	52 Quincy st	"	804 "	March 2, 1909
Mary E. Davin	66 Wayland st	"	996 "	Sept. 14, 1904
Mary G. Davis	93 Gainsboro st	"	996 "	Oct. 24, 1904
Delia E. Donahue	Medford	"	996 "	April 11, 1904
Florence P. Donelson	35 Lyndhurst st	"	996 "	Sept. 23, 1895
Mary I. Donlan	7 Hawes ave	"	852 "	April 9, 1907
Helen M. Ekstrom	Franklin Square House	"	852 "	Sept. 11, 1907
William A. England	Cambridge	"	996 "	March 1, 1901
Solvi Greve	25 Michigan ave	"	996 "	Sept. 7, 1897
Blanche S. Hall	31 Bowdoin st	"	804 "	" 21, 1908
Martha E. Hall	32 Greenville st	"	804 "	" 21, 1908
Grace E. Hayden	169 St. Botolph st	"	948 "	Feb. 1, 1906
Elise Jonsson	48 Astor st	"	948 "	Sept. 13, 1905
Alice L. Lanman	17 Concord sq	"	996 "	" 18, 1895
Charlotte M. Maloney	44 Beech st	"	948 "	" 13, 1905
Josephine May	15 Pearl st	"	996 "	" 10, 1902
Nellie N. Nolan	Cambridge	"	804 "	Feb. 16, 1909
Effie Owen	99 Dale st	"	996 "	Sept. 14, 1904
Katharine Robinson	Cambridge	"	996 "	" 11, 1901
L. Gertrude Sprague	20 Cumberland st	"	996 "	" 9, 1903
Anna S. Streijffert	48 Astor st	"	996 "	" 9, 1903
Helen F. Veasey	28 Shatter st	"	996 "	Oct. 24, 1900
Sarah I. Wilson	14 Rockville pk	"	948 "	Sept. 13, 1905
Ellen F. Coffin	275 Walnut ave	Substitute	2.00 day	" 16, 1908

Department of Household Science and Art.

Name.	Residence.	Designation.	Compensation.	Date of Election or Appointment.
Josephine Morris	61 Monument ave	Supervisor	$1,356 yr	Dec. 1, 1906

Teachers of Cookery.

Name.	Residence.	Designation.	Compensation.	Date of Election or Appointment.
Grace D. Batchelder	9 St. James ave	Teacher	$936 yr	Nov. 6, 1894
Mary W. Cauley	68 Baldwin st	"	552 "	Oct. 6, 1908
Sarah L. Cauley	68 Baldwin st	"	600 "	Dec. 1, 1907
Elizabeth D. Chadwell	West Lynn	"	696 "	Jan. 2, 1906
Catherine F. Clifford	22 Savin st	"	696 "	Feb. 13, 1906
Josephine W. Cowan	59 Copeland st	"	552 "	Oct. 1, 1908
Julia T. Crowley	63 Rutland st	"	936 "	Dec. 1, 1896
Roberta M. Cummins	11 Monument sq	"	888 "	Oct. 1, 1901
Mary Cunningham	Auburndale	"	936 "	Sept. 6, 1898
Annie M. Eaton	West Somerville	"	936 "	Feb. 1, 1899
Anna U. Foley	61 Murdock st	"	744 "	Sept. 14, 1904
Mary T. Galvin	14 Selden st	"	648 "	Dec. 4, 1906
Mary A. Geary	7 Waverley st., Bri	"	600 "	Sept. 11, 1907
Annie F. Gray	22 Woodbine st	"	888 "	Jan. 6, 1902
Emily H. Hawes	Arlington	"	936 "	Dec. 1, 1898
Margaret W. Howard	Newton	"	936 "	Sept. 8, 1896
Julia A. Hughes	78 Bowdoin st	"	936 "	" 7, 1897
Mary E. Kinsley	498 Adams st	"	600 "	" 11, 1907
Althea W. Lindenberg	178 Walnut ave	"	936 "	" 26, 1887
Alice R. Merrick	671 Washington st., Dor.	"	792 "	" 13, 1905
Mary C. Mitchell	61 Monument ave	"	936 "	Jan. 4, 1892
Anna E. Muldoon	2 Romsey st	"	696 "	Sept. 13, 1905
Ellen B. Murphy	557 Massachusetts ave	"	936 "	Feb. 14, 1894
Julia M. Murphy	Hotel Dale An'x.Regent st	"	936 "	Jan. 1, 1890
Grace B. Nichols	Reading	"	792 "	Sept. 14, 1903
C. Jane O'Brien	7 Fiske ter., Alls	"	600 "	" 16, 1907
Helen A. Parker	Reading	"	600 "	Oct. 14, 1907
Gertrude A. Power	415 W. Fourth st	"	552 "	Sept. 14, 1908
Emeline E. Torrey	23 Winthrop st	"	936 "	" 12, 1892
N. Florence Treat	Chelsea	"	936 "	" 5, 1894
Angeline M. Weaver	18 Claxton st	"	936 "	Feb. 2, 1892
Florence I. Brady	110 Canterbury st	Temporary Teacher	2.00 day	" 1, 1909
Margaret M. Downing	8 National st	"	2.00 "	Nov. 9, 1908

Teachers of Sewing.

Name.	Residence.	Designation.	Compensation.	Date of Election or Appointment.
Eldora M. S.Bowen	960 Morton st	Teacher	$936 yr	March 16, 1897
Harriet E. Browne	28 Downer ave	"	936 "	Sept. 23, 1884
Helen L. Burton	Brookline	"	936 "	April 10, 1882
Margaret C. Crane	25 Castlegate rd	"	936 "	Sept. 15, 1902

School Department.— Continued.

Name.	Residence.	Designation.	Compensation.	Date of Election or Appointment.

Teachers of Sewing.— Concluded.

Name.	Residence.	Designation.	Compensation.	Date of Election or Appointment.
Annie M. Cullen	3 Worthington st	Teacher	$936 yr	Oct. 18, 1899
Isabella Cumming	150 Chandler st	"	936 "	Sept., 1869
Mary L. Dermody	32 Batavia st	"	936 "	" 13, 1899
Mary F. Doherty	128 Devon st	"	936 "	April 16, 1902
Clara L. Dorr	12 Moultrie st	"	936 "	Sept. 15, 1894
M. Lillian Dunbar	21 Wheatland ave	"	936 "	" 25, 1895
Kate Farlin	Hyde Park	"	600 "	" 11, 1907
H. Clare Fisher	251 Lamartine st., J. P.	"	936 "	Jan. 16, 1905
Katharine E. Flanagan	80 Mt. Pleasant ave	"	600 "	Sept. 11, 1907
Anastasia Gannon	24 Monument sq	"	552 "	Oct. 6, 1908
Helen E. Hapgood	Wollaston	"	936 "	" 15, 1894
Mary T. Hassett	10 Woodbine st	"	936 "	Nov. 18, 1901
Sarah A. Horan	10 Woodbine st	"	936 "	Sept. 28, 1903
Katharine M. Howell	23 Thornley st	"	936 "	Oct. 1, 1897
Margaret A. Kelley	53 Forest st	"	936 "	Sept. 5, 1888
Annie L. Killion	180 Heath st	"	600 "	" 11, 1907
Marguerite S. King	Waverley	"	600 "	" 16, 1907
Ellen E. MacHugh	38 Union Park st	"	936 "	Oct. 17, 1904
Katharine M. Mahoney	Medford	"	696 "	Dec. 13, 1905
Annie F. Marlowe	239 Dorchester st	"	936 "	Nov. 5, 1896
Margaret T. McCormick	2 Worthington st	"	936 "	" 1, 1897
Mary L. E. McCormick	2 Worthington st	"	936 "	Jan. 16, 1905
Agnes E. McDonald	40 Wenham st., J. P.	"	936 "	Sept. 26, 1903
Margaret McDonald	7 Alpha rd	"	936 "	" 20, 1897
Mary J. McEntyre	19 Harvest st	"	936 "	Dec. 14, 1886
Annie S. Meserve	145 Eustis st	"	936 "	Sept. 6, 1893
Margaret G. Moore	392 Seaver st	"	600 "	" 11, 1907
Mary A. Mulvey	1368 Columbus ave	"	552 "	" 14, 1908
Margaret J. Murphy	107½ Main st	"	936 "	" 28, 1903
Adeline M. Norton	19 Olney st	"	552 "	" 14, 1908
Mary E. Patterson	61 Thomas pk	"	936 "	Feb. 1, 1877
Esther C. Povah	68 W. Sixth st	"	936 "	March 16, 1896
Ethel M. Rae	4 Dahlgren st	"	696 "	Dec. 13, 1905
Elizabeth L. Rogers	393 Main st	"	600 "	Sept. 24, 1907
Sara C. Selby	6 Louise pk	"	936 "	Feb. 1, 1904
Sarah A. Stall *	55 Brentwood st., Alls	"	468 "	March 20, 1876
Ella L. Thomas	11½ Spring Park ave., J. P.	"	936 "	Oct. 27, 1897
Lizzie A. Thomas	373 Commonwealth ave	"	936 "	Feb. 1, 1881
Frances Tully	28 Washington st., Chsn	"	936 "	Oct. 17, 1899
Nida F. Vesper	89 Waldeck st	"	936 "	Sept. 14, 1903
Florence I. Waitt	27 Florida st	"	936 "	Oct. 2, 1903
Emma A. Waterhouse	50 Kenilworth st	"	936 "	April 28, 1873
Emma G. Welch	61 Linden st	"	936 "	" 11, 1893
Ella Whiting *	Cambridge	"	420 "	Sept. 6, 1893
Ellen M. Wills	Franklin Square House	"	936 "	" 7, 1887
Henrietta L. Yelland	West Newton	"	936 "	Oct. 12, 1899
Ellen M. Wight	69 Bowdoin st	Temporary Teacher	2.00 day	Dec. 1, 1908

Department of Music.

Name.	Residence.	Designation.	Compensation.	Date of Election or Appointment.
James M. McLaughlin	56 Bowdoin st	Director of Music	$3,000 yr	Jan. 2, 1900
Grant Drake	Melrose Highlands	Assistant Director	2,436 "	Sept. 1, 1902
Leonard B. Marshall	48 Lyndhurst st	"	2,652 "	" 1, 1902
Albert G. Mitchell	16 Francis st	"	2,436 "	" 1, 1902
John A. O'Shea	20 Wales st	"	2,436 "	" 1, 1902
Helen A. Brick	147 Draper st	Assistant	1,236 "	" 1, 1902
Laura F. Taylor	75 Waldeck st	"	1,236 "	" 1, 1902
Blanche Tibbitts	25 Greenough ave., J. P.	"	1,188 "	May 2, 1904
Nellie L. Woodbury	16 Leyland st	"	1,236 "	Sept. 1, 1902

Department of School Hygiene.

Name.	Residence.	Designation.	Compensation.	Date of Election or Appointment.
Thomas F. Harrington, M.D.	310 Commonwealth ave	Director of School Hygiene	$3,756 yr	Sept. 11, 1907
Nathaniel J. Young	442 Saratoga st	Assistant Director of Physical Training and Athletics	2,400 "	Oct. 8, 1901
Gordon Trowbridge	Weymouth	Assistant Director of Physical Training and Athletics	2,040 "	" 15, 1902
Ernst Hermann	Foxboro	Assistant Director of Physical Training and Athletics	1,800 "	April 30, 1909
John D. O'Reilly	79 Olney st	Instructor in Athletics	1,356 "	Sept. 1, 1906

* Leave of absence on half pay to September 1, 1909.

School Department.—Continued.

Name.	Residence.	Designation.	Compensation.	Date of Election or Appointment.

Department of School Hygiene.—Concluded.

Name.	Residence.	Designation.	Compensation.	Date
James H. Crowley	20 Decatur st	Asst. Instructor in Athletics	$900 yr.	May 19, 1908
Leo H. Leary	936 Broadway	" "	900 "	19, 1908
William C. Matthews	Cambridge	" "	900 "	19, 1908
Fred L. O'Brien	81 Brooks st	" "	900 "	19, 1908
John J. O'Donnell, Jr.	106 Byron st	" "	900 "	19, 1908
M. Joseph Redding	165 W. Ninth st	" "	900 "	19, 1908
George H. Benyon	209 W. Springfield st	Instructor in Military Drill	2,004 "	April 12, 1899
Charles H. Reardon	117 Wayland st	Armorer	1,050 "	8, 1895
Arthur C. Jelly, M. D.	10 Arlington st	Medical Inspector of Special Classes	1,008 "	Sept. 1, 1906
Margaret E. Carley, M. D.	483 Beacon st	Supervising Nurse	1,284 "	11, 1907
Laura H. Barbrick	60 Seymour st., Ros.	Assistant Nurse	648 "	Oct. 20, 1908
Mary F. Buckley	965 Canterbury st	"	696 "	Feb. 3, 1908
Sarah M. Cahoon	726 E. Third st	"	696 "	Sept. 11, 1907
Mary Callaghan	65 Westland ave	"	696 "	" 11, 1907
Elizabeth R. R. Card	Everett	"	696 "	" 11, 1907
Edith S. Cooke	475 Columbia rd	"	696 "	" 11, 1907
Miriam H. Crowell	6 Windermere rd	"	696 "	" 11, 1907
Helena M. Daly	44 Hartford st	"	696 "	Feb. 3, 1908
Mary A. Didham	Lynn	"	696 "	Sept. 11, 1907
Jennie R. Dix	Cliftondale	"	696 "	" 11, 1907
Mary S. Doherty	320 Warren st	"	696 "	" 11, 1907
Mary F. Donovan	521 Massachusetts ave	"	648 "	May 1, 1908
Ellen M. Dwyer	479 Massachusetts ave	"	696 "	Feb. 17, 1908
K. Josephine Ellis	32 Westland ave	"	696 "	Oct. 14, 1907
Alice B. Felton	40 Berkeley st	"	696 "	Feb. 3, 1908
Katharine Fitz Gerald	521 Massachusetts ave	"	696 "	3, 1908
Frances Z. Flannery	4A Forest st	"	696 "	March 2, 1908
Amalia H. Grover	Reading	"	696 "	Feb. 3, 1908
Annie I. Hollings	Clement pk	"	696 "	Sept. 11, 1907
Mabel A. Hunter	60 Seymour st., Ros.	"	696 "	11, 1907
Mary G. Kenny	Somerville	"	648 "	Jan. 19, 1909
Mary Martin	Cambridge	"	696 "	Sept. 11, 1907
Helen F. McCaffrey	33 Adams st	"	696 "	" 11, 1907
Katherine O'Callaghan	2418 Washington st	"	696 "	" 11, 1907
Agnes I. Quirk	114 Havre st	"	696 "	Feb. 3, 1908
Anna Regan	33 Webster ave., Alls.	"	696 "	3, 1908
Sadie G. Reynolds	929 E. Fourth st	"	696 "	Sept. 11, 1907
Harriet A. Shaw	Cambridge	"	648 "	Nov. 1, 1908
Edith W. Sheehan	374 Dorchester st	"	696 "	Feb. 3, 1908
Emily A. Snow*	31 Upton st	"	696 "	Sept. 11, 1907
Alice M. Sweeney	60 Waverley st	"	696 "	" 11, 1907
Alma Taylor	1164 Washington st	"	696 "	" 11, 1907
Hulda H. Tingley	Lynn	"	696 "	Feb. 3, 1908
Blanche Wildes	Cambridge	"	648 "	" 16, 1909
Catharine C. Marks	2 Roseland st	Temporary Nurse	2.00 day	March 15, 1909
Helen L. Golden	167 Princeton st., E. B.	Stenographer	840 yr.	Sept. 15, 1902

Special Instructors.

Name.	Residence.	Designation.	Compensation.	Date
Caroline D. Aborn	Medford	Director of Kindergartens	$1,800 yr.	Dec. 1, 1906
Mary C. Mellyn	11 Mayfair st	Supervisor of Substitutes	3,060 "	Sept. 12, 1906
Maurice J. O'Brien	36 Sherman st	Director of Evening and Vacation Schools	2,100 "	March 1, 1908
Frances A. Neilson	141 Draper st	Teacher, School on Spectacle Island	552 "	Sept. 28, 1908

Truant Officers.

Name.	Residence.	Designation.	Compensation.	Date
George Murphy	70 Bowdoin st	Chief Truant Officer	$1,900 yr.	March 24, 1885
George W. Bean	42 Sagamore st	Truant Officer	1,400 "	April 17, 1893
Henry M. Blackwell	107 Brook ave	"	1,400 "	Sept. 1, 1887
James Bragdon	1790 Columbia rd	"	1,400 "	Jan. 22, 1878
John S. Clark	20 Gleason st	"	1,400 "	Oct. 22, 1906
Maurice F. Corkery	28 Longfellow st	"	1,400 "	Nov. 13, 1900
Philip Davis †	112 Salem st	"	1,400 "	Jan. 15, 1907
Frank A. Dothage	627 Massachusetts ave	"	1,400 "	Nov. 13, 1900

* Leave of absence, no pay, to September 1, 1909.   † Supervisor of Licensed Minors.

School Department.— Concluded.

Name.	Residence.	Designation.	Compensation.	Date of Election or Appointment.

Truant Officers.—Concluded.

Name.	Residence.	Designation.	Compensation.	Date of Election or Appointment.
John T. Hathaway	21 Mendum st	Truant Officer	$1,400 yr	Sept. 7, 1897
Timothy J. Kenny	296 W. Fifth st	"	1,400 "	Oct. 9, 1900
David F. Long	286 Bunker Hill st	"	1,400 "	April 17, 1893
John McCrillis	514 Park st	"	1,400 "	Oct. 14, 1896
William A. O'Brien	421 Meridian st	"	1,400 "	" 22, 1906
Richard F. Quirk	564 E. Broadway	"	1,400 "	Jan. 15, 1907
George A. Sargent	15 Pinckney st	"	1,400 "	" 3, 1908
Amos Schaffer	695 Washington st	"	1,400 "	Dec. 23, 1890
William B. Shea	119 Radcliffe st	"	1,400 "	Sept. 1, 1887
Warren J. Stokes	1850 Centre st., W. R	"	1,400 "	" 12, 1876
John J. Sullivan	22 Alcott st	"	1,080 "	Jan. 25, 1909
Richard W. Walsh	5 Woodville st	"	1,400 "	Sept. 13, 1881
John H. Westfall	24 Ashford st	"	1,400 "	Feb. 1, 1895
Charles B. Wood	619 Columbus ave	"	1,400 "	Nov. 22, 1892

Sinking Funds Department.

Name.	Residence.	Designation.	Compensation.	Date of Election or Appointment.
Nathaniel J. Rust	488 Commonwealth ave	Chairman	None	April 28, 1890
Frank G. Webster	167 Commonwealth ave	Commissioner	"	Dec. 27, 1898
Joseph H. O'Neil	122 Seaver st	"	"	May 8, 1899
Horatio G. Curtis	179 Marlboro st	"	"	" 3, 1905
James T. Wetherald	50 Fenway	"	"	" 3, 1906
Israel A. Ratshesky	232 Commonwealth ave	"	"	" 7, 1907
J. Alfred Mitchell	796 E. Fourth st	Secretary	$700 yr	Nov. 25, 1904
Charles H. Slattery	520 E. Broadway	Treasurer	200 "	May 7, 1906
George H. Dana	28 Cummings rd	Bookkeeper	800 "	Nov. 20, 1904

Soldiers' Relief Department.

Name.	Residence.	Designation.	Compensation.	Date of Election or Appointment.
John E. Gilman	13 Schuyler st., Rox	Commissioner	$3,500 yr	April 2, 1901
Ellen M. Reilley	176 Walnut ave., Rox	Chief Clerk	1,300 "	Dec. 16, 1890
John F. O'Brien	42 Ditson st., Dor	Settlement Clerk and Visitor.	1,500 "	June 1, 1905
Henry B. Lovering	460 Geneva ave., Dor	Clerk	1,500 "	Oct. 18, 1907
Emily F. Dore	40 Howland st., Rox	Clerk and Visitor	1,100 "	Dec. 27, 1892
Mary E. Mulvee	4 Stafford st., Rox	" "	1,100 "	March 2, 1892
Louise C. Newbury	192 Dartmouth st	" "	1,100 "	Feb. 1, 1896
Elizabeth F. Whalen	19 Harvest st., Dor	" "	1,100 "	May 1, 1891
Mary E. Slattery	31 Shafter st., Dor	Clerk	800 "	" 1, 1899
Mary E. Crowley	4 Henchman st	Stenographer & Typewriter.	800 "	April 23, 1907
Elizabeth V. Wilkie	59 Monument ave., Chsn	Matron	600 "	Oct. 15, 1906

Statistics Department.

Name.	Residence.	Designation.	Compensation.	Date of Election or Appointment.
B. Rodman Weld	155 Forest Hills st	Chairman	None	April 12, 1897
William Jackson	136 Academy Hill rd., Bri	City Engineer, Trustee *ex officio*	"	" 12, 1897
Gordon Abbott	240 Beacon st	Trustee	"	June 12, 1899
William D. C. Curtis	7 Highland ave., Dor	"	"	May 28, 1906
Foy Spencer Baldwin	42 Newcastle rd., Bri	"	"	" 4, 1908
Edward M. Hartwell	4 Parley vale, J. P	Secretary	$3,000 yr	Sept. 1, 1897
William T. Seeger	227 Park st., Rox	Editorial Clerk	1,200 "	April 15, 1907
Carrie E. Taylor	7 Linden st., Alls	Stenographer & Typewriter.	720 "	May 15, 1899
John H. Glover	112 D st., S. B	Temporary Clerk	.50 hr	March 24, 1909

Steamer "Monitor."

Name.	Residence.	Designation.	Compensation.	Date of Election or Appointment.
Fred D. Cook	26 Princeton st	Captain	$1,600 yr	Oct. 1, 1904
Edward W. Bates	350 Columbus ave	Mate	1,200 "	" 1, 1904

Steamer " Monitor." — Concluded.

Name.	Residence.	Designation.	Compensation.	Date of Election or Appointment.
Philip F. Shaw	1½ Russell st	Engineer	$1,400 yr	Aug. 14, 1905
Edward Walsh	45 Saratoga st	Assistant Engineer	1,000 "	May 1, 1905
Augustus Calkins	77 Burt st	Fireman	900 "	" 2, 1905
George E. Johnson	250 Kilton st	"	900 "	Dec. 2, 1904
Humphrey J. Donovan	7 Phipps pl	Seaman	900 "	March 1, 1904
John Putwain	62 Elm st	"	900 "	June 15, 1896
Jefferson D. Sheldon	13 Windsor st	"	900 "	Jan. 4, 1909
John Hollingsworth	109 Liverpool st	Night Watchman	960 "	June 16, 1887
Ellias Boudrot	108 E. Brookline st	Assistant Watchman	720 "	Jan. 4, 1909
Dennis J. Driscoll	1823 Dorchester ave	Wharfinger	720 "	April 4, 1908
Catherine M. Dale	78 Clifton st	Stewardess	480 "	May 1, 1900

Street Department.

Central Office.

Name	Residence	Designation	Compensation	Date
Guy C. Emerson	4 Brewer st	Superintendent of Streets	$7,500 yr	April 14, 1908*
Benjamin B. Tremere	23 Burroughs st	Chief Clerk	2,500 "	" 6, 1908*
Patrick J. A. Murphy	24 Athelwold st	Clerk	2,250 "	May 1, 1882
Alva C. Peck	122 Rosseter st	Clerk and Stenographer	1,800 "	" 1, 1891
William J. McGlinchy	38 Calumet st	Clerk	1,500 "	Oct. 1, 1895
Peter T. Costello	59 Rosseter st	Messenger and Clerk	1,200 "	May 1, 1891
Daniel R. Murray	149 Charles st	Civil Service Clerk	1,200 "	Dec. 12, 1902
John J. Connelly	16 Parnell st	Clerk	800 "	July 3, 1903
Daniel F. Murphy	103 Union Park st	Office Boy	1.75 day	March 27, 1903
John P. Meehan	8 Child st	Chauffeur	3.00 "	Jan. 29, 1909*

Bridge Division.

Name	Residence	Designation	Compensation	Date
Thomas H. Sexton †	105 Hutchings st., Rox	Engineer of Bridges	$2,000 yr	April 4, 1908
Joseph H. Stack ‡	51 McLellan st., Dor	Clerk and Stenographer	1,200 "	Dec. 22, 1898
John F. Doyle	3 Oak st., Chsn	Messenger	800 "	April 16, 1896
Peter O'Neil	153 Princeton st., E. B	Supervisor of Construction	1,820 "	Jan 27, 1902

Drawtenders and Assistants.

ATLANTIC AVENUE BRIDGE.

Name	Residence	Designation	Compensation	Date
Dennis J. O'Connor	102 Tyler st	Drawtender	$1,200 yr	Sept. 15, 1905
William C. Donovan	50 St. Margaret st	First Assistant	960 "	Jan. 1, 1895
James F. Cooper, Jr	663 E. Eighth st	"	960 "	Oct. 7, 1904
Richard H. Alexander	131 Hudson st	Assistant Drawtender	800 "	Nov. 24, 1902
Patrick J. Crowley	10 Sussex st	"	800 "	March 27, 1903
William H. Dowd	10 Nightingale st., Dor	"	800 "	June 13, 1902
William Hyde	32 Wendell st	"	800 "	Nov. 7, 1902
Edward T. Landers	13 Sumner st., Dor	"	800 "	June 3, 1907
Hugh F. Tolan	21 Harvard st	"	800 "	" 3, 1907

BROADWAY BRIDGE.

Name	Residence	Designation	Compensation	Date
Patrick H. Boyle	27 Emerald st	Drawtender	$1,200 yr	Nov. 15, 1879
Thomas W. Cogger	25 Union st., Chsn	First Assistant	960 "	March 29, 1902
James J. McNamara	208 Hampden st	"	900 "	June 21, 1895
James F. Berger	34 Richfield st	Assistant Drawtender	800 "	" 3, 1907
Edward J. Broughan	57 W. Sixth st	"	800 "	" 8, 1901
Benjamin M. Campbell	333 Neponset ave	"	800 "	Nov. 2, 1906
Richard A. Coleman	39 Cambridge st	"	800 "	June 3, 1907
John J. McKenna	37 Lyon st	"	800 "	May 1, 1896
Joseph F. O'Neil	172 W. Fourth st	"	800 "	Jan. 30, 1904

* Previously in the service of the department.
† Previously in the Engineering Department.
‡ See, also, Cambridge Bridges Division.

Street Department (Bridge Division).— Continued.

Name.	Residence.	Designation.	Compensation.	Date of Election or Appointment.

Drawtenders and Assistants.— Continued.

CHARLESTOWN BRIDGE.

Henry A. Bolan	19 Stonehurst st	Drawtender	$1,200 yr	Sept. 10, 1880
Joseph R. Downey	393 Charles st	First Assistant	900 "	June 11, 1886
James J. Sweeney	212 Endicott st	"	900 "	" 5, 1891
James R. Coyle	18 Dorrance st	Assistant Drawtender	800 "	" 23, 1905
Albert J. Donovan	50 St. Margaret st	"	800 "	July 1, 1907
John J. Foley	140 Elmo st., Dor	"	800 "	March 21, 1902
James J. Galvin	74 Eustis st	"	800 "	June 14, 1901
John A. Lynch	53 Green st., Chsn	"	800 "	Oct. 7, 1904
Dennis J. Manning	28 Winslow st	"	800 "	Sept. 18, 1903
James J. Meany	35 Elton st	"	800 "	April 16, 1902
James P. Mulcahy	6 Marion st., Chsn	"	800 "	Nov. 2, 1906
William C. Tirrell	55 Mt. Vernon st., Dor	"	800 "	Oct. 7, 1904

CHELSEA NORTH BRIDGE.

Michael H. Enwright	56 Oak Square ave	Drawtender	$1,200 yr	April 22, 1887
William J. Doherty	4 Sprague st., Chsn	First Assistant	900 "	May 7, 1892
Martin J. Griffin	160 Chelsea st., Chsn	"	900 "	Jan. 15, 1882
Frank E. Kaveney	14 Causeway st	Assistant Drawtender	800 "	June 30, 1902
Miles J. Koen	49 Chestnut st	"	800 "	Nov. 20, 1903
Dennis C. Mahoney	70 Decatur st., Chsn	"	800 "	Sept. 2, 1892
Francis F. Morse	187 Bunker Hill st	"	800 "	Nov. 2, 1906
George W. Pike	37 Falcon st	"	800 "	Jan. 3, 1901
Daniel J. Shea	81 Warren st., Chsn	"	800 "	March 7, 1902

CHELSEA SOUTH BRIDGE.

Thomas F. Cloney	46 Tonawanda st., Dor	Drawtender	$1,200 yr	Aug. 21, 1888
Benjamin F. Arey	2 Polk st., Chsn	First Assistant	900 "	May 1, 1882
John J. McCabe	26 Decatur st., Chsn	"	900 "	April 15, 1879
John Carney	11 Ellwood st., Chsn	Assistant Drawtender	800 "	Dec. 29, 1899
Patrick W. Cummings	45 Lawrence st	"	800 "	Nov. 21, 1899
James Gallagher	71 W. Cedar st	"	800 "	March 20, 1896
Frank W. Harvey	280 Bunker Hill st	"	800 "	Oct. 21, 1902
William J. Lynch	18 Vine st., Chsn	"	800 "	Jan. 20, 1909
William L. Waterman	13 Monument sq	"	800 "	Oct. 7, 1904

COMMERCIAL POINT BRIDGE.

Morton Alden	23 Beaumont st	Drawtender	$50 yr	1887

CONGRESS STREET BRIDGE.

Cornelius J. Callahan	187 W. Third st	Drawtender	$1,200 yr	Sept. 19, 1884
Charles J. Thompson	823 Dorchester ave	First Assistant	900 "	May 10, 1907
John J. Dunn	7 Charles st	"	900 "	July 3, 1891
Timothy A. Harkins	19 Dorset st	Assistant Drawtender	800 "	March 1, 1879
Thomas E. Neary	1081 Tremont st	"	800 "	June 13, 1902
Jeremiah Scanlan	1A Sharon st	"	800 "	May 16, 1902
William S. O'Brien	75 Tudor st., S. B	"	800 "	Jan. 26, 1909
Cornelius S. O'Connor	21 Rawson st	"	800 "	July 2, 1902
Thomas F. O'Donnell	41 Melville ave	"	800 "	March 7, 1903

DORCHESTER AVENUE BRIDGE.

Daniel J. Holland	41 Melville ave	Drawtender	$1,200 yr	April 6, 1879
Francis R. Hickey	95 Savin Hill ave	First Assistant	900 "	Feb. 26, 1902
Timothy J. Shea	161 Silver st	"	900 "	May 1, 1896
John Collins	211 W. Second st	Assistant Drawtender	800 "	March 21, 1902
Jeremiah A. Healy	67 Bower st	"	800 "	April 16, 1902
John J. Nelligan	10 Mather st	"	800 "	March 24, 1909
Joseph P. Shea	561 E. Fifth st	"	800 "	Feb. 27, 1903
Frank E. Welch	10 Bellflower st	"	800 "	Oct. 29, 1897
Thomas A. Gookin	120 W. Third st	Engineer	800 "	Feb. 13, 1891

DOVER STREET BRIDGE.

Francis O'Brien	88 F st	Drawtender	$1,200 yr	April 15, 1883
William Murray	90 W. Sixth st	First Assistant	900 "	Jan. 1, 1895
John Rick	4 Hawthorne pl	"	900 "	June 5, 1901
Edward F. Cotter	20 Ward st	Assistant Drawtender	800 "	Jan. 22, 1909
Daniel J. Donovan	90 W. Sixth st	"	800 "	July 2, 1902

Street Department (Bridge Division).— Continued.

Name.	Residence.	Designation.	Compensation.	Date of Election or Appointment.

Drawtenders and Assistants. — Continued.

Name.	Residence.	Designation.	Compensation.	Date of Election or Appointment.
Lawrence H. Dunn	736 South st	Assistant Drawtender	$800 yr	June 3, 1907
Jeremiah Gallivan	17 Madison pl	"	800 "	Sept. 15, 1884
Michael H. McCarthy	195 Sydney st	"	800 "	June 15, 1885
Timothy Myron	166 Kneeland st	"	800 "	Dec. 30, 1901

GRANITE BRIDGE.

Name.	Residence.	Designation.	Compensation.	Date of Election or Appointment.
George G. Pike	Granite Bridge Station	Drawtender	$240 yr	Feb. 3, 1909

L STREET BRIDGE.

Name.	Residence.	Designation.	Compensation.	Date of Election or Appointment.
James T. Nunan	190 Emerson st	Drawtender	$1,200 yr	June 4, 1894
John H. Wallace	343 K st	First Assistant	900 "	" 23, 1905
Charles E. Paget	158 M st	"	900 "	" 4, 1894
Patrick J. Donovan	176 L st	Assistant Drawtender	800 "	March 1, 1907
Thomas J. Fitzgerald	506 E. Broadway	"	800 "	Feb. 26, 1902
Michael S. Green	12 Marion st	"	800 "	March 29, 1909
Daniel J. Lane	569 First st	"	800 "	June 5, 1903
John F. McKeon	639 E. Seventh st	"	800 "	Dec. 15, 1899
Thos. J. Sullivan	44 Templeton st	"	800 "	March 29, 1902

MALDEN BRIDGE.

Name.	Residence.	Designation.	Compensation.	Date of Election or Appointment.
Hugh H. McNerlin	426 Bunker Hill st	Drawtender	$1,100 yr	May 1, 1874
James O. Brown	91½ Russell st., Chsn	First Assistant	900 "	Sept. 30, 1892
Timothy J. Murphy	40 Adams st	"	900 "	May 3, 1892
James E. Crogan	89 Chelsea st., Chsn	Assistant Drawtender	800 "	Nov. 12, 1895
John Haggerty	36 Adams st	"	800 "	Feb. 27, 1903
Hampton V. Hayward	27 Copeland st	"	800 "	June 11, 1904
Morris Jacobs	10 Williams st	"	800 "	" 5, 1904
James E. Rourke	78 Rutland st	"	800 "	Dec. 23, 1898
Patrick J. Welch	395 Bunker Hill st	"	800 "	" 7, 1903

MERIDIAN STREET BRIDGE.

Name.	Residence.	Designation.	Compensation.	Date of Election or Appointment.
Daniel McFarland	56 Sumner st	Drawtender	$1,100 yr	May 31, 1888
Jeremiah Fitzgerald	105 Lexington st	First Assistant	900 "	" 2, 1891
Benjamin P. Hodgkins	1 Monmouth	"	900 "	Aug. 9, 1895
Edmund Cussen	9 Atlantic st	Assistant Drawtender	800 "	Jan. 22, 1909
John J. Graham	153 Princeton st	"	800 "	Nov. 20, 1903
Warren K. Ince	584 E. Fifth st	"	800 "	Dec. 2, 1907
Dennis Kelleher	29 Grove st	Steam and Elec. Engineer	800 "	Feb. 28, 1902
John F. Morrison	9 Falcon st	Assistant Drawtender	800 "	Jan. 21, 1909
Harry H. White	305 E. Eagle st	"	800 "	June 4, 1901

NEPONSET BRIDGE.

Name.	Residence.	Designation.	Compensation.	Date of Election or Appointment.
Daniel Procter	103 Minot st	Drawtender	$400 yr	Oct. 5, 1900

NORTHERN AVENUE BRIDGE.

Name.	Residence.	Designation.	Compensation.	Date of Election or Appointment.
James E. Murray	525 E. Seventh st	Drawtender	$1,200 yr	Feb. 15, 1891
Robert E. Burrill	103 Union Park st	First Assistant	900 "	Nov. 6, 1902
John F. Collins	108 Broadway	"	900 "	March 21, 1902
William J. Condon	143 Court st	Assistant Drawtender	800 "	July 1, 1907
Matthew L. Kelly	8 Russell st., Chsn	"	800 "	Dec. 2, 1907
Michael F. Doyle, Jr.	519 E. Third st	"	800 "	Nov. 2, 1906
John J. Hastry	278 E. Ninth st	"	800 "	Dec. 29, 1905
William T. O'Neill	619 E. Second st	"	800 "	Nov. 20, 1903
William M. Tracey	610 E. Seventh st	"	800 "	Jan. 13, 1902
James F. Cummings	106 Dresser st	"	800 "	" 27, 1909

SUMMER STREET BRIDGE.

Name.	Residence.	Designation.	Compensation.	Date of Election or Appointment.
John F. Kinnaly	622 E. Sixth st	Drawtender	$1,200 yr	Dec. 18, 1894
John T. Cosgrove	37 Decatur st., Chsn	First Assistant	900 "	Nov. 20, 1900
William J. Sullivan	24 Everett st	"	900 "	Dec. 8, 1897
Dennis M. Clifford	8 Endleigh st	Assistant Drawtender	800 "	April 18, 1907
John F. Coffey	568 E. Sixth st	"	800 "	Feb. 26, 1902
Charles M. Coakley	428 W. Second st	"	800 "	Jan. 27, 1909
Matthew J. McBreen	49 Homes ave	"	800 "	Nov. 2, 1906
Thomas C. McCarthy	364 W. Fourth st	"	800 "	July 17, 1899
Joseph Mullins	154 W. Sixth st	"	800 "	April 19, 1902

Street Department (Bridge Division).—Continued.

Name.	Residence.	Designation.	Compensation.	Date of Election or Appointment.

Drawtenders and Assistants.—Continued.

WARREN BRIDGE.

Name.	Residence.	Designation.	Compensation.	Date of Election or Appointment.
William J. Alcorn	155 Bunker Hill st	Drawtender	$1,200 yr	Oct. 15, 1881
Thomas B. Pollard	152 Bunker Hill st	First Assistant	900 "	May 29, 1891
Augustine P. Turnbull	47 Corey st., Chsn	"	900 "	July 22, 1895
Samuel B. Edgeworth	8 Wrenthan pk	Assistant Drawtender	800 "	Oct. 4, 1889
John E. Fitzgerald	470 Commercial st	"	800 "	July 4, 1902
Patrick Harvey	197 Shawmut ave	"	800 "	" 22, 1895
Timothy Sheehan	427 Bunker Hill st	"	800 "	Feb. 1, 1909
Daniel Sullivan	34 Monument sq	"	800 "	Dec. 29, 1905
Edward J. Sullivan	121 Marcella st	"	800 "	June 3, 1907
James J. Linnehan	38 Nashua st	Engineer	800 "	" 11, 1902

WESTERN AVENUE TO WATERTOWN AND NORTH BEACON STREET.

Name.	Residence.	Designation.	Compensation.	Date of Election or Appointment.
William A. Kelley	506 Western ave	Drawtender	$400 yr	Feb. 21, 1903

WINTHROP BRIDGE.

Name.	Residence.	Designation.	Compensation.	Date of Election or Appointment.
Herbert W. Tewksbury	12 Pleasant st., Winthrop	Caretaker	$100 yr	Sept. 16, 1905

Mechanics, Yard and Stable Force.

Name.	Residence.	Designation.	Compensation.	Date of Election or Appointment.
Frederick H. Spring	426 Columbus ave	Clerk	$2.50 day	Oct. 26, 1866
George F. Coleman	39 Cambridge st	Janitor	3.00 "	Feb. 7, 1902
Joseph V. Maddock	14 Causeway st	Electrician	3.60 "	Jan. 27, 1902
Parker V. Coburn	69 Staniford st	Sub-foreman	3.50 "	July 11, 1902
Augustine S. Quinn	4 Decatur st., Chsn	"	3.50 "	" 21, 1900
Michael J. Renison	897 Broadway	Sub-foreman of Carpenters	3.50 "	" 1, 1895
George E. Hanlon	6 Ward ct	Carpenter	3.50 "	April 18, 1900
Joseph A. Coyle *	635 Saratoga st	"	3.00 "	Jan. 8, 1909
Michael J. Sullivan *	752 Broadway	"	3.00 "	" 8, 1909
Daniel Crowley	44 Hudson st	"	2.75 "	May 15, 1889
Michael J. Harkins	16 Hulbert st	"	2.75 "	July 23, 1900
Henry D. Gay	80 Bragdon st	Painter	3.00 "	June 21, 1895
John B. Walsh	28 Telegraph st	"	3.00 "	April 3, 1900
John B. Bowler	24 No. Russell st	"	2.50 "	June 24, 1889
Jeremiah A. Crowley	11 Parmenter st	Watchman	2.25 "	May 8, 1891
Dennis J. Donohue	30 Emerson st	"	2.25 "	Dec. 5, 1902
Charles A. Leete	24 Ruggles st	"	2.25 "	June 4, 1901
James J. Lyng	45 Chelsea st	"	2.25 "	April 19, 1907
James F. McIntyre	14 Charles st	"	2.25 "	June 4, 1901
Jeremiah Brosnahan	98 W. Third st	Teamster	2.50 "	Feb. 7, 1902
John Friel	3 Lathrop pl	"	2.25 "	May 15, 1900
John J. Green	68 Decatur st	"	2.75 "	April 14, 1905
Walter J. Holland	11 Coleman st	Driver	2.75 "	" 13, 1906
Hugh McLaughlin	56 Washington st	Stableman	2.25 "	June 28, 1901
James Pendergast	28 W. Fifth st	Hostler	2.25 "	April 26, 1889
Patrick F. Murphy †	11 Mt. Vernon st., Dor	Machinist	3.52 "	May 22, 1908

Cambridge Bridges. ‡

Name.	Residence.	Designation.	Compensation.	Date of Election or Appointment.
Guy C. Emerson	4 Brewer st., J.P.	Commissioner	None	May 1, 1908
Joseph H. Stack §	51 McLellan st	Secretary	$200 yr	May 15, 1908
John H. Holt	Cambridge	Clerk	50 "	Feb. 13, 1908
Patrick J. Henebury †	871 Albany st	Laborer	2.25 day	April 9, 1909
William Rogers ‖	86 Neponset ave	"	2.25 "	Feb. 26, 1908
Timothy Sullivan ¶	9 Devens st	"	2.25 "	Oct. 4, 1908

CAMBRIDGE BRIDGE.

Name.	Residence.	Designation.	Compensation.	Date of Election or Appointment.
Walter B. Hoitt	165 Charles st	Custodian	$500 yr	Dec. 21, 1907
John J. Kelleher	Cambridge	Bridge Cleaner	360 "	" 21, 1907
William G. England	Cambridge	"	360 "	" 21, 1907
Michael Gibbons	93 Endicott st	"	360 "	" 21, 1907
Frank J. Welch	24 Valentine st	"	360 "	" 21, 1907

* From Paving Division.   † From Ferry Division.
‡ Amounts paid by City of Boston; equal amounts paid by City of Cambridge.
§ See, also, Bridge Division.   ‖ Stableman, April 27, 1900.
¶ Stableman, June 12, 1908.

Street Department (Bridge Division).—Concluded.

Name	Residence.	Designation.	Compensation	Date of Election or Appointment.

Drawtenders and Assistants.— Concluded.

HARVARD BRIDGE.

Name	Residence.	Designation.	Compensation	Date of Election or Appointment.
James A. Gorman	Cambridge	Drawtender	$550 yr	Aug. 1, 1892
Peter Boodro	265 Gold st	"	400 "	Oct. 1, 1907
John H. Tukey	Cambridge	"	400 "	Jan. 4, 1903
John Brogan	Cambridge	First Assistant	400 "	Aug. 16, 1890
Patrick A. Berkeley	Cambridge	Motorman	400 "	June 27, 1904
Cornelius McHugh	Cambridge	"	400 "	Sept. 1, 1906

PRISON POINT BRIDGE.

Name	Residence.	Designation.	Compensation	Date of Election or Appointment.
Nathaniel E. Story	103 Warren st	Drawtender	$500 yr	May 15, 1874
Charles P. Nolan	Cambridge	First Assistant	400 "	Dec. 1, 1900
John A. Solari	198 Chambers st	"	400 "	April 1, 1884
Hugh J. Mullen	Cambridge	Assistant Drawtender	400 "	1, 1900
Thomas F. Toomey	Cambridge	"	400 "	Nov. 1, 1900
Frank H. Waitt	Cambridge	"	400 "	8, 1902

NORTH HARVARD STREET BRIDGE.

Name	Residence.	Designation.	Compensation	Date of Election or Appointment.
Donald McNaughton	50 Forbes st., J. P.	Drawtender	$400 yr	Sept. 3, 1907

CAMBRIDGE STREET AND WESTERN AVENUE BRIDGE.

Name	Residence.	Designation.	Compensation	Date of Election or Appointment.
Thomas J. Murphy	Cambridge	Drawtender	$500 yr	Nov. 10, 1897
William H. Blanchard	273 Shawmut ave	"	400 "	July 23, 1888
Howard B. Burgess	Cambridge	"	400 "	March 1, 1899
Timothy Crowley	Cambridge	"	400 "	Feb. 20, 1903

Ferry Division.

Name	Residence.	Designation.	Compensation	Date of Election or Appointment.
Henry P. Christiernin	26 London st	Deputy Superintendent	$3,000 yr	Jan. 20, 1908*
Joseph F. Low	47 Falcon st	Chief Clerk	1,800 "	Sept. 4, 1902*
Daniel T. S. Leland	8 Bowdoin st	Clerk	1,400 "	3, 1895
John A. Sullivan	211 Webster st	Cashier	1,200 "	Jan. 24, 1902
Theodore H. Card	259 Webster st	Captain	1,320 "	1, 1896
William R. Clark	11 Winthrop st	"	1,320 "	March. 1875
Andrew A. Greer	9 Jeffries st	"	1,320 "	Dec. 20, 1907*
John P. Jacobson	94 Falcon st	"	1,320 "	May 22, 1895*
Francis P. Joy	163 Saratoga st	"	1,320 "	April 1, 1870
James J. Kelly	5 Lamson st	"	1,320 "	June 23, 1908*
Harry King	120 Princeton st	"	1,320 "	Nov. 1, 1892*
Dennis McCarthy, 2d	314 Saratoga st	"	1,320 "	Jan. 1, 1905
Adin C. Small	426 Meridian st	"	1,320 "	July 1, 1895*
John A. Wheeler	17 Dixwell st	"	1,320 "	1, 1895*
George H. Varney	8 Westminster st	Foreman Engineer	1,560 "	Feb. 19, 1909*
Oscar O. Bucknam	68 Marion st	Engineer	1,320 "	July 28, 1908
Thomas Cragin	1027 Bennington st	"	1,320 "	28, 1908
Henry Currie	648 Saratoga st	"	1,320 "	28, 1908
John A. Johnson	119 Trenton st	"	1,320 "	28, 1908
Michael McDonough	118 Falcon st	"	1,320 "	Dec. 22, 1899*
Daniel F. Rowan	7 Lamson ct	"	1,320 "	Jan. 1, 1909*
Helmer G. Skonberg	57 Homer st	"	1,320 "	July 28, 1908
Charles Stomberg	299 Maverick st	"	1,320 "	28, 1908
Charles R. Brown, Jr	17 Hinckley st	"	17.00 wk	28, 1908
Benjamin Williams	220 Brooks st	Temporary Engineer	1,320 yr	Aug. 11, 1908*
John J. Belton	121 Havre st	Quartermaster	900 "	Jan. 22, 1904
John H. Flynn	14 Moulton st	"	900 "	May 1, 1896
Frederick Graeme	24 Border st	"	900 "	April 28, 1905
Edward R. Gray	29 Bennington st	"	900 "	28, 1905
Thomas W. LeRay	92 Meridian st	"	900 "	Feb. 15, 1902
Michael J. Murphy	207 Havre st	"	900 "	Dec. 20, 1907*
Nicholas J. Ryan	499 Sumner st	"	900 "	Jan. 29, 1902
Richard L. Searle	93 Everett st	"	900 "	22, 1904
Timothy A. Toohig	260 Maverick st	"	900 "	Feb. 14, 1902
James Young	13 Haynes st	"	900 "	Jan. 22, 1904
Charles F. Crocker	658 Saratoga st	Temporary Quartermaster	900 "	Oct. 30, 1908
Abiel A. Howard	62 Princeton st	"	900 "	Dec. 10, 1908
George Bussey	256 E. Eagle st	Captain	1,320 "	June 1870
Charles A. Estey	96 Falcon st	Tollman	1,080 "	Sept. 1874

* Previously employed in this division.

Street Department (Ferry Division).— Continued.

Name.	Residence.	Designation.	Compensation.	Date of Election or Appointment.
Charles H. Godbold	150 Trenton st	Tollman	$1,080 yr	July, 1874
Francis A. Griffin	235 E. Eagle st	"	1,080 "	Sept., 1871
Fred C. Horner	20 Eutaw st	"	1,080 "	Nov. 22, 1907*
Charles W. Keen	24 Maverick sq	"	1,080 "	Feb. 1, 1899*
John D. Mahoney	65 Perrin st	"	1,080 "	Oct. 29, 1907*
William A. McCarthy	670 Bennington st	"	1,080 "	" 23, 1903*
Michael J. O'Brien	250 Princeton st	"	1,080 "	" 23, 1903*
John P. Riley	29 Monument sq	"	1,080 "	July, 1879
Nathan S. Walker	98 Falcon st	"	1,080 "	" 1873
Charles A. Wentworth	3 Belmont sq	"	1,080 "	June 15, 1908*
Charles S. Colby	84 Falcon st	Gateman	960 "	July, 1874
John J. Cronin	746 Saratoga st	"	960 "	Feb. 26, 1909
William G. Greenall	106 Meridian st	"	960 "	Nov. 29, 1907
LaForest W. Hall	281 Lexington st	"	960 "	April, 1887
William H. Harding	13 Winthrop st	"	960 "	June, 1874
John F. Labohn	62 Condor st	"	960 "	Dec., 1881
Robert W. Cook	182 Leyden st	"	960 "	June 7, 1887
Thomas F. Lynch	613 Bennington st	"	960 "	" 19, 1905*
Henry H. McCarthy	569 Bennington st	"	960 "	Dec. 2, 1904*
Phillip McLaughlin	51 Maverick sq	"	960 "	May 23, 1899
William P. Murphy	24 Brooks st	"	960 "	Dec. 2, 1904*
Walter H. Noyes	38 Monmouth st	"	960 "	July 1, 1895
Michael F. Powers	256 Paris st	"	960 "	Dec. 2, 1904*
William J. Timmins	61 Marion st	"	960 "	Nov. 29, 1907
Wilber F. Wilder	43 Chelsea st	"	960 "	April 25, 1901
Frank L. Westman	10 Central sq	"	900 "	May, 1875
Edward S. Gray	62 Maverick sq	Gate Watchman	900 "	Aug., 1879
Richard Boland	16 Mt. Vernon st	Deckhand	840 "	Nov. 8, 1907
John E. Brown	235 Webster st	"	840 "	Jan. 22, 1904
Walter L. Brown	318 Sumner st	"	840 "	" 22, 1904
Lawrence Collins	55 Havre st	"	840 "	" 7, 1908
James D. Coughlin	396 Chelsea st	"	840 "	April 28, 1905
Edward Delehunty	37 Decatur st	"	840 "	March 25, 1902
Thomas Doyle	1 Lamson st	"	840 "	April 28, 1905
John F. Driscoll	125 Bolton st	"	840 "	Jan. 7, 1908
Charles Hadley	5 Drakes pl	"	840 "	April 28, 1905
Patrick Hickey	84 W. Eagle st	"	840 "	Jan. 7, 1908
William J. Ivers	134 Falcon st	"	840 "	" 22, 1904
Joseph Joy	163 Saratoga st	"	840 "	April 1, 1873
Michael J. O'Neil	203 London st	"	840 "	" 11, 1902
Owen Shields	110 Marginal st	"	840 "	Jan. 22, 1904
John H. Sullivan	63 Havre st	"	840 "	Oct. 31, 1906
Florence W. Sullivan	24 Decatur st	"	840 "	June 30, 1905
Charles A. Stafford	80 Paris st	"	840 "	Jan. 22, 1904
John H. Tyrer	197 Trenton st	"	840 "	March, 1885
Alfred N. Wesberg	22 Maverick st	"	840 "	April, 1887
Theodore F. Paquet	24 Border st		840 "	Sept. 7, 1906
Edward J. Wilkie	67 Marion st	Temporary Deckhand	840 "	Feb. 2, 1909
Dennis Long	73 Chelsea st	Gateman	960 "	May 4, 1906
Peter Moran	107 Homer st	"	960 "	Dec. 22, 1899*
Thomas L. Cody	354 Sumner st	Deckhand	840 "	Jan. 22, 1904
Edward P. Donohue	296 Maverick st	Oiler	17.00 wk	April 22, 1897
Patrick V. Mackey	358 Sumner st	"	17.00 "	Oct. 22, 1904
Charles E. McGunigle	6 Sumner pl	"	17.00 "	May 24, 1901
James L. Murphy	89 Webster st	"	17.00 "	Jan. 22, 1904
Daniel McLaughlin	24 Havre st	"	17.00 "	Aug., 1876
Morgan J. Sullivan	65 Havre st	"	17.00 "	March 3, 1900
James M. Walsh	250 Maverick st	"	17.00 "	April 28, 1905
Francis J. Wehrle	147 Brooks st	"	17.00 "	Dec. 2, 1895
Jeremiah P. Casey	279 Webster st	Fireman	17.00 "	April 28, 1905
Michael Crahan	292 Ruggles st	"	17.00 "	March 1, 1907
Francis M. Donohue	333 Maverick st	"	17.00 "	Jan. 22, 1904
Thomas J. Doren	11 Hooten ct	"	17.00 "	" 22, 1904
Michael Driscoll	585 Bennington st	"	17.00 "	" 24, 1902
James B. Gallagher	412 Sumner st	"	17.00 "	Feb. 28, 1902
John Gallagher	16 Chapman st	"	17.00 "	Nov. 18, 1907
Phillip F. Gallagher	59 Brooks st	"	17.00 "	Sept. 19, 1899
Dennis Hannigan	191 Sumner st	"	17.00 "	April 28, 1905
George W. Holmes	23 Chelsea st	"	17.00 "	May 2, 1907
Dennis F. Horgan	698 Parker st	"	17.00 "	Feb. 10, 1908
John F. Keefe	496 Sumner st	"	17.00 "	Jan. 22, 1904
Michael J. Kennedy	265 Eustis st	"	17.00 "	Nov. 1, 1907
Charles C. Llewellyn	283 Princeton st	"	17.00 "	Dec. 20, 1907

* Previously employed in this division.

Street Department (Ferry Division).— Concluded.

Name.	Residence.	Designation.	Compensation.	Date of Election or Appointment.
Henry T. McConell	41 White st	Fireman	$17.00 wk	Dec. 20, 1907
Patrick McGuigan	87 Cottage st	"	17.00 "	" 22, 1899
John McQuade	148 Falcon st	"	17.00 "	" 23, 1907
Franklin B. Metcalf	21 White st	"	17.00 "	March, 1890
James Mooney	155 Everett st	"	17.00 "	April 28, 1905
Owen Moore	38 Fuller st	"	17.00 "	Nov. 16, 1908
Patrick Morrissey	64 Centre st	"	17.00 "	Oct. 9, 1907
Thomas Murphy	67 Meridian st	"	17.00 "	March 3, 1907
Maurice H. Neville	28 W. Sixth st	"	17.00 "	April 18, 1900
John H. Nolan	111 Chelsea st	"	17.00 "	" 18, 1905
Henry E. Pingree	259 Havre st	"	17.00 "	July 28, 1908
Patrick Riley	64 Bremen st	"	17.00 "	Dec. 22, 1899
John Seaman	351 Chelsea st	"	17.00 "	Nov. 15, 1907
Richard J. Shaw	129 Byron st	"	17.00 "	Oct. 22, 1899*
Thomas P. Shea	5 Grimes st	"	17.00 "	Dec. 20, 1907
William J. Smith	24 Paris st	"	17.00 "	Feb. 10, 1892
Michael Sullivan	24 Boyd st	"	17.00 "	" 21, 1908
John Turvanen	228 Princeton st	"	17.00 "	July 28, 1908
Mrs. Mary Duggan	229 Bennington st	Janitress	480 yr	April 24, 1907
Mrs. Ellen C. Green	193 Marion st	"	480 "	" 14, 1905
Mrs. Jennie F. Hughes	663 Saratoga st	"	480 "	Jan. 17, 1908
Mrs. Bridget McKenney	169 Bennington st	"	480 "	March, 1883
Mrs. Daphne Sullivan	277 Paris st	"	480 "	Dec. 22, 1907
Timothy Harrington	6 Meridian st	Stockkeeper	900 "	Jan. 28, 1902
James Kerly	269 Sumner st	Rigger	1,080 "	April 4, 1902
William Kissock	242 Princeton st	Lamplighter	840 "	Sept., 1874
Dennis McCarthy	42 Bennington st	"	840 "	April, 1887
Horatio L. Nelson	1 Short st	Laborer	840 "	" 14, 1905
Christopher T. Leonard	78 Chelsea st	"	2.25 day	March 20, 1908
James A. McLaughlin	3 Seaver st	"	2.50 "	Dec. 23, 1905
Henry C. Barnard	213 Trenton st	"	2.25 "	June 25, 1908
Patrick Henry	368 Bremen st	"	2.25 "	April 21, 1902
Joseph O. White	32 Haynes st	"	2.25 "	Jan. 22, 1904
Francis A. Whealan	29 Maverick sq	Boat Watchman	2.25 "	Dec. 7, 1903
Daniel F. Harrigan	12 Chelsea st	Janitor	2.25 "	May 22, 1893
Charles A. Kelly	73 Maverick st	"	2.25 "	April 25, 1902
Michael E. Rice	33 Maverick sq	"	2.25 "	Jan. 22, 1904
J. Herbert Sullivan	104 Eutaw st	"	2.25 "	March, 1881
William H. Wise	153 Leyden st	"	2.25 "	Jan. 23, 1897
Stephen D. Snow	19 Torrey st	Boilermaker	3.00 "	Nov., 1876
Henry J. Callahan	191 London st	"	3.00 "	April 11, 1902
George W. Emery	250 Shawmut ave	Painter	3.16 "	May 9, 1900
John A. Buckley	462 Saratoga st	"	3.00 "	Jan. 22, 1904
Jeremiah F. Coleman	49 Meridian st	"	3.00 "	Dec. 30, 1902
James E. Doyle	440 Saratoga st	Boss Joiner	4.00 "	April 13, 1900
Marshall Brown	120 London st	Joiner	3.50 "	Feb. 2, 1904
John H. Claney	186 Webster st	"	3.50 "	April 11, 1902
Michael E. Moran	218 Webster st	Boss Ship Carpenter	3.50 "	Jan. 22, 1904
John E. Burke	13 London st	Ship Carpenter	3.50 "	Nov. 22, 1907
Jeremiah J. Donovan	177 Franklin st	Roofer	3.25 "	June 7, 1907
James A. Douglass	579 Saratoga st	Electrician	3.60 "	Sept. 30, 1907
John J. Hassett	35 Batchelder st	Machinist Helper	2.75 "	Feb. 27, 1906

Lamp Division.

Name.	Residence.	Designation.	Compensation.	Date of Election or Appointment.
Edward C. Wade	87 Bellevue st	Deputy Superintendent	$2,000 yr	April 14, 1908†
George H. Rymill	10 Perham st	Clerk	1,800 "	" 14, 1889
Michael T. Callahan	16 Charles st	Messenger	1,040 "	" 4, 1896
Edgar O. Haddock	14 Edson st	Inspector	900 "	May 1, 1907
Lawrence Kennedy, Jr.	53 Parsons st	"	2.50 day	Sept. 8, 1905
John F. Mahoney	67 Baldwin st	"	900 yr	May 13, 1902
Thomas A. Lynch	14 School st	"	900 "	" 1, 1907
James McHugh	25 E. Cottage st	"	2.25 day	" 1, 1907

Paving Division.

Office.

Name.	Residence.	Designation.	Compensation.	Date of Election or Appointment.
James H. Sullivan	10 Longfellow st	Deputy Superintendent	$3,500 yr	Sept. 14, 1900
Bernard C. Kelley	15 Gates st	Chief Clerk	2,500 "	April 30, 1888
John F. Brennan	22 Pleasant st., Chsn	Clerk	1,500 "	July 25, 1898

* Previously employed in this division.
† Promoted to present position on date given. Previously in the department.

Street Department (Paving Division).— Continued.

Name.	Residence.	Designation.	Com-pensation.	Date of Election or Appointment.

Office.— Concluded.

Chester E. Tarbell	343 Washington st., Dor	Clerk	$1,400 yr	June 9, 1899
Andrew A. O'Dowd	17 Ruthven st	"	1,200 "	" 6, 1891
Henry J. McGuiness	57 W. Eagle st	"	800 "	July 7, 1908
Edward J. Houghton	51 Bowdoin st	"	800 "	" 21, 1908
Alfred J. Hannon	76 Dorchester st	"	3.50 day	June 22, 1900
Joseph H. Mellyn	11 Mayfair st	Stenographer	1,400 yr	Oct. 14, 1898
Robert J. Mason	4 Anderson st	Messenger	2.50 day	May 7, 1896
Arthur H. Davison	337 Talbot ave	Examining Physician	1,500 yr	Dec. 1, 1908

Permit Office.

Storrs S. Durkee	194 Quincy st	Permit Clerk	$1,800 yr	Oct. 26, 1908
Luke H. Leonard	131 Franklin st., Bri	Clerk and Inspector	1,100 "	Jan. 9, 1897
James H. Madden	36 Linden Park st	" "	3.50 day	Aug. 13, 1891
John F. Doyle	34 Greenwich pk	Clerk	800 "	" 6, 1897
Patrick C. Kelly	7 Cordis st	Street Numbering Inspector,	1,200 "	" 7, 1897
John J. Hayes	26 Mapleton st., Bri	"	3.00 day	July 18, 1902
Edward M. Richardson	78 Surrey st., Bri	Inspector of Property	4.00 "	" 3, 1908
William Lawless	1 Louise pk., Rox	Inspector	3.50 "	Sept. 23, 1896
Francis H. Maloney	1413 Washington st	"	3.50 "	May 29, 1891
Frederick A. Breen	259 Silver st	"	3.00 "	Sept. 12, 1899
John F. Cullen	27 Clifton st., Rox	"	3.00 "	Dec. 14, 1906
John P. Dinand	59 Bowdoin ave., Dor	"	3.00 "	Aug. 16, 1900
Walter Jenkins	51 River st., Dor	"	3.00 "	May 12, 1900
James H. Keveney	66 L st., S. B	"	3.00 "	Aug. 6, 1897
William J. Kilduff	38 Norfolk st., Rox	"	3.00 "	Jan. 29, 1897
Edward A. McGrath	2 Savin st	"	3.00 "	July 16, 1900
Michael F. O'Brien	24 Edgewood st	"	3.00 "	Feb. 25, 1903
Frederick C. Power	16 Glenwood st	"	3.00 "	Sept. 17, 1902
Ralph E. Reardon	673 Saratoga st	"	3.00 "	Aug. 11, 1900
John J. Mullen	62 Forest st., Rox	Aid	3.50 "	March 23, 1892
James A. Sugrue	81 Franklin st., Bri	Chauffeur	3.50 "	" 26, 1907

Engineers.

Joshua Atwood, 3d	280 Foster st., Bri	Chief Engineer	$3,000 yr	Jan. 24, 1902
Dwight L. Hubbard	645 Washington st., Bri	Junior Assistant Engineer	4.50 day	Sept. 14, 1900
Hiram R. Chubbuck	523 Park st., Dor	"	4.50 "	" 14, 1900
Edwin T. Hoisington	25 Clement ave	"	4.00 "	Jan. 12, 1904
Frank O. Holmes	1343 Blue Hill ave., Dor	Instrumentman	3.50 "	Aug. 6, 1903
George L. Grainger	218 Princeton st., E. B	"	3.00 "	Oct. 15, 1903
John V. Corbett	45 Speedwell st	Rodman	2.50 "	May 13, 1901
James J. Doyle	26 Monument st., Chsn	"	2.50 "	July 22, 1908
James C. Gallagher	96 Mt. Pleasant ave	Clerk	1,200 yr	May 29, 1901
George R. Starkey	46 Vose st., Dor	"	800 "	July 16, 1908
Thomas W. H. Kelly	241 Columbus ave	Inspector	4.00 day	Sept. 23, 1896
Lloyd H. Chase	45 Clarendon st	"	3.00 "	May 11, 1900
Patrick H. Connolly	113 Warren st., Rox	"	3.00 "	Sept. 24, 1897
Edmund J. Fitzgerald	2 Gore st., Rox	"	3.00 "	Aug. 22, 1902
James D. Gorman	107 Hancock st., Dor	"	3.00 "	June 10, 1904
Frank J. Hasson	16 Fairbury st	"	3.00 "	Sept. 24, 1897
George W. Jepson	23 Congreve st	"	3.00 "	Aug. 2, 1904
William J. Lynch	286 E. Ninth st	"	3.00 "	Oct. 4, 1898
Frank E. Martin	328 Centre st., J. P	"	3.00 "	Sept. 21, 1896
Frank A. Corcoran	96 Erie st	Sub-foreman	3.00 "	Oct. 24, 1902
Thomas Ring	8 Winship st	Coachman	2.50 "	March 4, 1905
Frank Lynch	37 Mercer st	Axeman	2.50 "	April 22, 1902

District No. 1.— South Boston.

William A. Fitzgerald	609 E. Ninth st	Foreman	$1,800 yr	May 5, 1890
John Barry	64 Telegraph st	Sub-foreman	3.50 day	Oct., 1878
John J. Devlin	570 E. Second st	"	3.50 "	Dec. 5, 1902
Alexander T. King	729 Washington st., Dor	"	3.00 "	" 14, 1906
William Thomas	442 E. Sixth st	"	3.50 "	Oct. 16, 1896
John J. McGinn	178 I st	Inspector	3.50 "	April 17, 1902
Michael T. Harrington	636 E. Fifth st	Laborer	2.25 "	Aug. 4, 1902
Jeffrey Eager	609 E. Ninth st	Messenger	3.00 "	Feb. 8, 1895
Peter B. Mooney	713 E. Fifth st	Carpenter's Helper	2.75 "	Dec., 1883
Michael Mulkern	256 Bowen st	"	2.25 "	July, 1884
Daniel Bresnahan	132 Abbott st	Patchpaver	2.75 "	Oct., 1873
Patrick Hartnett	102 I st	"	3.00 "	June, 1865

Street Department (Paving Division). — Continued.

Name.	Residence.	Designation.	Compensation.	Date of Election or Appointment.

District No. 1. — South Boston. — Concluded.

Name.	Residence.	Designation.	Compensation.	Date of Election or Appointment.
Dennis Looney	26 Bellflower st	Patchpaver	$3.00 day	Aug., 1877
Andrew O'Shaughnessy	213 E. Eighth st	Paver	3.00 "	Sept., 1884
John Connell	82 Baxter st	"	2.75 "	April, 1902
Dennis Crowley	512 E. Fourth st	Stonecutter	3.00 "	May 2, 1891
John D. Quinn	39 Dwight st	Wharfman	2.50 "	March 8, 1907
John Kirby	152 W. Third st	Blacksmith's Helper	2.25 "	April 13, 1904
Richard A. Delaney	6 W. Sixth st, pl	Rammer	2.25 "	Nov. 30, 1897
Cornelius J. Harrington	725 E. Seventh st	"	2.50 "	Sept. 18, 1903
Nicholas Lynch	63 Dorchester st	"	2.25 "	April 21, 1906
Daniel J. McNamara	39 Howell st	Laborer	2.25 "	Aug., 1884
Patrick F. McNamara	589 E. Second st	"	2.25 "	Sept. 30, 1905
John T. McCarthy	537 E. Fourth st	Rammer	2.75 "	Jan. 22, 1904
John Clancy	12 I st	Teamster	2.25 "	July, 1883
Martin Devine	484 E. Fifth st	"	2.25 "	April, 1884
John Dinneen	212 E st	"	2.25 "	Oct., 1879
Michael J. Lynch	4 W. Fifth st	"	2.25 "	Jan. 8, 1904
William J. Lyons	3 Wellington pl	"	2.25 "	May 1, 1879
John J. Maher	262 W. Broadway	"	2.25 "	Sept. 16, 1904
Cornelius McCarthy	730 E. Second st	"	2.25 "	" 1884
Jeremiah Ryan	592 E. Fourth st	"	2.25 "	March, 1876
Michael H. Sheedy	208 W. Seventh st	Stableman	2.25 "	Aug., 1884
Melvin D. Brackett	98 F st	Laborer	2.25 "	May, 1883
Luke Burns	56 H st	"	2.25 "	April, 1887
Patrick J. Curran	287 C st	"	2.25 "	Oct. 9, 1903
John M. Dacey	149 Bowen st	"	2.25 "	May 22, 1903
Patrick Devlin	324 W. Fourth st	"	2.25 "	1876
Edward Dempsey	159 W. Sixth st	"	2.25 "	Sept. 13, 1895
John Donahoe	22 Ward st	"	2.25 "	July, 1882
Edward Emmett	121 L st	"	2.25 "	June, 1863
Matthew Foley	204 E. Ninth st	"	2.25 "	Oct., 1883
John Freeland	70 Sagamore st	"	2.25 "	Sept. 10, 1900
Timothy A. Hayes	3 Saxton st	"	2.25 "	June 8, 1906
Arthur Hickey	431 E. Third st	"	2.25 "	July 30, 1906
Elmer H. Kendall	581 E. Ninth st	"	2.25 "	Dec. 3, 1901
Edward J. Lane	19 Knowlton st	"	2.25 "	Aug. 21, 1903
Andrew Moynihan	154 C st	"	2.25 "	Oct. 4, 1892
Patrick O'Donnell	930 E. Fourth st	"	2.25 "	April 2, 1895
John Smith	611 E. Seventh st	"	2.25 "	Oct. 2, 1900
Thomas J. Sullivan	19 I st	"	2.25 "	" 23, 1895
Michael Tierney	45 Crescent ave	"	2.25 "	" 15, 1892
James J. Willock	759 Columbia rd	"	2.25 "	Sept. 11, 1897
John W. Woods	10 Beckler ave	"	2.25 "	April 4, 1901

District No. 2. — East Boston.

Name.	Residence.	Designation.	Compensation.	Date of Election or Appointment.
James Maguire	41 Collins st	Sub-foreman	$3.50 day	April 14, 1899
Eugene F. Sullivan	297 Maverick st	"	3.50 "	Nov. 8, 1897
William F. Delehanty	266 Princeton st	Clerk	3.00 "	April 17, 1902
Charles J. Regan	357 W. Fourth st	Inspector	3.50 "	Aug. 6, 1897
Horace Sias	37 Wordsworth st	"	3.50 "	May 9, 1900
John C. King	227 Trenton st	Hoisting and Portable Eng.	3.50 "	April 24, 1906*
Bernard J. McGovern †	75 Chelsea st	Engineer	3.00 "	" 30, 1906
Daniel A. McDonald	104 Bennington st	Carpenter	3.50 "	Nov. 3, 1904
John Dobbin	317 Paris st	Patchpaver	3.00 "	May, 1883
Thomas McColgan	467 Sumner st	"	3.00 "	April 18, 1902
James O'Malley	240 Maverick st	"	3.00 "	Aug. 7, 1903
Michael Sullivan	229 Bennington st	"	3.00 "	May 20, 1898
Dennis Buckley	30A Bunker Hill st	Stonecutter	3.50 "	Feb. 19, 1902
Walter W. Delehanty	56 Sumner st	"	3.00 "	March 10, 1902
John J. Crowley	70 London st	Stableman	2.75 "	" 24, 1902
Richard F. O'Niel	430 Bennington st	"	2.25 "	" 3, 1905
Timothy Boyan	304 Chelsea st	Teamster	2.25 "	" 8, 1907
William E. Cronan	351 Chelsea st	"	2.25 "	Oct. 25, 1890
Thomas Cunningham	214 Bennington st	"	2.25 "	Aug. 9, 1905
John Ryan	460 Bremen st	"	2.25 "	July 5, 1895
William F. Gallagher	466 Saratoga st	Laborer	2.25 "	April 17, 1902
Joseph F. Berry	320 Chelsea st	"	2.25 "	Sept., 1899
Nicholas Brennan	620 Saratoga st	"	2.25 "	July, 1879
Thomas Boyan	552 Bennington st	"	2.25 "	Nov. 9, 1899
Cornelius Donovan	487 Chelsea st	"	2.25 "	May, 1872
Jeremiah T. Donahoe	14 Havre st	"	2.25 "	Oct. 9, 1908

* Previously in the department.   † Transferred from Ferry Division.

Street Department (Paving Division).— Continued.

Name.	Residence.	Designation.	Compensation.	Date of Election or Appointment.
District No. 2.—East Boston.— Concluded.				
Timothy F. Donovan	225 Paris st	Laborer	$2.25 day	March 19, 1909
Michael Doyle	153 Falcon st	"	2.25 "	May 19, 1891
James E. Fitzpatrick	246 Havre st	"	2.25 "	June 12, 1908
Edward Gallinaugh	189 Havre st	"	2.25 "	April 28, 1902
John E. Harrington	461 Sumner st	"	2.25 "	Feb. 17, 1902
John Healey	704 Saratoga st	"	2.25 "	April 18, 1896
Richard I. Howard	108 Byron st	"	2.25 "	Aug. 8, 1902
George McCarthy	431 Frankfort st	"	2.25 "	" 10, 1895
Thomas McCullogh	525 Bennington st	"	2.25 "	Nov. 10, 1899
Michael J. Ryan	300 Paris st	"	2.25 "	Sept. 8, 1898
Daniel Smith	154 Putnam st	Watchman	2.25 "	April 11, 1904
Patrick Sullivan	149 Trenton st	Laborer	2.25 "	May, 1874
Michael Sweeney	97 Bennington st	"	2.25 "	Aug. 23, 1900
District No. 3.— Charlestown.				
John F. Owen	251 Princeton st., E. B.	Foreman	$1,800 yr	June 16, 1908
James J. McElaney	11 Park st	"	3.00 day	April 14, 1902
Charles J. Gabriel	9 Polk st	Sub-foreman	3.50 "	May, 1868
John F. Toomey	103½ High st	"	3.50 "	Jan. 5, 1905
John F. Donovan	87 Elm st	Clerk	3.00 "	June, 1883
Joseph Dowd	29 Green st	Carpenter	3.50 "	Dec. 30, 1902
Daniel Green	4 Princeton st	Carpenter's Helper	2.75 "	Jan. 27, 1902
Richard Doherty	26 Princeton st	Stonecutter	3.00 "	May 22, 1893
Thomas F. Flynn	47 High st	"	3.00 "	June, 1884
Patrick T. Gill	61 Walnut st	Laborer	2.25 "	Dec. 4, 1897
Hugh Canny	45 Pearl st	Patchpaver	2.50 "	May 23, 1902
John Devlin	48 Tremont st	"	3.00 "	" 29, 1907
John J. Galvin	11 Park st	"	3.00 "	Aug. 24, 1900
Patrick Kelly	38 Everett st	"	3.00 "	June 20, 1882
Charles Logue	16 Common st	"	3.00 "	Oct. 29, 1897
Peter Mellen	8 Everett st	"	2.75 "	April 13, 1903
Jeremiah C. O'Donovan	2 Riorden pl	"	3.00 "	Feb. 1, 1902
Daniel McKenna	82 Monument st	Laborer	2.25 "	Dec. 29, 1905
Thomas E. Burns	339 Bunker Hill st	Rammer	2.25 "	May 1, 1891
Daniel J. Callaghan	5 Holden row	"	2.25 "	March 14, 1902
Timothy Sullivan	55 High st	Laborer	2.25 "	" 18, 1904
James Gilday	81 Elm st	Tallyman	2.25 "	June 21, 1905
Charles J. Jacobs	32 Austin st	Stableman	2.75 "	July 3, 1908
John D. Miller	42 Bunker Hill st	"	2.25 "	Nov. 15, 1897
John F. McCormack	92 Henley st	"	2.25 "	Oct. 7, 1904
John Conroy	47 Allston st	Teamster	2.25 "	July 15, 1889
Michael Doyle	40½ Bunker Hill st	"	2.25 "	May 1, 1901
Joseph R. Everett	69 Monument st	"	2.25 "	" 1, 1891
William Kelly	38 Moulton st	"	2.25 "	July 2, 1898
John Welch	85 Alford st	"	2.25 "	June 4, 1906
Cornelius J. Collins	21 Cook st	Laborer	2.25 "	Jan. 1, 1895
Simon J. Cullinane	39 Auburn st	"	2.25 "	May 28, 1897
Daniel Doherty	6 Short street pl	"	2.25 "	Sept. 24, 1895
Timothy Doherty	92 Decatur st	"	2.25 "	Oct. 2, 1908
James Fitzgibbons	41 Washington st	"	2.25 "	April 3, 1902
Edward Harrington	31 School st	"	2.25 "	Oct. 10, 1902
Michael C. Horgan	4 Roughan rd	"	2.25 "	March 8, 1901
Daniel C. Kelley	4 Hill st	"	2.25 "	Aug. 19, 1908
John J. Kelley	Rutherford ave. cor. Arrow	"	2.25 "	" 19, 1908
Hugh Keenan	37 Soley st	"	2.25 "	May 1, 1891
Timothy F. Leonard	27 Albion pl	"	2.25 "	April 30, 1898
James T. Mahan	51 Tufts st	"	2.25 "	March 19, 1909
William J. McNulty	30 Pearl st	"	2.25 "	Aug. 19, 1908
Edward Moss	322 Medford st	"	2.25 "	July 22, 1895
Bernard McCabe	26 Decatur st	"	2.25 "	May 2, 1891
Dennis Nihan	79 Austin st	"	2.25 "	Aug., 1884
Edward Rogers	11 Marion st	"	2.25 "	July 3, 1908
Thomas H. Rorke	3 Mystic st	"	2.25 "	Jan. 24, 1906
Mortimer J. Sullivan	65 School st	"	2.25 "	May 1, 1891
John E. Tierney	372 Bunker Hill st	"	2.25 "	June 23, 1908
District No. 4.— Brighton.				
Dennis A. Kennedy	30 Greenwich pk	Foreman	$1,800 yr	Jan. 14, 1908*
James P. Coyle	60 Parsons st	Sub-foreman	3.50 day	Feb. 26, 1906
James E. McCullum	100 Devon st	"	3.50 "	" 19, 1902

* Previously in department.

Street Department (Paving Division).— Continued.

Name.	Residence.	Designation.	Compensation	Date of Election or Appointment.

District No. 4.— Brighton.— Concluded.

Name.	Residence.	Designation.	Compensation	Date of Election or Appointment.
John T. Sweeney	11 Hobart st	Sub-foreman	$3.50 day	March 14, 1902
Arthur F. Murphy	709 E. Broadway	Acting Sub-foreman	2.25 "	May 11, 1896
Elisha N. Brady	227 Roxbury st	Clerk	800 yr.	Nov. 7, 1908
J. Francis Chickey	88 Parsons st	"	800 "	April 30, 1900
William A. McDevitt	38 Pratt st	Inspector	3.50 day	June 24, 1896
Arthur T. Wilson	65 Dunboy st	"	3.50 "	May 22, 1908
William Mullen	9 Shannon st	Blacksmith	3.50 "	Dec. 6, 1894
Kirk W. Caldwell	81 Chestnut Hill ave	Carpenter	3.50 "	June 23, 1891
James J. Sullivan	44 Bennett st	"	3.50 "	April 27, 1896
Patrick Conly	215 L st	Engineer	3.50 "	May 20, 1896
James B. Dolan	12A New Heath st	"	3.50 "	Jan. 10, 1897
John Hickey	94 Murdock st	"	3.50 "	June 11, 1902
William Concannon	51 Shannon st	Patchpaver	3.00 "	Nov. 15, 1904
Michael Doyle	13 Raymond st	"	3.00 "	" 6, 1902
James Byrne	23 Winship st	"	2.75 "	July 11, 1899
Michael Maher	222 Hemenway st	Stonecutter	3.00 "	Nov. 13, 1900
Andrew T. Roach	47 Greenwich pl	Weigher	2.50 "	Feb. 20, 1903
Patrick Phelan	38 Harriet st	Steamdriller	2.25 "	July, 1874
Daniel Finn	210 C st	Yardman	2.25 "	June, 1871
William McLaughlin	246 Washington st., Bri	Stableman	2.25 "	Aug. 8, 1876
Patrick Vericker	691 Shawmut ave	"	2.25 "	Dec. 11, 1902
Frank Burns	71 Garden st	Teamster	2.50 "	Oct. 22, 1902
Jeremiah Connors	43 Snow st	"	2.25 "	May 22, 1891
James Cullen	rear 54 Lincoln st	"	2.25 "	March, 1884
Dennis Donovan	43 Snow st	"	2.25 "	May 4, 1895
William P. Igoe	30 Winship st	"	2.25 "	" 3, 1895
Neil McAnulty	14 Shannon st	"	2.25 "	" 4, 1895
James McKenney	9 Shannon st	"	2.25 "	" 1, 1883
John Ring	8 Winship st	"	2.25 "	July 18, 1874
Michael Tighe	80 Foster st	"	2.25 "	May 4, 1895
Wallace R. Marie	302 Washington st., Bri	Watchman	2.25 "	" 25, 1900
John J. Tatten	8 School st	"	2.25 "	Jan., 1888
John Welch	40 Colwell ave	"	2.25 "	" 2, 1902
Thomas Akin	rear 25 Shepard st	Laborer	2.25 "	March, 1874
Bartley Barrett	38 Shannon st	"	2.25 "	Jan., 1873
Michael Burke	49 Spring st	"	2.25 "	May 6, 1895
Michael Byrne	20A Winship st	"	2.25 "	" 6, 1883
Neil Campbell	33 Sheridan st	"	2.25 "	March 22, 1899
Thomas Cleary	12 Portsmouth st	"	2.25 "	May 6, 1895
Patrick Costello	22 Belmont st	"	2.25 "	July, 1889
John Cox	365 Market st	"	2.25 "	" 16, 1888
William Cox	8 Peaceable st	"	2.25 "	May 4, 1895
Edward Davis	La Rose pl	"	2.25 "	Dec. 29, 1905
Dennis Desmond	5 Baldwin pl	"	2.25 "	April 22, 1895
Patrick Divan	27 Shannon st	"	2.25 "	" 22, 1895
Thomas Flynn	Warren st. cor Com. ave	"	2.25 "	" 22, 1895
Patrick Foley	34 Windham st	"	2.25 "	Jan. 2, 1900
Patrick Ford	rear Warren block	"	2.25 "	July 16, 1888
John Gleason	12 Sharon st	"	2.25 "	May, 1895
James Hickey	249 N. Beacon st	"	2.25 "	March, 1885
Patrick Hickey	21 Shannon st	"	2.25 "	May, 1883
George A. Hurley	107 Calumet st	"	2.25 "	Nov. 30, 1906*
John Kelley	37 Snow st	"	2.25 "	May 6, 1895
William Kelly	449 Main st	"	2.25 "	Aug. 19, 1908
Eben E. Kimball	rear Monument st	"	2.25 "	" 27, 1908
Daniel King	12 Rena st	"	2.25 "	Sept. 4, 1901
Edward Lennon	136 N. Harvard st	"	2.25 "	May, 1881
John G. Meserve	99 E. Canton st	"	2.25 "	Nov. 15, 1907
John McCann	487 Washington st., Bri	"	2.25 "	June, 1882
John McCarthy	309 Washington st., Bri	"	2.25 "	Aug. 1, 1884
John McCarthy, 2d	22 Shannon st	"	2.25 "	April 4, 1901
John McGrail	414 Washington st., Bri	"	2.25 "	May 13, 1901
Joseph McLean	24 Arlington st	"	2.25 "	Dec. 29, 1905
Patrick Neville	28 Newton st	"	2.25 "	May, 1884
John J. Noonan	94 N. Beacon st	"	2.25 "	Nov. 20, 1904
Patrick Powers	47 Waverley st	"	2.25 "	July 16, 1902
Edward Russell	9 Peaceable st	"	2.25 "	Sept. 12, 1873
John Russell	8 Newton st	"	2.25 "	" 18, 1873
John Ryan	8 Whitney st	"	2.25 "	July 22, 1895
Michael Shine	4 Eastburn st	"	2.25 "	Aug. 23, 1900
John P. Sweeney	133 Roxbury st	"	2.25 "	June 16, 1905

* Previously in the department.

Street Department (Paving Division).— Continued.

Name.	Residence.	Designation.	Compensation.	Date of Election or Appointment.

District No. 5.— West Roxbury.

Name.	Residence.	Designation.	Compensation.	Date of Election or Appointment.
Thomas H. Duffy	27 Ballard st	Foreman	$1,800 yr.	Feb. 10, 1900
John H. Loughlan	327 Walk Hill st	"	3.00 day	Sept. 14, 1906
Thomas Comdry	68 Keyes st	Sub-foreman	3.50 "	May, 1884
Michael T. Cuddy	129 Sycamore st	"	3.50 "	Dec. 26, 1905
William R. Jeffrey	41 Mozart st	"	3.50 "	July 17, 1900
James Kehoe	58 Heath st	"	3.50 "	Feb. 4, 1902
George H. Kelley	3379 Washington st	"	3.50 "	Sept., 1897
Patrick J. O'Neill	59 Ashland ave	"	3.50 "	March 11, 1903
Henry A. Holden	53 Olney st	Clerk	2.50 "	Aug. 18, 1900
William L. Carty	73 Dudley ave	Inspector	3.00 "	" 18, 1897
Patrick J. Kyle	6 Mt. Vernon ave	"	3.00 "	Jan. 25, 1897
George W. Zeigler	170 Amory st	"	3.00 "	Sept., 1896
Timothy J. O'Connell	46 Newbern st	Weigher	2.75 "	June 4, 1908
Joseph A. Hennessy	19 Myrtle st	Carpenter	3.50 "	Jan. 22, 1904
Thomas H. Waters	1 Union ave	"	3.50 "	Aug. 28, 1891
John H. Lang	34 Goldsmith st	Engineer	3.50 "	June 27, 1895
Thomas H. Glennon	182 Keyes st	Patchpaver	2.50 "	Sept. 5, 1902
Michael McDonald	106 Child st	"	2.50 "	" 5, 1902
Martin Thornton	72 Child st	"	2.50 "	" 16, 1904
John C. Woodward	101 Carolina ave	Painter	2.25 "	Jan. 1, 1902
Edward Donlon	65 Penfield st	Stableman	2.25 "	June, 1889
Michael Cady	59 Jamaica st	Teamster	2.25 "	May, 1873
William S. Clancy	26 Custer st	"	2.25 "	" 18, 1891
Edward Cook	53 South st	"	2.25 "	June, 1883
John English	25 St. Rose st	"	2.25 "	May, 1881
Michael Fitzgerald	34 Jamaica st	"	2.25 "	March, 1873
William J. Galvin	93 Paine st	"	2.25 "	Jan. 21, 1902
James Glynn	9 Ballard st	"	2.25 "	Sept. 28, 1891
Michael C. Heaney	97 Call st	"	2.25 "	Aug. 19, 1895
Daniel Murray	68 Seaver st	"	2.25 "	May, 1891
Patrick Murray	33 Jamaica st	"	2.25 "	Aug., 1882
Timothy S. Lyons	30 Jamaica st	Harnessmaker	2.25 "	May 10, 1907
Daniel J. Dooling	36 Goldsmith st	Driver	2.25 "	Oct. 6,1905
Martin Coy	20 Ray st	Powderman	2.50 "	Jan., 1874
Timothy McLaughlin	63 Johnson st	"	2.25 "	Dec. 28, 1896
John Kelley	104 Keyes st	Ledgeman	2.25 "	May 18, 1903
Cornelius O'Neil	12 Adams st	"	2.25 "	June 7, 1907
Michael Harney	37 Keyes st	Watchman	2.25 "	May, 1882
William C. Porter	58 Child st	"	2.25 "	" 1874
Henry M. Carroll	25 Belle ave	Laborer	2.25 "	" 29, 1891
Peter Carty	12 Haverford st	"	2.25 "	Aug., 1884
Michael Conway	357 Baker st	"	2.25 "	Sept. 2, 1892
Edward Dolan	25 Ballard st	"	2.25 "	" 3, 1873
Michael Dolan	37 Custer st	"	2.25 "	July 18, 1902
Patrick Dolan	3 Ballard pl	"	2.25 "	Dec. 28, 1900
Patrick Downing	Williams st., J. P.	"	2.25 "	May, 1884
Patrick Finnerty	97 Child st	"	2.25 "	July 18, 1889
James H. Fitzgerald	23 Woodman st	"	2.25 "	May 8, 1891
Martin Gateley	31 St. Rose st	"	2.25 "	June 18, 1899
John Gardner	41 Ballard st	"	2.25 "	April, 1873
John Godvin	11 Carolina ave	"	2.25 "	Dec. 7, 1895
Timothy Griffin	Pond st., J. P.	"	2.25 "	May 18, 1891
John Healey	149 Orange st	"	2.25 "	Dec. 10, 1900
Edward F. Hines	4 Mills st	"	2.25 "	March 18, 1904
Michael Hughes	270½ Centre st	"	2.25 "	April 4, 1900
Bernard J. Kelley	90 Jamaica st	"	2.25 "	May, 1889
Michael Kelley	22 Byron st	"	2.25 "	June, 1895
William Kelley	30 Alaric st	"	2.25 "	Nov., 1890
Thomas F. Kinahan	122 Day st	"	2.25 "	March 2, 1904
John Leonard	50 Keyes st	"	2.25 "	May, 1882
Patrick Leonard	119 Hyde Park ave	"	2.25 "	" 18, 1891
William H. Leonard	63 Keyes st	"	2.25 "	Dec. 8, 1905
Jeremiah S. Long	31 Hyde Park ave	"	2.25 "	Oct. 8, 1892
Edmund Lynch	97 Paine st	"	2.25 "	July, 1895
John W. Lynch	1980 Centre st	"	2.25 "	Aug. 10, 1895
Patrick C. Mahoney	11½ Woodlawn st	"	2.25 "	" 29, 1905
Hubert W. May	316 Amory st	"	2.25 "	July, 1889
Timothy J. Mullins	82 E. Newton st	"	2.25 "	Feb. 7, 1908
William H. Mulrey	39 Keyes st	"	2.25 "	June, 1881
Patrick J. McCarron	206 Endicott st	"	2.25 "	" 20, 1902
George J. McCormack	222 Keyes st	"	2.25 "	Sept. 5, 1902
William McLaughlin	961 Canterbury st	"	2.25 "	Aug. 21, 1908

Street Department (Paving Division). — Continued.

Name.	Residence.	Designation.	Compensation	Date of Election or Appointment.
District No. 5.— West Roxbury. —Concluded.				
William T. Noonan	95 Child st	Laborer	$2.25 day	Aug. 6, 1908*
William Osborn	3 Germania st	"	2.25 "	Sept. 12, 1892
Jeremiah Phillips	7 Smith ct	"	2.25 "	Aug. 28, 1895
Timothy Reardon	184 Spring st	"	2.25 "	Jan. 1, 1908
Thomas Reynolds	8 Perkins st	"	2.25 "	March 11, 1902
James Stewart	102 Call st	"	2.25 "	May 18, 1891
John J. Tarpey	17 Keyes st	"	2.25 "	" 1891
John B. Tighe	63 Wachusett st	"	2.25 "	Dec. 17, 1897
James Walsh	20 Hyde Park ave	"	2.25 "	March 9, 1909
Lawrence B. Welch	102 Sheridan st	"	2.25 "	June, 1899
District No. 6.— Dorchester.				
Benjamin A. Ham	15 Salcombe st	Foreman	$1,800 yr	June 22, 1908
Patrick J. Brannan	35 Holiday st	Sub-foreman	3.50 day	Nov. 27, 1903
Alonzo C. H. Laws	71 Wheatland ave	"	3.50 "	April 30, 1900
William F. Sullivan	34 Church st	Messenger	1,000 yr	" 2, 1902
James F. Clifford	81 Barry st	Carpenter	3.50 day	Dec., 1890
Thomas Cawley	109 River st	Engineer	3.50 "	July 15, 1903
Thomas Gagin	14 Leedsville st	Paver	3.00 "	March 27, 1891
Daniel O'Connell	20 East st	"	3.00 "	May, 1877
Michael Crosby	272 Norfolk ave	"	2.50 "	Sept. 5, 1902
Patrick Duggan	64 Edwin st	"	2.50 "	May 5, 1902
Thomas N. Mulvey	27 Vaughan ave	Stonecutter	2.75 "	Sept. 5, 1902
Thomas Fallon	159 Bowdoin st	Watchman	2.50 "	Nov. 16, 1900
Simon P. Nolan	89 Freeport st	"	2.25 "	Sept. 5, 1891
John Barry	22 Winter st	Ledgeman	2.25 "	May 31, 1901
Patrick Tierney	60 Hecla st	"	2.25 "	July 8, 1895
Daniel Murphy	5 Lyons st	Stableman	2.25 "	May 29, 1903
James Lally	11 St. Margaret st	"	2.25 "	April 4, 1904
Robert Adams	1286 Dorchester ave	Teamster	2.25 "	May, 1895
Richard Cameron	58 Linden st	"	2.25 "	July 5, 1895
John H. Flanders	7 Payson ave	"	2.25 "	Aug., 1880
John Holloran	215 Hancock st	"	2.25 "	" 1887
John Lane	30 Highland st	"	2.25 "	May 5, 1891
Dennis O'Neil	12 Highland st	"	2.25 "	July 18, 1895
Thomas Ryan, 2d	115 Adams st	"	2.25 "	May, 1891
Michael Shaughnessy	2 Clayton pl	"	2.25 "	July 17, 1895
Timothy Callahan	259 Hancock st	Laborer	2.25 "	Sept. 7, 1900
John E. Carney	222 Bowen st	"	2.25 "	Aug. 14, 1908
Patrick Cunningham	57 Greenwich st	"	2.25 "	1872
John Devlin	290 Hancock st	"	2.25 "	Dec. 29, 1897
Dennis Doherty	18 School st., W. R	"	2.25 "	April 4, 1901
Stephen Donohoe	232 W. Fourth st	"	2.25 "	Aug. 25, 1908
John Downey	162 Hancock st	"	2.25 "	May 20, 1901
Thomas Egan	14 Sullivan pl	"	2.25 "	Aug. 16, 1895
Joseph Ennis	36 Chadwick st	"	2.25 "	May, 1885
James Gibbon	413 Bowdoin st	"	2.25 "	Oct. 16, 1895
Michael Hart	15 Dacia st	"	2.25 "	Aug., 1876
Dennis Higgins	124 Quincy st	"	2.25 "	" 1873
John Hopkins	6 Marshfield st	"	2.25 "	1876
Elias Kingsley	22 Margaret st	"	2.25 "	July 16, 1901
John Lally	8 Fenwick st	"	2.25 "	Dec. 10, 1897
Cornelius Minahan	107 Freeport st	"	2.25 "	Aug. 16, 1895
Martin Meehan	Mt Vernon st	"	2.25 "	June, 1884
Timothy Minahan	1243 Dorchester ave	"	2.25 "	July 18, 1895
Michael McDonald	51 Lyons st	"	2.25 "	Sept., 1873
William McGovern	1284 Dorchester ave	"	2.25 "	1878
Patrick Mulrey	181 Bowdoin st	"	2.25 "	Aug. 15, 1895
James H. Noonan	35 Coleman st	"	2.25 "	Oct. 23, 1895
James P. O'Meara	221 W. Ninth st	"	2.25 "	Feb. 12, 1903
Patrick Shea	29 Dacia st	"	2.25 "	July 28, 1905
Bartholomew Spelman	38 Dickens st	"	2.25 "	Dec. 20, 1897
Thomas Welch	25 Lyons st	"	2.25 "	June, 1882
Robert H. J. Wilcox	12 Tuckerman st	"	2.25 "	Aug. 27, 1908
District No. 7.— Roxbury.				
James K. Crowley	7 W. Cottage st	Foreman	$1,800 yr	Feb. 1, 1902
John H. Cassidy	40 Tower st	Sub-foreman	3.50 day	" 4, 1902
John J. Connell	78 Fisher ave	"	3.50 "	Nov. 14, 1896
Constantine Doherty	126 Conant st	"	3.50 "	June, 1880

* Previously in the department.

Street Department (Paving Division).— Continued.

Name.	Residence.	Designation.	Compensation.	Date of Election or Appointment.

District No. 7.— Roxbury.— Continued.

Name.	Residence.	Designation.	Compensation.	Date of Election or Appointment.
John J. Murphy	357 W. Fourth st	Sub-foreman	$3.50 day	Aug. 6, 1907
John H. McCarthy	644 Dudley st	"	3.50 "	April 11, 1902
Patrick H. Fallon	39 Darling st	"	2.50 "	Dec. 26, 1905
William A. Ryan	198 Vernon st	"	2.50 "	" 20, 1905
James M. Hewitt	7 Warwick st	Inspector	3.00 "	Sept. 24, 1897
Francis P. Aieta	8 Barry pk., Dor	Clerk	2.50 "	June 24, 1907
Charles E. Fitzgerald	42 Liverpool st., E. B.	"	800 yr	Nov. 20, 1908
John J. Finneran	6 Abbotsford st	Messenger	2.50 day	April 30, 1906*
James J. Flynn	6 Longmeadow st	Weigher	3.00 "	July 12, 1902
Francis A. Johnson	74 Weld Hill st	"	2.50 "	Feb. 19, 1900
Cornelius J. Donovan	34 Francis st	Blacksmith	3.00 "	Sept., 1889
John White	54 Chadwick st	Tool Sharpener	3.16⅔ "	March 3, 1905
Charles H. Bannister	2 Centre st	Carpenter	3.50 "	Dec. 14, 1896
Thomas M. Cotton	2842 Washington st	"	3.50 "	July, 1859
Anthony McAnulty	26 Clarence st	"	3.50 "	March 2, 1906
John T. Kelley	24 Gardner st	Carpenter's Helper	2.50 "	July 22, 1895
John F. Merrigan	10 Akron st	"	2.25 "	April 28, 1902
Edward P. Blanchard	1 Calder pl	Engineer	3.50 "	June, 1875
Lorenzo Mitchell	293 Centre st	"	3.50 "	May 13, 1891
Patrick McCann	20 Marmion st	"	3.50 "	" 20, 1896
John A. Osborne	1417 Tremont st	"	3.50 "	June, 1888
Daniel F. Madden	18 Codman pk	"	2.50 "	Sept. 16, 1904
James J. Broggie	21 Cranston st	Paver	3.00 "	June 12, 1903
Mark F. Foley	2 Farnum pl	"	3.00 "	" 16, 1902
James Hunt	519 Dudley st	"	3.00 "	March 13, 1902
Dennis B. McLaughlin	480 Brookline ave	"	3.00 "	April, 1882
William Dwyer	502 Parker st	"	2.50 "	June 23, 1902*
Walter McNally	86 Marcella st	"	2.50 "	July 22, 1895
James E. McNulty	10 Chestnut ave	"	2.50 "	Feb. 4, 1902
Andrew Allgaier	9 Leon st	Paver's Helper	2.50 "	Nov. 3, 1902
Thomas Muldoon	2892 Washington st	"	2.25 "	April 9, 1872
Edward B. Sheehy	9 Leon st	"	2.25 "	Feb. 4, 1899
Timothy H. Driscoll	21 Bucknam st	Stonecutter	3.00 "	July 30, 1897
John E. O'Brien	120 Heath st	"	3.00 "	Nov. 22, 1907
Patrick F. Jones	17 Smith st	"	2.50 "	June 28, 1901
Andrew McGann	1 Dewey st	Driver	800 yr	Feb. 19, 1900
Michael H. Killion	228 Highland st	"	2.50 day	" 21, 1902
Cornelius Mee	1473 Columbus ave	Stableman	2.25 "	June 5, 1900
Thomas F. Norton	169 Thornton st	Feeder	2.25 "	April 24, 1902
Patrick Kelley, 4th	820 Parker st	Powderman	3.00 "	June 20, 1874
Patrick Tracey	1003 Columbus ave	"	2.25 "	May 16, 1902
Thomas Nugent	23 Forbes st	Steam Driller	2.25 "	1889
George D. Currie	4 Plant ave	Ledgeman	2.25 "	Aug. 18, 1900
Patrick Gilmore	31 Dacia st	"	2.25 "	May 23, 1907
William Lally	28 Ray st	"	2.25 "	June 20, 1901
John McCarthy	25 Cornwall st	Watchman	2.75 "	Oct. 29, 1897
Patrick Sheehan	23 Walpole st	"	2.75 "	Sept. 16, 1895
John Clabby	27 Leon st	"	2.25 "	March 29, 1901
James Cosgrove	15 Taber st	"	2.25 "	May, 1874
Patrick O'Brien	21 Mansur st	"	2.25 "	July 22, 1895
John Shanney	4 Centre pl	"	2.25 "	Aug. 26, 1895
James F. Sullivan	25 Sunnyside st	"	2.25 "	July 19, 1895
Dennis Cronin	1 St. Alphonsus ave	Teamster	2.25 "	Jan. 5, 1901
Malachi Culahan	113 St. Alphonsus st	"	2.25 "	June, 1884
John Doherty	6 School st	"	2.25 "	Jan. 23, 1899
Francis Griffin	948 Parker st	"	2.25 "	July 22, 1895
Martin Horan	3 Thornton pl	"	2.25 "	June, 1871
Patrick Kelley, 2d	47 Marcella st	"	2.25 "	" 1875
John Moore, 2d	77 Bromley st	"	2.25 "	Sept., 1871
James Murray	28 Wensley st	"	2.25 "	Feb. 8, 1901
Michael Stretch	1 Carlow st	"	2.25 "	July 22, 1895
Timothy Sullivan	98 Lawn st	"	2.25 "	" 1888
Thomas E. Tirrell	269 Highland st	"	2.25 "	May, 1870
Patrick Collins	137 W. Fifth st	Tagman	2.25 "	Dec. 20, 1905
John Atkinson	1013 Columbus ave	Laborer	2.25 "	June, 1890
Peter Ball	943 Parker st	"	2.25 "	Sept. 23, 1895
Michael Bolan	29 Howell st	"	2.25 "	Oct., 1883
Joseph Buckley	5 Crosby pl	"	2.25 "	Sept. 9, 1895
Timothy J. Buckley	1 Wise st	"	2.25 "	Aug. 23, 1900
Patrick H. Burke	169 Heath st	"	2.25 "	Sept. 21, 1900
William Carson	55 Roxbury st	"	2.25 "	Oct. 6, 1900

*Previously in the department.

Street Department (Paving Division).— Continued.

Name.	Residence.	Designation.	Compensation	Date of Election or Appointment.

District No. 7.— Roxbury.— Concluded.

Name.	Residence.	Designation.	Compensation	Date of Election or Appointment.
Neil Cassidy	8 Carmel st	Laborer	$2.25 day	Feb. 8, 1904
Thomas Cloren	21 Forbes st	"	2.25 "	Oct. 26, 1896
Michael Costello	117 Smith st	"	2.25 "	July 22, 1895
Patrick Costello	120 Quincy st	"	2.25 "	" 1889
Patrick Curley	332 Amory st	"	2.25 "	May 9, 1895
Patrick Dennehy	710 Shawmut ave	"	2.25 "	Feb., 1883
John Dolan	261 Heath st	"	2.25 "	May 15, 1903
Thomas J. Dolan	1 Folsom ave	"	2.25 "	Jan. 4, 1906
John J. Donnelly	62 Station st	"	2.25 "	Feb. 26, 1902
Michael Donnelly	596 Parker st	"	2.25 "	Sept. 17, 1895
William Donovan	14 Phillips st.	"	2.25 "	June 18, 1899
Andrew J. Doran	33 Heath ave	"	2.25 "	March 13, 1902
Peter Doran	1436 Columbus ave	"	2.25 "	May, 1891
William F. Doyle	4 Batchelder ter	"	2.25 "	Aug. 7, 1896
John Driscoll	985 Harrison ave	"	2.25 "	July 20, 1895
Michael Finn	20 Washington pl	"	2.25 "	" 30, 1895
William J. Finn	178 W. Ninth st	"	2.25 "	March 13, 1900
John P. Finneran	131 Centre st	"	2.25 "	April 1, 1902
Thomas Flanagan	102 Heath st	"	2.25 "	Aug., 1875
Joseph S. Goodnow	189 Boylston st., J. P	"	2.25 "	" 24, 1900
John Grady	16 Terrace st	"	2.25 "	July 20, 1895
John J. Green	59 Circuit st	"	2.25 "	Jan. 14, 1899
Thomas F. Guinan	9 Forbes st	"	2.25 "	Sept. 29, 1905
John Guinee	6 Palmer pl	"	2.25 "	Feb. 24, 1899
John Hanley	94 Calumet st	"	2.25 "	May 24, 1907
John Haverty	140 Howard ave	"	2.25 "	" 6, 1901
Charles J. Hennrikus	14 Byron ct	"	2.25 "	April 9, 1901
Joseph Herbert	8 Conant st	"	2.25 "	Aug. 16, 1900
Thomas Hoar	24 Clarence st	"	2.25 "	July 20, 1895
Dennis J. Holland	320 Ruggles st	"	2.25 "	Aug. 11, 1900
Frederick Howe	4 Terrace st	"	2.25 "	Sept. 16, 1895
John Keegan	53 Marshfield st	"	2.25 "	July, 1874
John Kelley, 1st	208 Highland st	"	2.25 "	Nov., 1871
John Kelley, 2d	26 New Heath st	"	2.25 "	Aug., 1889
Andrew Kenney	803 Parker st	"	2.25 "	June 19, 1905
Michael Kenney, 2d	20 Harwood st	"	2.25 "	" 20, 1901
Dennis Lyons	4 Dove st	"	2.25 "	July 22, 1895
Daniel Meagher	21 Dudley st	"	2.25 "	May 19, 1891
Stephen F. Merrigan	6 Dearborn pl	"	2.25 "	Aug., 1885
Michael Mellon	940 Parker st	"	2.25 "	Sept. 14, 1900
Michael Mitchell	36 Rockwood	"	2.25 "	May, 1875
Owen Mullaney	429 Walnut ave	"	2.25 "	Aug. 17, 1900
Patrick Mulloy	15 Boston st	"	2.25 "	June 9, 1905
Patrick Murray, 2d	62 Cornwall st	"	2.25 "	Dec. 19, 1897
Daniel McCarthy	133 St. Alphonsus st	"	2.25 "	June, 1895
John McElaney	28 Hawthorn	"	2.25 "	Aug. 20, 1895
John McFarland	68 Bromley st	"	2.25 "	March 5, 1909
James McGregor	219 Cabot	"	2.25 "	Sept., 1885
William McGovern	1142 Columbus ave	"	2.25 "	" 12, 1895
James McLaughlin	128 Havre st	"	2.25 "	" 12, 1895
John J. Niland	170 St. Alphonsus st	"	2.25 "	Feb. 12, 1908
John O'Neil	15 Dorr st	"	2.25 "	Aug. 12, 1895
Oliver Penny	136 Moreland st	"	2.25 "	July 22, 1895
Dennis Quinn	603 E. Second st	"	2.25 "	Aug. 16, 1895
Michael Quinn	1379 Columbus ave	"	2.25 "	June, 1889
Timothy Reddington	273 Highland st	"	2.25 "	" 1874
Michael J. Rooney	51 Regent st	"	2.25 "	Nov. 13, 1900
John Rowan	80 Calumet st	"	2.25 "	May 15, 1903
Patrick F. Sennott	35 Ray st	"	2.25 "	April 20, 1899
William F. Shaughnessy	26 Belden st	"	2.25 "	July 11, 1902
George H. Simpson	15 Bickford st	"	2.25 "	" 22, 1895
Augustus H. Stardigle	776 Columbus ave	"	2.25 "	Feb. 27, 1908*
John Towle	943 Parker st	"	2.25 "	July 19, 1897
John H. Tully	34 Dacia st	"	2.25 "	Feb. 4, 1905
James H. Ward	2664 Washington st	"	2.25 "	Aug. 12, 1896
Henry J. Wagner	157 Highland st	"	2.25 "	April 4, 1902
John Watson	29 Vaughan ave	"	2.25 "	Aug., 1875
William T. Watson	2467 Washington st	"	2.25 "	May 15, 1903
Thomas Welch	237 Cabot st	"	2.25 "	" 1884
John J. Woods	rear 89 Norfolk ave	"	2.25 "	July 19, 1895

* Previously in the department.

Street Department (Paving Division).— Continued.

Name.	Residence.	Designation.	Compensation.	Date of Election or Appointment.

District No. 8. — South End.

Name.	Residence.	Designation.	Compensation.	Date of Election or Appointment.
John J. Costello	11 Linden st	Foreman	$1,800 yr	June, 1885
William H. Condry	15 Brook ave	Sub-foreman	3.50 day	Feb. 6, 1902
James Burton	11 Chauncy pl	"	3.50 "	March 31, 1902
Dennis V. Driscoll	226 Shawmut ave	"	3.50 "	Feb. 5, 1902
John J. Norton	23 Belvidere st	"	2.50 "	Dec. 22, 1905
John J. Killion	52 Forbes st	Clerk	1,000 yr	March 5, 1902
Thomas M. Lannon	1562 Tremont st	"	800 "	Aug. 28, 1908
John W. Halpin	106 Moreland st	Inspector	3.50 day	April 17, 1902
Dennis C. Crowley	71 Palmer st	"	3.00 "	" 17, 1902
James F. Whooley	8 Clarkson st	"	2.50 "	Feb. 20, 1904
Thomas Manning	106 Fellows st	Weigher	2.25 "	July 19, 1895
James J. Sullivan	586 Tremont st	Messenger	3.00 "	Dec. 15, 1905
Patrick Clancy	30 Middle st	Blacksmith	3.00 "	March 13, 1900
John A. McKee	53 Clifton st	"	3.00 "	June, 1890
Bernard Duffy	86 Westminster st	Blacksmith's Helper	2.25 "	July, 1870
Thomas F. Grant	704 Parker st	Carpenter	3.50 "	Nov. 18, 1902
Lawrence F. Sheeley	319 W. Fourth st	"	3.50 "	Aug., 1883
Eugene Sweeney	38 Sharon st	"	3.50 "	Nov. 16, 1906
James P. Feeley	32 Border st	Carpenter's Helper	2.50 "	Feb. 18, 1902
Charles E. Flynn	668 Harrison ave	"	1.50 "	Dec. 9, 1903
Michael H. Murray	28 Ball st	Engineer	3.50 "	June, 1884
Albert J. Rymes	74 Tuttle st	"	3.50 "	March 22, 1895
Thomas F. Scanlon	7 Vinton st	"	3.50 "	June, 1889
William H. McFarland	42 Auburn st	"	2.25 "	" 14, 1897
John Follen	219 Cabot st	Paver	3.00 "	July, 1883
Patrick Manning	23 Baxter st	"	3.00 "	May 15, 1891
Patrick Mulcahy	44 Woodward st	"	3.00 "	Oct., 1884
Philip McEntee	1688 Washington st	"	3.00 "	Aug. 1, 1902
Lawrence O'Connor	219 Cabot st	"	3.00 "	March 13, 1902
Thomas Kilroy	39 E. Canton	"	2.75 "	May 2, 1902
Patrick J. King	36 A st	"	2.75 "	Dec. 19, 1905
Peter Cleary, Jr.	47 Conant st	"	2.50 "	July 23, 1906*
William J. Donahue	138 K st	Rammer	2.25 "	Nov. 7, 1904
James Butler	46 E. Brookline st	Stonecutter	3.00 "	June 1, 1906*
Michael H. Dwyer	25 Chadwick st	"	3.00 "	Oct. 2, 1896
Daniel Kearney	49 Delle ave	"	3.00 "	Feb. 19, 1904
Martin Mulroney	653 Harrison ave	"	3.00 "	" 13, 1898
Thomas S. O'Toole	317 Blue Hill ave	"	3.00 "	Oct. 12, 1897
John J. Magee	71 Dover st	Janitor	2.50 "	" 14, 1903
John T. Sullivan	35 Carver st	Painter	2.50 "	Feb. 14, 1904
Patrick McDonnell	1 Miller pk	Tool Sharpener and Granite Cutter	2.25 "	Nov. 22, 1907
Charles W. Liscomb	35 Roxbury st	Tallyman	2.25 "	Aug. 28, 1900
Patrick Feeley	33 Vaughan ave	Powderman	2.25 "	" 1868
Peter Queenan	20 Ormond ter	Ledgeman	2.25 "	May 2, 1896
Patrick Kearns	15 Dacia st	Steam-driller	2.25 "	July, 1892
Bernard Tansey	23 Areola st	"	2.25 "	May, 1889
John J. Cronin	79 W. Lenox st	Stableman	2.50 "	June 24, 1901
Michael Dillon	10 Elder st	"	2.25 "	Aug. 24, 1906
John J. Clancy	673 Albany st	Teamster	2.50 "	Oct. 23, 1899
Lawrence Sullivan, 1st	804 E. Third st	"	2.50 "	June, 1890
Thomas Walsh	300 Eustis st	"	2.50 "	July, 1875
Patrick Connell	8 Church pl	"	2.25 "	March 4, 1901
Hugh Cosgrove	28 Fifield st	"	2.25 "	Jan. 26, 1900
John Donahue	110 Hunneman st	"	2.25 "	Feb. 5, 1904
John Lynch	131 Hampden st	"	2.25 "	Sept. 4, 1889
Michael J. Maguire	3 Andrews st	"	2.25 "	April 17, 1903
Patrick A. Murray	25 Downing st	"	2.25 "	May 17, 1902
Eugene D. McCauley	162 Cabot st	"	2.25 "	Nov. 17, 1897
James O'Toole	9 Vernon pl	"	2.25 "	Aug. 5, 1904
Lawrence Sullivan, 2d	45 Randall st	"	2.25 "	Sept., 1881
John Taaffe	23 Malden st	"	2.25 "	March 1, 1904
Joseph Baxter	51 Dale st	Watchman	2.50 "	June, 1884
Nicholas P. Walsh	89 E. Canton st	"	2.25 "	April 1, 1901
John O'Brien	5 Nawn st	Laborer	2.50 "	May 18, 1906
Edward F. Simpson	8 Conant st	"	2.50 "	March 16, 1901
Daniel Anglin	112 W. Lenox st	"	2.25 "	April 22, 1902
Thomas Attridge	118 Malden st	"	2.25 "	March 5, 1909
Edward J. Balfe	431 E. Sixth st	"	2.25 "	July 19, 1895
Jeremiah Barry	79 Preble st	"	2.25 "	May 16, 1895
Patrick Breen	66 Fayette st	"	2.25 "	April 21, 1902

* Previously in the department.

Street Department (Paving Division.)—Continued.

Name.	Residence.	Designation.	Compensation	Date of Election or Appointment.

District No. 8.— South End.— Concluded.

Name.	Residence.	Designation.	Compensation	Date of Election or Appointment.
William F. Brennan	36 Vineland st	Laborer	$2.25 day	May 16, 1895
Martin J. Burke	156 F st	"	2.25 "	March 8, 1902
Thomas Burke	16 Orchard pk	"	2.25 "	1884
Thomas Carroll	25 W. Dedham st	"	2.25 "	Sept. 3, 1895
John T. Cashman	677 Parker st	"	2.25 "	Nov. 3, 1902
Kophman Clark	27 Ingleside st	"	2.25 "	Dec. 22, 1900
Jeremiah Coleman	139 St. Alphonsus st	"	2.25 "	June 28, 1895
John Collins	29 Reed st	"	2.25 "	May 27, 1907
Daniel P. Connor	106 Conant st	"	2.25 "	April 1, 1902
Patrick J. Conley	236 Gold st	"	2.25 "	Sept. 23, 1895
Daniel Conroy	16 Laconia st	"	2.25 "	May 5, 1891
Dennis Cronin	32 Oneida st	"	2.25 "	June, 1881
John Crosby	92A Burrell st	"	2.25 "	July, 1871
Michael T. Craven	174 Fisher ave	"	2.25 "	Aug. 30, 1900
Dennis Crowley	25 W. Dedham st	"	2.25 "	1874
Daniel Crowley	877 Harrison ave	"	2.25 "	Dec. 18, 1896
Charles A. Devine	298 Neponset ave	"	2.25 "	July 18, 1895
Patrick A. Dolan	49 Judson st	"	2.25 "	22, 1895
Michael Donahue	817 Tremont st	"	2.25 "	March 13, 1900
John Donovan	2 Malden ct	"	2.25 "	April 17, 1896
Robert Downing	731 Tremont st	"	2.25 "	May 9, 1895
Joseph H. Flannigan	2 Rochester st	"	2.25 "	July, 1889
James E. Flynn	406 E. Third st	"	2.25 "	April 28, 1902
John J. Flynn	467 E. Third st	"	2.25 "	Oct. 31, 1894
Thomas F. Flynn	9 Gloucester pl	"	2.25 "	April 1, 1902
James Gaffney	14 Patterson st	"	2.25 "	March 22, 1901
Thomas Gallin	24 Waterford st	"	2.25 "	Aug. 23, 1900
Daniel J. Gleason	66 Cabot st	"	2.25 "	5, 1904
Thomas J. Graham	313 Dudley st	"	2.25 "	Nov. 3, 1905
Josiah R. Hallowell	27 Union pk	"	2.25 "	Jan. 6, 1908
John Hannon	99 Union pk	"	2.25 "	Nov. 1884
John Hayes	41 Newland st	"	2.25 "	Aug. 11, 1899
George Hill	1782 Washington st	"	2.25 "	March 8, 1907
Frederick O. Hinckley	479 Dudley st	"	2.25 "	May 5, 1902
Edward Hoben	8 Prescott st., Rox	"	2.25 "	July 6, 1895
Martin Hogarty	23 Vernon st	"	2.25 "	May, 1891
Michael Hurley	2 Oriental ct	"	2.25 "	Sept. 12, 1907
William Hurley	572 E. Second st	"	2.25 "	April 6, 1909
Patrick T. Kinsella	139 W. Fifth st	"	2.25 "	July, 1884
Thomas Lane	46 Fellows st	"	2.25 "	Aug., 1882
Daniel J. Leary, 1st	24 Bradford st	"	2.25 "	April 9, 1904
Patrick J. Lucid	178 Pleasant st	"	2.25 "	June 5, 1901
George A. Lynch	43 Emerald st	"	2.25 "	Oct. 18, 1902
Thomas Martin	29 Weston st	"	2.25 "	March 20, 1903
Bernard Meehan	1077 Columbus ave	"	2.25 "	July, 1895
Michael Moran	170 Norfolk ave	"	2.25 "	Sept., 1882
Thomas Moran	9 Andrews st	"	2.25 "	Oct. 2, 1900
James Murphy	13 Malden st	"	2.25 "	May 17, 1901
Patrick D. Murphy	12 Rollins st	"	2.25 "	April 29, 1902
William J. Murphy	1 Robinson pl	"	2.25 "	Dec. 6, 1897
Edward Murray	27 Vaughan ave	"	2.25 "	July 16, 1895
James Murray	39 E. Canton st	"	2.25 "	June 8, 1906
John E. Mulvee	40 Chadwick st	"	2.25 "	March 31, 1905
Martin J. McCarthy	63 Albany st	"	2.25 "	Aug. 8, 1900
Michael McDonald	13 Andrews st	"	2.25 "	Feb. 6, 1905
Philip McGathgan	219 Cabot st	"	2.25 "	April 10, 1902
Frank McKeever	989 Harrison ave	"	2.25 "	June, 1884
Edward McManus	9 Chesterfield st	"	2.25 "	March 1, 1901
John J. McNamara	40 Wensley st	"	2.25 "	Oct. 10, 1902
Joseph H. Norris	646 Shawmut ave	"	2.25 "	May 13, 1901
John W. O'Connell	40 Mercer st	"	2.25 "	April 9, 1909
Daniel O'Keefe	37 E. Canton st	"	2.25 "	Oct. 30, 1906
Timothy O'Sullivan	19 Melrose st	"	2.25 "	July 14, 1908
John Rafferty	674 E. Broadway	"	2.25 "	June 26, 1905
Thomas Ratchford	929 Albany st	"	2.25 "	April 5, 1901
Patrick Ronan	26 Langdon st	"	2.25 "	June 8, 1906
John F. Sheehan	9 Ringgold st	"	2.25 "	Jan. 26, 1904
Timothy Sugrue	88 Dover st	"	2.25 "	Sept. 14, 1905
Dennis J. Sullivan	71 E. Brookline st	"	2.25 "	Aug. 3, 1906
Maurice M. Sullivan	22 B st	"	2.25 "	Sept. 4, 1908
Patrick Thornton	2 Orange ct	"	2.25 "	May 8, 1902

Street Department (Paving Division.) — Continued.

Name.	Residence.	Designation.	Compensation.	Date of Election or Appointment.

District No. 9.— Ashmont.

Name.	Residence.	Designation.	Compensation.	Date of Election or Appointment.
Maurice Condon	19 Charles st., Dor.	Foreman	$1,800 yr.	April 24, 1903
Edward S. Coyle	55 Samoset st.	Sub-foreman	3.50 day.	Feb. 10, 1902
Florence Crowley	155 Geneva ave	"	3.50 "	July 25, 1904
Lawrence Flanagan	1185 Dorchester ave	"	3.50 "	Feb. 19, 1902
John H. Murphy	133 Walnut st.	Inspector	3.00 "	Sept. 24, 1897
Francis D. Carmody	588 Park st	Clerk	800 yr.	July 21, 1908
James J. Chute	296 Neponset ave	Weigher	2.75 day.	May 15, 1891
William T. Brady	227 Roxbury st.	Carpenter	4.00 "	July 18, 1900
Daniel J. Regan	27 Page st.	"	3.50 "	Nov. 5, 1897
Thomas F. Maher	641 E. Sixth st.	Engineer	3.50 "	Aug. 16, 1902
Patrick J. Cantwell	58 Boston st.	Patchpaver	3.00 "	June 16, 1902
Amos V. Sargent	6 Trent st	Stonecutter	3.00 "	May 14, 1895
John T. O'Hearn	301½ Broadway	Tallyman	2.50 "	Jan. 26, 1904
John M. Conboy	6A Melbourne st.	Laborer	2.25 "	Feb. 13, 1906
Jeremiah Ahern	34 Dix st.	Teamster	2.25 "	July 17, 1895
Andrew T. Brown	20 Avondale st.	"	2.25 "	Aug. 15, 1895
Patrick Casey	138 Marsh st.	"	2.25 "	Oct. 31, 1895
Richard T. Fitzgerald	331 Freeport st.	"	2.25 "	July 17, 1895
John Murray	40 Greenwich pl.	"	2.25 "	June 24, 1901
John Sheehan	45 Hecla st.	"	2.25 "	1871
Michael Walsh	19 Fuller st.	"	2.50 "	June, 1883
Daniel Hurley	56 Tolman st.	Stableman	2.25 "	Sept. 30, 1892
Thomas Culnan	23 Beach st.	Watchman	2.25 "	1875
Nathan Hopkins	526 W. Park st.	"	2.25 "	May 13, 1904
Thomas J. Clark	107 Granite ave	Laborer	2.25 "	16, 1895
Neil Devlin	4 Dever st.	"	2.25 "	Nov., 1897
James F. Donovan	501 E. Third st.	Teamster	2.25 "	July 2, 1908
Michael Dorsey	93 Clarkson st.	Laborer	2.25 "	June, 1880
James Dunphy	11 Minot pl.	"	2.25 "	Aug., 1879
David Fitzgerald	13 Kimball st.	"	2.25 "	April 22, 1904
Henry J. Gunning	1 Fenton st.	"	2.25 "	" 5, 1901
John Henderson	2 Patterson st.	"	2.25 "	Aug. 18, 1908
John P. Leach	73 Burt st.	"	2.25 "	Oct. 17, 1895
Charles Maguire	4 Eaton st.	"	2.25 "	June, 1874
Michael Murphy	11 Coffey st.	"	2.25 "	May 16, 1895
John J. Moore	10 Hutchinson st.	Watchman	2.25 "	Oct. 23, 1895
Daniel McCarthy	125 Wrentham st.	Powderman	2.25 "	May, 1871
James McCormack	1351 Dorchester ave	Laborer	2.25 "	March 29, 1901
Patrick McGarrahan	1084 Washington st.	"	2.25 "	Nov. 18, 1900
Hugh C. McGovern	3 Fenton st.	"	2.25 "	Oct. 23, 1895
Stephen McGrail	250 Westville st.	"	2.25 "	July 17, 1895
David McQuinn	26 Cedar st.	"	2.25 "	Aug. 6, 1890
Daniel Queeney	5 Brooks st.	"	2.25 "	Oct. 18, 1895
James Sheehan	29 Sturbridge st.	"	2.25 "	Aug. 13, 1900
John F. Sullivan	181 Bunker Hill st.	"	2.25 "	" 3, 1908

District No. 10.— North End.

Name.	Residence.	Designation.	Compensation.	Date of Election or Appointment.
Timothy F. Murphy	21 Allen st.	Foreman	$1,800 yr.	March 4, 1904
William J. Donohue	174 Webster st.	Sub-foreman	3.50 day.	Feb. 6, 1902
Patrick J. Haley	6 Pacific st.	"	3.50 "	Sept. 30, 1895
Florence Stacey	34 Prospect st.	"	3.50 "	July, 1870
Jacob Gediman	23 Temple st.	Clerk	800 yr.	" 21, 1908
Michael Sinnott	70 Bernard st.	Messenger	2.50 day.	March 18, 1902
Jerome O'Neil	297 Columbus ave	Inspector	3.50 "	Dec. 23, 1902
Michael F. Barry	55 S. Margin st.	"	3.00 "	Oct. 6, 1902
Isiah H. Beals	46 Dartmouth st.	"	3.00 "	July 26, 1901
Ariel M. Cain	26 Harley st.	"	3.00 "	May 24, 1901
James Crowley	70 Ferrin st.	"	3.00 "	March 27, 1905
John J. Hoey	40 Auburn st.	"	3.00 "	Aug. 24, 1900
John Seiberlich	2 Woodville pk.	Blacksmith	3.00 "	May, 1872
Christopher O'Brien	521 Commercial st.	Wharfinger	3.00 "	Aug. 13, 1897
John Clark	176 Endicott st.	Patchpaver	3.00 "	March, 1874
George Doherty	182 Endicott st.	"	3.00 "	Nov. 12, 1897
Joseph Finamore	23 Rogers st., S. B.	"	3.00 "	May, 1873
John Mahoney	43 Charter st.	"	3.00 "	March 11, 1903
William J. Mealley	139 H st.	"	3.00 "	July 22, 1904
John McGovern	71 Green st.	"	3.00 "	June, 1883
Daniel Riley	237 Bennington st.	"	3.00 "	" 16, 1902
Patrick S. Sullivan	23 Boston st.	"	2.50 "	Feb. 10, 1902
Michael McLaughlin	228 Main st.	Paver's Helper	2.25 "	April 18, 1902
Patrick O'Dowd	56 Auburn st.	Rammer	2.25 "	Nov. 30, 1904

Street Department (Paving Division).— Concluded.

Name.	Residence	Designation.	Compensation	Date of Election or Appointment.

District No. 10.— North End.— Concluded.

Name.	Residence	Designation.	Comp.	Date
John H. Barry	153 Richmond st	Stonecutter	$3.00 day	Aug. 10, 1896
Patrick Heffernan	62 Beach st	"	3.00 "	May 8, 1896
Edward O'Keefe	37 Bennet	Janitor	2.50 "	Feb. 1, 1905
Alexander Rosatto	9 Monument st	Yardman	2.25 "	Aug. 7, 1899
James Lennon	87 Brook ave	Teamster	2.50 "	May 16, 1895
Michael Devlin	93 Endicott st	"	2.25 "	Sept. 5, 1905
Michael Fanning	36 Nashua st	"	2.25 "	April, 1876
James M. Magee	3282 Washington st	"	2.25 "	" 26, 1904
Daniel O'Rourke	34 Havre st., E. B.	"	2.25 "	Jan. 6, 1896
Thomas Flesk	436 Commercial st	Watchman	2.25 "	March 29, 1904
Abraham Moss	25 Allen st	"	2.25 "	Nov. 16, 1904
Neil Bonner	24 Virginia st	Stableman	2.25 "	June, 1871
James J. Barry	12 Cedar st., Chsn	Laborer	2.25 "	Sept. 4, 1908
Domenico Botte	84 Bremen st	"	2.25 "	Oct. 27, 1905
John Brennan	8 Sumner st	"	2.25 "	May, 1875
Charles F. Caffrey	391 Charles st	"	2.25 "	Oct. 16, 1905
Timothy Callahan	19 Charter st	"	2.25 "	Dec. 30, 1899
Dennis Cary	59 Chambers	"	2.25 "	Oct. 14, 1905
Patrick J. Clougherty	11 Topliff st	"	2.25 "	Nov. 24, 1904
Dominick Crane	6 Melrose st	"	2.25 "	July 10, 1908
Thomas Curley	3223 Washington st	"	2.25 "	June 6, 1902
Daniel F. Dailey	134 C st	"	2.25 "	Dec. 1, 1905*
Michael Devine	513 Hanover st	"	2.25 "	Oct. 27, 1903
Owen Devlin	164 Endicott st	"	2.25 "	June 1, 1904
Patrick Doherty	9 Bridge ct	"	2.25 "	April, 1874
Roger Doherty	47 Park st	"	2.25 "	July 31, 1895
Richard E. Dooley	34 Chestnut st., Chsn	"	2.25 "	Dec. 31, 1902
John Dowd	157 Leverett st	"	2.25 "	July 7, 1892
William F. Downey	60 Nashua st	"	2.25 "	March 1, 1904
William A. Duffy	67 Brighton st	"	2.25 "	Aug. 18, 1900
Peter Francis	48 Monument st	"	2.25 "	Nov. 16, 1894
Edward Glynn	7 Allen st	"	2.25 "	June, 1871
John Golden	78 Poplar st	"	2.25 "	July 29, 1903
Edward W. Gordon	67 W. Cedar st	"	2.25 "	May 13, 1907
John W. Green	3 Garden ct. st	"	2.25 "	Oct. 25, 1900
Michael Haggerty	36 Nashua st	"	2.25 "	May, 1873
Richard Jones	39 Blossom st	"	2.25 "	" 19, 1891
John Lane	134 Charles st	"	2.25 "	Feb. 6, 1902
John F. Leonard	68 Causeway st	"	2.25 "	Dec. 29, 1905
Thomas Malone	58 Billerica st	"	2.25 "	June 29, 1891
Thomas Mandeville	6 Walk Hill st	"	2.25 "	Jan. 21, 1896
Henry P. Minard	67 Brighton st	"	2.25 "	July 21, 1897
Edward F. Moffitt	3 Endicott st	"	2.25 "	April 23, 1902
James W. Morrow	16 Emerald st	"	2.25 "	May, 1885
George Morong, Jr	31 Causeway st	"	2.25 "	July 3, 1895
Thomas Mullary	22 Billerica st	"	2.25 "	Aug. 18, 1900
Andrew Murphy	5 Fleet st	"	2.25 "	May, 1890
Maurice Murphy	23 Blossom st	"	2.25 "	April, 1875
Timothy J. Murphy	23 Everett st	"	2.25 "	" 1884
Patrick McCaffrey	85 Washington st., Chsn	"	2.25 "	" 1872
Patrick S. McCarthy	3 K st. pl	"	2.25 "	June 16, 1908
Francesco S. Penta	353 Hanover st	"	2.25 "	Aug. 17, 1899
George L. Robinson	52 Phillips st	"	2.25 "	Sept. 12, 1895
Daniel H. Ryan	6 Burnham pl., S. B	"	2.25 "	June 16, 1908
Daniel Spellman	10 Conant st	"	2.25 "	April, 1883
Thomas J. Sruhan	3 St. Alphonsus st	"	2.25 "	Oct. 29, 1907*
John A. Sweeney	40 Nashua st	"	2.25 "	" 27, 1895

Sanitary Division.

Office.

Name	Residence	Designation	Comp.	Date
George H. Foss	17 DeWolf st	Deputy Superintendent	$3,500 yr	May 7, 1908
Thomas A. Dolan	35 Alban st	Chief Clerk	1,800 "	Oct. 3, 1902*
Thomas P. Roe	19 Wharf st	Clerk	1,400 "	Feb. 7, 1902*
Edward O. Risem	15 Lansing st	"	800 "	July 24, 1908
Christopher D. A. Hourin	1577 Columbus ave	Chief Inspector	1,600 "	Aug. 17, 1906*
Vincent H. Jacobs	641 Huntington ave	Stenographer	800 "	Feb. 12, 1909*
Cornelius Lee	20 Champney st	Chauffeur	21.00 wk	" 12, 1909*
Bessie Goldstein	5 Gannett st	Sanitary Inspector	2.50 day	" 19, 1909

* Dates of present positions. Previously in the service.

Street Department (Sanitary Division).— Continued.

Name.	Residence.	Designation.	Compensation.	Date of Election or Appointment.

District Nos. 1 and 6.

Name.	Residence.	Designation.	Compensation.	Date of Election or Appointment.
John F. Wade	204 L st	Foreman	$1,400 yr	April 3, 1896
Joseph P. Keyes	79 Glenway st	Inspector	3.00 day	" 23, 1903
John Mahoney	488 E. Seventh st	"	3.00 "	Sept. 30, 1896
Frank J. Nagle	188 Highland st	"	3.00 "	" 21, 1900
Daniel J. O'Brien	510 Third st	"	3.00 "	Aug. 4, 1899
Antonio Silva	44 Pearl st	"	3.00 "	Feb. 2, 1903
Patrick H. Shaughnessey	71 Woodcliff st	Provisional Inspector	3.00 "	April 21, 1900
Bartholomew Sullivan	39 Bainbridge st	"	3.00 "	Aug. 3, 1900
Michael Wade	493 E. Seventh st	Stableman	2.50 "	Oct. 18, 1899
Peter Burns	20 Gates st	"	2.25 "	May 1, 1891
Andrew Sullivan	278 Bowen st	"	2.25 "	" 11, 1891
Thomas J. Lane	218 E st	Dumper	2.25 "	" 5, 1905
Matthew J. Barrett	298 E. Eighth st	Teamster	2.25 "	Feb. 7, 1899
Edward Condon	754 E. Fourth st	"	2.25 "	May 1, 1891
John V. Curran	592 E. Second st	"	2.25 "	Aug. 9, 1897
Daniel Dillon	5 B st	"	2.25 "	June 22, 1895
William J. Dwyer	1443 Columbia rd	"	2.25 "	Aug. 6, 1896
John T. Kane	115 H st	"	2.25 "	May 1, 1891
Matthew Kelley	162 D st	"	2.25 "	Nov. 25, 1893
James Meade	564 E. Second st	"	2.25 "	Jan. 1, 1900
Patrick C. Sheehan	501 E. Third st	"	2.25 "	Dec. 19, 1899
Garrett Stapleton	10 O st	"	2.25 "	July 22, 1899
John Stapleton	596 E. Third st	"	2.25 "	Aug. 24, 1906
William H. Tatten	365 E st	"	2.25 "	May 6, 1895
Patrick J. Toomey	76 Oak st	"	2.25 "	" 5, 1905
Michael Walsh	24 Lincoln st	"	2.25 "	April 28, 1895
Michael Barrett	47 H st	Helper	2.25 "	Aug. 22, 1899
William Carr	7 Blackinton st	"	2.25 "	Dec. 21, 1899
Timothy J. Conners	301 E. Eighth st	"	2.25 "	May 16, 1905
John Dobbins	260 D st	"	2.25 "	" 1, 1891
John Dowdal	24 O st	"	2.25 "	Nov. 16, 1899
Matthew Doyle	22 Gates st	"	2.25 "	Jan. 30, 1889
John Flannery	374 W. Second st	"	2.25 "	" 1, 1902
John J. Gorman	1 Sayward pl	"	2.25 "	April 29, 1904
David H. Hurley	90 W. Eighth st	"	2.25 "	May 2, 1904
Patrick J. Lally	361 E. Eighth st	"	2.25 "	March 26, 1897
William J. McCarthy	81 F st	"	2.25 "	May 2, 1904
Patrick O'Toole	114 F st	"	2.25 "	April 22, 1904
James Scully	403 W. Second st	"	2.25 "	March 7, 1902
John Costello	296 Bolton st	Regular Extra Laborer	2.25 "	Sept. 26, 1906
Bernard F. Devine	298 W. Second st	" "	2.25 "	Aug. 24, 1906
Francis E. Donnellon	789 E. Sixth st	" "	2.25 "	Aug. 25, 1906
Bernard Donogher	284 Bolton st	" "	2.25 "	Oct. 16, 1906
Dennis Donovan	508 E. Third st	" "	2.25 "	Dec. 3, 1906
Daniel Dwyer	92 Mercer st	" "	2.25 "	Aug. 24, 1906
Bartholomew Foley	591 E. Fourth st	" "	2.25 "	Nov. 12, 1906
Bartholomew F. Griffin	384 W. Second st	" "	2.25 "	Aug. 24, 1906
Patrick J. Keely	21 Gates st	" "	2.25 "	" 24, 1906
Dennis Kenneally	40 O st	" "	2.25 "	Oct. 22, 1906
Ernest W. McEldowney	330 W. Third st	" "	2.25 "	Jan. 3, 1908
Frank L. Shea	34 Shannon st	" "	2.25 "	Oct. 5, 1906
David D. Wade	133 E st	" "	2.25 "	Sept. 27, 1906
Benjamin J. Magoun	73 Bromley st	Reserve Laborer	2.25 "	April 24, 1905
Florence J. O'Sullivan	426 W. Broadway	"	2.25 "	" 28, 1905

District No. 2.

Name.	Residence.	Designation.	Compensation.	Date of Election or Appointment.
Daniel Flanagan	62 Washington st	Provisional Inspector	$3.00 day	July 2, 1900
James A. Guthrie	638 E. Seventh st	"	3.00 "	Jan. 9, 1899
Michael Winston	107 Bennington st	Helper	2.25 "	Sept. 2, 1891

District No. 3.

Name.	Residence.	Designation.	Compensation.	Date of Election or Appointment.
Benjamin J. A. Green	32 Oak st	Foreman	$1,400 yr	Dec. 23, 1904
Cornelius J. O'Brien	337 Bunker Hill st	Sub-foreman	3.00 day	May 1, 1896
John Green	58 Pearl st	Stableman	2.25 "	" 1, 1859
George McColgan	19 Harvard st	"	2.25 "	March 16, 1906
Daniel E. McInnis	3 Seminary st	"	2.25 "	Feb. 8, 1905
John O'Brien	21 Eden st	"	2.25 "	Aug. 2, 1907
Daniel Powers	34 Haverhill st	"	2.25 "	" 2, 1907
Bartholomew E. Spellman	67 W. Seventh st	Dumper	2.25 "	June 26, 1908
William F. Blake	104 Rutherford ave	Teamster	2.25 "	May 1, 1891

Street Department (Sanitary Division).—Continued.

Name.	Residence.	Designation.	Compensation	Date of Election or Appointment.
District No. 3.—Concluded.				
Arthur W. Blankenburg	5 Lynde st	Teamster	$2.25 day	April 28, 1905
John B. Carr	28 Monument ct	"	2.25 "	May 1, 1891
John F. Conners	101 Bartlett st	"	2.25 "	March 23, 1906
John Cullinane	6 Reardon pl	"	2.25 "	April 28, 1905
John J. Doherty	110 Water st	"	2.25 "	Oct. 18, 1897
Patrick Toomey	3 Hancock st	"	2.25 "	May 6, 1888
John Wilson	7 Gray st	"	2.25 "	" 16, 1887
Patrick J. Callahan	11 Benedict st	Helper	2.25 "	March 2, 1891
Charles Cullinane	35 Bartlett st	"	2.25 "	1886
Neil Harkins	8 Monument st	"	2.25 "	May 1, 1883
Edward F. Lafayette	2 Auburn pl	"	2.25 "	April 24, 1905
James McGaffigan	141 Chelsea st	"	2.25 "	" 24, 1905
Daniel McGuigan	5 Gilbert ave	"	2.25 "	" 25, 1905
Patrick McGuinness	5 Hill st	"	2.25 "	Oct. 5, 1891
William J. O'Brien	21 Eden st	"	2.25 "	April 24, 1905
William F. Powers	34 Haverhill st	"	2.25 "	" 24, 1905
Timothy Quinlan	422 Bunker Hill st	"	2.25 "	July 9, 1899
Patrick Burke	51 Essex st	Regular Extra Laborer	2.25 "	Aug. 24, 1906
Henry Clark	24 Washington st	" "	2.25 "	Dec. 13, 1906
James Farrell	11 Salem street ave	" "	2.25 "	March 22, 1907
Daniel Gallagher	77 Russell st	" "	2.25 "	Nov. 2, 1906
Daniel Mahoney	37 Cook st	" "	2.25 "	Aug. 24, 1906
Michael A. McCann	40 Soley st	" "	2.25 "	Oct. 19, 1906
Dennis McGonagle	100 Henley st	" "	2.25 "	Aug. 24, 1906
Charles E. McLaughlin	7 Mystic pl	" "	2.25 "	Oct. 26, 1906
John J. Murphy	60½ Moulton st	" "	2.25 "	Nov. 5, 1906
John F. Nagle	13 Frothingham ave	" "	2.25 "	Dec. 12, 1906
James O'Donnell	20 Moulton st	" "	2.25 "	" 5, 1906
James T. O'Neil	3 N. Quincy pl	" "	2.25 "	Aug. 24, 1906
Samuel A. Wright	11 Salem st	" "	2.25 "	Dec. 5, 1906
District No. 4.				
William F. Brogie	78 Parsons st	Inspector	$3.00 day	Feb. 20, 1902
Peter F. Gerrity	86 Day st	"	3.00 "	June 22, 1906
Charles A. Gilman	Washington and Market sts., Washington Building	Messenger	450 yr	May 29, 1900
Districts Nos. 5 and 7.				
William Clark	18 Frederick st	Foreman	$1,400 yr	Jan. 30, 1902
Michael J. Clark	2 Andrew pl	Inspector	3.00 day	Sept. 30, 1896
John H. Finneran	306 Centre st	"	3.00 "	Aug. 16, 1906
James H. Keenan	29 Shirley st	"	3.00 "	Sept. 30, 1896
Dominick Murray	2976 Washington st	"	3.00 "	Nov. 15, 1905
Patrick J. Sullivan	7 Freeland st	"	3.00 "	Jan. 30, 1902
James Regan	18 Linden Park st	Provisional Inspector	3.00 "	June 9, 1891
Florence A. Sullivan	16 Tremont st	Inspector	2.50 "	March 3, 1907
John Gallagher	46 Fisher ave	Stableman	2.50 "	Sept. 30, 1892
Thomas Doyle	9 Round Hill st	"	2.25 "	July 29, 1898
Martin Gibbons	268 Centre st	"	2.25 "	" 10, 1897
George Ruck	24 W. Walnut pk	"	2.25 "	1878
Robert Welch	177 Centre st	"	2.25 "	1872
Patrick Craven, 1st	31 Chestnut ave	Watchman	2.25 "	1891
Michael Jesso	27 Codman pk	"	2.25 "	1884
Joseph J. Downing	41 Sharon st	Dumper	2.50 "	Dec. 28, 1906
Thomas F. Good	37 Edison green	"	2.25 "	May 11, 1886
John Sullivan	61 Marcella st	Dumpman	2.50 "	1873
Michael Curley	137 Centre st	"	2.25 "	May 1, 1871
Charles W. Bleiler	29 Lamartine st	Teamster	2.25 "	April 29, 1905
Michael Brennan	942 Parker st	"	2.25 "	Dec. 7, 1894
Patrick Cass	131 Marcella st	"	2.25 "	1879
Thomas Cleary	251 Highland st	"	2.25 "	April 11, 1891
Arthur P. Connor	21 Langdon st	"	2.25 "	Feb. 22, 1907
John E. Cox	251 Highland st	"	2.25 "	June 15, 1891
Patrick H. Cunningham	30 Dacia st	"	2.25 "	Aug. 5, 1896
Eugene J. Dailey, Jr.	56 Ottawa st	"	2.25 "	April 20, 1904
William Doherty	164 Norfolk ave	"	2.25 "	July 3, 1900
Dennis Donlan	26 Bower st	"	2.25 "	May 1, 1884
Michael J. Dorsey	181 Centre st	"	2.25 "	April 13, 1900
Morris A. Downey	49 Shirley st	"	2.25 "	Dec. 4, 1886
Patrick J. Downey, 1st	190 Fisher ave	"	2.25 "	Aug. 2, 1900
Patrick J. Downey, 2d	287 Highland st	"	2.25 "	May 14, 1900

Street Department (Sanitary Division).— Continued.

Name.	Residence.	Designation.	Compensation.	Date of Election or Appointment.
Districts Nos. 5 and 7.— Continued.				
James E. Fay	29 Adams st	Teamster	$2.25 day	June 27, 1905
John H. Finnerty	112 Brookside ave	"	2.25 "	April 27, 1905
William Flaherty	16 Barnes st	"	2.25 "	March 11, 1909
Michael J. Gately	51 Vale st	"	2.25 "	1887
William Gordon	1 Albert st	"	2.25 "	Sept. 7, 1895
James Kiley	49 Atherton st	"	2.25 "	March 20, 1890
William Knightley	104 Marcella st	"	2.25 "	May 1, 1891
James Lynch	45 Delle ave	"	2.25 "	Aug. 9, 1901
Patrick D. Monahan	28 Vale st	"	2.25 "	May 22, 1900
Keiran A. Mulvey	47 Delle ave	"	2.25 "	Jan. 1, 1900
Joseph J. McGonagle	78 Fulda st	"	2.25 "	Feb. 24, 1902
Thomas McGrath	57 Walden st	"	2.25 "	1878
Daniel H. Prior	259 Cabot st	"	2.25 "	July 3, 1901
David Pyne	93 Roxbury st	"	2.25 "	Aug. 6, 1896
John Shannon	1479 Columbus ave	"	2.25 "	" 6, 1900
John Skehan	121 Addison st	"	2.25 "	April 24, 1905
Patrick Slaman	69 Marcella st	"	2.25 "	July 1, 1893
John J. Walsh	7 Texas st	"	2.25 "	March 18, 1907
Charles Blessington	153 Minot pk	Helper	2.25 "	March 11, 1909
James J. Burns	29 Webber st	"	2.25 "	1881
John Carroll	1168 Adams st	"	2.25 "	Aug. 5, 1896
John Carty	176 Blue Hill ave	"	2.25 "	April 12, 1889
Jeremiah Casey	22 Fisher ave	"	2.25 "	1881
Michael Coffee	88 Fisher ave	"	2.25 "	Dec. 4, 1891
Thomas P. Conboy	24 Armandine st	"	2.25 "	April 24, 1905
William P. Connelly	93 George st	"	2.25 "	Aug. 21, 1899
Patrick Craven, 2d	285 Cabot st	"	2.25 "	May 28, 1900
Louis Davidmeyer	14 Ashley st	"	2.25 "	Nov. 22, 1895
Philip Doherty	12 Letterfine ter	"	2.25 "	May 22, 1891
John Donnelley	171½ Centre st	"	2.25 "	Nov. 16, 1888
Patrick Doyle	74 George st	"	2.25 "	May 21, 1895
Edward Fleming	279 Highland st	"	2.25 "	1884
Daniel J. Flynn	53 Vale st	"	2.25 "	June 25, 1887
Thomas Flynn	23 St. Joseph st	"	2.25 "	Jan. 17, 1901
John Gormley	7 Sewall st	"	2.25 "	Aug. 3, 1900
Timothy Hayes	3 Echo st	"	2.25 "	1897
Martin J. Hughes	83 Lamartine st	"	2.25 "	May 9, 1902
Stephen A. Hughes	11 Wise st	"	2.25 "	Sept. 15, 1899
Frank A. Keenan	157 Westville st	"	2.25 "	Aug. 7, 1896
Peter Kelley	29 Boynton st	"	2.25 "	May 31, 1901
John J. Kenney	41 W. Walnut pk	"	2.25 "	Oct. 19, 1892
Daniel L. Kilroy	103 Hampden st	"	2.25 "	Aug. 13, 1896
Andrew J. Muldoon	179 Vernon st	"	2.25 "	Nov. 30, 1900
Edward Mulvaney	32 Chestnut ave	"	2.25 "	1883
Humphrey McCarthy	2 Bromley st	"	2.25 "	Aug. 6, 1900
James P. McDonald	3 Darling st	"	2.25 "	Nov. 26, 1895
Augustus E. McLaughlin	219 Highland st	"	2.25 "	March 19, 1895
Martin Norton	14 Lambert st	"	2.25 "	1883
James J. Powers	1299 Columbus ave	"	2.25 "	June 21, 1898
William H. Quinn	1899 Columbus ave	"	2.25 "	1882
John Riley	429 Walnut ave	"	2.25 "	May 31, 1890
Thomas Stanton	12 Ritchie st	"	2.25 "	April 22, 1902
James Sullivan	1 Merton pl	"	2.25 "	" 17, 1888
James Vaughan	3 Elmwood pl	"	2.25 "	1878
Patrick Burke	12 Whittier st	Laborer	2.25 "	Aug. 29, 1889
John J. Dempsey	135 Sterling st	"	2.25 "	June 5, 1900
Thomas Dolan	51 Custer st	"	2.25 "	" 6, 1900
John Enwright	22 Smith st	"	2.25 "	" 27, 1892
John Gaffney	8 Highland st	"	2.25 "	" 26, 1900
Michael Grady	8 Oswald st	"	2.25 "	Aug. 3, 1900
Michael J. Murphy	4 Conant st	"	2.25 "	June 8, 1906
John Smith	574 Freeport st	"	2.25 "	" 25, 1900
James F. Brennan	16 Speedwell st	Reserve Laborer	2.25 "	May 1, 1905
John F. Considine	161 Freeport st	"	2.25 "	April 24, 1905
James H. Dolan	637 Parker st	"	2.25 "	" 24, 1905
Charles Folan	23 Centre st	"	2.25 "	May 26, 1905
Richard J. Higgins	647 Bennington st	"	2.25 "	April 24, 1905
John T. Hughes	262 Cabot st	"	2.25 "	" 27, 1905
Thomas H. Kelly	293½ Highland st	"	2.25 "	" 27, 1905
James J. Maguire	1336 Columbus ave	"	2.25 "	" 27, 1905
Frank L. McMann	204 Lamartine st	"	2.25 "	" 27, 1905
William F. Merrick	65 Northfield st	"	2.25 "	" 27, 1905

Street Department (Sanitary Division).— Continued.

Name.	Residence.	Designation	Compensation	Date of Election or Appointment.

Districts Nos. 5 and 7.— Concluded.

Name.	Residence.	Designation	Compensation	Date of Election or Appointment.
Walter E. Moore	28 Halleck st	Reserve Laborer	$2.25 day	Aug. 27, 1905
John H. Murray	12 Dracut st	"	2.25 "	Aug. 13, 1909
Timothy J. Sheehan	914 Albany st	"	2.25 "	April 27, 1905
Thomas Carr	34 Bennett st	Regular Extra Laborer	2.25 "	Feb. 16, 1909
Daniel Casey	81 Chestnut ave	" "	2.25 "	Nov. 13, 1906
Patrick Coffey	30 Walden st	" "	2.25 "	Sept. 20, 1906
Martin J. Connelly	60 Dickens st	" "	2.25 "	Nov. 16, 1906
John J. Connors	27 Chestnut ave	" "	2.25 "	Sept. 20, 1906
Bartholomew Costello	1 Loftus pl	" "	2.25 "	" 20, 1906
James F. Craffey	18 Whitney st	" "	2.25 "	" 20, 1906
William Croke	69 W. Lenox st	" "	2.25 "	Nov. 2, 1907
Dennis J. Cronin	158 Ward st	" "	2.25 "	Jan. 17, 1908
James L. Cronin	114 Heath st	" "	2.25 "	Nov. 4, 1907
Edward J. Forbes	21 E. Canton st	" "	2.25 "	Dec. 26, 1906
James Garrity	17 Geneva ave	" "	2.25 "	" 4, 1906
John Hasson	2057 Centre st	" "	2.25 "	Sept. 20, 1906
James F. Kelly	1 Weston pl	" "	2.25 "	" 20, 1906
Owen Kelly	49 Bickford st	" "	2.25 "	Dec. 27, 1907
John J. Kilroy	19 Conant st	" "	2.25 "	" 4, 1906
Thomas W. Lee	794 Saratoga st	" "	2.25 "	" 25, 1906
James J. Lynch	7 Newark st	" "	2.25 "	Aug. 29, 1906
Edward J. Maher	114 Moore st	" "	2.25 "	" 24, 1906
William H. Mahoney	33 Newman st	" "	2.25 "	March 11, 1907
John Mitchell	16 Fenwick st	" "	2.25 "	Oct. 23, 1906
John Moore	2 Vernon pl	" "	2.25 "	Aug. 31, 1906
James J. Moroney	237 Washington st	" "	2.25 "	Nov. 1, 1906
James Murtagh	45 Terrace st	" "	2.25 "	Sept. 20, 1906
Edward J. McGoldrick	328 Amory st	" "	2.25 "	" 20, 1906
Dennis J. McKeon	25 Newhall st	" "	2.25 "	Nov. 25, 1907
Owen McNulty	2 Sunny ct	" "	2.25 "	Sept. 20, 1906
Henry R. Nickerson	33 Valentine st	" "	2.25 "	" 4, 1906
George W. Penson	138 Ward st	" "	2.25 "	Dec. 27, 1907
Thomas F. Reddish	9 Smith st. pl	" "	2.25 "	" 23, 1907
James Reidy	140 Moreland st	" "	2.25 "	Sept. 20, 1906
James Reynolds	171½ Centre st	" "	2.25 "	Oct. 15, 1906
Dennis F. Shea	93 Broadway	" "	2.25 "	Feb. 6, 1907
Thomas Sheerin	31 Woodward ave	" "	2.25 "	Oct. 29, 1907
Charles Shepperd	33 Minden st	" "	2.25 "	Sept. 20, 1906

District No. 8.— Shop.

Name.	Residence.	Designation	Compensation	Date of Election or Appointment.
Morris B. Rowe	279 Eustis st	Foreman	$1,400 yr	April 4, 1854
John H. Crowley	8 Summer st	Clerk	800 "	March 12, 1909
Thomas Butler	37 Hillside st	Wheelwright	3.00 day	July 22, 1898
Charles J. Burns	7 Caldwell st	"	2.75 "	May 12, 1902
Edward Giroux	2 Howe ct	Wheelwright's Assistant	2.75 "	Oct. 22, 1897
William J. Magee	1363 Washington st	Carpenter	3.50 "	Aug. 5, 1902
Thomas R. Every	34 Tonawanda st	Blacksmith	3.50 "	June 23, 1908
Owen Foley	22 E. Springfield st	"	3.50 "	March 12, 1900
John E. Gillespie	4 Patterson st	"	3.00 "	April 13, 1900
Edville Sanford	7 Madison st	"	3.00 "	Oct. 22, 1888
Aaron Stackpole	45 Forest st	"	3.00 "	May, 1877
David M. Tobin	35 Tolman st	"	3.00 "	Jan. 1, 1906
Joseph Wolter	251 Highland st	"	3.00 "	April 14, 1902
Roger J. Berran	291 Highland st	Blacksmith's Assistant	2.50 "	Feb. 8, 1904
William A. Mahoney	10 Dacia ter	"	2.50 "	July 6, 1900
Thomas M. O'Leary	913 Albany st	"	2.50 "	May 16, 1902
Patrick F. Silk	260 D st	"	2.50 "	Dec. 27, 1899
John R. Wall	1582 Tremont st	"	2.50 "	Aug. 6, 1900
James R. Crozier	18 Minton st	Carriage and Wagon Painter	3.50 "	July, 1908
Maurice Greenwood	131 W. Concord st	Sign Painter	3.50 "	Dec. 20, 1902
Timothy J. McCarthy	9 Gloucester pl	"	3.50 "	April 26, 1909
Thomas Lundy	312 E. Eighth st	Painter	3.50 "	March 14, 1902
Daniel P. O'Sullivan	81 Mercer st	"	3.00 "	April 9, 1909
Thomas A. Gilbody	2070 Dorchester ave	"	2.75 "	June 20, 1898
George Bloom	20 E. Springfield st	"	2.50 "	May 1, 1882
Eugene Cox	78 Alexander st	"	2.50 "	" 1, 1871
Cornelius L. Sullivan	761 Norfolk st	"	2.50 "	Nov. 16, 1903
William J. Cronin	495 E. Seventh st	Foreman Harnessmaker	3.00 "	July 14, 1905
Patrick Keevan	11 Winthrop st	Harnessmaker	3.00 "	May 1, 1891
James J. Sullivan	75 Clifton st	Carriage Trimmer and Harnessmaker	3.00 "	Aug. 15, 1895
Thomas F. McCarthy	17 Laurel st	Harnessmaker's Assistant	2.50 "	Jan. 3, 1899

Street Department (**Sanitary Division**).— Continued.

Name.	Residence.	Designation.	Compensation.	Date of Election or Appointment.

Districts No. 8 — Shop. — Concluded.

Name.	Residence.	Designation.	Compensation.	Date of Election or Appointment.
Michael F. Danihy	16 Bennington st	Horseshoer	$3.16⅔ day.	May 3, 1907
William H. Gallagher	16 Everett st	"	3.16⅔ "	April 19, 1907
Jeremiah P. O'Leary	1215 Dorchester ave	"	3.16⅔ "	Dec. 18, 1899
Michael C. Roche	16 Sharon st	"	3.16⅔ "	Oct. 31, 1902
Benjamin Rose	63 Sanford st	Mechanic	3.50 "	March 22, 1909
Charles Downing	5 W. Canton st	Blanket Repairer	2.25 "	May 1, 1892
Timothy Moriarty	54 Wayland st	Laborer	2.25 "	April 13, 1875

Districts No. 8 and 9.

Name.	Residence.	Designation.	Compensation.	Date of Election or Appointment.
Michael J. Carmody	13 Malden st	Foreman	$1,400 yr.	Jan. 1, 1899
Simon J. Cavanagh	181 Norfolk ave	Inspector, Prov'l	3.00 day.	Nov. 9, 1906
John Duggan	53 Dennis st	"	3.00 "	June 7, 1886
Hugh Curran	38 E. Canton st	"	3.00 "	July, 1858
William H. Dolan	45 Burrell st	"	3.00 "	" 27, 1906
John B. Donahoe	32 Whitney st	"	3.00 "	April 13, 1900
Patrick Geoghegan	32 E. Dedham st	"	3.00 "	" 18, 1902
Marshall E. Mills	24 Worcester sq	"	3.00 "	Sept. 30, 1896
Joseph P. Ripley	49 Idaho st	"	3.00 "	March 10, 1902
Patrick T. Sullivan	90 Milton ave	"	3.00 "	April 2, 1900
Walter H. Rowe	663 Tremont st	Clerk	2.75 "	Oct. 8, 1900
Daniel P. Walker	38 Clifton st	Clerk, Prov'l	2.50 "	Dec. 5, 1882
Daniel Connor	122 Eustis st	Stableman	2.50 "	Aug. 27, 1897
James J. Flanagan	650 Albany st	"	2.50 "	May 14, 1888
James O'Halloran	17 Sargent st	"	2.50 "	Aug. 6, 1896
Dennis J. Donovan	13 Andrews st	Watchman	2.25 "	July 14, 1905
Murty Fitzgerald	108 E. Canton st	Stableman	2.25 "	Aug. 5, 1885
Martin J. Gately	46 George st	"	2.25 "	" 2, 1889
Michael King	6 Carlow st	Feeder	2.50 "	April 22, 1902
John Cooney	47 Shirley st	Watchman	2.25 "	July 26, 1907
William Cotter	10 Elder st	"	2.25 "	May 3, 1905
Garrett T. J. Culhane	85 W. Rutland sq	Janitor	2.50 "	Aug. 29, 1905
Arthur B. Murphy	177 Winthrop st	"	2.25 "	April 15, 1902
James E. Crowley	64 Parsons st	Wharfinger	3.00 "	" 6, 1907
Henry J. Hart	21 Essex st	Dumper	2.50 "	Sept. 14, 1908
John C. Fitzgerald	328 Shawmut ave	"	2.25 "	Jan. 27, 1905
Edward Breen	48 E. Brookline st	Teamster	2.25 "	Oct. 9, 1895
Thomas Burke	1A Sharon st	"	2.25 "	1880
Peter Callahan	36 Mystic st	"	2.25 "	1881
William F. Carmody	112 Union Park st	"	2.25 "	Dec. 20, 1907
Michael Cochrane	29 E. Dedham st	"	2.25 "	1879
Jeremiah Collins	43 Sharon st	"	2.25 "	Sept. 27, 1895
Lawrence Conroy	89 Village st	"	2.25 "	March 25, 1902
William Corcoran	68 E. Canton st	"	2.25 "	April 18, 1887
Hugh Crossen	9 Malden lane	"	2.25 "	1882
James Crowley	47 Island st	"	2.25 "	April 11, 1888
George W. Currier	12 Forest st	"	2.25 "	May 1, 1891
William Dwyer	49 Hunneman st	"	2.25 "	" 30, 1875
Garrett Fitzgerald	27 Hamburg st	"	2.25 "	March 11, 1890
Patrick W. Fox	86 E. Canton st	"	2.25 "	Oct. 14, 1887
Stephen A. Gaffey	46 Fellows st	"	2.25 "	May 1, 1891
William P. Greaney	42 Randall st	"	2.25 "	April 15, 1895
William Guinan	76 Williams st	"	2.25 "	" 15, 1895
Patrick Hafferty	96 E. Newton st	"	2.25 "	" 29, 1904
Daniel J. Harrington	113 Hampden st	"	2.25 "	Oct. 21, 1895
Thomas Harrington	669 Albany st	"	2.25 "	July 11, 1901
James Harris	20 Adams pl	"	2.25 "	Oct. 17, 1898
Matthew J. Kelley	89 C street	"	2.25 "	Dec. 20, 1897
John Kerrigan	1A Sharon st	"	2.25 "	June 24, 1895
Patrick J. Leahy	6 Mt. Pleasant ave	"	2.25 "	May 25, 1906
Patrick J. Lennon	284 Eustis st	"	2.25 "	June 30, 1900
Timothy J. Luddy	916 E. Fourth st	"	2.25 "	March 17, 1887
William Mackell	113 Hampden st	"	2.25 "	Jan. 2, 1893
James Manning	92 Draper st	"	2.25 "	1872
Patrick Murphy	104 E. Canton st	"	2.25 "	1873
Timothy H. McAuliffe	1 Clifton st	"	2.25 "	Sept. 23, 1892
Charles W. McCance	20 Forbes st	"	2.25 "	1872
Richard McCarron	3 Andrews st	"	2.25 "	1874
James McCarthy	31 Hamburg st	"	2.25 "	*April 15, 1895
Lawrence McCarthy	80 E. Brookline st	"	2.25 "	Dec. 24, 1895
Patrick McGeever	806 Shawmut ave	"	2.25 "	1882
Patrick J. Nolan	111 Winthrop st	"	2.25 "	Oct. 30, 1891
Hugh O'Connor	2161 Dorchester ave	"	2.25 "	1880

Street Department (Sanitary Division).— Continued.

Name.	Residence.	Designation.	Compensation.	Date of Election or Appointment.

Districts Nos. 8 and 9.— Continued.

Name.	Residence.	Designation.	Compensation.	Date of Election or Appointment.
Martin O'Mealley	19 Hamburg st	Teamster	$2.25 day	Sept. 27, 1892
Charles F. Rand	8 Gifford pl	"	2.25 "	May 11, 1896
John E. Reardon	121 Brook ave	"	2.25 "	April 27, 1896
James Rooney	109 Union Park st	"	2.25 "	May 2, 1891
Daniel Scannell	27 Malden st	"	2.25 "	Sept. 27, 1892
Dennis Shea	28 Magdala st	"	2.25 "	May 18, 1900
Edwin O. Spencer	1434 Washington st	"	2.25 "	April 15, 1895
Cornelius Sullivan	128 Shirley st	"	2.25 "	Sept. 8, 1887
Samuel J. Thompson	494 Tremont st	"	2.25 "	Nov. 2, 1896
George M. Tully	80 Middlesex st	"	2.25 "	Jan. 30, 1900
Edward F. Wehle	65 Centre st	"	2.25 "	Aug. 23, 1899
Maurice White	59 W. Canton st	"	2.25 "	April 15, 1895
John Byrne	125 Zeigler st	Helper	2.25 "	1873
John Conley	11 E. Canton st	"	2.25 "	1873
John A. Desmond	24 Sturbridge st	"	2.25 "	Oct. 29, 1897
John J. Dolan	3 Weston pl	"	2.25 "	Nov. 14, 1901
Florence Donovan	60 Hunneman st	"	2.25 "	1874
Laurence Farrell	58 Cabot st	"	2.25 "	May 1, 1891
Edmund Fortier	19 Sargent st	"	2.25 "	1877
Patrick Gorham	118 W. Sixth st	"	2.25 "	1873
Gustave H. Gotthardt	5 Orange ct	"	2.25 "	Oct. 8, 1887
William Harrold	98 W. Brookline st	"	2.25 "	May 11, 1886
Arthur Hennessey	36 Dennis st	"	2.25 "	June 20, 1899
Timothy Hurley	599 Harrison ave	"	2.25 "	May 1, 1881
Thomas E. Keenan	42 Woodward ave	"	2.25 "	1, 1891
William Lynch	1455 Washington st	"	2.25 "	16, 1887
Dennis Mahoney	37 E. Canton st	"	2.25 "	1881
James Malley	16 Huckins st	"	2.25 "	1873
James Maloney	8 Newhall pl	"	2.25 "	Sept. 19, 1898
James F. Maloney	120 Malden st	"	2.25 "	Feb. 27, 1891
Michael Moran	1A Sharon st	"	2.25 "	1883
Richard Morrison	258 Ruggles st	"	2.25 "	Jan. 27, 1888
Michael Mulholland	49 Adams st	"	2.25 "	June 1, 1887
Daniel Murphy	9 Albion st	"	2.25 "	1888
Thomas McCabe	110 E. Brookline st	"	2.25 "	1884
John McCarter	10 Ball st	"	2.25 "	1872
Florence T. McCarthy	14 Norwood st	"	2.25 "	Feb. 13, 1909
Daniel J. McCormick	828 Parker st	"	2.25 "	March 18, 1898
James McKeon	279 Norfolk ave	"	2.25 "	May 4, 1886
Peter O'Hea	17 Oak Grove ter	"	2.25 "	4, 1888
John J. O'Neil	3 Oakland ave	"	2.25 "	March 14, 1902
Patrick J. O'Toole	47 Moseley st	"	2.25 "	May 8, 1896
Patrick Raughan	271 Eustis st	"	2.25 "	1881
William J. Reagan	683 E. Seventh st	"	2.25 "	Jan. 3, 1895
Eugene F. Sullivan	9 Winthrop st	"	2.25 "	April 3, 1908
Bartholomew F. Swan	123 P st	"	2.25 "	March, 1909
John J. Talbot	45 Melrose st	"	2.25 "	Feb. 27, 1901
John Travis	38 Northampton st	"	2.25 "	May 1, 1891
George E. Ward	96 Burrell st	"	2.25 "	1876
John W. White	480 Tremont st	"	2.25 "	18, 1905
James Barry	44 Dearborn st	Laborer	2.25 "	March 15, 1892
Patrick J. Barry	52 Reed st	"	2.25 "	June 11, 1900
John Chambers	1326 Dorchester ave	"	2.25 "	March 6, 1900
Patrick Colleran	2 Tremont ct	"	2.25 "	June 12, 1891
James F. Dempsey	9 Burke st	"	2.25 "	May 5, 1899
John J. Desmond	28 Weston st	"	2.25 "	June 5, 1900
Timothy Flaherty	134 W. Eighth st	"	2.25 "	March 11, 1909
John Freany	2 Griffin ct	"	2.25 "	Nov. 30, 1898
William T. Godfrey	48 Reed st	"	2.25 "	May 28, 1900
Edward A. Millen	119 W. Seventh st	"	2.25 "	Dec. 8, 1898
Martin F. Mulligan	128 Shirley st	"	2.25 "	May 1, 1891
Jeremiah McCarthy	10 Nassau st	"	2.25 "	June 5, 1900
William T. Norton	1007 Harrison ave	"	2.25 "	Sept. 28, 1908
John D. O'Brien	339 Codman st	"	2.25 "	March 11, 1909
John H. O'Brien	47 Batchelder st	"	2.25 "	May 18, 1898
Philip O'Reilley	43 Sydney st	"	2.25 "	Sept. 22, 1892
John D. Rollo	12 Tudor st	"	2.25 "	May 8, 1897
John C. Smith	61 Hillside st	"	2.25 "	Dec. 2, 1893
Thomas Watson	37 Tabor st	"	2.25 "	Sept. 14, 1908
James M. Blake	73 Village st	Reserve Laborer	2.25 "	April 24, 1905
John J. Burke	38 Compton st	"	2.25 "	24, 1905
John P. Byrne	32 Sharon st	"	2.25 "	27, 1905
Michael J. Cahill	62 Leonard st	"	2.25 "	24, 1905

Street Department (Sanitary Division).— Continued.

Name.	Residence.	Designation.	Compensation.	Date of Election or Appointment.

Districts Nos. 8 and 9.— Continued.

Name.	Residence.	Designation.	Compensation.	Date of Election or Appointment.
Dennis Collins	89 E. Canton st	Reserve Laborer	$2.25 day	April 24, 1905
James J. Curran	38 E. Canton st	"	2.25 "	" 24, 1905
Michael Doherty	44 Union Park st	"	2.25 "	" 24, 1905
Thomas F. Dolan	45 Burrell st	"	2.25 "	" 24, 1905
Daniel J. Donovan	2 Malden ct	"	2.25 "	" 24, 1905
Edward J. Dunlea	356 Harrison ave	"	2.25 "	" 24, 1905
Maurice Ferris	56 E. Dedham st	"	2.25 "	" 24, 1905
Michael C. Flynn	71 Yeoman st	"	2.25 "	1884
Malachi Hart	38 Compton st	"	2.25 "	" 24, 1905
John L. Hennessey	105 E. Newton st	"	2.25 "	" 24, 1905
Joseph M. Higgins	46 Hampden st	"	2.25 "	" 24, 1905
Andrew F. Maguire	88 E. Canton st	"	2.25 "	" 24, 1905
John J. Mahoney	39 E. Springfield st	"	2.25 "	" 24, 1905
Patrick J. Mahoney	105 E. Dedham st	"	2.25 "	" 24, 1905
James Moran	100 E. Canton st	"	2.25 "	" 24, 1905
John McCarthy	4 Oneida st	"	2.25 "	" 20, 1904
William J. McDermott	22 Tyler st	"	2.25 "	" 24, 1905
John Norton	33 Webber st	"	2.25 "	" 24, 1905
Edmund O'Connell	6 Huckins st	"	2.25 "	" 24, 1905
Isreal Sternberg	24 Rose st	"	2.25 "	" 20, 1904
James F. Welch	263 Shawmut ave	"	2.25 "	Dec. 29, 1905
Joseph Wilmouth	665 Albany st	"	2.25 "	April 24, 1905
William J. Barrett	290 Shawmut ave	Regular Extra Laborer	2.25 "	Jan. 2, 1908
Hugh J. Barry	264 Eustis st	" "	2.25 "	Oct. 31, 1907
Martin Beatty	58 Silver st	" "	2.25 "	Dec. 2, 1906
Albert H. Brown	99 Hunneman st	" "	2.25 "	" 4, 1906
Patrick Burns	276 Eustis st	" "	2.25 "	Nov. 9, 1906
David A. Byrnes	110 George st	" "	2.25 "	Sept. 20, 1906
Frederick Calbag	22 Chadwick st	" "	2.25 "	Oct. 5, 1906
Bernard Callahan	165 Putnam st	" "	2.25 "	Nov. 1, 1906
Eugene Canney	7 Andrews st	" "	2.25 "	" 9, 1906
John J. Carroll	70 Bunker Hill st	" "	2.25 "	Aug. 24, 1906
Dennis E. Coakley	355 Athens st	" "	2.25 "	" 24, 1906
John T. Connelly	968 Parker st	" "	2.25 "	Sept 20, 1906
Patrick Connelly	38 Mercer st	" "	2.25 "	Aug. 24, 1906
John F. Copell	572 Shawmut ave	" "	2.25 "	Dec. 27, 1907
John M. Coyne	135 C st	" "	2.25 "	Oct. 22, 1906
Michael J. Cremin	20 Ormond ter	" "	2.25 "	Dec. 14, 1906
Timothy J. Cunniff	111 George st	" "	2.25 "	Nov. 9, 1906
Michael F. Dolaher	70 E. Dedham st	" "	2.25 "	Dec. 27, 1906
Jerome C. Dolan	129 Moreland st	" "	2.25 "	March 19, 1907
James Dumphy	59 Magazine st	" "	2.25 "	Oct. 5, 1906
Michael Finn	42 Troy st	" "	2.25 "	Dec. 21, 1906
James Finneran	1158 Harrison ave	" "	2.25 "	" 21, 1906
Edward D. Fitzgerald	27 Blue Hill ave	" "	2.25 "	Oct. 5, 1906
Michael F. Fitzgerald	87 Athens st	" "	2.25 "	Dec. 19, 1906
Andrew J. Flanagan	50 Webber st	" "	2.25 "	" 7, 1906
Patrick Flynn	188 Keyes st	" "	2.25 "	Sept. 5, 1906
William Gately	278 Eustis st	" "	2.25 "	Oct. 5, 1906
Michael Gilmore	15 Dacia st	" "	2.25 "	Dec. 5, 1906
Patrick Glynn	1011 Columbus ave	" "	2.25 "	Oct. 5, 1906
John Grady	1 Colony st	" "	2.25 "	Nov. 29, 1907
Herman Griffith	35 Billings st	" "	2.25 "	Feb. 10, 1906
George E. Hayes	12 Greenmount st	" "	2.25 "	Dec. 7, 1906
Dennis J. Healy	140 M st	" "	2.25 "	Feb. 17, 1909
John Horgan	4 Medford ct	" "	2.25 "	Dec 6, 1906
Arthur E. Jacobs	25 Rose st	" "	2.25 "	" 27, 1907
James T. Jordan	41 Webber st	" "	2.25 "	Nov. 23, 1906
Richard Kelly	Havre st	" "	2.25 "	Aug. 24, 1906
Hugh L. Kenney	10 Phillips st	" "	2.25 "	Dec. 7, 1906
James Kerrigan	43 Chadwick st	" "	2.25 "	" 31, 1907
Patrick C. Manning	48 Magazine st	" "	2.25 "	Sept. 20, 1906
Timothy Mulcahy	109 W. Lenox st	" "	2.25 "	Dec. 7, 1906
Patrick J. Muldoon	41 Cabot st	" "	2.25 "	Oct. 15, 1906
John J. Mullin	339 Adams st	" "	2.25 "	Jan. 1, 1907
Michael McCarthy	35 E. Lenox st	" "	2.25 "	Aug. 24, 1906
John McCormack	912 Harrison ave	" "	2.25 "	Feb. 12, 1909
Patrick F. McCormick	105 Union Park st	" "	2.25 "	Dec. 7, 1906
John L. McDonough	602 E. Seventh st	" "	2.25 "	Feb. 16, 1909
Lawrence McGahan	45 Emerald st	" "	2.25 "	" 10, 1908
Henry McLaughlin	972 Harrison ave	" "	2.25 "	Oct. 5, 1906
William T. McLaughlin	50 Malden st	" "	2.25 "	Nov. 9, 1906
Bernard F. McNulty	656 Harrison ave	" "	2.25 "	Sept. 27, 1906

Street Department (Sanitary Division).— Continued.

Name.	Residence.	Designation.	Compensation.	Date of Election or Appointment.

Districts Nos. 8 and 9.-- Concluded.

Name.	Residence.	Designation.	Compensation.	Date of Election or Appointment.
Jeremiah F. O'Leary	8 Whitney st	Regular Extra Laborer	$2.25 day	Nov. 22, 1907
Francesco Petrocelli	1042 Harrison ave	" "	2.25 "	" 12, 1907
Joseph J. Reid	259 Hancock st	" "	2.25 "	Dec. 30, 1907
Mark E. Smith	16 Concord sq	" "	2.25 "	Oct. 5, 1906
John J. Spillane	283 Hancock st	" "	2.25 "	Nov. 9, 1906
James Stewart	9 Douglas st	" "	2.25 "	Dec. 15, 1906
Dennis Sullivan	2784 Washington st	" "	2.25 "	Sept. 20, 1906
Michael Sullivan	19 Willow pk	" "	2.25 "	March 18, 1907
James W. Tracey	140 George st	" "	2.25 "	Oct. 5, 1906
Edward White	54 Reed st	" "	2.25 "	" 5, 1906

District No. 10.

Name.	Residence.	Designation.	Compensation.	Date of Election or Appointment.
James J. Sullivan	1 Akron pl	Foreman	$1,400 yr	May 8, 1908
Joseph F. Avers	415 Columbus ave	Inspector	3.00 day	Nov. 22, 1901
Dennis T. Mahoney	395 Charles st	"	3.00 "	" 30, 1896*
James J. Mullen	23 Pleasant st	"	3.00 "	" 30, 1896*
Francis Quinn	5 Causeway st	"	3.00 "	April 12, 1897
Michael Reardon	41 McLean st	"	3.00 "	Sept. 30, 1896
George H. O'Donnell	110 Draper st	Provisional Inspector	2.75 "	" 12, 1899
Martin A. Hernan	53 Allen st	Inspector	800 yr	Jan. 24, 1902
Charles McCarthy	131 Staniford st	Janitor	2.25 day	Feb. 13, 1903
John F. Coffey	32 N. Grove st	Stableman	2.50 "	March 19, 1902
Patrick Gallagher	45 Mead st	"	2.25 "	Feb. 28, 1901
Henry J. Savage	10 Milton st	"	2.25 "	June 30, 1905
Edward F. Sweeney	2818 Washington st	Watchman	2.25 "	1885
Joseph H. Boyle	59 Washington st	Horse-shoer	3.16⅔ "	Feb. 5, 1904
John J. Murray	90 W. Sixth st	"	3.16⅔ "	Dec. 19, 1902
William H. Bragg	1761 Washington st	Blacksmith	3.16⅔ "	May 17, 1899
John S. Crowley	461 Charles st	"	3.00 "	April 29, 1903
Frank P. Tully	708 Columbus ave	"	3.00 "	Nov. 27, 1908
John Dilworth	142 Leverett st	Lockman	2.25 "	Dec. 28, 1905
Thomas Ambrose	179 Cambridge st	Teamster	2.25 "	July 5, 1885
Samuel Blair	4 N. Anderson st	"	2.25 "	May 25, 1899
Patrick Carroll	62 Troy st	"	2.25 "	Aug. 22, 1899
John Conlan	11 Staniford st	"	2.25 "	May 4, 1888
Timothy Dwyer	8 Mt. Vernon st	"	2.25 "	Aug. 30, 1903
Daniel Harkins	94 Bartlett st	"	2.25 "	May 1, 1875
Peter A. Havlin	183 Chambers st	"	2.25 "	Sept. 13, 1897
Martin Heffernan	91 Burrill st	"	2.25 "	" 6, 1895
Richard J. Landy	35 Charter st	"	2.25 "	Aug. 30, 1905
Henry Mullen	141 Leverett st	"	2.25 "	May 1, 1884
Frank J. Munster	5 Cambridge street pl	"	2.25 "	Jan. 15, 1904
John Murray	22 Billerica st	"	2.25 "	June 25, 1892
Michael F. McGrath	117 W. Ninth st	"	2.25 "	May 26, 1899
John F. O'Brien	14 Blossom st	"	2.25 "	Nov. 21, 1895
Thomas O' Connor	4 Hancock st	"	2.25 "	Sept. 16, 1901
Martin Quirk	358 Hanover st	"	2.25 "	July 31, 1899
John Smith	11 Maiden lane	"	2.25 "	1873
John L. Sullivan	63 Longwood ave	"	2.25 "	May 1, 1889
Patrick Sullivan	rear 34 Lynde st	"	2.25 "	" 1, 1887
Philip J. Toland	65 Staniford st	"	2.25 "	Jan. 19, 1899
Charles Carey	38 Cabot st	Helper	2.25 "	April 16, 1896
Felix Certisimo	21 Cooper st	"	2.25 "	" 24, 1905
William Coughlin	304A Bunker Hill st	"	2.25 "	May 1, 1877
William Fleming	3 Lawrence pl	"	2.25 "	Jan. 1, 1900
Daniel Gallagher	7 Allston pl	"	2.25 "	Dec. 30, 1901
James E. Gavin	11 Charter st	"	2.25 "	May 1, 1879
Patrick H. Good	14 Gurney st	"	2.25 "	Dec. 19, 1899
John J. Harrington	177 Rutherford ave	"	2.25 "	Sept. 28, 1898
Patrick Horty	40 Pleasant st	"	2.25 "	May 1, 1884
Eugene Leonard	395 Charles st	"	2.25 "	" 1, 1868
John Little	5 Dever st	"	2.25 "	Nov. 25, 1893
Dennis D. Mahoney	78 Poplar st	"	2.25 "	May 1, 1891
Thomas Mulvey	44 Bower st	"	2.25 "	" 1, 1879
Bernard McCool	21 Edgeworth st	"	2.25 "	" 1, 1884
Antonio Penta	1 Webster pl	"	2.25 "	" 12, 1905
Patrick Riordan	34 Emerald st	"	2.25 "	April 29, 1902
Augustus Rogers	31 Cooper st	"	2.25 "	Dec. 6, 1897
Luigi Selvitella	21 Moon st	"	2.25 "	Aug. 9, 1903
Edward Welch	47 McLean st	"	2.25 "	May 1, 1873

* Previously in the department.

Street Department (Sanitary Division).— Continued.

Name.	Residence.	Designation.	Compensation.	Date of Election or Appointment.

District No. 10.— Continued.

Name.	Residence.	Designation.	Compensation.	Date of Election or Appointment.
William M. Allen	202 Norfolk ave	Laborer	$2.25 day	May 8, 1895
James J. Bradley	146 Richmond st	"	2.25 "	Jan. 2, 1902
Michael Brennan	3 Warren st	"	2.25 "	Dec. 29, 1899
William J. Brogan	187 Webster st	"	2.25 "	April 22, 1892
John Devlin	93 Endicott st	"	2.25 "	Sept. 12, 1899
John Doherty	18 Thatcher st	"	2.25 "	Dec. 30, 1901
James Flynn	29 Mt. Vernon st	"	2.25 "	Oct. 23, 1901*
Simon Goldberg	19 Auburn st	"	2.25 "	Nov. 15, 1901*
William F. Griffin	25 Eaton st	"	2.25 "	May 10, 1897
James Hannon	162 Franklin st	"	2.25 "	June 16, 1891
Thomas J. Hannon	442 Dudley st	"	2.25 "	April 18, 1895
Miles Heffernan	26 Portsmouth st	"	2.25 "	May 3, 1892
John Higgins	228 Commercial st	"	2.25 "	Aug. 27, 1906
John McCool	22 Tufts st	"	2.25 "	Jan. 10, 1900
Daniel F. McLaughlin	181 Endicott st	"	2.25 "	Nov. 18, 1892
Patrick J. Nagle	2 Revere st. pl	"	2.25 "	" 13, 1897
John O'Brien	82 W. Canton st	"	2.25 "	" 16, 1898
Michael B. O'Brien	52½ Washington st	"	2.25 "	Oct. 4, 1895
Francis J. O'Connor	102 Tyler st	"	2.25 "	June 9, 1900
William O'Hagan	22 Park st	"	2.25 "	May 19, 1891
William Waters	10 Mt. Vernon st	"	2.25 "	Nov. 25, 1893
Patrick F. Bergen	47 Poplar st	Reserve Laborer	2.25 "	April 29, 1905
James E. Burns	70 Poplar st	"	2.25 "	" 29, 1905
Guiseppe Capozza	18 Charter st	"	2.25 "	May 15, 1905
James J. Carney	96 Bartlett st	"	2.25 "	" 2, 1904
Pasquale Cataldo	88 Cottage st	"	2.25 "	" 15, 1905
Elmer E. Caverley	8 Bridge ct	"	2.25 "	" 29, 1905
Joseph F. Cavinaro	3 Mechanics ct	"	2.25 "	" 16, 1905
Thomas H. Connelly	75 Horace st	"	2.25 "	April 24, 1905
Thomas Donovan	53 Leverett st	"	2.25 "	" 24, 1905
John F. Dunn	16 Kennard ave	"	2.25 "	" 24, 1905
Cornelius Fitzpatrick	43 Allen st	"	2.25 "	" 24, 1905
Joseph Fleischer	301 Bennington st	"	2.25 "	June 25, 1900
William J. Garnett	7 Cypress st	"	2.25 "	April 24, 1905
Charles J. Haley	22 Lynde st	"	2.25 "	" 24, 1905
Benigno Iandoli	355 Hanover st	"	2.25 "	June 25, 1900
John J. Kilduff	125 Centre st	"	2.25 "	Jan. 1, 1900
Edward S. Lucas	10 Revere st	"	2.25 "	April 24, 1905
Patrick Moran	10 Bridge ct	"	2.25 "	" 29, 1904
James J. McCluskey	28 S. Russell st	"	2.25 "	" 24, 1905
Owen A. McDonald	17 Irving st	"	2.25 "	" 24, 1905
Philip J. McLaughlin	5 Bridge ct	"	2.25 "	" 29, 1904
Ansell Nichols	16 N. Anderson st	"	2.25 "	" 20, 1904
Michael J. O'Laughlin	69 Bromley st	"	2.25 "	" 24, 1905
Michael C. O'Hare	rear 365 Sumner st	"	2.25 "	" 22, 1904
Lamont Powers	17 Parkman st	"	2.25 "	May 29, 1904
Thomas Prendible	68 Poplar st	"	2.25 "	April 28, 1904
Buonaventure Raimondi	6 Sheafe st	"	2.25 "	" 29, 1904
Patrick W. Sheehan	126 Bunker Hill st	"	2.25 "	" 24, 1905
Thomas F. Walsh	7 Cypress st	"	2.25 "	" 24, 1905
Thomas P. Cahill	253 E. Eighth st	Regular Extra Laborer	2.25 "	Jan 4, 1907
Michele Cardillo	22 Chelsea st	" "	2.25 "	Sept. 11, 1906
Robert H. Creighton	163 W. Second st	" "	2.25 "	Dec. 10, 1906
Frank Cunningham	30 Blossom st	" "	2.25 "	Dec. 5, 1906
William F. Danehy	86 Hudson st	" "	2.25 "	Aug. 27, 1906
Raffaele Dello Russo	13 Charter st	" "	2.25 "	Sept. 7, 1906
John Doherty	32 N. Anderson st	" "	2.25 "	Aug. 24, 1906
Dennis Donovan	508 E. Third st	" "	2.25 "	Dec. 3, 1906
Patrick Egan	172 C st	" "	2.25 "	March 15, 1907
John Ferry	1 Quincy pl	" "	2.25 "	Aug. 24, 1906
William A. Hammond	3 Russell pl	" "	2.25 "	Oct. 15, 1906
William Hanlon	247 Bennington st	" "	2.25 "	Jan. 13, 1908
James E. Hart	52 Austin st	" "	2.25 "	Feb. 3, 1908*
John Holloran	45 Chambers st	" "	2.25 "	Dec. 31, 1907
John Glennon	86 Marcella st	" "	2.25 "	Oct. 15, 1906*
Frank J. Kane	6 Thatcher st	" "	2.25 "	Dec. 28, 1906
John Kennedy	515 Hanover st	" "	2.25 "	Aug. 24, 1906
Henry Kent	rear 200 Cambridge st	" "	2.25 "	March 5, 1908
Daniel J. Liddy	23 Highland st	" "	2.25 "	Aug. 27, 1906
John J. Lindsay	42 Nashua st	" "	2.25 "	Sept. 6, 1906
Owen McDermott	92 Neponset ave	" "	2.25 "	Aug. 24, 1906

* Previously employed in the department.

Street Department (Sanitary Division).— Concluded.

Name.	Residence.	Designation.	Compensation.	Date of Election or Appointment.

District No. 10.— Concluded.

Name.	Residence.	Designation.	Compensation.	Date of Election or Appointment.
John F. McNamara	1 Bridge ct	Regular Extra Laborer	$2.25 day	Nov. 1, 1907
Lawrence J. Noel	13 Sewall st	" "	2.25 "	Sept. 20, 1906
Edward C. Ralph	12 Mill st	" "	2.25 "	Aug. 24, 1906
Daniel Regan	412 W. Fourth st	" "	2.25 "	Feb. 23, 1909
John Roche	31 Hano st	" "	2.25 "	Aug. 24, 1906
John A. Roe	8 Marbury st	" "	2.25 "	Oct. 15, 1906
Fierorante Ruggiero	336 Commercial st.	" "	2.25 "	" 19, 1906
Daniel Shea	1466 Washington st.	" "	2.25 "	Sept. 6, 1906
John Shea	12 Hamlin st	" "	2.25 "	Nov. 5, 1907
James J. Sullivan	155 Albany st	" "	2.25 "	Oct. 15, 1906
Edward J. Tighe	94 Hammond st	" "	2.25 "	Aug. 27, 1906
Thomas Turley	101 Charles st	" "	2.25 "	Dec. 28, 1907
Francesco Zirpollo	47 Chelsea st	" "	2.25 "	Aug. 24, 1906

District No. 11.

Name.	Residence.	Designation.	Compensation.	Date of Election or Appointment.
John A. Dillon	13 Richmond st	Foreman	$3.50 day	March 3, 1905
Alexander Helsten	21 Dracut st	Watchman	2.25 "	Dec. 4, 1895
James E. Quinn	45 W. Second st	"	2.25 "	May 1, 1905
Michael F. Sullivan	46 Dover st	Boatman	2.50 "	Jan. 2, 1905
Martin T. Folan	14 W. Broadway	Scowman	2.25 "	July 1, 1902
John F. Bromfield	363 Maverick st	Dumper	2.25 "	Aug. 10, 1896
Owen Callahan	3 Sawyer st	"	2.25 "	May 11, 1891
William F. Ryan	18 Sturbridge st	"	2.25 "	April 6, 1899
James J. Barry	241 Havre st	Reserve Laborer	2.50 "	" 24, 1905
Edmund J. Hardy	83 Fulton st	"	2.50 "	Aug. 18, 1908
Daniel W. Kearns	18 Stanton st	"	2.50 "	April 24, 1905
William Hansbery	60 Sanford st	"	2.25 "	" 24, 1905
Augustine G. Kerrigan	226 Highland st	"	2.25 "	" 27, 1905
John Reagan	61 W. Lenox st	Regular Extra Laborer	2.25 "	Sept. 20, 1906
George A. Ham	161 Sydney st	Captain	1,200 yr.	Jan. 2, 1888
Michael J. McCarthy	408 Summer st	Engineer	3.50 day	Oct. 11, 1897
Henry E. Pingree	9 Frankfort st	"	3.50 "	April 24, 1909
Joseph Nelson	346 Bremen st	Emergency Engineer	3.50 "	" 14, 1909
Daniel J. Collins	94 Mercer st	Mate	3.00 "	May 8, 1907
James Kelly	34 Tolman st	Fireman	17.00 wk.	Dec. 30, 1896
James Reilly	261 Webster st	"	2.83¼ day	April 14, 1905
Charles E. Anderson	19 Decatur st	Deckhand	2.25 "	Feb. 12, 1908
Martin Clancy	7 W. Third st	Sailor	2.25 "	Nov. 23, 1907

Sewer Division.

Office.

Name.	Residence.	Designation.	Compensation.	Date of Election or Appointment.
C. Barton Pratt	25 Huntington ave	Deputy Superintendent	$3,500 yr.	Feb. 1, 1909*
Edgar S. Dorr	213 Savin Hill ave	Chief Engineer	3,000 "	March 26, 1891*
Henry W. Sanborn	69 Chestnut Hill ave	Executive Engineer	3,000 "	Jan. 2, 1888
John J. Quinn	292 Temple st	Chief Clerk	2,500 "	April 27, 1906*
William P. Willard	19 Granville st	Clerk	2,400 "	Nov. 1888*
William N. Irving	221 Corey st	Bookkeeper	1,800 "	Aug. 29, 1900
Peter J. Rooney	41 Angell st	Clerk	1,600 "	May 2, 1896
Harry J. Rockett	49 Bowdoin st	"	1,400 "	Aug. 29, 1892
Thomas H. Copell	7 Bynner st	"	1,200 "	May 11, 1896
Fred J. Steele	124 Calumet st	"	1,000 "	April 17, 1907
James J. McNamee	417 Main st	"	800 "	July 30, 1906
Erasmus F. Smith	485 Poplar st	"	4.00 day	Sept. 30, 1887
Edward J. McMinnie	326 Shawmut ave	"	17.50 wk.	July 21, 1896
Lawrence N. Shaw	621 E. Third st	"	2.50 day	April 1, 1906*
Hugh McCarron	71 Grove st	Stenographer	1,400 yr.	" 7, 1899
Joseph P. Hutchinson	16 Kerwin st	"	800 "	Aug. 31, 1908
Isaiah D. Barnett	28 Porter st	Messenger	800 "	Feb. 5, 1902
Thomas F. Bowes	42 Sycamore st	Assistant Engineer	6.00 day	July 10, 1900*
George W. Hamilton	143 W. Canton st	"	6.00 "	" 1, 1898*
Alexander L. Kidd	43 Sagamore st	"	6.00 "	" 1, 1898*
Edward F. Murphy	898 Adams st	"	6.00 "	Feb. 7, 1902*
Charles H. Dodd	7 Meredith st	Junior Engineer	5.00 "	Sept. 1892
Carl S. Drake	45 Dustin st	"	4.00 "	Aug. 12, 1902*
John E. Hartnett	1699 Washington st	"	4.00 "	March 16, 1904
James Hurley	19 Joy st	"	4.00 "	Sept. 21, 1904*
Fred A. Lovejoy	28 Wren st	"	4.00 "	" 3, 1895

* Previously employed in the department.

Street Department (Sewer Division).— Continued.

Name.	Residence.	Designation.	Compensation.	Date of Election or Appointment.
Office.— Continued.				
John E. L. Monaghan	319 Fourth st	Junior Engineer	$4.00 day	June 30, 1906
Owen Monahan	38 Lambert st	"	4.00 "	July, 1898*
John M. Shea	19 Myrtle st	"	4.00 "	May 11, 1891
William A. Johnson	173 Millet st	"	3.50 "	Oct. 5, 1903
Daniel J. Lynch	763 Columbia rd	"	3.50 "	" 2, 1907*
Warren A. Rogers	31 Bradbury st	"	3.50 "	Nov. 2, 1897
Ernest M. Young	26 Bentley st	"	3.50 "	May 30, 1903*
Mark E. Pitman	22 Gladstone st	"	3.00 "	Oct. 2, 1903
Edward Barnwell	18 Bowdoin st	Instrument Man	3.50 "	Nov., 1889
Thomas A. Finneran	28 Fisher ave	"	3.50 "	Oct. 29, 1903
Henry A. Sherman	1697 Washington st	"	3.50 "	May 13, 1904*
Francis A. Garvin	67 Fairbanks st	"	3.00 "	Oct. 10, 1903
Cyrus C. Howland	592 Park st., Dor	"	3.00 "	Sept. 27, 1895
Bertram A. Williams	48 Sanford st., Dor	"	3.00 "	Feb. 10, 1905*
Fred G. Daniels	1196 Dorchester ave	Rodman	2.75 "	Aug. 1, 1895
James A. Ackland	87 Hamilton st	"	2.50 "	" 12, 1896
James A. Bell	8 Fifield st	"	2.50 "	April 13, 1896
Francis J. Corbett	8 Fuller st., Dor	"	2.50 "	June 12, 1896
William H. Cunningham	226 Cambridge st	"	2.50 "	April 12, 1897
Fred M. Dacey	8 Lexington st	"	2.50 "	March 11, 1907*
Douglas C. Fagin	48 Mercer st	"	2.50 "	April 30, 1896
Thomas J. Ganley	65 Chestnut ave	"	2.50 "	Oct. 12, 1896
William V. P. Hoar	33 Dennis st	"	2.50 "	June 21, 1907
Henry C. Hoppe	468 Southampton st	"	2.50 "	" 3, 1902
Harry H. Hughes	19 Hamlet st	"	2.50 "	Oct. 9, 1895
John J. Lane	33 Sargent st	"	2.50 "	Nov. 8, 1895
Frank H. Lonergan	121 Mill st	"	2.50 "	Dec. 4, 1895
William B. Roche	116 Minot st., Dor	"	2.50 "	May 26, 1900
John J. Scollard	21 Marshfield st	"	2.50 "	April 29, 1896
Timothy F. Spillane	47 E. Dedham st	"	2.50 "	Sept. 2, 1896
William H. Bland	92 Pearl st	"	2.25 "	Oct. 7, 1896
Thomas J. Downey	11 Ruggles st	"	2.25 "	Jan. 30, 1897
Edward J. Logan	12 Fisher ave	"	2.25 "	" 21, 1896
George H. Sloan	317 Quincy st	"	2.00 "	Oct. 7, 1896
Frank J. Gately	5 Wenham st	"	1.75 "	May 3, 1905
John J. Burke	7 Sherwood st	"	1.25 "	July 17, 1907
Michael J. Morris	51 Magazine st	"	800 yr	Nov. 27, 1906
Richard J. McNulty	30 Newport st	Draughtsman	4.00 day	April 28, 1904
William J. Watkins	30 Collins st	"	4.00 "	Oct. 5, 1898
J. Philip O'Connell	257 Metropolitan ave	"	3.75 "	Sept. 16, 1903
Rudolph J. Thanisch	151 Park st., W. Rox	"	3.75 "	March 20, 1909
William M. Coombs	16 Paris st	"	3.50 "	Aug. 2, 1892
Charles A. Herbert	53 Moulton st	"	3.50 "	Sept. 11, 1903*
Daniel L. Mahoney	84 Ferrin st	"	3.50 "	" 16, 1896
Richard F. Ritchie	764 Broadway	"	3.50 "	Feb. 11, 1903
Walter L. Flanagan	35 Mt. Vernon st., Dor	"	3.00 "	Oct. 3, 1903
John J. Cusick	217 H st	"	3.00 "	July 8, 1902
John Connor	34 High st., Chsn	"	900 yr	Oct. 22, 1902
Fred A. Fales	189 Highland st	House Inspector	3.50 day	May 1, 1887
William F. Finneran	74 Smith st	"	3.50 "	Sept. 4, 1903
John M. Hurley	29 Wenham st	"	3.50 "	May 21, 1891
Randall E. Young	77 Callender st	"	3.50 "	April 26, 1900
James J. Conway	19 Beethoven st	Chief Inspector	1,800 yr	Nov. 21, 1898
James A. Berrill	101 Walnut ave	Inspector	5.00 day	" 30, 1895
James E. Coyne	35 Sherman st	"	5.00 "	July 10, 1906*
Lucius M. S. Horton	118 White st., E. B	"	5.00 "	Aug. 7, 1908
John F. McCarthy	409 Sumner st	"	5.00 "	" 6, 1896
Charles L. Weeks	rear 471 Columbus ave	"	4.00 "	April 1, 1901
Walter I. Brown	110 Park st	"	3.50 "	Feb. 13, 1903
Frank C. Gillooly	6 Washington st., Chsn	"	3.50 "	Aug. 26, 1896
Timothy J. Gunning	226 Lamartine st	"	3.50 "	Oct. 8, 1906*
William A. Moore	38 Atherton st	"	3.50 "	" 26, 1893
John W. O'Neil	23 Barry st	"	3.50 "	Dec. 1, 1892
Edward J. Ryan	136 Walnut ave	"	3.50 "	" 16, 1904*
John C. Sargent	2 Elbert st., Rox	"	3.50 "	Oct. 10, 1899
Michael J. Tehan	54 F st	"	3.50 "	Dec. 4, 1903*
Chester A. Young	25 Henshaw st	"	3.50 "	March 3, 1902
John L. Barry	23 Medford st	"	3.00 "	Dec. 29, 1905*
James A. Mitchell	7 Cardington st	"	3.00 "	Nov. 27, 1899
George E. Phalan	33 Cross st., Chsn	"	3.00 "	Aug. 20, 1897
Charles E. Sheehe	69 High st	"	3.00 "	June 13, 1902

* Previously employed in the department.

Street Department (Sewer Division).— Continued.

Name.	Residence.	Designation.	Compensation.	Date of Election or Appointment.

Office.— Concluded.

Name.	Residence.	Designation.	Compensation.	Date
Austin C. Woodside	86 W. Eagle st	Inspector	$3.00 day	Aug. 2, 1896
Patrick McBride	17 Temple st., Dor	Driver	3.00 "	Feb. 6, 1902
Joseph F. Burke	121 Heath st	"	17.50 wk	April 8, 1900
Daniel Connor	86 Fenwood rd	Blue Printer	2.25 day	March 23, 1896
Charles F. Ryan	76 Dale st	Cement Tester	2.75 "	April 28, 1902
Harry J. Reidy	138 Fisher ave	Chauffeur	21.00 wk	Aug. 23, 1906
Joseph P. Crotty	37 Stanley st	Laborer	2.75 day	July 15, 1897

District No. 1.— South Boston.

Name	Residence	Designation	Compensation	Date
William F. Lowe	60 Allen st	Foreman	$1,800 yr	Oct. 2, 1900*
James F. Granlee	14 S. Russell st	Inspector	3.75 day	May 1, 1887
William S. Halstrick	200A Hampden st	Clerk	800 yr	" 1, 1887
John H. Gibbard	121 Charles st	Mason	5.60 day	" 1, 1895
John Drillio	703 E .Broadway	Steam Engineer	.50 hr	Dec. 24, 1891
James P. Hurley	55 Dewey st	"	.50 "	April 1, 1892
John H. McGee	16 South st	"	.50 "	Sept. 12, 1907
Thomas F. McManaman	13 Ireland st	"	.50 "	May 28, 1905
John Cassidy	254 Ninth st	Carpenter	2.50 day	" 22, 1887
Patrick J. Barry	189 J st	Stableman	2.25 "	Oct. 29, 1889
Maurice Fitzgerald	11 Beckler ave	Watchman	2.25 "	Dec. 19, 1898
Michael McEtterick	9 Malden st	"	2.25 "	April 4, 1888
James McGrady	314 E st	"	2.25 "	May 1, 1887
Michael Monaghan	68 C st	"	2.25 "	Sept. 13, 1900
Dennis Callaghan	16 F st	Bracer	2.50 "	" 14, 1897
Michael F. Conley	75½ F st	"	2.50 "	May 23, 1888
Edward Flaherty	199 Second st	"	2.50 "	April 8, 1897
Walter McDonough	82 Third st	"	2.50 "	June 25, 1897
Robert Noonan	635 Sixth st	Laborer	2.50 "	Dec. 28, 1905
John J. Barry	1 Union ave	"	2.25 "	April 15, 1903
Patrick Brobson	56 Gold st	"	2.25 "	Oct. 4, 1892
Coleman Conley	68 Gold st	"	2.25 "	Feb. 6, 1899
Michael F. Connelly	632 E. Eighth st	"	2.50 "	May 20, 1889
Stephen Connolly	364 Second st	"	2.25 "	Aug. 26, 1896
John H. Connor	26 Ward st	"	2.25 "	Nov. 19, 1897
William J. Coughlin	214 C st	"	2.25 "	Aug. 2, 1897
James Dooley	153 Second st	"	2.25 "	Jan. 12, 1898
Andrew T. Flaherty	169 Athens st	"	2.25 "	May 26, 1891
Martin Foley	175 Bowen st	"	2.25 "	Oct. 26, 1898
John Gorham	42 Third st	"	2.25 "	May 10, 1907
John Joyce	87 Bowen st	"	2.25 "	" 7, 1907
Peter J. Keenan	1 Hayden pl	"	2.25 "	" 11, 1907
William H. Keevan	8 Yeoman st	"	2.25 "	June 25, 1906
John King	14 Sixth st	"	2.25 "	Oct. 15, 1892
Michael King	193 C st	"	2.25 "	June 23, 1891
Michael King, 2d	13 Gate st	"	2.25 "	" 6, 1897
Patrick King	5 Chestnut pl	"	2.25 "	Sept. 13, 1897
William R. Lomasney	75 Poplar st	"	2.25 "	Dec. 28, 1905
Christopher McDonough	161 Sixth st	"	2.25 "	June 20, 1891
James McDonough	22 B st	"	2.25 "	April 4, 1897
Michael McMahon	33 Devon st	"	2.25 "	Dec. 2, 1891
Owen Malloy	43 Fifth st	"	2.25 "	Oct. 14, 1889
Patrick Mungovern	686 Eighth st	"	2.25 "	" 15, 1902
William J. Neville	177 Fifth st	"	2.25 "	" 22, 1897
John O'Connor	12 Howe ave	"	2.25 "	Aug. 4, 1890
Michael O'Keefe	50 A st	"	2.25 "	June 22, 1895
James Patten	39 Palmer st	"	2.25 "	July 6, 1891
James F. Regan	272 Bowen st	"	2.25 "	" 2, 1890
Jeremiah Sheehan	184 I st	"	2.25 "	Aug. 3, 1892
Michael J. Smart	511 Third st	"	2.25 "	Feb. 7, 1899
Daniel J. Spain	69 Telegraph st	"	2.25 "	Sept. 22, 1897
John F. Traynor	631 Sixth st	"	2.25 "	Jan. 30, 1905
Michael J. Welch	19 Rawson st	"	2.25 "	" 5, 1899

District No. 2.— East Boston.

Name	Residence	Designation	Compensation	Date
John M. Conry	157 Webster st	Foreman	$1,800 yr	Feb. 5, 1902*
Robert J. Pumphret	1092 Bennington st	Sub-foreman	3.50 day	Oct. 24, 1902*
William J. Wickett	217 Webster st	Steam Engineer	.50 hr	July 7, 1907
Charles Carroll	423 Bennington st	Carpenter	3.50 day	Aug. 7, 1903
Robert Jeffers	67 Liverpool st	"	3.50 "	May 21, 1902
Frank J. Johnson	56 Wadsworth st	Yardman	2.50 "	April 1, 1902

* Previously employed in the department.

Street Department (Sewer Division).— Continued.

Name.	Residence.	Designation.	Compensation.	Date of Election or Appointment.
District No. 2.— East Boston.— Concluded.				
John H. Barry	244 Princeton st	Watchman	$2.25 day	Aug. 10, 1896
Thomas McIrney	7 Putnam st	"	2.25 "	Aug. 6, 1896
Roger Doherty	27 Chaucer st	Bracer	2.50 "	May 25, 1891
Michael Donnelly	12 Nicholson ct	"	2.50 "	April 6, 1897
Daniel Donohue	77 Byron st	"	2.50 "	July 17, 1888
John J. Price	11 Glendon pl	"	2.50 "	Dec. 7, 1897
Edward Grant	24 Chambers st	Laborer	2.50 "	Nov. 22, 1897
John P. Cady	101 Maverick sq	"	2.25 "	May 11, 1898
Patrick Cummings	170 Putnam st	"	2.25 "	Sept. 26, 1902
John Donohue	788 Saratoga st	"	2.25 "	Feb. 1, 1897
John Kennedy	148 Putnam st	"	2.25 "	May 10, 1907
Frank Kilbride	366 Meridian st	"	2.25 "	Sept. 25, 1888
James S. Knox	430 Bennington st	"	2.25 "	May 18, 1891
Michael E. Matthews	314 Bennington st	"	2.25 "	Jan. 6, 1908
Patrick McGee	331 Bennington st	"	2.25 "	Nov. 8, 1890
Bernard McGee	519 Bennington st	"	2.25 "	Oct. 25, 1890
Charles McCarthy	125 Farrington st	"	2.25 "	April 18, 1891
Bernard McLaughlin	91 Morris st	"	2.25 "	May 1, 1897
Jeremiah Moynihan	168 Putnam st	"	2.25 "	" 1, 1887
John Murray	18 Thwing st	"	2.25 "	Sept. 2, 1896
Michael Fitzgerald	143 Everett st	"	2.25 "	July 17, 1888
William Love	444 Bennington st	"	2.25 "	Oct. 4, 1890
Charles McGovern	80 Chelsea st	"	2.25 "	" 27, 1890
William T. Whalen	42 Everett st	"	2.25 "	April 7, 1902
John Bradley	242 Everett st	"	2.25 "	May 1, 1887
John Glavin	48 Jeffers st	"	2.25 "	July 20, 1898
John P. Queenan	185 Havre st	"	2.25 "	Oct. 24, 1895
District No. 4.— Brighton.				
Alfred Pitts	18 Bennett st	Foreman	$1,800 yr	Sept. 4, 1896*
William J. Nutley	24 Edwin st	Inspector	5.00 day	June 8, 1891
Patrick Grace	6 Garden st	Mason	.70 hr	Aug. 1, 1887
Joseph E. Brown	20 Exchange st	Steam Engineer	.50 "	July 29, 1899
John F. Fitzpatrick	18 Hitchborn st	Watchman	2.25 day	Jan. 30, 1894
Dennis Burke	15 Mackin st	Laborer	2.50 "	Oct. 24, 1899
Jeremiah Doyle	43 Oakland st	"	2.50 "	March 21, 1899
John Driscoll	31 Winship st	"	2.50 "	May 3, 1902
Robert Cameron	26 Cypress rd	"	2.25 "	Nov. 19, 1897
John Cawley	rear 32 Shepard st	"	2.25 "	" 25, 1893
Michael Coleman	7 Snow st	"	2.25 "	May 20, 1891
Patrick F. Collins	24 Shannon st	"	2.25 "	Nov. 25, 1893
John Connors	14 Winship st	"	2.25 "	" 25, 1893
Patrick W. Cotter	14 Holiday st	"	2.50 "	April 12, 1902
Michael J. Coyne	337 Market st	"	2.25 "	Aug. 11, 1887
Luke J. Curley	6 Cypress rd	"	2.25 "	Sept. 9, 1892
Cornelius Driscoll	33 Snow st	"	2.25 "	May 2, 1892
Owen Fitzgerald	54 Lincoln st	"	2.25 "	Nov. 25, 1893
John Flynn	54 Portsmouth st	"	2.25 "	" 25, 1893
Thomas Fogarty	8 Spring st	"	2.25 "	May 1, 1896
James Foley	339 Market st	"	2.25 "	" 22, 1902
Thomas P. Good	156 Heath st	"	2.25 "	Sept. 3, 1897
John T. Henry	238 Market st	"	2.25 "	May 1, 1891
Coleman Kane	20 Smith st	"	2.25 "	Dec. 2, 1893
John Kelliher	160 N. Beacon st	"	2.25 "	May 9, 1892
Bart McCarthy	Seager ct	"	2.25 "	June 25, 1890
Charles McElaney	14 Winship st	"	2.25 "	Sept. 11, 1892
John McFarland	950 Parker st	"	2.25 "	April 26, 1887
Thomas Morrison	176 N. Beacon st	"	2.25 "	June 2, 1893
Dennis O'Keefe	109 Dustin st	"	2.25 "	Nov. 25, 1893
John O'Neil	12 Waverly pl	"	2.25 "	May 5, 1892
Daniel D. Quill	33 Snow st	"	2.25 "	Jan. 2, 1903
David H. Rines	178 N. Beacon st	"	2.25 "	May 1, 1883
James Shea	3 Crossland pl	"	2.25 "	" 20, 1902
Daniel Sullivan	27 Litchfield st	"	2.25 "	Nov. 25, 1893
Thomas Tevenan	25 Snow st	"	2.25 "	" 25, 1893
John J. Tumblety	2 Conant pl	"	2.25 "	July 17, 1888
Michael Ward	12 Peaceable st	"	2.25 "	June 3, 1893
District No. 5.— West Roxbury.				
John Kelly	30 Boylston st	Foreman	$1,800 yr	Nov., 1893*
John J. Collins	4 Centre pl	Inspector	3.50 day	" 8, 1895

* Previously employed in the department.

Street Department (Sewer Division).— Continued.

Name.	Residence.	Designation.	Compensation.	Date of Election or Appointment.
		District No. 5.— West Roxbury.— Continued.		
John H. Driscoll	73 Walter st	Inspector	$3.50 day	Dec. 1, 1892
William O'Brien	19 Spring Park ave		4.25 "	May, 1895
Joseph Timilty	5 Crowley st	Mason	.70 hr	July 22, 1898
John J. Foley	2212 Centre st	Steam Engineer	.50 "	Feb. 18, 1898
Thomas Cunningham	21 Bradstreet ave	Blacksmith	3.00 day	May 23, 1895
William P. Barrett	95 Child st	Blacksmith's Helper	2.25 "	1, 1896
Charles J. Gallagher	61 Maywood st	Carpenter	3.75 "	Jan. 2, 1899
Daniel W. Moore	6 Holborn pk	Clerk	3.00 "	Dec. 12, 1899
Robert Stafford	5 Sanford pl	Yardman	2.25 "	May 11, 1887
John Barrett	164 Heath st	Teamster	2.25 "	Dec. 23, 1898
William H. Duffy	4 Elmwood ct	"	2.25 "	May 1, 1896
George W. Gilmore	2 Terry st	"	2.25 "	July 17, 1899
John F. Graham	36 Goldsmith st	"	2.25 "	May 14, 1891
Bernard Brady	26 Rosemary st	Stableman	2.25 "	1, 1883
Frank McMurrough	7 Rosemary st	"	2.25 "	14, 1891
John E. Boyle	31 Boylston st	Watchman	3.00 "	April 20, 1900
Patrick Egan	13 Anson st	"	2.25 "	Sept. 12, 1892
George Faul	10 Mechanic st	"	2.25 "	July 12, 1899
Michael F. Gilraine	48 Temple st	"	2.25 "	May 29, 1891
Timothy F. Sullivan	125 Bolton st	"	2.25 "	Dec. 29, 1899
Patrick J. Barrett	159 Green st	Laborer and Bracer	2.50 "	2, 1898
Patrick Cronin	12 Cherokee st	"	2.50 "	May 1, 1887
James Daley	1177A Tremont st	"	2.50 "	Oct. 23, 1895
Michael Donnelly	498 Parker st	Fireman	2.50 "	1, 1898
Thomas J. Early	38 Norfolk ave	Pipe Layer, Bracer and Laborer	2.50 "	May 21, 1891
Michael E. Foley	976 Parker st	Pipe Layer, Bracer and Laborer	2.50 "	Sept. 3, 1889
Thomas Giblin	101 Smith st	Pipe Layer, Bracer and Laborer	2.50 "	May 1, 1887
Cornelius J. McDonough	83 Call st	Bracer, Powderman and Laborer	2.50 "	Sept. 29, 1892
Hugh Shannon	214 Poplar st	Laborer, Bracer and Rigger	2.75 "	June 5, 1890
Daniel Brady	512 Hyde Park ave	Laborer	2.50 "	Aug. 23, 1895
Frank A. Brothers	32 Valentine st	"	2.50 "	March 2, 1906
James P. Barrett	116 Keyes st	"	2.25 "	Nov. 28, 1898
James Coyne	75 Maywood st	"	2.25 "	June 11, 1872
James Cunningham	93 Brookside ave	"	2.25 "	May 11, 1896
James J. Cusick	324½ Amory st	"	2.25 "	1, 1896
John Craven, 1st	33 Conant st	"	2.25 "	July 25, 1880
Michael Carty	21 Ballard st	"	2.25 "	Sept. 12, 1892
Michael Conway	668 Canterbury st	"	2.25 "	May 11, 1907
Patrick Carthy	87 Jamaica st	"	2.25 "	Aug. 26, 1893
Thomas Cox	169 Norfolk ave	"	2.25 "	July 24, 1897
William Clancy	5 Crosby pl	"	2.25 "	May 1, 1889
Andrew Doyle	71 Walk Hill st	"	2.25 "	1, 1896
Edward Dillon	96 Keyes st	"	2.25 "	Nov. 25, 1893
John Dolan	58 Call st	"	2.25 "	Oct. 18, 1897
Thomas Devny	651 Parker st	"	2.25 "	May 1, 1896
William Dunlea	50 E. Dedham st	"	2.25 "	6, 1904
Michael A. Flynn	5 Tremont ct	"	2.25 "	Oct. 7, 1896
Peter F. Fay	1122 Columbus ave	"	2.25 "	May 15, 1891
James Gibbons	151 Centre st	"	2.25 "	1, 1891
John Galvin	107 Carolina ave	"	2.25 "	Aug. 22, 1895
Luke Glennon	38 Dunlow st	"	2.25 "	Feb. 28, 1900
Patrick Gately	948 Parker st	"	2.25 "	June 14, 1883
Thomas Gavin	63 Wensley st	"	2.25 "	Oct. 15, 1889
Michael Hanley	384 Amory st	"	2.25 "	May 1, 1896
Patrick Higgins	121 Linden Park st	"	2.25 "	Nov. 25, 1893
Daniel Kenny	246 Cabot st	"	2.25 "	July 24, 1895
Michael Kelley	37 Goldsmith st	"	2.25 "	Nov. 25, 1893
Thomas Kelly	24 Day st	"	2.25 "	May 19, 1891
Frank J. Leslie	56 Lawn st	"	2.25 "	April 15, 1885
Garret Leahy	22 Weston st	"	2.25 "	Oct. 4, 1892
Richard Leonard	61 Child st	"	2.25 "	May 5, 1896
Charles McCarey	66 Gardner st	"	2.25 "	Nov. 25, 1893
Edward McShane	49 Smith st	"	2.25 "	April 23, 1892
Frank McCormack	39 Leon st	"	2.25 "	Dec. 31, 1892
Joseph McMahon	16 Rosemary st	"	2.25 "	June 5, 1885
John Mulloy	102 William st	"	2.25 "	July 9, 1897
Michael Murray	102 Williams st	"	2.25 "	1889
Michael B. McGarry	46 Union Park st	"	2.25 "	April 27, 1904

Street Department (Sewer Division).— Continued.

Name.	Residence.	Designation.	Compensation.	Date of Election or Appointment.

District No. 5.— West Roxbury.— Concluded.

Name.	Residence.	Designation.	Compensation.	Date of Election or Appointment.
Patrick J. Murrin	7 Texas st	Laborer	$2.25 day	July 13, 1897
William P. Malloy	277 Centre st	"	2.25 "	Oct. 31, 1904
John Maguire	191 Green st	"	2.25 "	May 2, 1896
Patrick Norton	3 Ballard pl	"	2.25 "	Sept. 8, 1896
Peter O'Rourke	25 Chestnut ave	"	2.25 "	" 23, 1892
Thomas O'Toole	27 Cabot st	"	2.25 "	Aug. 6, 1897
Charles Quigley	5 Tremont ct	"	2.25 "	Aug. 6, 1897
Joseph Rafferty	5 Crosby pl	"	2.25 "	Oct. 12, 1897
John Ryan	1188 Columbus ave	"	2.25 "	Jan. 2, 1898
Patrick Redden	324½ Amory st	"	2.25 "	Aug. 8, 1890
Michael Sheridan	27 Keyes st	"	2.25 "	Nov. 25, 1893
James Waters	7 Alden pl	"	2.25 "	Aug. 2, 1888
James Williamson	3540 Washington st	"	2.25 "	May 11, 1896
John Lawlor	95 Keyes st	"	2.25 "	Jan. 20, 1909*
John W. Murphy	Adams pl	"	2.25 "	April 17, 1889
Patrick Flynn	58 Call st	"	2.25 "	Sept. 24, 1895
John P. Sullivan	46 Baldwin st	"	2.25 "	Jan. 1, 1904

District No. 6.— Dorchester.

Name.	Residence.	Designation.	Compensation.	Date of Election or Appointment.
William Park	624 Dudley st	Foreman	$1,800 yr	May 1, 1900
John J. Crowley	13 Wrentham st	Inspector	5.00 day	Oct. 4, 1898
James F. Lucas	60 Astoria st	"	5.00 "	April 4, 1888
James C. Coleman	357 Seaver st	Clerk	3.50 "	May 1, 1885
John F. McMorrow	322 Adams st	Inspector and Carpenter	3.50 "	Jan. 11, 1904
Dennis Brennan	60 Fuller st	Mason	.70 hr	Oct. 10, 1898
William Finneran	9 Catawba st	"	.70 "	June 18, 1898
Matthew Taylor	13 Hecla st	Carpenter	2.25 day	Nov. 29, 1907*
Thomas McDonald	176 Westville st	Yardman	2.50 "	May 1, 1882
John Cain	73 Yeoman st	Steam Driller	2.50 "	" 1, 1888
John H. Riley	9 Bloomington st	Stonecutter	3.00 "	Oct. 1, 1899
Martin L. Boyle	1 Minot pl	Stableman	2.25 "	May 17, 1902
Patrick Thornton	35 East st	"	2.25 "	Nov. 25, 1898
James Farrell	1582 Dorchester ave	Watchman	2.25 "	June 26, 1895
Thomas H. Kelly	15 Plain st	"	2.25 "	Sept. 23, 1898
John Sullivan	10 Greenmount st	"	2.25 "	May 1, 1875
Martin F. O'Melia	1 Hammett st	"	2.25 "	" 11, 1892
Robert W. Sullivan	70 W. Cedar st	"	2.25 "	" 1, 1885
John Delaney	2082 Dorchester ave	Teamster	2.25 "	Sept. 7, 1892
Daniel Cotter	21 Roach st	Bracer	2.50 "	Aug. 5, 1896
Patrick Gorman	31 Dickens st	"	2.50 "	July 11, 1891
James Lee	43 W. Seventh st	"	2.50 "	May 31, 1898
Patrick Foley	18 B st	Pipe Layer	2.50 "	" 1, 1876
Patrick Curran	54 Beach st	Laborer	2.50 "	Oct. 14, 1897
Michael Graham	24 Greenwich st	"	2.50 "	" 5, 1896
Robert Amrouck	68 Grainger st	"	2.25 "	Nov. 30, 1898
Patrick J. Bennett	130 Draper st	"	2.25 "	Oct. 4, 1892
George Buchanan	87 1st	"	2.25 "	June, 1887
Patrick Burke	126 Eighth st	"	2.25 "	May 1, 1891
James Clancy	78 Taylor st	"	2.25 "	Oct. 2, 1895
Patrick Clougherty	161 Sixth st	"	2.25 "	" 11, 1897
Stephen Connolly	74 Middle st	"	2.25 "	May 25, 1896
Thomas Connolly	9 Ellsworth st	"	2.25 "	" 18, 1891
Stephen Costello	767 Dorchester ave	"	2.25 "	Aug. 22, 1895
Patrick Craven	700 Parker st	"	2.25 "	Aug. 23, 1897
John Dolan	419 Neponset ave	"	2.25 "	Nov. 1, 1897
James F. Fagan	60 Newhall ave	"	2.25 "	June 27, 1907
Peter Fahey	23 Fuller st	"	2.25 "	Aug. 6, 1890
Michael Flaherty	14 Fifth st	"	2.25 "	Sept. 10, 1890
Edward Galvin	5 Bertram st	"	2.25 "	Oct. 18, 1897
Daniel Higgins	22 Ellet st	"	2.25 "	Dec. 5, 1898
Patrick Higgins	22 Ellet st	"	2.25 "	July 11, 1891
Daniel Hurley	280 Neponset ave	"	2.25 "	May 5, 1896
Martin Joyce	124 Gold st	"	2.25 "	Oct. 8, 1889
Patrick Keating	37 Fremont pl	"	2.25 "	Aug. 5, 1896
James P. Keelan	82 Thetford ave	"	2.25 "	July 19, 1906
William J. Kelly	8 Preston ct	"	2.25 "	" 14, 1891
Timothy Leary	6 Fenton pl	"	2.25 "	Oct 25, 1889
James Lynch	111 Heath st	"	2.25 "	" 12, 1897
Stephen Manning	66 B st	"	2.25 "	Sept. 18, 1889

* Previously employed in the department.

Street Department (Sewer Division).— Continued.

Name.	Residence.	Designation.	Com- pensation.	Date of Election or Appointment.

District No. 6.— Dorchester.— Concluded.

Name.	Residence.	Designation.	Com- pensation.	Date of Election or Appointment.
Patrick J. McKenna	1155 Dorchester ave	Laborer	$2.25 day	Nov. 26, 1895
Michael Mecleedy	64 Pierce ave	"	2.25 "	June 16, 1902
Richard F. Moore	22 Bailey st	"	2.50 "	May 7, 1902
James Mulvaney	54 Terrace st	"	2.25 "	July 25, 1895
Thomas McParthn	20 Fenton st	"	2.25 "	April 20, 1904
Patrick Muldoon	46 Fuller st	"	2.25 "	Aug. 5, 1896
William Mullin	22 Ellet st	"	2.25 "	Dec. 19, 1898
Cornelius O'Brien	320 Adams st	"	2.25 "	Sept. 30, 1895
Jeremiah O'Brien	54 Cedar st	"	2.25 "	Dec. 5, 1898
Michael O'Brien	6 Loring st	"	2.25 "	May 11, 1897
John H. Peters	35 Jenkins st	"	2.25 "	Feb. 4, 1905
Thomas Phalen	13 Patterson st	"	2.25 "	May 10, 1902
Daniel Reiley	56 Grainger st	"	2.25 "	Dec. 9, 1898
Patrick Ronan	521 Ashmont st	"	2.25 "	Aug. 14, 1897
Martin Sheehan	46 Greenwich st	"	2.25 "	Nov. 8, 1889
John Sweeney, 1st	22 Greenwich st	"	2.25 "	Oct. 3, 1895
Daniel C. Doherty	12 Fenton st	"	2.25 "	July 24, 1897
Thomas McGovern	283 Hancock st	"	2.25 "	Dec. 29, 1887
Dennis Calnan	138 Pleasant st	"	2.25 "	Jan. 11, 1891
James H. McCarthy	76 Hudson st	"	2.25 "	Dec. 29, 1905
Nathan Gilman	1 Causeway st	"	2.25 "	" 26, 1905
Thomas Dury	34 Hampshire st	"	2.25 "	" 13, 1897
John Flynn	32 Tolman st	"	2.25 "	Aug. 3, 1896
John L. J. Flynn	94 E. Newton st	"	2.25 "	May 13, 1907
Abraham Minisky	27 Rochester st	"	2.25 "	Jan. 9, 1899
Richard Murray	2½ Clayton pl	"	2.25 "	April 10, 1897
Thomas Mullen	22 Langdon st	"	2.25 "	Oct. 26, 1898
Patrick Lilly	1 Elm st	"	2.25 "	May 26, 1891
Peter Blessington	49 Torrey st	"	2.25 "	Oct. 18, 1895
Boynton Harris	8 Fellows st	"	2.25 "	Dec. 22, 1897
Thomas Galvin	182 Norfolk ave	"	2.25 "	" 7, 1896
Dennis Glynn	5 Whitten st	"	2.25 "	July 12, 1897
Michael Donegan	8 Riverside st	"	2.25 "	Aug. 9, 1897
Thomas F. Ford	49 Weston st	"	2.25 "	Oct. 28, 1897
Patrick Kenney	812 Parker st	"	2.25 "	July 11, 1907
William T. Marshall	926 Albany st	"	2.25 "	Sept. 20, 1898
George H. Caswell	24 Hammond st	"	2.25 "	Jan. 3, 1898
William L. Johnson	42 Vernon st	"	2.25 "	Aug. 10, 1897
John Shannon	512 Third st	"	2.25 "	May 14, 1891
Cornelius J. Murphy	247 Kilton st	"	2.25 "	Nov. 20, 1907
Andrew H. Legere	206 Emerson st	"	2.25 "	Jan. 17, 1899
Murphy Henry	221 Webster st	Mason	.70 hr.	Dec. 7, 1896

Districts Nos. 7 and 8.— South End and Roxbury.

Name.	Residence.	Designation.	Com- pensation.	Date of Election or Appointment.
Patrick F. Kelley	109 Fenwood rd	Foreman	$5.00 day	May 8, 1908*
William J. Gormley	30 Cobden st	Inspector	3.50 "	April 30, 1903
Dennis Walsh	23 Chambers st	"	3.75 "	May 1, 1884
Edward J. Ryan	115 Adams st	Clerk	3.50 "	July 13, 1895
Patrick Broder	44 Hillside st	Mason	.70 hr.	Dec. 1, 1889
Michael Green	28 Walden st	Carpenter	2.75 day	May 1, 1877
Joseph H. Rorke	19 Adams st	"	3.50 "	Nov. 30, 1906
Ernest E. Cummings	1109 Harrison ave	Carpenter's Helper	2.75 "	March 10, 1902
Michael Duffee	253 Highland st	Steam Engineer	3.00 "	May 28, 1890
Oscar C. Holden	6 Sumner pl	Stableman	2.25 "	Nov. 23, 1891
Joseph P. Morley	109 E. Newton st	"	2.25 "	May 19, 1891
Thomas W. Coughlin	503 Harrison ave	Watchman	2.25 "	June 5, 1903
Jeremiah Ford	641 Eighth st	"	2.25 "	" 4, 1890
Patrick Hayes	28 Clarence st	"	2.25 "	" 5, 1902
Thomas Kelley	30 Boylston st	"	2.25 "	May 1, 1896
Dennis O'Sullivan	55 E. Newton st	"	2.25 "	" 1, 1887
Nathan F. O'Neill	24A Wakulla st	Teamster	2.50 "	Oct. 19, 1888
John F. Breen	43 Palmer st	"	2.25 "	Jan. 4, 1899
Thomas F. Casey	21 Winslow st	"	2.25 "	Oct. 3, 1892
William Downey	48 Cedar st	"	2.25 "	Sept. 13, 1897
Thomas F. Gillespie	656 Harrison ave	"	2.25 "	" 19, 1888
Edward J. Walsh	42 Sharon st	"	2.25 "	" 15, 1897
James Giblin	1248½ Tremont st	Bracer	2.50 "	May, 1887
Thomas McLaughlin	57 Roseclair st	"	2.50 "	" 10, 1887
Michael Neary	16 Halleck st	"	2.50 "	July 25, 1895
John P. Bogan	5 King st	Laborer	2.50 "	May 26, 1891

* Previously employed in the department.

Street Department (Sewer Division).— Continued.

Districts Nos. 7 and 8.— South End and Roxbury.— Concluded.

Name.	Residence.	Designation.	Compensation.	Date of Election or Appointment.
Michael Brady	876 Harrison ave	Laborer	$2.25 day	May 29, 1896
Allen Brydie	231 Bunker Hill st	"	2.25 "	Sept. 13, 1897
Timothy Carney	179 Heath st	"	2.25 "	May 1, 1872
James Clancy	56 Northampton st	"	2.25 "	Dec. 31, 1896
Hugh Clark	199 Vernon st	"	2.25 "	May 14, 1907
William Cluff	3 Champney pl	"	2.25 "	Sept. 22, 1890
Patrick Curley	264 Eustis st	"	2.25 "	Aug. 19, 1895
Patrick Daley	12 Lamont st	"	2.25 "	May 1, 1885
Thomas F. Daley	136 Marcella st	"	2.25 "	June 29, 1889
Stephen Desmond	14 Winship st	"	2.50 "	Sept. 14, 1896
Thomas H. Doherty	890½ Harrison ave	"	2.25 "	Nov. 3, 1898
Patrick Donohue	51 Sawyer st	"	2.25 "	Sept. 15, 1887
James F. Fagen	8 Riverside st	"	2.25 "	May 26, 1891
Henry Fitzgerald	38 Clapp pl	"	2.25 "	Sept. 21, 1896
Thomas Foley	5 Minden st	"	2.25 "	Oct. 3, 1892
Edmund J. Gallagher	1223 Tremont st	"	2.25 "	July 21, 1890
Martin Gallagher	910 Harrison ave	"	2.25 "	Feb. 2, 1906
James P. Hogan	1 Victor st	"	2.25 "	June 8, 1900
William F. Hughes	7 Bromley st	"	2.25 "	" 15, 1891
John J. Lamb	43 Hampshire st	"	2.25 "	May 13, 1907
Edward Lee	90 Sixth st	"	2.25 "	" 1, 1877
Luke Lyons	57 Gates st	"	2.50 "	" 1, 1880
Michael P. Lyons	14 Whitney st	"	2.25 "	Nov. 7, 1907
Patrick J. Madden	5 Conant st	"	2.25 "	Aug. 20, 1897
Patrick Murray	24 Conant st	"	2.25 "	May 1, 1887
John McCarthy	23 Walpole st	"	2.25 "	" 1889
James McFarland	155 K st	"	2.25 "	" 10, 1897
James McGee	1495 Columbus ave	"	2.25 "	" 24, 1897
Michael O'Toole	27 Cabot st	"	2.25 "	April 10, 1897
Timothy Reardon	69 Cabot st	"	2.50 "	Aug. 23, 1897
John L. Stanton	6 Whitney st	"	2.25 "	Oct. 4, 1892
Jeremiah F. Sullivan	31 Batchelder st	"	2.25 "	May 9, 1902
Dennis Toland	82 Williams st	"	2.25 "	1889
Owen Winn	42 Dunlow pl	"	2.25 "	Sept. 15, 1890
Daniel F. Sullivan	12 Vineland st	"	2.25 "	May 13, 1907
Daniel Coleman	23 Downing st	"	2.25 "	April 7, 1897
Florence J. Hartnett	317 Dudley st	"	2.25 "	June 16, 1902

Districts Nos. 9 and 10.— North and West Ends.

Name.	Residence.	Designation.	Compensation.	Date of Election or Appointment.
Francis E McCarthy	142 St. Alphonsus st	Foreman	$1,800 yr	Feb. 8, 1908
Thomas Glennon	16 St. Rose st	Inspector	3.50 day	June 24,.1908*
John J. McKenna	167 Hamilton st	"	3.50 "	Oct. 26, 1906*
Francis P. McGuinness	9 Ohio st	Mason	.70 hr	April 11, 1892
Thomas Keane	7 Exeter pl	Engineer	.50 "	June 3, 1898
John Ring	27 Eulila ter	"	.50 "	March 16, 1895
Edward P. Sullivan	Willis st	"	.50 "	" 29, 1907
John M. McCann	52 Rockland st	Carpenter	3.75 day	Feb. 12, 1897*
William R. G. Doyle	432 Bennington st	Clerk	2.50 "	May 9, 1902
John Flaherty	98 Old Harbor st	Yardman	2.50 "	July 17, 1888
Timothy Driscoll	327 Hanover st	Watchman	2.25 "	Aug. 7, 1896
Thomas J. Griffin	96 Bunker hill st	"	2.25 "	Nov. 20,.1889
Malachi A. Hanley	350 Amory st	"	2.25 "	Oct. 18, 1899
Sylvester G. Maloney	13 Everett st	"	2.25 "	April 5, 1897
Thomas Toomey	11 Union st., Chsn	"	2.25 "	Feb. 27, 1899
Lawrence F. McNamara	11 Washington st., Chsn	"	2.25 "	Aug. 7, 1899
John T. Dunn	9 Mt. Vernon st., Chsn	Teamster	2.25 "	May 21, 1891
Timothy Kennedy	267 Silver st	"	2.25 "	Dec. 26, 1905
James McNabb	107 Charter st	"	2.25 "	March 19, 1895
Martin J. Tynan	3 Hillside pl	"	2.25 "	June 16, 1898
Willis West	180 F st	"	2.25 "	" 12, 1898
Owen Kelly	1569 Tremont st	Driver	2.25 "	Sept. 14, 1896
Daniel Doherty	43 Bartlett st., Chsn	Bracer	2.50 "	May, 1882
Edward Doherty	55 Rutherford ave	"	2.25 "	Oct. 19, 1887
Thomas Flaherty	193 Silver street	"	2.50 "	April 7, 1897
Bernard Gibbons	11 Adams st	"	2.50 "	June 8, 1874
James King	17 Newark st	"	2.50 "	April 7, 1897
James Mulhern	185 Highland st	"	2.75 "	Nov. 4, 1897
Thomas Burke	5 Union ave., J. P.	Laborer	2.25 "	Jan. 9, 1899
Thomas Burston	45 Grove st	"	2.25 "	" 26, 1906
Robert Butland	1 Thompson st., Chsn	"	2.25 "	Sept. 13, 1895

* Previously employed in the department.

Street Department (Sewer Division).— Continued.

Name.	Residence.	Designation.	Com- pensation.	Date of Election or Appointment.

Districts Nos. 9 and 10.— North and West Ends. - Concluded.

Name.	Residence.	Designation.	Com- pensation.	Date of Election or Appointment.
Michael Cain	38 Heath st	Laborer	$2.25 day	Sept. 15, 1890
John Cassano	88 Endicott st	"	2.25 "	Nov. 11, 1897
John Creedon	1 Reisse pl	"	2.25 "	Aug. 4, 1882
John F. Curley	40 Charles st	"	2.25 "	June 21, 1907
John Devlin	93 Endicott st	"	2.25 "	Oct. 23, 1906
Patrick Doherty	14 Everett st	"	2.25 "	Sept. 20, 1898
William Donnelly	8 Mystic pl., Chsn	"	2.25 "	" 28, 1889
Robert B. Dunlap	747 Shawmut ave	"	2.25 "	May 29, 1891
Patrick Flaherty	33 Hyde Park ave	"	2.25 "	June 24, 1907
Martin Flynn	1 Grotto Glen rd	"	2.25 "	Dec. 1, 1896
James Gallagher	202 Cambridge st	"	2.25 "	May, 1887
Patrick Glennon	95 St. Alphonsus st	"	2.25 "	June 22, 1895
John Guinee	491 Maitland st	"	2.25 "	May 22, 1891
Daniel Hart	8 Riverside st	"	2.25 "	June 8, 1880
Michael Hourihan	108 Conant st	"	2.25 "	Sept. 5, 1897
Thomas Hughes	18 Posen st	"	2.50 "	July 7, 1897
John Joyce	41 A st	"	2.25 "	Oct. 4, 1892
Martin Kelly	76 Longwood ave	"	2.25 "	May 9, 1892
Thomas Kirby	35 Centre st	"	2.25 "	Dec. 2, 1891
Peter Lally	37 Taber st	"	2.25 "	Aug. 23, 1897
John McAteer	334 Amory st	"	2.25 "	Dec. 16, 1897
Patrick McDermott	126 Terrace st	"	2.25 "	Aug. 26, 1897
John A. McDonald	906 Columbus ave	"	2.25 "	June 27, 1907
Terence McFarland	938 Parker st	"	2.25 "	May 18, 1885
Thomas McHugh	28 Bromley pk	"	2.25 "	" 27, 1891
Michael McKenna	5 Union ave., J. P	"	2.25 "	July 12, 1897
Michael Mulvey	166 Norfolk ave	"	2.25 "	Sept. 22, 1890
James J. Murphy	81½ Warren st., Chsn	"	2.25 "	Feb. 28, 1906
Patrick Noonan	65 Staniford st	"	2.25 "	Aug. 31, 1898
Michael Patten	20 Smith st	"	2.25 "	" 7, 1896
Thomas H. Patten	166 Market st	"	2.25 "	June 10, 1902
Thomas Reddington	17 Kent st., Rox.	"	2.25 "	Jan. 5, 1896
Joseph H. Reed	37 Everett st., Chsn	"	2.25 "	Oct. 4, 1895
John Short	9 McLean st	"	2.25 "	Aug. 17, 1899
Daniel Sullivan	167 Hamilton st	"	2.25 "	April 7, 1897
Peter Tumblety	3 Culbert pl	"	2.50 "	Jan. 17, 1888
James J. Walsh	41 Dover st	"	2.25 "	Dec. 14, 1891
Thomas Walsh	29 Reed st	"	2.25 "	Sept. 22, 1890
Thomas W. Fitzpatrick	23 Oakley st	"	2.50 "	June 27, 1902
William H. Joyce	344 Hanover st	"	2.25 "	Dec. 9, 1898

District No. 11.— Main Drainage.

Name.	Residence.	Designation.	Com- pensation.	Date of Election or Appointment.
Edward McLaughlin	456 Parker st	Foreman	$1,800 yr.	May 1, 1882
Humphrey J. Moynihan	699 Massachusetts ave	Inspector	3.50 day	Dec. 29, 1905
James Brayden	121 Boston st	Sub-foreman	3.00 "	Jan. 2, 1888
Leonard J. Rollins	6 Concord sq	Clerk	2.50 "	April 1, 1891
Michael J. Conley	34 Worthington st	Machinist	3.52 "	Jan. 26, 1907
Peter Ducie	3 Fielding pl	Watch and Stableman	2.50 "	" 12, 1894
Matthew Cannaven	12 Dennis st	"	2.25 "	" 15, 1894
Jeremiah Savage	73 Middlesex st	Yardman	2.25 "	April 1, 1902
William H. Anderson	17 Weston st	Laborer	2.25 "	May 13, 1907
Thomas Bragan	44 Charles st	"	2.25 "	June 5, 1904
Melville F. Battis	22 Hanson st	"	2.25 "	April 28, 1900
Joseph P. Driscoll	289 Shawmut ave	"	2.50 "	Jan. 24, 1903
Patrick Fay	88 Marcella st	"	2.25 "	June 16, 1891
Thomas A. Hogan	97 Hunneman st	"	2.25 "	May 10, 1907
James Kelley	2 Prescott pl	"	2.25 "	June 25, 1906
Patrick Murray	9 Centre st	"	2.25 "	May 19, 1891
Michael Riordan	33 Middle st	"	2.25 "	Aug. 1, 1890
Michael Wade	203 K st	"	2.25 "	May 1, 1887
Matthew Walsh	224 Ninth st	"	2.25 "	June 22, 1895

Pumping Station.

Name.	Residence.	Designation.	Com- pensation.	Date of Election or Appointment.
Bliss W. Robinson	61 Grampian way	Superintendent	$2,500 yr.	Jan. 11, 1909
Joseph A. Rourke	1699 Washington st	Mechanical Engineer	2,000 "	July 26, 1906*
Charles C. Carroll	29 Claxton st	Draughtsman	3.00 day	Aug. 5, 1899
Edward W. Crotty	59 Chelsea st	"	3.00 "	April 7, 1902
William F. Chadwick	15 Mt. Vernon st., Dor	Clerk	3.00 "	Nov. 15, 1897
George W. Emerson	30 Saxton st	Assistant Engineer	4.66⅔ "	Dec. 17, 1888

* Previously employed in the department.

Street Department (Sewer Division).— Continued.

Name	Residence.	Designation.	Compensation.	Date of Election or Appointment.

Pumping Station.— Concluded.

Name	Residence.	Designation.	Compensation.	Date of Election or Appointment.
James H. Finn	15 Mt. Vernon st., Chsn	Assistant Engineer	$4.66⅔ day	Jan. 2, 1888
Charles R. Palmer	21 Edison green	"	4.66⅔ "	" 2, 1888
Richard Sliney	600 Dorchester ave	"	4.66⅔ "	Nov. 26, 1898
Bernard Barry	633 Dorchester ave	Oiler	3.25 "	July 11, 1887
Jeremiah Clifford	596 Seventh st	"	3.25 "	June 5, 1889
Daniel L. Doherty	71 Clarkson st	"	3.25 "	Jan. 2, 1888
William DuWors	299 Sumner st	"	3.25 "	Feb. 28, 1902
John Farley	580 Dorchester ave	"	3.25 "	April 26, 1899
James Fitzgerald	22 Lark st	"	3.25 "	Nov. 7, 1897
John Hennessey	47 Kimball st	"	3.25 "	Aug. 2, 1887
John J. Jordan	478 Eighth st	"	3.25 "	June 19, 1906
Charles A. Kelly	19 Torrey st	"	3.25 "	Feb. 26, 1906
Edward A. Kennedy, Jr.	12 Fifield st	"	3.25 "	Jan. 15, 1906
James McDonough	233 E st	"	3.25 "	" 2, 1888
James H. McNeil	16 Roach st	"	2.50 "	" 2, 1888
John F. Powell	794 Sixth st	"	3.25 "	March 19, 1898
Timothy Scully	122 Boston st	"	3.25 "	Jan. 15, 1906
Joseph Sullivan	15 Edison green	"	3.25 "	March 31, 1902
Thomas Sullivan	19 Sudan st	"	3.25 "	Jan. 2, 1888
Albert P. Wood	14 Quincefield st	"	3.25 "	" 29, 1896
David A. Kurriss	6 Linden st	Oil Tester	2.91⅓ "	July 25, 1902
Andrew Calnan	7 Leroy st	Fireman	3.25 "	Aug. 23, 1897
Jeremiah C. Delaney	16 Leedsville st	"	3.25 "	Nov. 30, 1898
Thomas Donohue	73 Romsey st	"	3.25 "	April 30, 1896
John Flynn	10 Hecla st	"	3.25 "	Dec. 8, 1898
Thomas M. Mahoney	30 Newport st	"	3.25 "	April 14, 1905
Martin P. Mullen	47 Torrey st	"	3.25 "	" 7, 1897
Patrick O'Melia	245 Cabot st	"	3.25 "	" 7, 1897
John Sullivan	67 Granger st	"	3.25 "	Oct. 28, 1889
John F. Ahern	94 Dresser st	Coal Passer	2.75 "	April 18, 1902
John Francis	458 Eighth st	"	2.75 "	Feb. 5, 1903
Philip Lamb	13 Water st	"	2.75 "	April 17, 1897
Patrick Murray	10 Preston ct	"	2.75 "	May 10, 1907
Thomas Naughton	161 Third st	"	2.75 "	Sept. 27, 1897
Michael J. Reilly	48 Fuller st	"	2.75 "	May 19, 1902
James F. Slattery	245 Dorchester st	"	2.75 "	" 24, 1907
Richard J. Tobin	69 Granger st	"	2.75 "	Dec. 9, 1898
Thomas Howe	1064 Dorchester st	Blacksmith	3.00 "	March 8, 1888
James R. Wiley	58 Baxter st	Blacksmith's Helper	2.25 "	Aug. 10, 1896
Michael J. Hughes	151 Sidney st	Machinist	3.52 "	" 3, 1898
Daniel Leary	382 Columbia rd	"	3.52 "	July 18, 1898
George B. Sherry	96 Templeton st	"	3.52 "	Jan. 18, 1906
Edward E. Hasenfus	42 Union Park st	Machinist's Helper	2.50 "	April 10, 1903
Thomas F. Regan	139 Mt. Pleasant ave	"	2.50 "	Feb. 26, 1906
John Slattery	28 Fairbury st	Storekeeper	3.00 "	Jan. 2, 1888
Richard H. Shannon	184 E st	Wireman	4.00 "	Oct. 6, 1905
Peter J. Mullen	94 I st	Carpenter	3.50 "	Nov. 1, 1899
Patrick Nolan	32 Sudan st	"	3.50 "	" 2, 1897
James McNamara	93 Buttonwood st	Sub-foreman	2.75 "	Jan. 2, 1888
Patrick J. Foley	23 Champney st	Teamster	2.50 "	May 18, 1891
Bartholomew F. Lally	62 Romsey st	Stableman	2.50 "	April 22, 1904
Thomas Condon	27 Dorchester ave	Watchman	2.50 "	Oct. 11, 1897
Daniel Murnane	1185 Dorchester ave	Sewer Cleaner	2.50 "	May 18, 1891
Patrick Thornton	482 Eighth st	"	2.50 "	" 5, 1888
John T. Shea	62 Allen st	Mason	.70 hr	April 5, 1902
Maurice Ahern	94 Dresser st	Laborer	2.25 day	Jan. 2, 1888
James Blessington	20 Fenton st	"	2.25 "	Aug. 23, 1897
Walter H. Burgess	101 Concord st	"	2.25 "	" 30, 1900
William J. Edwards	98 Pleasant st	"	2.25 "	Jan. 2, 1888
Patrick Fitzpatrick	134 Eighth st	"	2.25 "	June 22, 1895
Peter Fitzpatrick	68 Middle st	"	2.25 "	Aug. 5, 1896
Michael Harrison	51 Speedwell st	"	2.50 "	Jan. 2, 1888
John Henshou	60 Pierce ave	"	2.25 "	Nov. 30, 1898
Thomas Lavin	5 Roach st	"	2.25 "	Oct. 19, 1897
William Plane	15 Jenkins st	"	2.25 "	Sept. 18, 1895
John Reilly	56 Granger st	"	2.25 "	Oct. 19, 1897
Dudley Sullivan	150 Dorchester st	"	2.25 "	Jan. 2, 1888
John Sweeney	20 Roach st	"	2.25 "	Aug. 23, 1897

Moon Island.

Name	Residence.	Designation.	Compensation.	Date of Election or Appointment.
Timothy F. Callahan	Quincy	Foreman	$1,800 yr	Jan. 2, 1883
Cushing Baker	27 Kenwood st., Dor	Engineer	2.91⅓ day	Sept. 1, 1888

Street Department (Sewer Division).— Concluded.

Name.	Residence.	Designation.	Compensation.	Date of Election or Appointment.

Moon Island.— Concluded.

Name.	Residence.	Designation.	Compensation.	Date of Election or Appointment.
Robert Harding	Quincy	Gateman	$2.91½ day	Jan. 2, 1888
Daniel Madden	153 Winthrop st., Rox	"	2.91½ "	Nov. 25, 1898
Timothy Nagle	318 Adams st	"	2.91½ "	Sept. 18, 1895
Felix McConn	3069 Wash'n st., W. R	"	2.50 "	Feb. 23, 1906
Cornelius Collins	320 Adams st., Dor	Teamster	2.25 "	July 30, 1888
Christopher Kenney	5 Bear-e ave	Laborer	2.25 "	May 8, 1902
Daniel Murphy	320 Adams st	"	2.25 "	Oct. 12, 1892

Street Cleaning and Watering Division.

Name.	Residence.	Designation.	Compensation.	Date of Election or Appointment.
John A. Brant	315 Paris st	Clerk	$1,300 yr	Feb. 1, 1907
Thomas B. Harty	15 Fenno st	"	1,200 "	March 25, 1895
Arthur Neilson	131 Newbury st	"	1,200 "	April 26, 1900
William E. Bennett	35 Mt. Vernon st	"	1,000 "	" 4, 1906

District No. 1.— South Boston.

Name.	Residence.	Designation.	Compensation.	Date of Election or Appointment.
Bartholomew Haley	850 Broadway	Foreman	$1,400 yr	April 6, 1891
Joseph F. Mello	116 W. Seventh st	Sub-foreman	2.50 day	Dec. 25, 1908
Richard Wallace	108 Emerson st	"	3.00 "	March 3, 1892
Michael J. Hurley	577 E. Second st	Yardman	2.25 "	Sept. 15, 1905
John F. Johnson	700 E. Sixth st	Stableman	2.25 "	Aug. 21, 1895
Cornelius Moynihan	105 W. Ninth st	"	2.25 "	April 11, 1891
John A. English	234 D st	Machine Driver	2.33⅓ "	" 22, 1907
William M. Gorman	505 E. Third st	"	2.33⅓ "	May 1, 1905
John J. Welsh	4 I st	"	2.33⅓ "	April 28, 1905
Benjamin J. Fitzpatrick	175 W. Broadway	Inspector	3.00 "	Aug. 15, 1908
Thomas Dahill	596 E. Second st	Teamster	2.25 "	Oct. 28, 1902
Daniel J. Donovan	27 H st	"	2.25 "	April 25, 1905
James Kearney	497 E. Sixth st	"	2.25 "	Feb. 1, 1897
Philip Lonergan	298 W. Third st	"	2.25 "	May 22, 1891
Alexander McCarthy	658 E. Sixth st	"	2.25 "	April 25, 1905
John Sullivan, 1st	6 Willis st	"	2.25 "	March 20, 1891
John Conley	137 W. Eighth st	Helper	2.25 "	April 23, 1895
Dennis J. Cronan	2 Lawrence ct	"	2.25 "	June 19, 1896
John Fitzgerald	292 W. Fifth st	"	2.25 "	" 11, 1897
Michael Kelly	314 W. Fourth st	"	2.25 "	Oct. 19, 1891
Jeremiah J. Moynihan	719 Second st	"	2.25 "	Feb. 21, 1901
Peter Mulvey	294 W. Fourth st	"	2.25 "	April 27, 1901
Thomas O'Malley	624 E. Third st	"	2.25 "	" 24, 1902
Stephen Whalen	29 Old Harbor st	"	2.25 "	Sept. 15, 1891
William Cassell	104 E. Canton st	Laborer	2.25 "	Dec. 5, 1903
James Condon	496 E. Eighth st	"	2.25 "	" 8, 1899
Daniel Dempsey	35 Woodward st	"	2.25 "	March 27, 1891
William A. Doherty	407 W. First st	"	2.25 "	Sept. 25, 1891
John Fitzsimmons	35 Woodward st	"	2.25 "	March 20, 1891
Thomas F. Foley	608 E. Third st	"	2.25 "	May 2, 1904
John Harrington	503 E. Sixth st	"	2.25 "	Nov. 23, 1891
William Kestle	496 E. Sixth st	"	2.25 "	May 21, 1891
Michael Lane	415 W. First st	"	2.25 "	" 4, 1891
James McDermott	44 Mt. Vernon st	"	2.25 "	Sept. 14, 1892
William McDonough	141 Bowen st	"	2.25 "	Feb. 1, 1906
Denis McGrath	730 E. Third st	"	2.25 "	March 20, 1891
John J. O'Hearn	54 I st	"	2.25 "	April 28, 1905
Patrick Organ	16 Dorchester ave	"	2.25 "	Oct. 23, 1891
Henry Waldron	321 Dorchester st	"	2.25 "	" 12, 1892
Hugh Timmins	6 Rozella st	Watchman	2.25 "	June 27, 1892
James Dahill	774 E. Seventh st	Regular Extra Laborer	2.25 "	Sept. 6, 1906
Edward P. Keller	164 E. Third st	" "	2.25 "	April 22, 1907
Sylvester McCarthy	24 Dixfield st	" "	2.25 "	" 22, 1907
John T. Slattery	249 W. Second st	" "	2.25 "	Sept. 24, 1906
Cornelius Sullivan	34 L st	" "	2.25 "	" 5, 1906
William Spleen	31 Old Harbor st	Laborer	2.25 "	April 13, 1891

District No. 2.— East Boston.

Name.	Residence.	Designation.	Compensation.	Date of Election or Appointment.
Michael J. Pumphret	249 Princeton st	Foreman	$1,400 yr	Dec. 29, 1899
Harry Keenan	391 Chelsea st	Sub-foreman	3.00 day	June 28, 1904
Daniel D. Flaherty	445 Bennington st	Yardman	2.25 "	April 28, 1902
William Grant	353 Chelsea st	Machine Driver	2.33⅓ "	Jan. 1, 1900
Edward F. Henneberry	132 Webster	"	2.33⅓ "	" 2, 1902
Cornelius E. Sutton	20 Paris	Stableman	2.25 "	Sept. 25, 1903
Martin Gill	158 Chelsea st	Teamster	2.25 "	April 25, 1905

Street Department (Street Cleaning and Watering Division).— Continued.

Name.	Residence.	Designation.	Compensation.	Date of Election or Appointment.

District No. 2.— East Boston.— Concluded.

Name.	Residence.	Designation.	Compensation.	Date of Election or Appointment.
James McGlinchy	307 E. Eagle st	Teamster	$2.25 day	April 25, 1905
Daniel A. Diamond	610 Bennington st	Laborer	2.25 "	Oct. 12, 1903
Richard J. Donnelly	15 Border st	"	2.25 "	Jan. 12, 1900
Joseph E. Hanley	177 Everett st	"	2.25 "	June 26, 1908
John F. Hickey	290 Chelsea st	"	2.25 "	April 25, 1905
Daniel J. Hyde	510 Sumner st	"	2.25 "	" 25, 1905
Herbert S. Lawrence	80 Chelsea st	"	2.25 "	" 29, 1904
Timothy Mahoney	262 Paris st	"	2.25 "	" 25, 1905
James W. Morris	17 New st	"	2.25 "	Sept. 25, 1903
John Murray	363 Sumner st	"	2.25 "	April 22, 1907
John J. Murray	119 Porter st	"	2.25 "	" 25, 1905
Michael J. O'Connell	505 Orleans st	"	2.25 "	Dec. 29, 1908
Daniel Cosgrove	57 Bennington st	Regular Extra Laborer	2.25 "	July 22, 1907
Joseph H. Jeffrey	26 Decatur st	" "	2.25 "	Aug. 24, 1906
Owen Kelly	439 Bennington st	" "	2.25 "	" 24, 1906
James M. McGovern	93 London st	" "	2.25 "	Sept. 8, 1906
John Riley	33 Cottage st	" "	2.25 "	Dec. 6, 1907
James Roach	167 Lexington st	" "	2.25 "	Aug. 24, 1906

District No. 3.— Charlestown.

Name.	Residence.	Designation.	Compensation.	Date of Election or Appointment.
Thomas O'Leary	74 Washington st	Foreman	$1,400 yr	May 4, 1891
James H. Devine	72 Washington st	Sub-foreman	3.00 day	March 20, 1891
Timothy Conway	1 Pearl street pl	Machine Driver	2.33⅓ "	April 29, 1904
Richard J. Leonard	27 Albion pl	"	2.33⅓ "	March 20, 1891
Jeremiah O'Leary	14 Linwood pl	Stableman	2.25 "	Sept. 22, 1892
Edward Linehan	57 Decatur st	Teamster	2.25 "	June 16, 1902
Charles Monagle	7 Mystic pl	"	2.25 "	July 27, 1893
Cornelius J. Crowley	535 Medford st	Helper	2.25 "	April 25, 1905
Michael J. Donahue	329 Bunker Hill st	"	2.25 "	" 25, 1905
James McGinnis	17 Mt. Vernon st	"	2.25 "	May 4, 1891
Bernard McShane	19 Hudson st	"	2.25 "	July 25, 1899
Charles Gould	20 Miller st	Laborer	2.25 "	" 22, 1899
John J. Griffin	5 Foss st	"	2.25 "	March 26, 1894
John C. Hourihan	7 Chestnut ct	"	2.25 "	April 22, 1907
Patrick Leary	79 Russell st	"	2.25 "	May 4, 1891
Lawrence McAvoy	20 Vine st	"	2.25 "	April 22, 1907
Eugene P. McCarthy	508 Medford st	"	2.25 "	" 22, 1907
Peter McDonald	3 Princeton st	"	2.25 "	May 4, 1891
John Murphy	20 Concord st	"	2.25 "	Oct. 24, 1893
Daniel Sheehan	9 Lexington st	"	2.25 "	May 4, 1891
Bartholomew Coyne	44 Austin st	Regular Extra Laborer	2.25 "	Sept. 1, 1906
Daniel Davis	102 Medford st	" "	2.25 "	Aug. 25, 1906
Francis Madden	9 Freemont ct	" "	2.25 "	" 27, 1906
Martin F. Sullivan	8 Edgeworth st	" "	2.25 "	" 27, 1906
John J. Wade	43 Austin st	" "	2.25 "	Oct. 19, 1906
James Leonard	4 Mystic st	Yardman	2.50 "	April 1, 1902

District No. 6.— Dorchester.

Name.	Residence.	Designation.	Compensation.	Date of Election or Appointment.
Thomas Reagan	40 Magnolia st	Sub-foreman	$3.00 day	May 4, 1891
Patrick Cronin	8 Bloomington st	Laborer	2.25 "	April 29, 1904
Timothy Downey	19 Kimball st	"	2.25 "	Jan. 20, 1899
Michael J. Hill	43 Chickatawbut st	"	2.25 "	Oct. 24, 1895
Dennis Crowley	70 Newhall ave	Regular Extra Laborer	2.25 "	Aug. 27, 1906
Patrick J. Hardiman	8 Duncan pl	" "	2.25 "	" 27, 1906
Peter Keon	10 Middleton st	" "	2.25 "	Dec. 4, 1906
James M. McKenna	61 Hiawatha rd	" "	2.25 "	Nov. 27, 1906
David Welch	12 Fenton st	" "	2.25 "	April 23, 1907
Peter McManus	60 Pierce ave	" "	2.25 "	" 24, 1907

District No. 7.— Roxbury.

Name.	Residence.	Designation.	Compensation.	Date of Election or Appointment.
James P. Craffey	9 Washington pl	Foreman	$1,400 yr	Jan. 28, 1902
John P. Kelley	27 Neponset ave	Inspector	3.00 "	May 5, 1905
Richard Wood	86 Humboldt ave	"	3.00 "	April 25, 1900
Thomas Cook	171 Heath st	Stableman	2.25 "	Oct. 24, 1892
Joseph H. Patterson	4 Merton pl	Machine Driver	2.33⅓ "	Sept. 12, 1892
John F. Craffy	108 Cedar st	Teamster	2.25 "	Aug. 7, 1896
James Galvin	12 Heath pl	"	2.25 "	Jan. 23, 1901
Michael S. Healy	30 Creighton st	"	2.25 "	June 5, 1897
Michael Dooley	10 Halleck st	Helper	2.25 "	May 6, 1892
Thomas Marshall	926 Albany st	"	2.25 "	" 6, 1895

Street Department (Street Cleaning and Watering Division).— Continued.

Name.	Residence.	Designation.	Com. pensation.	Date of Election or Appointment.

District No. 7.— Roxbury.— Concluded.

Name.	Residence.	Designation.	Com. pensation.	Date of Election or Appointment.
Michael A. Page	32 Elmwood st	Helper	$2.25 day	April 22, 1907
John Cavanagh	245 Cabot st	Laborer	2.25 "	Nov. 30, 1894
John Coy	156 Boylston st	"	2.25 "	Oct. 23, 1894
John Craffey	14 Washington pl	"	2.25 "	5, 1892
William Davis	18 Wise st	"	2.25 "	Nov. 17, 1894
Francis J. Dowd	157 Leverett st	"	2.25 "	April 22, 1907
James Duffley	6 Dillon st	"	2.25 "	Jan. 1, 1909
William J. Hayes	35 Rand st	"	2.25 "	Feb. 10, 1899
Oscar Johnson	60 Clifton st	"	2.25 "	Jan. 30, 1900
James G. McIntyre	23 Newark st	"	2.25 "	May 1, 1891
John H. Malloy	17 Batchelder st	"	2.25 "	Dec. 11, 1900
John J. Mellyn	39 Langdon st	"	2.25 "	Aug. 3, 1900
John Powers	1467 Tremont st	"	2.25 "	June 12, 1908
Michael J. Brogan	7 Chesterfield st	Regular Extra Laborer	2.25 "	Sept. 21, 1906
John F. Cunningham	1211 Dorchester ave	" "	2.25 "	Nov. 5, 1906
Thomas Griffin	1 Plymouth ct	" "	2.25 "	June 15, 1908
Richard Kelley	306 Ruggles st	" "	2.25 "	Sept. 1, 1906
William J. Kelly	216 Cabot st	" "	2.25 "	Jan. 27, 1909
Barney McLaughlin	11 Jess st	" "	2.25 "	Oct. 11, 1906
James Murphy	40 Jamaica st	" "	2.25 "	Sept. 25, 1906
William H. O'Connor	37 Smith st	" "	2.25 "	May 15, 1908
Michael Reilly	8 Pontiac st	" "	2.25 "	Oct. 11, 1906
Patrick J. Keefe	8 Church pl	Teamster	2.25 "	April 22, 1907

District No. 8.— Down Town.

Name.	Residence.	Designation.	Com. pensation.	Date of Election or Appointment.
William E. Reardon	177 Wayland st	Foreman	$1,400 yr	Jan. 28, 1902
Louis O. Cloudman	9 Richfield st	Sub-foreman	3.00 day	April 23, 1902
Michael J. Concannon	7 Gustin st	"	3.00 "	23, 1902
Michael F. Daly	35 Washburn st	"	3.00 "	March 25, 1902
Nicholas Bergh	59 Julian st	Inspector	3.00 "	April 28, 1905
John Fitzgerald	102 E. Canton st	Machine Driver	2.33⅓ "	Jan. 2, 1906
William T. Graham	39 Worcester sq	"	2.33⅓ "	Sept. 6, 1899
John J. Kelligrew	50 Crescent ave	"	2.33⅓ "	July 31, 1899
John Kirby	37 Orchard st	"	2.33⅓ "	March 20, 1891
Patrick J. Nee	92 E. Newton st	"	2.33⅓ "	Nov. 20, 1891
Thomas Rice	11 Marshfield st	"	2.33⅓ "	13, 1906
Stephen A. Sawyer	35 Thorndike st	"	2.33⅓ "	March 20, 1891
Patrick Sweeney	30 Forest st	"	2.33⅓ "	Aug. 10, 1903
John F. Brown	909 Albany st	Teamster	2.25 "	April 25, 1905
Patrick Breen	5 Brewster st	Helper	2.25 "	Dec. 20, 1897
Joseph H. Donnellan	717 E. Seventh st	"	2.25 "	April 25, 1905
James Finnerty	11 Lansing st	"	2.25 "	Nov. 24, 1902
Patrick McCarron	209 Athens st	"	2.25 "	June 26, 1896
James J. O'Connor	85 B st	"	2.25 "	April 25, 1900
William J. O'Malley	179 N st	"	2.25 "	May 5, 1905
Frank E. Taylor	31 Washington st	"	2.25 "	March 3, 1909
Thomas F. Walsh	22 Faxon st	"	2.25 "	April 22, 1907
James J. Bruen	414 E. Eighth st	Laborer	2.25 "	Dec. 11, 1891
John Holland	5 Mt. Vernon st	"	2.25 "	Nov. 20, 1902
Jeremiah J. Keating	8 Shawmut st	"	2.25 "	Jan. 25, 1909
Bartholomew T. Mahoney	5 Shawmut st	"	2.25 "	Nov. 17, 1902
Thomas Martin	512 Third st	"	2.25 "	Oct. 7, 1892
John Meehan	257 E. Ninth st	"	2.25 "	Sept. 25, 1900
John H. Quinn	729 Parker st	"	2.25 "	April 22, 1907
Patrick Sliney	34 Troy st	"	2.25 "	May 8, 1891
Daniel Toohey	926 Harrison ave	"	2.25 "	April 22, 1907
Philip Welch	4 B st	"	2.25 "	Aug. 28, 1902
Michael H. Williams	24 Jenkins st	"	2.25 "	April 22, 1907
Patrick Coyle	1367 Dorchester ave	Regular Extra Laborer	2.25 "	Aug. 24, 1906
Patrick D. Casey	833 Third st	" "	2.25 "	Dec. 23, 1907
Thomas B. Gately	9 Larkin st	" "	2.25 "	Feb. 24, 1909
Patrick F. Glynn	137 Terrace st	" "	2.25 "	Jan. 8, 1907
Cornelius A. Haley	15 Cedar st	" "	2.25 "	Dec. 24, 1907
John Lally	13 Roach st	" "	2.25 "	April 22, 1907
Thomas A. Landrigan	98 H st	" "	2.25 "	Dec. 30, 1907
Brian McGowan	28 Dunmore st	" "	2.25 "	Nov. 13, 1906
Patrick McLaughlin	34 E. Dedham st	" "	2.25 "	19, 1906
Michael McManus	26 Arklow st	" "	2.25 "	May 7, 1907
Theodore C. Ryan	7 O st	" "	2.25 "	Sept. 21, 1906
Miles Rynn	32 Carson st	" "	2.25 "	Aug. 31, 1906

Street Department (Street Cleaning and Watering Division).— Continued.

Name.	Residence.	Designation.	Compensation.	Date of Election or Appointment.
District No. 8.— Up Town.				
Daniel Leonard	66 Blue Hill ave	Foreman	$1,400 yr	March 20, 1891
John Fee	311 Dudley st	Sub-foreman	3.00 day	June 8, 1891
Laurence M. Felch	55 Mattapan st	"	3.00 "	May 21, 1900
James Cassell	99 E. Canton st	Machine Driver	2.33½ "	Dec. 5, 1903
Peter King	109 E. Newton st	"	2.33½ "	March 20, 1901
Daniel H. Callahan	22 Haskins st	Teamster	2.25 "	April 6, 1891
Charles F. Pike	25 Magazine st	"	2.25 "	" 22, 1907
John Sullivan	82 Shirley st	"	2.25 "	Nov. 17, 1891
John Dacey	909 Albany st	Helper	2.25 "	May 17, 1895
Michael Dolan	128 Vernon st	"	2.25 "	Dec. 8, 1897
Henry J. Domigan	10 Plymouth st	"	2.25 "	Nov. 30, 1891
William J. Flynn	3 Vernon ct	"	2.25 "	Sept. 15, 1891
Daniel Fallon	177 Vernon st	"	2.25 "	Aug. 27, 1894
Jeremiah Hartin	1 Walnut ct	"	2.25 "	March 14, 1898
James Hegarty	36 Randall st	"	2.25 "	April 22, 1907
Joseph A. Brown	99 Hunneman st	Flushing	2.33½ "	" 2, 1909
Patrick Norton	1462 Tremont st	"	2.33½ "	March 26, 1909
Daniel Sullivan	109 Union Park st	"	2.33½ "	" 19, 1909
John J. Connors	27 Chestnut ave	"	2.25 "	April 19, 1909
Samuel Blaisdell	1508 Washington st	Laborer	2.25 "	March 20, 1901
John J. Curley	274 Eustis st	"	2.25 "	" 20, 1891
Francis Garaughty	141 Harvard ave	"	2.25 "	July 7, 1903
Bernard C. Harkins	29 W. Canton st	"	2.25 "	Dec. 23, 1904
Thomas Kelly	200 Norfolk st	"	2.25 "	Sept. 11, 1891
Patrick J. O'Callaghan	12 Daniel st	"	2.25 "	" 29, 1900
Edward Rogan	734 Harrison ave	"	2.25 "	Feb. 18, 1902
Martin Ryan	65 Marcella st	"	2.25 "	Nov. 26, 1904
James Watterson	1508 Washington st	"	2.25 "	June 20, 1896
Michael Driscoll	71 Baxter st	Regular Extra Laborer	2.25 "	Sept. 24, 1906
Alfred M. Reynolds	98 Mt. Pleasant ave	" "	2.25 "	Nov. 3, 1906
Peter Connors	15 Dacia st	Teamster	2.25 "	April 20, 1891
Daniel Gillen	102 Marcella st	"	2.25 "	March 20, 1891
Michael Green	1 Duncan st	"	2.25 "	Nov. 28, 1891
Lawrence Sullivan	46 Troy st	"	2.25 "	" 19, 1897
District No. 8.— South Stable.				
Patrick J. O'Daly	599 Shawmut ave	Clerk	$800 yr	March 9, 1896
William Batts	24 Ellery st	Stableman	2.25 day	June 22, 1891
James Gillen	32 Forest st	"	2.25 "	March 20, 1891
William Glass	610 E. Sixth st	"	2.25 "	" 14, 1899
Bartholomew Kilkelly	35 W. Seventh st	"	2.25 "	" 22, 1907
Patrick McMorrow	9 Preston ct	"	2.25 "	Dec. 30, 1901
Michael Mullen	569 Freeport st	"	2.25 "	Aug. 25, 1906
John Doherty	31 E. Dedham st	Watchman	2.25 "	Nov. 16, 1899
John Brown	8 Perch st	Laborer	2.25 "	May 16, 1895
District No. 9.— Back Bay.				
John H. O'Brien	17 Wakullah st	Foreman	$1,400 yr	March 28, 1902
John J. Carey	493 Harrison ave	Sub-foreman	3.00 day	May 22, 1895
Thomas L. Tucker	12 Upham ave	"	3.00 "	March 28, 1902
William Moore	43 Island st	Machine Driver	2.25 "	Sept. 1, 1904
Richard L. Costello	34 Hamburg st	Teamster	2.25 "	April 29, 1904
Patrick J. Kellard	64 Tudor st	Helper	2.25 "	Oct. 15, 1892
John J. Rogers	11 Lansdowne st	"	2.25 "	April 28, 1905
Frank Shalley	26 E. Canton st	"	2.25 "	" 27, 1897
Michael J. Walsh	109 Charter st	"	2.25 "	June 26, 1908
James Hart	5 Prescott pl	Laborer	2.25 "	March 20, 1891
Cornelius L. Hayes	50 Grainger st	"	2.25 "	May 13, 1895
Michael J. Otis	19 Conant st	"	2.25 "	March 15, 1892
Robert Barrett	169 W. Fourth st	Regular Extra Laborer	2.25 "	Oct. 3, 1906
George S. Magoun	2 Dimock st	" "	2.25 "	Sept. 4, 1906
Jeremiah O'Callahan	851 Broadway	" "	2.25 "	" 4, 1906
John O'Toole	55 Silver st	" "	2.25 "	" 11, 1906
Michael F. Greene	6 Penryth st	" "	2.25 "	March 29, 1909
John W. Kelley	14 Fenwick st	" "	2.25 "	" 29, 1909
John Ring	145 Union st	Helper	2.25 "	Sept. 15, 1892
Michael J. O'Brien	935 Dorchester ave	Extra Teamster	2.25 "	April 26, 1909
District No. 10.— West End.				
Thomas F. Gargan	10 Cypress st	Inspector	$3.00 day	Feb. 14, 1902
Jonas Hoff	318 Hanover st	"	3.00 "	Sept. 14, 1906

Street Department (Street Cleaning and Watering Division).— Continued.

Name.	Residence.	Designation.	Compensation	Date of Election or Appointment.

District No. 10.— West End.— Concluded.

Name.	Residence.	Designation.	Compensation	Date
Maurice Cashman	73 Allen st	Machine Driver	$2.33⅓ day	Oct. 13, 1906
Charles Noon	54 Monument st	"	2.33⅓ "	May 14, 1902
Thomas F. Stanton	45 Allen st	"	2.33⅓ "	Sept. 25, 1900
Bernard J. Burgess	53 Chambers st	Teamster	2.25 "	Dec. 20, 1905
Dominick Conlin	24 Monument sq	"	2.25 "	Oct. 30, 1893
James J. McDonald	212 Chambers st	"	2.25 "	May 2, 1899
John T. Toohey	14 Causeway st	"	2.25 "	April 29, 1904
John Welsh	30 Causeway st	"	2.25 "	" 14, 1902
Patrick O'Shea	56 Nashua st	Helper	2.25 "	" 27, 1900
Carl Zimmerman	99 Chambers st	"	2.25 "	Sept. 21, 1897
Thomas Barry	298 Paris st	Laborer	2.25 "	Feb. 1, 1899
Michael J. Cahill	99 Chambers st	"	2.25 "	Oct. 6, 1897
Patrick Canney	53 Hull st	"	2.25 "	Dec. 4, 1899
Frederico D'Ambrosio	6 Sheafe st	"	2.25 "	April 28, 1905
James Doherty, 2d	105 Poplar st	"	2.25 "	Oct. 4, 1893
John F. Donaher	75 Chambers st	"	2.25 "	Dec. 30, 1905
Joseph J. Patterson	125 Charles st	"	2.25 "	April 25, 1905
Leopoldo Ciccone	27 Sheafe st	Regular Extra Laborer	2.25 "	Oct. 22, 1907
Michael Doherty	210 Endicott st	" "	2.25 "	" 17, 1906
Richard J. Fife	32 Rawson st	" "	2.25 "	" 23, 1906
Timothy T. Flynn	138 Medford st	" "	2.25 "	Sept. 18, 1906
Peter Griffin	92 Gold st	" "	2.25 "	Oct. 22, 1906
John A. Henry	114 George st	" "	2.25 "	Dec. 23, 1907
Michael McDonough	392 Commercial st	" "	2.25 "	Oct. 12, 1906

District No. 10.— North End.

Name.	Residence.	Designation.	Compensation	Date
Patrick J. Maguire	55 Joy st	Foreman	$1,400 yr	March 4, 1904
Frank Di Pesa	18 Charter st	Sub-foreman	3.00 day	May 13, 1908
John J. Murphy	333 Charles st	"	3.00 "	" 4, 1891
Frederick W. Annis	39 Blossom st	Machine Driver	2.33⅓ "	March 20, 1891
David Punch	82 Paris st	"	2.33⅓ "	Aug. 12, 1899
John B. Sullivan	261 Bowen st	"	2.33⅓ "	" 24, 1906
Edward J. Gallagher	21 Middlesex st	Teamster	2.25 "	" 31, 1894
William Gibbons	93 Endicott st	"	2.25 "	Nov. 9, 1903
Daniel McColgan	25 Washington st	"	2.25 "	May 4, 1891
John Sullivan	158 Chelsea st	"	2.25 "	July 21, 1891
James Toland	28 Washington st	"	2.25 "	June 5, 1902
Neil Doherty	27 Parkman st	Helper	2.25 "	April 15, 1891
Jeremiah Donahue	54 Nashua st	"	2.25 "	Dec. 22, 1905
Michael McSweeney	17 Parkman st	"	2.25 "	Aug. 19, 1896
John J. Myers	22 N. Anderson st	"	2.25 "	Dec. 26, 1905
Michael Allen	33 School st	Laborer	2.25 "	May 15, 1907
Thomas Gallagher	21 Moore st	"	2.25 "	Aug. 27, 1898
Abraham Ferino	463 Main st	"	2.25 "	" 27, 1898
Thomas Loughlin	36 Nashua st	"	2.25 "	Jan. 1, 1906
John McClair	55 Cooper st	"	2.25 "	April 22, 1907
Cornelius D. Murray	66 Green st	"	2.25 "	" 25, 1905
Bernard Doherty	12 Rutherford ave	Regular Extra Laborer	2.25 "	Oct. 1, 1906
John J. Glynn	6 Smith pl	" "	2.25 "	Sept. 11, 1906
Michael F. Hurley	1339 Dorchester ave	" "	2.25 "	Aug. 24, 1906
James O'Connor	17 Mercer st	" "	2.25 "	" 24, 1906
Joseph Picardi	22 Fleet st	" "	2.25 "	Jan. 23, 1908
John Kelly	22 Union st	" "	2.25 "	Oct. 1, 1906
James J. Maguire	181 Fifth st	" "	2.25 "	" 3, 1906

District No. 10.— Patrol.

Name.	Residence.	Designation.	Compensation	Date
Patrick J. McNulty	217 Cambridge st	Inspector	$3.00 day	March 5, 1907
Jeremiah Canty	6 Woodville pk	Laborer	2.25 "	Nov. 27, 1891
John H. Deane	57 Hancock st	"	2.25 "	Dec. 30, 1905
Michael Doherty	14 Monument ave	"	2.25 "	Oct. 4, 1893
John Donahue	68 Callender st	"	2.25 "	July 10, 1891
Patrick Gilmartin	2 Seminary st	"	2.25 "	March 20, 1891
Patrick Higgins	1 McLean ct	"	2.25 "	Sept. 24, 1897
Jeremiah Keohane	58 Oak st	"	2.25 "	Oct. 27, 1908
James Malvey	14 Milton st	"	2.25 "	April 11, 1896
Jeremiah McCarthy	212 Chambers st	"	2.25 "	Dec. 26, 1905
Edward McGuinness	177 Endicott st	"	2.25 "	Oct. 13, 1893

District No. 10.— West Stable.

Name.	Residence.	Designation.	Compensation	Date
Daniel J. McLaughlin	62 Brighton st	Inspector	$2.50 day	June 28, 1904
Humphrey J. McCarron	204 Bowdoin st	Watchman	2.50 "	May 25, 1899

Street Department (Street Cleaning and Watering Division).— Continued.

Name.	Residence.	Designation.	Compensation.	Date of Election or Appointment.

District No. 10.— West Stable.— Concluded.

Name.	Residence.	Designation.	Compensation.	Date of Election or Appointment.
Charles P. Hobbs	76 Allen st	Stableman	$2.50 day	March 20, 1891
Joseph M. Kenney	175 Chambers st	"	2.25 "	Dec. 30, 1905
Henry McGuiness	40 Blossom st	"	2.25 "	March 27, 1891
Patrick J. Rinn	58 Allen st	"	2.25 "	Dec. 15, 1898
Harry Singer	68 Allen st	"	2.25 "	April 14, 1902
Frank H. Wilson	403 Charles st	"	2.25 "	Jan. 10, 1898
John J. Toomey	49 L st	Yardman	2.25 "	Feb. 7, 1902

District No. 11.— Patrol System.

Name.	Residence.	Designation.	Compensation.	Date of Election or Appointment.
Cornelius Owens	3 Sumner pl	Foreman	$1,400 yr	May 21, 1906
John J. Dolan	14 Melrose st	Inspector	3.00 day	April 13, 1905
Bernard J. McMackin	61 Bunker Hill st	"	3.00 "	July 7, 1906
Edward J. Noonan	170 Boston st	"	3.00 "	May 11, 1906
Richard Welch	32A Winship st	"	3.00 "	Feb. 13, 1902
Cornelius J. Scanlan	137 Dakota st	"	2.50 "	May 17, 1907
John Curran	78 Phillips st	Teamster	2.25 "	July 21, 1908
John H. Hurley	589 Shawmut ave	"	2.25 "	Nov. 28, 1894
James J. Lavin	53 Chambers st	"	2.25 "	Dec. 30, 1905
Michael J. Stanford	36 Billerica st	"	2.25 "	April 24, 1901
Michael Galvin	34 Pierce ave	Watchman	2.25 "	Sept. 15, 1906
John Norton	524 Fifth st	"	2.25 "	May 9, 1902
George W. Egan	731 Sixth st	Helper	2.25 "	April 18, 1902
Daniel E. McCarthy	266 Shawmut ave	Boy	1.00 "	Feb. 2, 1905
Thomas Baggott	42 Shannon st	Laborer	2.25 "	Jan. 16, 1903
Daniel J. Barrett	157 Albany st	"	2.25 "	April 19, 1893
John Barry	67 Newman st	"	2.25 "	March 26, 1892
Thomas Bride	1427 Columbus ave	"	2.25 "	Nov. 26, 1906
Patrick F. Carey	34 Linden Park st	"	2.25 "	Sept. 13, 1898
Patrick Connolly	306 Dorchester ave	"	2.25 "	June 27, 1892
Dominick Connors	75 Chambers st	"	2.25 "	April 27, 1901
Paul J. Cuddy	29 Clapp st	"	2.25 "	May 29, 1891
John J. Cunningham	829 Albany st	"	2.25 "	" 31, 1902
Patrick J. Curley	75 Gates st	"	2.25 "	March 27, 1891
William Devin	50 Oak st	"	2.25 "	" 27, 1891
John F. Dillon	17 Eldora st	"	2.25 "	April 26, 1902
James F. Fay	5 Auburn st	"	2.25 "	July 12, 1904
James J. Farrell	72 Hillside st	"	2.25 "	May 12, 1902
John Fitzgerald	741 Broadway	"	2.25 "	April 2, 1902
Patrick Francis	14 Chestnut ave	"	2.25 "	Sept. 30, 1891
Patrick Gaffney	267 Hanover st	"	2.25 "	March 20, 1901
Charles Gale	62 Mt. Vernon st	"	2.25 "	July 20, 1891
John Harkins	197 Endicott st	"	2.25 "	Nov. 28, 1898
Daniel Holland	111 Lenox st	"	2.25 "	Oct. 17, 1902
Patrick Joyce	314 Princeton st	"	2.25 "	May 11, 1895
Patrick F. Joyce	448 Dudley st	"	2.25 "	Dec. 29, 1902
Morgan J. Kane	22 Henchman st	"	2.25 "	Oct. 3, 1902
John Kelly	9 Dresden st	"	2.25 "	April 3, 1891
Michael Kenney	8 Carmel st	"	2.25 "	Nov. 13, 1897
Gaetano Laurano	20 Chelsea st	"	2.25 "	" 14, 1908
William Lavender	11 Chesterfield st	"	2.25 "	May 1, 1891
Thomas McCarthy	41 Dorchester st	"	2.25 "	Aug. 2, 1899
Michael J. McCormick	4 Estey st	"	2.25 "	May 22, 1897
Peter Massa	2 Haynes st	"	2.25 "	Sept. 11, 1900
Francis Murphy	1 Butterick pl	"	2.25 "	Nov. 10, 1897
John McGonigle	211 W. Fourth st	"	2.25 "	May 15, 1891
Edward J. Orann	122 W. Sixth st	"	2.25 "	March 20, 1891
John O'Toole	8 Humboldt pl	"	2.25 "	July 22, 1899
Michael Pendergast	38 Cherokee st	"	2.25 "	March 27, 1891
John S. Plunkett	374 W. Second st	"	2.25 "	Feb. 1, 1900
James H. Powers	212 Chambers st	"	2.25 "	April 21, 1899
Nicholas Powers	37 E. Canton st	"	2.25 "	May 13, 1907
John Quilty	8 Blackwell st	"	2.25 "	Dec. 21, 1906
Daniel J. Ring	36 Rochester st	"	2.25 "	June 18, 1904
John Robertson	67 W. Dedham st	"	2.25 "	Dec. 6, 1897
Michael Rogan	33 Monument ave	"	2.25 "	May 1, 1891
John Ryan	877 Fourth st	"	2.25 "	July 10, 1893
David Sheehan	17 Bruce st	"	2.25 "	May 4, 1891
Daniel J. Sweeney	40 Nashua st	"	2.25 "	Jan. 1, 1906
Edward Sweeney	4 Woodcliff st	"	2.25 "	Oct. 5, 1891
Patrick Toole	150 Athens st	"	2.25 "	March 27, 1891
Thomas Walsh	5 Rogers ave	"	2.25 "	Nov. 21, 1899
Martin Welch	73 Middlesex st	"	2.25 "	May 1, 1891

Street Department (Street Cleaning and Watering Division). — Concluded.

Name.	Residence.	Designation.	Compensation.	Date of Election or Appointment.

District No. 11. — Patrol System. — Concluded.

Name.	Residence.	Designation.	Compensation.	Date of Election or Appointment.
John J. Winters	39 Vineland st	Laborer	$2.25 day	Oct. 4, 1897
John Woods	101 Rutherford ave	"	2.25 "	June 1, 1903
Jacob H. Yeagle	12 Newman st	"	2.25 "	May 12, 1905
Edward Collins	196 W. Sixth st	Regular Extra Laborer	2.25 "	Aug. 24, 1906
Peter Conaty	9 Elmwood st	" "	2.25 "	Oct. 13, 1906
Michael Connolly	2 Hampshire ct	" "	2.25 "	Sept. 5, 1906
Patrick Finn	318 Adams st	" "	2.25 "	Oct. 1, 1906
Festus J. Gavin	197 Silver st	" "	2.25 "	April 5, 1907
James P. Golden	28 Blaine ave	" "	2.25 "	Aug. 24, 1906
James F. Healy	8 Sullivan pl	" "	2.25 "	" 27, 1906
Thomas Hickey	485 E. First st	" "	2.25 "	Sept. 27, 1906
Patrick H. Hogan	645 Third st	" "	2.25 "	Aug. 24, 1906
Charles McColgan	385 Neponset ave	" "	2.25 "	April 17, 1907
James E. McCormack	48 Fellows st	" "	2.25 "	" 4, 1908
William H. White	17 Union st	" "	2.25 "	Aug. 25, 1906
James Gallagher	249 E. Eighth st	" "	2.25 "	April 5, 1909
Richard J. Sullivan	255 Gold st	" "	2.25 "	" 2, 1909
Jeremiah Carroll	81 Centre st	Clerk	1,000 yr.	Jan. 9, 1903

Street Watering.

Name.	Residence.	Designation.	Compensation.	Date of Election or Appointment.
Joseph F. O'Brien	224 W. Seventh st	Inspector	$1,400 yr.	March 13, 1908
Thomas J. Watson	818 Parker st	"	3.00 "	Jan. 29, 1909
John D. Costello	88 Regent st	"	3.00 "	March 26, 1909
Patrick F. Logan	117 W. Second st	"	2.50 "	" 29, 1909
John L. Carven	377 Bunker Hill st	"	3.00 "	April 2, 1909
David Cronin	13 G st	"	2.50 "	March 29, 1909
Thomas J. Flanagan	64 Newhall ave	"	3.00 "	Aug. 24, 1906
Robert H. Hill	487 E. Third st	"	2.50 "	March 29, 1909
John P. Hurley	2 Mears st	"	2.50 "	" 29, 1909
Patrick J. McLaughlin	185 Endicott st	"	3.00 "	April 2, 1909
Nunziato F. Mondello	2 Hildreth pl	"	2.50 "	" 2, 1909
James F. Mullen	76 Dorchester st	"	3.00 "	Oct. 26, 1906
William V. Quinn	291 E st	"	2.50 "	March 29, 1909
John H. Riley	63 Heela st	"	2.50 "	" 29, 1909
Richard Sheehan	45 Heela st	"	2.50 "	" 29, 1909
Thomas Burden	365 Centre st	Fireman	2.83½ "	" 24, 1909
Thomas Collins	23 Downing st	"	2.83½ "	" 19, 1909
Thomas Griffin	19 George st	"	2.83½ "	April 2, 1909
John E. Patts	27 Randolph rd	"	3.25 "	June 24, 1908
Michael Tirrell	15 Ballard st	"	2.83½ "	March 19, 1909
John E. Brophy	27 Shepard st	Laborer	2.25 "	Aug. 13, 1898
Patrick J. Cronin	665 Albany st	"	2.25 "	March 29, 1909
Timothy H. Dacey	890 Brookline st	"	2.25 "	April 10, 1909
Patrick Fallon	28 Custer st	"	2.25 "	" 12, 1909
Dennis J. Griffin	105 W. Brookline st	"	2.25 "	" 28, 1902
William C. Hughes	246 Lamartine st	"	2.25 "	March 3, 1909
Jeremiah J. Rohan	3 Vernon pl	"	2.25 "	Jan. 23, 1909
John Whelton	38 Church st	"	2.25 "	April 2, 1909
John J. Holland	5 B st	"	2.25 "	" 22, 1909
Patrick Cunningham	303 Highland st	"	2.25 "	" 23, 1909
James J. Shea	80 Wyman st	Driver	2.25 "	June 23, 1902

Street Laying=Out Department.

Name.	Residence.	Designation.	Compensation.	Date of Election or Appointment.
Salem D. Charles	286 Chestnut ave	Chairman	$4,500 yr.	Jan. 2, 1899
James A. Gallivan	353 W. Fourth st	Commissioner	4,000 "	" 7, 1901
John H. Dunn	897 E. Broadway	"	4,000 "	" 4, 1909
John J. O'Callaghan	10 Monument sq	Secretary	3,000 "	" 6, 1902
Mary Agnes Mahan	154 Willow st	Clerk	1,200 "	July 2, 1895
Edward H. Costello	20 Fenwood rd	Assessment and Abatement Agent	1,500 "	April 4, 1898
John F. McDermott	87 Condor st	Messenger	800 "	May 28, 1896
Frank L. Murphy	242 W. Third st	Clerk and Constable	1,200 "	Aug. 8, 1898
Joseph L. Cox	495 E. Broadway	Office Boy	364 "	Sept. 3, 1907

Street Laying=Out Department.— Concluded.

Name.	Residence.	Designation.	Compensation.	Date of Election or Appointment.

Assessment Division.

Name.	Residence.	Designation.	Compensation.	Date of Election or Appointment.
Joseph F. Sullivan	6 Prospect st	Chief	$2,200 yr	Aug. 22, 1902
John J. Cadigan	92 Cottage st	Clerk	1,200 "	April 28, 1898
Edward G. Gillooly	298 Neponset ave	"	1,000 "	" 28, 1898
Joseph T. Towle	20 Bromley pk	"	1,000 "	March 26, 1899
Thomas W. Malone	30 Auburn st	"	1,000 "	" 28, 1898

Surveying Division.

Name.	Residence.	Designation.	Compensation.	Date of Election or Appointment.
Frank O. Whitney †	175 Humboldt ave	Chief of Division	$3,500 yr	June 1, 1899*
Irwin C. Cromack ‡	8 Elm Lawn	Assistant to Chief	2,800 "	" 23, 1899*
John F. Connell	538 E. Eighth st	Assistant Engineer	5.00 day	Feb. 13, 1897
William H. Foss	147 Foster st., Bri	"	4.75 "	June 24, 1891
Neil J. Holland	863 Blue Hill ave	"	4.50 "	April 6, 1896
Michael D. O'Farrell	60 Dustin st	"	4.25 "	Sept. 15, 1892
Laurence J. Monahan §	24 Havre st	"	4.00 "	June 23, 1891
Thomas J. Duane	168 Webster st	Draughtsman	1,300 yr	Sept. 10, 1892
Henry L. Wightman	5 Russell st	"	3.50 day	Feb. 6, 1896
James J. Kelly	124A Dorchester st	"	1,000 yr	April 4, 1896
William Warren §	33 Chestnut Hill ave	Transitman	3.50 day	" 21, 1892
Michael J. Driscoll	506 E. Third st	"	3.50 "	July 1, 1895
William N. Carroll	134 W. Third st	"	3.25 "	Jan. 31, 1900
Patrick J. Dolan §	188 Chelsea st	"	3.25 "	Nov. 16, 1896
Charles F. Hatton	358 Bunker Hill st	"	3.25 "	June 1, 1894
Frank P. McCarty §	38 Milford st	"	3.25 "	Sept. 1, 1895
George L. Philpott	85 Ferrin st	"	3.25 "	May 16, 1898
Henry A. Brawley	37 Hillside st	"	3.00 "	Dec. 28, 1899
Thomas F. Sullivan	97 N. Harvard st	"	3.00 "	June 20, 1893
Timothy J. McCarthy	207 Bowdoin st., Dor	"	2.75 "	Feb. 1, 1897
James S. Murray §	113 Trenton st., E. B	"	2.75 "	" 3, 1896
Francis D. Sullivan §	30 Everett st., Chsn	Rodman and Conveyancer	3.50 "	June 11, 1891
John H. Duane, Jr	168 Webster st., E. B	Assistant Conveyancer	3.00 "	May 10, 1907
Edward E. Hannan	2 Westmoreland st	"	3.00 "	Dec. 10, 1906
Joseph W. A. Oliver	131 W. Seventh st	"	3.00 "	Oct. 3, 1902
Frank J. McNulty	21 Calumet st	"	2.75 "	Aug. 20, 1907
Frank N. Dunnels	Waverley House, Chsn	"	2.50 "	Dec. 28, 1900
Charles F. Scheele	78 Middlesex st	"	2.50 "	Oct. 24, 1902
John J. Bradley §	41 Randolph rd	Rodman	2.50 "	Sept. 10, 1895
Bartholomew F. Clougherty	11 Topliff st	"	2.50 "	Aug. 1, 1898
John T. Daly	36 Forbes st	"	2.50 "	Feb. 13, 1897
Michael H. Drinkwater	48 Chelsea st., E. B	"	2.50 "	Aug. 4, 1896
Joseph J. Grady	54 Bayswater st	"	2.50 "	" 5, 1896
David P. Harrigan	74 Bunker Hill st	"	2.50 "	June 12, 1891
Francis M. Killion	129 Templeton st	"	2.50 "	May 26, 1899
Thomas F. Lynch	34 Washington st., Chsn	"	2.50 "	Nov. 16, 1896
Joseph McCabe §	23 Hancock st	"	2.50 "	Dec. 6, 1893
Michael J. McCarron §	212 Chambers st	"	2.50 "	Nov. 22, 1894
James E. Morrow	152 Howard ave	"	2.50 "	July 6, 1896
John Quirk §	31 Billerica st	"	2.50 "	Feb. 2, 1893
John J. Russell	58 F st	"	2.50 "	March 13, 1903
Alfred M. Shevlin	384 Hyde Park ave	"	2.50 "	Feb. 3, 1896
Mortimer F. Toomey §	2418 Washington st., Rox	"	2.50 "	July 6, 1896
Henry A. Crowley	11 Dracut st	"	2.00 "	June 12, 1908*
James W. Glynn	37 Hillside st	Tape Repairer and Custodian of Instrument Room	3.00 "	July 24, 1891
Charles E. Townsend	21 Trenton st., Chsn	Map Mounter and Electrical Blue Printer	3.00 "	June 2, 1899
Charles F. Bogan	261 Bunker Hill st	Caretaker of Instruments	3.00 "	Oct. 19, 1899
Patrick J. Fitzgerald	121 G st	" "	3.00 "	Sept. 27, 1899
Charles S. O'Connor	14 Frederick st	" "	3.00 "	Aug. 26, 1899
William F. Glennon	65 Regent st	Clerk	2.00 "	Sept. 11, 1899
Andrew F. Fitzpatrick	24 Glendon st	Messenger	2.50 "	Oct. 7, 1898
Martin J. Foley	236 Athens st	"	2.50 "	May 30, 1902
John F. Sullivan	43 Decatur st., Chsn	Axeman	3.00 "	Nov. 16, 1899
John C. Tobin, Jr	792 Parker st	"	2.50 "	May 22, 1899
Frank R. Gillespie	334 Harrison ave	Boy	11.50 wk	May 12, 1899

* Previously employed in the department.
† Salary, $3,500; $2,100 paid by Street Laying-Out Department and $1,400 paid by Engineering Department.
‡ Salary, $2,800; $1,400 paid by Street Laying-Out Department and $1,400 paid by Engineering Department.
§ Detailed for service upon sewerage works and paid from Sewerage Works Appropriation.

Supply Department.

Name.	Residence.	Designation.	Compensation.	Date of Election or Appointment.
J. Edward Mullen	16 Arundel st	Purchasing Agent	$2,500 yr.	Aug. 27, 1908
John T. Caulfield	338 Centre st	Assistant Purchasing Agent	1,600 "	Feb. 1, 1985
George E. Carroll	34 Quincy st	Clerk and Stenographer	1,400 "	Jan. 6, 1908
William W. Kee	157 Temple st	Weigher	1,000 "	Oct. 8, 1900
Francis P. Rock	19 Marshfield st	Clerk	360 "	Sept. 26, 1907

Treasury Department.

Name.	Residence.	Designation.	Compensation.	Date.
Charles H. Slattery † §	520 E. Broadway	City Treasurer	$5,000 yr.	May 1, 1906
Benjamin S. Turner ‡	33 Elm Hill ave	Cashier	4,000 "	July 16, 1881
Ellison B. Cushing	92 Ridge rd	Teller	3,000 "	" 8, 1870
John D. Carty	6 Kensington st	Paymaster	2,700 "	Oct. 15, 1882*
John T. McNary †	566 E. Seventh st	"	2,500 "	Feb. 14, 1902*
George H. Dana †	28 Cummings rd.	Bookkeeper	1,900 "	Dec. 1, 1904*
Edward J. Sullivan	357 K st	Paymaster	2,500 "	May 7, 1902*
Horton G. Ide ‡	37 Ridgemont st	Draft and Trustee Clerk and Paymaster	2,300 "	" 7, 1902*
Edward C. Seates	11 Elko st	Paymaster	2,300 "	Nov. 1, 1904*
Arthur L. Stevens	6 Harvard pl., Bri.	"	2,300 "	Dec. 1, 1904*
Charles E. Bartlett	57 Rutland sq	Bond and Interest Clerk and Paymaster	2,000 "	May 7, 1902*
Dennis H. Mahony ‡	11 Rutland st	County Clerk and Paymaster	1,600 "	Dec. 1, 1904*
Thomas F. Brophey	90 Foster st	Pay Roll Clerk and Paymaster	1,800 "	" 1, 1904*
Russell S. Hyde	24 Greenough ave	Asst. Bookkeeper and Clerk	1,500 "	Nov. 28, 1904
Patrick Henry Fahey	14 Lexington st	General Clerk	1,100 "	Dec. 22, 1905
Maurice J. Power	14 Chestnut st	"	1,400 "	Nov. 1, 1906
Walter W. Foley	50 Rockland st	Messenger	900 "	Sept. 17, 1906

Water Department.

Water Commissioner's Office.

Name.	Residence.	Designation.	Compensation.	Date.
William E. Hannan	32 Milwood st	Water Commissioner	$5,000 yr.	April 27, 1908
Walter E. Swan	110 Richmond st	Chief Clerk	3,000 "	July 9, 1874
Joseph W. Swan	21 Carruth st	Assistant Clerk	2,000 "	June 24, 1875
Walter E. Welch	88 Elm st	Clerk and Messenger	1,200 "	Dec. 28, 1899
Michael A. Horigan	28 Howell st	Stenographer	1,400 "	May 23, 1908
George F. W. Stevens	60 Norfolk st	Chauffeur	3.00 day	Sept. 21, 1908

Income Division.

Name.	Residence.	Designation.	Compensation.	Date.
Joseph H. Caldwell	2 Franklin st	General Superintendent	$3,000 yr.	July 1, 1895*
Timothy V. Sullivan	31 Johnston rd	Assistant Superintendent	2,000 "	Jan. 16, 1902*
John H. Flynn	31 Marcella st	Deputy Superintendent	2,000 "	" 16, 1897*
Robert W. Wilson	551 Saratoga st	"	1,600 "	April 9, 1909*
Gustave DeCock	200 Willow st	Clerk	1,600 "	May, 1873
Frank Donnelly	62 Wenham st	"	1,600 "	March 27, 1876
Benjamin F. Drown	50 Milwood st	"	1,600 "	Dec. 23, 1895
William B. Dunlevy	15 Greenock st	"	1,600 "	Oct. 22, 1894
John A. Finnegan	4 Roseland st	"	1,600 "	May, 1880
Henry A. Fisher	966 South st	"	1,600 "	March 18, 1895
Benjamin T. Hall	337 Main st	"	1,600 "	May, 1878
Charles Raymond	17 Cross st	"	1,600 "	Aug. 13, 1895
Thomas H. Connelly	343 Bowdoin st	Clerk and Stenographer	1,400 "	May 4, 1906
John H. Dougherty	680 Tremont st	Clerk	1,400 "	" 12, 1896
John J. McAuliffe	180 Norfolk st	"	1,400 "	July 13, 1883
John J. McGrath	14 Clive st	"	1,400 "	March, 1885
George W. Nason	36 Bromfield st	"	1,400 "	Aug. 1, 1895
Wendell P. Lee	416 Adams st	"	1,100 "	Dec., 1881
James J. Waters	6 Bowdoin ave	"	1,100 "	Jan. 3, 1899
Charles G. Kelley	11 Speedwell st	"	1,000 "	July 3, 1907
John J. Ahern	6 Salutation st	"	800 "	June 12, 1908

* Promotion on date given. Previously in department.
† See County of Suffolk and Sinking Funds Department.
‡ See County of Suffolk. § See School Department.

Water Department.— Continued.

Name.	Residence	Designation.	Compensation.	Date of Election or Appointment.

Income Division.— Continued.

Name.	Residence	Designation.	Compensation.	Date of Election or Appointment.
Arthur E. Gaygin	1043 Dorchester ave	Clerk	$800 yr	June 15, 1908
John J. McCarty	318 Beach st	Foreman	1,600 "	April 26, 1907
James F. Anderson	765 Columbia rd	"	1,200 "	Sept. 18, 1899
James L. Sweeney	140 London st	"	1,100 "	June 1, 1906*
Edward F. Lynch	19 Alexander st	"	3.00 day	March 15, 1909
Theodore L. Kelly	813 Broadway	Chief Inspector	1,800 yr	Dec., 1864
John T. Gaffney	32 Allen st	Asst. Chief Inspector	1,100 "	March 16, 1909*
John B. Hassett	20 Lawrence st	Inspector	1,200 "	May 1, 1889
John C. McDonough	314 Bunker Hill st	"	1,200 "	Nov. 28, 1898
Michael J. O'Brien	16 Franklin st	"	1,200 "	Feb. 3, 1905
Isaac Soloman	315 Huntington ave	"	1,200 "	Dec. 23, 1905
George L. Almeder	193 Neponset ave	"	1,100 "	May 1, 1895
Joseph E. Cahill	717 Massachusetts ave	"	1,100 "	April 20, 1899
Myer Daniels	28 Burgess st	"	1,100 "	March 13, 1903
Michael F. Edmonds	13 Gay Head st	"	1,100 "	July 13, 1883
John W. Fraser, Jr.	271 Normandy st	"	1,100 "	June, 1888
Francis M. Gray	21 Harwich st	"	1,100 "	Sept. 22, 1907
John A. Haley	14 Wenham st	"	1,100 "	July 1, 1883
John H. Lally	39 Walnut st	"	1,100 "	Dec. 9, 1898
Thomas M. Lane	113 M. st	"	1,100 "	July, 1893
John H G. Munro	14 Whittemore st	"	1,100 "	Aug. 1, 1895
John J. Murphy	439 Shawmut ave	"	1,100 "	1889
Joseph B. Neagle	108 W. Concord st	"	1,100 "	May 8, 1896
James M. Paige	97 Eustis st	"	1,100 "	Aug. 1, 1895
Charles F. T. Schwaar	28 Falcon st	"	1,100 "	July 1, 1894
James S. Shepard	19 Nonquit st	"	1,100 "	Aug. 1, 1895
William H. Townsend	88 Ferrin st	"	1,100 "	Sept. 22, 1902
John B. Fitzpatrick	360 K st	"	1,000 "	May 9, 1907
William J. Doherty	18 Gaston st	"	3.00 day	Sept. 25, 1906
Patrick Slane	6 Sagamore st	"	3.00 "	May 15, 1896
John W. Magoon	81 Williams st	"	2.50 "	Nov 25, 1907
E. Rich Dwight	54 Aldie st	Meter Inspector	1,100 yr	April, 1876
Lawrence P. Furlong	16 Pearl st	"	1,100 "	July, 1883
William Hickey	20 Prince st	"	1,100 "	August, 1871
Patrick R. Kenney	7 Faneuil st	"	1,100 "	1892
John J. Regan	11 Gaylord st	"	1,100 "	July, 1883
William Williams	2 W. Concord st	Sealer	3.00 day	" 26, 1898
John J. Hennessey	139 Bunker Hill st	"	2.90 "	May 16, 1898
Patrick Higgins	15 Allen st	"	2.90 "	June 30, 1893
Michael H. Leary	1675 Washington st	Messenger	2.50 "	July 1, 1895
Patrick Connolly	75 South st	"	2.25 "	Oct. 8, 1895
Martin J. Flaherty	72 Waverley st	Inspector of Work	2.75 "	March 10, 1898
James J. Curtis	82 Bunker Hill st	"	2.25 "	" 23, 1909
William H. Donnelly	81 Cottage st	"	2.25 "	April 2, 1909*
Bernard Magee	103 Conant st	Carpenter	3.50 "	May 21, 1888*
James Martin	25 Mystic st	Storekeeper	3.25 "	1885
John J. Norton	11 Leyland st	Plumber	3.25 "	March 1, 1885
Michael Bowen	2 S. Worthington st	"	3.00 "	Feb. 19, 1907
John C. Clark	573 Dudley st	"	3.00 "	March 24, 1909
John H. Cullen	30 Gurney st	"	3.00 "	April 5, 1909
Michael H. Fenton	95 Norfolk st	"	3.00 "	May 9, 1890
Owen J. Gilloon	46 Brook st	"	3.00 "	March 15, 1909
Daniel J. Rull, Jr.	507 E. Seventh st	"	3.00 "	Feb. 12, 1909
Thomas J. Sullivan	224 Chelsea st	"	3.00 "	Feb. 15, 1909
Patrick J. Gateley	214 Ruggles st	"	2.75 "	Aug. 26, 1898
Patrick J. McCarthy	56 Nashua st	"	2.75 "	Sept. 8, 1905
Michael P. Welch	104 E. Newton st	"	2.75 "	" 18, 1889
Dennis J. Sullivan	41 W. Second st	Engineer	3.00 "	Jan. 22, 1897
John J. Connor	212 Chambers st	Repairer	2.90 "	July 16, 1896
James Gilroy	77 St. Alphonsus st	"	2.25 "	1877
William Hughes	8 Hill st	"	2.25 "	March 11, 1895
Robert J. Connorton	299 Bunker Hill st	Meter Tester	2.50 "	Jan. 11, 1897
Francis B. Lang	22½ Causeway st	"	2.50 "	Nov. 27, 1898
Joseph Rice	667 Harrison ave	"	2.50 "	July 18, 1894
Edward H. Gilmore	67 Cabot st	"	2.25 "	Aug. 26, 1898
Michael J. Dinneen	10 Fifield st	Plumber's Helper	2.25 "	June 2, 1889
Cornelius Fitzgerald	11 Chesterfield st	"	2.25 "	April 28, 1886
Thomas H. Green	117 Baldwin st	"	2.25 "	Sept. 18, 1899
William Kelley	48 Elmwood st	"	2.25 "	Aug. 6, 1909
Michael M. Kenney	5 Whittier st	"	2.25 "	May 13, 1895
James J. Mahoney	60 Oak st	"	2.25 "	Jan. 30, 1900

* Promoted to present position on date given.   Previously in department.

Water Department. — Continued.

Name.	Residence.	Designation.	Com- pensation.	Date of Election or Appointment.

Income Division.— Concluded.

Name.	Residence.	Designation.	Com- pensation.	Date of Election or Appointment.
George A. Murphy.	93 Worthington st	Plumber's Helper	$2.25 day	Sept. 4, 1903
Thomas J. Ratchford	74 L st	"	2.25 "	Jan. 8, 1903
James J. Roche	16 Chadwick st	"	2.25 "	April 10, 1886
John J. Shea	2 Melbourne st	"	2.25 "	Sept. 26, 1904
Patrick J. Clougherty	22 W. Third st	Teamster	2.25 "	July 22, 1895
Edmund Mahoney	347 W. Fourth st	"	2.25 "	Sept. 19, 1885
Thomas McAuliffe	27 Pleasant st	"	2.25 "	Oct. 11, 1897
Michael M. McGrath	366 W. Second st	"	2.25 "	July 11, 1900
Michael Mulkern	36 Mercer st	"	2.25 "	21, 1887
Patrick A. Russell	42 Chadwick st	"	2.25 "	May 28, 1895
Michael Hogarty	17 Orchard st	Laborer	2.50 "	July 1, 1895
Andrew Ahern	18 Cliff st	"	2.25 "	Sept. 20, 1901
Thomas Blake	15 Albion st	"	2.25 "	1884
Edward F. Breslin	69 Bunker Hill st	"	2.25 "	May 28, 1896
John T. Butler	35 Everett st	"	2.25 "	July 8, 1896
Francis J. Cadigan	393 Bunker Hill st	"	2.25 "	June 12, 1896
John Callahan	2 E. Newton st	"	2.25 "	May 8, 1888
Patrick Callan	1858 Washington st	"	2.25 "	" 28, 1895
James H. Connorton	570 E. Second st	"	2.25 "	Jan. 6, 1903
Michael J. Curran	121 W. Ninth st	"	2.25 "	Nov. 25, 1898
Edward Doherty	9 Stone st	"	2.25 "	July 8, 1895
John J. Doherty, 1st	8 Edgeworth st	"	2.25 "	April 17, 1894
Michael Doherty	22 Ray st	"	2.25 "	" 25, 1888
John Dooley	3171 Washington st	"	2.25 "	Sept. 8, 1896
John B. Fitch	81 Paris st	"	2.25 "	July 1, 1895
Michael J. Greeley	82 Joy st	"	2.25 "	April 23, 1893
Michael Hughes	1 Orchard st	"	2.25 "	March 29, 1891
Walter C. Huntress	6 Heath st	"	2.25 "	July 1, 1895
Edward Kelley	361 Charles st	"	2.25 "	May 25, 1895
Patrick Leary	4 Maywood ter	"	2.25 "	June 12, 1899
Dennis Lynch	18 Sackville st	"	2.25 "	Feb. 9, 1897
Jeremiah Madden	40 Everett st	"	2.25 "	April 25, 1888
Philip McCaffrey	38 Leverett st	"	2.25 "	July 1, 1895
Thomas McKenney	17 Dorchester st	"	2.25 "	March 16, 1899
Charles Monagle	13 E. Canton st	"	2.25 "	June 3, 1895
John H. Murphy	65 Lawrence st	"	2.25 "	Jan. 5, 1898
Michael O'Connor	362 Silver st	"	2.25 "	March 7, 1899
Matthew J. O'Neil	24 Williams st	"	2.25 "	May 8, 1895
Timothy Riley	32 W. Fifth st	"	2.25 "	Dec. 17, 1897
Timothy Scully	53 Sterling st	"	2.25 "	May 24, 1886
Daniel Sullivan	337 Harrison ave	"	2.25 "	April 11, 1899
Jeremiah Sullivan	16 Garland st	"	2.25 "	May 28, 1895
Patrick Sullivan	29 Tufts st	"	2.25 "	March 22, 1897
Martin Twomey	362 Athens st	"	2.25 "	June 20, 1895

Distribution Division.

Name.	Residence.	Designation.	Com- pensation.	Date of Election or Appointment.
George H. Finneran	197 St. Botolph st	Superintendent	$3,000 yr	March 1, 1909*
Adam McClure	125 Pembroke st	Assistant Superintendent	2,000 "	July 3, 1908*
John W. Leahon	98 Albion st	"	2,000 "	Jan. 28, 1909*
George A. Pratt	632 Washington st	Chief Clerk	1,400 "	March 17, 1909*
Cornelius J. McNaughton	40 Chelsea rd	Clerk	1,300 "	Sept. 23, 1888
Robert F. Denvir, Jr	22 Coolidge rd	"	1,200 "	April 16, 1891
James F. Cloney	486 Warren st	"	1,100 "	Sept. 3, 1897
Harold G. Gallagher	96 Franklin st	"	1,000 "	March 29, 1909
Thomas H. Carr	627 Dorchester ave	"	800 "	April 16, 1909
William D. Nagle	32 Union st	"	800 "	June 29, 1908
Joseph J. Wilson	16 Sullivan st	"	800 "	" 15, 1908
William J. Green	8 Nonquit st	"	2.75 day	April 7, 1908*
William A. O'Connor	61 Storey st	"	2.50 "	Dec. 4, 1908*
Edward P. Fogarty	83 Olney st	Stenographer	1,100 yr	May 28, 1908*
John Hurley	121 Calumet st	Messenger	1,000 "	April 7, 1896
Jeremiah P. Maloney	26 Cordis st	"	900 "	Feb. 21, 1895
Theodore Leutz	70 Paul Gore st	"	2.75 day	" 28, 1908*
John J. Maguire	195 Hamilton st	Yardmaster	1,800 yr	April 10, 1896
Samuel J. Hallett	253 Park st	Inspector of Gates	1,600 "	July 3, 1908*
Edward J. Bachelder	116 Evans st	Master Machinist	1,600 "	" 5, 1885
John R. Brooks	4394 Washington st	Patternmaker	1,300 "	Dec. 17, 1901
William T. Lenehan	15 Stratton st	Foreman	1,600 "	Oct. 3, 1894*
Bernard F. Rogers	11 Marion st	"	1,200 "	Nov. 1, 1898*

* Previously in the department.

Water Department.— Continued.

Name.	Residence.	Designation.	Compensation.	Date of Election or Appointment.

Distribution Division.— Continued.

Name.	Residence.	Designation.	Compensation.	Date of Election or Appointment.
Walter B. Wood	6 Dunford st	Foreman	$1,100 yr	Aug. 3, 1903*
Jacob F. Mayo	24 Pond st	"	800 "	May, 1853
Richard F. Neagle	42 Moulton st	"	4.00 day	Nov. 9, 1908*
George J. Coyle	22 Hendry st	"	3.00 "	Sept., 1883
James Doherty, 1st	78 E. Canton st	"	3.00 "	April 1, 1908*
Thomas F. Donovan	10 Sumner ter	"	3.00 "	Dec. 1, 1904*
Michael Durand	27 Baxter st	"	3.00 "	April 1, 1908*
James F. Hurley	24 Monument ave	Inspector of Castings	4.00 "	" 16, 1903
Matthew Brennan	120 Buttonwood st	Inspector of Work	3.00 "	" 1, 1908*
Michael McCarthy, 1st	41 Chadwick st	"	3.00 "	" 1, 1908*
Patrick J. Kelly	126 D st	"	2.95 "	June 20, 1905*
William J. Carr	79 Elm st	"	2.75 "	Dec. 20, 1907*
Richard P. Collins	60 Pleasant st	"	2.75 "	April 16, 1909*
Patrick F. Mullen	122 D st	"	2.75 "	Feb. 2, 1907*
Jeremiah P. Scanlon	1 Auburn st	"	2.25 "	April 7, 1908*
William Abbott	284 Bunker Hill st	Engineer	3.00 "	May 8, 1896
Patrick Cooney	34 Dennis st	Fireman	2.83¼ "	Aug. 3, 1882
John J. Doherty	5 Union ct	Carpenter	3.50 "	Feb. 20, 1903
John H. Finnerty	16 Magazine st	"	3.50 "	July 15, 1895
Joseph Hayes	10 Summer st	"	3.50 "	May 7, 1897
Daniel W. Lyons	14 Winthrop st	"	3.50 "	Aug. 31, 1897
Dennis M. Murphy	114 Bowdoin st	"	3.50 "	" 11, 1891
William E. Murphy	2 Leeds st	"	3.50 "	April 5, 1897
Philip Nagle	39 Soley st	"	3.50 "	Aug. 23, 1903
William O'Keefe	66 Adams st	"	3.50 "	May 8, 1893
Charles H. Trask	146 Byron st	"	3.50 "	Sept. 9, 1895
Charles A. Dale	78 Clifton st	Concrete Worker	3.00 "	Nov. 10, 1906
Patrick H. Bates	159 Dorchester st	"	2.50 "	Sept. 21, 1899
William T. Loring	26 Worcester sq	Mason	2.75 "	" 19, 1899
Joseph Dunbar	27 Jefferson ave	Stone Cutter	2.50 "	July 20, 1895
George W. Callahan	12 Upton st	Machinist	3.00 "	April 6, 1897
Hugh Green	92 Newland st	"	3.00 "	July 12, 1895
Timothy F. Harrington	61 Yeoman st	"	3.00 "	April 20, 1894
Michael A. McCarthy	77 Fuller st	"	3.00 "	Oct. 16, 1897
Joseph Nunan	190 Emerson st	"	3.00 "	June 25, 1888
Alfred H. Stewart	55 Corey st	"	3.00 "	May 13, 1896
Neil J. Tolan	47 Woodbine st	"	3.00 "	Sept. 13, 1889
True Thuerson	13 Telegraph st	"	3.00 "	" 11, 1888
Timothy J. Kelleher	121 L st	"	2.75 "	June 7, 1898
John Sullivan, 1st	370 E st	"	2.75 "	Sept. 14, 1888
Patrick Sullivan, 1st	122 Malden st	"	2.75 "	Oct. 23, 1895
Michael Watson	31 Reading st	"	2.75 "	April 26, 1887
William Carr	627 Dorchester ave	"	2.50 "	" 6, 1886
Daniel H. Curley	71 Yeoman st	"	2.50 "	May 4, 1887
John F. Doolan	6 Kent st	"	2.50 "	June 1, 1895
Charles J. McLaughlin	66 Northfield st	"	2.50 "	April 14, 1873
James J. Murray	1 Exeter pl	"	2.50 "	Nov. 13, 1897
John Ganley	38 Ward st	Driller	2.75 "	Oct. 25, 1886
Bradford E. Treat	94 W. Newton st	Elevatorman	2.25 "	July 21, 1901
Edward J. Ryan	14A Blue Hill ave	Blacksmith	3.50 "	May 15, 1899
John E. Grant	915 Albany st	"	3.00 "	" 13, 1895
John Cassell	53 W. Dedham st	Blacksmith's Helper	2.50 "	March 16, 1883
Michael Desmond	17 Chadwick st	"	2.25 "	April, 1865
Edward McFall	92 Charles street pl	"	2.25 "	" 26, 1896
John B. Jeffers	39 Cambridge st	Electrolysis Investigator	1,100 yr	Oct. 12, 1896
Thomas R. Melville	79 Pearl st	Plumber and Electrician	3.00 day	Aug. 7, 1903
Thomas Devlin	171 Princeton st	Plumber	3 00 "	June 5, 1906
Robert J. Doyle	16 Meade st	"	3.00 "	Oct. 5, 1896
Patrick G. Finnerty	1 Dayton ave	"	3.00 "	Sept. 10, 1895
Charles Hines	41 Batchelder st	"	3.00 "	March 20, 1874
Joseph T. Ryan	21 Northfield st	"	3.00 "	Nov. 20, 1899
Thomas J. Dolan	10 Alleghany st	"	2.75 "	Feb. 24, 1897
Charles M. Driscoll	506 Third st	"	2.75 "	Aug. 18, 1904
Timothy H. Colgan	29 Everett st	Plumber's Helper	2.25 "	May 3, 1888
Thomas F. Crowley	6 Hammett st	"	2.25 "	April 10, 1905
Michael Downey	31 Winthrop st	"	2.25 "	" 6, 1899
Martin Dunlap	88 Springfield st	"	2.25 "	Dec. 6, 1897
Patrick J. Lawless	601 Shawmut ave	"	2.25 "	Sept. 2, 1903
Timothy F. Murphy	93 Henley st	"	2.25 "	March 4, 1904
Thomas F. Hayes	8 Tuckerman st	Painter	2.75 "	Jan. 8, 1903

* Previously in the department.

Water Department.— Continued.

Name.	Residence.	Designation.	Compensation.	Date of Election or Appointment.

Distribution Division.— Continued.

Name.	Residence.	Designation.	Compensation.	Date of Election or Appointment.
John E. Curry	6 Wesley st	Painter	$2.50 day	Feb. 6, 1904
Robert Donnelly	58 Chadwick st	"	2.40 "	April 22, 1896
John J. Broderick	62 Tremont st	"	2.25 "	Sept. 25, 1902
Richard T. Lambert	53 Russell st	"	2.25 "	Nov. 29, 1898
James B. Connolly	25 Blanche st	Yardman	3.00 "	July 20, 1889
Thomas F. Golding	88 Winthrop st	"	2.75 "	Nov. 30, 1884
John W. Sullivan	148 N st	Storekeeper	3.00 "	April 12, 1886
Thomas A. Gorman	52 Nashua st	Stock and Tool Keeper	2.75 "	June 16, 1896
Thomas J. Denny, 1st	601 Seventh st	" "	2.50 "	Feb. 17, 1893
Michael Reddy	7 Allston st	" "	2.50 "	Sept. 8, 1903
John J. Austin	11 Prospect st	Watchman	2.25 "	May 14, 1895
Charles J. Parks	20 Dunmore st	"	2.25 "	April 16, 1887
Frank T. McCarthy	10 Weston st	"	2.25 "	Oct. 4, 1898
Robert A. Barry	Parker Hill ave	Custodian Parker Hill Res'r.	2.25 "	March 19, 1906
Peter Dolan	397 Charles st	Janitor	2.25 "	June 9, 1905
James A. McCaffrey	15 Davis st	"	2.25 "	April 27, 1886
Michael F. Burke	41 Rutherford ave	Teamster	2.50 "	July 9, 1884
Patrick A. Curran	290 K st	"	2.50 "	Oct. 11, 1898
Jeremiah J. McLaughlin	12 Tufts st	"	2.50 "	Jan. 25, 1899
Matthew I. Nolan	11 Raven st	"	2.50 "	March 2, 1885
Thomas Bowen	59 Oak st	"	2.25 "	June 20, 1895
Michael J. Carney	61 Telegraph st	"	2.25 "	May 15, 1893
Raffael Curcio	44 Lexington st	"	2.25 "	Feb. 26, 1897
Michael Hines	127 Hampshire st	"	2.25 "	Sept. 21, 1885
David Leo	72 Sawyer st	"	2.25 "	Oct. 4, 1898
Moses McCue	14 Adams st	"	2.25 "	Sept. 24, 1895
Thomas Magee	11 Palmer st	"	2.25 "	July 12, 1894
Timothy Noonan	1155 Dorchester ave	"	2.25 "	Sept. 17, 1895
John J. O'Brien	607 E. Third st	"	2.25 "	July 12, 1895
Edward A. Pyne	124 Cabot st	"	2.25 "	May 27, 1895
John P. Regan	31 Bellflower st	"	2.25 "	June 24, 1895
Michael Ronan	11 Elder st	"	2.25 "	Oct. 31, 1887
John C. Thompson	3 Salvisberg ave	"	2.25 "	April 8, 1886
Thomas Williams	1828 Washington st	"	2.25 "	June 11, 1883
Edward A. McGonagle	40 Lexington st	Driver	2.50 "	Nov. 4, 1898
John J. Callahan	156 K st	"	2.25 "	Aug. 7, 1899
John A. Keyes	352 Columbus ave	"	2.25 "	Dec. 23, 1896
Jerome H. Moore	6 Bridge ct	"	2.25 "	Aug. 25, 1902
Harry Novograbelsky	6 Parkman st	"	2.25 "	Dec. 10, 1903
Rinaldo Eldridge	33 Worcester sq	Superintendent of Stables	1,000 yr	July 1, 1900
James J. Connors	5 Hunneman pl	Stableman	2.75 day	Aug. 16, 1898
Thomas Broderick	9 Leyland st	"	2.25 "	July, 1883
John Cahill	32 Spring Garden st	"	2.25 "	Nov. 12, 1885
William Carroll	31 Lexington st	"	2.25 "	June 11, 1895
James Donovan	153 Bunker Hill st	"	2.25 "	May 31, 1895
Martin F. King	265 Bolton st	"	2.25 "	Oct. 30, 1899
John C. McCarthy	24 Day st	"	2.25 "	Feb. 12, 1898
John F. McCauley	15 Newbern st	"	2.25 "	Oct. 26, 1898
Michael Noonan	44 Tufts st	"	2.25 "	May, 1878
Daniel J. Sullivan	69 Dorchester st	"	2.25 "	" 27, 1895
Thomas Douglas	3 Leyland st	Emergency Man	3.00 "	Sept. 12, 1887
John Doherty	283 Eustis st	"	2.25 "	" 10, 1895
Morgan Donahue	103 Eighth st	"	2.25 "	Oct. 15, 1884
Patrick A. Foley	123 Brown ave	"	2.25 "	April 10, 1886
Charles J. McKenna	44 Union pk	"	2.25 "	Sept. 21, 1896
Robert McLaughlin	51 Burrell st	"	2.25 "	May, 1881
Michael F. White	25 Barry st	"	2.25 "	Aug. 23, 1899
Walter Kelly	982 Harrison ave	Paver	3.00 "	April 21, 1886
Philip McDevitt	107 Ninth st	"	3.00 "	" 22, 1886
James McEttrick	53 Woodward ave	"	3.00 "	May 8, 1895
Lawrence E. Murphy	4 Nassau st	Repairer	3.00 "	Oct. 1, 1897
Hugh Campbell	100 Heath st	"	2.50 "	Sept. 13, 1888
John Campbell	34 Vine st	"	2.50 "	Jan. 17, 1893
William Collins	117 Buttonwood st	"	2.50 "	April, 1883
Patrick Douglas, 1st	19 Harvard st	"	2.50 "	March, 1872
Patrick Douglas, 2d	284 Eustis st	"	2.50 "	May 5, 1896
Patrick Heffernan	132 Union Park st	"	2.50 "	" 27, 1895
Hugh McKenney	70 Charter st	"	2.50 "	1853
Michael McLaughlin	8 Darling st	"	2.50 "	April 9, 1889
Isaac Saperstein	146 Paris st	"	2.50 "	Oct. 15, 1886
Michael C. Sullivan	749 Washington st	"	2.50 "	May 8, 1895
Michael Welch	75 Bolton st	"	2.25 "	April, 1865
John Begley	510 Third st	Pipe Layer	2.75 "	May 11, 1895

Water Department.— Continued.

Name.	Residence.	Designation	Compensation.	Date of Election or Appointment.

Distribution Division.— Continued.

Name.	Residence.	Designation	Compensation.	Date of Election or Appointment.
Martin Burke	156 Sixth st	Pipe Layer	$2.50 day	April 11, 1895
Hugh Cauley	152 Keyes st	"	2.50 "	" 1885
Arthur Christie	106 Sumner st	"	2.50 "	Sept. 19, 1898
John Geary	233 Fifth st	"	2.50 "	June 11, 1894
Patrick Lonergan	65 Ferrin st	"	2.50 "	Sept. 20, 1887
Daniel J. McCallion	133 Winthrop st	Gateman	2.50 "	July 9, 1895
Terrence T. McNulty	31 School st	"	2.50 "	Sept. 12, 1902
Douglas Forbes	31 Welles ave	Gate Marker	2.40 "	" 19, 1895
Patrick J. Barry	rear 135 Harrison ave	Laborer	2.25 "	March 29, 1895
John W. Brown	62 Bolton st	"	2.25 "	May 4, 1899
John Carey	38 Troy st	"	2.25 "	Jan. 19, 1897
John J. Carey	8 Tyler st	"	2.25 "	May 29, 1894
Thomas Carey, 2d	134 Vernon st	"	2.25 "	Dec. 28, 1897
John Concannon	8 Marshfield st	"	2.25 "	April 17, 1894
John Connolly, 1st	210 Second st	"	2.25 "	" 26, 1886
Martin H. Connolly	534 E. Sixth st	"	2.25 "	July 12, 1895
Timothy Connolly	47 Fifth st	"	2.25 "	Nov. 20, 1872
John Cook	12 Yale st	"	2.25 "	" 1884
Thomas F. Corcoran	12 Boston pl	"	2.25 "	April 3, 1894
Mark Cunniff	29 Whitney st	"	2.25 "	June 1, 1895
Morgan Curran	701 Sixth st	"	2.25 "	July 16, 1894
Michael F. Daley, 2d	6 Bucknam st	"	2.25 "	Aug. 10, 1903
Dennis J. Delaney	8 Island st	"	2.25 "	June 1, 1894
Thomas J. Denney, 2d	17 Reed's ct	"	2.25 "	March 24, 1899
Nicholas F. Deveraux	1251 Washington st	"	2.25 "	April 16, 1897
Edward A. Ditmus	67 Phillips st	"	2.25 "	March 29, 1895
Michael Donahue	33 B st	"	2.25 "	Oct. 10, 1886
Thomas Donahue	245 Eighth st	"	2.25 "	March 3, 1894
Daniel J. Douglas	4 Fremont ave	"	2.25 "	July 6, 1894
John F. Doyle	555 Medford st	"	2.25 "	Aug. 30, 1888
Florence Driscoll	3 Wapping st	"	2.25 "	June 10, 1898
Thomas F. Ducey	330 Bunker Hill st	"	2.25 "	April 22, 1890
Patrick Duffy	162 Endicott st	"	2.25 "	Oct. 26, 1897
Patrick Durand	219 Sixth st	"	2.25 "	Sept. 29, 1885
Daniel Fallon	31 Woodward ave	"	2.25 "	May 27, 1895
Patrick Fallon	12 Gurney st	"	2.25 "	April 27, 1895
William Fallon	216 Northampton st	"	2.25 "	June 3, 1895
Edward S. Farmer	9 Daniel st	"	2.25 "	" 3, 1895
John Farren	1 Buttrick pl	"	2.25 "	Oct. 26, 1897
Patrick Farrey	10 Roswell st	"	2.25 "	Sept. 11, 1895
John Fay, 1st	113 Longwood ave	"	2.25 "	June 4, 1880
Thomas Feeley	4 Tufts street ave	"	2.25 "	March 29, 1895
Michael J. Flaherty	124 Eighth st	"	2.25 "	July 6, 1887
Patrick Flaherty	134 Eighth st	"	2.25 "	May 14, 1888
Michael Fleming	41 Palmer st	"	2.25 "	July 12, 1895
Charles J. Forster	19 Marion st	"	2.25 "	June 6, 1895
John Furey	18 Boynton st	"	2.25 "	Oct. 10, 1898
John J. Gallagher	15 Preble st	"	2.25 "	Feb. 12, 1896
Michael Galvin	31 Eustis st	"	2.25 "	Dec. 8, 1893
Patrick Gorham	8 Baxter st	"	2.25 "	June 9, 1895
Michael Grady	190 Harrison ave	"	2.25 "	" 3, 1895
Patrick Griffin	389 Shawmut ave	"	2.25 "	July 13, 1894
Patrick Gurry	107 South st	"	2.25 "	May 29, 1895
Patrick Hannon	44 Francis st	"	2.25 "	April 18, 1893
Thomas Hannon	1517½ Tremont st	"	2.25 "	June 9, 1894
Charles Harkins	43 Sharon st	"	2.25 "	Sept. 10, 1895
Michael Healey	10 Langdon st	"	2.25 "	June 20, 1895
John Hill	38 Mystic st	"	2.25 "	July 10, 1895
Patrick Hurley	15 Hammond st	"	2.25 "	Sept. 10, 1895
Michael Jackson	45 Middle st	"	2.25 "	June 9, 1895
Patrick Joyce	29 Clayton st	"	2.25 "	July 20, 1885
John M. Kelliher	3 Payson pl	"	2.25 "	April 13, 1896
Coleman Kelly	298 Eighth st	"	2.25 "	March 1, 1886
Daniel P. King	13 Bower st	"	2.25 "	July 12, 1895
Thomas Larkin	504 Seventh st	"	2.25 "	" 19, 1887
John A. Lane	96 W. Concord st	"	2.25 "	Oct. 29, 1897
Thomas Lavery	207 D st	"	2.25 "	June 9, 1895
Michael Leonard, 1st	27 Charter st	"	2.25 "	Aug. 12, 1895
George H. Linnell	62 Pearl st	"	2.25 "	May 19, 1896
James Logue	12 Gerard st	"	2.25 "	July 16, 1894
William Lonergan	267 Eustis st	"	2.25 "	April 26, 1899
Jeremiah Looney	26 Boston st	"	2.25 "	March 27, 1885
Edward Lucey	122 C st	"	2.25 "	July 11, 1895

Water Department.— Continued.

Name.	Residence.	Designation.	Compensation.	Date of Election or Appointment.

Distribution Division.— Continued.

Name.	Residence.	Designation.	Compensation.	Date of Election or Appointment.
Daniel P. Lynch	64 Penfield st	Laborer	$2.25 day	March 1, 1873
John P. Lynch	1 Ambrose st	"	2.25 "	Sept. 25, 1888
James Lyons, 2d	15 Station st	"	2.25 "	April 23, 1886
James A. McAuley	526 Dorchester ave	"	2.25 "	June 3, 1895
Bernard McCarron	206 Endicott st	"	2.25 "	July 19, 1895
Hugh T. McCarthy	18 Franklin st	"	2.25 "	Nov. 13, 1896
John McCarthy, 1st	3 Buttonwood st	"	2.25 "	May 5, 1888
John McCarthy, 2d	26 Whitney st	"	2.25 "	Aug. 9, 1887
Michael McCarthy, 2d	96 E. Canton st	"	2.25 "	May 27, 1895
James E. McConnell	55 E. Concord st	"	2.25 "	June 4, 1897
Michael J. McDonough	343 Bowdoin st	"	2.25 "	Dec. 1, 1902
James McGee	44 Belmont st	"	2.25 "	July 13, 1894
Patrick McGinnis	139 Dover st	"	2.25 "	April 13, 1896
John McKay	3536 Washington st	"	2.25 "	July 11, 1895
William H. McKenna	182 London st	"	2.25 "	March 27, 1895
Cornelius McLaughlin, 2d	10 Fellows st	"	2.25 "	Feb., 1885
Daniel McLaughlin	93 Baldwin st	"	2.25 "	Dec. 11, 1897
Hugh McLaughlin	8 Edgeworth st	"	2.25 "	May 1, 1897
Patrick McLaughlin, 3d	219 Boylston st	"	2.25 "	Sept. 13, 1897
James McMullen	45 Pearl st	"	2.25 "	Dec. 5, 1896
James Martin, 2d	439 Shawmut ave	"	2.25 "	Sept. 4, 1896
Thomas Miley	118 Elmo st	"	2.25 "	July 20, 1894
Coleman Mullen	43 Mercer st	"	2.25 "	Oct. 31, 1887
John Mullen, 2d	170 Ninth st	"	2.25 "	Aug. 8, 1887
William J. Mullen	72 Northfield st	"	2.25 "	July 16, 1894
Michael Mulloy	14 Halleck st	"	2.25 "	Oct. 29, 1897
Martin Murray	45 Woodward st	"	2.25 "	Nov. 13, 1895
John W. Murphy	394 Shawmut ave	"	2.25 "	June 3, 1895
Thomas G. Nicholson	9 Stonehurst st	"	2.25 "	Sept. 10, 1895
Thomas O'Brien	15 Howes st	"	2.25 "	June 14, 1897
Timothy O'Brien	12 Pontiac st	"	2.25 "	Dec. 30, 1896
Joseph O'Connor	25 Oakley st	"	2.25 "	Aug. 16, 1897
Patrick F. O'Connor	146 K st	"	2.25 "	Feb. 28, 1899
Daniel O'Donnell	15 Elder st	"	2.25 "	May, 1884
Patrick O'Donnell	1041 Dorchester ave	"	2.25 "	1870
Bartholomew O'Leary	640 Ninth st	"	2.25 "	April 18, 1887
Daniel O'Neil	24 Leon st	"	2.25 "	June 1, 1894
Thomas O'Neil	675 Albany st	"	2.25 "	" 20, 1895
John D. Porter	51 Telegraph st	"	2.25 "	Oct. 31, 1903
Franz J. Protz	81 Lamartine st	"	2.25 "	" 29, 1887
John J. Quann	111 Tudor st	"	2.25 "	Jan. 1, 1901
Charles Quigley	60 Longwood ave	"	2.25 "	April 23, 1886
Jeremiah Quirk	33 Alexander st	"	2.25 "	" 29, 1887
Thomas D. Reardon	4 Concord st	"	2.25 "	Oct. 22, 1896
Timothy Reardon	886½ Harrison ave	"	2.25 "	June 21, 1895
John Rogers	17 Chambers st	"	2.25 "	" 8, 1887
James V. Russell	522 Seventh st	"	2.25 "	May 8, 1895
Daniel Ryan	15 Coleman st	"	2.25 "	July 13, 1887
Timothy Scully, 2d	284 Eustis st	"	2.25 "	May 29, 1895
Jeremiah Shea	9 Bond st	"	2.25 "	April 17, 1888
John Sheehan	129 Minden st	"	2.25 "	May 28, 1895
Patrick M. Sheehan	6 Lincoln pk	"	2.25 "	" 8, 1895
Eugene T. Shea	4 Clapp pl	"	2.25 "	Jan. 20, 1897
Daniel Shields	436 Commercial st	"	2.25 "	May 28, 1895
George Spillane	4 Carnes pl	"	2.25 "	July 14, 1899
Cornelius Sullivan	10 Kenney st	"	2.25 "	June 9, 1895
Jeremiah Sullivan, 1st	526 Seventh st	"	2.25 "	April 25, 1885
Peter Sullivan, 1st	12 Lamont st	"	2.25 "	May 8, 1895
Thomas D. Sullivan	273 Bunker Hill st	"	2.25 "	April 25, 1888
Thomas J. Toolin	166 O st	"	2.25 "	June 11, 1895
Edward J. Trainor	9 Olney st	"	2.25 "	Dec. 23, 1905
John Victor	26 Grove st	"	2.25 "	June 5, 1895
John Wall	918 Albany st	"	2.25 "	" 20, 1895
Francis T. Ware	23 Washburn st	"	2.25 "	July 20, 1896
John J. Welch	121 Bolton st	"	2.25 "	Oct. 30, 1896
Benjamin Bowden	48 Sharon st	"	1.50 "	Aug. 23, 1880
John Brennan	123 Dorchester ave	"	1.50 "	May 13, 1895
Matthew Burns	104 E. Canton st	"	1.50 "	April 18, 1887
William H. Connolly	51 Linden st	"	1.50 "	June 20, 1895
Edward Devlin	48 Auburn st	"	1.50 "	May 17, 1888
John Fay, 2d	6 Ward st	"	1.50 "	June 20, 1895
James Hurley	26 Delle ave	"	1.50 "	May 23, 1881
Patrick J. Hall	389 Bunker Hill st	"	1.50 "	Nov. 12, 1897

Water Department.— Continued.

Name.	Residence.	Designation.	Com-pensation.	Date of Election or Appointment.
Distribution Division.— Concluded.				
John Kane	116 Bartlett st	Laborer	$1.50 day	Nov. 12, 1885
Patrick Mullen	134 Vernon st	"	1.50 "	Sept. 10, 1895
William Smyrle	4 Weston pl	"	1.50 "	Oct. 1, 1888
Frank Quinn	45 Randall st	Boy	1.00 "	May 27, 1907
Brighton District.				
Thomas Neville	16 Harriet st	Foreman	$1,200 yr	May 15, 1905*
Thomas H. Palmer	40 Field st	Plumber	3.00 day	Oct. 15, 1895
David McCarthy	74 Chestnut ave	Gateman	2.50 "	Sept., 1867
James M. Synnott	279 Market st	"	2.50 "	June 19, 1891
Patrick H. Burke	133 St. Alphonsus st	Repairer	2.25 "	May 12, 1896
Thomas Cullen	33 Winship st	Stableman	2.25 "	April, 1873
Daniel J. Donovan	776 Cambridge st	Watchman	2.25 "	" 28, 1887
Dennis McCarthy	5 Baldwin pl	"	2.25 "	Nov. 9, 1895
Humphrey D. Sullivan	5 Westville st	"	2.25 "	April 29, 1904
Peter Welch	20 Academy Hill rd	Teamster	2.25 "	Nov. 20, 1874
Thomas Barrett	29 Snow st	Laborer	2.25 "	Oct. 29, 1897
John Coyne, 1st	1 Crossland pl	"	2.25 "	April 4, 1883
John Farrell	rear 24 Winship st	"	2.25 "	Oct. 29, 1897
Dennis Griffin	290 Ninth st	"	2.25 "	Feb. 15, 1898
Daniel F. Hanley	5 Norman st	"	2.25 "	June 7, 1899
Timothy Hayes	15 Shannon st	"	2.25 "	Feb. 23, 1898
John Murphy	1 Call st	"	2.25 "	April 27, 1896
Andrew B. Toomey	31 School st	"	2.25 "	March 4, 1904
Charlestown District.				
Patrick Kelly	83 Pearl st	Foreman	$1,200 yr	April 20, 1905*
John Gallagher	58 Lexington st	Paver	3.00 day	July 8, 1896
Bernard E. Flanagan	375 Bunker Hill st	Plumber	3.00 "	June 8, 1896
John Buckley	33 Cordis st	Watchman	2.25 "	March 27, 1885
James J. Hayes	1 Crystal pl	"	2.25 "	July 26, 1902
William P. Kilty	140 Medford st	Yardman	2.25 "	Feb. 2, 1898
Patrick Dacy	8 Lexington st	Stableman	2.25 "	July, 1889
Edward P. Sullivan	14 Princeton st	Teamster	2.25 "	Oct. 2, 1893
Michael Conway	138 Medford st	Laborer	2.25 "	July 11, 1896
John Coyne, 2d	11 School st	"	2.25 "	" 9, 1895
Cornelius Hegarty	22½ Union st	"	2.25 "	Sept. 12, 1898
William Kenny	38 Corey st	"	2.25 "	1874
Michael Leonard, 2d	4 Green's block	"	2.25 "	Aug. 8, 1887
Patrick McCormick	7 Wellington pl	"	2.25 "	1874
Patrick McGrath	30 Tremont st	"	2.25 "	Sept. 1, 1896
John Mahan	30 Winthrop st	"	2.25 "	Aug. 25, 1902
Timothy Murray	77 Warren st	"	2.25 "	Oct. 25, 1897
George J. O'Donnell	89 Baldwin st	"	2.25 "	April 25, 1888
Patrick Ryan	120 High st	"	2.25 "	1868
Peter Sullivan, 2d	90 Elm st	"	2.25 "	July 9, 1895
Dorchester District.				
Timothy Casey	8 Lorraine st	Foreman	$1,200 yr	July 3, 1908*
Alexander Thompson	47 Norton st	Plumber	3.00 day	March 27, 1885
Daniel O'Brien	185 Ninth st	Pipe Layer	2.50 "	Sept. 14, 1885
Daniel J. Buckley	17 Lincoln st	Watchman	2.25 "	July 25, 1902
Patrick J. Gorman	117 Howard ave	"	2.25 "	June 26, 1899
John McDonald	47 Fenton st	Teamster	2.25 "	May 19, 1893
John J. Barry	102 E. Cottage st	Laborer	2.25 "	" 15, 1895
Thomas Coyne	128 Cushing ave	"	2.25 "	Nov. 3, 1897
Timothy Donovan	80 Topliff st	"	2.25 "	June 10, 1895
James Gulliver	578 Dorchester ave	"	2.25 "	March 20, 1905
Peter Halligan	125 Quincy st	"	2.25 "	Nov. 9, 1895
Martin King	72 Fifth st	"	2.25 "	July 10, 1895
Timothy J. Leary	238 Dorchester st	"	2.25 "	Aug. 24, 1904
James P. McKenney	384 Neponset ave	"	2.25 "	" 9, 1904
John McNulty	1 Parkman pl	"	2.25 "	Sept. 11, 1895
Edward Quigley	53 Freeport st	"	2.25 "	June 14, 1898
Dennis Shea	35 Vaughan ave	"	2.25 "	Sept. 24, 1885
Patrick Sheedy	300 Fourth st	"	2.25 "	July 6, 1887
John Walsh	212½ D st	"	2.25 "	April 13, 1888

* Previously in the department.

Water Department.— Concluded.

Name.	Residence.	Designation.	Compensation.	Date of Election or Appointment.

East Boston District.

Name.	Residence.	Designation.	Compensation.	Date of Election or Appointment.
William F. O'Donnell	429 Saratoga st	Foreman	$1,200 yr.	July 27, 1906*
Dennis Regan	221 Bennington st	"	3.50 day	June 23, 1908*
John Cummings	110 Bennington st	Repairer	2.75 "	1881
James F. Donovan	153 Bunker Hill st	Watchman	2.25 "	May 8, 1896
Patrick H. McCarthy	28 Shelby st	"	2.25 "	Jan. 9, 1900
William Regan	219 Bennington st	"	2.25 "	Sept. 10, 1888
Daniel Sweeney	107 Falcon st	Stableman	2.25 "	April 18, 1886
John McCormick	191 Paris st	Teamster	2.25 "	Oct. 3, 1901
John F. Callahan	39 Pleasant st	Laborer	2.25 "	June 8, 1895
Patrick Canney	1 Parkman pl	"	2.25 "	April 26, 1886
Thomas Carey, 1st	38 Collins st	"	2.25 "	June 9, 1895
Michael Daly	133 London st	"	2.25 "	July 25, 1886
Timothy J. Driscoll	185 Chelsea st	"	2.25 "	Nov. 21, 1895
Jeremiah J. Fenton	90 Wordsworth st	"	2.25 "	June 4, 1895
Edward M. Houghton	179 Marion st	"	2.25 "	July 13, 1894
John McLaughlin	313 Chelsea st	"	2.25 "	June 10, 1895
Thomas F. Meade	31 Pleasant st	"	2.25 "	May 4, 1897
Francis Nelligan	10 Mather st	"	2.25 "	June 12, 1895
Michael Sullivan, 3d	4 Melrose pl	"	2.25 "	July 13, 1894

West Roxbury District.

Name.	Residence.	Designation.	Compensation.	Date of Election or Appointment.
Thomas C. McDonald	20 Rosemary st	Foreman	$1,200 yr.	Feb. 10, 1905*
Patrick J. Feeney	3 Hunneman pl	Inspector of Work	2.75 day	Dec. 20, 1907*
George Greer	33 Hyde Park ave	Repairer	2.50 "	May 28, 1895
James F. Black	60 Yeoman st	"	2.50 "	27, 1895
Peter O'Hare	1 Crosby pl	"	2.50 "	April 10, 1895
Michael O'Leary	62 Tower st	Stableman	2.25 "	Sept. 25, 1895
John Egan	31 Ballard st	Teamster	2.25 "	Oct. 11, 1886
James Murphy	91 Gardner st	"	2.25 "	April 28, 1899
Patrick Cassidy, 1st	16 Anson st	Watchman	2.25 "	July 10, 1895
Michael H. Dwyer	117 O st	"	2.25 "	Nov. 24, 1897
Thomas F. Callahan	12 Bradstreet ave	Laborer	2.25 "	June 27, 1907
James Griffin	3 Tyler st	"	2.25 "	Oct. 3, 1887
Lawrence A. Hillary	188 Bunker Hill st	"	2.25 "	April 26, 1897
James C. Killackey	32 Chestnut ave	"	2.25 "	July 19, 1887
Thomas Lyden	33 Woodman st	"	2.25 "	June 11, 1895
William Lyden	322 Amory st	"	2.25 "	March 27, 1876
Patrick J. Lynch	2 Meade st. ter	"	2.25 "	Jan. 5, 1897
Philip P. Lynch	29 Johnson st	"	2.25 "	Sept. 22, 1885
Dennis McGowan	66 Day st	"	2.25 "	May 9, 1884
Daniel McHugh	70 Brookside ave	"	2.25 "	Sept. 17, 1895
James McMahon	104 Williams st	"	2.25 "	Oct. 11, 1886
John Riley	131 Boylston st	"	2.25 "	Sept. 10, 1895
Patrick Smith	30 Phillips st	"	2.25 "	July 29, 1895
Patrick H. Walsh	3 Pleasant st	"	2.25 "	Aug. 15, 1905

Weights and Measures Department.

Name.	Residence.	Designation.	Compensation.	Date of Election or Appointment.
Charles B. Woolley	Hotel Comfort	Sealer	$3,000 yr.	May 1, 1908
John E. Ansell	64 W. Cedar st	Deputy Sealer	1,600 "	" 1, 1902
Jeremiah J. Crowley	4 Henchman st	"	1,600 "	" 1, 1902]
Louis Hertgen	59 Reading st	"	1,600 "	Sept. 23, 1908]
Frank L. Harney	266 Ruggles st	"	1,600 "	" 23, 1908]
Benjamin P. Hutchinson	6 Wendover st	"	1,600 "	" 23, 1908
Julius Meyer	2 Seneca st	"	1,600 "	" 23, 1908
James A. Sweeney	109 Hudson st	"	1,600 "	Aug. 6, 1904
Charles O. Sikora	139 Lauriat ave	"	1,600 "	Sept. 23, 1908
Fred A. Thissell	197 Green st	"	1,600 "	" 23, 1908
Charles E. Walsh	53 Thomas pk	"	1,600 "	May 1, 1906
Philip F. Leonard	444 E. Third st	Laborer	940 "	June 21, 1897]

Wire Department.

Head of Department.

Name.	Residence.	Designation.	Compensation.	Date of Election or Appointment.
James E. Cole	64 Perham st	Commissioner	$5,000 yr.	June 15, 1908*

* Previously in the department.

Wire Department.— Concluded.

Name.	Residence.	Designation.	Compensation.	Date of Election or Appointment.

Office.

Frank H. Rice	22 Saunders st	Chief Clerk	$1,600 yr	Oct. 5, 1900
John F. Flanagan	8 Adams st	Stenographer	1,000 "	Nov. 24, 1905
Agnes T. Fetherston	252 Dudley st	Telephone Operator	600 "	Dec. 31, 1900

Interior Division.

Walter J. Burke	41 Hillside st	Inspector	$1,500 yr	Aug. 4, 1894
John M. Costello	108 I st	"	1,200 "	June 17, 1904
Jeremiah A. Field	174 Sycamore st	"	1,500 "	Aug. 4, 1894
George W. Fuller	409 Warren st	"	1,200 "	April 5, 1901
Thomas F. Haley	328A Longwood ave	"	1,100 "	Sept. 1, 1905
Timothy F. Holland	30 Ophir st	"	1,200 "	July 27, 1900
John J. Kelleher	11 Danforth st	"	1,100 "	March 20, 1903
Charles P. Lynch	46 Bailey st	"	1,500 "	Dec. 26, 1894
Eugene C. McCarthy	99 Howard ave	"	1,500 "	Feb. 25, 1898
Francis J. Murray	28 Columbia rd	Clerk & Deputy Inspector	700 "	Aug. 5, 1903
Augustine C. Neville	12 Neptune ave	Deputy Inspector	800 "	July 20, 1906
William F. Peters	75 Dorchester st	Clerk and Inspector	1,400 "	April 26, 1897
James J. Ward	46 Clarence st	Inspector	1,000 "	Dec. 16, 1907

Exterior Division.

William H. Godfrey	43 G st	Chief Inspector	$2,000 yr	Aug. 4, 1894
James T. Ball	39 Rosedale st	Engineer	1,500 "	" 4, 1894
Arthur E. Clark	60 Hollander st	Stenciller	1,000 "	July 16, 1907
James W. Collins	3 Auburn st	Inspector	1,000 "	Jan. 28, 1902
Patrick Crilley	35 Washington st	Driver	1,000 "	Aug. 15, 1894
Terrence Desmond	67 Elm st	Inspector	1,200 "	" " 4, 1894
James Friel	36 Billerica st	"	1,200 "	" 4, 1894
J. Paul Haynes	27 Withington st	Engineer	1,500 "	Sept. 28, 1894
David Isaacs	24 Engleside st	Inspector	1,100 "	May 1, 1896
John M. Kenney	530 Fifth st	"	1,000 "	Jan. 28, 1901
James F. Kenneally	628 Sixth st	"	1,000 "	March 24, 1905
Patrick H. Kilroe	97 Hyde Park ave	"	1,100 "	June 30, 1905
Patrick J. Larkin	49 Dennis st	"	1,100 "	March 20, 1903
Thomas J. Lythgoe	81 Mapleton st	"	1,200 "	Jan. 30, 1895
Patrick F. McMahan	45 Tufts st	"	1,200 "	Oct. 21, 1897
Robert W. O'Toole	15 Hamlet st	"	1,000 "	Jan. 28, 1901
Charles D. Reagan	240 W. Fifth st	Driver	1,000 "	March 20, 1903
William J. Reagan	100 Wheatland ave	Inspector	1,200 "	Nov. 15, 1896
James W. Reid	776 Weld st	"	1,100 "	April 5, 1901
John A. Richardson	63 Forest st	"	1,000 "	" 5, 1901
Oliver P. Ricker	80 Van Winkle st	Clerk	1,200 "	Jan. 28, 1901
Martin F. Ryder	24 Hanover ave	Inspector	1,200 "	Sept. 7, 1898

COUNTY OFFICIALS AND EMPLOYEES.

County Buildings.

Name.	Residence.	Designation.	Compensation.	Date of Election or Appointment.
Roxbury Court House.				
William C. Moore	339 Savin Hill ave	Custodian	$1,000 yr	June 1, 1908
Henry W. Childs	28 Forest st	Janitor	750 "	May 1, 1888
John H. Banks	732 Shawmut ave	"	750 "	June 12, 1907
Michael Bath	914 Albany st	"	750 "	May 1, 1901
Hannah Driscoll	16 Downing st	Cleaning	.20 hr	June 30, 1902
Lillian Mulranan	19 Conant st	"	.20 "	July 23, 1902
Ellen Welch	44A Linden Park st	"	.20 "	" 2, 1902
West Roxbury Court House.				
Frank Kelly	90 Marcella st	Janitor	$600 yr	April 25, 1902
Nora A. Hurley *	90 Call st	Janitress	10.00 mo	Sept. 15, 1905
East Boston Court House.				
James J. Donnelly	45 Lamson st., E. B	Janitor	$720 yr	Sept. 6, 1904
Brighton Court House.				
William S. Arnaud †	325 Washington st., Bri	Janitor	$600 yr	Dec. 31, 1901
Jennie A .O'Connell †	19 Union st., Bri	Cleaning	180 "	May 2, 1908
Dorchester Court House.				
John F. Halligan ‡	365 Quincy st	Janitor	$600 yr	Feb. 11, 1902
Mary A. Donovan †	313 W. Third st	Cleaning	.20 hr	" 27, 1902
South Boston Court House.				
John B. Dooley §	204 W. Eighth st	Janitor	$600 yr	Feb. 6, 1902
Mary A. Donovan †	313 W. Third st	Cleaning	.20 hr	" 27, 1902
Charlestown Court House.				
Patrick Malloy	319 W. Fourth st	Janitor	$720 yr	Oct. 15, 1908
Sarah A. Ryan	3 Buttrick pl	Cleaning	300 "	July 4, 1902
Jury Waived Session. Room 10, Old Court House.				
William J. Hagerty	62 Savin st	Janitor	$2.50 day	Oct. 5, 1903
Helena Gaffney †	30 Newman st	Cleaning	.20 hr	" 5, 1903

Suffolk County Court House.

Fred H. Seavey *	215 Charles st	Custodian	None	May 24, 1900
Solomon B. Stebbins	862 South st	Superintendent	$2,000 yr	Jan. 1, 1895
John R. McCausland	Beachmont	Engineer	1,680 "	" 1, 1895
Edward B. McMartin	142 W. Concord st	Assistant Engineer	1,200 "	" 1, 1895
John Ridge	144 Bowen st	Fireman	2.50 day	" 1, 1895
John H. Madden	33 Newport st	"	2.50 "	" 1, 1895

* See Police Department; employed here only during winter season.
† See Public Buildings Department.
‡ See Library Department.
§ See School Department.

Suffolk County Court House.— Concluded.

Name.	Residence.	Designation.	Compensation.	Date of Election or Appointment.
Gustav T. Peterson	107 Sheridan st	Fireman	$2.50 day	Jan. 1, 1895
Peter V. Fernandez	15 Knox st	"	2.50 "	April 22, 1906
John Welch	Chelsea	"	2.50 "	Dec. 25, 1907
Edmund Doherty	Yeoman st	"	2.50 "	April 13, 1908
Peter A. Peterson	57 Brentwood st	Janitor	780 yr.	Jan. 1, 1895
Americus A. Bordman	63 Falcon st	"	2.50 day	" 1, 1895
William S. Foster	4 Allston st	"	*780 yr.	" 1, 1895
Guilford D. Saunders	31 Lawrence st	"	780 "	" 1, 1895
John J. Murray	24 Pleasant st	"	2.50 day	" 1, 1895
Bernard S. Remick	24 Myrtle st	Janitor and Watchman	3.00 "	" 1, 1895
Joseph H. Bonner	245 Saratoga st	Janitor and Floor Officer	1,000 yr	" 1, 1895
William A. Norcott	272 E. Cottage st	"	1,000 "	Oct. 22, 1900
Coleman Madden	51 Farrington st	Janitor and Elevator Relief	960 "	Jan. 1, 1895
John Quane	566 E. Seventh st	"	900 "	Oct. 20, 1897
Charles F. Leahy	523 E. Fourth st	Janitor	900 "	Dec. 4, 1896
Edward J. Pigeon	26 Dean st	"	900 "	Oct. 17, 1898
James J. Doherty	10 St. Germain st	"	2.50 day	Dec. 12, 1903
Richard H. Walsh	8 Willard st	Gateman	2.00 "	May 14, 1906
Dennis McGuire	26 Somerset st	Elevator Man	2.00 "	Jan. 1, 1895
Timothy W. Gunning	226 Lamartine st	"	2.00 "	Sept. 9, 1907
William H. Collins	Revere	"	2.00 "	Nov. 20, 1908
James J. McShane	9 Park st., Chsn	Watchman	2.50 "	Feb. 23, 1897
Charles H. Reinhardt	78 Middlesex st	"	2.50 "	Aug. 31, 1906
George A. Marks	Revere	Carpenter and Jobber	939 yr.	Jan. 31, 1899
John Collins	Revere	Electrician	939 "	" 1, 1895
Catherine Farren	21 Allston st	Forewoman	2.00 day	" 1, 1895
Annie Doherty	2 Poplar st	Cleaner	1.17 "	" 1, 1895
Elizabeth Sheehan	162 Endicott st	"	1.17 "	Aug. 10, 1898
Mary Barr	46 Chelsea st	"	1.17 "	" 24, 1900
Ellen Healey	41 Woodward st	"	1.17 "	" 18, 1903
Ellen Murphy	119 Kendall st	"	1.17 "	Feb. 26, 1906
Annie E. Ware	39 N. Russell st	"	1.17 "	Nov. 6, 1906
Mary Smith	137 Endicott st	"	1.17 "	Dec. 2, 1906
Margaret Barry	19 Sheafe st	"	1.17 "	Feb. 4, 1907
Julia McCarthy	37 Union st	"	1.17 "	" 13, 1907
Catherine Chipman	835 Albany st	"	1.17 "	March 22, 1907
Ellen McGonagle	110 Endicott st	Laundry	30.00 mo	May 1, 1905
Edmund Belben	12 Roach st	Cleaning Windows and Jobbing	.25 hr	Sept. 1, 1904
Florence A. Coops	Canton	Telephone Operator	1.58 day	March 31, '906

Suffolk County Jail.

Name	Residence	Designation	Compensation	Date
Fred H. Seavey†	215 Charles st	Jailer	$1,000 yr	May 24, 1900
Edmund P. Kelly	72 Westville st	Chief Officer	1,800 "	Nov., 1906
John Burke	86 Foster st	First Inside Officer	1,350 "	" 1896
John J. Reardon	215 Charles st	Second Inside Officer	1,250 "	May, 1885
Thomas J. Kelley	23 Monument sq	Third Inside Officer	1,250 "	Jan., 1895
Charles M. Hunter	65 Chestnut st	Officer and Watchman	1,200 "	Dec. 1893
Henry A. Simpson	Revere	" "	1,200 "	Nov., 1900
Joseph A. Singler	89 Templeton st	" "	1,200 "	" 1900
Edwin C. Crafts	Chelsea	"	1,200 "	April, 1901
Thomas Fallon	59 Clifton st	"	1,200 "	Dec., 1907
George W. Brown	231 Belgrade ave	Van-Driver	1,200 "	1893
Arthur R. Towle	Winthrop	Clerk	1,200 "	Feb., 1906
George A. Sargent	46 Hereford st	Physician	1,000 "	Jan., 1901
John P. Hatch	44 Tuttle st	Watchman	1,000 "	Oct., 1903
William B. Hussey	20 Paris st	"	1,000 "	Feb., 1906
Joseph F. Devonshire	257 Westville st	"	1,000 "	" 1906
Kasper Zimmerman	178 Boylston st	"	1,000 "	Oct., 1906
John Evans	1 Yeoman pl	Watchman and Engineer	1,000 "	Jan., 1907
Joseph O. Nelson	15 Hunnewell ave	" "	1,000 "	Feb., 1909
Timothy J. Hannon	28 Arcadia st	Steward	1,350 "	Jan., 1907
Moses H. Richardson	6 Henley st	Officer and Watchman	900 "	Oct., 1903
Charles S. Robinson	Chelsea	" "	900 "	Feb., 1908

NOTE.— By virtue of chapter 453 of the Acts of the Legislature for 1894, the care and custody of the Suffolk County Court House is vested in the Supreme Judicial Court, who fix the number of persons to be employed and their compensation.

* William S. Foster receives in addition from the Register of Probate $600 per year for messenger service.
† See Jail and Miscellaneous.

Suffolk County Jail.— Concluded.

Name.	Residence.	Designation.	Compensation.	Date of Election or Appointment.
Grant McIntosh	55 Joy st	Officer and Watchman	$900 yr	Sept. 21, 1908
George H. Gilmore	6 Magdella st	"	900 "	March 3, 1909
Edgar J. Helms	59 Patten st	Chaplain	600 "	May, 1904
Jeremiah E. Millerick	6 Allen st	"	600 "	1904
Belle A. Floyd	215 Charles st	Matron	720 "	Oct., 1900
Helen M. Mott	215 Charles st	Assistant Matron	600 "	Dec., 1902
Sarah O. Bain	215 Charles st	"	480 "	Sept., 1903
Alice Whitcomb	215 Charles st	"	480 "	Dec., 1904
Lilly P. Egan	215 Charles st	"	480 "	April, 1906
Pauline Pastene	215 Charles st	"	480 "	" 1908

Supreme Judicial Court.

Name.	Residence.	Designation.	Compensation.	Date of Election or Appointment.
Walter F. Frederick	30 Puritan ave	Clerk	†$5,000 yr	June 16, 1908*
John H. Flynn	421 Meridian st	Assistant Clerk	‡3,000 "	Nov. 12, 1908*
May I. Everett	62 Cliff st	Recorder	1,062 "	Feb. 23, 1870
Margaret V. Garrity	77 Gainsboro st	Office Clerk	1,000 "	Sept. 1, 1893
Josie M. Murphy	11 Grant st	Charge of Records and Files	880 "	April 1, 1889
Christie A. Scheele	78 Middlesex st	Office Clerk	750 "	Feb. 1, 1909
Helen G. Connor	920 E. Fourth st	Recording	580 "	March 15, 1904
Madeline Connors	181 Foster st	"	580 "	May 16, 1899
Catherine T. A. Flannery	80 Revere st	"	580 "	Jan. 1, 1897
Alice G. Keenan	41 McLean st	"	580 "	8, 1903
Nellie T. Kenneally	170 Sixth st	"	580 "	May 15, 1905
Annie E. Murray	70 W. Cedar st	"	580 "	Sept. 19, 1905
Lillie S. Dowd	50 Ruggles st	Stenographer	580 "	May 1, 1906
Philip J. Feinberg	7 Hancock st	Messenger	500 "	Jan. 1, 1909

Work on Early Court Files.

Name.	Residence.	Designation.	Compensation.	Date of Election or Appointment.
Katherine G. Brennan	256 E. Cottage st	Indexing	$540 yr	Jan. 15, 1906

Superior Court.— Civil Session.

Name.	Residence.	Designation.	Compensation.	Date of Election or Appointment.
Francis A. Campbell	8 Kinross rd	Clerk	$6,000 yr	Nov. 8, 1904
Henry E. Bellew	9 Beacon st	Assistant Clerk, Equity‡	4,500 "	April 9, 1892
William Gilchrist	427 Meridian st	1st Assistant Clerk	3,000 "	Feb. 1, 1903
George E. Kimball	40 Welles ave	2d "	3,000 "	June 10, 1895
Allen H. Bearse	Melrose	3d "	2,500 "	April 30, 1897
Stephen Thatcher	Cambridge	4th "	2,500 "	June 15, 1899
Guy H. Holliday	26 Fountain st	5th "	2,500 "	Sept. 1, 1901
George P. Drury	Waltham	6th "	2,500 "	Oct. 1, 1901
Edward A. Willard	8 Arden st	7th "	2,500 "	Feb. 21, 1877
Flourence J. Mahoney	Hopkinton	8th "	2,500 "	Sept. 1, 1903
Charles J. Hart	187 Dudley ave	9th "	2,500 "	March 2, 1904
John F. Volk	Cambridge	10th "	2,500 "	Sept. 6, 1904
Francis P. Ewing	56 Lawrence ave	11th "	2,500 "	April 28, 1906
Fred W. Card	11 Chestnut sq., J. P.	Stenographer, 1st Session	2,500 "	Sept. 3, 1895
Lucius W. Richardson	3 Aldie st., Alls.	" 2d "	2,500 "	April 1, 1904
Frank H. Burt	Newton	" 3d "	2,500 "	Feb. 1, 1894
Florence Burbank	14 Peverell st	" 4th "	2,500 "	April 1, 1904
Alice E. Brett	173 Maple st., W. R.	" 5th "	2,500 "	Oct. 1, 1902
Clarissa L. Hill	3 Chestnut st	" 6th "	2,500 "	" 1, 1903
Saidee M. Swift	50 Pinckney st	" 7th "	2,500 "	" 1, 1903
Wells H. Johnson	70 Shepton st	Stenographer, Session Without Jury	2,500 "	" 1, 1904
John P. Foley	Peabody	Stenographer, Equity Session, 1st Division	2,500 "	April 10, 1909
William N. Todd	5 Schuyler st	Stenographer, Equity Session, 2d Division	2,500 "	Oct. 8, 1906

* Previously in the department.
† $1,500 additional from Commonwealth.
‡ $500 additional from Commonwealth.

Superior Court, Civil Session.— Concluded.

Name.	Residence.	Designation.	Compensation.	Date of Election or Appointment.

Law Division.

Name.	Residence.	Designation.	Compensation.	Date of Election or Appointment.
Albert E. Macdonald	56 Mapleton st	Chief Clerk	$1,920 yr	Feb. 1, 1903
Edmund S. Phinney	23 Rexhame st	Execution Clerk	1,620 "	May 2, 1898
F. Howard Hallett	1058 Washington st., Dor.	Assistant Execution Clerk	900 "	April 1, 1903
Alice M. Cashman	94 Princeton st	Secretary	1,620 "	June 1, 1901
Emily F. Epps	9 Irving pl	Appeal Clerk	1,500 "	" 8, 1897
Flora M. Parrish	46 Adams st., Dor.	Entry Clerk	1,200 "	Aug. 1, 1896
Agnita J. Curry	824 Blue Hill ave	Copyist	780 "	Sept. 1, 1905
Katharine M. Bulger	174 Third st	"	780 "	Feb. 1, 1908
Elizabeth N. Harris	Cambridge	Recording Clerk	1,200 "	June 1, 1884
Mary M. Fitzsimmons	15 Bullard st	Assistant Recording Clerk	1,200 "	Dec. 23, 1893
Anna S. Norton	524 Fifth st	" "	1,200 "	" 13, 1898
Katherine T. Flynn	1047 Saratoga st	" "	1,080 "	Feb. 1, 1900
Ella A. Dugan	134 Devon st	" "	720 "	May 1, 1905
Marion A. Shea	616 Dudley st	" "	720 "	Oct. 9, 1905
Margaret Hayes	316 E st	" "	720 "	April 9, 1906
Helen V. Cullen	45 Kingsdale st	" "	600 "	Dec. 1, 1906
Helen R. O'Brien	76 Washington st., Chsn.	" "	720 "	March 4, 1907
Mary A. Condon	20 Folsom st	" "	600 "	Dec. 10, 1907
T. Donald Adair	194 Quincy st	Index Clerk	780 "	March 11, 1904
Charles E. Barnett	274A Shawmut ave	File Clerk	1,020 "	Oct. 1, 1906
James F. McDermott	2 Tyler st	Docket Clerk	1,020 "	Feb. 11, 1907
John L. Kelly	224 Webster st	Messenger	1,400 "	March 1, 1906
Michael F. Hart	57 Hancock st	Office Clerk	1,200 "	May 7, 1906
George A. Scheele	78 Middlesex st	File Clerk	480 "	Feb. 11, 1907
John L. McCubbin	742 E. Eighth st	Boy	216 "	Oct. 5, 1908

Equity Division.

Name.	Residence.	Designation.	Compensation.	Date of Election or Appointment.
Rosa B. Torrey	30 Welles ave	Entry and Recording Clerk	$1,500 yr	May 1, 1888
Adeline D. Elkins	26 Granville st	Assistant Entry and Recording Clerk	960 "	" 1, 1892
Agnes Louise Malone	62 Allen st	Assistant Entry and Recording Clerk	900 "	Nov. 20, 1902
Mary Donovan	10 Corona st	Assistant Entry and Recording Clerk	720 "	May 7, 1906
Katherine A. Dowling	1 Wigglesworth st	Assistant Entry and Recording Clerk	720 "	" 21, 1906

Divorce Division.

Name.	Residence.	Designation.	Compensation.	Date of Election or Appointment.
Lila F. Roberts	28 Union Park	Entry and Recording Clerk	$1,200 yr	Dec. 29, 1902
Katherine M. Hatton	358 Bunker Hill st	Assistant Entry and Recording Clerk	720 "	March 1, 1906

Superior Court.— Criminal Session.

Name.	Residence.	Designation.	Compensation.	Date of Election or Appointment.
John P. Manning	56 Moreland st	Clerk	$6,000 yr	Nov. 30, 1874
John R. Campbell	31 Everton st	Assistant Clerk	3,000 "	Aug. 15, 1876
Julian Seriack	496 Massachusetts ave	"	2,960 "	Oct. 1, 1884
Martin L. Curley	38 Woodville st	Clerk	2,100 "	Sept. 1, 1891
Mary F. Welch	10 Dayton ave	"	1,140 "	May 1, 1899
Mary A. B. Maher	162 Harvard st	"	960 "	March 1, 1893
Grace N. Caiger	11 Baker ct	"	900 "	June 1, 1903
Alice E. O'Brien	105 Howland st	"	900 "	July 1, 1904
Theresa G. Sheridan	6 Waterlow st	"	900 "	Jan., 1904
Charles F. Mahony	200 Northampton st	Temporary Clerk	18.00 mo	June, 1906
Kate Good	68 Blue Hill ave	"	10.00 wk	Oct., 1907
A. Mabel Cook	145 Highland st	"	10.00 "	Jan., 1909
Richard Keefe	76 Mapleton st	Probation Officer	2,100 yr	April 13, 1909*
James F. Wise	65 Brent st	"	2,000 "	Jan. 18, 1907
Charles M. Warren	250 Neponset ave	"	2,000 "	" 18, 1907
Alice M. Power	22 Howland st	"	1,700 "	Nov. 21, 1906
Kate M. Reilly	43 Norton st	"	1,700 "	" 21, 1906
Frances McCormick	8A Auburn st	"	1,200 "	May 20, 1907
John H. Farley †	11 Bicknell st	Court Stenographer	2,500 "	June, 1896

* Previously in the department.
† And fees.

Superior Court, Criminal Session.—Concluded.

Name.	Residence.	Designation.	Compensation.	Date of Election or Appointment.

District Attorney's Office.

Hugh J. Doherty	30 Worthington st	Clerk	$1,200 yr.	Feb. 25, 1909
Henry P. Fielding	14 Lawrence rd	Stenographer	1,200 "	March 9, 1909

County of Suffolk Court Officers.

Robert Herter*	15 Catawba st	Supreme Court Messenger	$1,600 yr.	Jan., 1884
James J. Lyons*	5 Royal st	Supreme Court Officer	1,300 "	Feb., 1888
James F. McCarthy*	7 Adams st	" "	1,300 "	May, 1888
Michael F. Meagher*	593 E. Eighth st	" "	1,300 "	Jan., 1908
Richard J. Murray*	70 W. Cedar st	" "	1,300 "	Nov., 1886
Daniel H. Ryan*	61 Maverick sq	" "	1,300 "	Oct., 1892
Charles F. Dolan†	55 W. Cedar st	Superior Court Messenger and Clerical Assistant	2,000 "	Nov., 1892
Daniel A. Cronin†	117 Dale st	Superior Court Officer	2,000 "	Jan., 1884
William O. Armstrong†	2989 Washington st	" "	1,700 "	April, 1893
Howard R. Bowers†	10 Ridgemont st	" "	1,700 "	Oct., 1903
William Burns†	11 Cottage st	" "	1,700 "	May, 1897
Irving W. Campbell†	Winthrop	" "	1,700 "	Jan., 1890
William W. Campbell.†	45 Dwight st	" "	1,700 "	Feb., 1885
Dennis J. Collins†	47 McLean st	" "	1,700 "	April, 1895
William F. Clerke†	2 St Botolph st	" "	1,700 "	Jan., 1891
John F. Cook†	Chelsea	" "	1,700 "	" 1886
Andrew J. Crotty†	52 Devon st	" "	1,700 "	Oct., 1894
Martin F. Donnellon†	Hotel Langham	" "	1,700 "	Nov., 1895
James H. Donovan†	110 Porter st	" "	1,700 "	Oct., 1903
Caleb D. Dunham†	58 Sawyer ave	" "	1,700 "	Feb., 1895
John A. Finley†	409 E. Seventh st	" "	1,700 "	April, 1908
James A. Haliburton†	65 Selwyn st	" "	1,700 "	Oct., 1902
Willard W. Hibbard†	115 Richmond st	" "	1,700 "	1903
Thomas P. Hurley†	167 W. Third st	" "	1,700 "	" 1898
James A. Hussey†	73 Knoll st	" "	1,700 "	Jan., 1886
Frederick P. Knapp†	25 Fairview st	" "	1,700 "	Oct., 1894
William J. Leonard†	15 Cohlberg ave	" "	1,700 "	Jan., 1901
Peter McCann†	Chelsea	" "	1,700 "	Oct., 1903
William A. McDevitt, Jr.†	263 Columbus ave	" "	1,700 "	Feb., 1902
Michael J. McDonough†	4A Allston st	" "	1,700 "	May, 1893
Robert M. McLeish†	394 K st	" "	1,700 "	Oct., 1903
William C. Morey†	38 Esmond st	" "	1,700 "	1896
George F. Mitchell†	20 Dustin st	" "	1,700 "	Dec., 1892
John R. Murray†	27 McLean st	" "	1,700 "	Oct., 1903
Thomas A. Murray†	28 Columbia rd	" "	1,700 "	1893
William J. Nawn†	46 Creighton st	" "	1,700 "	" 1903
Daniel Noonan†	23 Hillside st	" "	1,700 "	April, 1879
Joseph S. Paine†	307 Cambridge st	" "	1,700 "	Oct., 1888
John B. Patterson†	464 Norfolk st	" "	1,700 "	April, 1895
Frank C. Pierce†	9 Harold st	" "	1,700 "	Feb., 1907
John R. Rea†	68 Brent st	" "	1,700 "	Jan., 1886
Charles F. Riley†	53 Clarkwood st	" "	1,700 "	1893
Forrest E. Starr†	593 Tremont st	" "	1,700 "	" 1891
Henry A. Silver†	45 Palmer st	" "	1,700 "	1893
Oscar L. Strout†	31 Wendover st	" "	1,700 "	Oct., 1901
George W. Thompson†	41 High st	" "	1,700 "	Jan., 1903
Archibald A. Turner†	9 Abbott st	" "	1,700 "	April, 1893
Francis H. Wall†	15 Magnolia sq	" "	1,700 "	Jan., 1890
Frank B. Willson†	556 Broadway	" "	1,700 "	May, 1897
George O. White†	42 Green st	" "	1,700 "	Oct., 1903
Patrick J. Donnelly	124 Fisher ave	" "	3.00 day	Feb., 1908
James McComiskey	47 W. Cedar st	" "	3.00 "	1907
Peter H. Reinstein	25 Ransom st	" "	3.00 "	April, 1908
Edward F. Tracy	3 Bartlett ter	" "	3.00 "	Jan., 1904
Frederick J. Finnegan†	Chelsea	Probate Court Officer	1,700 yr	1, 1904
Frank W. Brown	57 Hancock st., Dor	" Messenger	1,500 "	1, 1904
Adolphus G. McVey†	200 Hancock st., Dor	Municipal Civil Court Officer	1,500 "	March 5, 1885
Thomas Hall†	62 Chelsea st., E. B	"	1,500 "	June, 1868
Thomas J. Gorman	27 Pearl st., Dor	Municipal Civil Court Officer and Messenger	1,700 "	March 28, 1906

* $100 additional allowed for uniform, and $400 from Commonwealth.
† $100 additional allowed for uniform.

County of Suffolk Court Officers.— Concluded.

Name.	Residence.	Designation.	Com-pensation.	Date of Election or Appointment.
Ambrose H. Abbott*.......	24 Pratt st............	Mun. Criminal Court Officer	$1,700 yr...	April 16, 1889
Albert S. Buswell*..."....	69 Moreland st...........	" " "	. 1,700 "..., " 16, 1889	
Peter F. Hanley*.........	17 Dorset st...........	" " "	. 1,700 "...May 6, 1893	
James F. McKenzie*......	652 Columbia rd.........	" " "	. 1,700 "...June 13, 1902	
James F. Mitchell*.......	180 Maple st...........	" " "	. 1,700 "...Sept. 26, 1883	
William H. Powers*......	5 Cross st.............	" " "	. 1,700 "...Nov. 5, 1908	

Registry of Probate and Insolvency.

John J. Burke..........	Chelsea...............	Clerk...............	$1,500 yr...Aug.	1, 1898
Louis V. Jennings........	72A Clifton st.........	"	1,500 "...Sept.	11, 1896
Mary E. Garrity.........	77 Gainsboro st.........	"	1,320 "...Oct.,	1885
Gertrude M. Smith.......	362 Geneva ave........	"	1,260 "...Sept.	21, 1893
Sarah A. Gallagher.......	22 High Rock way.......	"	1,200 "...Oct.,	1876
Sarah E. Lyon..........	Newton Lower Falls......	"	1,200 "...Jan.,	1886
Ada M. Noble..........	36 Myrtle st..........	"	1,080 "...June	7, 1893
Katherine L. Lappen......	1 Normandy st.........	"	900 "...May,	1893
Arthur W. Sullivan.......	258 Webster st........	"	900 "...March	18, 1907
Evelyn G. Collins........	45 Allen st..........	"	840 "...Feb.	11, 1896
Margaret Hayes.........	39 Seneca st..........	"	840 "... "	6, 1893
Mary F. Meehan........	5 LaGrange pl.........	"	840 "... "	6, 1893
Julia J. Williams........	69 Clifford st.........	"	840 "...Sept.	21, 1893
Sarah F. Cullen........	45 Kingsdale st........	"	780 "...May	1, 1893
Estelle E. Dealey........	624 Bennington st......	"	780 "...Feb.,	1902
Mabel Lapworth........	62 Clifton st..........	"	780 "...July	11, 1897
Katherine E. Lyons......	32 Albion pl..........	"	780 "...June	8, 1903
Katherine F. O'Brien.....	30 Allston st.........	"	780 "...Nov.	1, 1902
Carrie B. Williams.......	64 Auckland st........	"	780 "...Jan.	27, 1896
Margaret V. Cashman....	Beachmont	"	720 "...Sept.	1, 1908
Mary W. Daly..........	76 Blue Hill ave........	"	600 "...April	12, 1909
William B. Foster.......	4A Allston st..........	Messenger †	600 "...Jan.	1, 1904

Old Records.

Helen G. Mitchell........	45 Moulton st..........	Clerk...............	$660 yr...April	1, 1908

Justices of the Municipal Court of the City of Boston.

Wilfred Bolster..........	137 Ruthven st........	Chief Justice..........	$5,000 yr...Sept.	19, 1906
William J. Forsaith......	372 Longwood ave......	Associate Justice........	4,500 "...March	8, 1882
Frederick D. Ely........	Dedham...........	"	4,500 "...Oct.	1, 1888
John H. Burke.........	Brookline	"	4,500 "...Feb.	12, 1891
George L. Wentworth.....	South Weymouth........	"	4,500 "...May	12, 1899
James P. Parmenter......	Arlington.............	"	4,500 "...Jan.	29, 1902
William Sullivan........	Brookline............	"	4,500 "...Dec.	17, 1902
Michael J. Murray.......	45 Robinwood ave......	"	4,500 "... "	19, 1906
John A. Bennett........	18 St. James ave........	Special Justice..........	‡15.00 day..May	24, 1899
John Duff	19 Seaverns ave........	"	‡15.00 " ..Sept.	26, 1906

Municipal Court, Civil Session.

Orsino G. Sleeper........	Newton	Clerk...............	$3,500 yr...June	1, 1894
Oscar F. Timlin.........	67 Maywood st........	First Assistant Clerk......	2,500 "...Nov.	12, 1883
Henry R. W. Browne.....	22 Blagden st..........	Second Assistant Clerk.....	2,000 "...April	11, 1892
Warren C. Travis........	Framingham..........	Third Assistant Clerk.....	1,800 "...Feb.	1, 1891
Herbert C. Blackmer.....	20 Saranac st.........	Fourth Assistant Clerk.....	1,800 "...Dec.	1, 1893
Clesson S. Curtice.......	Malden..............	Fifth Assistant Clerk......	1,500 "...June	11, 1906
George B. Stebbins......	Everett..............	Copyist..............	1,300 "... "	17, 1899
Arthur W. Ashenden.....	37 Evelyn st.........	"	1,200 "...Dec.	1, 1897

* $100 additional allowed for uniform.
† See Court House.   ‡ Per diem for actual service.

Municipal Court, Civil Session.— Concluded.

Name.	Residence.	Designation.	Compensation.	Date of Election or Appointment.
Volney D. Caldwell	60 Idaho st	Copyist	$800 yr	Feb. 18, 1901
George B. Frost	Medford	"	750 "	" 16, 1903
Louis B. Torrey	30 Welles ave	"	650 "	March 18, 1904
James F. Tobin	54 Bower st	"	400 "	Sept. 21, 1906

Municipal Court, Criminal Session.

Frederic C. Ingalls	1 Larchmont st	Clerk	$3,500 yr	Dec. 12, 1886
Edward J. Lord	Melrose	First Assistant Clerk	2,500 "	" 23, 1886
Sidney P. Brown	Newton	Second Assistant Clerk	2,000 "	" 23, 1886
John F. Barry	14 Elmont st	Third Assistant Clerk	1,800 "	Aug. 1, 1896
Harvey B. Hudson	39 Parsons st., Bri	Fourth Assistant Clerk	1,600 "	Sept. 30, 1898
Henry R. Blackmer	Medford	Fifth Assistant Clerk	1,600 "	April 22, 1908
Albert R. Brown	76 Barry st., Dor	Sixth Assistant Clerk	1,600 "	June 4, 1908
Richard J. Lord	Melrose	Copyist	1,300 "	April 20, 1908
Charles T. Willock	23 Gates st	"	800 "	Jan. 1, 1909
Michael H. Travers	24 Blackstone st	"	1,200 "	Dec. 12, 1906
Albert J. Sargent	72 Wellington Hill st	Probation Officer	2,200 "	March 11, 1909*
Charles E. Grinnell	101 Dale st	Assistant Probation Officer	2,000 "	July 1, 1893
Albert J. Fowles	106 Stoughton st	" "	2,000 "	April 14, 1909
Richard J. Walsh	20 Nazing st	" "	2,000 "	Jan. 10, 1893
Frank L. Warren	16 Silloway st	" "	2,000 "	March 15, 1906
James F. Wilkinson	9 Mascot st	" "	2,000 "	Nov. 1, 1893
Elizabeth A. Lee	858 Albany st	" "	1,200 "	May 1, 1907
Mary A. Maynard	3 Austin st	" "	1,700 "	April 20, 1897
Elizabeth L. Tuttle	66 Chestnut st	" "	1,700 "	June 1, 1895
Eugene J. Callanan	30 Pond st., Dor	Clerk	1,200 "	April 30, 1908

Municipal Court, Charlestown District.

Henry W. Bragg	282 Berkeley st	Justice	$2,200 yr	Dec. 7, 1886
Joseph J. Corbett	14 Monument sq	Special Justice	†7.19 day	" 13, 1905
William H. Preble	291 Bunker Hill st	"	†7.19 "	Sept. 11, 1901
Mark E. Smith	7 Forest pl	Clerk	1,500 yr	July 16, 1902
John M. Pitman	387 Main st	Clerical Assistant	500 "	Oct. 28, 1907
Nathaniel Leonard	5 Prescott st	Probation Officer	1,500 "	July 1, 1891
Frank B. Cotton	30 Oak st	Court Officer	1,000 "	March 22, 1899
Henry Fox	30 Oak st	"	1,000 "	Oct. 23, 1888

East Boston District Court.

Albert E. Clary	441 Meridian st	Justice	$2,500 yr	May 6, 1903
Joseph H. Barnes	206 Lexington st	Special Justice	†8.17 day	Aug. 16, 1899
Frank E. Dimick	225 Lexington st	"	†8.17 "	July 24, 1903
Thomas H. Dalton	189 Trenton st	Clerk	1,500 yr	Sept. 11, 1903
Lubell E. Gallagher	Winthrop	Clerical Assistant	700 "	April 27, 1903
George E. Harrington	27 Monmouth st	Court Officer	1,300 "	Nov. 30, 1898
Charles F. Taylor	24 Maverick sq	Probation Officer	1,500 "	May 12, 1904

Municipal Court, South Boston District.

Joseph D. Fallon	789 Broadway	Justice	$2,750 yr	May 25, 1893
Adrian B. Smith	416 Fifth st	Clerk	1,650 "	March 20, 1907
Harry W. Park	645 Sixth st	Assistant Clerk	1,100 "	Sept. 3, 1907
George N. Parker	437 Fourth st	Probation Officer	1,800 "	May 25, 1893
Ellen McGurty	1677 Washington st	Asst. Probation Officer	1,200 "	April 20, 1905
William L. Droban	8A Bellflower st	Court Officer	1,300 "	June 1, 1895
Thomas J. Condon	754 Fourth st	"	1,300 "	Sept. 1, 1899
Josiah S. Dean	15 Lanark rd	Special Justice	†8.99 day	May 25, 1893
Edward L. Logan	560 E. Broadway	"	†8.99 "	March 20, 1907

* Previously in the department.   † Per diem for actual service.

Municipal Court, Dorchester District.

Name.	Residence.	Designation.	Compensation.	Date of Election or Appointment.
Joseph R. Churchill	32 Percival st	Justice	$3,000 yr	Jan. 1, 1871
George M. Reed	256 Ashmont st	Special Justice	*9.80 day	1872
Michael H. Sullivan	48 Hewins st	"	*9.80 "	1909
Frank J. Tuttle	43 Beaumont st	Clerk	1,800 yr	March 13, 1907
Alvin I. Phillips	3 Freeman st	Court Officer	800 "	June, 1881
Alvin I. Phillips	3 Freeman st	Probation Officer	800 "	July 29, 1881

Municipal Court, Roxbury District.

Name.	Residence.	Designation.	Compensation.	Date of Election or Appointment.
A. Nathan Williams	153 Ruthven st	Justice	$4,000 yr	March 15, 1907
Joseph N. Palmer	Newton	Special Justice	*13.07 day	May 27, 1897
Abraham K. Cohen	90 Walnut ave	"	*13.07 "	March 20, 1907
Maurice J. O'Connell	16 Wyoming st	Clerk	2,400 yr	Nov. 14, 1893
Fred E. Cruff	21 Montrose st	Assistant Clerk	1,600 "	Dec. 7, 1893
Joseph H. Keen	9 Don st	Probation Officer	2,000 "	Feb. 15, 1909
John D. Regan	27 Stratton st	Clerical Assistant	600 "	May 1, 1908
Celia S. Lappen	42 Lambert st	Asst. Probation Officer	1,200 "	July 5, 1905
George H. Nason	25 Rockville pk	Court Officer	1,200 "	Aug. 1, 1895
Joseph Houghton	18 Perrin st	"	1,200 "	Jan. 1, 1902

Municipal Court, West Roxbury District.

Name.	Residence.	Designation.	Compensation.	Date of Election or Appointment.
John Perrins, Jr.	87 Sedgwick st	Justice	$2,000 yr	Jan. 12, 1905
Henry Austin	Cottage ave	Special Justice	*6.53 day	Oct. 22, 1890
J. Albert Brackett	Hemenway Chambers	"	*6.53 "	April 29, 1894
Edward W. Brewer	263 Pond st	Clerk	1,200 yr	June 11, 1887
Charles H. D. Stockbridge	259 Harold st., Rox	Probation Officer	1,200 "	Jan. 13, 1894
Thomas H. Staples	26 Clive st	Court Officer	1,000 "	" 1909
Caroline M. Adams	Burroughs st	Clerical Assistant	†	May, 1908
Dorothy E. Brewer	263 Pond st	"	†	" 1908

Municipal Court, Brighton District.

Name.	Residence.	Designation.	Compensation.	Date of Election or Appointment.
Charles A. Barnard	45 Parsons st	Justice	$1,600 yr	Feb. 5, 1902
Henry P. Kennedy	669 Cambridge st., Bri	Clerk	900 "	July 1, 1874
Henry P. Kennedy	669 Cambridge st., Bri	Probation Officer	800 "	June 24, 1891
B. Franklin Sanborn	41 Milford st	Officer	1,000 "	" 11, 1894
Harry C. Fabyan	21 Sparhawk st	Special Justice	*5.23 day	Jan. 7, 1903
Robert W. Frost	47 N. Beacon st	"	*5.23 "	Nov. 19, 1902

Boston Juvenile Court.

Name.	Residence.	Designation.	Compensation.	Date of Election or Appointment.
Harvey H. Baker	Brookline	Justice	$3,000 yr	July 13, 1906
Frank Leveroni	32 Hull st	Special Justice	*9.80 day	" 13, 1906
Philip Rubenstein	11 Michigan ave	"	*9.80 "	" 13, 1906
Charles W. M. Williams	223 W. Canton st	Clerk	1,500 yr	" 13, 1906
Clarence E. Fitzpatrick	32 Sigourney st	Probation Officer	1,800 "	Jan. 1, 1907
Roy M. Cushman	42 Pinckney st	"	1,800 "	" 1, 1908
Evelyn E. Gould	West Somerville	Stenographer	15.60 wk	Sept. 1, 1908

Police Court, Chelsea.

Name.	Residence.	Designation.	Compensation.	Date of Election or Appointment.
Albert D. Bosson	Chelsea	Justice	$2,500 yr	July 13, 1892
Samuel R. Cutler	Revere	Special Justice	*8.17 day	April 29, 1897
George M. Stearns	Chelsea	"	*8.17 "	Jan. 28, 1903
Joseph M. Curley	Chelsea	Clerk	1,500 yr	May 11, 1892
Cora V. Morris	Chelsea	Assistant Clerk	600 "	Aug. 1, 1906
Eben Hutchinson, Jr.	Chelsea	Probation Officer	1,500 "	July 1, 1891
John F. Sullivan	Chelsea	Constable	1,000 "	May 9, 1904
James J. Trainor	Chelsea	Janitor	300 "	Oct. 1, 1904

* Per diem for actual service.
† No fixed compensation. Court is allowed $600 for extra clerical assistance.

Registry of Deeds.

Name.	Residence.	Designation.	Compensation.	Date of Election or Appointment

Central Administration Department.

Name.	Residence.	Designation.	Comp.	Date
William T. A. Fitzgerald	137 Walnut ave., Rox	Register	*$5,000 yr.	1906
Stephen A. Jennings	32 Humphreys st., Dor	Assistant Register	2,500 "	1908
John W. Johnson	146 Massachusetts ave	Second Assistant Register	30.00 wk.	1892
Patrick F. Brogan	98 Endicott st	Clerk	18.00 "	1907
Gertrude A. Donovan	117 Pembroke st	Superintendent of Work	20.00 "	1881
Sidney Dunn	36 Minot st., Dor	Clerk	25.00 "	1902
Daniel E. Harrington	32 Oak st	"	30.00 "	1907
George A. Holmes	Cambridge	"	7.00 "	1857
Alberta Jefferson	22 Greenwich st., Rox	Coat Room	7.00 "	1903
Frank J. McCarthy	367 Cambridge st	Clerk	15.00 "	1900
Angelina McKenna	11 E. Newton st	Stenographer	15.00 "	1907
Francis J. Reddy	98 Albion st	Clerk	12.00 "	1907
Mary E. Graham	23 E. Concord st	Entry Clerk	18.00 "	1895
Josephine A. Small	55 Corbett st	"	20.00 "	1870

Recording Department.

Name.	Residence.	Designation.	Comp.	Date
John A. Bruen	27 Sargent st	Reference Clerk	$6.00 wk.	1894
Angela B. Curry	824 Blue Hill ave	Comparer	18.00 "	1907
Susan M. Dyer	776 Norfolk st., Mat	"	18.00 "	1886
Ellen Egan	144 Bowdoin st	"	18.00 "	1868
Mabel E. Mansfield	305 Havre st	"	18.00 "	1907
A. Grace Small	36 Millwood st	Clerk Register Land	20.00 "	1903
Margaret G. King	19 Copley st., Rox	Indexer	15.00 "	1902
Elizabeth V. Sullivan	43 Decatur st., Chsn	"	15.00 "	1907
Cecilia F. Egan	144 Bowdoin st	Pager	15.00 "	1880
Jane J. Martin	335 K st	"	15.00 "	1907
Bertha M. D. Carleton	Chelsea	Copyist	†	1907
Jane F. Connelly	31 Hillside st	"	†	1905
Mary T. Curley	512 Dorchester ave	"	†	1907
Mary J. Doherty	804 Blue Hill ave	"	†	1902
Mary M. Donahue	11 Central ave	"	†	1905
Gertrude A. Drey	18 E. Canton st	"	†	1906
Katheryn V. Feehan	20 Harvest st	"	†	1906
Gertrude M. Fleming	6 Thornton st	"	†	1907
Mary C. Gallagher	15 Bromley pk	"	†	1902
Mary E. Galvin	15 Mt. Vernon st., Dor	"	†	1907
Cora M. Getchell	88 Worcester st	"	†	1890
Sadie V. Green	117 Baldwin st	"	†	1908
Annie Grimm	79 Webster st	"	†	1907
Elizabeth M. Hennessey	137 Marcella st., Rox	"	†	1905
Jeanette G. Hunter	5 Sumner pl	"	†	1907
Mary Lane	32 K st	"	†	1907
May E. Mackay	23 Sudan st	"	†	1906
Lillian B. Newton	260 Broadway	"	†	1907
Gertrude A. Norton	7 Olney st	"	†	1907
Anna E. Pearsall	1289 Massachusetts ave	"	†	1892
Emma L. Tuttle	13 Oakman st	"	†	1892
Annie L. Voigt	53 Hancock st., Dor	"	†	1892
Ruth E. Washburn	11 S. Munroe ter	"	†	1906
Ethel Wright	83 Walnut st., Nep	"	†	1905

Miscellaneous.

Name.	Residence.	Designation.	Comp.	Date
Charles H. Slattery ‡	520 E. Broadway	County Treasurer	8800 yr.	May 1, 1906
Thomas J. O'Daly	11 Stockton st	Paymaster	3,600 "	" 7, 1902
Dennis H. Mahony §	11 Rutland st	Clerk	400 "	Dec. 1, 1904
Benjamin S. Turner §	33 Elm Hill ave	Cashier	200 "	July 1, 1885
George H. Dana ‖	28 Cummings rd	Bookkeeper	100 "	Dec. 1, 1904
Horton G. Ide §	37 Ridgemont st	Clerk	100 "	" 1, 1904
J. Alfred Mitchell ¶	796 E. Fourth st	County Auditor	800 "	Nov. 23, 1904
Fred H. Seavey **	215 Charles st	Sheriff	3,000 "	May 24, 1900
John J. Hennessey ††	247 Millet	Clerk, Collecting Dept	400 "	Jan. 23, 1897
Cornelius J. Bresnahan	21 Waumbeck st	Prison Van Driver	24.00 wk.	" 24, 1902
Jeremiah J. Gilman	21 Eaton st	"	24.00 "	March 30, 1908

* $1000 additional as Assistant Recorder, Land Court.
† Copyists paid by the fold, earning from $10 to $15 a week.
‡ See Treasury Department Sinking Funds Department and Schools.
§ See Treasury Department.
‖ See Treasury Department and Sinking Funds Department.
¶ See Auditing Department and Sinking Funds Department.
** See Jail and Court House.   †† See Collecting Department.

Medical Examiners.

Name.	Residence.	Designation.	Compensation.	Date of Election or Appointment.

Northern District.

George B. Magrath, M. D..	274 Boylston st	Examiner	$4,000 yr	Jan. 18, 1907
William E. Patten	408 Columbus ave	Clerk	1,020 "	April 21, 1908
Rebecca M. Sullivan	Harcourt, St. Botolph st	Stenographer	900 "	" 21, 1908

Southern District.

Wm. G. Macdonald, M. D..	Centre st., J. P.	Examiner	$4,000 yr	July 1, 1905
Richard Currie	44 E. Brookline st	Clerk	900 "	" 24, 1908
Timothy Leary, M. D	17 Grovenor rd	Associate Examiner	666 "	" 23, 1908

Penal Institutions Department.

Central Office.

Vernon V. Skinner	2849 Washington st	Commissioner	$5,000 yr	March 2, 1908
Herbert S. Carruth	152 Beaumont st	Asst. Commissioner	3,500 "	May 5, 1902
Hubert Pope	132 Chiswick rd	Secretary	2,500 "	July 1, 1895
William J. Graham*	42 Holmes ave	Clerk of Accounts	2,000 "	Nov. 10, 1896
William A. Prescott	Chelsea	Clerk	1,900 "	Aug. 11, 1876
Henry M. Quinn	223 South st	"	1,100 "	Feb. 1, 1909
D. Joseph Linehan	146 Blue Hill ave	Probation Clerk	1,300 "	Sept. 1, 1901
George F. H. Murray	29 G st	Asst. Probation Clerk	1,100 "	Nov. 1, 1904
Katherine Berran	21 Bainbridge st	" "	900 "	Sept. 1, 1896
Eva L. Connor	106 Mt. Pleasant ave	Stenographer	780 "	" 14, 1903
G. Arthur Tappan	90 Maywood st	Messenger	600 "	Oct. 12, 1908

House of Correction.

James H. Cronin	Deer Island	Master	$2,500 yr	Nov. 1, 1907
William Hendry	"	Deputy Master	1,500 "	" 1, 1907
Bernard F. McGaffigan	"	Physician	1,650 "	April 24, 1907
Charles F. Mahoney	"	Assistant Physician	600 "	Feb. 24, 1908
Paul Carson	"	"	650 "	Dec. 7, 1896
John C. Bossidy	419 Boylston st	Consulting Physician	None	" 10, 1906
William T. Councilman	78 Bay State rd	"	"	Nov. 6, 1902
William H. Devine	595 Broadway	"	"	" 6, 1902
Charles G. Dewey	539 Talbot ave	"	"	" 6, 1902
George F. Jelly	69 Newbury st	"	"	" 6, 1902
James G. Mumford	Haddon Hall	"	"	" 6, 1902
Edward M. Plummer	5 Adams st., Chsn	"	"	" 6, 1902
Charles S. Whitney	Deer Island	Clerk	$1,000 yr	May 8, 1907
William B. Mahar	647 Third st	Assistant Clerk	700 "	June 1, 1907
Henry J. Lund	Deer Island	"	600 "	May 5, 1908
Fred W. Dahl	25 Walnut ave	"	480 "	Jan. 1, 1909
William J. Graham	42 Holmes ave	Clerk	125 "	Nov. 15, 1901
John P. Riley	229 Marion st., E. B	Engineer	1,200 "	July 1, 1908
John Fay	411 E. Seventh st	Assistant Engineer	3.50 day	Dec. 1, 1902
Burt H. Candage	25 Elinor st	"	780 yr	Sept. 3, 1889
Clarence P. Greene	Deer Island	"	900 "	Dec. 23, 1884
James Shea	31 White st., E. B	"	3.50 day	" 24, 1904
Howard W. Wheeler	Winthrop	"	3.50 "	March 2, 1901
Frederick C. Brughts	78 London st	Fireman	600 yr	June 1, 1907
Bernard Cassidy	Deer Island	"	600 "	Dec. 11, 1907
John S. Flanders	"	"	600 "	Nov. 3, 1908
Jerome Hurley	267 Bunker Hill st	"	600 "	Dec. 12, 1907
Michael McNulty	2 Florence st	"	600 "	Nov. 1, 1907
Orrin A. Webster	5 Sunnyside st	"	600 "	Aug. 5, 1908
Patrick Harkins	4 Pleasant street ct	"	600 "	March 9, 1907
John S. Averill	Deer Island	Officer	660 "	July 16, 1889
James E. Barnett	"	"	660 "	March 12, 1903
William Barrett	150 Broadway	"	660 "	July 29, 1907
George G. Brown	Winthrop	"	660 "	March 15, 1892
Herman Call	Deer Island	"	660 "	Jan. 1, 1901
Peter H. Cooper	"	"	660 "	Aug. 1, 1900
Thomas A. Costello	455 W. Fourth st	"	660 "	Sept. 1, 1907
Harry L. Currier	22 Upton st	"	660 "	Aug. 1, 1900

* See, also, Deer Island.

Penal Institutions Department.—Continued.

Name.	Residence.	Designation.	Compensation.	Date of Election or Appointment.

House of Correction.— Continued.

Name.	Residence.	Designation.	Compensation.	Date of Election or Appointment.
Samuel C. Dunne	Winthrop	Officer	$660 yr	March 8, 1901
Patrick J. Fitzgerald	8 Bridge ct	"	660 "	Sept. 1, 1906
John B. Grady	Deer Island	"	660 "	Jan. 6, 1894
John A. Hearn	"	"	660 "	March 9, 1905
Martin A. Hollaran		"	660 "	Jan. 26, 1893
John H. Kelly	Winthrop	"	660 "	July 19, 1903
George A. Kenison	Deer Island	"	660 "	March 6, 1895
Edward L. Kenney	907 E. Fourth st	"	660 "	Oct. 15, 1906
Llewllyn Lincoln	Winthrop	"	660 "	April 28, 1895
Bernard F. Mellen	23 Medford st., Chsn	"	660 "	July 16, 1903
Thomas Mulligan	800 Third st	"	660 "	Nov. 2, 1906
Albert S. Nason	Deer Island	"	660 "	Oct. 27, 1893
John W. Nolan	21 Woodward ave	"	660 "	Dec. 26, 1906
David J. Stapleton	549 E. Third st	"	660 "	March 20, 1907
Elihu L. Vaughn	Deer Island	"	660 "	Feb. 3, 1896
Joel F. Vinal	"	"	660 "	March 12, 1895
Anthony White	"	"	660 "	Oct. 3, 1892
Joseph A. Wiggin	"	"	660 "	March 4, 1893
George S. Carr	20 Harvard st., Chsn	"	600 "	June 4, 1908
William J. Cronin	60 St. James st	"	600 "	March 1, 1908
Timothy J. Hourihan	80 W. Dedham st	"	600 "	July 3, 1908
Lawrence D. Lindquist	Deer Island	"	600 "	June 23, 1908
Andrew Petitti	182 Main st., Chsn	"	600 "	Oct. 5, 1908
Thomas W. Plunkett	828 Adams st	"	600 "	Dec. 11, 1907
John H. Seeley	3286 Washington st	"	600 "	Aug. 5, 1908
John H. Doherty	341 K st	Machinist	600 "	May 15, 1908
Joseph F. Wilson	Deer Island	Librarian	660 "	Oct. 3, 1902
Robert F. Kernachan	43 Westwood st	Shoemaker	660 "	Dec. 1, 1902
Patrick Minton	784 E. Third st	Farmer	840 "	April 16, 1908
Richard McKeown	800 E. Third st	Steward	790 "	Oct. 15, 1902
James H. McManus	451 Beach st., Ros	Receiving Officer	780 "	April 20, 1908
Peter Bay	67 Windsor st., Rox	Baker	780 "	Sept. 3, 1889
Charles Noll	877 Parker st	Assistant Baker	780 "	April 16, 1883
Daniel J. Barry	212 Emerson st	Officer	480 "	Nov. 4, 1908
Charles Bowman	Deer Island	"	480 "	" 16, 1908
James L. Callahan	541 Medford st	"	480 "	Jan. 1, 1909
John Callanan	3 Frederick ter	"	480 "	Dec. 1, 1908
James J. Garrity	16 Fifield st	"	480 "	" 5, 1908
Walter I. Mason	30 Huntington ave	"	480 "	March 12, 1909
William McCreight	761 Broadway	"	480 "	Dec. 1, 1908
Thomas E. Robinson	40 Wendover st	"	480 "	" 1, 1908
Augustine D. Russell	20 Downing st	"	480 "	March 15, 1909
Lester L. Whitehead	176 Coolidge st	"	480 "	Dec. 19, 1908
Robert H. Davison	Deer Island	"	540 "	Aug. 11, 1895
John R. Dunlap	"	Messenger	240 "	Sept. 17, 1906
Michael W. Fitzgibbon	"	Cutter	960 "	March 7, 1887
William L. Moore	258 Chestnut ave	Assistant Cutter	480 "	April 3, 1909
Thomas F. Fitzpatrick	23 Oakley st	Instructor	960 "	March 16, 1887
John H. Forger	53 Augusta ave	Overseer	840 "	Feb. 9, 1892
Thomas F. Keefe	2 Woodville pk	Painter	840 "	June 25, 1897
William F. Kyle	1294 Dorchester ave	Carpenter	780 "	" 1, 1907
George E. Stokes	Winthrop	Chaplain	600 "	" 19, 1908
William J. Scanlon	St. Mary's Church	"	600 "	Jan. 1, 1907
Clara W. Baker	Somerville	Organist	360 "	Sept. 1, 1890
Ellie L. Donahue	Everett	"	360 "	Jan. 1, 1905
Margaret E. O'Neill	Deer Island	Chief Matron	600 "	Nov. 1, 1907
Nancy B. Davis	"	Head Cook	600 "	Sept. 15, 1878
Lena A. Ackford	"	Matron	360 "	July 12, 1895
Nancy E. Collins	"	"	360 "	March 14, 1881
Addie F. Gunn	"	"	360 "	June 12, 1907
E. Maud Harriman	"	"	360 "	March 1, 1891
Hulda E. Heitman	"	"	360 "	Oct. 9, 1891
Katherine Hickey	"	"	360 "	July 31, 1902
Susan H. Keefe	"	"	360 "	May 1, 1908
Margaret E. Armstrong	"	"	325 "	" 10, 1900
Carrie E. Bowman	"	"	325 "	Sept. 1, 1886
Catherine Douglass	"	"	325 "	Oct. 21, 1907
Emma B. Ford	"	"	325 "	May 8, 1905
Catherine Hally	"	"	325 "	Nov. 25, 1907
Marvill M. Lee	"	"	325 "	May 1, 1894
Jennie M. Morris	"	"	325 "	April 12, 1900
Mary F. O'Neil	"	"	325 "	Nov. 24, 1903
Ellen Stafford	"	"	325 "	" 16, 1901

Penal Institutions Department.— Concluded.

Name.	Residence.	Designation.	Compensation.	Date of Election or Appointment.

House of Correction.— Concluded.

Name.	Residence.	Designation.	Compensation.	Date of Election or Appointment.
Sarah Stevens	Deer Island	Matron	$325 yr	Oct. 6, 1905
Sarah Dempsey	"	"	300 "	June, 1908
Marion M. Hix	"	"	300 "	July 1, 1908
Clara E. Reed	"	"	300 "	Aug. 5, 1908
Mary E. Dempsey	"	Head Nurse	420 "	July 18, 1907
Adelaide C. Haley	"	Nurse	325 "	Jan. 1, 1905
Anna O'Connor	"	"	325 "	May 17, 1904
Winifred Dillon	"	"	300 "	Feb. 1, 1908
Elizabeth Doggett	"	"	300 "	April 1, 1908
Elizabeth Fitzgerald	"	"	300 "	Aug. 18, 1908
Mary Flemming	"	"	300 "	" 19, 1908
Olive E. Saunders	"	"	300 "	Dec. 5, 1908
Adeline M. Tucker	"	"	300 "	April 1, 1908
Elizabeth Sullivan	"	"	300 "	March 1, 1909

NUMBER OF PAID OFFICIALS AND EMPLOYEES.

	April 30, 1905.	April 30, 1906.	April 30, 1907.	April 30, 1908.	April 30, 1909.
Mayor's Office............................	8	7	10	11	10
Board of Aldermen........................	14	14	14	14	14
Common Council...........................	78	78	78	77	78
Art Department...........................	—	—	—	—	1
Assessing Department.....................	146	145	146	156	152
Auditing Department......................	18	16	16	16	16
Bath Department..........................	139	177	198	159	141
Building Department......................	61	61	69	67	61
Board of Appeal..........................	3	3	3	6	6
Cemetery Department......................	91	92	93	95	88
Children's Institutions Department........	93	106	97	106	104
City Clerk Department....................	33	32	32	31	29
City Messenger Department................	27	30	30	32	30
Clerk of Committees Department...........	9	9	9	8	8
Collecting Department....................	62	61	83	54	59
Consumptives' Hospital Department........	—	—	3	20	58
Election Department......................	33	33	33	37	33
Engineering Department...................	83	82	82	80	82
Finance Commission.......................	—	—	—	7	—
Fire Department..........................	834	950	961	970	961
Health Department........................	136	140	176	170	197
Hospital Department......................	543	576	563	607	613
Insane Hospital Department *.............	163	152	148	176	—
Institutions Registration Department.....	13	13	13	13	12
Law Department...........................	15	14	15	15	15
Library Department.......................	453	492	514	483	484
Market Department........................	7	7	7	7	7
Music Department.........................	2	2	7	7	2
Overseeing of the Poor Department........	35	35	32	48	35
Park Department..........................	285	338	316	348	327
Pauper Institutions Department †.........	138	145	146	147	136
Police Department........................	1,356	1,355	1,346	1,486	1,552
Licensing Board..........................	—	—	12	13	14
Printing Department......................	124	134	120	83	99
Public Buildings Department..............	113	122	131	118	103
Public Grounds Department................	143	138	168	109	119
Registry Department......................	25	25	26	27	27
Schoolhouse Department...................	30	27	31	35	44
School Department........................	2,918	2,979	3,036	3,128	3,251
Sinking Funds Department.................	3	3	3	3	3
Soldiers' Relief Department..............	11	11	10	11	11
Statistics Department....................	4	3	4	4	4
Steamer "Monitor".......................	13	13	14	14	13
Street Department:					
Central Office.........................	9	—	—	7	10
Bridge Division.......................	197	193	182	192	193
Ferry Division........................	174	186	172	175	164
Lamp Division.........................	6	7	7	149	8
Paving Division.......................	975	973	953	787	813
Sanitary Division.....................	699	739	782	764	673
Sewer Division........................	918	912	976	850	638
Street Cleaning Division..............	412	} 496	489	446	438
Street Watering Division..............	23	}			
Street Laying-Out Department.............	67	75	78	70	74
Supply Department........................	—	5	4	4	5
Treasury Department......................	16	17	17	17	17
Water Department.........................	686	670	650	601	562
Weights and Measures Department..........	13	13	13	13	12
Wire Department..........................	41	43	46	40	39
	12,558	12,949	13,174	13,108	12,645
County of Suffolk........................	536	550	579	571	577
	13,094	13,499	13,753	13,679	13,222

* Taxes by Commonwealth Dec. 1, 1908.
† Boston Infirmary Department from April 15, 1908.

INDEX.

	Page.
Aldermen, Board of	3
Almshouse, Charlestown	14
Art Department	6
Assessing Department	6
Auditing Department	8
Bath Department	8
Board of Aldermen	3
Board of Appeal	15
Boston Almshouse and Hospital	12
Boston Infirmary Department	11
Boston Juvenile Court	214
Brighton Municipal Court	214
Bridge Division	151
Building Department	14
Cambridge Bridges	154
Cemetery Department	16
Charlestown Municipal Court	213
Children's Institutions Department	17
Charlestown Almshouse	14
Chelsea Police Court	214
City Clerk Department	19
City Messenger Department	20
Clerk of Committees Department	20
Collecting Department	20
Common Council	3
Consumptives' Hospital Department	21
County Buildings	207
County of Suffolk	207
County of Suffolk, Miscellaneous	215
Court House	207
Court Officers	211
Dorchester Municipal Court	214
East Boston District Court	213
Election Department	22
Engineering Department	23
Ferry Division	155
Fire Department	24
Health Department	41
Hospital Department	44
House of Correction	216
Institutions:	
Children's Institutions Department	17
Placing Out and Office Division	18
Parental School	17
Suffolk School for Boys	19
Boston Infirmary Department	11
Boston Almshouse and Hospital	11, 12
Almshouse, Charlestown	14
Office Expenses	12
Steamer "John Howard"	14
Institutions Registration Department	54
	Page.
Jail	208
"John Howard" Steamer	14
Justices, Municipal Court	212
Juvenile Court	214
Lamp Division	157
Law Department	54
Library Department	55
Licensing Board	65
Market Department	65
Mayor	3
Medical Examiners	216
"Monitor" Steamer	150
Music Department	66
Municipal Court, Civil	212
Criminal	213
Brighton	214
Charlestown	213
Dorchester	214
Justices	212
Roxbury	214
South Boston	213
West Roxbury	214
Office Expenses of Penal Institutions	216
Overseeing of the Poor Department	66
Parental School	17
Park Department	66
Paving Division	157
Penal Institutions Department	216
Placing Out and Office Division	18
Police Court, Chelsea	214
Police Department	71
Printing Department	93
Probate Court	212
Public Buildings Department	95
Public Grounds Department	97
Register of Probate and Insolvency	212
Registry of Deeds	215
Registry Department	99
Roxbury Municipal Court	214
Sanitary Division	169
School Department	100
Schoolhouse Department	99
Sewer Division	179
Sinking Funds Department	150
Soldiers' Relief Department	150
South Boston Municipal Court	213
Statistics Department	150
Steamer "John Howard"	14
Steamer "Monitor"	150
Street Department	151
Central Office	151

Page.

Street Department.—*Concluded.*
   Bridge Division...................... 151
   Ferry Division...................... 155
   Lamp Division...................... 157
   Paving Division 157
   Sanitary Division.................. 169
   Sewer Division 179
   Street Cleaning and Watering Division 189
Street Laying-Out Department........ 195
Suffolk County 207
           Court House.......... 207
           Jail................... 208

Page.

Suffolk Registry of Deeds............. 215
Suffolk School for Boys.............. 19
Superior Court, Civil................. 209
                Criminal............. 210
Supply Department................... 197
Supreme Judicial Court.............. 209
Treasury Department................. 197
Water Department.................... 197
Weights and Measures Department.... 205
West Roxbury Municipal Court....... 214
Wire Department..................... 205

Lightning Source UK Ltd.
Milton Keynes UK
UKHW031124020720
365926UK00009B/524